Herrick

# INSIDE THE MIDDLE EAST

BY THE SAME AUTHOR

---

*Inside India Today*
*The Untouchables of India*
*Black British, White British*
*A Triangular View (A novel)*
*To Anchor a Cloud (A play)*
*Apply, Apply, No Reply* and *A Clean Break (Two plays)*
*Interior, Exchange, Exterior (Poems)*

DILIP HIRO

# INSIDE THE MIDDLE EAST

**McGraw-Hill Book Company**

New York St. Louis San Francisco Bogotá Guatemala
Hamburg Lisbon Madrid Mexico Montreal Panama
Paris San Juan São Paulo Tokyo Toronto

Reprinted by arrangement with Routledge & Kegan Paul Ltd.

First U.S. edition

1234567890DODO8765432

ISBN 0-07-029055-5 {H.C.}
0-07-029056-3 {PBK.}

**Library of Congress Cataloging in Publication Data**
Hiro, Dilip.
Inside the Middle East.
Bibliography: p.
1. Near East—Politics and government. 2. Near East—Economic conditions. I. Title.
DS63.H55 1982 956 82-15195
ISBN 0-07-029055-5 AACR2
0-07-029056-3 (pbk.)

# CONTENTS

# ABBREVIATIONS

| | |
|---|---|
| AHC | Arab Higher Committee |
| AIOC | Anglo–Iranian Oil Company |
| AIPAC | American–Israeli Public Affairs Committee |
| ANM | Arab Nationalist Movement |
| APNU | Alliance of the Progressive Nationalist Unionists |
| APOC | Anglo–Persian Oil Company |
| Aramco | Arabian American Oil Company |
| ARCECS | All Russian Central Executive Committee of the Soviets |
| ASP | Arab Socialist Party |
| ASU | Arab Socialist Union |
| Awacs | Airborne Warning and Control Systems |
| Bapco | Bahrain Petroleum Company |
| BBC | British Broadcasting Corporation |
| bpd | barrels per day |
| BSO | Black September Organisation |
| CFDP | Compagnie Française des Pétroles |
| CIA | Central Intelligence Agency |
| Comintern | Communist International |
| CPI | Communist Party of Iraq |
| CPL | Communist Party of Lebanon |
| CPP | Communist Party of Palestine |
| CPS | Communist Party of Syria |
| CPSL | Communist Party of Syria–Lebanon |
| CPSU | Communist Party of the Soviet Union |
| DFLP | Democratic Front for the Liberation of Palestine |
| DLF | Dhofari Liberation Front |
| EEC | European Economic Community |
| FLOSY | Front for the Liberation of the Occupied South Yemen |
| GCC | Gulf Cooperation Council |

| | |
|---|---|
| GDP | Gross Domestic Product |
| GNP | Gross National Product |
| IDF | Israel Defence Forces |
| IEA | International Energy Authority |
| IPC | Iraq Petroleum Company |
| ISO | Israeli Socialist Organisation |
| JNF | Jewish National Fund |
| KDP | Kurdish Democratic Party |
| KOC | Kuwait Oil Company |
| LNL | League of National Liberation |
| MDLN | Mouvement Démocratique de Libération Nationale |
| Nato | North Atlantic Treaty Organisation |
| NCC | National Cultural Club |
| NDF | National Democratic Front |
| NDP | National Democratic Party |
| NLF | National Liberation Front |
| NLP | National Liberal Party |
| NRP | National Religious Party |
| OAPEC | Organisation of Arab Petroleum Exporting Countries |
| OPEC | Organisation of Petroleum Exporting Countries |
| PASC | Palestine Armed Struggle Command |
| PDP | Popular Democratic Party |
| PDRY | People's Democratic Republic of Yemen |
| Petromin | Petroleum and Minerals Organisation |
| PFLO | Popular Front for the Liberation of Oman |
| PFLOAG | Popular Front for the Liberation of the Occupied Arab Gulf (1968–71); Popular Front for the Liberation of Oman and the Arab Gulf (1971–4) |
| PFLP | Popular Front for the Liberation of Palestine |
| PLO | Palestine Liberation Organisation |
| PNC | Palestine National Council |
| PNF | Palestine National Front |
| PNF | Progressive National Front |
| RCC | Revolutionary Command Council |
| RDF | Rapid Deployment Force |
| SAM | Surface to Air Missile |
| SAS | Special Air Services |
| Socal | Standard Oil Company of California |
| Socony | Standard Oil Company of New York |
| Texaco | Texas Company |
| TPC | Turkish Petroleum Company |
| UAE | United Arab Emirates |
| UAR | United Arab Republic |
| UN/UNO | United Nations Organisation |

| | |
|---|---|
| UNEF | United Nations Emergency Force |
| UNESCO | United Nations Educational, Scientific and Cultural Organisation |
| UNF | United National Front |
| UNSCOP | United Nations Special Commission on Palestine |
| US/USA | United States of America |
| USSR | Union of Soviet Socialist Republics |
| VIP | Very Important Person |
| WZO | World Zionist Organisation |

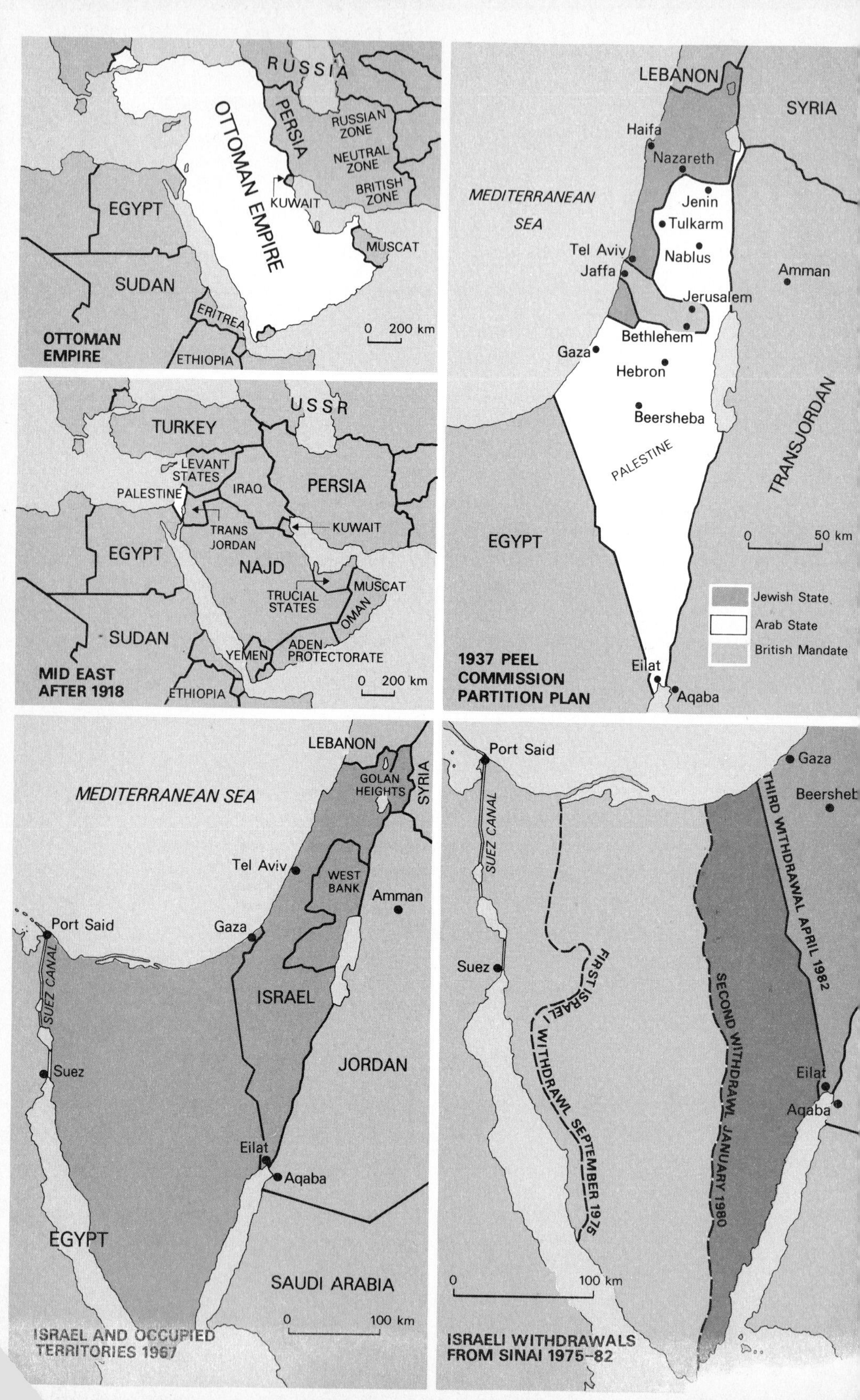
RUSSIA
OTTOMAN EMPIRE
PERSIA
RUSSIAN ZONE
NEUTRAL ZONE
BRITISH ZONE
KUWAIT
EGYPT
MUSCAT
SUDAN
ERITREA
ETHIOPIA
0 200 km
OTTOMAN EMPIRE
USSR
TURKEY
LEVANT STATES
PALESTINE
IRAQ
PERSIA
TRANS JORDAN
KUWAIT
EGYPT
NAJD
MUSCAT
TRUCIAL STATES
OMAN
SUDAN
YEMEN
ADEN PROTECTORATE
ETHIOPIA
0 200 km
MID EAST AFTER 1918
LEBANON
SYRIA
Haifa
Nazareth
MEDITERRANEAN SEA
Jenin
Tulkarm
Tel Aviv
Nablus
Jaffa
Amman
Jerusalem
Bethlehem
Gaza
Hebron
Beersheba
PALESTINE
TRANSJORDAN
EGYPT
0 50 km
Jewish State
Arab State
British Mandate
Eilat
Aqaba
1937 PEEL COMMISSION PARTITION PLAN
LEBANON
MEDITERRANEAN SEA
GOLAN HEIGHTS
SYRIA
Tel Aviv
WEST BANK
Amman
Port Said
Gaza
SUEZ CANAL
ISRAEL
Suez
JORDAN
Eilat
Aqaba
EGYPT
SAUDI ARABIA
0 100 km
ISRAEL AND OCCUPIED TERRITORIES 1967
Port Said
Gaza
Beershe
SUEZ CANAL
THIRD WITHDRAWAL APRIL 1982
Suez
FIRST ISRAELI WITHDRAWAL SEPTEMBER 1975
SECOND WITHDRAWAL JANUARY 1980
Eilat
Aqaba
0 100 km
ISRAELI WITHDRAWALS FROM SINAI 1975–82

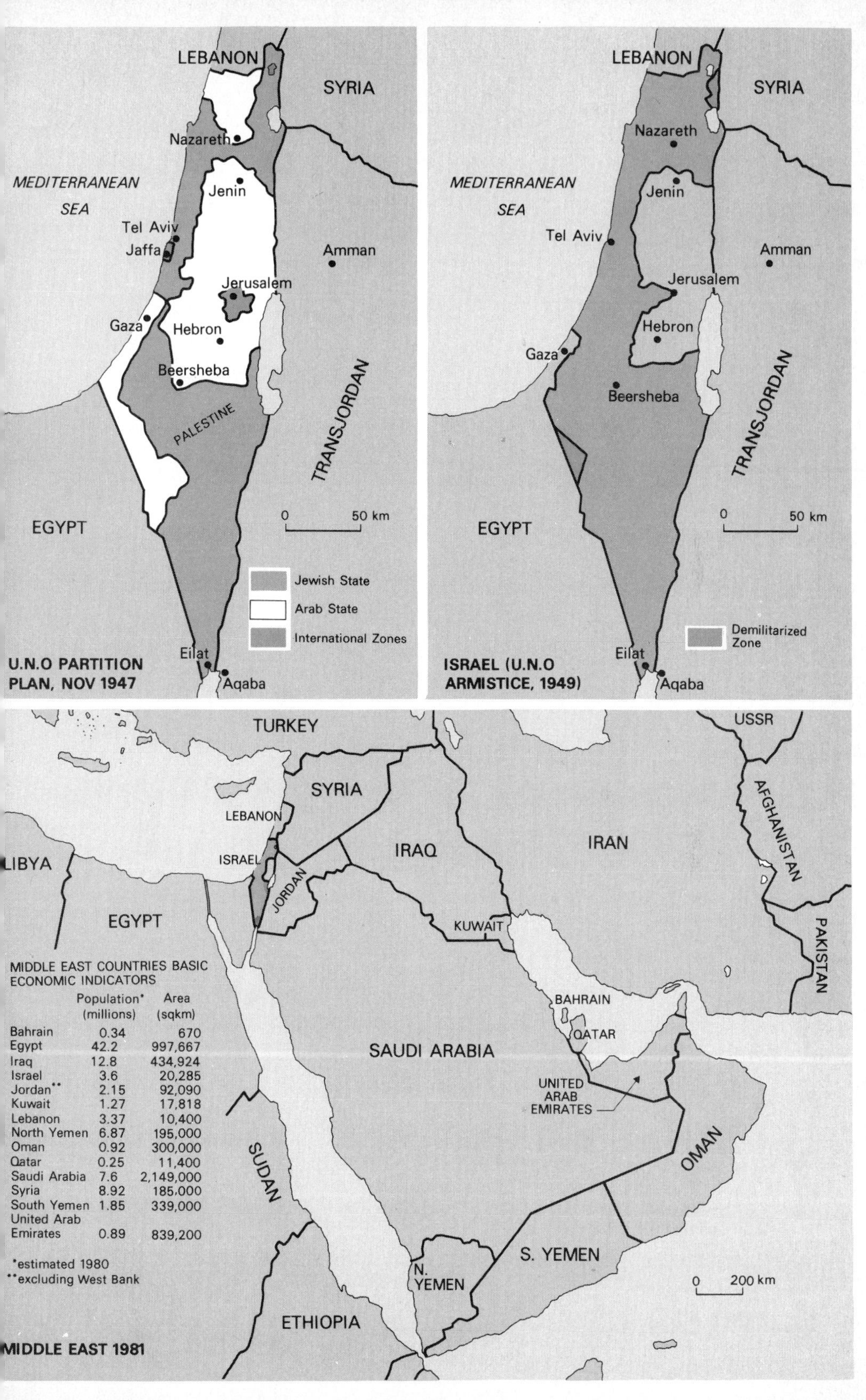


MIDDLE EAST COUNTRIES BASIC ECONOMIC INDICATORS

| | Population* (millions) | Area (sqkm) |
|---|---|---|
| Bahrain | 0.34 | 670 |
| Egypt | 42.2 | 997,667 |
| Iraq | 12.8 | 434,924 |
| Israel | 3.6 | 20,285 |
| Jordan** | 2.15 | 92,090 |
| Kuwait | 1.27 | 17,818 |
| Lebanon | 3.37 | 10,400 |
| North Yemen | 6.87 | 195,000 |
| Oman | 0.92 | 300,000 |
| Qatar | 0.25 | 11,400 |
| Saudi Arabia | 7.6 | 2,149,000 |
| Syria | 8.92 | 185,000 |
| South Yemen | 1.85 | 339,000 |
| United Arab Emirates | 0.89 | 839,200 |

*estimated 1980
**excluding West Bank

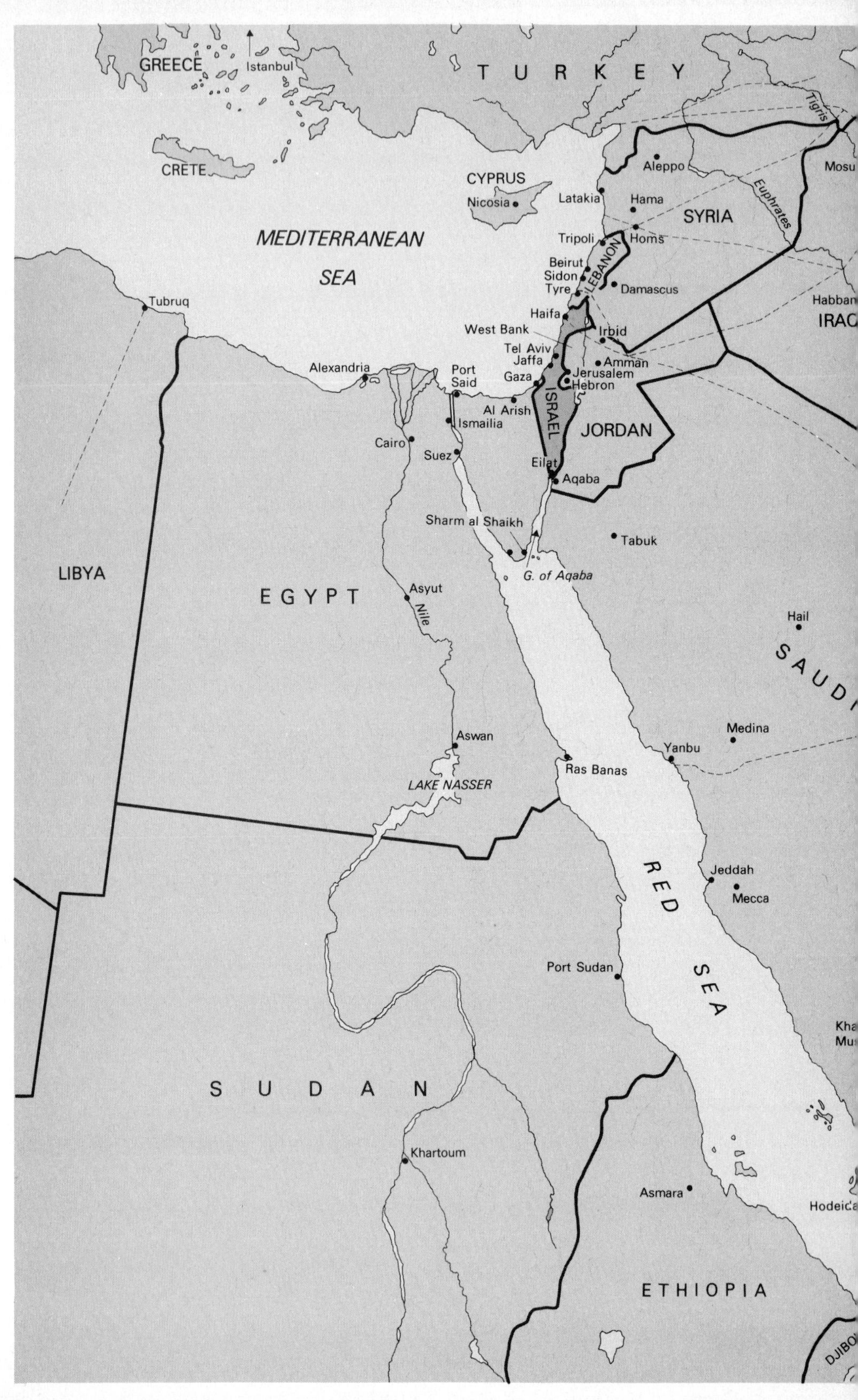
GREECE
Istanbul
TURKEY
CRETE
CYPRUS
Nicosia
Aleppo
Latakia
Hama
SYRIA
Tripoli
Homs
MEDITERRANEAN
SEA
Beirut
Sidon
Tyre
LEBANON
Damascus
Tubruq
Haifa
West Bank
Irbid
Tel Aviv
Jaffa
Amman
Jerusalem
Hebron
Alexandria
Port Said
Gaza
Al Arish
Ismailia
ISRAEL
JORDAN
Cairo
Suez
Eilat
Aqaba
Sharm al Shaikh
Tabuk
G. of Aqaba
LIBYA
EGYPT
Asyut
Nile
Hail
Medina
Aswan
Yanbu
Ras Banas
LAKE NASSER
RED SEA
Jeddah
Mecca
Port Sudan
SUDAN
Khartoum
Asmara
ETHIOPIA
Tigris
Euphrates
Mosu
Habban
IRAC
SAUDI
Hodeida
DJIBO

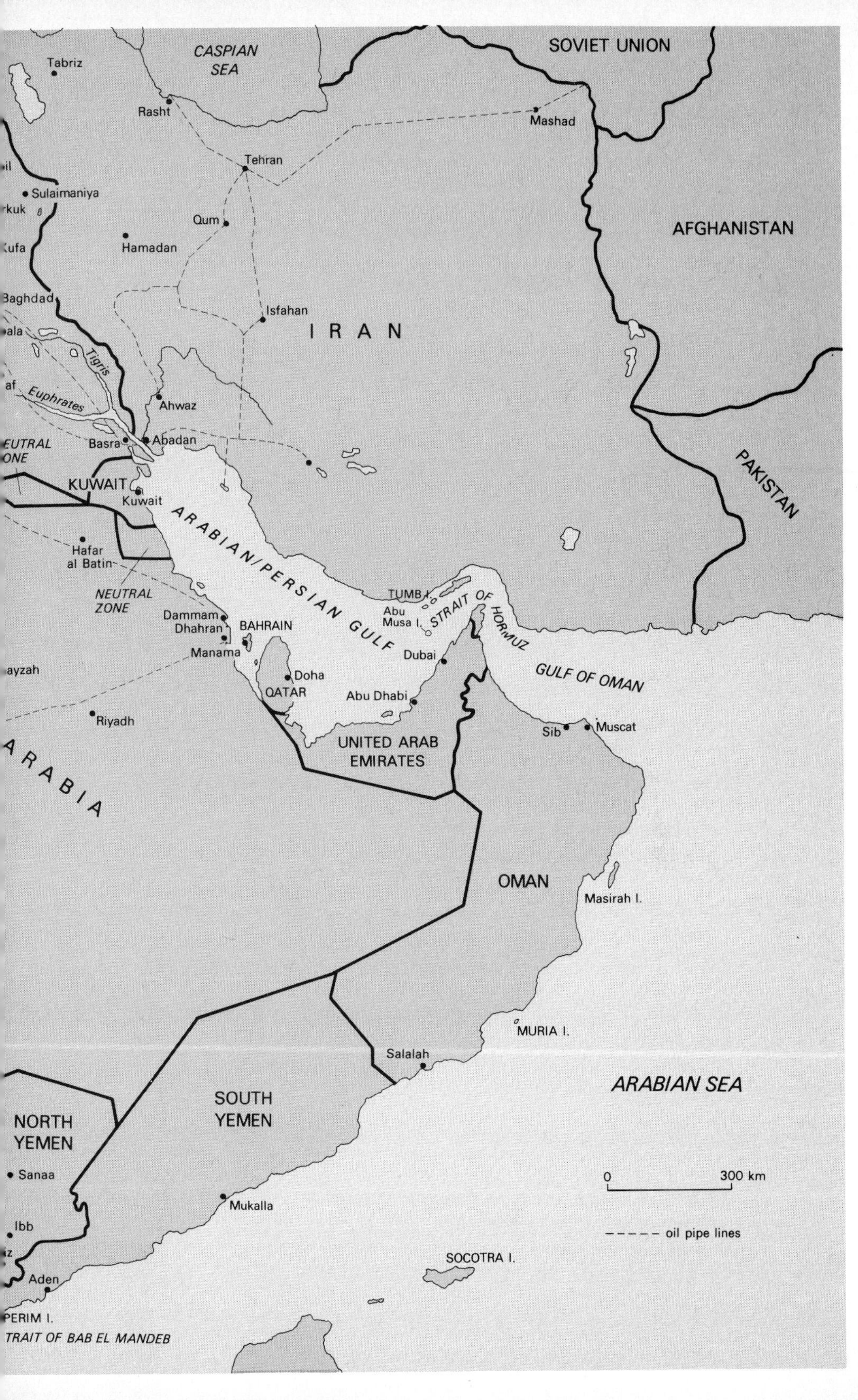
CASPIAN SEA
SOVIET UNION
Tabriz
Rasht
Mashad
Tehran
Sulaimaniya
Qum
Hamadan
AFGHANISTAN
Baghdad
Isfahan
I R A N
Tigris
Euphrates
Ahwaz
Basra
Abadan
KUWAIT
Kuwait
PAKISTAN
ARABIAN/PERSIAN GULF
Hafar al Batin
NEUTRAL ZONE
TUMB I.
Abu Musa I.
STRAIT OF HORMUZ
Dammam
Dhahran
BAHRAIN
Manama
Dubai
GULF OF OMAN
Doha
QATAR
Abu Dhabi
Sib
Muscat
Riyadh
UNITED ARAB EMIRATES
ARABIA
OMAN
Masirah I.
MURIA I.
Salalah
ARABIAN SEA
SOUTH YEMEN
NORTH YEMEN
Sanaa
0
300 km
Mukalla
Ibb
oil pipe lines
SOCOTRA I.
Aden
PERIM I.
TRAIT OF BAB EL MANDEB

# GLOSSARY OF ARABIC WORDS

abu: father
adha: nearest
ahali: masses
ahd: covenant
ahram (sing., haram): pyramids
al/el/ul: the
Alawi: follower of Ali
alem (pl., ulema): religious–legal scholar
amal: labour
amr: command
assifa: storm
ayatollah: sign or token of Allah
baath: renaissance
bedouin (sing., bedu): nomads
bin: son
daawa: call
dar: house or realm
dhimmi: the state of being a non-Muslim under Islamic rule
eid: festival
Eid al adha/Eid ul adha: the nearest (to the time of hajj) festival
Eid al fitr/Eid ul fitr: the festival of 'breaking the fast'
emir/amir: one who gives amr (command); commander
Falastine: Palestine
fatah: conquest
fatwa: legal deduction
fedayeen;(sing., fedayee): (lit.) self-sacrificers; (fig.) commandos or guerrillas
fellaheen (sing., fellah): peasants
fitr: breaking the fast
hajj: pilgrimage (to Mecca)
hijra: migration, flight

hojatalislam: one who conducts debate on Islam
ibn: son
ikhwan: brotherhood
imam: (lit.) one who leads prayers in a mosque; (fig.) religious leader
islam: state or act of submission (to the will of Allah)
jaish: army
jehad: (lit.) struggle in the name of Allah; (fig.) holy war or crusade
kataeb (sing., katiba): battalions or phalanxes
koran/quran: recitation
maghreb: west
mehdi: one who is guided by Allah
mohammed: praiseworthy or blessed
mojahed (pl., mojahedeen): (lit.) one who volunteers for jehad; (fig.) combatant
mufti: one who delivers a fatwa; religious–legal jurist
mujtahid: one who forms opinions on Islamic jurisprudence; expert on Islamic law
mukhabarat: intelligence service
mumineen: faithful
muslim: one who accepts islam – the state of submission (to the will of Allah)
mustaqabal: future
muttawi (pl., muttaween): (lit.) one who enforces compliance; (fig.) religious police
qadi: religious judge
rasul: messenger
sahafi: journalist
salaf: (lit.) roots; (fig.) ancestors
salafi: one who wishes to follow ancestral customs
shaab: people
shahada: (lit.) act of religious witness; (fig.) central precept (of Islam)
shaikh: (lit.) old man; (fig.) a title of respect accorded to a wise man
sharara: spark
sharia: Islamic law
sharif: noble
shia: partisan
sultan: ruler
sunna: tradition
sunni: one who follows sunna (tradition)
sura: chapter
takfir: (lit.) act of declaring somebody unbeliever; (fig.) repentance
tareeq: road
ulema: body of religious–legal scholars
umma: nation
waqf: religious trust

# GLOSSARY OF HEBREW ACRONYMS AND WORDS

aguda/agudat: community
aharonot: last or latest
ahdut: unity
al: on
aliyah (pl., aliyot): (lit.) ascent – to Palestine/Israel; (fig.) immigration wave
artzi; national or countrywide
Ashkenazi (pl., Ashkenazim): (lit.) Jew from central Europe; (fig.) European Jew
avoda; labour
ba-be: in
boker: morning
dati/datit: religious
emunim: faithful
eretz: land
Gahal: Gush Herut-Liberalim
gedolei: (lit.) great men; (fig.) sages
gush: bloc
ha: the
hadash: new
haganah: defence
hashomer: guard
hayesod: foundation
herut: freedom
histadrut: federation
hovevei (sing., hovev): lovers
ihud: union or unity
irgun: organisation
Ivriim: Hebrew
kayemet: current
keren: fund

kibbutz (pl., kibbutzim): collective agricultural settlement
kippur: atonement
klaliyim (sing., klali/klalit): general
knesset: parliament or assembly
kvutza (pl., kvutzot): collective group
le: for
Lehy: Lohamey Herut Y'Israel
leumi/leumit: national
likud: consolidation
lohamey (sing., loham): fighters
maarach: alignment
maariv: evening
Mafdal: Mifleget Datit Leumit
Maki: Miflaga Kommunistit Israelit
Mapai: Mifleget Poalei Israel
Mapam: Mifleget Poalim Meuhedet
matzpen: compass
merkaz: centre
meuhedet: united
miflaga/mifleget: party
Mizrahi: Merkaz Rouhani
moetzet: council
Mopsi: Mifleget Poalim Sozialistim
moshav (pl., moshavim): cooperative settlement
mossad: (lit.) institution; (fig.) intelligence service
ovdim: workers
poal (pl., poalim/poale): worker
rabbi: (lit.) my great one; (fig.) Jewish teacher of doctor of the law
Rafi: Reshima Poalei Israel
Rakah: Reshima Kommunistit Hadash
reshima: list
rouhani: spiritual
Sephardi (pl., Sephardim): (lit.) Jew from Spain; (fig.) Oriental/Arab Jew
shel: of
Siah: Smol Israel Hadash
smol: left
tenuat: movement
tzair: young
tzvai: military
yediot: news
Yishuv: Jewish community in Palestine (before the founding of Israel in 1948)
yom: day

# GLOSSARY OF RUSSIAN ABBREVIATIONS AND WORDS

agentstvo: agency
flot: fleet
i: and
iskra: spark
izvestia: news
krasnaya: red
mezhdunarodnie/mezhdunarodnaya: international
MiG: Mikoyan i Gurevitz*
mirovaya: world
novoe: new
otnosheniya: relations
pravda: truth
rubezhom: boundary
sevodnya: today
soyuza: union
sovietski/sovietskovo: soviet
Tass: Telegraphanoe Agentstvo Sovietskovo Soyuza
trud: labour
vremia: times
za: beyond
za rubezhom: abroad
zhizn: life
zvezda: star

*The names of the military aircraft's designers

# PREFACE

There is no standard definition of the Middle East. Some authors apply the term to the geographical area extending from Morocco to Pakistan, and Turkey to Sudan, including the island republic of Cyprus; others restrict it to the Arabic-speaking section of the region, and thus leave out Turkey, Cyprus, Iran, Afghanistan, and Pakistan. Still others narrow it further by excluding Arab North Africa – Morocco, Tunisia, Algeria, and Libya – and Sudan. I use the term in its narrowest sense.

The above definitions fit neatly into the concept that the Middle East consists of a core and peripheries. The core, often called the Arab East, includes the Fertile Crescent, comprising Lebanon, Jordan, Syria, and Iraq; the Arabian Peninsula, consisting of Saudi Arabia, North Yemen, South Yemen, Oman, the United Arab Emirates, Qatar, Bahrain and Kuwait; and Egypt. To the south of the core lies Sudan; to its west the Arab West – the Maghreb – made up of Libya, Algeria, Tunisia, and Morocco; and to its north and east the non-Arab countries of Cyprus, Turkey, Iran, Afghanistan, and Pakistan.

This book is a political and economic survey of the core countries of the Middle East. Since Israel is a geographical part of the Fertile Crescent, and has had a profound impact on the Arab East, it has been included in the survey; and so are the (presently stateless) Palestinians. It is the result of extensive research and study, spread over a period of three years; and is addressed to the general reader.

I did my fieldwork during the winter and spring of 1977–8, when I travelled widely in the Middle East, and again in January 1979, when I paid a short visit to the region. (Ten months later I visited Iran, and stayed there until the end of the year.) Having been born and brought up in the Islamic milieu of Pakistan, I felt at ease with the social environment of the Middle East in more ways than one. This feeling was reciprocated by the people I interviewed, whether they were local journalists, academics, students, workers, shopkeepers, or religious functionaries. In every country I visited I read the local press avidly, and listened to the radio. My intention was to familiarise myself as much as I could with the contemporary politico-economic scene in order to understand the past better.

I have divided the book into five parts. Part I begins with an introduction which establishes the unifying factors of the Arab world: Islam and the Arabic language. The historical survey which follows shows inter alia that events in one country have profoundly affected the fate of others. In fact, once the states have been classified as monarchies and republics, the survey covers the countries in an order which is dictated by the flow of the historical narrative – and not by geographical contiguity or alphabetical order. While the chapter on monarchies ends with Jordan, that on republics concludes with the (stateless) Palestinians; and this leads, logically, to the next chapter: Israel.

In Part II I outline the socio-economic context in which each of the Arab countries exists today, and go on to discuss the elements I have used to categorise various forces in the Arab world as conservative, centrist, or leftist. I then provide a survey of the conservative forces in the Arab Middle East, moving from one country to the next on the basis of a common sub-theme. Since I define Islamic republicanism as a centrist ideology I qualify the centrist forces, described in chapter 7, as 'secular and religious'. The leftist forces surveyed in the following chapter are all Marxist: lack of space precluded a description of the non-Marxist left.

Part III deals with Israel, and covers its internal politics and economics, as well as its relations with the international power blocs. It has a unity of its own, and can be read in conjunction with the earlier chapter on Israel. Part IV begins with a Soviet view of the Arab East as a whole, and then focuses on the relationship between an individual Arab state and the Soviet bloc in an order which is once again decided by the thrust of the narrative. The same approach prevails in the next chapter, which deals with the Arabs and the West, and which includes the history of Western involvement in Middle East oil since 1908.

The final part of the book analyses the past in social, economic and political terms, and discusses the various possibilities that the future holds for the region.

While each chapter is related to the one before it and after, it is sufficiently self-contained to merit being read on its own. Given the very wide scope of the book, and its complex structure, cross references to important events are inevitable, with a concomitant risk of repetition. I have avoided that risk by stressing different aspects of an event in different chapters. For instance, I have mentioned the September 1970 fighting between the Palestinian commandos and the Jordanian army four times: on p. 24, p. 54, p. 221, and pp. 322–3. But the first of these pages carries a brief reference to the event; the second gives the duration and casualties of the conflict; the third states Israel's stance on it; and the final ones describe the American involvement in it.

A word about the names of the countries, and the spellings of Arabic words. Since 1952 Egypt has undergone two name changes: the United Arab Republic, and the Arab Republic of Egypt; and so have Syria and the two sections of (historic) Yemen. The northern segment of Yemen, once called the Yemen, is now officially known as the Yemen Arab Republic. The southern part has had two names since independence in 1967: the People's Republic of South Yemen, and the People's Democratic Republic of Yemen. For the sake of simplicity and consistency I have respectively used the names: Egypt, Syria, North Yemen, and South Yemen. I have, however, included the other names in the index.

Similarly, while I have used the term 'the Gulf' for the gulf which divides Iran from the Arabian Peninsula, I have listed the two other names in vogue – the Arabian Gulf and the Persian Gulf – in the index.

Spelling an Arabic name can be a nightmare: there are fifty-two different ways of spelling Hussein. What I have done is to select one of the most widely used spellings in the English-speaking world, and stick to it – except when the spelling of a book author differs from mine. There I have simply reproduced the published spelling. For instance, Mohammed Heikal appears as Mohamed Heikal when he is mentioned as the author of, say, *The Road to Ramadan*. (The same principle applies to Hebrew and Russian names.) A particular difficulty arises when different spellings of a proper name, or an object, begin with a different letter. The most common examples are: Kassem and Qassem; Koran and Quran. I have solved this problem by using one spelling in the text but including both in the index.

In general I have tried to be simple and consistent. Instead of writing 'á', I have chosen 'aa'; and instead of following the example of authors who write Shiite and Alawite (but never Sunnite), I have stuck to Shia, Alawi, and Sunni. However, to help the reader, I have listed both variations of the terms in the index. Following the same principles in an altogether different context I have throughout used the exchange rate of two American dollars to one British pound.

The reader is advised to remember that the following Arabic and Hebrew words are used as religious or secular titles: ayatollah, emir, hojatalislam, imam, rabbi, shaikh, and sultan. He is also advised to take a periodic look at the notes, listed at the back, and to try to read the explanatory ones along with the text.

June 1981

Dilip Hiro

Postscript. While President Sadat's assassination in October 1981 is mentioned briefly in the text, the events leading up to it are described and analysed in the Postscript.

1 June 1982

DH

# PART I

# THE MIDDLE EAST:
## A HISTORICAL SURVEY

# 1

# INTRODUCTION

Although divided into thirteen sovereign states, the eighty-nine million inhabitants of the Arab East are remarkably homogeneous. They share a common language, culture and – excepting parts of Lebanon – religion. They believe in the concept of the Arab Nation (Umma al Arabiya), and are proud of the predominance enjoyed by the Arabs in Islam and Islamic history. 'The principal dimensions of Arab nationhood appear to be a collective awareness of a common history, a distinctive language and culture (literature, art, folkways), a degree of similarity in appearance – which is not racial since the Arabs are an amalgam of races and do not practise racial exclusivity – and a historic, geographic homeland', states Michael C. Hudson, an American specialist on the Middle East.[1]

Arabic is a major unifying factor; and all those who speak it are regarded as part of the Arab Nation. Spoken Arabic varies widely from area to area, but the literary language is more or less the same throughout the Arab Middle East. 'Arabic is the holy language of Islam, and specifically – in its classical form – the language of the Koran', notes David Holden, a British author and journalist. 'Its meanings and symbols are woven into the entire fabric of Arab life, providing, as it were, a common nervous system through a complex inheritance of linguistic and religious cross-references.'[2]

The symbols and sounds of Islam are to be found everywhere in the Arab East: in the mosques with minarets, the call of the muezzin, the arabesque decorations and Koranic inscriptions on buildings, religious and secular. At a less dramatic but more significant level, the constitutions of all the Arab East countries, excepting Lebanon, specify Islam as the official or state religion.

Islam is more than religion, since it embraces a whole social system composed of Muslims: all those who have submitted to Allah, the one and only God. (Islam, in Arabic, means the state of submission, and Muslim is the one who has submitted.) By putting all believers on an equal footing – of submission to Allah – Islam, which originated in western Arabia during the seventh century, created a confraternity above the traditional bonds of clan and tribe. The faithful were united in their belief in Allah and his precepts, as conveyed through Mohammed (literally, praiseworthy), his messenger.

Mohammed was born in 571 to Abdullah of the Hashem clan of the Quraish tribe in Mecca – a trading post and a place of pilgrimage for the worshippers of idols at the sanctuary of Kaaba, in western Arabia. When he was about forty he began preaching revelations in Arabic that purportedly came to him from the archangel Gabriel. (These utterances, delivered in rhythmic prose, were noted down and compiled into 114 suras (chapters) of varying lengths to form a book – the Koran[3] – a few years after Mohammed's death.)

The early revelations concerned mainly the omniscience and omnipotence of Allah, the compassionate; the evils of idol worship; and the concept of divine judgment. Since Mohammed's monotheistic teachings were antithetical to the idol worship practised at Kaaba, they angered the merchants of Mecca who profited by the arrival of pilgrims.

In 622 local hostility drove Mohammed and a dozen of his followers out of Mecca to Medina, an oasis town, about three hundred miles to the north-east. Here the feuding tribes of Aus and Khazraj welcomed Mohammed as an arbiter. The subsequent acceptance of Islam – the faith by then being preached by Mohammed – enabled the Medinese tribes to rise above their feuding and live in peace as Muslims. Mohammed became the military and civil governor of Medina. This is reflected in the later (Medinese) part of the Koran, which deals with daily problems of administration.

By the time he died in 632 Mohammed had brought most of western Arabia, including Mecca, under his control. From Medina he ruled an umma (community)[4] that had a dual character. 'On the one hand the umma was a political organism, a kind of new tribe with Mohammed as its shaikh,[5] and with Muslims and others as its members,' states Bernard Lewis, a historian of Islam. 'Yet at the same time it had a basically religious meaning. It was a religious community, a theocracy. Political and religious objectives were never really distinct in Mohammed's mind or in the minds of his contemporaries. This dualism is inherent in Islamic society of which the umma of Mohammed is the germ.'[6]

The later Islamic empires that were to emerge in Damascus (Ummayad, 661–750), Baghdad (Abbasid, 751–1258), Cairo (Mameuke, 1260–1517), and Constantinople (Ottoman, 1517–1918) followed the model of Mohammed's umma in Medina. The Ottoman empire which, until its dissolution in 1918, included the contemporary Arab East, was guided by the Koranic ideology which does not separate the realm of God from that of Caesar. 'Politically, the interpreters of the Law of Islam, the Sharia, have always been close to the centres of dynastic power: the formal separation of church and state was until recent times inconceivable,' notes Hudson. 'Even today, although secular-minded rulers have to a large extent succeeded in reducing the power of the religious leaders, the reaction of the Muslim judges and scholars, as well as masses of the faithful, to secular reforms is still significant.'[7] There are countless instances of Islamic leaders in the present-day Arab East referring to political matters in their sermons at the mosque, and even urging political action for or against the state.

The social impact of Islam is equally strong. It is to be seen in such institutions as religious schools and brotherhoods, and the existence of waqfs, charitable property trusts. The practice of Muslim children learning the Koran by heart, as part of their primary education, is another example of a continuing Islamic tradition.

Since the Koran covers not only politics and economics, but also interpersonal relationships, worship, and rituals, the impact of Islam is felt by the believer in his day-to-day life. The five obligations enjoined upon the faithful are simple and direct. A Muslim should often recite the shahada, the central precept (la ilaha illallah, mohammedun rasulullah – There is no god but Allah, Mohammed is the messenger of Allah); pray at five specific times of the day; abstain from food and sex between sunrise and sunset during the month of Ramadan; give anonymously one fortieth of his fixed annual income as charity; and make the pilgrimage to Mecca at least once in his lifetime, if he can afford it.

'Islam in the Arab world differs from religion in Western society: it permeates the daily life of the individual with its ritualistic obligations,' states Hudson. 'It is an important part of socialization; it affects personal status; it plays a political role. Islam also serves to integrate Arab society by inculcating a sense of the Muslim's special relationship with God and in the brotherhood and mutual obligations of all believers. . . . It is thus a powerful force for social and cultural stability.'[8]

Within the general framework of Islam there are certain minority sects, the most important being the Shias (literally, partisans). The roots of Shiaism go back to the first civil war in the Dar al Islam (Realm of Islam) which occurred in 656. After prophet Mohammed's death his father-in-law, Abu Bakr, was chosen as his successor or deputy (khalifa in Arabic; caliph in English). Abu Bakr died in 634, and was followed by Umar. By the time Umar was assassinated by an Iranian slave a decade later the Dar al Islam included not only Arabia but also Syria, Iraq and Egypt. Uthman, who succeeded Umar as the caliph, belonged to the powerful Ummayad family of Mecca. It was his murder by rebellious tribesmen in 656 that led to the first violent upheaval in the realm.

The claim of Ali, the cousin and son-in-law of Mohammed, to the caliphate was challenged by the Ummayads as well as by Aisha, the prophet's widow. Ali overpowered his adversaries on the battlefield, conquered Iraq, and moved the capital from Medina to Kufa, in Iraq. But the second major battle between the two sides at Siffin in 659 proved indecisive. Ali agreed to arbitration; and this went in favour of his rival, Muawiya, the Ummayad governor of Syria. Ali was murdered two years later; and his son, Hassan, who became the ruler of Iraq, was persuaded to abdicate. He died in Medina in 699.

Those who remained loyal to Ali and his descendants, and did not accept Muawiya as the caliph, came to be called the Shias, as against the Sunnis who did: the people of sunna (custom). By the time Muawiya died in 680 the Shias had emerged as a well-organised group dedicated to the idea that the Dar al Islam should be ruled by an imam: a born leader, a human imbued with part of Allah's divinity. Following Muawiya's death, Hussein, the second son of Ali, led a revolt against the Ummayads. This failed, and Hussein and his followers were massacred at Karbala in southern Iraq. Hussein came to be recognised as the third imam of the Shias, the first two being Ali and Hassan.

The majority of present-day Shias believe in the existence of twelve imams, and are called the Twelvers, or simply the Imamis.[9] They are concentrated in Iran, Bahrain, southern Iraq, and south-eastern Lebanon. There are others who regard Zaid, a great-grandson of Ali, as the fifth and the last imam: they are known as the Zaidis. By the end of the ninth century they had established their rule in North Yemen, then a Sunni region. Today the Zaidi tribes are a major force in that country. There are still others who regard Ismail – a son of the sixth imam – as the last imam, and dispute the Twelvers' accusation against him of unseemly behaviour. They are called the Ismailis or Seveners.

The Ismailis played an important role in the founding of the Fatimid caliphate in North Africa in 910. During the Fatimid rule – which, later exercised from Cairo, continued until 1171 – Ismaili missionary zeal helped incorporate two sects into Islam without their shedding some non-Islamic practices and concepts: the Alawis (literally, followers of Ali) and Druzes.

Like the Ismailis, the Alawis believe in seven imams,[10] to whom they attribute divine and miraculous qualities. They hold Ali in higher esteem than any of the earlier prophets mentioned in the Koran: Adam, Noah, Moses, Jesus, and Mohammed. They follow certain rituals derived mainly from Christianity, including the celebration of Easter and Christmas. Since they have been traditionally concentrated in the Ansarieh mountains of north-western Syria, they are also known as Nusairis.

The Druzes derive their name from Darazi, an eleventh-century Ismaili missionary, whose followers regarded Hakim, a Fatimid caliph, as a 'hidden imam'. They do not feel bound by two of the five obligations enjoined upon Muslims: fasting during Ramadan and pilgrimage to Mecca. Persecution by the Sunnis drove them to the mountainous regions of Syria–Lebanon–Palestine. They are now to be found in the Druze mountains of southern Syria, the mountainous area of south Lebanon, and Israel.

Taking the Arab East as a whole, the Shias (including the Alawis) and Druzes are no more than 15 per cent of the population. But they are a majority in Iraq and Bahrain, and an influential minority in Syria, Lebanon, North Yemen, and Kuwait. In contrast the Sunnis are 77 per cent of the Arab East's population.

All Sunni Muslims are Arab, excepting the two and a half million Kurds in Iraq. As descendants of the Indo-European tribes that settled in south-eastern Turkey, northern Iran, and north-eastern Iraq, the Kurds trace their distinct history as mountain people to the seventh century B.C. It was not until fourteen centuries later that they embraced Islam, the religion of their conquerors: the Arabs from the plains. While retaining their language and their way of life, the Kurds proved to be as devout Muslims as the Arabs. In fact Saladin (Salah al Din al Ayubi), the famous Muslim warrior who expelled the Crusaders from Jerusalem in 1187, was a Kurd.

This expulsion was a setback for the Christians, both abroad and at home. Christianity had been implanted into the Arab East, in the fifth century, as the official religion of the Byzantine empire. That it thrived is apparent from the fact that the majority of the inhabitants of Greater Syria during the eleventh century were Christian. With the ascendancy of Islam in the region the Christians, both Orthodox and Latin (i.e. Maronite Catholic), were treated as dhimmi – the state of being a non-Muslim under Islamic rule – and accorded personal and religious tolerance, but not equality before the law.

Excepting today's Lebanon, the Christians are a small minority in the Fertile Crescent: 5 per cent in Iraq, 6 in Jordan, 8 in Syria, and an estimated 12 per cent among the Palestinians. 'The Christians have become integrated in the predominantly Muslim populations without losing their religious identity or communal tradition,' states Hudson. 'It is noteworthy that the 2.5 to 3 million Eastern Orthodox Arabs of today take pride in their pre-Islamic identity and indigenous presence and claim that they are co-equal members with Muslims in the Arab nation.'[11] This is equally true of the 3.5 million Christians in present-day Egypt, known as Copts, a derivative of the Greek term Aigyptios that was applied to all Egyptians before the Arab conquest in 640. The six million followers of Christianity in the Arab East are therefore generally considered to be Christian Arabs.

Not surprisingly Lebanon, ruled by a Christian president, played a significant role in founding the League of Arab States in March 1945, along with Egypt, Syria, Transjordan (now Jordan), Saudi Arabia and North Yemen.[12] Following its recognition by the United Nations as a regional body in 1958, the Arab League has been acting inter alia as the Arab regional United Nations Educational, Scientific and Cultural Organisation, and World Health Organisation. It has been instrumental in creating an Arab postal union, an Arab union of wireless communication and telecommunication, a nationality code, and an Arab cultural treaty[13] – as well as instituting an economic boycott of Israel since its founding in 1948. It is the headquarters of seventeen Arab unions, including the union of iron and steel workers, and physicians and veterinarians; and it now has eleven specialised ministerial councils and seventeen permanent technical committees.[14]

Shared concepts of Arabism have helped foster common objectives in politics, culture and economics. The Arab states are united in their support for the liberation of Palestine, the only part of the Arab homeland still in non-Arab hands. Culturally they are committed to working for the resurgence of Arab civilisation.

Their economic objective is to safeguard Arab oil and secure the best possible price for it. The Organisation of Arab Petroleum Exporting Countries was formed in 1968 for this purpose. Unlike the Organisation of Petroleum Exporting Countries, OAPEC does not exclude political considerations from its decision-making process. It used oil exports as a political weapon during the October 1973 war in the Middle East. By so doing it helped to project the Arabs as a major economic and political power in world affairs.

All Arab states are committed to the goal of rapid economic and social development. The oil-rich states have been assisting those with lesser natural resources through governmental and private channels. Besides the investment banks in such countries as Kuwait, Saudi Arabia, the United Arab Emirates, and Qatar, the Arab Fund for Social and Economic Development and the Arab Bank for Agricultural and Industrial Development have been active in this field.

Depending on the economic and human resources available, the Arab governments are modernising their societies – that is, increasing production, both agricultural and industrial; literacy; exposure to mass media; and urbanisation. This is as true of the traditional monarchies as it is of the republics.

2

# ARAB MONARCHIES

The traditional regimes in the Middle East can be subdivided into kingdoms and emirates (principalities) since Saudi Arabia, Oman, and Jordan are ruled by kings, while Kuwait, Bahrain, Qatar and the United Arab Emirates by emirs.[1] All these states came into being between 1921 and 1971 – and always with the active help of Britain, then the leading imperialist power in the region.

Excepting Jordan, all the kingdoms and emirates are in the Arabian Peninsula, the least populated part of the Arab East, which until the late 1960s was also the least economically developed. Since then a dramatic rise in oil revenues has financed unprecedently fast economic development, and transformed these countries into some of the richest in the world. Yet the social system in these states is unevenly developed.

Although all are monarchies, the way authority is exercised by the ruler varies. 'Some monarchies like Saudi Arabia and the smaller Arabian emirates are patriarchal in a distinctly familial way; others like Jordan are more bureaucratically developed,' states Hudson. 'Fabulous petroleum wealth has transformed several of these kingdoms into advanced welfare states, yet they remain governed by medieval structures and values.'[2]

The most medieval of them all is the Sultanate[3] of Oman, the second largest state in the Arabian Peninsula. Oman was part until 850 of the Dar al Islam (which emerged in the Peninsula of the seventh century). In that year the Omani tribes, loyal to the Ibadhi school within the Khariji[4] movement – which rejected the idea of having a caliph – broke away from the Abbasid caliphate of Baghdad, and set up an independent domain in the plateau of Jebel Akhdar (Green Mountain).

In 1507 Omani independence suffered a blow when the port of Muscat was lost to the invading Portuguese, who were to be followed by the Dutch and finally the British. It was not until 1650 that the Omanis, led by the Yaruba family, regained Muscat. A century later the Yarubas were displaced by Al Bu Saids as the ruling family. The power of this dynasty reached its peak in the 1850s when the Omani empire extended to the eastern shores of Africa. The collapse of this empire in the following decade so weakened the ruling family that it was overpowered by tribes from the mountainous interior. In 1871 the British attacked Muscat and restored the Al Bu Saids to power. Oman thus became a de facto colony of Britain.

Forty years later the traditional rivalry between the coast and the hinterland came to the surface again, with the leader of the tribes of the interior, the Imam, challenging the suzerainty of the Sultan of Muscat. Imperial Britain stepped in again, on behalf of the Sultan. The result was a compromise, formalised in the Treaty of Sib of 1920. It allowed the Imam to rule the interior in consultation with the tribal chiefs while the Sultan, aided by British arms and money, controlled the coastal area.

Britain exercised its imperial authority in 1932 by deposing Sultan Taimur on the grounds of fiscal irresponsibility and placing his son, Said, on the throne. Sultan Said ibn Taimur was challenged twice in the 1950s by the Imam, Ghalib ibn Ali, who went so far as to proclaim the independent state of Ibadhi in 1954. On both occasions the rebellion was put down by the Omani troops, armed and led by the British.

The next challenge to Sultan Said came in 1963 from the inhabitants of the south-western province of Dhofar, comprising nearly half of the kingdom, an area of 82,000 square miles, which had been annexed by the sultanate in 1879. The Dhofaris felt neglected and exploited; and their secessionist movement gradually turned into an armed national liberation struggle. The victory of the leftist forces in the adjoining South Yemen, on the eve of the British withdrawal in November 1967, boosted the morale of the Dhofari revolutionaries. This, and the total inflexibility of Sultan Said, infamous for his insularity and the repression of his subjects, made the British apprehensive. They therefore engineered a coup in July 1970 which replaced Sultan Said[5] with his only (British-trained) son, Qaboos.

Implacably opposed to progress, Sultan Said had prevented his subjects from using, for instance, patent medicines, trousers, radios, books, and even spectacles. Towards the end of his rule he was considering closing the three primary schools he had allowed earlier. 'The reign of Sultan ibn Taimur during the eventful period from 1932 to 1970 was marked by a degree of absolutism and isolationism probably without parallel,' states Hudson. 'It was one of the most successful and resolute efforts by any ruler to prevent modernization.'[6] He was such a miser that he left practically all of the oil revenue, which climbed from £8 million in 1967 to £44 million in 1970, untouched.[7]

Sultan Qaboos ended Oman's isolation by successfully seeking membership of the Arab League and the United Nations. He removed the ban on smoking, dancing, use of modern medicines, and wearing of western dress. Aided by rising oil production – which reached a peak of 400,000 barrels per day in the mid 1970s – he spent large sums on building or expanding the infrastructure of roads, electric power plants and communications, and providing social services to its estimated

800,000 inhabitants. The dramatic jump in economic development, social services and defence can be gauged by the fact that the state budget increased ninety-five-fold between 1971 and 1976. However, half of the 1976 budget of 606 million Omani riyals (£730 million) went to defence.[8] This was the case after the government had – with massive foreign assistance in men, money, and weapons – succeeded in defeating the Dhofari rebels in late 1975.

By then the modernisation of the governmental system, begun soon after the 1970 coup, had been completed. It had created a council of ministers and such specialist bodies as the Development Council, the Foreign Affairs Council and the Defence Council. But these bodies are advisory; and the members, appointed directly by the Sultan, are responsible to him. All laws and decrees are issued personally by the Sultan; and all international agreements and treaties are signed by him.

In other words, despite an impressive and rapid expansion of governmental functions and the economy, the political system basically remains that of an absolute monarchy, as it did in the days of Sultan Said, and before. There is no written constitution, and no (fully or partially nominated) legislative or consultative assembly.

The only other Arab East state that rivals Oman in the autocracy of its monarch is Saudi Arabia. In fact there the ruler combines the roles of the Sultan and the Imam (religious leader): the two figures in the Omani history who often fought each other. Saudi Arabia is a theocracy with an absolute monarch at the top who is not only the head of the royal family and the chief of state and its commander-in-chief, but is also the leader of all tribal chiefs (shaikh al mashaikh) and the supreme religious leader (imam). Furthermore, as the commander of the faithful (emir al mumineen), Saudi Arabia's ruler is required to safeguard the holy places of Islam, as well as the Islamic community scattered throughout the world. (Ironically, the Saudi Arabian regime itself is based on a narrow base of loyalty – to the House of Saud: the very name of the state carries the Saudi stamp.)

The history of Saudi Arabia goes back to the mid-eighteenth century when Mohammed ibn Abdul Wahhab (1703–87), a militant alem (religious–legal scholar), led a puritanical movement for the abolition of the elaborate Islamic structure which had evolved over the past millennium, and which was being perpetuated by the ruling Ottoman caliph in Constantinople. He called for a return to the simplicity of the Islam of the prophet Mohammed's days, and the strict application of the Sharia, the Islamic law. In 1744 he allied himself with Mohammed ibn Saud, the leader of the Saudi tribe from Najd in central-eastern Arabia; and this gave considerable military muscle to his movement.

By the early nineteenth century a coalition of tribes, fired by the tenets of Wahhabism and led by Mohammed ibn Saud, had conquered a large part of the Arabian Peninsula. Further advances by these tribes were checked by the British – who controlled the Peninsula's coastline from Bahrain to Aden – and the Ottomans. The latter then went on the offensive, and pushed the leading Saudi tribe into its home territory of Najd. In 1891 the Rashedis, acting as clients of the Ottomans, sent the Saudis into exile to Kuwait.

It was not until 1902 that Abdul Aziz ibn Abdul Rahman al Saud (1881–1953) ventured out of Kuwait to regain Riyadh, the capital of Najd. Within the next decade he had extended his domain to the rest of Najd as well as the eastern province of Hasa. He prepared to attack the western province of Hejaz (containing the holy cities of Mecca and Medina), then ruled by Sharif Hussein ibn Ali. But his plans were interrupted by the outbreak of the First World War during the course of which Sharif Hussein formed an alliance with the British against the Ottoman Turks.

Abdul Aziz now took to settling his bedouin (nomadic) followers on land in the Ikhwan (Brotherhood) colonies. By the early 1920s some 200 Ikhwan settlements, scattered around the Wahhabi territory in the peninsula, provided him with a military force of several thousand armed men, eager to expand their domain. Their chance came in 1924 when, following the abolition of the institution of the caliphate by the secularist Mustapha Kemal Ataturk in Turkey, Sharif Hussein of Hejaz declared himself the caliph. An incensed Abdul Aziz attacked Hejaz in 1925 and captured it. The following year he assumed the title of King of Hejaz; and in 1932 he combined his realms in the east and the west and named the new state – covering about 80 per cent of the 745,000 square miles of the Arabian Peninsula – Saudi Arabia.

The Saudi kingdom was founded at a time when its ruler was facing an economic crisis caused by a severe drop in the number of pilgrims to Mecca (and thus in the pilgrimage tax payable to the government) due to a worldwide economic depression. It was against this background that Abdul Aziz granted an oil concession to Standard Oil Company of California in 1933 for £50,000 paid in gold, as advance against future royalties on actual oil production. Exploration began immediately in Hasa, and modest commercial extraction ensued five years later.

The Second World War interrupted oil production, but once it was over, it jumped from 50,000 to 900,000 barrels per day in 1951. The subsequent boom in the economy overstretched the rudimentary institutions of the state, supervised by the king and some of his close relatives. Yet it was not until October 1953 – a month before his death – that King Abdul Aziz issued a decree establishing a council of ministers as an advisory body.

Five more years passed before the ruler, King Saud ibn Abdul Aziz, gave executive and legislative powers to the ministers. He did so only because by then (1958) the country's administration, lacking any budget or even an accounting system, had come to a virtual halt,[9] and Crown Prince Feisal ibn Abdul Aziz had been put in overall charge of state affairs. In 1960 a draft constitution, declaring Islam to be the state religion, private property and capital as 'fundamental values of natural wealth' and specifying the creation of a national assembly of 90 to 120 members – two thirds elected and the rest nominated by the monarch – was presented to King Saud for approval. He rejected the document, stating, 'The Koran is the oldest and the most efficient of the world's constitutions.'[10]

But the overthrow of the monarchy in neighbouring North Yemen in September 1962 undermined the smugness of the Saudi royal family. Two months later Crown Prince Feisal issued a ten-point programme covering the constitutional, religious, judicial, social and economic aspects of the state. It declared its commitment to the improvement of 'the lot of the average citizen' through intensified economic development and the implementation of 'social legislation'. It promised the issuance of a 'Basic Law' (i.e. constitution), based on the Koran and the Sharia, which would provide for the citizen's fundamental rights, 'including the right to freely express his opinion within the limits of Islamic belief and public policy'. It also pledged to reform the existing Committees for Public Morality in accordance with the Sharia, and establish a Judicial Council of twenty members – drawn from the ulema (religious–legal scholars) and the muftis (religious–legal jurists)[11] – to reconcile the legal problems of a modern society with the rules laid down by prophet Mohammed.[12]

The stress laid on the religious-cum-legal system stems from the fact that the constitutional basis of the government is rooted in the Sharia, the Islamic law.[13] The religious hierarchy is interwoven with secular authority at all levels in the kingdom. Locally, the religious establishment – composed of the imam, the ulema, and the qadi (religious judge) – works in conjunction with the government administrator. The ulema are a link between the imam and the faithful. Their task is to study and interpret the Sharia as well as advise the imam on how to safeguard the purity of the faith and ensure adherence to the Islamic obligations by Muslims. The muttaween, religious police, execute the imam's decisions. They see to it that Islamic practices are observed. They also instruct the faithful at educational institutions, and outside, on the observance of Islamic edicts. At the national level the king, who is the chief imam, is assisted by the minister of religion/justice (traditionally a direct descendant of Mohammed ibn Abdul Wahhab), the chief qadi, and the grand mufti.

The authority of the religious establishment is formalised in the Wahhabi Religious Council, consisting of ulema, qadis and muftis. Parallel to this there exists the Council of Senior Princes, drawn from the six main branches of the House of Saud. A decision on such a subject as abdication/enthronement, or the appointment of the Crown Prince, by the Council of Senior Princes is not valid unless it is endorsed by the

Wahhabi Religious Council through a fatwa (legal deduction) issued by the grand mufti.

It was for instance the Wahhabi Religious Council's decision, announced by the grand mufti, that legitimised in March 1964 the transfer of power from King Saud to Crown Prince Feisal, decided earlier by the Council of Senior Princes. Disapproving of King Saud's extravagant and luxurious lifestyle, the religious establishment had all along favoured Feisal, well known for his piety and asceticism. Eight months later, Feisal became King; and Saud went into exile. As king, Feisal failed to keep his promise to offer his subjects a written constitution and 'fundamental rights', including freedom of expression, contained in the ten-point programme he had proclaimed as crown prince in November 1962. On the contrary he muzzled even the mildest of critics. This drove the opposition underground. In the end King Feisal fell victim to the bullets of a young American-educated royal prince in March 1975.

Soon after his accession King Khaled ibn Abdul Aziz considered establishing a consultative assembly, but nothing came of it. Indeed the Saudi royal family encouraged – successfully – the rulers of neighbouring Kuwait and Bahrain to suspend or dissolve the popularly elected parliaments that existed there. In mid-1978 Crown Prince Fahd opposed public participation in the Saudi government on the ground that elections would not confer leadership on the country's most qualified people: the young Saudis who had been educated abroad. 'We have invested heavily in educating these young men, and now we want to collect a dividend on our investment,' he told *Time* magazine. 'But if we were to have elections . . . the winners would be rich businessmen.'[14]

But the overthrow of the dictatorial Mohammed Reza Shah of Iran by a popular Islamic republican movement in February 1979 cracked the face of confidence presented by the House of Saud to the outside world. Nine months later the royal family's prestige suffered a severe blow when its authority was challenged by several hundred armed commandos who took over the Grand Mosque of Mecca for a fortnight.

The Mecca uprising was eventually crushed; but the experience left the ruling family shaken. King Khaled appointed a nine-man committee, presided by his half-brother Prince Nayef ibn Abdul Aziz, the interior minister, to draft laws for a consultative assembly and a governmental system.[15] All in all, it had taken the House of Saud eighteen years to take initial steps towards transforming a promise, first made in 1962, into reality.

During that period the economic face of the kingdom had been altered beyond recognition. Annual oil revenue had zoomed from $302 million to $70,000 million. Whereas the First Five Year Plan (1970–5) had cost $8,000 million, the Second Plan amounted to $142,000 million. More than 80 per cent of the Plans' funds had been invested in building or expanding the infrastructure of roads, communications and power plants. These unprecedently ambitious plans had been realised only by importing a vast pool of foreign labour, skilled and unskilled. It had been drawn from all over the Arab world as well as the Indian subcontinent, Taiwan and South Korea.

Although forming only about 30 per cent of the country's total population of seven million, the foreign residents estimatedly constitute 70 per cent of the workforce.[16] The reasons for the low Saudi proportion in the national labour force are: 10 per cent of the five million Saudi nationals, being nomadic,[17] are outside the organised economy; an estimated half of the settled Saudis are below the working age of eighteen; social-religious laws bar women from taking up jobs except as teachers and nurses (in all-female establishments); and the Armed Forces, the National Guard, the police, and the muttaween claim a substantial percentage of Saudi nationals. The overdominance of foreigners in the Saudi workforce is regarded by the ruling family as undesirable. Yet the Third Five Year Plan costing $250,000 million cannot be fully realised without a further import of hundreds of thousands of foreign workers into the kingdom.

A similar situation exists in the adjoining, oil-rich state of Qatar: there an estimated two thirds of the labour force is foreign.[18] Parallels between the two neighbours go beyond the economic profile. Qatar's reigning Thani family feel close to the House of Saud since both the ruling families follow the strict Hanbali code of the Wahhabis.[19] The intermeshing of the religious establishment with the state administration is almost as tight in Qatar as it is in Saudi Arabia.

But unlike the Saudi royal family, the Thanis began political reform as early as 1964 when they appointed an advisory council with authority to issue laws and decrees for 'the fundamental principles and basic rules of overall policy'.[20] They did so under pressure applied partly by the National Unity Front's popular agitation (in 1963) for a proper state budget, a representative council, and for curbs on the unlimited prerogatives of the ruling family; and partly by the British government.

Ever since its intervention in the Qatari–Bahrain battles of 1867–8, Britain had been the dominant foreign influence in Qatari politics. The end of the Ottoman suzerainty over Qatar in 1916 brought the ruling Thani family closer to Britain. They signed a treaty with London, whereby Britain guaranteed Qatar's territorial integrity against external aggression while Qatar promised not to cede any rights to a third party without British consent.[21]

With oil output reaching commercial proportions in 1949, the importance of Qatar increased – as did British interference in its internal affairs. In 1951 and again in 1960 the rulers were made to abdicate, at London's behest, with the second abdication creating a crisis which could only be resolved by the new monarch, Shaikh Ahmed ibn Ali al Thani, sharing power with his cousin, Shaikh Khalifa ibn Hamad, the crown prince.

The ruler's extravagance, which cost the country half of its considerable oil revenue,[22] and his long absences abroad, were the prime reasons behind the outbreak of popular discontent in 1963. The work of the advisory council, appointed the following year, did not reach fruition until 1970, when the ruler promulgated a provisional constitution. While describing the regime as 'democratic', the constitution named the al Thanis the country's hereditary ruling family, and invested the ruler with 'the supreme authority under the law'.[23] It specified a ten-member council of ministers, appointed and led by the ruler, to be the chief executive authority. The ministers were to be the additional members of the twenty-three-strong consultative assembly, whose twenty members were to be chosen by the ruler out of forty popularly elected representatives. Shaikh Ahmed appointed a cabinet of ten – with seven ministers drawn from the Thani family – but did nothing to establish the consultative assembly, even after the country had become independent in September 1971.

Five months after independence Crown Prince Shaikh Khalifa, assisted by the army, overthrew the monarch in a bloodless coup while the latter was abroad. As ruler, Shaikh Khalifa introduced a proper state budget and called to session the first consultative assembly, but this was not constituted as specified in the constitution: the members, drawn from the royal family and local notables, were all nominees of the monarch. The assembly is purely advisory, offering recommendations on subjects referred to it by the ruler.

Yet demands for a representative government have been comparatively muted. This is so not only because the state's intelligence and repressive machines are efficient, but also because some of the benefits of the dramatic jump in oil revenue – running at $3,600 million in 1976[24] – have percolated down; the country, being only 4,200 square miles in area, is easily governable; its population is small (200,000, of whom only about 40,000 are Qatari nationals) and concentrated (with 70 per cent living in the state capital); and the large size of the ruling family – 1,000 strong in the mid 1970s[25] – has a stabilising effect. Despite the dramatic events of 1979 in Iran and Saudi Arabia the regime has not felt pressured either to step forward and hold elections or move backward and abolish the consultative assembly.

In contrast the experience of the United Arab Emirates – the only other state of the Arabian Peninsula with a fully nominated consultative assembly, called the federal national assembly – has been different. During 1978 the federal assembly overstepped its bounds and invited the cabinet to form a joint committee to examine immigration into the Emirates. In early 1979 it invited the cabinet to its sessions; and together they issued the joint memorandum of March 1979 which combined a call for parliamentary democracy with stronger federal control over individual emirates.

Although the federation of the seven principalities along the littoral of the Peninsula – Abu Dhabi, Dubai, Sharjah, Ajman, Umm al Qualwain, and Fujaira – materialised in July 1971, under British aegis,[26] the first step in this direction had been taken in 1952. In that year Britain, which had established its hegemony over the region in the 1890s, formed the Trucial States Council, composed of the seven emirs, as an advisory body.

However, the Trucial States Council did not start meeting regularly until 1960, when oil was found in Abu Dhabi, the largest of the emirates. With substantial oil exports commencing two years later, British interest in Abu Dhabi rose. When its ruler Shaikh Shakhbut ibn Sultan al Nahyan refused to spend oil revenue on economic development, he was overthrown by the British in 1966, and replaced by his brother Shaikh Zaid. Abu Dhabi then underwent rapid economic transformation, but only with the aid of a foreign workforce: a fact reflected in the dramatic population leap, from 17,000 in 1966 to 300,000 a decade later.

A similar development occurred in Dubai, the second most important emirate. However, here the rise in population and prosperity had more to do with the boom in trade – imports of £3 million in 1958 rose to over £200 million in 1975 – than with oil production, which started in 1969 and which, at 317,000 bpd in 1976, was only about one fifth of Abu Dhabi's.[27]

It was primarily Abu Dhabi's booming oil revenue that encouraged the five small poor emirates to agree to a federation some months before the scheduled British departure in December 1971, and it has been oil income that has enabled Abu Dhabi to meet 90 per cent of the federal expenses since the federation was formed.

The provisional constitution of 1971 provides for a Supreme Council of Emirs (Commanders), a federal council of ministers, a federal national assembly, and federal judiciary. The Supreme Council (of seven emirs) deals with defence, foreign affairs, economic development and education. On an important issue a decision is reached only if five rulers, including those of Abu Dhabi and Dubai (who are respectively the federation's president and vice-president), support it. The twenty-seven ministers are drawn from all the emirates, with the largest, Abu Dhabi, providing eight, and the smaller ones two each. The technocrat ministers are often outnumbered by those with a ruling-family background by one to two. All the forty members of the federal assembly are nominated (by respective emirs), and tend to be the younger educated sons of the leading families. The constitution assigns the assembly an advisory role: to offer opinions to the Supreme Council on matters referred to it by the cabinet.

But, as stated earlier, the assembly took unprecedented initiatives in 1978–9. The joint memorandum of March 1979, issued in conjunction with the cabinet, proposed that the existing inter-emirate boundaries be abolished and the emirates' individual revenues centralised. Moreover, the document recommended that the federal assembly should cease to be a 'consultative council' and instead become a 'true legislative authority' with full legislative powers.[28] The boldness of the assembly stemmed partly from the deep division among the emirs on the degree of centralisation to be effected, that had paralysed the Supreme Council for many months, and partly from the success of the revolutionary, republican movement across the Gulf in Iran.

Unwilling to yield to these demands, the Supreme Council acted swiftly to first put its house in order, with Shaikh Zaid of Abu Dhabi and Shaikh Rashed ibn Said al Maktum of Dubai ending their personal rivalry, which had bedevilled the federation since its inception. The Supreme Council asked Shaikh Rashed to become the prime minister. Thus charged, Shaikh Rashed went about defusing the political situation, and had some success. But various factors, political and non-political, point towards an unsettled future.

Apart from its strategic position in the Gulf, its substantial area (30,000 square miles) and fast increasing population (already 1.2 million in 1979),[29] the UAE has vast oil resources currently being pumped out at the rate of about two million bpd. What makes the UAE unusually vulnerable are lack of cohesion among its constituent emirates, heavy dependence on foreign labour which accounts for 80 per cent of its workforce,[30] and its traditional trade and kinship links with Iran. These ties are particularly strong in the case of Dubai, the largest trading port in the Gulf with a substantial Shia population.

However, the Arab East state where the pull of Shia Iran is probably strongest is Bahrain, the majority of whose 317,000 inhabitants are Shia.[31] Bahrain, an archipelago of thirty-three islands (of which only three with an area of 210 square miles are occupied), was ruled by the Shia dynasty of Iran from 1603 until 1783, when the local (Sunni) Khalifa family overthrew the Iranian authority. But the Khalifas' independence lasted only a few decades: they came under British influence in 1820. A series of treaties signed by them with Britain in 1861, 1880 and 1892 turned Bahrain into a British protectorate. The deposing of Shaikh Issa al Khalifa in 1923, and the appointment of Sir Charles Belgrave as adviser to the ruler Shaikh Hamid al Khalifa, set the final seal on British control of Bahrain. This continued until August 1971.

Bahrain was spared the worst effects of the collapse of its important pearling industry – caused by the arrival of cheap, artificial Japanese pearls in the early 1930s – by the timely discovery of oil. With the development of an oil industry came organised labour which first resorted to strike action in 1938 to gain inter alia trade union rights. This failed. Nearly a generation later, at the height of the Arab nationalist movement led by Gamal Abdul Nasser of Egypt, the Bahrainis mounted massive demonstrations against the Anglo–French–Israeli attack on Egypt in November 1956.

The accession of the young Shaikh Issa ibn Salman in 1961 was followed by demonstrations and a strike by secondary school teachers a year later. In 1965 the workers of the western-owned Bahrain Petroleum Company struck. In each case the ruler acted with a heavy hand against the strikers. It was not until early 1970 that he showed the first signs of temporising when he appointed a twelve-member advisory Council of State.

As the British prepared to leave in August 1971 the ruler transformed the Council of State into the council of ministers, and charged it with framing a constitution that would provide for limited popular participation in the government. But before the cabinet could complete its task the country was rocked by severe rioting and strikes in March 1972, and again in September. As a result the ruler compromised by agreeing to have twenty-one of the forty-two members of the proposed constituent assembly elected by voters. These elections were held on limited franchise in December.

The constituent assembly finished drafting the constitution in June. The ruler approved the document, and ordered elections six months later. Although the franchise was restricted to only 30,000 males, the nationalist–leftist Popular Bloc list won twenty-one of the thirty (elected) seats in the forty-two member national assembly. (The rest of the seats were filled by the twelve-member cabinet appointed by the ruler and responsible to him.) The nationalist–leftist coalition members pressed for the introduction of income tax, granting of trade union rights, and nationalisation of (predominantly western-owned) large companies.

The ruler responded by promulgating a law on state security in October 1974, which empowered the interior minister to detain 'any suspect' without being charged for up to three months. An impasse ensued when the assembly refused to endorse the law. In August 1975 the ruler arrested many leftist leaders, dissolved the national assembly, and suspended the constitution. This drove all opposition underground where it remained until the Iranian revolution in early 1979.

Aware of the popularity of the Iranian revolution and its leader, Ayatollah Ruhollah Khomeini, particularly among the Shia majority – composed of workers, civil servants and merchants – the ruler banned all news on the subject. The security forces broke up a massive demonstration on Jerusalem Day (15 May) with 900 arrests. Undaunted, forty ulema issued a twelve-point charter demanding inter alia that Bahrain be declared an Islamic republic, that the state security law be reviewed, and unemployment lowered. The ruler's response was to suppress the demonstrations by students and others in support of these demands, and to expel Said Hadi al Modaresi, the Shia leader.[32]

Although only 20 per cent of the indigenous population, the Shias in nearby Kuwait had, by virtue of their backing for the Iranian revolution, become so much of a threat as to lead the ruler to expel the leading Shia preacher, and ban private meetings of more than twenty people.[33] Encouraged by the events in Iran, the Shias had taken to meeting at the Shabaan mosque in Kuwait city, where the theme of discussions had gradually moved from Shia–Sunni relations to 'the real problems of wages, prices, rents, the political situation, and corruption'.[34] In a way, the mosque came to replace the national assembly, dissolved in 1976, as a forum for the expression of popular grievances. The dissolution of the national assembly had marked a major setback to the development of the democratic institutions which dated back to 1921, when the ruling Sabah family was successfully persuaded to share some of its power.

The Sabahs were members of the Anaza tribal federation which had been in occupation of the area since 1710, and which had developed trading facilities at Kuwait port. The region was then under the nominal suzerainty of the Ottoman Turks. The incursion of the British into the area, marked by the opening of a base by the (British) East India Company in 1776, began to undermine the Turkish authority.

In the late nineteenth century – when Kuwait had become a centre of rivalry between Turkey, Britain, Russia and Germany – the British were alarmed by the German plans to extend the proposed Berlin–Baghdad railway to Kuwait. The railway project fell through when the pro-British Shaikh Mubarak al Sabah became emir in 1896, after murdering his two half-brothers. Intent on ending the Ottoman overlordship, Shaikh Mubarak gave Britain in 1899 the right of exclusive presence in Kuwait, for an annual sum of £15,000, thus turning Kuwait into a British protectorate.[35]

When the Ottoman empire fell in 1918 the Kuwaiti ruler, Shaikh Salem al Sabah (1917–21), tried to expand his realm at the expense of the adjoining Hasa province, then controlled by Abdul Aziz al Saud. The attempt failed. In fact the subsequent offensive by the Saudi forces robbed the Sabahs of much of their own domain. Britain intervened actively in 1922–3 and had the lost territory returned to the Kuwaiti emir, Shaikh Ahmed al Sabah (1921–50).

It was during Shaikh Ahmed's reign that the first step toward political reform was taken. The local merchants were inducted into the governmental system in 1921 through the device of an elected twelve-member advisory committee. However, the ruler soon ended the practice. In the early 1930s Kuwait's considerable pearling industry faced crippling competition from the cheap, artificial Japanese pearls. Although oil exploration, which started in 1934, relieved the situation somewhat, the continuing economic downturn led to popular demonstrations in 1938 for political-economic reform.

The ruler yielded by asking the Merchant Society to select a fourteen-member council, and then directing the council to produce a constitution. The draft constitution specified a popularly elected legislative assembly with powers to veto 'all internal concessions and lease monopolies as well as external agreements and treaties'. Since this would have interfered with Britain's colonial administration of Kuwait and, more importantly, the British companies' objective of extracting the best possible terms for oil concessions, London disfavoured the constitution. Shaikh Ahmed therefore rejected the document and dissolved the council.

Production of oil, which had begun in 1938, was interrupted by the Second World War. It was only after 1946 that oil extraction and exports reached commercial proportions. The closing down of the oil industry in neighbouring Iran during the period 1951–3 led to a rapid increase in Kuwait's oil output. In 1955, during the rule of Shaikh Abdullah al Salem al Sabah, Kuwait became the leading oil exporter in the region, and maintained this position for the next decade.

The economic boom provided the backdrop against which political liberalisation was carried out. Elections to local councils – charged with education, health and administration of waqfs – were held in 1954. The National Cultural Club, founded by Ahmed Khatib, did well in these elections. In mid-1955 the NCC revived the pre-war demand for a legislative assembly. By mounting successful popular demonstrations against Anglo–French–Israeli aggression towards Egypt in late 1956, in the capital, the NCC showed itself to be the chief political force in the country.

But the ruler's promise to offer his subjects a constitution and a national assembly did not come until 1960, when claims by the republican regime of Iraq on Kuwait, and the scheduled exit of Britain in the following year, compelled the ruler to take steps to give the populace some stake in the system. Yet it was only after Iraq had reiterated its claims in strong terms after the British withdrawal from Kuwait, in June 1961, that the ruler finally appointed a constituent assembly in December.

The constitution was promulgated in November 1962. While giving 'pre-eminence' to Islam and the Islamic law, the Sharia, the constitution guarantees 'complete freedom for all sections of the population'. It also guarantees 'personal liberty' and 'the freedom of the press', and allows the citizen 'freedom to join trade unions or contract out of them'. It assigns the task of safeguarding these freedoms to an independent judiciary.[36]

Elections to the fifty seats in the national assembly (whose membership is automatically extended to the council of ministers appointed by the ruler), first held in January 1963, were repeated three times at the stipulated four-year interval. Although the electoral system, including the demarcation of the five-member constituencies, was tailored to favour the ruling family; political parties were disallowed; the franchise was limited to about 10 per cent of the citizens;[37] and the national assembly lacked executive power;[38] over the years it established itself as an independent body, voicing popular views on many internal and external matters. It provided 'an institutional means of expression and access to the main socio-political elements in contemporary Kuwait – the nomadic and sedentary tribes, the urban merchants and businessmen, and the politicised intellectuals and professionals'.[39]

This statement applies only to Kuwaiti nationals who in 1975 were about 44 per cent of the population, estimated at one million.[40] Among the non-Kuwaitis, the quarter million Palestinians were the largest single group. Due to their disproportionately high presence in educational institutions, the civil service, and the mass media, the Palestinians have had considerable influence on Kuwaiti public opinion and thus on the national assembly. For instance, the national assembly, reluctant to endorse the Egyptian–Israeli agreement of September 1975 (often known as the Sinai II agreement) opposed aid to Egypt. The intervention of the Syrian forces in June 1976 in the Lebanese civil war against the leftist Lebanese–Palestinian alliance angered most Palestinians, and created tension in Kuwait. Disruption of the press in Beirut, regarded as the freest in the Middle East, encouraged the Kuwaiti papers (largely staffed by Palestinians) to provide uncensored news in the Arab East. This alarmed and angered not only the Kuwaiti ruler, Shaikh Sabah al Sabah, but also the royal family of neighbouring Saudi Arabia.

Accusing the national assembly members of wasting time on debating legislation and indulging in 'malicious behaviour', the ruler suspended the house in August 1976. He also restricted press freedom and suspended four important articles of the constitution.[41] This action was taken in close collaboration with the House of Saud, who had earlier encouraged the Bahraini ruler to suspend the parliament there. The dissolution of the Kuwaiti national assembly by the emir in September 1977 signalled the end of the era of democratic reform that had begun, haltingly, in 1921.

The totally unexpected success of the republican revolution in Iran in February 1979 changed the situation almost overnight. The Iranian event was viewed favourably not only by the Shia minority, composed of bedouins, poor urban dwellers, and merchants, but also by the Palestinians. The latter noted the warmth with which Yasser Arafat, the Palestine Liberation Organisation leader, was received in Tehran by Ayatollah Khomeini, and learnt that the PLO had actively helped the Iranian revolutionaries in their struggle against the Shah.

Shaikh Jaber al Sabah, the Kuwaiti emir, resorted to tough action against the protesters by further restricting press freedom and banning discussion of public affairs at (even) private meetings of less than twenty people.[42] Then, in February 1980, he moved to placate the populace by appointing a constitutional commission of thirty-five members (including eight Shias) to recommend amendments to the constitution, with a view to reviving the institution of an elected assembly of some kind. By the end of the next February, the constitution had been amended, and elections to the national assembly held under it.

The impact of the surge for democracy, in the wake of the Iranian revolution, was felt as far as the Hashemite Kingdom of Jordan, where the house of representatives, dissolved in late 1974, was resurrected as a (nominated) consultative council in the spring of 1979. Significantly, at least half of the 2.9 million people of Jordan[43] are of Palestinian origin. This was the result of the wars in Palestine/Israel since 1948, which determined the boundaries and the composition of the population of contemporary Jordan: a country ruled by the Hashemi dynasty since 1923.

Jordan's reigning dynasty is part of the Hashem clan of the Quraish tribe to which prophet Mohammed belonged. The Hashemis became the ruling family of Mecca and the surrounding province of Hejaz in the tenth century. This continued until 1517 when – following the Ottoman Sultan Salem I's victory over the Mamelukes in Egypt – the head of the Hashemi ruling family, known as the Sharif (noble), sent an emissary to present the keys of Mecca to the Ottoman Sultan and offer him the title of Protector of the Holy Places. The Ottoman Sultan accepted both.

In 1893 Sultan Abdul Hamid II exiled Sharif Hussein ibn Ali of Mecca – the thirty-seventh in line of descent from prophet Mohammed – by 'inviting' him to live in Constantinople with his family. His exile ended only when the Sultan was removed in 1908 by the Young Turks. As stated earlier, during the First World War, Sharif Hussein ibn Ali allied himself with the British against the Ottoman Turks.[44] In June 1916 he led the Arab rebellion with the help of his sons: Ali, Abdullah, Feisal I, and Zaid.

After Turkey's defeat in 1918 Sharif Hussein declared himself the king of Hejaz. The Syrian National Congress, meeting in Damascus in February–March 1920, proclaimed the independence of Greater Syria, and the formation of a national government under Feisal ibn Hussein as a constitutional monarch. A similar gathering in Baghdad declared Iraq to be independent under the constitutional reign of Abdullah ibn Hussein as monarch. These declarations were rejected by the victors of the First World War: Britain and France.

The Supreme Council of the League of Nations, meeting in San Remo, Italy, in April 1920 gave France the mandate for Greater Syria, minus Palestine (which went to Britain), and Britain the mandate for an undivided Iraq. The French drove out Feisal I and his forces from Greater Syria. Feisal then accepted the throne of Iraq offered to him by his younger brother Abdullah, who prepared to attack the French forces. Abdullah was dissuaded from executing his plan by the British who carved out land east of the river Jordan, called it Transjordan, and presented it to him.

In April 1923 Britain announced that it would recognise the 'independence' of Transjordan under Abdullah's rule if a constitutional regime were established and a preferential treaty with London signed. The next month Abdullah declared Transjordan 'independent', but it was not until April 1928 that a constitution, stipulating that legal and administrative authority should be exercised by the ruler through a legislative council, was proclaimed. This nominated body was quite powerless. It was only in 1939 that it was transformed into a cabinet and given some powers.

Full independence came in 1946 when Abdullah proclaimed himself king, and promulgated a new constitution. A revised treaty signed between Transjordan and Britain stipulated mutual assistance in the event of war. In the Arab–Israeli war of 1948 the Arab Legion, founded in the mid-1920s and British trained and led, occupied the West Bank and east Jerusalem in what was then Palestine. Two years later King Abdullah formally merged these areas into his kingdom and renamed his country Jordan. Assassinated in May 1951, Abdullah was succeeded by his son Talal, who issued a new constitution in January 1952. His abdication seven months later, on grounds of ill-health, brought his son Hussein to the throne.

The 1952 constitution specifies a parliament made up of a fully nominated senate of thirty, and an elected house of representatives of sixty. The normal four-year tenure of the two chambers can be extended by a year or more by the king. In theory legislative powers are shared between parliament and the king; in practice parliament's authority is minimal. It is the king who issues all laws and decrees, signs foreign treaties, and nominates the prime minister and his cabinet. Political parties, allowed during the mid 1950s, have remained banned. During the first two decades of the constitution the country was placed under martial law for over eleven years.[45]

The loss of the West Bank and east Jerusalem in the June 1967 Arab–Israeli war had a traumatic effect on the ruler and his subjects. An increase in the number of refugees from these territories, and rising militancy among the Palestinians in Jordan, led to fighting between the Palestinian commandos and the Jordanian army in September 1970, in which the latter won.

Although King Hussein ibn Talal refused to join the Arab–Israeli war of October 1973, he continued to press for Israel's evacuation of the occupied territories of the West Bank and east Jerusalem. This ceased only when a summit conference of the Arab League, in October–November 1974, recognised the Palestine Liberation Organisation as 'the sole and legitimate representative of the Palestinian people', and supported 'the right of the Palestinian people to establish an independent national authority on any liberated territory (of Palestine)'.

Having (reluctantly) accepted the Arab League revolution, King Hussein had parliament authorise him to dismiss individual senators, and postpone 'the legislative elections' for up to one year (at a time) 'in case the holding of elections is rendered impossible by virtue of extraordinary circumstances'. He then dissolved both houses of parliament. A week later he renominated the senate, reducing the number of members with a Palestinian background from fifteen (in the dissolved chamber) to seven.[46]

However, by refraining from suspending or abrogating the constitution, and instead choosing to approach parliament to amend it (if only to further increase the ruler's powers), the king indirectly acknowledged the supremacy of parliament. Such behaviour was in direct contrast to the pattern dominant among the monarchies of the Arabian Peninsula.

But, as Hudson points out, 'Jordan is more thoroughly socially mobilised than the other monarchies: its stock of educated people, its exposure to modern political values, and its political experience in the maelstrom of conflict and revolution have intensified the salience of democracy as a legitimising principle. . . . The fact that the king and the ruling circles have themselves gone so far in giving the kingdom a constitutional and parliamentary *form* of government is indicative of the importance attached to participatory values.'[47]

In fact one of the main features that generally distinguishes monarchies from republics is the importance attached to democratic and participatory values and practices (however ritualistic or hypocritical, sometimes) by republics.

# 3

# ARAB REPUBLICS AND THE PALESTINIANS

The Arab East republics came into existence as the result either of the withdrawal of a European imperialist or mandatory power, or of the violent overthrow of the indigenous monarchy. Syria, Lebanon and South Yemen fall into the first category; and Egypt, Iraq and North Yemen into the second.

Egypt, one of the oldest nation-states in the world, has the longest history of modernisation in the Arab East, dating back to the period 1798–1801, when it was occupied by Napoleon Bonaparte of France. This was followed shortly thereafter by the rule of Mohammed Ali, an Albanian soldier of the Ottoman empire, which lasted until 1845. However, French influence remained strong, and manifested itself when a French company received the concession in 1854 – during the reign of Said, one of Mohammed Ali's sons – to construct the Suez canal. By the time the canal was built fifteen years later, Egypt was being governed by Said's nephew, Ismail, who was notorious for his extravagance.

Ismail's financial incompetence turned Egypt into a heavily indebted country. To stay solvent, he had to sell his own 44 per cent share of the Universal Suez Maritime Canal Company to the British government in 1875. Four years later, at the instigation of London and Paris, the Ottoman emperor forced Ismail to abdicate in favour of his son Tawfiq. This humiliating interference in their country's internal affairs enraged the Egyptians, and prepared the ground for a nationalist uprising – headed by army officers under the leadership of Colonel Ahmed Arabi Pasha, and supported by the civilian National Party – which occurred in 1882. Britain intervened directly with its troops, quelled the uprising, and occupied Egypt.

Oddly enough this did not alter Egypt's position as a nominal viceroyalty of the Ottoman empire. This anomalous situation continued until the outbreak of the First World War, when Britain declared Egypt its protectorate and used it as such. After the war the Egyptian people, anxious to regain independence, backed the nationalist Wafd party. But Wafd's negotiations with the British government on the subject proved sterile. It was only after the Egyptian masses had rioted and demonstrated on a large scale that London conceded some form of independence in 1922. Britain ended Egypt's status as its protectorate, but retained control in Egypt of communications with the British empire (then extending to India, south-east Asia, and Australasia), and the authority to act as sole defender in case of foreign aggression, and to safeguard the interests of Sudan as well as foreigners and minorities in Egypt.

The first parliamentary election held under the 1923 constitution brought the Wafd to power; and increased the already high anti-imperialist feeling among the people, determined to secure full independence. Over the years a complex relationship evolved between the Wafd, King Fuad, and the British embassy in Cairo, with Britain exercising the ultimate authority. The situation changed in 1936 when the outbreak of the Italian–Ethiopian war put London in a conciliatory mood, and led to the signing of an Anglo–Egyptian treaty (to last twenty years) and Egypt's membership of the League of Nations. The treaty signified a formal end to the presence of British troops outside the Suez Canal zone; but this did not happen since withdrawal to the canal zone was conditional upon Egypt's building up its defence capabilities sufficiently. Britain retained the right to take over all of the country's defence and communications facilities in case of war – which came three years later.

Although Egypt refrained from declaring war against Germany it found itself under military occupation by Britain. Italy's entry into the war on the side of Germany in May 1940 complicated matters, since King Farouk had many close Italian friends and advisers. In February 1942, while German troops were advancing on Egypt from Libya, and Farouk was considering appointing a new prime minister known to be anti-British, the British ambassador in Cairo ordered tanks to surround the king's palace and then gave him the choice of abdicating or appointing the pro-British Wafd leader, Nahas Pasha, as prime minister. Farouk invited Nahas Pasha to form a government. While this secured the Allies' position in Egypt for the rest of the war, it destroyed the king's prestige among his subjects, and thus paved the way for his downfall a decade later.

Farouk's popular standing suffered a further setback when, following the British withdrawal from Palestine in May 1948, the Egyptian army joined the Arab war effort against the newly formed state of Israel, and did badly, mainly due to the incompetence and corruption of its senior officers, the obsolescence of its (British-supplied) arms, and irregular and inadequate supplies of food and medicine.

Anxious to restore the nation's wounded pride, Farouk came to terms with the Wafd leaders, and held a general election in early 1950. The poll put the Wafd firmly in power. Reflecting the popular mood which sought to avenge the humiliation suffered in the Palestine war of 1948–9, the Wafd government pressed Britain to withdraw its troops from Egypt. When London stonewalled, Cairo unilaterally abrogated the 1936

Anglo–Egyptian treaty (valid until 1956) in October 1951. The ensuing official non-cooperation, reinforced by popular guerrilla actions, made the British base in the Suez canal zone virtually inoperative. A confrontation between the local police and British troops in the Suez city of Ismailia on 25 January 1952 left fifty Egyptian policemen dead. The next day angry crowds in Cairo burned down the city centre. King Farouk dismissed the Wafd government and thus further destabilised the political situation.

It was against this background that the Free Officers group in the army, led by Brigadier Mohammed Neguib and Colonel Gamal Abdul Nasser seized power on 23 July, deposed King Farouk, and declared a republic. The original objective of the Free Officers' fifteen-man executive council – renamed the Revolutionary Command Council – was to act as a caretaker body until honest civilians, untarnished by the corruption of previous administration, had been found.

However, within six months this plan had been quietly discarded, the 1923 constitution suspended, political parties (with the exception of the Muslim Brotherhood) banned, and martial law imposed. In 1953 the Liberation Rally was formed as the officially backed political party with the unannounced purpose of destroying opposition to the revolution. By the end of the following year Neguib, who was the president and prime minister of the republic, was displaced by his deputy Nasser as the supreme leader: a position Nasser retained as long as he lived.

Nasser lifted martial law in 1956, when he promulgated a constitution. This was accompanied by the dissolution of the Liberation Rally, and the creation of the National Union, charged with the task of forging national unity. Elections to the national assembly were held in July 1957. Syria's decision to merge with Egypt to form the United Arab Republic the following year gave a boost to the National Union and Nasser: the move was seen as the first step towards unity of all Arab lands from the Gulf to the Atlantic. But the UAR ran into trouble and Syria seceded in September 1961.

Reacting to the Syrian disaster, Nasser offered the Charter of National Action to the Egyptian people in 1962, and followed this up with a provisional constitution two years later. Without altering the all-powerful position of the republic's president, as specified in the earlier constitution, the 1964 document introduced the office of prime minister, to be filled by presidential appointment. Although the prime minister presides over cabinet meetings, the president can do so if he wishes to. The cabinet is appointed by the president, but is responsible to the national assembly which can reject it through a vote of no confidence. The (theoretical) power to choose the president also lies with the national assembly, which is elected by popular vote for five years.[1] The president is the commander-in-chief of the armed forces, and can issue decrees even in normal times provided these are later approved by the assembly. He is empowered to dissolve the national assembly whenever he wishes, but must call fresh elections within two months of dissolution.

The 1964 constitution declared Egypt to be a democratic, socialist state, based on an alliance of 'the working powers of the people . . . [these consisting of] farmers, workers, soldiers, intellectuals, and national capital'. The document guaranteed 'people's control' over, and supervision of, the three forms of ownership – state, cooperative and private – and allowed the government to impose limits on private ownership and insist on the private sector functioning 'without exploitation' and within the limits prescribed by the national economic plan.[2]

The promulgation of the constitution was a prelude to the establishment of the Arab Socialist Union in January 1965 as the political instrument through which socialism was to be achieved and consolidated. But defeat in the June 1967 Arab–Israeli war led to a radical reappraisal of state policies, and a general downgrading of socialism and socialist institutions. This trend was accelerated during the presidency of Mohammed Anwar Sadat which began in September 1970.

After dismissing leading leftist figures from their seats of power in May 1971, President Sadat promulgated a new constitution in September. While maintaining many of the parameters of the previous constitution, this document played down the socialist guidelines and the importance of the public sector. The preface to the constitution, signed by President Sadat, mentions the 23 July 1952 revolution as having been brought about by 'the alliance of the working forces of our militant people', but states later on that, 'The alliance of the active popular powers is not a means for social strife leading towards historical development . . . [but] is a safety valve, protecting the unity of the working powers in the country and eliminating, through democracy, any contradictions.'[3] Significantly, the new constitution does not spell out the elements of 'the alliance of the active popular powers' or 'the working powers' as the previous one had done.

When it came to the actual working of the political institutions, Sadat made a clear break with the Nasserite past in 1976. He allowed the Arab Socialist Union to be split into three 'tribunes' – right, left and centre – and let the members of the national assembly (now renamed people's assembly) so label themselves. The Law for the System of Political Parties, which went into effect in June 1977 formalised the situation, and marked the beginning of a multi-party era in the republican history of Egypt. The parliamentary elections held two years later became the first to be contested on a multi-party system since 1950.

But this did not mean growing democratisation or decentralisation of power. For, a month before dissolving it, Sadat had the people's assembly – dominated by his own National Democratic Party – authorise him to pass laws without having them approved later by the assembly, and to dissolve existing parties or prevent the formation of new ones.[4] Sadat enhanced his power even further by nullifying the constitutional provision which limits the reelection of the president to one term of six years, through the device of a referendum in May 1980.[5]

In short, under Sadat, Egypt became a country which, while projecting an image abroad of a multi-party democracy, has assured its president lifelong tenure of office: a virtual monarchy. This was all the more ironic because the prime objective of the July 1952 revolution was to end monarchy in Egypt, and also because the success of the Free Officers of the Egyptian military (of whom Sadat was one) had inspired many nationalist, republican army officers in the Arab East's monarchies to revolutionary action.

An attempt by military officers to overthrow King Hussein of Jordan in 1957 failed. But an army coup led by the Free Officers of Iraq against his cousin Faisal II the following year succeeded. It was not the first time the Iraqi military officers had intervened in state affairs, since an earlier coup in 1936 had caused a change in the government,[6] although not in the political system. This was four years after Britain had ended its mandate over Iraq and allowed it to become a member of the League of Nations.

The British mandate over Iraq was the result of the Allies' victory in the First World War over the Central Powers – including the Ottomans who had been ruling Iraq since 1638 – and a decision by the League of Nations' Supreme Council in April 1920. By then, however, the Iraqi people, led by Al Ahd (The Covenant) group (dominated by nationalist Iraqi military officers opposed to Ottoman suzerainty over Iraq), had declared Iraq independent under the constitutional monarchy of Abdullah ibn Hussein. As stated earlier, Abdullah offered his throne to his brother Feisal I. The British established their authority in Iraq by crushing the popular movement against them, and then formalised their relations with Feisal I through a treaty which placed economic and military control of Iraq in their hands.

The Anglo–Iraqi treaty of 1922 was grudgingly ratified by the constituent assembly, convened by the monarch, two years later. By ratifying the constitution drafted by the assembly, and holding parliamentary elections, Feisal I legitimised his regime. This suited Britain, whose interest in Iraq was heightened by the discovery of oil in commercial quantities in 1927. Three years later Britain signed a new treaty with Iraq (to last twenty-five years) which obliged the Iraqi king to formulate a common foreign policy with Britain and allow the stationing of British forces in his country in exchange for a British guarantee to protect Iraq against foreign attack. This is the price London extracted from Baghdad before ending its mandate in October 1932.

Most Iraqis, whether civilian or military, considered their independence incomplete as long as British forces were posted in their country. Anti-British sentiment was widespread in the military hierarchy; and it prevented the pro-British prime minister Nuri al Said (who enjoyed unprecedented powers due to King Feisal II being under age) from declaring war against Germany when the Second World War broke out. In 1941 Rashed Ali Gailani, who succeeded Nuri al Said as prime minister, led a successful coup against the British. But he was unable to withstand a British counter-offensive. The triumphant British reinstalled Nuri al Said as prime minister; and he proclaimed war against Germany in 1943.

Following peace in 1945, Nuri al Said allowed political parties, excepting the Communists, to function freely. He played an active role in the formation of the Arab League, and sent troops to fight in the Palestine war of 1948–9. But they performed poorly. The disappointed Iraqis blamed the incompetence and corruption of the ruling oligarchy – headed by the Regent Abdul Ilah, King Feisal II's uncle – for the national humiliation on the battlefield.

Nuri al Said's increasingly dictatorial ways, his manipulation of the electoral system and elections, and the banning of political parties: all these widened the chasm between the rulers and the ruled which had been created by the Palestine War fiasco. By deciding to enrol Iraq into the British-sponsored Middle East Treaty Organisation in 1954, he showed utter disregard for the nationalist leanings of the military officer corps. His refusal to condemn Anglo–French–Israeli aggression against Egypt, a fellow-member of the Arab League, in November 1956, damaged the regime's popular standing beyond repair.

By then – as was to be revealed later – the Free Officers' group, commanding the loyalties of around 200 activists and 100 sympathisers,[7] had resolved to abolish the monarchy, and end Iraq's pro-West foreign policy in favour of non-alignment and the establishment of a genuine parliamentary democracy.

The first aim was achieved on 14 July 1958 when the Free Officers, led by Brigadier Abdul Karem Qassem and Abdul Salam Aref, assassinated the royal family as well as Nuri al Said. (The second aim was realised some months later when Iraq formally withdrew from the Western-sponsored Middle East defence pact, while the last aim was to remain unrealised for the next twenty-two years.[8]) A provisional constitution promulgated within a fortnight of the coup declared Iraq to be a republic with supreme executive and legislative authority invested in the three-member Sovereignty Council, assisted by a cabinet – until such time as a permanent constitution were to be framed by a popularly elected national assembly. A cabinet of fourteen, with ten civilians, was formed, with Qassem as prime minister. Without being formally named the republic's president, Qassem soon came to be regarded as the Sole Leader. He took no steps to convene a national assembly.

A tide of Arab nationalism then sweeping the Arab East had created the expectation that, once the pro-West Feisal II had been toppled, Iraq would rush to join the recently formed United Arab Republic of Egypt and Syria. But this was not to be. The Iraqi political parties were divided on the subject, with the Communists opposed to the union with the UAR, and the supporters of Nasser (Nasserites) and the Arab Baath Socialist Party (Baathists), in favour. Determined to hold on to power and maintain Iraq's separate identity, Qassem played the pro-unionist and anti-unionist camps against each other. In the process he became isolated, and paved the way for his own overthrow. This came in February 1963, and was accomplished by the Baathist supporters in the military.

Once in power, the Baathists fell out among themselves on the question of union with Egypt (since the UAR had by then broken up) and the degree of socialism to be achieved, thus allowing the prestigious but non-Baathist Abdul Salam Aref – one of the two leaders of the republican coup – to usurp total power as (provisional) president in November.

Under Aref's rule Iraq's relations with Egypt improved, with Aref and Nasser agreeing to lay the groundwork for an eventual political union of their countries. Following Nasser's lead in proclaiming the 'socialist' constitution of March 1964, Aref promulgated a provisional constitution for Iraq in May. This described Iraq as a socialist state, where private property was 'inviolable', and promised a permanent constitution within three years.[9] Aref also established the Arab Socialist Union in Iraq along the lines followed by Nasser. He made an attempt to gradually replace the military regime with a civilian one; but progress in that direction was cut short by his death in an accident in April 1966.

The cabinet and the national defence council appointed his brother Abdul Rahman Aref as president for a year, and then extended his term by another year. He continued the earlier policy of cooperation with Nasser's Egypt, and offered military aid to Egypt and Jordan during the June 1967 war. The defeat of the Arabs, led by Nasser, had an adverse effect on Aref's standing in Iraq. The long-simmering opposition now rallied around the demand for a popularly elected national assembly with powers to control the government.

Popular demonstrations in support of this demand led Aref to muzzle the press, and renege on his earlier promise to hold assembly elections by May 1968, by postponing these for two more years. The government's standing deteriorated rapidly as reports of corruption at the highest level, and a violent upheaval in the Kurdish region, gained currency. Following a split in the cabinet, prime minister Taher Yahya resigned on 15 July.

Two days later a group of old Baathist military leaders, who had been displaced from power in late 1963, mounted a successul coup against the Aref regime. A temporary constitution, promulgated in September, formalised the new political set-up. It provided for a parliamentary government with executive and legislative authority vested in the Revolutionary Command Council until the election of a national assembly (at an unspecified time). This document was amended four times before being replaced by a new constitution in July 1970, which stressed the nationalist and socialist principles of the ruling Arab Baath Socialist Party. It outlawed organisations opposing these principles or trying to stir up ethnic and sectarian antagonism. More importantly, the constitution institutionalised the intermeshing of the ruling Baath party with the state by specifying that the Revolutionary Command Council was to be appointed by the party's regional (meaning Iraqi) command,[10] and that the RCC was to remain the (exclusive) supreme authority until an elected national assembly had chosen the president.[11]

But ten years elapsed before these elections were held. During that period the regime had imbued the military officer corps with the Baathist ideology of nationalism and socialism while at the same time gradually lessening the military's dominance at the top. All of the five members of the RCC, formed in the wake of the July 1968 coup, held military rank, whereas only two of the five members of the re-formed RCC in mid-1977 did so. With the appointment of seventeen of the twenty-two members of the Baath regional command to the RCC in September, civilians became the predominant element in the RCC.[12] The resignation of Ahmed Hassan Bakr (a former major-general) as the republic's president, and the Baath regional command's general secretary, in July 1979, followed by the promotion of his deputy, Saddam Hussein, to these positions was the final step which underlined civilian control over the military.[13]

Since the seizure of power in July 1968 the Baath leadership has built up the party as the most pervasive factor in the country's secular life, with party activists occupying important positions in the military, police, intelligence, civil service, publicly and privately owned businesses, and educational institutions, as well as the trade unions, students' unions, and women's associations. Though none of the candidates for the 1980 national assembly election carried any party label, the fact remains that a large majority of the elected members are Baathists. As such the assembly's decision to elect Saddam Hussein as the republic's president was predictable.

To the extent that the Baath party had existed in Iraq long before the republican coup of 1958, and had gained supporters inside the military and outside, before seizing power first in 1963 and again in 1968, the history of Iraq is basically different from that of Egypt: there, all the parties existing prior to the 1952 republican coup were disbanded and the (essentially) military regime established a state-sponsored party which, although bearing different names at different times, was vaguely of Nasserite persuasion. But by 1980 the Arab East's two most populous and powerful republics had reached a point where each was ruled by a powerful figure who monopolised power by heading both the state and the ruling party, and where – as indicated by outside signs – the military had been brought under the firm control of the civilian authority.

Yet the military officers of both countries played an important – ideological – role in setting in motion a process that culminated in the republican coup of September 1962 in North Yemen. Ironically it was the ruler, Imam Ahmed (1948–62), himself who brought in officers from Egypt and Iraq to instruct Yemeni officer-cadets at the country's only military academy near Sanaa, the state capital. Despite a formal ban by the monarch against political education, these officers managed to plant republican ideology among many of their pupils. The 1962 coup ended the rule of a family that was related to the Rassed dynasty, founded by Yahya al Hadi il-al Haq in 898. Yahya was the imam of the Zaidas, a Shia sect, who had settled mainly in the northern and eastern highlands of Yemen, the south-western corner of the Arabian Peninsula.

Ottoman suzerainty over Yemen, established in 1517, was ended in 1636. The second period of the Ottoman overlordship, which began in 1849, was challenged by the local Zaidi ruler, Imam Yahya, in 1911, who was put down by Constantinople. The resulting treaty confined Imam Yahya to the highlands, leaving the Turks to rule the Shafeis, a Sunni sect,[14] in the Tihama coastal area and the southern hills bordering present-day South Yemen.

Following the collapse of the Ottoman empire in 1918, Imam Yahya immediately reasserted his authority over the Shafei region. He then tried to extend his domain beyond the southern hills, but was checked by the British, then in charge of southern Arabia. Later he attempted to re-establish control over Asir province to the north; and this brought him into conflict with King Abdul Aziz of Saudi Arabia. In the ensuing confrontation he lost. He was saved the humiliation of losing his own kingdom to Abdul Aziz by subtle but effective intervention by Britain, which was anxious to see that Abdul Aziz did not become the sole ruler of the whole Arabian Peninsula. By signing the Treaty of Muslim Friendship and Arab Fraternity with Abdul Aziz in 1934, Imam Yahya conceded the provinces of Asir, Jizan and Najran to the Saudi kingdom for forty years.[15] Relations between Sanaa and London improved to the extent that, though Yemen remained neutral during the Second World War, it interned the nationals of the Axis powers.

At home, Imam Yahya's autocratic rule, combined with his treatment of state revenue as his personal privy purse, caused widespread disaffection among his subjects. His death in 1948 aroused hopes that the situation would improve. It did not. His son Imam Ahmed continued Yahya's policies and style of government.

Imam Ahmed wanted to realise his father's ambition to create a Greater Yemen by annexing the British protectorate of Aden. Britain frustrated his plans, and this turned Ahmed militantly anti-British, and led him to befriend President Nasser who was then (1954) engaged in getting the British troops out of Egypt. In April 1956 he signed a mutual defence pact with Cairo which provided for a unified military command. Aware of the growing popularity of Nasser and Arab nationalism among his subjects, he offered to join the United Arab Republic soon after it was formed in early 1958. The resulting loose federation of Egypt, Syria and North Yemen was called the Union of Arab States. By then Imam Ahmed had signed friendship treaties with Moscow, Peking and other Communist capitals.

But pursuing a non-aligned policy and supporting Arab nationalism abroad made no difference to Ahmed's repressive style of government, which had driven a large number of politically conscious Yemenis into exile, to Aden and Cairo. As long as North Yemen was a (nominal) member of the Union of Arab States, Nasser felt inhibited from offering propaganda facilities to the anti-royalist Yemeni exiles in Cairo. However, once Ahmed had cut his country's ties with Egypt and attacked the Egyptian president for his 'revolutionary socialism' (after the Syrian secession from the UAR in September 1961), Nasser allowed the Yemeni exiles to use Cairo Radio to attack the monarch who, as it happened, was fast losing support among his subjects. His death on 18 September 1962 was received with widespread relief in the country.

His son, Mohammed al Badr, had occupied the throne for a mere eight days when Brigadier-General Abdullah Sallal, head of the royal bodyguard, carried out a successful coup against him. In this he had the active support of the secret Nasserite group among the military officers.[16] Imam Badr managed to escape unhurt, and later, with the active help of Saudi Arabia, he rallied his followers, and a civil war ensued. It lasted until 1970.

Sallal formed a Revolutionary Command Council and proclaimed the Yemen Arab Republic, which was soon recognised by Egypt, Iraq, Syria and the socialist bloc. Despite the civil war, Sallal promulgated a constitution in April 1964 which designated the president, prime minister and consultative council as the executive and legislative authorities of the state. In the civil strife the republicans – deriving their major support from the Shafei tribes which comprise 60 per cent of the national population[17] and inhabit the coastal plain and the southern hills – were aided by Cairo with arms and troops; while the royalists, with a solid base among the Zaidi tribes in the highlands adjoining Saudi Arabia, were similarly helped by Riyadh, Amman, and Tehran. Three years of intense fighting by the two sides were followed by a year of comparative lull. In mid-1966 the republicans, supported by Egyptian troops, launched an offensive to regain the areas lost to the monarchists. But the drive was interrupted by the Arab–Israeli war of June 1967, as a consequence of which Cairo decided to withdraw its forces from North Yemen by December.

This weakened the position of President Sallal, who had come to be regarded as a protégé of Egypt. He was overthrown in November by a group of leaders of the 'Third Force', who later constituted the five-member republican council, with Abdul Rahman Iryani as the president. Hopes that this would lead to peace were shattered when the royalists placed Sanaa under siege. Helped by emergency aid from the Soviet

Union, Syria and Algeria, the republicans ended the siege in February. A steady improvement in its standing at home encouraged the republican regime to appoint a sixty-eight-member national council in March 1969. By the end of the year the republican government had re-established its authority in most of the country. This helped to bring about a reconciliation between the warring sides at the Islamic foreign ministers' conference in Jeddah, Saudi Arabia, in March 1970. Saudi Arabia recognised the Yemen Arab Republic a few months later, thus signalling the final end of the civil war which had claimed an estimated 80,000 to 200,000 lives.[18]

A new constitution, promulgated in December, provided for a three-member republican council, elected for a five-year term by a consultative assembly, the council then choosing the republic's president. Of the 159 members of the consultative assembly, forty were to be appointed by the republican council, and the rest elected. Political parties were banned. During the following February and March, the assembly was formed through indirect elections, whereby each village appointed nominees who in turn participated in the election of a representative to the assembly. The consultative assembly elected Shaikh Abdullah al Ahmar, an eminent Zaidi tribal chief, as its chairman, and – through the republican council – confirmed Abdul Rahman Iryani as the republic's president. The first cabinet headed by the prime minister, elected by and responsible to the consultative assembly, was formed in May.

But this neat constitutional arrangement could not for long withstand the pulls and pressures of the arch-conservative House of Saud on the one hand and the leftist South Yemen on the other – not to mention the tensions created by the continued conflict between different tribes and classes within the country itself.

The emergence of a decidedly leftist government in South Yemen in June 1969 alarmed North Yemen and Saudi Arabia. In cooperation with the South Yemen émigrés in North Yemen and Saudi Arabia, Riyadh and Sanaa went on the offensive against Aden by leading a series of attacks along the South Yemen in September 1972. Mediation by the Arab League brought about a cease-fire, and a surprising agreement between the two states to work for political and economic unity. This upset Riyadh, which used its considerable economic and political leverage on Sanaa to nullify the agreement. As a result the government headed by prime minister Mohsen al Aini, a progressive, gave way to one led by Abdullah al Hijri, a pro-Saudi conservative.

Saudi pressure became so strong that President Iryani – an advocate of peaceful coexistence with the leftist opposition at home and South Yemen across the border – threatened to resign in August. He was persuaded to stay. Encouraged by the euphoric atmosphere created by the unprecedented Arab unity shown during and soon after the October 1973 Arab–Israeli war, Iryani invited South Yemen's president to Sanaa. Early next year he dismissed al Hijri as prime minister. But the conflict between the pro-Saudi conservatives and moderate North Yemeni nationalists, seeking close ties with Aden, was not properly resolved until mid-June.

On 13 June Colonel Ibrahim al Hamdi, assistant commander-in-chief, carried out a bloodless coup by securing the resignations of Shaikh Abdullah al Ahmar, the pro-Saudi conservative chairman of the consultative assembly, as well as the republican council – and assumed power as the head of the newly created Command Council. While maintaining close relations with Riyadh, Hamdi concentrated on consolidating his power base in the military and outside. Once he had secured his position at home, and dissolved the consultative assembly in October 1975, he moved to improve relations with Aden. During the South Yemeni president's visit to Sanaa in August 1977, the two heads of state agreed to work for the unification of their countries by 1981.[19] But two days before his scheduled departure for Aden in October 1977 to sign a mutual defence pact and ratify the common Yemeni state flag, Hamdi was assassinated (almost certainly by Saudi agents).

Hamdi was succeeded by Major Ahmed Hussein al Ghashmi, a pro-Saudi member of the command council. Ghashmi revived the consultative assembly and the republican council, and tried to mend fences with Abdullah al Ahmar, leader of the Hashed tribal federation, to which he himself belonged. His policies and actions alienated the progressive nationalist forces committed to seeing the two Yemens united. He was killed in June 1978 by the explosion of a bomb allegedly brought to his office in a suitcase by a special emissary of the South Yemeni president.

The reconstituted republican council elected Lieutenant-Colonel Ali Abdullah Saleh as the president. In October the regime survived an attempted coup by a section of the army. But the long-standing conflict between those who did not mind the Saudi rulers' domineering attitude towards North Yemen and those who wanted their country to assume a truly independent Yemeni identity grew worse. In February 1979 the nationalist-leftist forces, actively supported by Aden, assumed control of areas bordering South Yemen.

History repeated itself when the Arab League intervened, brought about a cease-fire, and the meeting of the heads of the warring states, arranged in Kuwait, resulted in an agreement to unify the two Yemens, within a year. Again, as in the past, the unity deadline was not met, but, following the South Yemeni prime minister's visit to Sanaa in October, travel and communications arrangements between the two countries improved considerably.[20] A return visit by the North Yemeni prime minister the following May resulted in a declaration that the two Yemens would undertake common economic projects.[21]

Evidently there is widespread support, at the popular level, for unity of the two Yemens; and this drives the rulers to undertake promises to that effect every so often. This is not surprising, because the Yemenis' sense of identity is strong and rooted in history that stretches back to antiquity. In modern times the domination by the Ottomans from 1517 to 1636, which left the territorial integrity of Yemen intact, did not cause a split in the Yemeni identity. The situation first changed with the arrival of the Europeans on the scene, and their colonisation of parts of the region.

The capture in 1839 of the port of Aden by the British, and their subsequent control of large tracts of southern Arabia, marked the formal end of Yemen's territorial integrity. Britain ruled Aden Colony through a governor attached to the India Office in London, and Aden Protectorate – consisting of twenty-three provinces – through local rulers (sultans). By playing up the antipathy of the (Sunni) Shafei inhabitants of this region towards the (Shia) Zaidi imams of the north, Britain consolidated its position, and easily frustrated Imam Yahya's attempt to annex parts of Aden Protectorate soon after the First World War. It tried to foster a distinctly local sense of identity by severing Aden Protectorate from the India Office in 1927, and doing the same to Aden Colony ten years later.

But it took another decade before political reform of sorts, in the guise of a fully nominated legislative council, was introduced in Aden Colony, and eight more years before four of the eighteen council seats were made elective. In 1962 plans were laid to form the Federation of South Arabia by knitting together the Colony and the twenty-three provinces of the Protectorate. Six sultans supported the plan immediately. While Britain was determined to make a success of its Federation plan, the anti-British forces, in the south as well as the north, were equally determined to frustrate it. North Yemen's ruler was dead set against it, since its success would have signified the end of his vision of the rebirth of the Greater Yemen of the past.

The decision of the Aden legislative council to join the Federation, a day before the republican coup was staged in North Yemen, accelerated the process of polarisation. Following the establishment of the Federation in January 1963, various nationalist groups, active in the south, held a congress in the North Yemeni capital of Sanaa. Here the radical Arab Nationalist Movement played a key role in welding the anti-imperialist groups into the National Front for the Liberation of South Yemen (commonly, but inaccurately, known as the NLF), which decided to achieve independence from Britain by waging an armed struggle.

An armed attack on 14 October by tribals, trained in North Yemen camps, on a security post in the Rafdan mountains marked the beginning of the anti-imperialist war. Within two years the armed guerrillas had opened up four fronts against the British forces, and taken their fight into Aden. The success of the militant tactics had driven the conservative and moderate nationalists – supporters of the South Arabian League and the People's Socialist Party respectively – to form the Organisation for the Liberation of the Occupied South Yemen (later to be called the Front for the Liberation of Occupied South Yemen, FLOSY), at the behest of President Nasser of Egypt.

The resulting competition between FLOSY and the NLF quickened the general tempo and intensity of the nationalist struggle against Britain to the extent that in early 1966 Britain declared its intention to leave by December 1968. This had the effect of sharpening the conflict between FLOSY and the NLF, each of them anxious to prove its primacy and thus establish its right to take over power from the departing British.

In the end the NLF emerged as the victor. By August 1967 it had not only occupied all of the vast eastern region of the Protectorate but also twelve provinces of the western region. Later it succeeded in beating FLOSY in Aden and winning the loyalty of the federal army. The British withdrawal on 29 November 1967 was therefore followed by the establishment of the People's Republic of South Yemen under the presidency of Qahtan al Shaabi, a leader of the NLF.

South Yemen was immediately menaced by its neighbouring conservative states – Saudi Arabia, North Yemen and Oman – which armed and trained South Yemeni exiles and encouraged them to attack the fledgling republic along its borders. At home the regime was divided on the question of tactics to be employed to bring about a socialist revolution: should the old, colonial machinery be retained and used for the purpose, or should it be dismantled and replaced by new state institutions with a popular base and dedicated to socialism?

In June 1969 President Qahtan al Shaabi, who advocated the moderate course, was ousted by the leftists within the ruling NLF, and replaced by a presidential council of five (later reduced to three), headed by Salem Robaye Ali. Six months later the NLF's general command, which had been exercising legislative powers since independence,[22] decided to provide the country with a constitution. A draft document was offered for public discussion, and the final version adopted in November 1970.

The constitution describes the workers, peasants, intellectuals and petty bourgeoisie as the classes to fulfil the national and democratic tasks required for transition to a socialist state. It states that 'the alliance of the people's democratic forces' finds 'its organisational embodiment' in the NLF, which 'leads all political activity within the masses and mass organisations, in the light of scientific socialism'. It specifies the Supreme People's Council of 101 members (eighty-six elected by local councils and fifteen by trade unions) as the legislative authority, and describes the NLF's central committee as 'the leading political organ of the country'. Its thirty-one members are chosen by the NLF's general congress which is held every three years and which is elected by members of the party cells (based on the workplace or geographical area) and section committees. The central committee selects a politbureau (political bureau) of seven, headed by the general secretary; and the politbureau runs parallel to the highest executive authority, the presidential council of three, which is elected by the Supreme People's Council.[23]

According to the constitution, Islam is the state religion, and the government is required to preserve the Islamic and Arabic culture. South Yemen's constitution is unique in the Arab East in so far as it combines the citizen's rights with their obligations. For instance, work is mentioned as not only a right of the citizen but also his obligation. Every citizen is required to 'protect and support public ownership as the essential material basis for the national democratic revolution'.[24]

The adoption of a leftist constitution was followed by the implementation of a radical land reform and the change of the country's name to the People's Democratic Republic of Yemen (PDRY). These moves made South Yemen all the more unpopular with its conservative neighbours. Border clashes became more frequent and bloodier, and finally led to a war between South Yemen and North Yemen in September 1972. The cessation of these hostilities, after a fortnight, led to a period of comparative calm for the radical republic: it lasted five years. The Arab–Israeli war of October 1973 helped to ease intra-Arab conflicts; and the seizure of power by Colonel Ibrahim al Hamdi in Sanaa augured well for improved relations between the two Yemens. Following the successful quelling of the Dhofari rebellion in Oman, by the end of 1975, Saudi Arabia recognised the Aden regime.

Hamdi's assassination in October 1977 caused rapid deterioration in Aden–Riyadh relations as well as Aden–Sanaa ties. A breaking-point was reached next June when, following President Ghashmi's murder, caused by a bomb explosion, allegations were made by Sanaa and Riyadh that an emissary of the South Yemeni president, Salem Robaye Ali, was responsible for the outrage.

Alleged South Yemeni involvement in Ghashmi's death brought to the surface the tension that had been building up between the factions led respectively by President Salem Robaye Ali and the NLF politbureau general secretary, Abdul Fatah Ismail. In the fight that ensued the leftist party faithfuls headed by Ismail emerged victorious. This, and the reports of South Yemeni complicity in the assassination of President Ghashmi (of North Yemen) impelled Saudi Arabia to urge the Arab League to impose sanctions against South Yemen. The Saudi proposal was adopted, except by Algeria, Libya, Syria and the PLO, which had refused to attend the Arab League meeting because it was being held in Cairo.

In any event the sanctions lasted only until November, when the Arab League summit conference in Baghdad – anxious to forge a united front against Cairo in retaliation to the Egyptian–Israeli accord of Camp David signed in September – decided to suspend them. Despite this, relations between Aden and Sanaa deteriorated rapidly. Indeed, with the North Yemeni nationalist-leftist forces occupying areas along the border with South Yemen, with the active aid of Aden, the two Yemens went to war again in February 1979. It was the intervention by Syria and Iraq (under the Arab League's aegis) that brought the hostilities to an end and paved the way for an agreement for the creation of a united Yemen.

Of the two mediators, Syria was considered pro-South Yemen, since both belonged to the Front of Steadfastness and Confrontation (against Israel). In addition Syria was notable for its long and consistent friendship with the Soviet Union: a super-power to which South Yemen had gravitated soon after its independence in 1967. Syria was the first Arab East republic to follow the example of South Yemen in coopting nationalist and progressive forces into the government – something the South Yemenis had achieved in the form of the National Liberation Front, whose origin went back to colonial days. There again the Syrians have a history of a long and violent struggle against France, which was given the mandate over their country soon after the First World War.

Following the collapse of the four-century-long Ottoman rule in 1918, Syria enjoyed a brief period of self-rule under Feisal I ibn Hussein. The delegates elected to the Syrian National Congress, convened in July 1919 in Damascus, unanimously opposed the mandate system or any other form of foreign control. Popular support for this resolution led to clashes between the Syrians and the French occupation forces during autumn and winter. On 8 March 1920 the Syrian National Congress declared Syria independent and chose a national government under the constitutional monarchy of Feisal I. Disregarding this, the League of Nations gave France a mandate over Greater Syria minus Palestine (i.e. Syria and Lebanon) in April. The Syrian National Congress retaliated by adopting a constitution in early July. Paris responded by giving an ultimatum to Feisal I to accept its authority unconditionally, and imposed its will by moving troops from the Mediterranean coastline to Damascus.

France enlarged the pre-war district of (Christian) Mount Lebanon by adding Muslim areas to its north, west and south, and naming the new province Greater Lebanon. It partitioned the rest of the mandate area into an 'independent' Latakia, or the state of the Alawis; an 'independent' Jebel Druze, inhabited mainly by Druzes; and the autonomous regions of Damascus and Aleppo. In December 1924 the French combined Damascus and Aleppo to form the state of Syria.

Contrary to the terms of the mandate, France seemed intent on perpetuating its control of Syria and Lebanon. Its appointment of generals, trained in its African colonies, as high commissioners was one indicator. The excessive military expenditure, which outstripped civilian expenditure by ten to one, was another.[25] It was not until January 1925 that Paris lifted martial law and allowed the formation of political parties.

Among these the People's Party was the most prominent. It lent support to the Druze rebellion that broke out in Jebel Druze in July, and helped to transform it into a nationwide armed struggle against the French. Despite resort to such drastic action as bombing Damascus and exiling all the People's Party leaders, the French took two years to pacify the nationalists.

An awareness of their unpopularity led the French to negotiate with the Syrian representatives; and this resulted in the convening of a national assembly in 1928. Dominated by the nationalist National Bloc, the assembly produced a constitution which refused to recognise the existence of the mandate. The French high commissioner dissolved the assembly and promulgated his own version of the constitution in 1930.

The parliament, elected under this constitution, reached an impasse with the French high commissioner on the terms of the treaty to replace the mandate, and was suspended. Frustrated nationalist aspiration expressed itself in popular protest, which closed down public services, schools, and bazaars for fifty days in early 1936. This compelled the French to enter negotiations with the nationalists, the success of which was assured by the installation of the leftist Popular Front government in Paris. The Franco–Syrian treaty, initialled in September, was similar to the 1930 Anglo–Iraqi treaty. That is, France agreed to grant Syria 'independence' in exchange for long-term military, political and economic privileges. The parliamentary elections held in November brought the National Bloc to power. A representative government was in office on the eve of the outbreak of the Second World War, when France suspended Syria's 1930 constitution (and with it the government in Damascus), and imposed martial law.

After the occupation of northern France by Germany, and the subsequent establishment of a pro-German regime in Vichy in southern France, control of the overseas French territories passed to the Vichy government. In mid-1941 the Vichy forces in Syria and Lebanon were attacked and defeated by the British, supported by the Free French troops under the command of General Charles de Gaulle (then operating from England). Prodded by London, the Free French authorities restored the suspended Syrian constitution and called parliamentary elections in 1943. The result was a National Bloc government with a comfortable majority. During the next year Syria won the recognition of Moscow as well as Washington. By declaring war against Germany in February 1945, Syria secured an invitation to the founding conference of the United Nations two months later. At the end of the Second World War France tried to reassert its authority in Syria through force, including the bombing of Damascus, but failed. Yet it was not until April 1946 that the last of the French troops left Syria.

Two years later Syria joined the Arab attempt to destroy the newly founded state of Israel, but in vain. This failure led to popular rioting against the government, and paved the way for an army coup which occurred in March 1949. Military rule lasted for five years under different military leaders, the last of whom was Colonel Adib Shishakli. His overthrow by the combined efforts of a section of the army and the political parties in February 1954 was followed by the restoration of parliamentary democracy.

The parliamentary poll of September 1954 was remarkable for being 'the first free election in the Arab world', with women accorded universal suffrage.[26] It marked the rise of radical, modernising groups at the expense of the well-established People's Party and the National Bloc which essentially represented the interests of the landed oligarchs, urban rich and the traditional 'notables'. The most important of the new groups was the Arab Baath Socialist Party, formed by the amalgamation of the Baath Party and the Arab Socialist Party in 1953.

Its cooperation with the Democratic Bloc, led by Khaled Azm, and the Communists during the next few years caused the political centre of Syrian politics – civilian as well as military – to move leftward. The appointment of Colonel Afif Bizri, regarded as a Communist sympathiser, as the commander-in-chief in August 1957 highlighted the ascendancy of the leftist-nationalist forces. It opened up the possibility of a coalition of the Baathists, Democrats and Communists assuming office. Unwilling to share power with the Communists, and equally unwilling to align with the traditional parties, the Baathists found a way out by proposing Syria's union with Egypt to President Nasser. The Egyptian leader agreed on condition that all political parties would be dissolved in the new state.

The United Arab Republic, consisting of Egypt and Syria, was inaugurated in February 1958 amidst high hopes for wider Arab unity and progress. But disillusionment set in among the Baathists when they were unable to dominate the National Union formed as the sole political party of the UAR. By the end of 1959 all of Baathist leaders had gone into voluntary exile in Lebanon. The UAR broke up in September 1961, following the arrest of Field-Marshal Abdul Hakim Amr, Nasser's deputy in Damascus, and the simultaneous announcement of Syria's secession from the union by a group of Syrian military officers.

A period of political instability followed. It lasted until 8 March 1963, when the pro-Baath Military Committee, in collusion with Major Zaid Hariri, a political neutral, seized power in a bloodless coup. The civilian and military Baathists formed a government in alliance with three minor Nasserite groups. Gradually, however, Nasserite groups were eased out of the government, as were Nasserite officers from the military. With this the incipient tension between the reformist, anti-Communist faction and the radical, pro-Marxist faction within the Baath came to the surface – particularly as the government had insisted on nationalising banks and carrying out radical land reform. In the resulting bloodletting that occurred in February 1966 the radicals headed by Colonel Saleh Jedid gained ascendancy.

The new regime suspended the provisional constitution of 1964, dissolved the (fully nominated) revolutionary council, and decided to pursue radical socio-economic reform at home, and opposition to the conservative Arab regimes abroad, as before. In the newly formed cabinet General Hafez Assad, who played a crucial role in ensuring the success of the 1966 coup, was made defence minister.

Though the regime successfully withstood whatever adverse effect its defeat in the June 1967 Arab–Israeli war had on its popular standing, the Baath leadership became divided on the subject of apportioning responsibility for the debacle. The faction led by Assad blamed the rival group headed by President Saleh Jedid. The conflict between the two sides came to a head in February 1969, with Assad tightening his grip over the military, and his rivals their control of the trade unions, students' associations, and the press.

The two sides then relapsed into an uneasy coexistence. This lasted until September 1970, when fighting broke out between the Jordanian troops and the Palestinian commandos in Jordan. As air force chief, Assad refused to give air support to the troops sent into Jordan by the Syrian government to help the Palestinian commandos; and this doomed the Palestinians' chances of winning. At the extraordinary congress of the party the Jedid group, supported by a majority of the delegates, demanded the resignation of Assad as defence minister. Assad ignored the call and carried out a bloodless coup on 16 November. He assumed the office of prime minister and party general secretary.

In order to broaden the popular base of his regime, Assad appointed a people's assembly in February 1971, where only 87 of the 173 members were Baathists, the rest being either independent, or belonging to other nationalist, progressive parties or worker/peasant unions. He formalised the Baath's power-sharing by including the Communists, Socialists, and Nasserites in the (ruling) Progressive National Front, on the basis of a common national charter, in March 1972.

Early next year the people's assembly drew up a constitution which won popular approval through a referendum. The constitution describes the Syrian Arab Republic as a 'democratic, popular, socialist state'. It invests the popularly elected people's assembly (where 51 per cent of the 186 deputies must be 'workers and peasants') with legislative authority, and the power to select a presidential candidate and offer him to voters. The president, elected for a seven-year term, is the chief executive, who can under certain circumstances legislate even when the people's assembly is in session, and who has the authority to dissolve the assembly when he wishes.

Notwithstanding the constitutional stipulations, the Regional (i.e. Syrian) Command of the Baath and the executive committee of the Progressive National Front are more important than the people's assembly: the former selects the presidential candidate, and the latter decides the broad working policies of the state. In the February 1973 parliamentary poll the PNF, which offered a common list of candidates, won 124 of the 186 seats. These were subdivided into: Baath, 104; Communists, 6; Arab Socialist Movement, 6; Unionist Socialist Movement, 4 and Arab Socialist Union, 4.[27] The second parliamentary election, held in August 1977, produced the following results: the PNF secured 159 out of the 195 seats – with 125 seats going to the Baath, 12 to the Unionist Socialist Movement, 8 to the Arab Socialist Movement, 8 to the Arab Socialist Union and 6 to the Communists. The remaining 36 seats were won by the Independents.

By the time the presidential election took place in February 1978, and Assad re-elected president for seven more years, he had consolidated his hold over the party and the civilian and military wings of the government. The fact that the military losses suffered during the fourth Arab–Israeli war were quickly offset by fresh arms supplies from the Soviet Union helped Assad's prestige in the armed forces. His consistent opposition to Sadat's unilateral moves to make peace with Israel – first highlighted by the Egyptian president's visit to Jerusalem in November 1977 – improved Assad's popularity. Syria's subsequent decision to found the Front of Steadfastness and Confrontation (against Israel) along with Algeria, Libya, the PLO and South Yemen won widespread public support.

In contrast, Assad's intervention in the Lebanese civil war of 1975–6 on the side of the Lebanese rightist Christians proved controversial. However, the end of the civil war in October 1976, accompanied by the stationing there of the Arab Deterrent Force, with Syria supplying the bulk of the troops, improved the Syrian president's image at home and abroad. The simmering antagonism among the Lebanese that the continued presence of the Syrian troops engendered was stilled in February 1980, when the Lebanese president – faced with the prospect of the Syrian peacekeeping forces' withdrawal – appealed to Assad to reconsider his decision.[28] This underlined the historical fact that the fortunes of Syria and Lebanon have been inextricably linked since the days of the French mandate – and before, when the two countries, along with Palestine, formed Greater Syria under the tutelage of the Ottoman Turks.

The French were bent on accentuating historical antagonism between Christians and Muslims, and favouring the former at the expense of the latter. The creation of Greater Lebanon by the addition of just enough Muslim-dominated areas to the Christian-dominated Mount Lebanon, to nevertheless leave Christians in the majority in a province three times the size of the Ottoman district of Lebanon, was a good example of French intentions translated into action. Having created a Christian territory of Greater Lebanon, Paris treated it favourably. Within two months of the mandate it formed a consultative council elected on male adult franchise. While violently suppressing the nationalist uprising of 1925–7 in adjoining Syria, Paris promulgated a republican constitution, drafted by a commission of the Lebanese consultative council, in 1926. This led to the creation of a parliament which elected the republic's president who then appointed the prime minister and his cabinet.

When the presidential contest between a Muslim candidate and a Christian became too heated in 1932, the French suspended the constitution and did not reinstate it until five years later. Meanwhile the installation of a leftist government in Paris had led to the signing of the Franco–Lebanese treaty of 1936, which was meant to pave the way for the end of the mandate. The outbreak of the Second World War saw the constitution suspended once again, and martial law imposed.

As stated earlier, the British and the Free French troops occupied Lebanon and Syria in 1941; and the Free French authorities, prodded by the British, restored the constitutions of the two countries in March 1943. General Edward Spears, the British representative in Beirut, mediated to resolve the conflict between Muslims (led by Riad al Solh) and Christians (led by Bishara al Khouri) regarding division of the parliamentary seats. Based on the 1932 census, which showed Christians to be 54 per cent of the population, Spears recommended six Christian seats to five Muslim. This was accepted by the prominent leaders of both communities as part of the National Pact, and then given official backing as a decree issued by the French Delegate-General in July. Elections were held in August. Later the six:five ratio was to apply to the posts in the civil service, judiciary and military.[29]

According to the National Pact, the Muslim leaders accepted the existing boundaries of Lebanon, and gave up their demand for a union with Syria to recreate the Greater Syria of the past, while their Christian counterparts agreed that Arabic should be the only official language of the republic, and that Lebanon should be free of any foreign (i.e. European) ties and present an Arab face to the world. The pact stipulated that the republic's presidency should go to a Maronite Christian,[30] prime ministership to a Sunni Muslim, parliament's chairmanship to a Shia Muslim, and parliament's vice-chairmanship to a Greek Orthodox Christian. Under the pact Bishara al Khouri became the country's president, and Riad al Solh its prime minister.

Following Lebanon's admission to the United Nations in 1945 – and the final departure of French troops from Lebanese soil in December 1946 – the republican constitution was altered to remove all reference to France. The amended document provides for a president who is both head of state and chief executive; for a single chamber of deputies, with legislative powers; and a cabinet which is responsible to the chamber. The president, who is elected by two thirds of the deputies for a six-year term, appoints the cabinet led by the prime minister. Parliamentary elections are to be held every four years on the basis of adult suffrage (which until 1952 excluded women).[31] Article 95 of the constitution sanctifies 'confessionalism' – that is, fixed communal representation – by stating that 'provisionally, and in order to promote harmony and justice, the communities will be equitably represented in government employment and in the composition of the ministry [cabinet] without jeopardising the good of the state'.[32]

The first parliamentary election held under the amended constitution in May 1947 gave a thumping 78 per cent majority to President Khouri's followers. This was achieved by the combined tactics of misusing the political machine built up by Khouri since 1943 – with the active backing of the traditional communal leaders drawn into it through patronage – and rigging the polls. Expectedly, the new chamber elected Khouri the republic's president for six years.

At the next parliamentary poll in 1951 Khouri's supporters manipulated the electoral system so thoroughly that even such opposition stalwarts as Kemal Jumblat found themselves defeated. This drove all the major opposition groups to coalesce under the aegis of the Socialist and Nationalist Front, and call a general strike in September 1953. Yielding to popular pressure, Khouri resigned two years before the end of his term and gave way to Camille Chamoun, the opposition's choice.

However, the nationalist and leftist elements in the country were soon disenchanted with President Chamoun because he pursued openly pro-West policies at a time when public opinion in the Arab East was rallying behind Nasser's pan-Arab, anti-imperialist stance. He upheld the Western-sponsored Baghdad Pact, whereas he refused to condemn Britain and France for their aggression against Egypt in late 1956. Consequently all those who opposed Chamoun sank their differences and united under the banner of the National Front. The formation of the United Arab Republic in February 1958 boosted the morale of the National Front.

By early spring the political atmosphere had become so surcharged that the assassination of Nasseb Metni, an opposition (Christian) newspaper editor, in May, led National Front supporters to paralyse the country in a three-day-long protest general strike. This triggered off a civil war in which the pro-West right-wing followers of Chamoun confronted the nationalist-leftist forces, with the army remaining neutral. The arrival of 10,000 American marines at the request of Chamoun, in July, marked an intensification of the war, which took a toll of 1,400 to 4,000 lives before coming to an end.[33]

The two sides compromised by dropping their own nominees for president and agreeing on General Fuad Chehab, the army commander-in-chief, as their common candidate. Supported by military officers and technocrats, President Chehab tried to modernise the Lebanese political-administrative machine – steeped in feudal values and sectarian cleavages – only to meet opposition from politicians, businessmen, and the civil service hierarchy, all intent on preserving their privileged positions built on interlocked networks of patronage. Chehab then used the civil and military intelligence apparatus to coerce the recalcitrant politicians; and this caused much resentment. Continued resistance to socio-political reform by well-entrenched interests brought the reformist drive of the late 1950s to a halt during the presidency of Charles Helou (1964–70).

During the latter half of its tenure, President Helou's administration found itself burdened with the problem of the Palestinian refugees, whose number soared in the wake of the Israeli occupation of the West Bank after the June 1967 war. Soon the Palestinian guerrillas took to launching armed actions against Israel from Lebanese territory; and this brought massive Israeli strikes – the most sensational being the Israeli commando action against Beirut on 28 December 1968 which destroyed several civilian aeroplanes on the ground.

Such reprisals soured relations between the Lebanese authorities and the Palestinian commando groups, and finally led to armed skirmishes between them, the first of which occurred in the spring of 1969. By the following November, however, a compromise was worked out with the help of Nasser in Cairo, whereby the Palestine Liberation Organisation was allowed to administer refugee camps and hold transit routes and certain positions in southern Lebanon, in return for its promise to respect Lebanese sovereignty.

Following the civil war in Jordan and Nasser's death, in September 1970, each side ignored the agreement as and when circumstances allowed. The presidency of Suleiman Franjieh (1970–6), therefore, witnessed a gradual deterioration in the political situation. The politico-military set-up which centred around the Palestinian refugee camps inspired and encouraged the radical, and largely underprivileged, Muslim groups of Lebanon, and crystallised their discontent with a system weighted in favour of the Maronite Christians, led by an oligarchy of businessmen and bankers. Franjieh's slow but definite adoption of the anti-Arab and anti-Palestinian policies advocated by the right-wing Maronite leaders added to existing anger and frustration among the pro-Palestinian, Arab nationalist Muslims as well as the middle-of-the-road Greek Orthodox Christians.

Threatened by a rising reformist tide, Franjieh turned to the army to control the Palestinians' activities. In the spring of 1973 the army launched an offensive against the Palestinian commando groups, which failed. This had the effect of further encouraging the Lebanese nationalist-leftists. But open confrontation between the opposing Lebanese forces was postponed by the outbreak of the fourth Arab–Israeli war in October.

Staying out of the Arab–Israeli war did not leave Lebanon's political life unaffected, since the conflagration had an important bearing on the fate of the Palestinians. The war brought the Palestinians and the Lebanese left closer together while their opponents – the right-wing Kataeb Party and the National Liberal Party – took to building up their armed militias. By the spring of 1975 the tension between the two camps had built up to the point where the gunning down of twenty-seven Lebanese and Palestinian Muslims, passing through a Christian suburb of

Beirut on a bus, by the (Kataebs') Phalange militias[34] on 13 April sparked off a civil war which raged for nineteen months.

During the first half of the civil war the Lebanese–Palestinian alliance emerged as the clear victor. In January 1976 the Lebanese army broke up, with the Muslim segment led by Lieutenant Ahmed Khatib taking charge of twenty-five garrisons and camps in the Muslim area. By March the Lebanese–Palestinian forces controlled two thirds of Lebanon: in fact practically all of the Muslim-dominated areas that France had added to the Christian Mount Lebanon in 1920 to create the present state.[35]

While the beleaguered Maronite militias began consolidating their hold over the 'Little Lebanon' by setting up public services there, the Assad regime in Syria prepared to intervene militarily in Lebanon. It did so in June, to dislodge the Lebanese–Palestinian forces from their positions and to help the right-wing Maronites, who were by then receiving substantial aid from Israel in men, money and war materials.[36] Having destroyed the supremacy of the leftist Lebanese–Palestinian alliance, the pro-West states of Saudi Arabia, Egypt and Kuwait moved, under the aegis of the Arab League, to end the strife, and succeeded in October. By then the civil war had caused the death of 60,000 to 80,000, injuries to another 130,000, and displaced 1.35 million people, in a country with an estimated population of 3.25 million.[37]

The stationing of the Arab-League-sponsored peacekeeping force in Lebanon was agreed to by the country's newly elected president, Elias Sarkis, who had the active backing of Damascus. Sarkis's main aims have been to strengthen the state's powers through the newly recruited military and police forces, and to maintain the unity of Lebanon, which is continually threatened by the rightist Maronite forces.

Following Palestinian commando action inside Israel on 11 March 1978, which caused thirty-two Israeli deaths, Tel Aviv attacked southern Lebanon four days later, using 20,000 troops, F-15 fighter planes, and cluster bombs.[38] Israel had occupied half of the Lebanese territory below the Litani river, caused the death of 700 people and made 160,000 homeless, before agreeing to the United Nations' cease-fire call on 20 March.[39] When it finally withdrew from Lebanon in June it handed over the strategic enclave along its border, with a population of about 100,000, to the Maronite forces commanded by Major Saad Haddad. Some weeks later Haddad declared the area 'independent', and refused to let the regular Lebanese army into the territory.

Haddad's actions had the tacit support of the Maronite forces controlling Christian areas in east Beirut and northern Lebanon, since they too had successfully barred entry to the Lebanese army into their territory. Fearing that the dramatic tilt in the Maronites' favour, underlined by the central government's failure to impose its will in southern Lebanon, would encourage the Maronites in the north to declare an independent Christian mini-state, the Syrian peacekeeping force launched an offensive against their strongholds in east Beirut in October. But the Maronite forces, dominated by the Phalange militiamen and aided once again by Israel, stood their ground.

Next spring, as Israel mounted intense air strikes against the Palestinian strongholds in the south – which were to leave 175,000 Lebanese and 50,000 Palestinians homeless by early August[40] – the Phalange, the largest of the Maronite militias, initiated a campaign to establish its supremacy in the Christian territory at the expense of the smaller National Liberal Party and the National Group (led by the pro-Syria former president Franjieh). This campaign reached its zenith in July 1980, when the Phalange launched a massive strike against the NLP, which left 350 NLP supporters dead and another 500 wounded.[41] The subsequent Phalange order that only the newly formed 'National Guard' (dominated by it) would in future wear uniforms and carry arms in the Christian areas confirmed its monopoly of power.

Neither the poorly led Lebanese army nor the Syrian peacekeeping force (weakened by President Assad's preoccupation with stemming violent opposition at home) acted to reverse the Phalange gain, which was widely seen as a step towards the declaration of an independent Christian state. This dismayed not only the Lebanese left but also the Palestinians, whose leaders detected the hand of Israel behind the latest development, which they regarded as amounting to 'declaring war on the Palestinians'.[42]

In their view the first hostile act against the Palestinians was taken by the British government, in November 1917, when its foreign minister, Arthur James (later Lord) Balfour, stated in a letter to Lord Rothschild, a British Jewish leader, that 'His Majesty's Government view with favour the establishment in Palestine of a National Home for the Jewish people, and will use their best endeavours to facilitate the achievement of this object'.[43]

As soon as the Arab leaders knew of the contents of what came to be known as the Balfour Declaration, they protested vehemently. They argued that Palestine was an integral part of the Ottoman Empire's Arab segment, which had been promised independence by Britain in its negotiations with Sharif Hussein of Hejaz (in 1916) to secure nationalist Arab backing against the Ottoman Turks. But nothing came of it, because Britain's promises to Sharif Hussein ran counter to the terms of the secret Sykes–Picot pact signed by London and Paris in May 1916.[44]

Following the Ottomans' surrender in October 1918, Britain and France carved up the former Arab empire of Turkey among themselves, and sanctified the operation in the form of mandates allotted by the League of Nations, dominated by them.[45] Palestine was separated from Greater Syria and placed under the British mandate, which came into effect in September 1923. Since the Balfour Declaration was incorporated into the mandate, it became the official policy of the British government to use its 'best endeavours to facilitate the achievement' of a

National Home for the Jewish people. This was an open encouragement to the Zionists – those Jews and non-Jews who believe in the 'ingathering' of world Jewry in the Biblical land of Israel – to settle foreign (mainly European) Jews into Palestine.

The Palestinian Arabs refused to accept either the British mandate or its corollary, Zionist colonisation. They repeatedly turned down London's offers of representative institutions in preparation for self-rule at some unspecified date in the future, and – like fellow-Arabs in Syria, Iraq and Lebanon – agitated for immediate, unconditional independence; but to no avail. Active Arab resistance to Zionist colonisation, which led to a major clash in 1921, gave way to passive non-cooperation with the Zionists, since the threat of Palestine, with a 92 per cent Arab population, becoming a Jewish state seemed far-fetched.

But the situation changed in 1929, when rapprochement between the Palestinian Zionists and the World Zionist Organisation (WZO), and the formation of the Jewish Agency, gave a dramatic boost to the Jewish settlement plans. The Arab–Jewish clashes in August left 133 Jews and 116 Arabs dead.[46] Arab fears were rekindled by the result of the 1931 census: it showed that the Jewish population had risen from 8 per cent in 1918 to 18 per cent in 1931. As economic depression deepened in the West, the monetary incentives offered to Jews by the WZO, and the persecution of German Jews by Adolf Hitler after 1933, brought an ever-increasing number of Jews to Palestine, and tension between the two communities rose perceptibly.

The discovery of an arms cache in a cement consignment for a Jewish builder in Jaffa, in the autumn of 1935, confirmed Arab suspicions that the Zionists were arming themselves illicitly. This, and the killing of a popular Arab leader, Shaikh Izzeddin Qassem, by the British in an encounter in November, led the different Arab factions to unite behind the Arab Higher Committee. When offered the British proposal for a legislative council, with fourteen Arab and eight Jewish members, the AHC turned it down because of the over-representation of the Jewish minority on it. The Zionist leaders rejected it too, as they feared that the proposed arrangement would make the Arab majority permanent.

With no further British move in prospect, the AHC called on its followers to stage a general strike on 1 April. They did; and the strike lasted until 12 October. A month later a British royal commission, headed by Lord Peel, visited Palestine. In July the Peel commission recommended partition, with a Jewish state in the coastal plain and Galilee, and an Arab state to the south and east, to be attached to Transjordan. This was rejected by the AHC, and led to a renewal of the Arab rebellion in 1938.

Despite heavy casualties inflicted on Arabs by 20,000 British troops, the rebellion did not end until the spring of 1939 – mainly because London finally put a limit on Jewish immigration. The three-year-long

Arab uprising claimed the lives of 3,232 Arabs (including 110 hanged by the British authorities), 329 Jews and 135 Britons.[47] Recognising the depth of the Palestinian Arabs' apprehension – and anxious to retain Arab goodwill in the region and access to the oilfields in Iraq, in the increasingly likely event of war with Germany – the British government's White Paper of May 1939 specified immigration of 75,000 Jews during the next five years, and offered an outline of a binational state within a decade.

Once Arab fears of an unlimited Jewish influx into Palestine were allayed, and Rashed Ali Gailani's anti-British regime in Iraq toppled in May 1941 – followed by the occupation of Vichy Syria and Lebanon by the British and Free French troops – the Palestinian Arabs in general cooperated with Britain in its war efforts.

After the Second World War the Anglo–American commission of enquiry on Palestine recommended in April 1946 that Britain should continue the mandate. In its talks with the AHC and the Jewish Agency (representing the Jews) during the summer, Britain tried to find common ground between the two parties, but failed. The decision of the World Zionist Organisation's twenty-second congress in December to demand an independent Jewish state in Palestine finally shattered whatever hopes Britain had of solving the problem on its own.

It therefore placed the issue before the United Nations in February. Seven months later the UN Special Committee's recommendation that Palestine be partitioned, with 40 per cent of its area going to the Arabs (who then formed 70 per cent of the population), won the required two thirds plurality in the UN General Assembly.

The Arabs were enraged by the UN resolution. Widespread fighting broke out between groups of armed Arabs and Jews, as Britain prepared to leave, and the Zionists forged plans to found the state of Israel. Responding to the Arab League call to resist the creation of Israel with war, 21,500 troops from Egypt, Syria, Iraq, Transjordan and Lebanon marched into Palestine as the British finally left on 14 May 1948.[48] Despite the United Nations' repeated efforts to secure a lasting cease-fire, fighting went on until January 1949. In the final phase of the Palestine War some 40,000 Arab troops faced 60,000 Israeli soldiers.[49] The Arab armies managed to retain only the enclave on the west bank of the river Jordan and the semi-desert Gaza strip along the Mediterranean coast: together these comprised about half of the area allocated to the Palestinian Arabs by the UN partition plan. The Arab presence in Israel – which now covered 79 per cent of the area of Palestine – was reduced from 750,000 to 165,000.[50]

While the Palestinian Arabs were represented by the Arab Higher Committee in exile in Beirut, and Hajj Amin al Husseini at the Arab League, they virtually lost their territorial identity in 1951, when King Abdullah of Transjordan, whose Arab legion had secured the West

Bank, incorporated the territory into his kingdom. However, the Gaza strip, secured by Egyptian troops and administered by Cairo, continued to have a distinct identity. In fact after the republican coup of July 1952, and particularly after the ascendancy of Nasser (who had fought in the Palestine War) in late 1954, the Gazans were allowed to undergo military training and launch guerrilla actions against Israel.

The occupation of the Gaza strip and the Sinai peninsula by Israel, following the 1956 Suez war, reinforced Palestinian identity among the Gaza residents. This came at a time of growing disillusionment among the Palestinians at large about the Arab states' ability to help them recover their lost land.

It was against this background that Fatah (literally, conquest)[51] was formed clandestinely by a group of young Palestinians, including Yasser Arafat, in Kuwait in 1958. Its basic credo was summarised thus: 'Revolutionary violence is the only means to liberate our homeland. It should be practised by the masses, and its objective is the liquidation of Zionism in all its forms.'[52] The success of revolutionary Arab nationalism over French imperialism in Algeria in 1962 boosted the morale of Fatah's founders.

Protesting against Israeli plans to build waterworks to pre-empt Lake Tiberias – an important source of the water supply to the Palestinian and Jordanian Arabs in the region – and thus consolidate its economic and military positions, the Arab League instructed its Palestinian representative, Ahmed Shukeiri, to create a 'Palestinian entity', with a view to involving the Palestinians in the impending Arab confrontation with Israel. In May 1964 the first Palestine National Council, attended by 350 delegates, met in (Arab) east Jerusalem and decided to form the Palestine Liberation Organisation.

Fatah, operating semi-clandestinely from headquarters in Damascus, launched its first attack against an Israel target on 1 January 1965. With the radical Baathists seizing power in Syria early next year, Fatah stepped up its guerrilla actions against Israel. To the extent that the Six Day Arab–Israeli conflagration highlighted Arab weakness in conventional war, and damaged the prestige of the regimes in Egypt, Syria and Jordan, it made Fatah and its guerrilla actions attractive to an increasing body of Palestinians. Fatah's success in March 1968 in the battle of Karameh (a Jordanian town) – when its commandos destroyed Israeli tanks and halted the incursion of an Israeli column into Jordan – turned it overnight into a popular organisation, which thousands of Palestinians volunteered to join.

For the next two and a half years the Palestinian resistance rode an unprecedented wave of popularity at both the popular and official levels. 'From March 1968 to September 1970, the Palestinians appeared to have seized the moral leadership and attained enormous influence over almost the entire Arab world – despite the fact that they still lacked a secure territorial base and possessed only minuscule fighting forces (not more than 15,000 guerrillas) and a rudimentary political infrastructure,' notes Hudson. 'Syria provided sanctuary; Egypt provided diplomatic support; Algeria supplied training and material; Saudi Arabia and the Gulf states provided money; Jordan and Lebanon almost provided a state.'[53]

During this period Fatah, the largest of the Palestinian parties, had affiliated to the PLO, and its leader, Arafat, had replaced Shukeiri as the PLO chairman. Besides Fatah, the PLO now included Saiqa (literally, Thunderbolt, supported by Syria), the Popular Front for the Liberation of Palestine, the Democratic Front for the Liberation of Palestine, and the Arab Liberation Front (backed by Iraq), as well as fourteen mass organisations representing trade unions, women, students, doctors, lawyers, etc.

Each of these bodies was represented on the Palestine National Council, the Palestinian parliament-in-exile, which assembles once a year. It elects a central committee and an executive committee. The central committee, which meets every three months, acts as an intermediary between the executive committee and the PNC, and decides broad policy lines.

The seventh PNC assembly session, held in Cairo in May–June 1970 and attended by all the commando groups, decided to form a single military command – the Palestine Armed Struggle Command – and appointed a Palestinian–Jordanian committee to iron out the problems that had arisen between the Palestinian commandos and the Jordanian authorities in the kingdom. But the committee failed in its task. In September fighting broke out between the 55,000 strong Jordanian military and some 40,000 Palestinian and Jordanian commandos. It lasted ten days, and claimed an estimated 1,500 to 5,000 dead, and up to 10,000 wounded – the casualties being mainly civilians living in the major Palestinian refugee camps.[54]

Following an agreement between Arafat and King Hussein, reached through the mediation of Nasser, the PLO/PASC moved all of its commandos out of the urban centres to the Jordanian–Israeli border area. The uneasy peace between the two sides proved temporary, as the royal troops kept up pressure against the Palestinian commandos. A major offensive launched by the Jordanian army in July 1971 pushed the last of the Palestinian commandos out of the kingdom – into Lebanon.

Reflecting the bitterness felt by the Palestinians against King Hussein, the tenth PNC assembly, meeting in April 1972, rejected the king's plan for a United Arab Kingdom, with the federated provinces of Jordan and Palestine, after Israel had withdrawn from the West Bank. Instead it reiterated its commitment to the Palestine National Charter, first adopted in 1964, which states: 'Palestine, with the boundaries it had during the British mandate, is an indivisible territorial unit.'[55]

However, following the Yom Kippur war, the PNC softened its stance.

The twelfth PNC assembly held in June 1974 called for the establishment of 'the independent combatant national authority for the people over every part of [the] Palestinian territory that is liberated', and that 'Once it is established, the Palestinian national authority will strive to achieve a union of the confrontation countries, with the aim of completing the liberation of all Palestinian territory.'[56] This was an indication that the PLO was ready to accept the mini-state of West Bank and Gaza, if only as a (theoretically) transient stage.

Its status was enhanced when Arab presidents and monarchs (including King Hussein of Jordan), meeting in Rabat, Morocco, in late October, unanimously recognised the PLO as 'the sole and legitimate representative of the Palestinian people'. A few weeks later the UN General Assembly invited Arafat to participate in a debate on the Palestinian issue, and followed this up by giving the PLO observer status at the United Nations Organisation, and passing a resolution which recognised 'the inalienable right of the Palestinians' to 'return to their homes and property from which they have been displaced and uprooted' and to 'national independence and sovereignty'.[57]

All this enhanced the already high popularity of the PLO among the Palestinians both inside and outside the Israeli-occupied West Bank and Gaza. By sponsoring the formation of the Palestine National Front in the occupied territories in 1973, the PLO had circumvented the Israeli ban on it, while providing its supporters with an organisation to rally around. The popularity of the PLO/PNF became apparent when the results of the local elections held in April 1976 in the occupied West Bank showed that almost all of the twenty-four mayors were PLO supporters 'in varying degrees'.[58] This was all the more remarkable because the PLO was at that time under a shadow due to its involvement in the civil war of Lebanon, where its forces were under attack by Syrian troops.

Sensing that the newly installed American President was receptive to the idea of reconvening the Middle East peace conference under United Nations auspices,[59] the thirteenth PNC assembly, meeting in March 1977, declared that, in view of UN General Assembly resolution of November 1974, the PLO was entitled to an invitation to such a conference. However, the possibility of such a conference materialising was dashed by President Sadat's visit to Jerusalem in November.

Mainly because Sadat's trip signified the breaking of Arab ranks when dealing with Israel, the PLO opposed the Egyptian president's move, and joined the Front of Steadfastness and Confrontation. It was a measure of the PLO/PNF's hold over the Palestinians that, despite immense pressures by Tel Aviv and Cairo, no Palestinian of substance cooperated with Egypt or Israel in their peace parleys, which led first to the Camp David accord in September 1978, and then to a peace treaty six months later. The failure of Tel Aviv and Cairo to reach an agreement on Palestinian autonomy – which is an important part of the Camp David accord – by the specified date of 26 May 1980 did not surprise or dismay the PLO, which had argued all along that as the almost universally recognised representative of the Palestinian people, only it had the necessary authority to negotiate on behalf of the Palestinians.

The widespread support which the PLO enjoys among the community of nations was underlined once more on 29 July, when 112 countries at the UN General Assembly, meeting in an emergency session, voted for the resolution which called on Israel to start withdrawing from the occupied Arab territories by 15 November so as to make way for the creation of a Palestinian state under the PLO.[60] Disregarding the fact that east Jerusalem is part of the Arab territories Israel occupied during the June 1967 war, the Israeli parliament passed the Jerusalem Basic Bill on 30 July, by sixty-nine votes to fifteen, which describes Jerusalem as the country's 'eternal and indivisible capital'.[61] The roots of the Israeli Jews' emotional attachment to Jerusalem can be traced back to the founding of the ancient kingdom of Eretz Israel about three thousand years ago.

4

# ISRAEL

Israel[1] was the name divinely received by Jacob, a Hebrew[2] patriarch, in the seventeenth century B.C. He was a grandson of Abraham, a leader of a nomadic Hebrew tribe from Mesopotamia who, according to the Book of Genesis of the Old Testament, had an encounter with the Lord God 'Jehovah'[3] when he was in the land of Haran, present-day southern Turkey. Jehovah promised to make Abraham's descendants His Chosen People, if he would go 'unto a land that I will show thee'.[4] As Abraham and his family passed Shechem (present-day Nablus), Jehovah appeared to Abraham, and said, 'Unto thy seed I will give this land'.[5] Shechem was then part of the land of the Canaanites, whose occupation of the region dated back to 4000 B.C.

Abraham finally settled near Hebron where he acquired some land. According to the Old Testament, Jehovah renewed His original promise, given to Abraham, to his son, Isaac, and his grandson, Jacob – who was later to be called Israel, and whose twelve sons were to become the originators of the Tribes of Israel. Jacob tried to settle in Shechem, but the local residents objected. Later, in the sixteenth century B.C., following a widespread famine in the area, the Tribes of Israel, led by Joseph, a favoured son of Jacob, migrated to the fertile Nile valley in Egypt.

Here the Israelite tribes tended their flocks and prospered for about four centuries, until a Pharaoh king began mistreating them and insisting that they do manual work. The Israelites objected to this. In the twelfth century B.C., led by Moses, they escaped into the Sinai desert. During their four-decade-long wanderings in the desert they were initiated into the worship of one God – Jehovah – by Moses. They then began entering the 'promised' land of Canaan from the east, under the leadership of Joshua, the successor to Moses.

They settled in the hilly area along the river Jordan, and encountered no barriers in intermixing with the Moabites, who lived in the surrounding region. But they came into conflict with the Philistines[6] – originally from Crete and the Aegean – whose steady expansion from the base of the coastal plain had, by the middle of the eleventh century B.C., given them control of most of the land of Canaan. Supported by the Hebrew tribes, who had stayed behind at the time of the great famine in the sixteenth century B.C., the Israelites began confronting the Philistines as one people.

Given their drive and religious fervour, dramatised in their worship of one God, Jehovah, the Hebrew-Israelites prevailed over the Philistines. In 1020 B.C. they consolidated their gains by founding a theocratic state based on the monotheistic religion of Jehovah, with Saul as king. David, his successor, destroyed the last bastion of the Philistinian power in the region, and established three more Hebrew provinces, to the east of the river Jordan. Taken together King David's domain was known as Eretz Israel (Land of Israel). During the reign of his son, Solomon, Eretz Israel became an important economic entity. After his death in 922 B.C. it split into the kingdoms of Israel in the north and Judah in the south. Israel lasted until 721 B.C., when it fell into the hands of the Assyrians, while Judah maintained its identity until 538 B.C., when it was conquered by the Babylonians.

The erection of an altar to Zeus, the Greek god, in the (Hebrew) Temple of Jerusalem in 168 B.C. by the Ptolemaic king Antiochus set off a revolt by the Jews,[7] led by Judas Maccabeus, which brought about the founding of the independent Maccabean Kingdom of Judah in the Judean hills two years later. This state, subsequently expanded to include Galilee and other parts, continued to exist until 63 B.C., when it was conquered by the Roman emperor Pompey, and renamed Judea.

After that the Jews made three major attempts (in A.D. 66, 115 and 135) to regain independence from Roman rule, but failed. Each failure brought massive reprisals. In A.D. 135 the Roman emperor Hadrian crushed the Jewish rebellion with an iron hand, banished the Jews from Jerusalem and its surroundings, and renamed Judea Syria-Palestina.[8] The Jews either moved west – to other parts of the Roman empire which then extended as far west as England – or east, to Babylon and Persia. After Hadrian's death in A.D. 137 the Jews were allowed to acquire Roman citizenship and return to Jerusalem. A period of benign tolerance ended in A.D. 325, when the Roman emperor Constantine embraced Christianity.

Following the division of the Roman empire into two sections, in 365, Syria-Palestina became part of the Byzantine empire. In the sixth century Syria-Palestina became a battleground for the competing Byzantine and (Persian) Sassanid empires. This led the Jews to emigrate in large numbers either to Italy, France and Germany (where they were invited to settle), or to the Arabian Peninsula. By the time Syria-Palestina was captured by the Muslim Arabs from the Peninsula in 640, the Jews had been reduced to a minority there.

The five-century-long Arab rule of Palestine was broken by the (Christian) Crusaders, who occupied the Holy Land in 1100. This lasted for almost two centuries, and was followed by the reign of the Mamelukes, who were based in Cairo. Their suzerainty was ended by the Ottoman Turks in 1517. By then the centre of Jewish life had shifted from east to west, with the Jews forming an important minority in such European countries as Italy, France, Germany, Spain and Poland. When, during the sixteenth and seventeenth centuries, Italy, Germany and other central European countries began to segregate Jews in ghettos, a large number of them migrated to Russia and Russian Poland. In contrast the size and the status of the Jewish minority in the Ottoman empire remained the same: treated as dhimmi, they were granted religious and other freedoms, but were required to pay the poll tax in lieu of rendering military service to the Islamic ruler.

With economic prosperity spreading in the wake of the colonisation of non-European lands during the eighteenth and nineteenth centuries, Western European societies became steadily less intolerant of the Jews. However, in the comparatively less developed economic order prevalent in east Europe and Russia, the Christian majority continued to be hostile towards them. This was particularly true of Russia and Poland, which between them accounted for nearly two thirds of world Jewry at that time.[9]

Centuries of persecution had helped to keep alive a yearning for Palestine, the (historic) Promised Land, among the Jews. In 1862 Moses Hess, a German Jew, published a book *Rome and Jerusalem* which advocated the return of the Jews to Palestine to create a spiritual centre there for the Jews dispersed throughout the world (the Jewish Diaspora). This was religious Zionism which called on the Jews to return to Zion (the name of the hill in Jerusalem with the royal palace, which was the ancient centre of Hebrew government, worship, and national life) for religious reasons. The idea was adopted by the Lovers of Zion (Hovevei Zion) societies that sprang up in Russia soon after the pogrom of 1881–2. They organised the first Jewish immigration wave into Palestine.

It was left to Theodor Herz, an Austrian Jewish journalist, to give a political dimension to the concept of Zionism. In his pamphlet *The Jewish State (Der Judenstaat)*, published in 1896, he argued for a Jewish state to be set up in Ottoman Palestine. This was the seed which was to yield the state of Israel in 1948.

In those fifty-two years Palestine's Jewish population went up thirty-eight times – from 20,000 to 771,000 – due to six waves of immigration (aliyot[10]) and natural growth. The first aliyah (1882–1903) took 25,000 Jews, mainly from Czarist Russia, to Palestine, and doubled the size of the local Jewish community, which was then equally divided between Sephardic Jews and Ashkenazi Jews.[11] The next two aliyot (1904–14 and 1918–23), concerned chiefly with Jews from Russia and Russian Poland, involved 76,000 people. As believers in socialism and the dignity of labour, these colonisers set up agricultural settlements (kibbutzim), cooperative villages (moshavim), and the general federation of labour

(Histadrut[12]). They also created an educational system, with Hebrew as the medium of instruction, and a host of self-governing institutions. They were encouraged in their endeavours by the Balfour Declaration of 1917, which was incorporated later into the British mandate.

The fourth aliyah (1923–6) brought 60,000 immigrants – principally middle-class Jews from Poland – to the Palestinian shores. With America ceasing to be an 'open' country from 1924, Jewish emigrants from Europe became more interested in Palestine than before. This, and the formation of the Jewish Agency (as a result of the rapprochement between the Palestinian Zionists and the World Zionist Organisation) to finance Jewish immigration and act as the political representative of the Jews in Palestine, laid the foundation for a bigger wave of immigration. The fifth aliyah, which lasted from 1932 to the publication of the British government's White Paper in May 1939, accounted for 225,000 immigrants. A third of them came from eastern Europe, and another third from Nazi Germany. They were chiefly middle-class professionals, and capitalists, and gave the vastly enlarged Jewish community in Palestine a distinctly European veneer. Despite their high birthrate, the Sephardic Jews were now reduced from the original 50 per cent of the total to 20.[13] The last aliyah (1945–8), which involved 120,000 Jewish refugees from Europe, tilted the balance further in favour of the Ashkenazim.

Conscious of the deep resentment felt by the Arabs against Jewish immigration, the Zionists set up a clandestine militia, Haganah (Defence), in 1920, and began arming it. Following the Arab–Jewish clashes of 1929 they accelerated the process of training and arming the Haganah with smuggled arms. It was the discovery of such arms, in the autumn of 1935, which triggered off the Arab rebellion in 1936. By then there were about 10,000 'well-trained and relatively well-equipped Haganah members'.[14]

As stated earlier, the Arab revolt consisted of two phases: before the Peel Commission report, and after. During the second phase – when the Arabs decided to attack not only British targets but also the Jewish settlements which had nearly quadrupled since 1922[15] – the Haganah was actively organised and armed by the British.[16] Not surprisingly, both the Haganah and the smaller, more militant Irgun Tzvai Leumi (National Military Organisation) went on the offensive against the Arabs; and this took a heavy toll of Arab life.

Whiie the British government actively aided the Jews in Palestine against the Arabs, it responded lukewarmly to appeals to allow Jewish refugees, pouring out of Germany, to settle in Britain. However, it was not alone in this. At the international conference on the Jewish refugee problem held in Evian, France, at the behest of the American president, Franklin D. Rooșevelt, other West European governments were as reluctant to render substantial help as the British, which had allowed in only 3,000 Jewish refugees during 1932–5.[17] Nor did such continental countries as America, Canada and Australia do any better. (In contrast, the small Dominican Republic in the Caribbean volunteered to take in 100,000 Jews.)

Against this background the Zionists considered the 1939 British White Paper, limiting Jewish immigration to an annual average of 15,000 for five years, all the more galling. But the Zionists could not remain anti-British once the Second World War had broken out in September. In fact they actively cooperated with the Allies. In Palestine 133,000 Jews volunteered to join the British Africa Corps; 30,000 were accepted. They fought as independent companies, and saw action in Libya, Crete and Syria. Many thousands more helped establish and run the munitions industry in Palestine. Simultaneously the Zionists actively sabotaged the 1939 White Paper by smuggling tens of thousands of Jews into Palestine.

With the USA entering the war in December 1941, and major American Zionist organisations passing a resolution at a conference in May 1942 favouring the founding of a Jewish commonwealth in all of Palestine, the international Zionist lobby focused its primary attention on America. After the war the Zionists narrowed their demands to the scrapping of the 1939 White Paper, and the immediate admission of 100,000 Jewish refugees (camped in Cyprus) into Palestine. In this they secured the backing of both the American president, Harry Truman, and Congress – the latter going so far as to call for unlimited Jewish immigration into Palestine, subject only to the physical and economic limitations of the country.

Aware that acceptance of these recommendations would irreparably damage its relations with the Arabs, in Palestine and elsewhere, Britain agreed to a proposal that a joint Anglo–American commission be appointed to study the whole Palestine problem. In its report, published in April 1946, the commission suggested that Britain should continue its mandate, that 100,000 Jewish refugees be let into Palestine immediately, and that all illegal militias – primarily the 65,000-strong Zionist irregulars, armed with weapons from the wartime munitions factories – be disbanded.

London agreed to continue the mandate only if Washington shared the responsibility, which the latter refused. For the rest, Washington stressed the need for the immediate admission of the Jewish refugees into Palestine, while London made this conditional on the prior disarming of the Zionist irregulars, whose violent activities posed an increasing threat to British life and property. The blowing up of Jerusalem's King David Hotel, then housing British civilian and military offices, in July by the Irgun members, which resulted in ninety-one deaths, underlined the seriousness of the problem.

As stated earlier, Britain was disheartened by its failure to find a negotiated solution, and by the WZO congress's resolution, endorsing its American affiliate's earlier call for an independent Jewish state in all of

Palestine. The result was the British referral of the problem to the United Nations in early 1947, and the subsequent recommendation of a partition plan, with Jerusalem as an internationally administered city, by the UN's Special Committee on Palestine, by thirty-three votes to thirteen, with ten abstentions (including Britain). The Zionists were doubly pleased. They were offered an independent Jewish state; and its area (55 per cent of Palestine) was nearly twice as large as the Jewish proportion of the population (30 per cent owning 6 per cent of the land). They accepted the UN plan enthusiastically; the Arabs rejected it angrily.

The inter-communal violence, which emerged immediately, intensified as Britain's withdrawal date – 14 May 1948 – approached. The skirmishes in Jerusalem and Haifa in March resulted in the deaths of 90 Jews and 230 Arabs. The disproportion between the casualities of the two sides was a reflection of the fact that the cohesive Jewish community was better armed and more disciplined than the loosely organised and poorly armed Arabs.

Conscious of the anomaly that the area about to constitute the Jewish state (according to the UN plan) had 10,000 more Arabs than Jews,[18] all the Zionist forces – the Haganah, the Irgun, and the Lehy (commonly known as the Stern Gang)[19] – concentrated on expelling as many Arabs from this area as possible. In this they were aided by the events of 9/10 April in the village of Deir Yassin near Jerusalem.

A joint force of 132 Irgun and Lehy militias, led by Menachem Begin, carried out an eight-hour-long attack on the village, during which they killed 254 men, women and children – two thirds of the total population – dynamited houses, looted, and raped.[20] From the Zionist viewpoint, the massacre and its reporting were to prove highly efficacious. 'Arab headquarters at [nearby] Ramallah broadcast a crude atrocity story, alleging indiscriminate massacre, by Irgun troops, of about 240 men, women and children in Deir Yassin,' wrote Begin in his memoirs. 'Arabs throughout the country, induced to believe wild tales of "Irgun butchery", were seized with limitless panic, and started to flee for their lives. This mass flight soon developed into a maddened, uncontrollable stampede.'[21] The result was that by the time the British ended their mandate, some 300,000 Arabs had fled from the areas expected to form the (planned) Jewish state.

Soon after the state of Israel was proclaimed on 15 May it was recognised by the US and the USSR. The state had 30,000 fully mobilised soldiers ready – supported by 32,000 reserves, 15,000 Jewish settlement police, and 32,000 home guards[22] – to face the 21,500 Arab troops who crossed over the borders of Palestine on the eve of the British withdrawal. Interspersed by three truces of varying lengths, the first Arab–Israeli war[23] continued until 7 January 1949. During the first fortnight the Arab forces managed to occupy a greater area than had been allocated to the Palestinian Arabs by the UN plan. But this did not last long. In a series of well-planned counter offensives the Israelis dislodged the Arabs from all areas, except the West Bank (2,200 square miles) and Gaza (135 square miles). In the process the Israelis suffered 30,000 casualties.[24] This was as much a reflection of the large Israeli forces involved in the fighting as of the ambition of the Israeli government to capture the maximum possible territory of Palestine.

When the war finally ended in early January, Israel controlled 24 per cent more of Palestine than had been allocated to it by the UN. Populated by 700,000 Jews and only 165,000 Arabs (down from the previous 750,000), Israel was now a truly Jewish state. A begrudging acceptance of its boundaries by an Arab neighbour came in February, when Egypt signed an armistice agreement with it. During the next five months Egypt's example was followed in succession by Lebanon, Transjordan, and finally Syria. (Iraq, which lacked common borders with Israel, did not sign an armistice agreement with the Jewish state.)

Internally, within a few weeks of the end of the war, the provisional government ordered an election, based on universal suffrage, to a constituent assembly. In February the constituent assembly passed the Transition Law, which declared Israel to be a republic, headed by the president – to be elected for a five-year term by the Knesset (Parliament), a single-chamber parliament of 120 members, by a simple majority. The Knesset itself is required to be elected by adult franchise, under the system of proportional representation, with the leader of the largest group to be invited by the president to become the prime minister and form the government, which exercises full executive powers. Having passed the Transition Law, and having decided to postpone (indefinitely) producing a written constitution, the constituent assembly transformed itself into the Knesset.[25]

A unique feature of Israel is its defence organisation. Known as the Israel Defence Forces, it is an integrated body covering land, sea and air – with a special section, Nahal, which combines military training with fieldwork in the agricultural settlements along the borders. It is a conscript force, and includes both males and females. Since its establishment Israel has built up the IDF, both in size and equipment, to the extent that in the late 1970s it consumed 26 to 30 per cent of the gross national product.[26] Its standing strength of some 170,000 can be bolstered to a fully mobilised 455,000 within forty-eight hours. For a country of 3.2 million Jews (with 600,000 non-Jews barred from joining the IDF), this is very impressive.

Military preparedness of the entire Jewish population has been the central theme of Israel since its founding. After the 1948–9 war Israel engaged in three major wars with its Arab neighbours: in October 1956, June 1967, and October 1973. The results of these conflagrations have had a profound effect on the evolution of Israel as a religious-national entity.

The armistice agreements with the Arab states did not lead to peace treaties. The Arabs insisted that Israel must first allow the Palestinian Arab refugees to return home (as recommended by the UN in December 1948) before they engaged in peace talks, while Israel maintained that the refugee problem should be discussed as part of the overall peace settlement.

By expressing their opposition to any attempt to alter the armistice boundaries in the Tripartite Declaration of May 1950, America, Britain and France guaranteed Israel's frontiers. In addition, the Declaration promised to supply arms to Israel and the Arab states only to the extent that did not create 'imbalance'. Given these guarantees, and the convulsions that shook the regimes of Egypt, Syria and Transjordan/Jordan in the wake of the Arab defeat in the 1948–9 war, Israel had a peaceful existence for the next few years.

However, once the political situation in these countries had settled down by late 1954, Israel experienced increased commando raids along its borders with Egypt, Syria and Jordan. It was also adversely affected by the continued naval blockade against it by Egypt in the Suez Canal and the Gulf of Aqaba since the Palestine war. But what alarmed Israel most was the public announcement made in September that Egypt's President Nasser had signed a major arms deal with Czechoslovakia. It tried to balance this by asking the signatories of the Tripartite Declaration to supply it with jet fighters and heavy weapons. Only France agreed to help, albeit clandestinely.

Franco–Israeli friendship deepened when, in July 1956, Nasser nationalised the Universal Suez Maritime Canal Company (with its headquarters in Paris), owned largely by the French and British governments. Together, Israel and France hatched a secret plan to occupy the Suez Canal, break the Gulf of Aqaba blockade, and compel Cairo to recognise Israel. Having failed to dislodge Nasser from power, or even to discredit him at home or abroad, Britain joined the Franco–Israeli plan.

The decision of the Jordanian king – taken in response to the wishes of the recently elected government – to form a joint military command with Egypt and Syria, in October, provided the triple alliance with a pretext to implement its secret plan. On 29 October Israel invaded the Sinai peninsula of Egypt; and two days later Britain and France followed with an attack on the Suez Canal. The unprovoked aggression caused an uproar in the community of nations, including America. At the promptings of the United Nations – strongly backed by the US and the USSR – Britain and France agreed to a cease-fire on 6 November, and to withdraw from the Suez Canal. By then Israel had occupied Gaza and most of Sinai. Although it agreed to withdraw from the occupied territories on 8 November, it did not actually do so until next March – and that too only after America had committed itself to stand by the Israeli right of passage through the Gulf of Aqaba, to ensure that Gaza was not used again for launching guerrilla attacks against the Jewish state, and to assist Israel (clandestinely) in its nuclear research programme.[27] Following the Israeli withdrawal, the United Nations Emergency Force was posted in Gaza and the Gulf of Aqaba in Egyptian territory.

Since its drive into Gaza and Sinai met little resistance, Israel suffered minimal losses in men and materials during the nine-day war: 134 dead and material loss of $400 million. In contrast 2,000 to 3,000 Egyptians were either killed or captured by the invading forces.[28] Of the three major war objectives of the triple alliance, only one was secured: ending the blockade of the Gulf of Aqaba. This provided Israel with direct maritime access to south and south-east Asia and the eastern seaboard of Africa.

The comparative peace of the 1957–66 decade allowed Israel to improve its position economically, socially, and diplomatically. Helped by large capital imports and the arrival of half a million Jewish immigrants – nearly half of them from east Europe and possessing professional skills – the country was able to transform its hitherto agrarian economy into an industrial one. This was manifested by the increase in per capita income, at constant prices, during the decade from 1,286 to 3,452 Israeli pounds.[29]

With their minds freed from fear for the survival of their state, the Israeli Jews turned increasingly to such social problems as discrimination against the Sephardic Jews, the vexed question of 'Who is a Jew?', and the degree to which the state should enforce Jewish religious taboos in everyday life.

Israel was active on the diplomatic front, winning recognition – particularly from the newly independent states in Africa – and offering economic and technical aid. It reinforced its already strong diplomatic and military links with France. It diversified its economic ties with West Germany – established with the signing of a reparations agreement with Bonn in 1953 – by arranging to receive heavy weapons from West Germany. Once the thorny problem of the occupied Arab territories had been resolved by March 1957, Israel's relations with America improved rapidly. In June Tel Aviv endorsed the Eisenhower doctrine which promised American economic and military aid to any Middle East country wishing protection against 'overt armed aggression from any nation controlled by international communism'. Israel played a subsidiary, but crucial, role in Anglo–American plans to contain the consequences of the overthrow of the pro-West monarchy in Iraq in July 1958.

With the Democrat John F. Kennedy assuming the office of American president in January 1961, the already friendly relations between Tel Aviv and Washington became cordial. Breaking past precedents, Kennedy publicly declared that Israel was an ally of America. The accession of Lyndon B. Johnson to the presidency, following Kennedy's assassination in November 1963, brought America and Israel even closer. Johnson authorised the sale of offensive weapons – tanks and fighter bombers – to Israel.

At just this time Israel's relations with her Arab neighbours began to deteriorate rapidly. This had primarily to do with the Israeli plans to divert the waters of the Jordan for irrigation and other purposes in the Negev desert in the south. Israel had disregarded Arab protests in the mid-1950s against this project (since it adversely affected their water resources) and had pressed ahead with it. As the operational date of Israel's National Water Carrier, scheduled for mid-1964, approached, Arab–Israeli tensions rose. The Arab League's response, expressed in terms of holding the first Palestine National Council in May 1964 in east Jerusalem, and establishing the Palestine Liberation Organisation, alarmed the Israelis. Their fears were confirmed when the Palestinian Fatah chose to announce its existence by blowing up the National Water Carrier's pipeline at Ein Bone.

At home the Israelis experienced their first economic recession in 1965 (made worse by a fall in immigration and foreign aid), which persisted for the next two years. Tension with Syria rose as the Palestinian commandos – encouraged by the radical Baathists who seized power there in early 1966 – stepped up their guerrilla actions against the Jewish state. The creation of the joint Egyptian–Syrian military command in November 1966 alarmed the Israelis. A series of bloody skirmishes on the ground and in the air, and the Israeli leaders' hostile statements in the spring of 1967, left little doubt that Tel Aviv wished to see the regime in Damascus changed. As tension between Egypt–Syria and Israel escalated, the Jordanian king joined the Egyptian–Syrian Cairo–Damascus military command on 30 May. Just as it had felt before (in late October 1956), Israel now judged that this was the opportune moment to strike against the Arabs, and did so.

On the morning of 5 June, in a surprise attack, Israeli planes bombarded all of Egypt's seventeen airfields, making them inoperative and knocking out two thirds of the Egyptian air force: 365 fighters and 69 bombers.[30] They then turned around and inflicted equally devastating damage on the air forces of Syria and Jordan. Disregarding the UN Security Council calls for an immediate cease-fire on 6 and 7 June, the Israeli forces moved forward on three fronts: Egypt's Sinai, Jordan's West Bank, and Syria's Golan Heights. It was not until 6p.m. (local time) on 10 June that Israel finally accepted the UN-sponsored cease-fire. By then it had occupied all of Gaza and Sinai, east Jerusalem and the West Bank, and the Golan Heights. At the price of 778 troops killed and 61 tanks lost, Israel had during the six days of war inflicted humiliating losses on her three Arab neighbours. Some 10,000 Egyptian troops died either in action or due to thirst; and another 1,000 Syrian soldiers and officers perished, with Jordan suffering an unknown number of casualties. All told, the Arab tank losses stood at 700, Egypt alone losing 550.[31]

This time the USA, in contrast to its behaviour during the Suez war, did not insist on an Israeli withdrawal to the pre-war borders as part of the UN's cease-fire demand. The subsequent UN Security Council resolution 242 (sponsored by Britain and backed by both the US and the USSR), passed in November, balanced the call for Israeli withdrawal from the occupied Arab territories with a de facto recognition of Israel by the Arab states. As had happened with the UN resolution of December 1948 on the Palestine war, Israel interpreted resolution 242 differently from others. It insisted that its withdrawal was to be part of the peace treaties to be negotiated with the Arab countries. In contrast others, Arab and non-Arab, considered an Israeli withdrawal a prerequisite before peace talks could begin.

The Six Day war victory ushered in a new era in Zionist history. Israel now possessed an Arab area four times its size. With the new borders running along such natural barriers as the Suez Canal, the Gulf of Aqaba, and the river Jordan, the Israelis felt more secure than ever before. But once their initial euphoria had subsided the Israeli Jews recognised that, by acquiring the West Bank and Gaza, they had enlarged the Arab population from about 400,000 within the pre-1967 borders to 1.4 million (as against a Jewish population of 2.4 million). This would pose a threat to the Jewish nature of their state, should the conquered territories be annexed, openly or stealthily, in the future.

That the military rule imposed on the West Bank and Gaza was unpopular became clear as the residents repeatedly resorted to demonstrations and strikes, while terrorist actions against Israeli targets increased dramatically, both inside the occupied territories and Israel proper. Arab resistance in the occupied territories became so severe that the Israeli government placed Gaza under emergency rule in 1968. A year later it did the same with the West Bank.

By then Tel Aviv's hopes, shared by Washington, that their humiliating defeat would lead the Arabs to the negotiating table had proved illusory. In fact, having re-equipped the Egyptian military to its pre-1967 level with Soviet help, Nasser initiated a war of attrition against the Israeli positions along the Suez Canal in March 1969. Israel responded by resorting to saturation bombing of Egyptian targets and deep penetration raids into Egypt. This drove Nasser further into the Soviet embrace. With a sophisticated Soviet-built air defence umbrella in operation by the spring of 1970, Egypt managed to curtail Israel's capacity for massive reprisals. It was against this background that Israel agreed to a cease-fire with Egypt and Jordan in early August 1970 as part of an American peace plan devised by the secretary of state, William Rogers, along the lines of UN resolution 242.

This caused the break-up of Israel's national unity government, which had been formed just before the Six Day war, and which had survived the October 1969 elections. The nationalist, conservative Herut[32] party, led by Menachem Begin, left the government in protest against the acceptance of the Rogers peace plan. The subsequent weakening of the government helped the hawks within the Labour-Mapam[33] Alignment – the dominant party in the administration – to prevail over the doves regarding the establishment of Jewish settlements in the occupied territories. Afraid that the hawks would break away from the Labour-Mapam Alignment, ally with the Herut party and the small religious parties, and bring down the government, the doves acquiesced to the annexionist policy of the hawks. The subsequent spurt in Jewish colonisation of the West Bank and Gaza, the Golan Heights, and north Sinai angered and alarmed the Arabs.

Following the successful Israeli involvement in the American plans to help the Jordanian king against the Palestinian commandos in September 1970, American aid to Israel went up dramatically. This added to Arab worries – as did the cavalier response of Tel Aviv to President Sadat's statement in February 1971 that Egypt was ready to sign a peace treaty with Israel, once it had vacated occupied Arab land. The Arabs were also dismayed by the fact that in order to strengthen the detente the two superpowers had decided to underplay the contentious and complex problem of peace in the Middle East. The joint American–Soviet communiqué issued after President Richard M. Nixon's visit to Moscow in June 1972 made no reference to the Middle East. Later Tel Aviv dismissed Sadat's statement that the Arabs might have to use 'shock tactics' to break the Middle East stalemate as a ploy to divert the Egyptian people's attention away from their mounting economic and social problems.

Israel was therefore genuinely surprised by the attack mounted against it on 6 October 1973 by Egypt and Syria. Since the offensive assault came on the eve of the three-day Yom Kippur (Day of Atonement) holidays, it took the Israel Defence Force seventy-two hours to get fully mobilised (as against the planned thirty-six hours). However, within eight days of mobilisation the IDF, with its arsenal of weapons bolstered by a continuous airlift of American arms, forced the Syrians back, and cut a wedge through the Egyptian front to establish a bridgehead on the western bank of the Suez Canal.

Now the two superpowers, who had so far refrained from pressing for a cease-fire, engaged in urgent consultations. The result was that resolution 338 of the UN Security Council, passed on 22 October, called for an immediate cease-fire, and endorsed the earlier resolution 242. Having accepted the cease-fire, Israel broke it soon after, in order to encircle Egypt's 20,000-strong Third Army on the western side of the Suez zone, from the rear. It was only after the Soviet Union had threatened unilateral action against Israel that Tel Aviv finally bowed to the UN Security Council resolution 340 of 25 October to return to the battle lines of three days earlier.

Both sides paid a heavy price for the fourth Arab–Israeli war. Egypt lost 7,700 fighting men, 650 tanks, and 182 planes; and Syria, 3,500 men, 600 tanks, and 165 planes. The Israeli losses were: 2,552 troops, 840 tanks and 114 aircraft.[34] It was by far the bloodiest confrontation between the Arabs and the Jews. By comparison, the Suez war of 1956 had been a bloodless affair. It had brought Israel military victory and the free passage of the Gulf of Aqaba, but the diplomatic price paid in terms of estrangement from America and condemnation by the world at large had been heavy. In contrast the June 1967 war had been an unqualified success, both militarily and politically. This time Israel was, on the whole, a loser. Although the military result was 'no victory, no defeat' for either side, politically and diplomatically Tel Aviv lost more than it gained.

Twenty-three African states severed diplomatic relations with Israel. The European Economic Community, comprising nine countries, issued a statement which supported UN Security Council resolution 242 in terms that were closer to the Arabs than the Israelis. By visiting the Arab Middle East in June 1974, President Nixon indicated that America was prepared to improve its political relations with the Arabs without jeopardising its special ties with Israel. By then, nudged by Henry Kissinger, the American secretary of state, Tel Aviv had signed separate armistice agreements with Cairo and Damascus.

A far more significant accord with Egypt, to be called the Sinai II agreement, came later – in September 1975. It required Israel to withdraw to the Mitla and Gidi passes in the Sinai desert. For this one-sided concession to Egypt, Israel obtained a series of commitments and assurances from America about its security and survival as well as its long-term military, economic and energy needs. As the most extensive undertakings that America had ever given to any nation, or group of nations, these guarantees underwrote the continued (prosperous) existence of Israel in the firmest possible terms.

Israel was helped further by the cleavage that the Sinai II accord created between Egypt and Syria, a development which in turn intensified the Lebanese civil war. All this was reassuring to Tel Aviv: and so was the American presidential campaign of the summer and autumn of 1976, when the two main contenders vied with each other in showing their pro-Israeli bias, in order to win crucial Jewish funds and votes.

Oddly enough, this improvement in the country's standing abroad came at a time of deepening crisis at home. More than a quarter century of power had left the Labour party – the leading force in the ruling coalition – smug and corrupt. Encouraged by the rising economic problems besetting the citizens, the conservative nationalist Likud (Consolidation)[35] bloc – composed of the Herut, the Liberals, and a few small parties – launched an offensive against Labour for its corruption and inefficiency. A series of financial scandals involving government ministers and top party officials, discovered during the latter half of 1976, gave additional punch to the Likud's attack. Not surprisingly, therefore, in the May 1977 poll Likud emerged as the largest single party in the Knesset, thus ending the pattern that had persisted since the founding of Israel. Its leader, Menachem Begin, was invited to form the government, and did so with the aid of the religious parties.

By stressing the private sector and free enterprise, the Begin administration gave the country's mixed economy a determined push in the direction of a free market economy. Later, popular attention was gripped by the arrival of President Sadat in Jerusalem in November, and the peace process initiated by the visit. Secure in his fundamentalist views about Israel and its Biblical boundaries, and his awareness of the Jewish state's current military superiority, Begin stuck firmly to his hardline position. Consequently the accord reached through the mediation of the American president, James Carter – at the presidential retreat of Camp David in the mountains of Maryland – was as much a reflection of Tel Aviv's military-economic strength as it was of Cairo's comparative weakness.

Preceding and following the signing of the Camp David accord in September 1978, both Israel and America had entertained high hopes that history would repeat itself – that other Arab states would once again follow the lead given by Egypt when it signed the armistice agreement with Israel in February 1949. But this was not to be. However, neither Israel nor Egypt was diverted from pursuing what had by then become a bilateral (and not the much-desired multi-lateral) path to peace in the Middle East. Israel had much to gain and little to lose by detaching Egypt from its sister Arab states. If nothing else, such a course guaranteed that the remaining Arab countries would be unable to wage a war against it. Yet the Begin government refused to conclude a peace treaty with Egypt until and unless it had obtained a further set of military, economic and diplomatic commitments for Israel from America. Once this was done it signed a peace treaty with Egypt in March 1979, thirty years after the first armistice agreement.

Within a year the two states had exchanged ambassadors, and Israel had returned nearly two thirds of Sinai to Egypt. But the next target of concluding an agreement on Palestinian autonomy by 26 May was not met. Begin stood uncompromisingly by his position that the West Bank and Gaza are part of historical Judea and Samaria, which together formed Eretz Israel, the Land of Israel. As such Jews have a historical right to settle anywhere in the presently 'Administered Territories' of West Bank and Gaza, and the autonomy to be granted to the Palestinian Arabs in these territories would apply only to people, and not to the land and natural resources which, by historical rights bestowed upon Jews by Jehovah, belong to the state of Israel.

In fact the Begin government had accelerated the process of Jewish colonisation in the occupied territories from the day it took office. The result was that by June 1980 there were 123 Jewish settlements (besides

Arab Jerusalem and its suburbs) in the occupied territories, with a Jewish population of 72,000 – or about 6 per cent of the total Arab population.[36] Most of the Jews lived in the Arab east Jerusalem and its suburbs, which were annexed into Israel within weeks of their capture by the Israeli military in June 1967, to form an 'undivided' city. The de facto existence of a united Jerusalem was given a de jure status through a parliamentary bill passed on 31 July.

The fears of the leftist opposition that this action was likely to arouse hostility throughout the Arab and Muslim world were borne out shortly. In a statement on Eid ul fitr,[37] on 12 August, Crown Prince Fahd of Saudi Arabia called for the liberation of Arab Jerusalem, the third holiest city of Islam, through a jehad, holy war, against Israel.[38]

It may seem odd; but barring their diametrically opposed stands on Arab Jerusalem, Fahd shares many of the political-economic views of Begin. Both leaders, for example, are deeply religious, believe in the sanctity of private property and free enterprise, and intensely hate leftist ideologies and the socialist bloc. But for their strong differences on Zionism, they would be in the same camp supporting conservative, free enterprise forces everywhere, and fighting leftist, radical ideas and regimes. In fact, the House of Saud is the single most important conservative force in the Arab East.

# PART II

# ARAB STATES AND THE PALESTINIANS: INTERNAL COMPOSITION

5

# SOCIO-ECONOMIC CONTEXT: AN OUTLINE

Political forces in the Arab East can be broadly categorised as conservative, centrist, or leftist. But since such forces are best understood in a socio-economic context, it is necessary to sketch a profile of the region in social and economic terms. The major socio-economic factors are: Islam; tribalism; natural resources, specially oil; the size of the population, indigenous and foreign; and the level of economic development.

While Islam is common to all the states, the stress laid on it by the political establishment varies. By and large the rulers emphasise Islam far more (and Islam evokes greater loyalty) in societies where tribal values are predominant – that is, in the states of the Arabian Peninsula – than elsewhere.

As it happens, all the Arabian Peninsula countries, excepting the two Yemens, are oil-producing. The steadily rising world demand for oil, and the dramatic jump in its price in 1973–4, have given an unparalleled boost to the economic development of the Peninsula, which in turn has had a profound impact on social values. But these socio-economic changes are not as yet fully reflected in the evolution of these countries' political institutions. As shown in chapter 2, the gap between the two is wide in Saudi Arabia, Oman and Qatar, and less so in Kuwait and Bahrain, with the United Arab Emirates falling somewhere in between.

The two Yemens do not fit the above canvas. Committed to liberating society from 'backward tribalism',[1] the leftist regime in South Yemen has gone a long way towards detribalising the community. This is all the more remarkable in that it is the result of ideological inspiration and education, rather than of rapid economic development and urbanisation. In North Yemen too the traditional tribal order is under attack but from different forces. There the power of tribal chiefs is being challenged by leaders of the rising urban commercial classes as well as the military officer corps drawn largely from rural and urban petty bourgeois families.

Egypt and the Fertile Crescent present a different picture. Here the tribal values are far less operative than in the Arabian Peninsula; and so too is the hold of Islam, in political terms. Jordan and Lebanon are the exceptions, but for different reasons. The original inhabitants of the East

Bank in Jordan and their descendants (a minority) are more aware of their tribal roots and more susceptible to visualising their loyalty to King Hussein in a religious context – in so far as the king is a direct descendant of prophet Mohammed – than others. In Lebanon, on the other hand, the office of president can be assumed only by a Christian.

As the state with the largest oil production (outside the Peninsula), Iraq has the fastest growing economy in this part of the Arab East, with an increasingly strong industrial sector. In 1976 oil and other industries contributed as much as 57 per cent to the gross domestic product.[2] Syria and Egypt too are oil-producing countries. But since the oil output there is not so high as it is in Iraq, the contribution made by oil and other industries to the gross domestic product is only about half as much.[3]

The predominant element in the Syrian economy is the tertiary sector, made up of transport and communication, trade, and public and private services: it accounts for more than half of the GDP.[4] In that sense Syria is nearer to Lebanon and Jordan where the tertiary sector accounts for three-fifths of the GDP. Given this, and the fact that the tertiary segment of the economy employs the largest proportion of labour (about 40 per cent),[5] it would be appropriate to say that the capitalist economies of these countries are dominated by commercial interests.

An examination of the distribution of labour within the economy shows that agriculture engages the highest proportion in the three most populous states of the Arab East – Egypt (forty million), Iraq (thirteen million), and Syria (nine million): about one-half of the total. But the contribution that agriculture makes to the GDP of these countries varies. It amounts to one sixth to one fifth in Syria and Iraq, but about one third in Egypt. The low ratio in Syria is explained by the highly developed tertiary sector, and that in Iraq by the dominance of the oil-based industrial sector. The much bigger ratio in Egypt is as much a measure of Egypt's poverty as it is of the comparative weakness of its non-agrarian sectors.

As a group, Egypt and the Fertile Crescent countries have much higher population densities than those prevailing in the Arabian Peninsula. They also have recorded histories stretching back into ancient times, and long-settled societies, with well-formed socio-economic classes. In contrast, the last of the nomadic tribes in the Gulf states are still in the process of settling down; and the indiginous social order, upset by the onrush of oil wealth, has yet to acquire a well-defined multi-class profile.

Due to their advanced socio-economic environment and higher political consciousness – engendered largely by the nationalist struggle against the Ottoman and European rulers – Egypt and the Fertile Crescent countries have been the main feeders of the movements for Arab nationalism, Arab socialism, and Marxism-Leninism. On the other hand the contribution made by the countries of the Arabian Peninsula (excepting South Yemen) to these movements has been negligible. Whatever political awareness exists there, and is allowed expression, is the result mainly of economic development, financed by oil revenue. Not surprisingly, Kuwait and Bahrain, with the longest history of oil production in the Peninsula, have the most politically conscious populations.

Wherever some form of representative government exists in the Arab East, under monarchical or republican aegis, the regime grants its citizens (at least on paper) such democratic rights as the freedom of speech and expression. In so far as freedom of association means forming political parties, this right is non-existent in the Arabian Peninsula, excepting South Yemen.[6] Most of the states of the Peninsula deny their workers and employees the right to form trade unions. In theory the republican constitutions of the Arab East guarantee both democratic and trade union rights. However, in practice these rights are allowed in varying degrees, Lebanon being the most liberal and Iraq the most authoritarian.

Heavily dependent on the extraction and export of oil, the economies of the Gulf states are capitalist. With the exception of exploitation of mineral resources, which is now assigned to state-run corporations, the Gulf rulers encourage private enterprise wherever possible. In the absence of a thriving agrarian sector (due to inhospitable land and climate) or a sizable industrial base (due to the smallness of the local market), the internal economies have developed large service sectors.[7]

Outside the Arabian Peninsula ideological commitment to private enterprise is to be encountered only in Jordan and Lebanon. Although Egypt still has a mixed economy, the government there has been moving unmistakably towards a free market economy since the mid-1970s. In Syria and Iraq too the economy is mixed, with the stress shifting fitfully from private sector to public, or the other way around, without any clear unambiguous pattern being followed. The only state to have an unmistakably Marxist-socialist economy, with the least possible role for private capital, is South Yemen. Thus the Arab East provides economic models which range from the laissez faire of Lebanese capitalism (much helped by the weakness of the state machinery) to the planned socialism of South Yemen.

A regime's socio-economic policies at home give some indication of its relationship with the superpowers. Expectedly, South Yemen has the closest links with the Soviet Union, and no ties at all with America. At the other end, Saudi Arabia has no links with the USSR, and its relations with America have always been very intimate and warm. There is of course one major foreign policy subject which is peculiar to the Arab states: Israel. Excepting Egypt, no Arab state as yet recognises Israel. Beyond that, antipathy towards Israel and Zionism varies from country to country. Leftist South Yemen has all along been uncompromisingly hostile towards Israel – on political ideological grounds, treating Zionism and its creature, Israel, as an integral part of the imperialist camp led by America. Saudi Arabia too has been consistently hostile towards Israel, but on purely religious grounds.

Policies towards the superpowers and Israel are just two of the criteria to be considered when deciding whether a political institution is conservative, centrist, or leftist. The other criteria are: attitude towards religion and religious establishment; policy towards tribalism and tribal organisations; preference for a free market economy or a socialist economic order; and commitment to democratic and trade union rights.

In view of the complex nature of these touchstones, some approximation needs to be used to label the numerous political institutions in the Arab East. Broadly speaking, the institutions fighting for the interests of the working classes have been termed leftist; those reflecting the interests of the rich, conservative; and those in sympathy with the middle stata, centrist. Whereas the conservative and leftist institutions tend to follow a fairly steady course in their policies, the centrist ones are inclined to fluctuate widely at home and abroad. The vacillation of the centrist forces reflects the behaviour of the middle classes: while they dislike and envy the rich, they tend to treat the poor either patronisingly or disparagingly. The history of the centrist forces in power in Egypt (after the overthrow of the monarchy in 1952), and Syria and Iraq (after the Baathist coups respectively in 1963 and 1968) – as described in chapter 7 – provides conclusive evidence.

6

# CONSERVATIVE FORCES

The monarchies of the Arabian Peninsula form a solid conservative bloc in the Arab East, with the vast, oil-rich kingdom of Saudi Arabia as their leader. Based on tribalism and adherence to the most orthodox and restrictive interpretations of the Koran and the Sharia, these regimes are as enthusiastic about encouraging private enterprise at home as they are reluctant to share power with the elected representatives of their subjects.

It is significant that the Saudi rulers are the followers of Mohammed ibn Abdul Wahhab, an eighteenth-century Islamic scholar who upheld, and propagated, the strict interpretation of the Koran and the Sharia as propounded by Ahmed ibn Hanbal of Baghdad in the mid-ninth century. 'Based on the Hanbali school of Islamic law, the Saudi regime is the strictest and most conservative of the regimes which still retain Islamic law,' notes Helen Lackner, a British specialist on Saudi Arabia. 'Within its structure the king is the Imam of Islam. . . . Wahhabism being a fundamentalist and proselytising creed, its supporters oppose any liberal tendencies within Islam both at home and abroad.'[1]

Their task is facilitated by the highly centralised and authoritarian structure of the government, which dates back to the founding of the kingdom in the late 1920s by Abdul Aziz al Saud. He consolidated his control over a conquered territory by marrying into the family of the subjugated tribal chief, thus leaving intact the traditional tribal system. In the process he acquired seventeen wives, and sired forty-four sons and 215 daughters.[2] Later he lavished his fast increasing oil revenue on the tribal chiefs, who had all along retained internal control over their members. He was careful to remain neutral between the feuding tribes; and by appointing expatriate Egyptians and Syrians as his personal advisers he managed this well. While he allowed the local religious figures and the secular governor to administer an area, he monopolised the ultimate religio-political authority, and ran a virtual one-man government from Riyadh.

Such a system, lacking any bureaucratic and financial institutions, proved inadequate to cope with the multitude of problems which followed the tenfold jump in oil production during the post-war years 1945–9.[3] As the royal family's personal fortunes soared, and as its members strayed from Wahhabi puritanism and took to extravagant life-styles, the moral authority of King Abdul Aziz was seriously undermined. Simultaneously a rapid injection of Western people and technology posed a threat to the traditional values of a bedouin society. A large influx of Palestinian, Egyptian and Yemeni immigrant workers brought into the kingdom the revolutionary idea of Arab nationalism, which was antithetical to Western dominance over the country's political economy. Inspired by Arab nationalism, 13,000 Arab workers of the American-owned and managed (Aramco) Arabian American Oil Company went on a two-week-long strike in October 1953.

An angry Abdul Aziz broke the strike by banishing the indigenous strike leaders to their home villages, and expelling their foreign colleagues. He then temporised by appointing a council of ministers to advise him. But they never got a chance to offer advice: Abdul Aziz died some weeks later, without having called a single ministerial meeting.

Continuing the policy of repressing opposition, his successor, King Saud, took to arresting and deporting 'radical' Palestinian oil workers in large batches. When Aramco employees struck in June 1956 he signed a decree outlawing strikes and prescribing long sentences for those defying it. At the same time he nudged the Aramco management towards improving working conditions and increasing employees' fringe benefits. But this was not enough to stem the tide of anti-authoritarian opposition which was rising, and which drew part of its strength from his inept style of government. The division within the royal family which became public in 1958 – when Saud was compelled to hand over executive authority to Crown Prince Feisal – helped the opposition.

In order to retrieve lost ground King Saud followed a twin-headed policy of cultivating the liberal 'Free Princes' and the leaders of the rising class of technocrat commoners, and securing the loyalties of the tribal chiefs by lavishing generous subsidies on them. His tactics paid off. Within two years he regained the supreme executive power. But once properly back in the saddle he refused to honour the promise made to the 'Free Princes' about reforming the political system into a constitutional monarchy, committed to guaranteeing civil rights (including trade union rights) to its subjects, and introducing a parliament with a two-third elected membership.[4]

King Saud in fact went further than merely to renege on his liberalisation promise. In 1961 he promulgated the State Security Act which prescribed the death penalty, or twenty-five years' imprisonment, for anybody convicted of an 'aggressive act' against the state or the royal family. Unable to accept the continued autocracy of the political system any longer, Prince Talal, leader of the 'Free Princes', flew to Cairo in August 1962, formed the Liberation Front of Arabia, and began broadcasting anti-royalist material on Cairo Radio. The republican coup in North Yemen in September boosted the morale of the liberal and democratic forces of Saudi Arabia. Nine Saudi pilots defected to republican North Yemen with their planes, and Prince Talal set up a government-in-exile in Cairo.

Recognising the seriousness of the challenge to the monarchical system, the Council of Senior Princes decided once again in November (during King Saud's stay in America for medical treatment), to invest Crown Prince Feisal with supreme executive power. Feisal immediately offered his Saudi subjects a ten-point programme, which not only promised a constitution and a consultative assembly, and the introduction of a new local government structure with its own regulations, but also the strengthening of both Islamic propaganda and the Committees for Public Morality – as well as increased capital investment and economic growth, based primarily on an intensive exploitation of the country's natural resources.

The multifarious programme was warmly received by the religious hierarchy, already well disposed to Feisal due to his personal asceticism; by the merchants who saw immense opportunities for themselves in the ambitious development plans to be launched; and by the growing body of educated Saudis, ready to man the expanding bureaucracy and play a part in shaping their country's development. With all these forces rallied behind him, Feisal had no trouble in defeating Saud's attempt in March 1964 to climb back into his old seat.

After he had assumed the formal title of king in November,[5] Feisal felt secure enough to disown the most important item in the ten-point programme: the transformation of the autocratic kingdom into a constitutional monarchy.[6] This confirmed the worst fears of the political dissidents, who became more active than ever before. They were helped by the fact that due to Saudi Arabia's involvement in North Yemen's civil war there was a thriving traffic of men and weapons across the borders; and that Nasser's Egypt, fighting alongside the republicans in North Yemen, was eager to aid, morally and materially, the anti-royalists of Saudi Arabia.

The opposition's activities reached a climax in 1966. While the Society for the Liberation of the Holy Soil openly distributed leaflets in Riyadh and Mecca announcing its founding, the older Union of the People of the Arabian Peninsula claimed responsibility for bomb explosions in such sensitive places as the defence ministry in Riyadh and the state security head office in Damman, in the eastern oil region.[7]

Feisal tried to meet the twin ideological challenge of Arab nationalism and republicanism by fostering Islamic spirit and solidarity in the form of the Islamic Alliance, open to the Muslim countries the world over, and by sponsoring programmes for the revival of orthodox Islam at home and abroad. He accelerated the process of expanding and modernising the armed forces and state intelligence – in active cooperation with the West – that he had initiated soon after the outbreak of the civil war in North Yemen. He carried out large-scale expulsions of the Palestinian, Egyptian and Yemeni immigrants, dismissed fifteen 'disloyal' army officers, and arrested fifty-five 'Communists'. Repression reached a peak in March 1967 when seventeen Yemenis were executed, some 750 Saudis arrested, and about 35,000 Yemenis deported.[8]

The Arab–Israeli war of June 1967 provided a chance for the opposition elements to show their strength, openly. Demonstrating against America's unqualified support for Israel, they attacked American clubs and recreation centres, as well as the military barracks in Dhahran, and called on the ruler to terminate all oil supplies to America and end repression at home.

Although they succeeded in getting the king to join the Arab oil boycott, the ill-effects of Egypt's defeat in the war rubbed off on them. The subsequent reconciliation between Nasser and Feisal, with the former promising to cease aiding the republican forces in the Arabian Peninsula, and the latter espousing the Palestinian cause, demoralised the Saudi opposition. Aware of this, Feisal hit out at his adversaries with renewed vigour.

Yet the anti-royalists remained active. Indeed in 1969 they twice attempted a coup. The first, in June, involved air force officers and leftist oil workers and teachers, and was aborted only a few hours before being executed by a tip-off from a government infiltrator. The second, a few months later, was instigated by some of the powerful, reformist families of Hejaz – traditional rivals to the House of Saud – in conjunction with high-ranking retired army officers, and was squashed in the early stages. As a result of these unsuccessful coups, 2,000 people were arrested, and scores of the conspiring air force officers executed.[9]

In the economic sphere Feisal regulated the speed of development to ensure that it did not corrupt his subjects, morally or materially, or outstrip their ability to actively participate in it. He authorised generous state funds to provide educational and health facilities to the public. He upheld the Islamic tradition by leading a spartan life, and fully backing the Committees for Public Morality. None the less he took issue with the religious hierarchy on such subjects as women's education and the introduction of television (in 1965) and wore down its resistance to change. By combining Islam with militant anti-communism, and backing it with enormous oil revenue, he won the support of many Muslim countries around the globe, and made Saudi Arabia a powerful force in the Arab East world.

The Yom Kippur war provided a further boost to Feisal and his regime. By giving an enthusiastic lead in imposing an Arab oil embargo on the countries supporting Israel, Feisal scored a double hit. He showed that he was an Arab nationalist, and at the same time he helped push oil prices up dramatically. The subsequent bonanza helped to strengthen the monarchical order in Saudi Arabia.

However, by then he had become too much of a hate figure among his adversaries to have any redeeming feature. Some of them had resorted to the desperate act of trying to kill him. These attacks invariably failed: it was not until March 1975 that one such attempt succeeded, and that only because the assassin, Feisal ibn Musaid, was a royal prince, with comparatively easy access to the monarch. His motives seemed both political and personal. The (later) discovery that he had received military training at one of the Palestinian camps in Lebanon showed that he was a radical of some kind. The fact that his brother had lost his life for having led an attack on the first television station in the kingdom indicated that the young prince was most probably motivated by a desire to avenge his brother's death.

Feisal's death, and Khaled's accession to the throne, came at a time when the ambitious Second Five Year Plan (1975–80), worth $142 billion, had just been launched, and the effects of a dramatic increase in economic activity, fuelled by the quadrupling of oil prices in late 1973, were being felt in all spheres of Saudi life. The unprecedented influx of foreign labour, from Arab and non-Arab countries, was rapidly turning the Saudi workforce into a minority, and undermining the puritanic, ultra-conservative socio-cultural fabric of Saudi society.

The reaction to this phenomenon varied among the senior princes. Although they and the king were all for economic progress and modern technology, they held different views on the speed of development and the extent to which to compromise with the orthodox Islamic values and practices. Those who advocated a slower pace of industrialisation and closer adherence to the teachings of the Koran and the Sharia at home were also the ones who stood for greater support for the Palestinians and a sharper struggle against Zionism abroad. Led by King Khaled and Prince Abdullah ibn Abdul Aziz, they came to be known as representatives of the Arab nationalist trend within the royal family. Those who stood for a fast pace of industrialisation, accompanied by greater religio-cultural liberalisation at home, advocated still closer ties with America, leading to the formal signing of a long-term security treaty with Washington. Headed by Crown Prince Fahd and Prince Sultan ibn Abdul Aziz, they came to be identified as representing the modernist-Americanist trend within the ruling family.

Fahd and Sultan are real brothers. As sons of Hussah al Sudeiri, the favourite among the seventeen wives of Abdul Aziz, they belong to the Sudeiri clan of the royal family. Of the seven Sudeiri brothers, three – Fahd, Sultan, and Nayef (inferior minister) – are in the cabinet. However, their powerful half-brothers, Khaled and Abdullah, belong to different clans: Khaled, a son of Jawhrah al Jiluwi, to the Jiluwi; and Abdullah, a son of Asi al Shureim, to the Shureim. In a move to balance the power of the Sudeiri princes, King Khaled allocated the foreign ministry to Prince Saud, a son of the late King Feisal, in late 1975.[10]

The king and these five most powerful princes sit at the apex of a pyramid which consists of over 4,000 princes. Half of them are direct descendants of Abdul Aziz, founder of the kingdom, and the rest, of his five brothers and cousins. The royal princes have all the provincial governorships and half of the cabinet posts, with a monopoly over all the most important ministries, except oil (which is run by Shaikh Ahmed Zaki Yamani). In addition, they occupy 200 of the top positions in the armed forces, police, coast-guard, and the central and provincial civil services. As government employees, they are barred from owning businesses. Of those who are not, some 800 are already multimillionaires.[11]

At the very top the modernist-Americanist Fahd and Sultan are balanced by the traditionalist-nationalist Khaled and Abdullah, with Khaled as the king, Fahd as the crown prince, Sultan as the head of the armed forces, and Abdullah the commander of the powerful National Guard. Although first established in 1946, the Saudi armed forces were a much neglected arm of the state until the republican coup (of September 1962) in North Yemen. Expansion and modernisation, initiated in the mid-1960s, were accelerated after the Yom Kippur war. During the period 1973–8, the annual defence budget rocketed from $1,700 million to $14,200 million (47,800 million Saudi riyals).[12] Most of the arms and training personnel came from America.

Yet, due to lack of loyalty to the House of Saud and familiarity with the recently acquired highly advanced weapons, the fighting abilities of the 61,000 men and officers[13] were rated low. 'Within Saudi Arabia itself, the regular armed forces are not trusted by the regime,' states Lackner. 'Within their ranks considerable dissent has been known to exist. . . . The Army is feared by the ruling family.'[14] Between mid-1977 and late 1978 an estimated 4,175 soldiers and officers were reported to have defected at different times and crossed over either into Jordan, Kuwait, or Iraq.[15]

Not surprisingly greater reliance is laid on the National Guard, a paramilitary force drawn from the most loyal of the tribes in the kingdom. It was established in 1932 as the White Guard, and had a liberal sprinkling of the former members of the Ikhwan (Brotherhood), after they had lost out in their clashes with Abdul Aziz, whom they had earlier accused of having strayed from the true path of Wahhabism. In the wake of the republican seizure of power in North Yemen the White Guard was placed under the command of Prince Khaled (later to become king) and renamed the National Guard. Its rearming and retraining were assigned to British military experts who were later joined by the Americans.

It was not long before the US, which already played the leading role in arming and training the Saudi military, became the prime source of arms supplies and military expertise to the National Guard. King Feisal was advised to merge the two forces but refused to do so, mainly because having two separate armed services in the kingdom enabled him to maintain a balance of power between the competing clans within the royal family.

By the late 1970s the 41,000-strong National Guard[16] had acquired a vast armoury of missiles, helicopters, artillery and armoured cars; and its members had reputedly become better trained than regular troops. Segregated from the populace at large, the National Guards are billeted outside urban centres, given extra privileges, and made to feel elitist. Their officers are the most pampered outside the royal family: they are in addition accorded social status on a par with that of the highly respected merchant families of Hejaz. Their commander, Prince Abdullah, is the second deputy prime minister, and thus next only to the king (who is also the prime minister) and the crown prince (who is the first deputy prime minister). As the regime's most reliable armed service, the National Guard is used to deal swiftly and mercilessly with anything that remotely threatens the House of Saud – be it a strike, demonstration, tribal revolt, or disaffection within the military.

Since July 1977, when an attempted military coup was foiled and 115 officers executed, the National Guard has been inordinately busy. Significantly, the rebellious officers' manifesto attacked the corruption rampant among the royal princes – which they associated with the rulers' intimate ties with America – and called for an Islamic republic which would truly abide by the basic values of the Koran and the Sharia.[17] This manifesto was thus a forerunner of the thinking that was to inspire the Islamic revolutionary forces in Iran a year later.

The failure of the July 1977 coup did not discourage a different group of military officers, led by the commander of an armoured brigade, to plan another. But this was discovered too, in October 1978, and led to the arrest of five princes and five leading army officers. While the princes were expelled from the country, the high-ranking military officers (along with twenty-one others of lower rank) managed to escape and, with the help of colleagues in the air force, flew to Libya.[18]

Nervous at these developments, Crown Prince Fahd (acting as regent in the absence of the king who was abroad for a heart operation) instructed the intelligence chief, Prince Turki, to put all military officers under surveillance. This was deeply resented by the officers, and led to strong protest by the chiefs-of-staff to Crown Prince Fahd. But the matter was not resolved until after the return of King Khaled to Riyadh in the middle of March 1979. The subsequent departure of Fahd a week later to a 'health farm' in Spain, along with his vast entourage, indicated that he had lost out.

In May there were reports of a planned coup by the commanders of the air force base at Jubail in the eastern region. One of the conspirators (who defected) allegedly produced evidence that the plotters had been in touch with Ayatollah Khomeini and the Iranian foreign minister Ibrahim Yazdi who promised to help destroy 'the tribal, feudal system' prevalent in Saudi Arabia, and replace it with 'a modern regime based on the teachings and practices of the Koran' along the lines being followed in the Iranian republic. Ending the American presence in Saudi Arabia, and radically altering the policies of Aramco, were the top priorities of the coup leaders.[19]

But what alarmed the ruling family most was the discovery that certain of the National Guard officers at Medina, Hail and Gassem had found the corruption in high places – and the excessive presence of Americans in the oil industry, the military and the National Guard[20] – so unbearable that they were driven to contemplate a coup against the regime. Following the murder of some ultra-loyalist National Guard officers at the above camps in early August, the government reportedly arrested 160 ranks and officers.[21]

It was against this background that the seizure of the Grand Mosque of Mecca by 400 well-armed guerrillas occurred at dawn on 20 November, which marked the start of the fifteenth century of the Islamic calendar. Led by Mohammed ibn Abdullah al Qahtani and Juheiman al Oteiba, the rebels put forward political and religious demands. Besides insisting that Qahtani, a brilliant twenty-seven-year-old former theological student at Riyadh's Islamic university, be accepted as the mehdi (one guided by Allah), they wanted the country to be declared an Islamic republic, its oil resources conserved, with an immediate halt to its export, and ties with the corrupt West, particularly America, severed.

The ranks of the rebels (who had won the cooperation of the army garrison at Mecca) contained dissident members of the military and the National Guard, and warriors from the Shammar and Oteiba tribes whose animosity to the House of Saud dated back to 1930, when Abdul Aziz, helped by the British, had crushed the Ikhwan. Their take-over of the holiest shrine of Islam was so well planned and thorough that the government had to muster a force of 10,000 men – including personnel from the military, National Guard, Emergency Force, and Special Security force, as well as Pakistani troops and French anti-terrorist experts[22] – and wage a fortnight-long battle to clear the mosque of the rebels.

According to official statements, the Mecca uprising led to the deaths of 127 troops, twenty-five pilgrims, and 117 rebels. Of the 170 guerrillas captured, 103 received long prison sentences, and the rest were beheaded by sword in public places in eight different cities of the kingdom (so as to discourage the citizens from mounting any such operation in the future).[23] There were reports that the occupation of the Grand Mosque at Mecca by the Islamic rebels was part of a wider revolt, with prophet Mohammed's mosque in Medina being occupied by local people with the connivance of dissident troops.[24] The claim, made by the clandestine Union of the People of the Arabian Peninsula, that about 7,000 people had been arrested during and after the Mecca uprising added credence to these reports.[25]

Encouraged by the general air of defiance engendered by the events in Mecca, the 300,000-strong Shia minority[26] – concentrated in the oil-rich region of Hasa – broke the long-established ban on the celebration of their festival of mourning, Ashura, on 27 November. To the alarm of the authorities, the Ashura processions turned into pro-Khomeini demonstrations in eight important towns of the oil region. The government pressed into action 20,000 security forces to break them up.[27] But sporadic demonstrations and pitched battles between the government forces and the Shia militants continued for about two months, and led to the deaths of fifty-seven members of the security forces and ninety-nine Shias. About six thousand people, including boys and old men, were arrested, often at random; and two thousand of them were still in jail six months later.[28]

Ayatollah Khomeini, an eminent Islamic personality particularly revered by the Shias, and renowned for his mastery of Koranic teachings, regards monarchy as un-Islamic, and maintains that when rulers become self-serving they deserve to be overthrown by their subjects. Available as taped cassettes and broadcasts on the Iranian state radio, his speeches on this and other subjects have reached large audiences in the Gulf states. He regards the Gulf monarchs as corrupt men who foster what he calls 'American Islam' or 'golden Islam'. He is scathing about the depleting of the valuable oil resources of their countries in order to satisfy the ever-growing demands of America, which he describes as the Great Satan, the number one source of corruption on earth. He denounces these rulers for denying their subjects any role in the decision-making process of the state. The creation of a representative system in Iran, with a popularly elected president and parliament – accomplished as a result of six referendums and elections in fifteen months – made his argument for republicanism attractive to the masses living in the Gulf states.

Finding itself increasingly on the defensive, the House of Saud has tried to refurbish its Islamic image. For instance, in the summer of 1979 the revitalised Committees for Public Morality closed all beauty parlours and hair-dressing salons for women, and forbade women to try on garments on the premises. Yielding to pressure from these Committees, the government banned all non-Islamic services, including Confirmation classes at foreign schools, in the kingdom. The sale of crosses, even as jewellery, was banned.[29]

While the royal family could impose such restrictions by the stroke of a pen, it had to grapple with something fundamental, and complex, when contemplating democratic reform of some kind in the kingdom. Its previous promises on the subject had come to nothing. Its basically cavalier attitude to political liberalisation was succinctly expressed by Prince Salman, the governor of Riyadh and one of the Sudeiri princes, in

June 1977. 'We don't want to set up such institutions [as a consultative assembly] so as to look good to the eyes of the world,' he told a British journalist. 'Anyone with ideas has only to come and discuss them with us.'[30]

But the overthrow of the Shah of Iran in February 1979, and more particularly the Mecca uprising, had a shattering effect on the ruling family's confidence. The reshuffling of seventeen top civilian and military positions, in the wake of the uprising, showed that the regime had taken a very serious view of this challenge to its religio-political authority. Unwilling to place its trust either in the military or the National Guard, the ruling family quietly initiated plans to use three specially trained Pakistani brigades (with a total strength of 12,000) as a special royal guard.[31] Simmultaneously steps were taken to reassure the populace that some sort of reform was being considered seriously. The king's appointment of a committee to produce a draft constitution was followed by an announcement by the crown prince that a consultative assembly of sixty to seventy nominated members would be established 'in the near future'.[32]

Yet, conscious of the fact that any concession to the democratic opposition would whet its appetite and result in further erosion of the royal prerogative – as had indeed happened in Iran in 1978 – the House of Saud intended to prolong the process of whatever liberalisation it meant to offer to its subjects, while maintaining all along that it had nothing to do with the challenge posed to its hegemony, as exemplified by the Mecca uprising. The Saudi ruling family knew that any explicit or implicit admission that its authority was waning would have a disastrous effect not only on the monarchical order in Riyadh but also in all of the remaining Arabian Peninsula's capitals, except Aden: it was only too aware of the big-brother status it enjoyed among its neighbours.

The Saudi rulers' influence is a derivative either of their economic power, as in the case of North Yemen, Bahrain, and Oman, or their close tribal or ideological ties with the neighbouring monarch, as in Qatar and Kuwait. Of all their neighbours, they attach particular importance to North Yemen. As an unstable republic, whose people are continually pulled southward and leftward in their quest for Yemeni unity, North Yemen is seen as a potential threat. While the three-quarter million Yemeni workers, performing some of the most menial tasks in the kingdom, are recognised as being crucial to the Saudi economy, they are also feared and distrusted as a possible fifth column.

Significantly, Riyadh's involvement in North Yemeni politics dates nearly as far back as the founding of the Saudi kingdom. It was the treaty of 1934 which placed the three Yemeni provinces in Saudi hands. Thereafter the House of Saud stood by the North Yemeni rulers, supporting them during the severe crises they faced, first in 1948 and then in 1955. The success of the republican coup of September 1962 came as a shock to the Saudi royal family. It did everything possible to help the deposed ruler, Imam Mohammed al Badr, to regain his throne. In fact it was Saudi aid in money, weapons, and training that enabled the royalist forces to regain half of North Yemen by August 1965.

The downfall of the monarch, and continued civil war, created an environment which helped the traditional tribal leaders to assume greater power than before. The two most important such leaders to emerge were Shaikh Naji al Ghadr, chief of the Bakel tribal confederation, and Shaikh Abdullah al Ahmar, head of the Hashed tribal confederation. (Between them the two tribal confederations accounted for 40 per cent of the national population.) Fattened on the subsidies received from different sources, primarily Saudi Arabia and Egypt, they raised large private armies, and this enhanced their bargaining power.

When the Egyptian troops, siding with the republicans, withdrew from North Yemen in December 1967, the royalists, backed by Riyadh, made a bid to capture Sanaa. They failed. However, following its success in lifting the siege of Sanaa, the tribal section of the republican forces took to attacking its erstwhile leftist colleagues, and weakened them considerably. This development encouraged Riyadh to drop its support of Imam Mohammed al Badr, and accept the much weakened republican regime in Sanaa. In March 1970 it agreed to cease its subsidies to the royalists. Responding to this, and the formal recognition bestowed upon them by Riyadh, the republican authorities expanded the forty-five-member consultative assembly by adding eighteen royalists to it, and included royalist ministers in a newly formed coalition government.

From then on Saudi influence on the regime in Sanaa rose steadily, and led to a war between the two Yemens in September 1972. However, the surprise end to this conflagration, with the two Yemens agreeing to unite, gave Riyadh a nasty shock. As stated earlier,[33] the House of Saud tried to frustrate this pact. It succeeded in having its nominee, Abdullah al Hijri, chosen as prime minister. During his visit to Riyadh in 1973 Hijri agreed to waive North Yemen's claims to the three Yemeni provinces annexed by Saudi Arabia in 1934, which were due to be returned to Sanaa in 1974. This accentuated the conflict which existed between Hijri and President Iryani, a Yemeni nationalist. It was not until early 1974 that this conflict was resolved – in Iryani's favour. But this made no difference to the power of Shaikh Abdullah al Ahmar, who continued to head the consultative assembly, dominated by pro-Saudi tribal leaders.

During the early days of his rule Colonel Ibrahim al Hamdi – who assumed power after a military coup in June 1974 – was in close touch with Riyadh. But as he followed up his dissolution of the consultative assembly with efforts to build a popular base for his regime, and pursue independent policies nationally and internationally, he fell foul of the tribal leaders at home and the Saudi royal family abroad. The disgruntled tribal chieftains attempted two coups in 1975 and one in early 1976, but in vain. Then, led by Mojahed Abu Shawareb, brother-in-law of Shaikh Ahmar, the tribals took to sabotage in their northern region.

Hamdi paid a secret visit to the north in January 1977, when he was presented with a charter of fourteen demands by the tribal leaders. These included the formation of a new government 'with tribal confidence' and, significantly, coordination of all North Yemeni policies with those of Saudi Arabia.[34] The negotiations between the two sides broke down when the former pro-Saudi prime minister Hijri was murdered in April in London. Shaikh Ahmar led 40,000 armed supporters to occupy the towns of Sadaa and Khamir in the north. Hamdi sent his air force and troops to the region, and quelled the tribal rebellion in July. Three months later, as he was preparing to leave for a state visit to South Yemen, he was assassinated – ostensibly by pro-Saudi elements.[35]

With the installation of the pro-Saudi Major Ghashmi as president, the conservative tribal forces of the north regained their ascendancy. The new government, reflecting the bias of the reconvened consultative assembly, dominated by the tribal chiefs, actively repressed the nationalist-leftist forces. The Saudi hold over the republic became stronger than ever before. 'The Saudi plenipotentiary (in North Yemen) is not the ambassador, who does not deign to spend much time in the country to which he is assigned, but the military attaché, Colonel Abdullah Gudayan, who maintains direct and automatic access to the officer corps,' reported David Hirst of the *Guardian*. 'Apart from its hold over the officer corps – maintained by handouts to key individuals along with the underwriting of almost the entire military budget – Saudi Arabia reinforces its grip through official contributions to Yemeni development, other subsidies and, above all, its cultivation of the tribal chieftains. . . . The great tribal confederations of the Hashed and Bakel . . . are an ever-ready instrument for sabotaging policies the Saudis don't like.'[36]

Since Ghashmi's violent death in mid-1978 was followed by the presidency of Ali Abdullah Saleh, who was once again a Saudi protagonist, there was little change in Sanaa–Riyadh ties. However it was not long before the nationalist-leftist forces, concentrated among the Shafei tribes in the south, mounted an armed rebellion, with the aid of South Yemen, in February 1979. The regular army of the republic performed poorly. It was helped by the northern tribals – now organised politically under the banner of the Islamic Front – who rushed south to join battle.[37] The North Yemeni government was also assisted by Saudi Arabia – diplomatically and, more importantly, financially. After putting its own forces on alert, Riyadh paid $387 million to Washington to airlift heavy weapons for North Yemen. In the end a cease-fire materialised after ten days of fighting. These events underlined once more the economic and political dominance of conservative Saudi Arabia over its neighbours.

Four years earlier, in somewhat less dramatic circumstances, Riyadh had granted a loan of $100 million to Sultan Qaboos of Oman to help him buy arms to quell the leftist-nationalist guerrillas operating in the province of Dhofar.[38] That the Omani Sultan needed to raise such a sizable loan – despite the large increase in state revenue due to a dramatic rise in oil prices – indicated that the counter-insurgency effort against the Dhofari rebels was proving to be a much tougher task than had been imagined by Qaboos when he ascended the throne in July 1970.

From early on, the objective of crushing the Dhofari rebellion was pursued in tandem with another: to build up basic infrastructures of a modern state, and provide such social services as education and health to its subjects, with special attention to be paid to those living in Dhofar. The rapid increase in both the non-military budget and the size of the civil service, up from 4,300 in 1971 to 19,123 in 1975,[39] showed that modernisation was being effected with great urgency.

Concurrently the state-controlled mass media tried to project Islam as an ideological antidote to atheistic Marxism, which was the main inspiration of the armed guerrillas inside Dhofar, and elsewhere. In 1973 Qaboos established a ministry of Waqf and Islamic Affairs to 'shoulder the responsibility for safeguarding the Muslim faith and spiritual values, and to ensure that the young were brought up in accordance with the beautiful teachings and principles of Islam'.[40]

The waging of an ideological war was accompanied by efforts to enlarge and modernise the military. Helped by a liberal intake of Pakistani recruits, the strength of the armed forces was raised to 15,000 in 1975.[41] While continuing to rely on London for military and counter-insurgency expertise, Qaboos cultivated close relations with the kings of Jordan and Saudi Arabia. But since neither of these monarchs could afford to provide him with fighting men to bolster his strength against the guerrillas, he turned to the Shah of Iran for extra troops, and got them. In late 1975, in conjunction with a division of Iranian troops and several hundred British military experts and Jordanian army engineers, the Sultan's forces launched a major offensive against the rebels in Dhofar. The operation was a success.

Yet this failed to secure the future of the monarchy. 'The continuing British presence, on the Masirah island base and in the officer corps of the Sultan's armed forces, cast a certain shadow over the regime's legitimacy, as did the sultanate's growing relationship with the American military and intelligence community,' stated Michael C. Hudson. 'Occasional acts of sabotage in the Muscat–Matrah area and reports of government arrests and executions indicated a degree of subversive ferment.'[42]

That was in early 1977. Since then Muscat's links with Washington have grown much stronger; and so have those with Cairo. As one of the two Arab League members to endorse the Camp David accord,[43] Oman became a special favourite of Egypt, which increased its supply of military personnel to the sultanate. This trend was accelerated when, following the Shah's downfall, the last of the Iranian troops left Oman by March

1979. Within months the Egyptian military presence in Oman, earlier put at 300 military advisers, had reportedly reached a strength of 'up to 8,000' troops.[44]

When in early 1980, Washington decided to set up a Rapid Development Force in the Indian Ocean, it approached the Gulf states for the use of local military bases. All of them refused – except Oman. Saudi Arabia played a crucial behind-the-scenes role in helping America. With the memory of the Mecca uprising still fresh, the Saudi rulers could not afford to compromise national sovereignty by leasing bases to a Western power, however friendly. At the same time they sincerely wanted to help America, their most staunch and powerful ally. So they found a way out. They encouraged Sultan Qaboos to give military facilities to the American forces:[45] something he did by signing a formal agreement in June. This was one more illustration of the power the Saudi monarchy wields to uphold the conservative forces of the Arab East.

Economics is one of the very important factors that determine the Omani ruler's international policies. The fast escalating military and civil expenditures of the state cannot be met out of the revenue from oil, because the output has been declining steadily since 1976,[46] and the new finds are apparently not keeping pace with the rate of extraction. Oman thus seems to be heading for the economic state of affairs prevalent in Bahrain, where the reserves are so low that production has been pegged to an insignificant 50,000 bpd,[47] and where three quarters of the crude oil processed at its refinery is supplied by Saudi Arabia.

The overall Saudi influence over Bahrain is reinforced by the fact that the ruling families of the two countries belong to the Anaza federation of tribes from the Najd region of the Arabian Peninsula. The migration of the Khalifas (of the Utab tribe) to Bahrain, and their subsequent success in overthrowing the Iranian overlords in 1783, was characteristic of the Anazas' daring behaviour. But the Sunni beliefs of the Khalifas were at odds with those of their predominantly Shia subjects. This schism has ever since been a source of weakness for the Bahraini monarchy.

However, the transformation of Bahrain into a British protectorate by the end of the nineteenth century softened the sectarian differences between the ruler and the ruled. By applying the British legal system to the large community of non-Bahrainis resident in the islands, and then extending it to many aspects of local administration, London weakened the traditional hold of Islam and Islamic law. These processes went hand in hand with a rise in literacy, which was financed by the oil revenue that began materialising in the mid-1930s. Rising consciousness among the islanders led to demands for a legislative council and replacement of Sir Charles Belgrave as the monarch's chief adviser.

These demands intensified after the Second World War, and were adopted in 1954 by the Committee of National Unity, which had been formed a year earlier in the wake of the sectarian riots between Sunnis and Shias. The dismissal of Sir John Bagot Glubb as commander-in-chief by the Jordanian king in March 1956 raised hopes that something similar would happen to Belgrave. It did not. The disaffected populace demonstrated in large numbers against the British foreign minister, when he visited Bahrain about that time, and followed it up with a general strike. This unnerved the ruler, who invited the Committee of National Unity for talks: these dragged on for months.

In November the Bahrainis took to the streets again, this time protesting at the British involvement in an attack on Egypt. Rioting broke out and was so serious that the ruling family abandonded its palace in Manama at the north-eastern tip of the main island, and moved to Rifaa al Gharbi, a secluded village to the south-west. Working in conjunction with the British representative, the ruler declared a state of emergency, and launched a determined counter-offensive against the protestors. Given the predominantly non-Bahraini composition of the police, officered largely by the British,[48] he had little difficulty in suppressing the challenge to his authority. He followed up the immediate ban on the Committee of National Unity with large-scale arrests and deportations. Having thus smashed the opposition front – which consisted of different social classes – he tried to win over the dissidents, and had some success, specially with the merchants' leaders.

The accession of the twenty-seven-year-old Shaikh Issa ibn Salman to the throne in 1961 aroused hopes of political reform. But these were soon dashed when, following a strike by schoolteachers in 1962, the young ruler ordered the immediate arrest of the strikers. But a far more serious challenge to his rule came in March 1965. Protesting against the sacking of a large number of workers, the employees of the Bahrain Petroleum Company went on strike: an action that snowballed into a general strike. Emboldened, the strikers added political aims to their economic demands, by calling for an end to the nine-year-old emergency, the granting of civil and trade union rights, and the introduction of a legislative assembly.

Uncomfortably aware that any concessions by the Bahraini ruler on these demands would encourage democratic forces in its own kingdom, the Saudi royal family strongly advised Shaikh Issa to move against the agitators, which he did by resorting to wholesale arrests of the strikers.

Following the British withdrawal from South Yemen in 1967 Bahrain became the headquarters of Britain's Middle East military command; and with this Bahrain's importance grew. Yet it failed to find a place within the federation of the British-protected principalities that was mooted after Britain had announced, in 1968, that it would withdraw from the Gulf within the next three years. The chief reason for Bahrain's exclusion was that many of the rulers of the Lower Gulf principalities had come to regard it as 'a potential source of subversion, radicalism, and decadence'.[49]

The result of the first parliamentary election to be held in independent Bahrain in December 1973 could only have confirmed the worst fears of these rulers: the nationalist-leftist Popular Bloc secured 70 per cent of the elected seats. The two and a half years of parliament's life were marked by frequent clashes between the deputies and the ruler, with the last one on the controversial state security law leading to an impasse. Alleging that the national assembly had held debates on 'ideas that are foreign to our principles and social structures', Shaikh Issa dissolved it in August 1975.[50] Riyadh was widely regarded as the prime force behind this action by the Bahraini ruler. In fact Mohsen Mahrun, a Popular bloc leader, openly accused Saudi Arabia of 'imposing the decision to dissolve the national assembly' on Shaikh Issa.[51]

Among those pleased by the strangling of democracy in Bahrain was the ruling Thani family in neighbouring Qatar. This relieved pressure on it to liberalise its own regime and transform the fully nominated consultative council into at least a partially elected assembly with legislative powers. As it was, it had taken two forced abdications and one palace coup, over a period of twenty-one years, for the Qatari monarchy to introduce such elementary practices as the state budget.

It had managed without one so far, primarily because of the steadily rising oil output, which increased from 32,000 bpd to nearly 600,000.[52] Moreover, the absence of a state budget allowed the large Thani clan to spend the money as it wished: Most of its members took to building palaces and maintaining huge fleets of cars. In the early 1960s, for instance, the ruler Shaikh Ahmed and his (recently deposed) father Shaikh Ali had a total of 452 cars between them.[53]

The blatant squandering of oil revenue by the Thanis, coupled with their iron grip over political and economic power, created widespread discontent among their subjects. The result was the formation of the clandestine National Unity Front in 1963, and a series of anti-regime demonstrations. Angered by these events, some of the Thanis advocated bombarding Khor, the town known to be a stronghold of the Front. Although the ruler turned down this suggestion, he initiated a policy of systematic repression of opposition, which proved quite effective, specially when it was fully backed by the fellow-Wahhabi House of Saud in the contiguous kingdom of Saudi Arabia.

By the time the idea of forming a federation of the British-protected shaikhdoms was aired in the late 1960s, Qatar was a placid country. Although wary of having Bahrain, with a radicalised population, as a constituent of the proposed federation, the Thanis participated in the early negotiations. Towards the end they insisted on being assured of a leading role in the union, in view of the large financial contribution expected of them, and having the details of the voting system and the federal capital settled before the founding of the federation. When these demands were refused they decided to stay out.

This disappointed the ruler of Dubai, Shaikh Rashed al Maktum – linked to the Thanis by marriage and commercial interests – who had counted on the wealthy Qatar to counter the influence of oil-rich Abu Dhabi in the proposed union. In the end he reluctantly accepted the number two role in the United Arab Emirates, which was headed by Shaikh Zaid of Abu Dhabi – with Rashed's son as the prime minister, and Zaid's as deputy prime minister.

To the detriment of the federation, personal rivalry between Rashed and Zaid persisted for many years. It was rooted as much in the differences between the personalities of the two men as between the varying economic bases of their respective principalities. An instinctive entrepreneur, Rashed had started building up Dubai as an entrepot ever since he became the emir in 1932, and had been successful.[54] In contrast, Zaid was a bedouin chief, who succeeded his elder brother – after he had been overthrown by the British in 1966 – to rule a shaikhdom whose importance lay exclusively in rising oil production, which had begun four years earlier.

As a cosmopolitan merchant, Rashed had maintained Dubai as a fairly relaxed, hospitable place, unencumbered by such Islamic strictures as a ban on alcohol. Zaid is an orthodox Muslim who believes in enforcing the traditional Islamic taboos. His allotment of $6 million in 1974 for the construction of new mosques in Abu Dhabi, a city of 200,000 people which already had 115 mosques, was a typical illustration of his Islamic fervour.[55] 'Islam is stressed, although the social impact is less evident in Abu Dhabi and especially Dubai than in Saudi Arabia,' notes Hudson. 'Not only is the piety of the ruling family taken for granted, Islam is the official religon . . . and the Islamic Sharia is the "principal source" of law.'[56]

Yet this did not make the UAE immune from the Islamic wind that blew from across the Gulf in the wake of the Shah's downfall in early 1979. The Iranian interpretation of Islam stressed elections and republicanism, both of which are missing in the UAE, and both of which seem to appeal to the younger citizens of the federation. Even the joint memorandum, issued in March by such establishment bodies as the (fully nominated) federal assembly and the cabinet, included the twin demands for parliamentary democracy and a unitary state.

That such demands posed a serious challenge to the existing order was recognised by all the seven members of the Supreme Council of Emirs. Not surprisingly, Zaid and Rashed sank their differences. Rashed was designated prime minister and assigned the task of forming the government. He clearly understood the seriousness of the threat implicit in the demands contained in the joint memorandum. 'A unitary state means no (internal) borders, and therefore no emirs,' he told a Kuwaiti newspaper. 'It means elections.'[57]

Apparently introducing elections was out of the question. Yet a proposal to hold parliamentary elections was first aired as early as 1976, when the provisional constitution of 1971 was to have expired. In order to make the federal assembly somewhat representative (in the proposed permanent constitution), it was suggested that its members be elected by an electoral college of one hundred from each of the emirates. One proposal recommended that the whole electoral college be nominated by the emir, and the other that only half of it be appointed, and the other half be elected by voters. Nothing came of these proposals, partly because the provisional constitution was extended for five more years, and partly because the proponents of popular elections were discouraged by the fact that, in August 1976, the first and longest parliament in the Gulf – the Kuwaiti national assembly – was suspended, and then dissolved altogether.

As in the case of Bahrain, this anti-democratic action by the Kuwaiti ruler was taken in consultation with the Saudi royal family, whose members had been particularly stung by the anti-Saudi statements made by sane Kuwaiti deputies in parliament, and reported in the local press. Close links between the Sabahs (of Kuwait) and the Sauds stem from their common membership of the Anaza tribal federation originally based in the Najd region. When Abdul Rahman al Saud (father of Abdul Aziz, the Saudi kingdom's founder) was expelled from Riyadh by the Rashedis, clients of the Ottoman Turks, he found sanctuary in Kuwait, with the Sabahs. And it was from Kuwait that Abdul Aziz set out to capture Riyadh in 1902; a venture in which he was successful.

However, the relationship between the two clans had its ups and downs. As stated earlier,[58] in the late 1910s the Sabahs tried to annex Hasa, then under the tutelage of Abdul Aziz, and paid dearly for it. Their defeat at the hands of the militant Ikhwan increased the Sabahs' dislike of Wahhabism, which they had always regarded as too harsh and puritanical. Given that their domain was centred around a port, and their inclination was mercantile, it was not surprising that they had come to be considered tolerant, even cosmopolitan, by their peers in the Arabian Peninsula. The presence of the British from 1899 onward, as their shaikhdom's protectors, helped the socially liberal streak within the clan.

This, and the existence of a cohesive body of merchants in the shaikhdom, wishing to dilute the absolute power of the Sabahs, provided the backdrop against which an explosion of education, financed by rocketing oil revenue in the 1950s, was to occur.[59] The consequent rise in political consciousness of the Kuwaitis made it increasingly difficult for the ruler to let London play the protector. Britain's position became virtually untenable when it was found to be one of the three countries to have attacked Egypt, the leader of Arab nationalism, in 1956. The overthrow of the pro-West monarchy in neighbouring Iraq in mid-1958 intensified popular demand for an end to British protection. Thus pressed, Shaikh Abdullah al Sabah, the ruler, initiated talks with London to abrogate the 1899 Anglo–Kuwaiti treaty.

Following Kuwait's independence in June 1961, and a renegotiated Anglo–Kuwaiti defence agreement, the British troops and tanks removed from Kuwait were stationed in Bahrain. The renewed and menacing claim by Abdul Karem Qassem of Iraq that Kuwait was an integral part of Iraq unnerved Shaikh Abdullah. He tried to meet the threat by rallying his subjects with the promise of a written constitution to be drafted by a constituent assembly, and by inviting back the British troops under a recently signed agreement. To the relief of the Kuwaitis, and their ruler, the new British presence ended within two months when Arab League forces arrived to guarantee Kuwait's territorial integrity.

It was under such circumstances that Shaikh Abdullah (1950–65) ratified the constitution which specified inter alia a fully elected national assembly of fifty. Although the constitution preserved the ruler's prerogative to appoint the council of ministers (who automatically became members of parliament), thus denying the assembly any executive authority, it gave parliament such powers as approving or disapproving the ruler's ministerial appointments, all official legislation, and the government's policies in defence, foreign affairs, oil and budget. While trade union rights were granted – to Kuwaiti nationals only[60] – political rights, in terms of forming of political parties, were not. On the other hand parliament was given the prerogative of choosing the crown prince (and thus the future ruler) out of a short list of three.

Having conceded a popularly elected parliament, Shaikh Abdullah and his successors tried to determine its composition by manipulating the electoral system, and by coopting the tribal and mercantile leaders into their scheme. The ten five-member constituencies were so demarcated that each had a large bedouin area; and an elector was allowed to vote anywhere he wished. An increasing number of (nomadic) bedouins were given the vote, and on polling day they were ferried en bloc to those constituencies where support for the ruler was known to be low.

Aided by such tactics and by the willing cooperation of the leaders of the dominant Ujman and Awazim tribes, Shaikh Abdullah had little difficulty in getting a parliament elected in January 1963 which was a virtual rubber-stamp. Yet several deputies found the new ministerial appointments made by Shaikh Sabah after his accession in 1965 so unacceptable that they resigned in protest. To forestall a repeat of such an embarrassing event in the future the ruler wished to see a totally pliant parliament elected at the next poll. The result was open vote-rigging in January 1967. The opposition protested, and demanded a re-run; but to no avail.

By comparison the election of 1971 was free, but hardly fair. As in the past, a large majority of seats went to the nominees of the monarch and his cabal of thirty to forty tribal leaders. The remainder were taken mainly by the nominees of the fifteen super-rich merchants, who stood at the apex of a 5,000-strong merchant community, with the rest – about half a dozen seats – going to the most politically conscious of the Kuwaitis: the nationalist-leftist professionals and intellectuals.

The Yom Kippur war, and particularly the use of oil as a diplomatic weapon by the Arab states (decided at a meeting in Kuwait), changed the situation in favour of the nationalist-leftist deputies led by Ahmed Khatib. Although the fourth parliament elected in 1975 continued to be dominated by the conservative tribal-merchant bloc, the tone of parliamentary debates became increasingly strident. The radical minority succeeded in having the majority back its demands that oil production be limited to a maximum of two million bpd, that the western-owned Kuwait Oil Company be fully nationalised, and that the press laws be liberalised.

Not surprisingly, the nationalist-leftists condemned the ruler's decision to dissolve parliament in September 1976, whereas the mercantile and tribal leaders endorsed it. Support from business quarters was to be expected. After all, by barring non-Kuwaitis from owning land or real estate, or the majority share in any business, in the early 1950s, the royal family had laid a firm foundation for the future prosperity of businessmen and real-estate owners. The oil price boom of late 1973, which in turn led to zooming imports and an accelerated economic activity, brought untold riches to this social class. For instance, by the mid-1970s private investments abroad of the top fifteen merchant families alone were estimated to be in the region of $6,000 million.[61]

Yet within a few years the merchants' endorsement of the strangling of parliament had soured into grumblings against the ruler. The reason was that, with the scrutinising gaze of parliament destroyed, the royal family had taken to stuffing its private coffers at the cost of both the state and the established merchants. 'Before [the dissolution of parliament] the Shaikhs were not really in business, but now they are everywhere,' said Ahmed, the American-educated forty-year-old son of an important merchant. 'Shaikh Mishaal, a brother of the ruler, who heads security, owns a factory for building material. It seems that a South Korean company won a contract on one condition: they would buy material from him. The Shaikhs get a cut from every contract, whether military or civil.'[62] That such complaints were widespread and well-founded became apparent when Abdullah al Nafisi – a political scientist who published a book which illustrated how the ruling family was making money at the expense of the state – was arrested and expelled.[63]

It was against this background that the revolution in Iran occurred: an event which was followed by relentless attacks by Ayatollah Khomeini on the corrupt and dictatorial ways of the Gulf rulers whom he often described as the 'mini-Shahs'.[64] Both individually and collectively they felt vulnerable. The Kuwaiti monarch felt all the more so, because in July a delegation of local Shia notables flew to Tehran to congratulate Khomeini, and thirty former parliamentary deputies petitioned the monarch to revive the national assembly and drop his plan to amend the constitution.[65]

The growing popularity of the protest movement, centred around the Shia mosques in the capital, added to the royal family's worries, apprehensive that the movement might encounter receptive minds among the substantial Shia segment within the armed forces. Over the years, while young local (Sunni) nomads, lured by lucrative job opportunities, had shunned the army, the authorities had come to rely increasingly on Shia nomads from southern Iraq as recruits. As stated earlier,[66] the ruler reacted sharply to these developments. He put further restrictions on press freedom and the right to free expression even in private meetings held at home. He initiated a policy of wholesale expulsion of 'undesirable' aliens: mainly Shia Iranians. It was carried out so efficiently that by early 1980 as many as 20,000 Iranians had been deported, and it was applied even to two Kuwaiti nationals – a Shia preacher and a Shia merchant – who were packed off to Iran.[67]

These actions were coordinated with regional guidelines on the reporting of Iranian events, laid down for the state-controlled mass media, which were decided unanimously by the information ministers of the Gulf states at a meeting in Riyadh. These guidelines stressed 'playing down the news from Tehran', and demoting 'the Iranian revolution from the status of an all-Muslim one to a purely Shia one, then to downgrade it to a purely Iranian Shia one'.[68] It is significant that Saudi Arabia was the main force behind calling the conference and shaping the strategy.

The House of Saud seemed to have realised that the Mecca uprising of Islamic militants – drawn partly from outside the kingdom – and the success of the Islamic revolutionary forces against the pro-West Shah had undermined its claim to be the spiritual leadership of the Islamic world, thus blunting one of its two most powerful weapons – the other being money. On the other hand by creating a shortage of oil, and thus pushing up its price, the Iranian revolution had inadvertently strengthened inter alia the economic muscle of Riyadh: its current-account surplus for 1980 was expected to top $40,000 million.[69] The steadily rising oil income, dating back to the early 1950s, had enabled the Saudi royal family not only to consolidate its influence over such neighbours as North Yemen but also to win over its longstanding rivals: the Hashem clan. The defeat inflicted on Sharif Hussein of Hejaz in 1925 by Abdul Aziz had left bitter feelings, particularly as Sharif Hussein, aware of his noble lineage (from the prophet), held the Sauds in low esteem.

Ever since its founding in 1923 Transjordan (later Jordan) has had to rely on massive foreign subsidies to survive. Initially it was Britain, the state's creator and guardian, which provided the funds – needed both to run the state and offer regular bribes to the leaders of the bedouin tribes, who then formed the bulk of the half a million Jordanians, to retain their loyalty. Later, particularly after the establishment of Israel,

America steadily became the leading donor. Between 1958 and 1965 it aided Jordan to the tune of $447 million.[70] But following the Six Day war – when Jordan lost the West Bank to Israel – Saudi Arabia and Kuwait began giving substantial grants and loans to Amman. Within a decade the Riyadh–Kuwaiti contribution had outstripped Washington's.[71]

Such assistance had been offered against the background of enterprising Palestinian refugees becoming a majority in the population. Not surprisingly the sixfold increase in the state's development expenditure during the period 1965–73[72] had been fairly well absorbed. 'But in terms of the non-material values associated with modernization . . . there was little progress made toward greater social justice or redistribution of wealth – no major land reform, no progressive taxation, and few curbs on private enterprise aside from the informal patronage and influence dispensed by the royal family itself and its closest retainers,' notes Hudson. 'The privileges of Jordan's wealthy commercial and landed class have been preserved, not tempered. Indeed, free enterprise . . . is one of the three main rights written into the Jordan constitution.'[73]

The royal family's power is underwritten by the military. Together, the politico-military establishment consists of the Hashemite family, the aides to the palace, the tribal chiefs, the topmost military and civil service officers, and wealthy families with extensive commercial and industrial interests. 'The military is manned largely by the bedouins who are indoctrinated with pro-royalist ideas since childhood, and then given intense training and excellent pay and fringe benefits, just like the National Guard in Saudi Arabia,' stated Tasleem, a Jordanian political researcher. 'The overall tribal loyalties are secured through the sums paid regularly by the king himself (often from the amounts received as aid from abroad), and by constant reiteration that disloyalty to the king, a descendant of prophet Mohammed, amounts to disloyalty to the prophet, and would lead the sinner to hell after death.'[74]

As early as 1933 the army, then functioning as the Arab Legion and led by British officers, had proved both its effectiveness and its loyalty to the Hashemite monarch by pacifying rebellious tribes in the kingdom. Fifteen years later, during the Palestine war, despite rapid expansion from 6,000 to 12,000,[75] it performed better than any other Arab force, and retained control of the West Bank and east Jerusalem. Steady enlargement, followed by a merger in 1956 with the (Palestinian-dominated) National Guard, raised its strength to 35,000.

The merger had been ordered by a popularly elected government, led by Suleiman Nabulsi, and had the sanction of the monarch. Following the dismissal of the British commander-in-chief, Sir John Bagot Glubb, by the king in March 1956, the military had acquired its first Jordanian chief, General Ali Abu Nawar. However, in April 1957 Abu Nawar became involved in a conspiracy to overthrow the monarchy. Aided by the loyal bedouin regiments the king mounted a successful coup against the conspirators, dismissed the government, and imposed martial law. This lasted until 1963.

About a year later the king made extensive use of the army to break up frequent demonstrations on the West Bank in support of the recently formed Palestine Liberation Organisation. But it was not until he had allowed the Palestinians to launch attacks on Israel from the West Bank that demonstrations and rioting finally ceased. When Palestinian actions resulted in severe Israeli reprisals he imposed martial law in late 1966 to put a stop to Palestinian activity. Following Jordan's defeat in the Six Day war he suspended the constitution, and undertook a slow but systematic purge of the Palestinians from the officer corps.

Evidently this policy helped the king to retain the loyalty of virtually the whole army, when his authority was seriously challenged by Palestinian commandos in September 1970. The commandos' hope that most of the Palestinians in the Jordanian army would defect and fight alongside them against the Hashemite monarch proved ill-founded. Barring insignificant defections, the 55,000-strong military remained loyal to the king, who won a victory over an alliance of Palestinian commandos and Jordanian radicals. He imposed martial law and continued it for six years.

By 1975 he felt sufficiently confident of the overall loyalty of his subjects – two thirds of whom were either Palestinians or their descendants – to introduce conscription from the following January: a step which bolstered the military's strength to 67,850 in 1977.[76] Such confidence was derived partly from the efficiency with which the military and civil intelligence had served the ruler. 'Few Jordanians (and even fewer Palestinians in Jordan) doubt the effectiveness of the *mukhabarat*, the royal intelligence apparatus,' notes Hudson.[77]

Jordan's intelligence is thorough, and has a history dating back to the early 1950s when, following the promulgation of a new constitution, political activity was legally allowed. This continued well into the late 1960s, with the secret service keeping track of all those involved in politics – a fact that has been corroborated by Moshe Ma'oz, an Israeli researcher, after a study of relevant Jordanian documents left behind by the Hashemite regime in east Jerusalem after the Six Day war. 'The Jordanian secret service maintained an extensive apparatus, trailing and reporting all the activities of party members, however insignificant,' states Ma'oz. 'Security service informers were planted in the cells of the various parties. . . . The secret service had comprehensive lists of members of parties and their main branches. These were periodically updated and were detailed enough to grade each member according to his importance in the party.'[78]

Although the Liberation Party did not express opposition to the monarchy, the king rejected its leaders' application for a licence to operate as a legal political entity in 1952. In the king's view, the party's stress on adopting Islam as a complete ideological-political system was divisive because Jordanian society had a 6 per cent Christian population, and its declaration that it was up to the faithful to choose the type of regime they wanted aimed at subverting the existing monarchical order.[79] However, he allowed it to function as a non-political 'Ottoman association'. Its 600 active members were drawn chiefly from traders and, more significantly, religious functionaries and teachers in schools.[80]

To stop radical Islamic ideas gaining ground through the mosque, the king promulgated the Law on Sermons and Guidance in Mosques in 1955. It specified that no sermon or instruction was to be delivered in a mosque unless it had been cleared by the chief qadi or one of his delegates (all of whom revered the monarch as a direct descendant of the prophet), and that those breaking the law would lose their licence to preach and serve a jail sentence of up to three months.

The law was directed as much at the Liberation Party as it was at the Muslim Brotherhood, which too was outlawed, and which enjoyed about the same degree of support from the same sections of society as did the Liberation Party.[81] The Muslim Brotherhood, originally founded in Egypt in 1928, had taken roots in Palestine during the mid-1930s mainly as a result of increasing Zionist colonisation. Not surprisingly in Jordan it now focused its attention primarily on the problem of Israel's existence.

Like the Liberation Party it considered Israel a creation of western imperialism, and held imperialism, and the Arab world's weakness, jointly responsible for its continued existence. In its view the Arabs' weakness was caused by their neglect of Islam. As such, it felt that only when the Arab nation had returned to the path of traditional Islam would it recover its lost strength, and regain that part of its homeland which had been usurped by the Zionists. All this, it recognised, would take time; and meanwhile it advised the Arab faithful to wage jehad against Israel.

Since it regarded any move which signified even implicit acceptance of Israel's existence as a betrayal of both Islam and Arab nationalism, it was angered by the reports of King Abdullah of Jordan having secret rendezvous with Israeli leaders. The subsequent assassination of Abdullah by an Islamic militant in May 1951 was well received by the Muslim Brotherhood in Jordan, and elsewhere in the Arab East, particularly Egypt.

Following the coup against King Farouk of Egypt in July 1952, the Egyptian Muslim Brotherhood was hopeful of being drawn into the republican regime. When this did not happen, and when in fact the party was banned by President Nasser in late 1954, it turned against Nasser and Nasserism. This determined the general policy line of the Muslim Brotherhood in different countries of the Arab East, including Jordan. Since Nasser waged an active campaign against Hussein, the Jordanian Brotherhood became less and less antagonistic towards King Hussein. Indeed when his throne was threatened by popular demonstrations, led by the Nasserites and leftists, it sided with him.[82]

Nasser's drift towards what the Brotherhood considered, 'atheistic socialism' led it to align itself increasingly with the Jordanian king. This trend was aided by the emergence of Saudi Arabia as the dominant force in the Arab East after Nasser's defeat in the June 1967 war. During the next decade, as King Hussein drew closer to the House of Saud for financial and ideological reasons, and as the local Brotherhood found itself often in agreement with his policies, the monarch reciprocated by coopting leading Brotherhood members into his regime.[83]

Given such rapport between the Brotherhood and the Jordanian monarch, it was not surprising that the Baathist authorities in Damascus – harassed by the violent activities of the Brotherhood in Syria during 1980 – should accuse King Hussein of giving sanctuary to its enemies. Hussein's denial proved hollow when a Syrian commando squad, assisted by PLO fighters, crossed into Jordan and captured twenty-seven Muslim Brethren at a training camp at Ajloun, near the Jordanian–West Bank border. Three days later, on 30 July, another Syrian task-force attacked a Brotherhood hideout in Amman, killed three activists, including Abdul Wahhab al Bakri, a leader of the Syrian Brotherhood, and then gave themselves up to the Jordanian authorities.[84]

What had driven the Syrian government to such extremes was the steady escalation of the Brotherhood's violent anti-government campaign, which by the middle of 1980 was claiming two victims a day – the targets being either prominent Baathists or Communists or Soviet military advisers. The Brotherhood had opposed the Arab Baath Socialist Party since its inception in 1953, and, before that, its predecessor the Arab Baath Party, founded a decade earlier. The fact that Michel Aflaq, one of the two founder leaders of the Baath movement, was a Christian had provided the Brotherhood with an emotive weapon.

The Muslim Brotherhood itself came into being in 1930, when Syrian students returning from Egypt began forming branches in different cities. The Brotherhood stood for an end to the French mandate, and for social and political reform along Islamic lines. Once the French had finally departed in 1946 it concentrated on socio-political issues, always stressing its opposition to secularism and communism. As in Jordan, it drew the bulk of its support from the urban Sunni petty bourgeoisie: traders, teachers, and religious functionaries.

It received a boost when, following a ban on the organisation in Egypt in 1954, many Egyptian activists took refuge in Syria. However, when Syria joined Egypt in early 1958 to form the United Arab Republic, and all political parties were outlawed, the Syrian Brotherhood too had to go underground. Growing disaffection with Nasser's presidency of the UAR among the Syrians helped the Brotherhood to expand its base. The result of the election held in December 1961, a few months after Syria's secession from the UAR, proved this. The Brotherhood won ten seats, nearly half as many as the older, established National Bloc.[85] In conjunction with other rightist elements it tried to counter the rising influence of the Baathists and leftists.

With the Baathist seizure of power in March 1963 the Brotherhood turned resolutely against the regime. During the next decade it came into open conflict with the authorities four times. Encouraged by popular discontent due to the economic downturn in early 1964, the Brotherhood stepped up its activities. In April, following anti-government rioting in Hama, a stronghold of the Sunni religious establishment, the muezzin issued the crusading cry of 'Islam or Baath' from the famous Al Sultan mosque. This brought the security forces to the neighbourhood. When they responded to the firing directed at them from the mosque and its surrounding quarter with shelling, they damaged one of the mosque's minarets. This inflamed the sensibilities of the faithful throughout the country: their protest took the form of widespread strikes in major cities. It was only after the government had formed the Workers' Militia, consisting of its proletarian supporters, and they had resorted to meting out summary rough justice to the Muslim Brothers that the uncoordinated protest fizzled out.

This experience had the effect of strengthening the hands of the radicals within the Baath Party. One result was the nationalisation of 106 private companies, with 12,000 employees, on 1 January 1965. The ulemas denounced the measure and called for a jehad against the atheistic Baath. The security forces' attempt to quell an anti-government demonstration outside the Ummayad mosque in Damascus led to the deaths of two people and injuries to many others. In protest the Brotherhood called for a general shutdown of the bazaars in the country; and the shopkeepers complied. The authorities responded by nationalising more industrial and commercial companies, and two thirds of import and export trade. And, aided by the Workers' Militia, the Baathist-dominated National Guard, and Communist militants, the army succeeded in breaking up the merchants' strike. Once this had happened the government released all the ulema it had arrested, but restored the right to preach to only those who promised to refrain from attacking it.[86]

The next round between the Sunni religious establishment and the Baathists came in early May 1967, in the wake of the humiliation inflicted upon the government (headed by left-wing Baathists since early 1966) by Israel on 7 April, when it shot down six Syrian planes. An emboldened opposition was goaded by clandestine radio broadcasts beamed from Jordan, which called for the 'overthrow of the atheist regime [in Damascus] hostile to Arabism and Islam', and 'deliverance of the country from Marxism and communism'.[87] In late April the chief alem, Shaikh Mohammed Habankah, seized upon an anti-religious sentence in an article published in *Jaish al Shaab* (The People's Army), the army's official journal,[88] and launched a bitter attack on the 'godless' Baath. Demonstrations against the government ensued and were accompanied by a merchants' strike in Damascus.

Once again the government rearmed the Workers' Militia, who played a major role in ending the traders' shutdown in the capital. It arrested the protestors' leaders, as well as the author of the offending article. After a summary trial he was sentenced to life imprisonment. It condemned Jordan and Saudi Arabia for conspiring to create religious troubles with a view to causing the regime's overthrow, and expelled three Saudi diplomats for allegedly colluding with the chief alem. And, as a warning to the merchants, it sequestrated sixty commercial firms.[89]

Soon after Hafez Assad assumed supreme authority in November 1970 he tried to placate those sections of urban society which had been alienated by the radical, secular policies of the past seven years. By easing import controls on consumer goods and encouraging small and medium-sized private enterprises, he lessened the hostility of merchants and small manufacturers, the traditional backbone of the Muslim Brotherhood, to his government. He tried diligently to project his image as a faithful Muslim by participating in prayers and other religious ceremonies in various mosques throughout the country, and by declaring publicly that he (an Alawi) prayed regularly and fasted during Ramadan. He replaced the secular presidential oath, 'I swear on my honour and my faith' with the traditional 'I swear by Allah the Great'.[90]

Yet the Sunni opposition's suspicion that the Baathists were intent on leading Syria away from its Islamic heritage persisted. When, in January 1973, the new constitution adopted by the people's assembly described the Syrian Arab Republic as a 'democratic, popular, socialist state', an influential group of pro-Muslim Brotherhood ulema attacked the constitution as being 'secular and atheistic', and demanded the insertion of an article declaring Islam to be the state religion. President Assad compromised by directing the assembly to specify that the head of the state must be Muslim; and the assembly did so.

Not satisfied with this concession, the ulema called for nationwide demonstrations. These were held and turned violent. Later they instructed their followers to abstain in the referendum on the constitution. Consequently the Sunni regions of the country registered low voter turnout. The agitation continued. Skirmishes between the security forces and the anti-government demonstrators in the northern Sunni strongholds of Aleppo, Homs and Hama, on the eve of the prophet's birthday in April, left twenty dead and sixty injured. The authorities accused Riyadh of complicity in organising the agitation, and of using Maruf Dawalibi – a former Syrian prime minister living in exile in Saudi Arabia – as an intermediary.[91]

Assad made an adroit use of the October 1973 war to reassert the Islamic credentials of his regime. 'Badr', the code word used for the Arab offensive on 6 October, was highly significant: it was the battle of Badr which had established the supremacy of the prophet's early followers over non-believers. In his radio broadcasts during the war Assad referred to the confrontation as a jehad against the 'enemies of Islam', and to the Syrian forces as the 'soldiers of Allah'.[92] Four months later, when he visited King Feisal of Saudi Arabia, he went to Mecca as well, to make a short hajj (pilgrimage); and this finally established him as a true believer.

As a result of this and the general amity that existed among the main Arab East states until the signing of the Sinai II agreement in September 1975, the activities of the Muslim Brotherhood subsided. The situation began to change early the following year when Assad started issuing statements against the alliance of Lebanese Muslims and Palestinians in the civil war in Lebanon. His intervention in the conflict on the side of the Christian forces in June angered the Brotherhood, which had already been critical of his growing dependence on Soviet arms and advisers.

Viewing Assad's move in Lebanon – and his earlier agreement with King Hussein for an economic union of their countries – as expansionist, Saudi Arabia ceased its economic aid to Syria. And reflecting Riyadh's displeasure with Damascus, the Muslim Brotherhood launched a campaign of assassinations and car bombings on 2 March 1977, when its member(s) murdered Mohammed Fadel, president of Damascus university, and a close aide of Assad. An attack on Rifaat Assad, the powerful brother of the president and head of the 36,000-strong Special Forces in the following February, by dissident army officers,[93] indicated that the Brotherhood enjoyed support in the officer corps.

Further evidence of this came in June 1979 when, aided by Captain Ibrahim Yusuf, the duty officer at the Aleppo military academy, Brotherhood militants killed nearly sixty cadets.[94] In a major swoop against the Brotherhood, the government arrested 300 of its activists, and mounted an anti-Brotherhood campaign in the state-controlled mass media. But there was no let up in the violent activities of the Brotherhood, whose victims now included not only military and intelligence personnel but also pro-government Sunni religious leaders. By murdering two eminent Alawis in Latakia, an Alawi stronghold, in late August, the Brotherhood showed that even the Alawi heartland was not immune from its assaults. However, the local Alawis retaliated by attacking Sunni homes and shops; and sectarian fighting ensued. When the Special Forces, led by Rifaat Assad, tried to enter the city they were assaulted by the Brotherhood militants. It was only after the security forces had sealed off the city that they could manage to restore order.[95]

These anti-governmental activities occurred against the background of rising discontent among the urban petty bourgeoisie due to inflation, housing shortages, and the maldistribution of daily necessities, in an atmosphere rife with stories of corruption among civilian and military leaders, and administrative inefficiency and bungling. The Sunnis among this class nursed a particular grievance. Their share of jobs in the police, intelligence, military officer corps, the presidential entourage, and the

Baathist hierarchy was nowhere near the two thirds mark to which their proportion in the population entitled them. They found the dominance of the Alawis – forming only one seventh of the populace – in these institutions unjust and unjustifiable.

Shaken by these incidents the (nominally) ruling Progressive National Front held a ten-day-long session under the chairmanship of Assad, and decided inter alia that 'corruption and the abuse of power and position should be stamped out . . . that the people's assembly should perform a supervisory function over the government, that the housing and supplies crises should be solved, and that the Front should be developed to represent a broader section of the population'.[96] However, important changes in the government and the Baath Party did not come until after the fortnight-long Baath Party congress in late December. Two thirds of the twenty-one-member national command of the party were replaced, with many of the seats going to such prominent Sunnis as Hikmat Shehabi, the army chief of staff, and Mahmoud Ayubi, a former prime minister. A new thirty-seven-member cabinet included a substantial number of Sunnis. The governors of the Sunni strongholds of Aleppo, Homs, and Hama lost their jobs, as did twenty-one top officials in public-sector enterprises. But none of this had much impact on the strategy or tactics of the Brotherhood.

This became apparent when on (or about) 10 March nearly half of Aleppo, the second largest city of the republic, was gripped by a near-insurrection. About the same time, following the fatal shooting by a traffic policeman of Bassam Arnaout, a Brotherhood leader in Hama, the local residents demonstrated, demanding the release of political prisoners, free elections, a liberalised economy, and a jehad for 'saving the pure faith from the filth of the enemies'.[97] Damascus had to send a force of 10,000 to Aleppo to end the insurrection. It was only after they had shot down about fifty protestors that the anti-government protest there fizzled out.[98] Once order had been restored in the two cities, some 6,000 people were arrested.

President Assad coupled these actions with promises to release political detainees and respect the rule of law. When these promises were not kept, Aleppo and Hama experienced renewed demonstrations and strikes in early April. The seesaw affair between Assad and the opposition (now encompassing secular as well as religious elements), with the initiative moving from one camp to the other and back again, came to an abrupt halt on 25 June, when an unsuccessful attempt was made to assassinate Assad in Damascus.[99] Now the government went all out to stamp out the Brotherhood.

By the time parliament passed a bill on 7 July making membership of the Muslim Brotherhood a capital offence, its security forces had reportedly executed more than a hundred Muslim Brothers.[100] During the next month, taking advantage of the government's clemency offer, 350

Brothers surrendered. An extension of the deadline until 5 September brought many more surrenders, as security forces continued their hunt, killing among others Hisham Jumbaz, the Brotherhood's military commander, while (as stated earlier) the Syrian commandos, assisted by the PLO fighters, flushed out the Brethren from two of their hideouts in neighbouring Jordan.

Soon after, the regime received a shot in the arm when Colonel Muammer al Gadhafi of Libya offered the merger of his country with Syria. This was readily accepted by Assad; and the two heads of state signed a formal agreement on 10 September. Allowing for the general apathy towards such hasty moves, this step could only have had the effect of softening the anti-regime stance of Syria's Sunni establishment, since Libya is a Sunni state, with impeccable Islamic credentials, and beholden neither to capitalism nor communism. What had driven Gadhafi to such an action was his (rather sudden) realisation that Libya had become a confrontation state in the same way as Syria had been (since 1948), because of its contiguity with Sadat's Egypt, where, in his view, 'Zionist and American peril lurks'.[101]

Among those opposing the Camp David accord and the Israeli peace treaty were the Islamic fundamentalists of Egypt, who were either members of the Muslim Brotherhood or of more militant groups. It was ironic that the Brotherhood, which had received official encouragement soon after Sadat assumed power in September 1970, should within a decade turn against his regime. The change had occurred due to the dramatic shift in Sadat's policies towards Israel and America in the mid-1970s. Such a turnabout had a parallel in Sadat's relationship with the Brotherhood in the past. Before the republican revolution of 1952 he was one of the leading Free Officers in close touch with its leaders. After the revolution, however, the Brotherhood fell foul of the military regime; and Sadat, a prominent member of the government, was apparently party to the anti-Brotherhood policies decided at the top.

Since its inception in 1928 the Muslim Brotherhood has had a chequered history. It was founded by Hassan al Banna, a schoolteacher, with the aim of reviving Islam as 'the guiding principle of life for all Muslim societies, and the reconstruction of these societies in accordance with the commandments of the Koran and its teachings'.[102] This politico-religious programme enabled it to function in both the religious and political fields. However, by opposing the Anglo–Egyptian treaty of 1936, and sending volunteers to support the 1936–9 Arab rebellion in Palestine, the Brotherhood emerged more as a political body than a religious one. It derived its following chiefly from the middle peasants, petty traders, civil servants, and artisans. Viewed as a counterforce to the nationalist Wafd party and the leftists, it was given a free rein by the king. By 1939 it had established 500 branches in the country,[103] and was running its own religious classes, hospitals, and schools where particular stress was laid on physical education (later military training) for its young members in order to wage a jehad.

During the Second World War its pro-Axis stance – stemming mainly from its hostility to the British occupation of Egypt – brought it into open conflict with the British. The dismissal of the Wafdist Prime Minister Nahas Pasha (regarded as sympathetic to the Brotherhood) in 1944 by the king, at the behest of the British, made the Brotherhood turn against all political parties and resort to subversion. Its alleged involvement in the murder of Prime Minister Ahmed Pasha in 1945, after his declaration of war against the Axis powers, alienated it further from the political establishment then dominated by the British.

All along, the Brotherhood remained anti-leftist. In 1946, when its claimed membership had passed the half million mark,[104] it set up the National Student Committee in opposition to the leftist National Centre of Students and Workers. Two years later it sent volunteers to fight alongside the Arab armies against the Israeli forces. The Arab effort failed. Holding the Egyptian political establishment responsible for the debacle, it resorted to subversive and terrorist activities. Prime Minister Nokrashi Pasha retaliated by promulgating martial law and disbanding the Brotherhood in December: an action which cost him his life. The Brotherhood activists were widely thought to have been responsible for the murder. Their supreme guide, Hassan al Banna, was assassinated next February, almost certainly by the political police.

It was not until 1950 that martial law was lifted and the Brotherhood allowed to function, if only as a religious body. However, after the election of Shaikh Hassan al Hudaybi as the supreme guide a year later, the Brotherhood returned to the political arena. Forming an anti-imperialist alliance with the leftists, it engaged in guerrilla actions against the occupying British forces. It played a significant role in the January 1952 riots in Cairo: an event which shook the monarchy and paved the way for an army coup six months later.

The Brotherhood expected to be coopted into the new regime, partly because it was one of the major political forces on the eve of the July 1952 coup, and partly because four of the eighteen-member Revolutionary Command Council (that is, Sadat and three others), which had assumed power after the coup, had been close to its leaders. The RCC was favourably disposed toward the Brotherhood, but not to the extent of accepting its proposal that Egypt be turned into an Islamic state with an Islamic constitution. Two months later differences arose between the Brotherhood and the regime, when it opposed the agrarian reform decree by insisting that the land ceiling be raised from 200 to 500 feddans.[105] Yet the RCC made an exception of the Brotherhood when dissolving all political parties in January 1953 by (conveniently) accepting its leaders' statement that it was a religious body.

It was only after Brotherhood members had attacked the supporters of the government-sponsored Liberation Rally in Cairo a year later that the RCC dissolved the Brotherhood and arrested its leaders. In October some Brotherhood militants made an unsuccessful attempt to assassinate Nasser, who had by then emerged as the supreme leader of the republic. This led to a full-scale repression of the organisation, with 4,000 of its activists being thrown into jail and many more put to flight to seek sanctuary in such countries as Lebanon, Syria and Saudi Arabia.

The repression of the Brotherhood continued for the next decade. In 1964, as part of a general amnesty, Nasser released its members with a view to coopting them into a reformed political set-up as a counterforce to the Communists, who were also freed. The ministry of culture and national guidance appointed Brotherhood members as editors of two government-financed magazines, with major stress on denouncing 'imported doctrines', a barely disguised reference to Marxism. As a body, the Brotherhood combined its traditional function of publishing the distributing religious works with denunciation of the 'atheists' for infiltrating the government-sponsored Arab Socialist Union, an all-embracing political entity.

But reconciliation between Nasser and the Brotherhood did not last long. Many of its leaders were found to be implicated in three plots to assassinate him, allegedly inspired and financed by the Saudi monarch, then engaged in a battle with the Egyptian president for supremacy in North Yemen and elsewhere in the Arab East. To Nasser's alarm, official investigators uncovered many secret cells of the Brotherhood in the army, police and universities. As a result, following the arrest of about a thousand Brethren, and the trial of 365, the top leaders were executed in August 1965.[106]

Egypt's defeat in the 1967 Arab–Israeli war severely damaged Nasser's popularity, thus enabling the Brotherhood, as well as other opposition forces, to recover some lost ground. The Brotherhood welcomed Sadat as president, because he held firm anti-communist views, and was regarded a pious enough Muslim to be chosen the secretary-general of the Islamic Congress, established by Cairo in the mid-1960s to rally Muslim opinion abroad behind Egypt. Sadat responded in kind. Promising that Islam would be the chief inspiration of future legislation in Egypt, he released all Brotherhood prisoners, including its supreme guide, Shaikh Hassan al Hudaybi.

After carrying out his 'corrective' coup against the left-leaning Ali Sabri group in May 1971, Sadat actively encouraged Islamic sentiment and groups as a counterweight to the leftist influence. He directed Abdul Moneim Amin, an army general with pro-Brotherhood sympathies, to establish, train and arm one thousand Islamic Committees in universities and factories, with the sole objective of fighting 'atheist Marxism'.

This programme proved so successful that the Islamic Committees soon acquired an independent existence. Their activities accentuated historic animosity between Muslims and Copts (i.e. Christians), and led to attacks on the Copts and their churches. This had the effect of undermining the regime's stability. When the government acted to discourage such activities, the Islamic committee members organised demonstrations to demand that Sadat should intensify the struggle against Israel.

The October 1973 Arab–Israeli conflict – described by Egypt's mass media as a victory for Cairo – produced a lull in the Islamic groups' activities. But this did not endure for long. The economic crisis that followed the war produced discontent, particularly among the middle and lower-middle classes, which provided a conducive environment for the growth of Islamic elements. An armed attack by the Islamic Liberation Group on the technical military academy in a Cairo suburb in June 1974, which left eleven people dead and twenty-seven injured,[107] came as a sharp reminder to the government that the Islamic forces were subterraneanly active.

Sadat's declaration of a general amnesty in 1975 – coupled with his decision a year later to allow a return to the multi-party system of the monarchical era – enabled the Brotherhood to reorganise its forces and reintegrate itself into Al Azhar university, the official centre of Islam, which had been purged of Brotherhood elements by the previous regime. But, because Sadat was apprehensive of the popular appeal of the Brotherhood, he frustrated its leaders' plan to have the organisation recognised as a distinct 'tribune' by the authorities, on the eve of the 1976 parliamentary poll. The Brethren therefore had no choice but to stand either as independents or members of the ruling (centrist) Arab Socialist Party. This suited Sadat, who was intent on dividing the Brotherhood and coopting its moderate section into the political establishment.

The six Brethren elected to parliament on the ruling party's ticket, and led by Saleh Abu Rokait, were treated favourably by the government, and allowed to publish a magazine, *Al Daawa* (The Call).[108] Although the Daawa group shared Sadat's anti-communist and anti-Nasserite views, it opposed his policy of leading Egypt into the American camp and subscribing totally to the American-sponsored peace plan for the Middle East. The nine independent Brethren in parliament, led by Said Ramadan, enjoyed much wider popular support and were more radical than the Daawa group. They offered to cooperate with the government only on the basis of their programme of Islamic action.

Then there were clandestine groups, such as the Denouncers of the Infidels, and the Repentance and the Flight (Takfir wal Hijra), which were totally opposed to the regime. Their members played a leading role in ransacking and burning the nightclubs along Cairo's 'golden strip' during the three days of rioting in January 1977. Six months later armed members of the Takfir wal Hijra caused a sensation by kidnapping the minister of waqfs and assassinating him when the government refused to release sixty of their imprisoned comrades. A large-scale hunt followed, resulting in 410 arrests. Of those arrested, twenty-three, including the leader Shukri Ahmed Mustapha, were executed.[109]

Having thus reasserted the authority of his regime, Sadat ordered that those clauses of the Egyptian law which were based on the Napoleonic code be replaced with appropriate ones from the Sharia. The state council announced that a bill to punish those found drinking or committing adultery was being studied, and that a presidential decree specifying the death penalty for those who renounce Islam was to be submitted to parliament.

These statements pacified the Islamic groups, but upset the Copts. They felt that the apostasy bill was directed against them, since they often convert to Islam to secure a quick divorce and then revert back to Christianity.[110] Led by their church the Copts undertook a four-day protest fast in September and declared that they would not submit to the apostasy bill if passed.

Faced with such opposition, Sadat dropped the idea of this law. Soon after he busied himself with a visit to Jerusalem, and talks with the Israeli prime minister. Since such moves ran counter to Islamic sentiment at home and abroad they widened the distance between the regime and the Islamic groups. This helped the Islamic movement, as a whole, to capitalise on the prevailing discontent and widen its base. 'The history of the Arab world is one of Islamic revival movements which appear in the aftermath of what is considered to be a great failure of the existing regime,' stated Saaduddin Ibrahim, sociology professor at Cairo university. 'The present cycle began in 1974–5. Students looked with alarm at the apparent rapprochement with Israel, and generally with the West. There were also the socio-economic dislocation of society, the frustration of the lower and middle classes.'[111] An important manifestation of this phenomenon was the support gained by the religious elements on the university campuses. In the spring 1978 elections for the students' union officials, the religious list won 60 per cent of the seats.[112]

The majority of present-day students come from rural petty bourgeois families, which have been the traditional backbone of the Muslim Brotherhood. Alienated by Sadat's recognition of Israel, and disgusted at the rising corruption, both material and spiritual, engendered by the regime's pro-capitalist economic policies, this section of society has turned against it. The formal rapprochement with Israel, signalled by the publication of the terms of the impending peace treaty between Cairo and Tel Aviv in March 1979, so angered the Islamic students that they mounted anti-government demonstrations at Alexandria and Asyut universities: a daring step, since it made the demonstrators liable to life imprisonment.[113] They coined such slogans as 'No peace with Israel', 'No privileges for the rich', 'An end to moral decadence', and 'No separation between Islam and the state'.[114] They had no doubt been cheered by the success of the Islamic forces in Iran about a month earlier.

Soon after the Shah's downfall a nervous Sadat had called on the Islamic leaders to reform the official Daawa group, and increase its staff of preachers. While the ministry of higher education had ordered the universities to make religious instruction compulsory, parliament, through the speaker, had promised that legislation based on Sharia, which had been kept in abeyance since July 1977, would be passed and enforced strictly.[115]

Having suffered severe government persecution in the wake of the anti-regime demonstrations, and finding themselves barred from expressing opposition to the Israeli peace treaty, the Islamic militants directed their energies against the Coptic minority. The result was attacks on Copts in Alexandria and Asyut, the cities with a substantial Coptic population. Following explosions in Coptic churches in Alexandria in January, anti-Coptic and anti-Sadat demonstrations were held in Upper Egypt cities in March. The Coptic pope, Patriarch Shenouda III, protested by retreating to a monastery and refusing to celebrate the Easter Mass. This in turn increased tension between Copts and Muslims, and led to widespread inter-communal clashes in Alexandria. Unnerved by these events, Sadat alleged that the Coptic pope and clergy were involved in a conspiracy to partition Egypt and set up a Christian state, with Asyut as its capital.[116]

Since no concrete evidence was offered to back up the charge, Sadat's statement was not meant to be taken seriously by objective observers. It was, however, true that over the years the Coptic church had become politicised. Ironically, this had come about as a result of Sadat's policies. Nearly a decade before the victory of Islamic fundamentalism in Iran, Sadat had encouraged Islamic groups in Egypt. His steps towards Islamisation, including partial prohibition – taken to counter Islamic militancy in the mid-1970s – had alienated the Copts. Having thus compromised the secularist ethos of the Nasserite era, Sadat undermined the main pillar of unity of the Egyptian people, irrespective of their religion – their struggle against the Zionist state – by visiting Jerusalem in late 1977. Deprived of a common national aim which had been actively pursued over the past three decades, the Copts became more aware of their religious identity.

Later, by strangling the secular, conservative neo-Wafd party, popular with the Copts, barely seven months after its formal founding in February 1978, Sadat robbed the Copts of an opportunity to actively participate in national politics. The ill-effects of Sadat's economic policies – accentuation of class differences and moral and material corruption – were felt as much by the Coptic petty bourgeoisie as the Muslim. Like their Muslim counterparts, therefore, the young Copts turned to religion to seek a new solution to a perplexing set of problems.

Finally there were the external influences – particularly that of Israel, which became more effective as relations between Tel Aviv and Cairo were normalised. 'Israel's ambition is for the whole area [of the Middle East] to be made up of small religious states,' said the author Milad Hanna, a (Copt) professor at Cairo university. 'Take the case of Lebanon, where Israel is supporting, arming and fighting for partition, and a purely Maronite Christian state.'[117]

In August 1978 there were persistent rumours of the rightist Lebanese Front planning to declare a Free Republic of Lebanon, and to sign a twenty-year defence treaty with Israel. Indeed three months earlier the National Group, led by the former president Suleiman Franjieh, had left the Lebanese Front in protest against such a move.[118] The Front was thus left with three constituents: the Kataeb Party,[119] the National Liberal Party, and the Order of the Maronite Monks: all of them right-wing and predominantly or exclusively Maronite.

The Maronites are the followers of Saint Maron, a Christian saint of the fourth century who lived in north-east Syria. Their migration to Mount Lebanon occurred in the seventh century, and was led by John Maron, a monk. With the persecuted Christians from the plains taking refuge in these mountains over the next few centuries, their ranks grew steadily. During the Crusades the Maronites sided with the Crusaders; and in 1180 their church acquired semi-autonomous affiliation with the Vatican, which allowed them to retain their own liturgy and have their own patriarch, resident in Lebanon.

A decade after the Ottoman conquest of the remainder of the Fertile Crescent, Iraq, in 1638, France proclaimed itself the protector of the Catholics in the Ottoman empire, and was so accepted. This was the beginning of a special relationship between Paris and the Maronites, which bloomed when Syria–Lebanon was placed under French mandate after the First World War. The Maronite and other Christian leaders cooperated actively with Paris in the creation of a Christian-dominated Greater Lebanon. France allowed the church to continue its near-monopoly over the educational system of the Christian Lebanese.

Centuries of isolation in the mountains, combined with successful resistance to direct control by Muslim overlords, had turned the Maronites into a community where religion and politics had become inextricably mixed. The first attempt to establish a Christian political organisation was not made until 1936. In that year Pierre Gamayel, inspired by the Nazi Youth Movement he had witnessed during his visit to the Berlin Olympics in Germany, founded the Kataeb Party. The party's motto was 'God, family, country'; and its following came chiefly from among the Christian youths of Mount Lebanon and Christian students of Beirut. It played an active role in the forging of the National Pact of 1943, which formalised Christian domination of the state apparatuses. With this the party adopted a new slogan: '1920 borders, 1926 constitution, 1943 National Pact'.

Following the full independence of Lebanon three years later, the party tried to widen its appeal to the Maronite masses. In this it was helped by the discovery in 1949 of a plot by the Syrian Popular Party to merge Lebanon with Syria, and the subsequent nationalist reaction that it aroused among Christians, determined to maintain Lebanon as an independent entity. Its pro-West stance, coupled with its opposition to Nasser and Arab nationalism, led it to back President Camille Chamoun in the civil war of 1958.

The party's initial support for President Chehab (1958–64) began to wane as he tried to strengthen the powers of the state at the expense of the financial and commercial oligarchs, who have been the Kataeb leaders since its inception. The reforming effort ceased altogether during the presidency of Charles Helou (1964–70) so that the state machinery reverted back to being 'little more than an instrument for the enrichment of the ruling class'.[120] Helped by the continuing prosperity of Lebanon – stemming mainly from its being a banking and tourist centre for the wealthy oil shaikhs of the Arab East – the party swelled its ranks with recruits from the Christian petty bourgeoisie. By aligning with Chamoun's National Liberal Party in the 1968 parliamentary elections, the Kataeb increased its share of seats from four to nine.[121]

However, with the economic boom petering out towards the early 1970s, disillusionment set in among the party members. This could have led the Kataeb's luminaries to critically examine the politico-economic system with a view to reforming it. But since such a course would inevitably have hurt the Christian oligarchy's interests, it was not pursued. Instead the leaders channelled the rising discontent among their followers against the Palestinians, whose presence in Lebanon had been increased by the June 1967 war and the Jordanian strife of 1970–1.

As an extreme example of militant Arab nationalism, the Palestinians were a perfect target for hatred by the Kataeb followers as well as the National Liberals. Both parties now began building up their militias: the Kataebites' Phalange, and the National Liberals' Tigers. At first the right-wing militias aided the Lebanese army in attacking the Palestinian commandos. Later, in 1973, they took to assaulting the Palestinian partisans on their own. By the summer of the following year the two militias were built up to the point where jointly they were a third as large as the 18,000-strong army.[122]

Tensions within Lebanese society were also building up. A succession of Israeli air attacks on southern Lebanon had driven tens of thousands of Muslim peasants into Beirut, and enlarged the disaffected urban Muslim constituency. The presence of the Palestinians had the effect of radicalising the (generally) underprivileged Muslim section of society. An overt manifestation of Muslim radicalism came in March 1975, when fishermen in the southern port of Sidon opposed the governmental plan to give the monopoly for offshore fishing to a company, and fought off the army. The slowly crystallising alliance of radical Lebanese and the Palestinians was considered a serious threat to the status quo by the rightist forces.

It was against this background that the killings by the Phalange in mid-April of twenty-seven Lebanese Muslims and Palestinians, returning by bus from a political rally in a Beirut suburb triggered off a civil war. The nineteen-month strife boosted the Kataeb's following. Its membership doubled to 40,000, with at least a quarter of them enrolled as militiamen. It allied with the National Liberals and two other Maronite bodies to form the Lebanese Front to fight the Lebanese National Movement, consisting of nationalist-leftist forces.

The conservative, anti-socialist Kataeb and the NLP were helped militarily not only by Israel and America but also by Jordan and France.[123] They received the most extensive and effective military aid before, during and after the civil war from Israel. And when, in the spring of 1976, they were squeezed into a tight corner by the Lebanese National Movement, Syria came to their rescue. By the time the civil war ended in October, Israel had by its own admission provided the Kataeb's Phalange and the NLP's Tigers with 110 tanks, 5,000 machine-guns, and 12,000 rifles.[124]

The NLP's Chamoun was closer to Tel Aviv than Kataeb's chief Gamayel. The National Liberal Party revolved chiefly around the personality of Camille Chamoun, who had established it soon after the 1958 civil war. The main pillars of its ideology have been Lebanese (as against Arab) nationalism, and 'economic liberalism based on private enterprise'.[125] Unlike the older and better organised Kataeb, the NLP was able to attract non-Maronite Christians. This had an important bearing on its strength in parliament. In the 1972 parliamentary poll it secured thirteen seats, the highest won by any party. It had fought that election, and the one before, in alliance with Kataeb. Its differences with Kataeb were described by Bashir Gamayel, the Phalange chief, as being 'more due to traditional rivalry rather than different political programme or philosophy'.[126]

The two parties worked together in building up the infrastructure of a modern state in the Christian area they held during the civil war: an airport, harbour, postal service, food distribution system, courts, police, and armed forces. They determinedly kept the Arab League peacekeeping force out of the region they controlled. In the political negotiations that followed the cease-fire they insisted on the 'decentralised unity' of Lebanon, which their opponents saw as another term for partition.

They strengthened their links with Israel. In July 1977 the NLP Tigers' commander announced that his men had carried out joint operations with the Israelis against the Palestinian positions in the south.[127] The Israeli invasion of southern Lebanon next March helped the right-wing Christians politically and militarily. It emptied the border area of all Muslims, leaving only about 20,000 Christians in occupation of the 29- by 5-mile strip. It enabled Tel Aviv to install a former Maronite army officer, Major Saad Haddad, as the military-political master of the Christian enclave along the border. His force of 2,000 to 3,000 men was armed, trained and financed by Israel.[128] The ties between Israel and the right-wing Christians became stronger and less inhibited. Gamayel and Chamoun visited Israel secretly in May, and reportedly signed an arms deal with the Israeli authorities. The presence of Israeli military advisers in the Christian mini-state increased to the extent that there were 1,500 such personnel in (Christian) east Beirut alone.[129]

In August President Elias Sarkis tried to reassert his authority over the Christian enclave in the south, and sent 700 troops to secure the strip. Haddad refused to yield, and was supported publicly inter alia by Chamoun. Aware of the comparative weakness of the Lebanese army (9,000 strong) vis-à-vis the joint strength of the Phalange and the NLP Tigers (at 12,000 to 15,000),[130] President Sarkis abstained from engaging Haddad's forces in battle.

Two months later the Christian militias frustrated the Syrian peacekeeping forces' plan to establish control over Asharfiya, a Beirut suburb, which links the capital with the 650-square-mile Christian hinterland to the north. Despite the Syrian blockade, Israel managed to send 300 tons of food and arms and ammunitions twice a week to the Christian-controlled port of Jounieh.[131]

Once the Kataeb and the NLP had jointly frustrated the plans of the central government and the Syrian peacekeeping troops, the simmering tension between the two parties came to the surface. Their differences centred around the issues of collecting levies from the populace, control over ports between Beirut and Jounieh,[132] and the overall policy towards Israel, the Syrian peacekeeping force, and the Lebanese Muslims. Pierre Gamayel, the Kataeb chief, wanted to play down links with Israel, and initiate talks with Damascus, whereas Chamoun wanted neither.

When their differences could not be ironed out behind closed doors, their militias took to street fighting. In one such incident in May 1979 ten militiamen were killed. Following this, a joint decision was taken by the two leaders to initiate talks for the merger of their parties. Nothing came of this, because the Kataeb leadership, commanding a heavily armed militia of 20,000 men,[133] was in no mood to compromise. The matter was finally settled in early July 1980 through force. In a three-day-long battle, which led to 850 casualties, the Phalange captured twelve offices and two garrisons of the NLP. Chamoun gave up and instructed his followers to disband.

With the NLP decimated, Kataeb emerged as the uncontested master of the Christian mini-state, with a population of under one million.[134] As early as the summer of 1978 it had established commissions on the economy, education, foreign relations, justice and information. Now it reiterated its intention to keep the Lebanese army out of the territory it controlled, and assigned internal security to the National Guard, to be composed of all the Christian militias in the area.

Having consolidated its hold over the Christian mini-state, Kataeb strengthened its ties with Israel. The process was now much simpler, since Israel had to deal with only one party. Thus reinforced, Kataeb tried to extend its influence to Zahle, a mainly Greek Orthodox city of 150,000, on the eastern slopes of Mount Lebanon, which bounded the Christian enclave in the north. Following the tactics they had used against the NLP the Kataeb–Phalange wiped out opposition elements in the city ruthlessly. In early 1981, assisted by Israeli military advisers, the Phalange fortified military posts on the hills surrounding Zahle, and started to build a military road from the mountain to the city.[135] The overall purpose was to transform Zahle into a strategic link between the Phalange forces in the north with those led by the Israeli-backed Major Saad Haddad in the southern strip along the Israeli border.[136]

Since Zahle is situated along the Beirut–Damascus road, the Syrian peacekeeping force in Lebanon could not allow it to develop into a 'dangerous enclave' in the (predominantly Muslim) Bekaa valley along the Lebanese–Syrian border. In early April Syrian forces attacked the Phalange positions in and around Zahle, and succeeded in dislodging them from the mountain posts and sealing off the city. Israel stepped in to help the Phalange. Its planes shot down two Syrian helicopter gunships on 28 April. Syria responded by bringing in SAM anti-aircraft missiles into the Bekaa valley. The Syrian–Israeli confrontation acquired an international dimension, with the two superpowers engaging in a diplomatic dialogue to defuse the situation.

One consequence of the crisis was that the Phalange emerged as a (publicly acknowledged) protégé of Israel. Reports that Israeli military advisers had been aiding the Phalange in Zahle and the Christian mini-state were given credence when Tel Aviv confirmed that the Israeli chief of staff, General Rafael Eitan had visited Jounieh – the capital of the Christian mini-state – on 1 April.[137] Some weeks later Prime Minister Begin's office confirmed that Israel had given a promise to the Phalange militia that if they were attacked by Syrian planes Israel would use its air force against the Syrians.[138]

The net result of the confrontation with the Syrian peacekeeping force, which its militia had invited, was a diminution in Kataeb's power in Lebanon. None the less, Kataeb remains the single most important political-military force in the Christian segment of society. It is therefore bound to influence the presidential elections due before September 1982. The new president chosen by the deputies who were elected in 1972 would lack the authority needed to make the central government's writ valid over all of the republic. In any case, following the present constitutional procedures for the presidential election, thus leaving the political set-up undisturbed, amounts to leaving the root cause of the two civil wars intact. Given this, and the artificiality of the country's boundaries, coupled with the almost even split in its citizens' religious loyalty, it is not surprising that the republic has undergone the most intense turmoil in the Arab East.

Where such factors are absent, as is the case with Egypt, the regimes have been comparatively stable, and internal upheavals minimal. In Egypt the people are imbued with a deep sense of national identity, which stretches back to antiquity; and they have been ruled by a strong, centralised authority. They are racially and religiously more homogeneous than the citizens of any other Arab East republic. These basic facts about Egypt were not altered by the republican coup of July 1952. If anything, the state became more centralised than before. Despite the apparent twists and turns in its internal and external policies, the Arab East's largest republic can be said to have followed a centrist course, oscillating between right-of-centre and left-of-centre positions.

# 7

# CENTRIST FORCES: SECULAR AND RELIGIOUS

Until the Law for the System of Political Parties was passed in June 1977, republican Egypt had been allowed only one political party. In 1953 it was called the Liberation Rally; in 1957, the National Union; and in 1962, the Arab Socialist Union. But no matter what name the organisation bore, it represented a wide spectrum of socio-economic interests, and followed an essentially centrist course.

The Liberation Rally stood for the removal of all foreign troops from Egyptian soil, 'the rights of the disfavoured classes to social protection and equality before the law',[1] and the land reform which had been decreed by the Revolutionary Command Council in September 1952. The agrarian reform involved reducing land rent, and imposing a ceiling of 300 feddans on land ownership. Since it affected only 10 per cent of the cultivated land,[2] its impact was limited. Its implementation was left to the state bureaucracy; and the landless and poor peasants were not organised to participate in the process and prepare the ground for further reform.

Although the land ceiling stipulation ended the monopoly on economic and political power that big landlords had enjoyed so far, it still left them the dominant class in the villages. 'The size of property they retained (up to 300 feddans, and often through legal subterfuge even larger areas of the best land), their experience with power, and their ideological influence, helped by the bureaucratic implementation of the reform, left them the major power in the countryside,' notes Mahmoud Hussein, an Egyptian author.[3]

Earlier, in August, the RCC had shown its opposition to the workers' militancy by crushing a strike at a textile mill in Kafr al Dawwar, near Alexandria, with tanks and troops. Over two hundred strikers were arrested and tried by a military court: two of their leaders, Mustapha Khamis and Mohammed Hassan al Bakari, were executed. The RCC followed up this action with a countrywide persecution of militant trade unionists and Communists.

Given this record of the RCC, and the general vagueness of the aims of the state-sponsored Liberation Rally, it was not surprising that the Rally began attracting many of the supporters of the ancien régime. As such, it failed to become a popular organisation, full of vitality. In any case, the politics of the republic were then dominated by rivalry between President Mohammed Neguib and his deputy, Gamal Abdul Nasser. This went on until October 1954, when the issue was settled in favour of Nasser.

By the time a republican constitution was promulgated in January 1956, Nasser had consolidated his position as the sole leader of the nation. He had also by then imbibed the virtues of socialism through his friendship with such international figures as Marshal Josip Tito of Yugoslavia and Jawaharlal Nehru of India, whom he had first met at the non-aligned nations' conference in Bandung, Indonesia, in April 1955. This was reflected in the new constitution. It provided for a National Union which, although composed of all political tendencies, stood for the abolition of 'feudalism and exploitation', and the reorientation of private property and its holders to serve the 'higher interests' of society. It believed in establishing 'socialist cooperative society', based on 'socialist laws'. An example of these laws was the official stipulation that workers must be taken into management, and that 25 per cent of the net profit be given to them, with 10 per cent in cash. However, on such important basic matters as the class composition of the national assembly there was hardly any socialism to show. Reflecting the class composition of the National Union, workers and employees formed only 3 per cent of the membership of the national assembly of 1957.[4]

Following the establishment of the United Arab Republic, consisting of Egypt and Syria, in February 1958, the concept of the National Union was extended to Syria, where all political parties were dissolved. With the rise of communist influence in post-revolutionary Iraq, then competing with Egypt for the Arab East's leadership, Nasser declared communism to be the main threat to the Arab nation. He therefore launched a virulent anti-communist campaign in 1959, and combined it with the tactic of adopting some of the policies advocated by them. In 1960 he nationalised Misr Bank, the main institution which financed the activities of Egypt's propertied classes. Blaming the 'negative aspects' of 'exploitative capital' for his regime's failures, he mounted a campaign against the urban rich.

A series of decrees issued during July 1961 introduced progressive income tax, nationalised Egypt's insurance, banking, and major industrial and commercial companies, and limited compensation to be paid to the nationalised companies' directors. The management of these establishments thus passed into the hands of the military bureaucracy, drawn largely from the petty bourgeoisie. In Syria these decrees resulted in full nationalisation of insurance, banking, and three industrial companies, and partial nationalisation of twenty-four other industrial firms. Unlike Egypt, where many of the expropriated capitalists were of foreign origin, in Syria all of those adversely affected were indigenous capitalists, with considerable socio-political influence. The alienation of this class of Syrians – who had earlier backed union with Egypt in order to forestall the rise of leftists in their country – prepared the ground for Syria's secession from the UAR, which came two months later.

Nasser was deeply disappointed, and blamed the National Union for the UAR's break-up. Declaring that 'internal reaction' had infiltrated it, and succeeded in 'dulling its revolutionary fervour', and reducing it to 'a mere organisational façade', he dissolved the National Union.[5] He then convened the preparatory committee of the National Congress of the Popular Forces to devise means of selecting representatives of the 'truly popular classes'. On the committee's recommendation, 1,750 representatives – 25 per cent peasants, 54 per cent workers and employees, and the rest from the remaining classes – were elected by trade unions, professional syndicates, and other voluntary bodies. After public discussion of the National Charter, drafted by Nasser, the National Congress unanimously adopted it, without any alteration, in June 1962.

The National Charter combined its belief in 'scientific socialism' and 'the struggle against exploitation and in favour of equal opportunities' with the aim of achieving the unity of 'all the working forces of the people', including the national capitalists – that is, manufacturers, contractors, businessmen, traders, and big landowners. The National Union was to be replaced with the Arab Socialist Union, which was described as 'the guardian of the values of true democracy'. Reflecting the thinking behind the National Charter, the ASU was conceived as an alliance of the five segments of the 'working forces': peasants, workers, intellectuals, soldiers, and national capitalists.

Arguing that the republican regime had successfully ended the exploitation that had existed in the monarchical era, Nasser stressed that relations between different socio-economic classes must now be peaceful. This was assured by the ASU's stipulation that its members were to act as individuals, and not as representatives of the class or organisation to which they belonged. 'Nasser's theory of the working forces was just a classification scheme of the population, not a recognition of the organisational autonomy for each group,' notes Iliya Harik, an American political scientist. 'Nasser acknowledged socio-economic differences in society but disavowed the Marxist doctrine of class warfare.'[6]

The ASU had a pyramidal structure: basic units of twenty at village, workplace or neighbourhood level, at the base, and the executive committee at the apex, with district and provincial committees in between. But the different tiers did not intermesh properly, mainly because the popular elections which were supposed to be held at different levels were not called, except for the provincial committees. Therefore, instead of emerging as the popular political body which would guide the state's executive arm, the ASU became subordinate to the state, assisting the civil and military bureaucracies to implement governmental policies decided by Nasser, his advisers, and the cabinet (many of whose members sat on the ASU's executive committee).

In rural areas the ASU was led by the village headman, rich farmers, and the educated with urban connections: the groups which in pre-revolutionary days had played second fiddle to the feudal lords. At the district and provincial levels the ASU leadership was composed of teachers, government bureaucrats, and other professionals: the very groups which could not blossom while the urban upper classes monopolised political-economic power, as they did in the monarchical era. By weakening the power of the traditional ruling classes – the feudal lords and urban rich – through the First and Second Agrarian Reform Laws (of 1952 and 1961),[7] and the nationalisation decrees of July 1961, the regime had enabled the petty bourgeoisie – that is, the professionals and the civil and military bureaucrats – to become the new leading class of Egypt.

Active governmental intervention in the economy led to a huge increase in the size of the bureaucracy. At the same time, without easy access to state officials, a citizen could not derive much benefit from the regime's new policies. The best way to secure the civil servants' cooperation was by achieving an important position in the ASU. (Even ordinary membership of the ASU was supposed to help with the bureaucrats: no wonder its membership soared to six million in four years.[8]) As a result a mutually supportive triad of the rich farmer, state bureaucrat, and urban professional grew up, and secured a monopoly of power.

Such a development ran contrary to the National Charter's basic intent that power should rest with the 'popular classes'. To be sure, the new ruling coalition did not question the National Charter's stipulation that 50 per cent of the national assembly members must be peasants (owning less than 25 feddans) and workers.[9] What it did was to promote clients among the peasants and workers to positions of leadership in the ASU, and thus to membership of the national assembly. Since these persons were elected as individuals, and not as representatives of the peasants' or workers' unions, there was no conflict of interests.

In their day-to-day work the industrial trade unionists often found the local ASU leaders sympathetic to their viewpoint. But at the national level the trade union leadership, deferential to the political establishment dominated by Nasser, lacked a credible independent identity. A series of nationalisation decrees affecting 300 private companies, issued in August 1963, was supported by the non-Marxist leftists in the ASU but disapproved by the rightists. However, no effort was made to resolve these differences, partly because ultimate power lay with one man, Nasser, and partly because the ASU was meant to embrace all political tendencies anyway. Its exceptionally broad base and lack of cohesion inhibited the ASU from becoming an active political agency able to bring about a socialist transformation of society.

Nasser himself realised this. In 1964 he began to toy with the idea of creating a revolutionary vanguard within the ASU. But since the vanguard was visualised as a secret body of dedicated partymen, the ASU leadership was faced with the difficult problem of devising a suitable method of selection.[10] Following the creation of the central committee of the ASU in July 1965, Nasser appointed Ali Sabri, the leftist-inclined prime minister, as the general secretary of the ASU, with a mandate to transform the organisation into a cadre-based party.

Sabri replaced the provincial and district committees with executive bureaus, and introduced the cadre concept in the form of a Leadership Group at the basic level. The first secretary to the provincial executive bureau was appointed by the central secretariat in consultation with the provincial governor. He in turn appointed the first secretaries to the district executive bureaus. Each district chief then named the secretaries to the Leadership Groups in the area. The ASU's district and provincial offices were soon manned by salaried functionaries, drawn from the civil service, business management, teaching and legal professions, landowning community, and factory floor, on the basis of 'personal evaluation by the top leadership elements of the ASU',[11] and trained at one of the three institutes of socialist studies.

Furthermore Sabri established the Socialist Youth Organisation as an auxiliary to the ASU, but with its own cadre, who were imbued with the ideology of Arab socialism and imparted organisational skills. He soon built up its strength to 20,000. Following Nasser's call in June 1966 to launch 'incessant struggle in every village and hamlet . . . to put an end to exploitation',[12] the Socialist Youth (aged sixteen to thirty-three) mounted a campaign against feudalism by exposing the misdeeds of big landlords.

Thus the ASU began to transform itself from being merely a collaborationist movement, helping the state apparatus to implement government policies and programmes, to being a popular mobilisation agency, with dedicated party activists replacing the local notables who had found a niche in it, creating much friction in the process.

ASU activists and Socialist Youth members played a crucial role in the popular demonstrations in Cairo on 9/10 June 1967 to persuade Nasser to reverse his decision to resign in the wake of Egypt's defeat in the Six Day war. Nasser stayed. But the war left his regime so shaken that he decided to re-establish the political consensus that had existed before the creation of the ASU cadre and the Socialist Youth. In October he dissolved the Socialist Youth Organisation. Eight months later he disbanded the Leadership Groups and changed the ASU's structure back to the one prevalent in the pre-Sabri days. (He even went on to establish a special reserve police force to quell protests at universities and factories.[13]) With this the displaced local notables of the past were back in their seats of power within the ASU framework. In the economic sphere the government began encouraging the private sector at the expense of the public.[14]

After Nasser's death in September 1970 there was a revival of the debate on the ASU's role. While the faction led by Ali Sabri advocated its continuation as an independent political entity, President Sadat proposed that it should be made subservient to the state executive. Sadat's line prevailed when he arrested the leading members of the Ali Sabri group, in May 1971, and appointed Mohammed Dakrory, a former secret service officer, as the ASU's general secretary. About a year later Sadat appointed a committee to propose changes in the ASU. In its report, submitted in March 1973, the committee recommended that the stipulation that anybody contesting a political or trade union office must be an ASU member should be dropped, and that the party machine be democratised.

Sadat did not act until after the October 1973 war when, in line with his new economic policy of 'open door' to foreign private capital, he tried to liberalise the political set-up. Following his instructions, parliament changed the law and made ASU membership voluntary for participants in a political or trade union election. Later Sadat appointed a commission to solicit public opinion on his proposal that each of the five constituents of the 'working forces' – peasants, workers, soldiers, intellectuals, and national capitalists – be allotted a tribune within the ASU to express its viewpoint. In January 1975 the commission proposed the formation of four tribunes within the ASU; and this was endorsed by the third congress of the ASU held in August.

A joint committee of the ASU and parliament was set up to examine the credentials of all the thirty-five tribunes which had staked a claim for official recognition. In May 1976 the joint committee decided to license only three: the centre tribune, represented by the Arab Socialist Party of Egypt led by the then prime minister Mamdouh Salem; the rightist tribune, represented by the Liberal Socialist Organisation, headed by Mustapha Kemal Murad; and the leftist tribune by the Alliance of the Progressive Nationalist Unionists, led by Khaled Mohieddin.

In the parliamentary poll of October–November 1976 the candidates were allowed to hold public meetings, and their statements published in the newspapers, which were all controlled by the ASU. Of the 342 elected seats,[15] 280 went to the centrist Arab Socialist Party, 12 to the rightist Liberal Socialists, 2 to the leftist Alliance of the Progressive Nationalist Unionists, and the rest to the independents.

Soon after these elections Sadat radically reduced the size and importance of the ASU. He dissolved the mass organisations affiliated to it, transferred all the district and provincial offices and officials to his Arab Socialist Party, and limited its role to supervising the activities of the three parties that were to be allowed to grow out of the existing tribunes. However, the ASU's position as the sole owner of all the major newspaper publishing companies was left undisturbed,[16] as was its exclusive authority to issue a licence for a new publication. Each of the three recognised parties was permitted to publish a weekly.

All this was sanctioned by the Law for the System of Political Parties passed in June 1977. This law also stipulated rules for licensing a new party: the support of at least twenty parliamentarians and evidence that, while believing in the general principles of 'democratic socialism', the new party offered a programme which was considerably different from those being advocated by the three existing parties.[17]

By early 1978 the leaders of the pre-revolutionary Wafd Party had secured a licence to establish the neo-Wafd Party. The new party organisation supported Sadat's peace moves with Israel, and promised to implement the policies of his regime with 'more efficiency' and 'less corruption'.[18] Encouraged by the enthusiastic response to the party by the secular, conservative sections of society, its leaders announced plans for publishing a weekly and a daily newspaper, to be printed at the party-owned press. At the other end of the spectrum, *Al Ahali* (The Masses), the APNU's weekly, had by late March gained a large circulation.

This was disturbing news to Sadat. At a public rally to celebrate the seventh anniversary of the 'correctionist' coup against the ASU leftists, on 14 May, he promised 'democratic crushing' of all those 'who create doubt in Egypt'.[19] He ordered a referendum on a complex set of guidelines for 'correcting' Egyptian democracy to be held within a *week*. Despite the boycott calls by the opposition parties, and doubts cast on the constitutional legality of the referendum by the Lawyers' Syndicate, it was carried out. According to the interior ministry, responsible for conducting elections and referendums, 85.4 per cent of the eleven million voters turned up at 23,000 polling stations; and 98.3 per cent of them voted 'Yes'. In practice, it meant marking a red circle (yes), or black (no), under the question: 'Do you agree to the six principles included in the referendum-presented speech delivered by the president of the republic on 14 May 1978 for protecting the home front and social peace?'.[20]

It is questionable whether such a method, used to measure opinion in a country where a third of all citizens are illiterate (the proportion among adult voters being still higher), is likely to reveal the true picture. Going by independent accounts, the official figures of the voter turnout and the favourable vote were both fabricated. 'On the referendum day, the BBC World Service reported that less than half the electorate had voted, and the samples taken by Reuter [news agency] at Cairo polling stations one and a half hours before they closed put the figures as low as 30 per cent,' wrote Faris Glubb of the *Middle East International*.[21]

Nevertheless, following the referendum parliament passed a law which specified various penalties for those who advocated 'an ideology that contradicts religion', or failed to respect 'the socialist democratic system of the state, social peace, and national unity', or spread 'unfounded rumours or defeatism', or had a record of belonging to 'the corruptive elements before or after the 1952 revolution'. In practical terms the new law set out to punish an exceptionally wide range of politicians and journalists: all those who believed in Marxism and class struggle as well as those who advocated laissez faire capitalism or the setting up of a religious state – and those who had led the Wafd Party in the past. Rather than face courts, or official dissolution, the neo-Wafd leaders disbanded their party. But, despite frequent confiscation of their publication and other forms of harassment, the leaders of the leftist APNU refused to dissolve their organisation.

In a public speech in August, Sadat threatened to 'birch' and 'flog' anybody who tried to disrupt his course of action,[22] which – as was revealed later – was to set up his own party, to be named the National Democratic Party. He invited Mustapha Khalil of the ASU to be its (nominal) leader. Even before the new party had published its programme 275 of the 300 parliamentarians belonging to the then ruling Arab Socialist Party lined up to join;[23] and this immediately assured the as yet unborn party political power.

Describing the party as 'national, democratic, socialist, scientific, faithful, popular, revolutionary, humanist and nationalist [i.e. pan-Arabist]', its programme listed the party's enemies: 'the followers of foreign ideologies' (i.e. Communists), 'those trying to take Egypt back to the pre-1952 era' (i.e. Wafdists), and 'the remnants of the totalitarian regime' (i.e. leftist Nasserites). It conceded that post-revolutionary attempts to rebuild Egyptian society had failed, and stated that this had happened because such attempts had been made in the shadow of a regime which was totalitarian, or at best pseudo-democratic, and bent on imitating 'the system and culture of foreign occupation': the reference to 'foreign' presumably meaning the Soviet Union. Outlining the party's socio-economic philosophy as 'socialist democracy, Arab Islamic and Christian values, and the principles of the 1952 revolution after being corrected', the programme stated that the public sector must be limited only to the projects which 'the people' felt should be assigned to it, and that the economic policy of the open door to foreign capital must remain.[24] These and other aspects of the National Democratic Party were aired at great length in the state-controlled mass media: radio, television, and newspapers.

Following the formation of the National Democratic Party, and the signing of the Camp David accord in September 1978, Sadat appointed a 'peace government' headed by Mustapha Khalil. For the next few months Sadat concentrated on meeting the Christmas deadline for a peace treaty with Israel. In this he failed. It was only after the American president had personally intervened in the negotiations, by travelling to Egypt and Israel, that the treaty was finally agreed on, and signed, in March.

There was considerable opposition to the unilateral peace treaty with Tel Aviv; but this was denied expression. Even what parliamentarians said against it in the House went unreported in the state-controlled media. Having secured parliament's endorsement of the treaty, Sadat placed it before the voters in the form of a referendum. But, as in the past, he attached minor disparate points to the main theme – such as the bill of rights, etc. – and offered a whole set of questions, to be answered with a single 'Yes' or 'No'.[25] On 19 April, polling day, 99.1 per cent of those voting said 'Yes'.

Next month, following his instructions, parliament authorised Sadat to make laws without having to secure subsequent parliamentary approval. This meant that the president now possessed an unqualified right to dissolve a political party, or authorise the founding of a new one, or disqualify a citizen from participating in public life. He amended the Law for the System of Political Parties so that only a party with a minimum support of ten parliamentarians could publish a newspaper. He then dissolved the people's assembly two years before its normal tenure and called a fresh poll in June.

These elections were rigged. For instance, when a leftist candidate in Alexandria managed to open a ballot box before polling began, he found it filled with 500 National Democratic Party ballots. At some places irate voters demonstrated against malpractices. But this did not help because the police (controlled by the interior ministry, which also conducted the elections) simply closed the polling stations.[26] Little wonder that the NDP won 302 of the 362 seats, with the leftist APNU wiped out altogether, the rightist Liberal Socialists reduced to 2 seats, and the newly formed 'honest' opposition, Socialist Labour, securing 26 seats. The results marked the end of the process of political liberalisation, which had been initiated two years earlier, with the Law for the System of Political Parties.

The brief period of liberalisation had done little to counter the deep-seated fear of criticising authority. This was particularly true of the rural areas where the majority of Egyptians live. 'You have to be careful here, even in a village of seven families and 500 people, since criticism of government policy can bring a fall from grace,' reported Caroline Tisdall, a British journalist visiting a village in the Valley of the Dead.[27]

The village poor had much to complain about. In June 1975 parliament had taken steps which favoured landlords and hurt the 1.5 million tenant peasants, who rented 43 per cent of all arable land.[28] Parliament increased the land tax and authorised landlords to receive rent in kind (something which had been abolished by the Nasserite land reform) and evict a tenant if he failed to pay rent within two months of the financial year (down from the previous period of three years). The intent of these amendments was to reduce the number of tenants and increase the size of the average landholding in order, ostensibly, to raise production.

It was not accidental that changes in land laws were proposed by Mahmoud Abu Wafia, chairman of the parliamentary committee on the 'open door' economic policy. Meant to attract capital from the Gulf states as well as the West, the policy was formally launched in early 1974.

However, it did not get going until April 1975, when laws ending state monopoly in foreign trade were passed. With individuals and private companies being allowed to import goods, Egypt witnessed the emergence of a new class of importers. Sadat's earlier policy of returning properties and businesses, sequestrated by Nasser, to the 600-odd owners brought back the 'White Egyptian' community of the monarchical days from its exile in Lebanon.[29] Helped by the enormous increases in house and business rents, the old rentier class entered into commercial partnership with the new class of importers and agents, as well as wealthy foreigners from the Gulf states. By 1976 the number of millionaires in the country had surpassed 500.[30]

Their number increased steadily as the Sadat administration pushed Egypt firmly on to a capitalist path, and the size and importance of the class of rentiers, merchants, importers, exporters, agents, and realtors grew. The systematic dismantling of the price mechanism of the Nasserite era, which accompanied this process, coupled with a ban on strikes and demonstrations, on pain of life imprisonment, imposed in February 1977, brought great hardship to the working and lower middle classes. While inflation ran at 30 to 40 per cent a year in the late 1970s, wage-earners had to manage with an annual income increase of 10 per cent.

In short, Sadat's policies increased differentiation within the middle class which had been the mainstay of the Nasserite regime. The top segment grew rich, allied itself with the (revived) urban bourgeoisie of the past, and the emerging kulaks. The resulting alliance became the single most powerful political-economic force. The bottom section – comprising among others the six million employees of the government and the publicly owned undertakings[31] – became weaker. It therefore swelled the ranks of opposition, secular and religious. This alarmed Sadat. But his massive strike against opposition on 3 September 1981 backfired: it intensified popular hatred of him, and paved the way for his murder on 6 October.

While Sadat moved Egypt to the right, internally and externally, his style of government was basically similar to his predecessor's. Like Nasser, he relied exclusively on the state machinery to implement his policies, and used the state-controlled mass media to gain popular acceptance of his actions and policies. Again, like Nasser, he changed course gradually, and presented his actions in pragmatic rather than ideological terms. It is noteworthy that it was not until April 1955 that Nasser first mentioned the term 'socialist society', in passing;[32] and that it was only in the wake of the Suez war of late 1956 – over four years after the July 1952 revolution – that he thought of giving an ideological underpinning to his regime.

This pattern – whereby a tightly knit group, led by a charismatic leader, produces an ideology, piecemeal, *after* it has assumed power – is quite different from the one which prevailed in Syria and Iraq. There the

Arab Baath Socialist Party, an organisation with a committed cadre and a well-defined political ideology, had emerged long before its leaders seized state power.

The roots of the Arab Baath Socialist Party go back to 1940, when Michel Aflaq and Zaki Arsouzi, both history teachers in Damascus, formed groups of nationalist students to agitate for independence from the French. Three years later the two leaders decided to merge their groups, and called the new body the Arab Baath Party. However, the formal, legal establishment of the party had to wait until after the final departure of the French in 1946.

At its first pan-Arab congress in Damascus in April 1947, delegates from Syria, Iraq, Lebanon, Transjordan, and Morocco adopted a constitution and a programme. The party's basic principles were described as: the unity and freedom of the Arab nation within its homeland; and a belief in the 'special mission of the Arab nation', the mission being to end colonialism and promote humanitarianism. To accomplish it the party had to be 'nationalist, populist, socialist and revolutionary'. While the party rejected the concept of class conflict, it favoured land reform; public ownership of natural resources, transport, and large-scale industry and financial institutions; trade unions of workers and peasants; the cooption of workers into management, and acceptance of 'non-exploitative private ownership and inheritance'.[33] It stood for a representative and constitutional form of government, and for freedom of speech and association, within the bounds of Arab nationalism.

In Syria the party drew its initial support either from the urban Sunni (Muslim) and Orthodox (Christian) petty bourgeoisie, or the rural notables, particularly those in the Alawi and Druze areas of Latakia. 'The party's social base remained the petit bourgeiosie of the cities, and in the countryside middle landlords with local social prestige,' notes Tabitha Petran. 'However, the Baath did not develop much in the cities. Most of the Sunni petit bourgeoisie, even in Damascus, was influenced by the Muslim Brotherhood and later also by President Nasser. But the Baath won a following among students and military cadets: future intellectuals and army officers.'[34]

The other party to draw support from the military cadets was the Arab Socialist Party, founded in January 1950 by Akram Hourani, a lawyer from Hama. His active participation in armed clashes with the French after the war had gained him respect and popularity in the officer corps of independent Syria. At his suggestion the Syrian government had instituted the egalitarian policy of disregarding the social background of the applicants to the only military academy at Homs. Since a military career was the only way a son of a poor or middle peasant could raise his social status, the Homs academy attracted many applicants from this section of society. Given the ASP's commitment to ending feudalism and distributing government land to the landless, and its leadership of peasant agitations, it was not surprising that it enjoyed considerable following among young cadets and officers.

Drawn together by their opposition to the dictatorial regime of Colonel Adib Shishkali, the leaders of the Baath and the ASP decided in September 1953 to form the Arab Baath Socialist Party: this was formally done six months later. The new party re-stressed the Baath's central slogan: 'Freedom, unity, socialism'. 'Freedom meant political, cultural, and religious liberty as well as liberation from colonial rule,' explains Peter Mansfield. 'Unity meant not only the political unification of the Arab peoples but (also) their regeneration through the release of their "hidden vitality" which is the true source of nationalism. . . . Socialism, which comes last in the Baath trinity, is less a set of socio-economic principles than a rather vague means of national moral improvement. . . . All they [Baathist leaders] said was that socialism was a means of abolishing poverty, ignorance, and disease, and achieving progress towards an advanced industrial society capable of dealing on equal terms with other nations.'[35]

None the less, the infusion of the ASP's predominantly peasant following into the new party gave it the militant mass base that the old urban-based party had lacked. Winning sixteen parliamentary seats in Hama, the ASP's stronghold, in the general election of September, strengthened the hands of the leftists in the party, and softened its anti-Communist stance, associated with the founders of the pre-merger Arab Baath Party. This, and the need to counter the external pressures on Syria to join the Western-sponsored Baghdad Pact, led the Baathists to cooperate with the Communists, headed by Khaled Bakdash. 'The Baath and the Communist Party shared control of the streets in a part of the world where the monopoly of power held by the traditional ruling class made street demonstrations a normal and necessary part of the political process,' states Tabitha Petran. 'Akram Hourani and Khaled Bakdash were acknowledged to be among the country's most able politicians. Demands for social reform went hand in hand with the left's anti-Baghdad Pact campaign.'[36]

The leftist alliance was helped by change in the composition of the military officer corps which had occurred since the Palestine war, and more particularly since the downfall of the Shishkali dictatorship, which was followed by a purge of many old, conservative officers, drawn from the upper classes and trained by the French. The quadrupling of the military[37] since the Palestine conflagration had led to a corresponding expansion in the officer corps, with many of the new officers coming from modest or middle-sized peasant families.

The rise in the leftists' influence alarmed rightist circles at home and abroad. A right-wing plot against the government, instigated by monarchical Iraq, was discovered in December 1956. The conspirators were put to trial before a military court, headed by Colonel Afif Bizri, known to be friendly with the Communists. In order to meet the rightist threat politically, the progressive forces banded together under the National Front, led by Khaled Azm, the defence minister. The Front's charter won the endorsement of 65 of the 142 parliamentarians.

In August another right-wing attempt (inspired this time by the USA) to overthrow the regime was aborted. Colonel Bizri's insistence that certain officers suspected of collusion with the USA be dismissed caused a split at the top, with the conservative chief-of-staff, Tawfiq Nizamuddin, and the president, Shukri Quwatli, opposing Bizri, and the prime minister, Sabri Asali, and the defence minister, Khaled Azm, supporting him. In the event Nizamuddin resigned. His job went to Bizri, mainly because he was 'a popular non-partisan officer who had held aloof from factionalism in the army'.[38]

But Bizri's appointment was presented by America and its close allies in the region – Turkey, Iraq, Jordan and Israel – as evidence that Syria had 'gone Communist'. A concerted drive was mounted by these countries to topple the regime. But, backed by the nationalist-leftist forces at home, and by Nasser abroad, the Syrian regime weathered the storm. However, once the external threat had subsided by early autumn, the National Front began to lose its cohesion. The Baathists turned cold toward the Communists, and refused to contest the impending local elections under the National Front banner. This virtually destroyed the Front.

The Baathist leaders were faced with an agonising dilemma, when Azm – appointed deputy prime minister in early December – began organising his own party with a view to forging an alliance with the Communists to win the parliamentary elections of 1958. They realised that the only way to defeat the Azm-led front would be by allying with the traditional conservative parties: ideologically a suicidal course. They therefore enthusiastically accepted Nasser's call for the 'total unity' of Egypt and Syria. Among those who supported the Baathist decision was the chief-of-staff Bizri: on 12 January he led a secret delegation of fourteen officers to Cairo to seek an immediate military union of the two republics.[39]

Once the United Arab Republic was formed in February, the Baath leaders reckoned that Nasser's anti-Communism would lead him to repress the Communists, and thus inadvertently leave the political field open for their followers – operating through the National Union, the only legal party of the UAR – to dominate. In the event Nasser suppressed both the Communists and the Baathists, while implementing the socio-economic programmes advocated by them with the exclusive help of the state bureaucracy.

The agrarian reform law, promulgated in September, attacked the inequitable situation whereby 70 per cent of all peasants were landless while 0.6 per cent of landlords owned 45 per cent of the irrigated and 30 per cent of the unirrigated land.[40] It lowered land rents and fixed a ceiling of 300 hectares for unirrigated land and 80 hectares for irrigated land. Its provisions were expected to affect 1.5 million hectares and benefit a third of all peasant families.[41] Although implementation was slow and the landlords were to be paid compensation (by the peasants), this measure turned feudal interests against the UAR government.

In the absence of a genuine political organisation the new regime was unable to turn the peasants' goodwill to its advantage, or counter the growing feeling among educated Syrians that their country/region, was being increasingly treated as the junior partner in the Union. The feeling of discrimination was heightened by the fact that Nasser had taken to appointing Egyptian officers to the top positions in the Syrian military, thus causing disaffection in the Syrian officer corps. As stated earlier, by nationalising all financial institutions and twenty-seven industrial companies, involving 17,000 shareholders (in July 1961) Nasser alienated the Syrian capitalists. This was the backcloth against which a successful coup was carried out against the Nasserite regime by a group of army officers and Syria taken out of the UAR.

However desirable, the Syrian secession ran counter to the pan-Arab aspirations of the Baath. The party's national command – consisting of representatives from Syria, Iraq, Lebanon, and Jordan – had considerable difficulty in hammering out a common stand on the subject. In the end it resolved to work for a reunion in the future, but along federal, not unitary, lines. This, and the weakness of the civilian government which followed the anti-Cairo coup, enabled the Syrian Baath to cooperate with the Nasserite groups, both inside the military and outside.

On 8 March 1963 the pro-Baath Military Committee seized power in Syria. Since then, despite a few dramatic upheavals, reflecting deep differences within the party leadership, the regime in Damascus has not ceased to describe itself as Baathist. Factionalism, a feature of the party since its inception, had been fortified by the party's clandestine existence during 1958–61, which encouraged secretiveness and curtailed communication between different groups within the party. By early 1963 three major streams had evolved in the Syrian party: an anti-Marxist, chiefly civilian, wing headed by Michel Aflaq; a Marxist faction led by Hamoud Shufi, a Druze; and a radical, primarily military, wing headed by General Saleh Jedid, an Alawi. (In contrast the Iraqi party, which seized power in February 1963, consisted mainly of the anti-Marxist right and the nationalist-progressive left, with the former in command.) The massacre of thousands of Iraqi Communists by the Baathists in power there had a divisive effect on the Syrian party, with the anti-Marxist faction endorsing the action and others condemning it.

At the Syrian regional congress of the party in September the new leftist wing, made up of younger and rural elements committed to the concept of class struggle, prevailed over the reformist old guard, and won a majority in the newly elected regional command. Something similar happened at the Iraqi regional congress. At the party's national congress, held in Damascus the following month, the leftists consolidated their position.

The newly adopted programme stated that the party's study of the economic and political situation in Syria and Iraq had led to the conclusion that 'the bourgeoisie is no longer capable of playing any positive role in the economic field, and [that] its opportunism has made it a new ally of imperialism'; and that a socialist revolution could only be brought about by the united effort of 'the workers, peasants, educated revolutionaries (military and civilian), and the petty bourgeoisie'. It advocated agrarian reform, leading to the formation of collective farms run by peasants, and workers' control of the means of production.[42] 'Resolutions inspired by Marxism, amounting to a new programme replacing that of 1947, were passed,' states Eric Rouleau. 'The ideas of scientific socialism, class struggle and international solidarity were subtly introduced into a text whose nationalist character was still not in doubt.'[43]

This programme inspired a burst of socialist measures which lasted seven years, and radically altered the ownership patterns in agriculture, commerce, and industry. The new agrarian law fixed lower, graduated ceilings for unirrigated and irrigated landholdings – 50 to 300 hectares, and 15 to 55 hectares respectively – depending on quality of land. More importantly, the Baath established the General Union of Peasants in December 1964 to 'promote the peasants' rights and socialist values in the countryside'.[44] The founding of the union of agricultural cooperatives in 1967 gave a boost to the rural cooperative movement. In the same year the government set up its first state farm. By 1969 an efficient implementation of land reform laws had enabled the government to distribute 643,000 hectares of the 1,513,000 hectares of excess land, recovered from the landlords, to the peasants. Steady progress in state farming and the rural cooperative movement had, by 1971, placed a quarter million hectares in the public sector of agriculture, and created 1,350 agricultural cooperatives.[45]

Not surprisingly, reform in agriculture and elsewhere met resistance from vested interests: the period 1963–70 was peppered with severe challenges to the regime by the propertied and professional classes, operating in league with the Sunni religious establishment. The government's renationalisation of banks in May 1963 resulted in a credit squeeze. This, and the flight of private capital, combined with lower governmental receipts leading to large cuts in civil servants' salaries, and the moderate Baathists' refusal to endorse the radical programme, had a damaging effect on the regime's popularity. Buoyed by this, the landlords resisted the peasants' legal demands and allied themselves with the urban Sunni traders and clergy to mount an attack on the government in religious terms. As stated earlier, widespread anti-governmental strikes and riots broke out in major cities in April 1964.[46]

What enabled the radical Baathists to withstand this threat was the active support of the militant peasants in the countryside and of the armed Workers' Militia in the cities – and, most importantly, the continued loyalty of the army led by an officer corps which, since the March 1963 coup, was being continually purged of urban Sunni officers and staffed with Alawi and Druze officers with peasant backgrounds (and thus hostile to the interests of the urban bourgeoisie, whether petty, middle or top).

Having crushed the conservative opposition in the spring of 1964, the government introduced a fresh set of radical decrees, starting on 1 January, which nationalised over 100 commercial and industrial companies as well as all the oil distribution firms and power plants, and most of the import and export trade. In order to meet the bourgeois reaction it imposed martial law and set up special courts. But these did not deter the opposition, led by the religious hierarchy, from launching a campaign of civil disobedience against the 'godless Baath'. Backed by the army, and aided by the National Guard, Workers' Militia, trade unionists, and Communist activists, the government succeeded in breaking down resistance to the reformation of the commercial and industrial sectors of the economy.

The appointment of Baathist supporters with a rural background to managerial positions in nationalised concerns helped to strengthen the ruling party's rural base. Not surprisingly, the radicals prevailed at the emergency party congress held in July, which adopted a phased programme of putting the republic on to the road to socialist transformation and a people's democracy.

The following month a ninety-five-member National Revolutionary Council was appointed to draft a new constitution. Little came of it. Reflecting the deep divisions within the ruling party, the Council failed to reach a consensus. The conflict between the opposing factions was not to be resolved until 23 February 1966 when the radicals, led by General Jedid seized total power in a violent coup, and drove one of the party's (moderate) founders – Michel Aflaq and Saleh Bitar – into exile, and put the other in jail.

Subsequent expulsion of Aflaq and Bitar from the party earned the coup leaders the label of 'neo-Baathists'. What contributed greatly to the radicals' victory over their rivals was the military support provided by General Hafez Assad, the Alawi commander of the air force. Not surprisingly, Assad, promoted to defence minister, emerged as one of the three most powerful men of the post-coup regime – the other two being General Jedid, appointed the party's assistant general secretary, and Prime Minister Yusuf Zayen. 'The new rulers of Syria were mainly of peasant origin and of Alawi, Druze and Ismaili religious and cultural affiliation,' notes Tabitha Petran. 'This was the source of their radicalism vis-à-vis the city, especially the city merchants, who dominated the agricultural economy, and the urban Sunni establishment. In the countryside their radicalism did not reach very deep. For they were not of the poor peasantry; they came from small and mainly middle landowning families and sometimes from families of local notables.'[47]

Lacking any base in urban areas the neo-Baathists accepted the support offered by the Communists, the only secular party with an organisation in every city. They appointed a Communist and two independent Marxists as cabinet ministers: an unprecedented step in Syrian history. 'The point of departure for the fulfilment of [Arab] unity is the struggle for socialism at home and the revolutionary struggle against imperialism and reaction abroad,' said Prime Minister Zayen.[48] The new regime combined its stance against imperialism and Arab reaction with attempts to create a united front of progressive Arab states. It made conciliatory overtures towards Nasser, who responded favourably, starting with the formal recognition of Syria as an independent entity and the resumption of diplomatic relations.

But this did not end the rivalry which had grown up between Damascus and Cairo as the fountainhead of progressivism in the Arab East since the Baathist coup of March 1963. By stepping up aid to the Palestinian commandos, then engaged in guerrilla attacks on Israel, the neo-Baathists showed themselves to be more militantly anti-Zionist than Nasser. Cairo disliked being seen to be lagging behind Damascus. The net effect of this rivalry was to raise Arab–Israeli tensions: a process which culminated in war in June 1967.

Although the Syrian regime withstood the shock of the defeat better than did Nasser's, it was not as unscathed by the experience as it claimed. In fact the defeat sowed the seeds of discord which were to mature into the 'correctionist' coup of November 1970. Following the defeat two factions emerged within the ruling party. The political wing, led by Jedid, the party's stalwart, stressed combining economic development with a sharper anti-Zionist struggle in the form of a people's war to liberate the Golan Heights (lost to Israel in the 1967 conflict), and fostering class struggle in major Arab states. In contrast the military faction, headed by General Assad, proposed sticking to conventional forms of warfare, and ending Syria's isolation by moderating the government's external as well as internal policies. Furthermore, the Assad camp questioned the party's authority to dictate a strategy to the military.

Using his position as defence minister, Assad curbed the influence of the political wing within the military, and ended party activities in the armed forces. In February 1969, taking advantage of an Israeli attack on a Damascus suburb, he took control of the strategic positions in the capital. But his plans to monopolise political power were foiled by demonstrations and strikes organised by the cadres of the party and its affiliated mass organisations. These events showed that neither side was strong enough to displace the other, but gradually the balance began to tilt in

Assad's favour as the urban bourgeoisie, attracted by the moderation of his views, began siding with his camp.

Conflict between the two sides reached a climax in September 1970 when Assad, in command of the air force, refused to provide air support to the Syrian/Palestine Liberation Army tank units sent into northern Jordan by Damascus to help the Palestinian commandos against the Jordanian troops. The Palestinians lost. An extraordinary congress of the party was held for a fortnight in November to resolve the crisis. It ended in failure. On 16 November, in a bloodless coup, Assad arrested top party and military leaders, and ordered the army to occupy the party offices. He then carried out a series of 'correctionist' measures.

In the economic field this meant reversing the trend towards enlarging the public sector, which had been the dominant characteristic of the Baathist regime since 1963, and which had driven an estimated 200,000 rich and middle-class Syrians into exile,[49] and instead encouraging private enterprise, thus conciliating the small and medium-sized businessmen and industrialists. In the political sphere it accelerated the process of coopting all the progressive forces into the government, something which had been haltingly initiated by the neo-Baathists. Not surprisingly the new cabinet included as many non-Baathists (i.e. Nasserite Arab Socialist Unionists, Akram Hourani's Arab Socialists, and Communists) as Baathists. Of the seventeen leaders of the Progressive National Front, formed in March 1972 on the basis of the National Action Charter, eight were non-Baathist. Furthermore, the holding of a referendum and two elections to approve Assad as president, and to elect the local government and the people's assembly, within the span of two years (March 1971–March 1973) was a point of departure in Baathist history.

But the Baath, with 20,000 activists on its rolls (compared to 400 in 1963)[50] had no intention of sharing its dominance of the military and civil organs of the government, and educational institutions, with any other party. The National Action Charter, the basic document of the Progressive National Front, therefore specifically barred all non-Baathist groups from conducting any political activity among the armed forces or the students.[51]

Aware of the Sunnis' numerical dominance in the republic, Assad extended his correctionist moves to the sectarian field. As described earlier,[52] he made it a point to be seen praying in different prominent mosques. Following his concession to the Sunni clergy to constitutionally limit the presidency to a Muslim, he cultivated close links with religious leaders. He offered them state honours and higher salaries. A declaration by the Shia leaders of Lebanon that Alawis are part of the Shia community helped to confirm Assad and his fellow-Alawis as Muslim. By describing the Arab offensive against Israel in October 1973 in Islamic terms, Assad reiterated his Muslim credentials.

After the war Assad discharged many Alawi army officers for poor performance on the front and replaced them with non-Alawis, thus broadening the military base of his regime. By then membership of the Baath had ceased to be a prerequisite for a rank in the armed forces. Outside of the military, however, the party faithful ruled supreme – be it in the state-controlled mass media, the police, intelligence, or in any other branch of state bureaucracy. They also controlled the General Union of Peasants and the General Federation of Trade Unions, as well as such popular organisations as the General Federation of Women and the General Union of Students.[53] Through these organisations the Baath reached out to the remotest part of countryside, which has been the party's mainstay since the early 1960s. Yet, as Moshe Ma'oz, an Israeli expert on Syria, put it, 'The regime does not depend solely opon the loyalty of Baath members in the party's organisations and upon the people's fear of the police and army; the loyalty and identification of additional groups of the population also exert considerable influence. There is no doubt that the masses of wage-earners, labourers and peasants favour the regime which has steadily improved their living conditions, raised their income level and provided them with social security. These feelings are also shared to some extent by the intellectuals and the urban proletariat.'[54]

However, the widespread support enjoyed by the regime began to wane when Assad intervened in the Lebanese civil war on the side of the right-wing Christian forces in June 1976. There were mutterings within the Baath itself; and Assad had to resort to arresting the dissenting Baathists to silence them. The end of the Lebanese conflict, followed by the stationing of the Arab Deterrent Force – to which Syria contributed the largest share of 30,000 troops – created another kind of problem for Damascus. Many of the Syrian officers posted in Lebanon became involved in clandestine commercial ventures, including smuggling goods into Syria from Lebanon. This happened against the background of a spurt in the economy, fuelled by aid from the oil-rich Arab states, and a general relaxation of economic controls, which in turn had given rise to a class of smugglers and middlemen operating in league with some of the top brass in the military, civil service, police and the president's entourage.

Recognising the gravity of the situation, Assad launched an anti-corruption drive in August 1977 with a donation of his own house and land to the state. The campaign led to some arrests but soon fizzled out, partly because powerful figures in the government and the Baath were against it, and partly because Sadat's visit to Jerusalem in November, and subsequent developments, diverted popular attention away from domestic ills to foreign events. With Syria emerging as the leader of the Front of Confrontation and Steadfastness, determined to resist the American-sponsored peace process, Assad's prestige rose at home and abroad. The rapprochement with Iraq, announced about a year later, further enhanced Assad's standing among the Syrians. Yet the problems of rising inflation, housing and other shortages, and administrative corruption and inefficiency, which particularly hurt the urban proletariat and petty bourgeoisie, remained unsolved.

The increasingly daring actions of the Muslim Brethren, highlighted by the massacre of scores of military cadets in Aleppo and the near-insurrection in Latakia during the summer of 1979, severely jolted the government. At the Baath congress, held in late December, Assad encouraged the 700 delegates to speak their minds freely, without fear, and they reportedly did so. While endorsing such governmental decisions as overhauling the wage scales in the public and private sectors to keep pace with inflation, the congress appointed a special inspection and control commission to ensure that no party member used his position for personal gain.[55]

By then any hope of unity with Baathist-ruled Iraq, as agreed in principle in October 1978, had been totally dashed. Part of the reason for this was that at the summit conference in June 1979, Saddam Hussein, then Iraq's vice-president, had suggested an immediate merger of the two Baathist parties, as a prelude to political and military union. The Syrian delegation had rejected the suggestion, because it was only too aware of the greater size and better organisation of the Iraqi Baath.[56]

Such disparity was all the more remarkable because the first party cells in Iraq were not established until 1952 in an environment which was hostile to political activity of any kind. Yet within two years the party acquired enough presence to be included in the anti-monarchical United National Front, composed of the anti-imperialist Istiqlal (Independence) Party, the liberal National Democratic Front, and the Communists. The party supported the republican coup carried out by the Free Officers, led by Brigadier Abdul Karem Qassem, since it was anti-imperialist and anti-feudal. With the elimination of the pro-West monarchy, the Baathist leaders hoped that the republican regime would seek union with Nasser's Egypt and thus help realise the popular pan-Arab aspirations.

When in fact the pan-Arabist Abdul Salam Aref, the number two man in the republican regime was eased out, Baathist leaders turned against Qassem. They tried to assassinate him in late 1959 but failed. Then, guided by Ahmed Hassan Bakr, the party resorted to establishing cells within the military. With Qassem's popularity declining rapidly in the early 1960s, the Baathists gained substantial support in the officer corps. This led finally to a successful coup against Qassem in February 1963.

Outside the armed forces the Baathists tried to appeal to the educated urban middle classes: students, teachers, and professionals. But unlike Syria, they faced tough competition from the Communist Party, which had existed since the early 1930s and had established its roots among these groups, as well as the peasants. Following the republican coup the Communists expanded their base rapidly. This, and the Communist stress on socialism rather than Arab unity, turned the Baathists against them. Although Communist influence was severely curtailed by Qassem during the latter part of his rule, they were the only party to fight alongside the pro-Qassem forces to defeat the Baathist attempt to seize power. No wonder they became the prime target of the countrywide attacks launched by the Baathist-dominated National Guard on their enemies.

Though the new cabinet was headed by Bakr, the presidency was offered to Abdul Salam Aref, who was not a party member. Soon differences arose among the Baath leaders on the speed and manner of unification with Egypt, and the continuing violent persecution of the Communists. At the regional party congress the leftists showed themselves to be stronger than the rightists led by Bakr. A similar pattern emerged at the party's pan-Arab congress in Damascus in October. As stated earlier, this assembly adopted a programme which subtly incorporated the ideas of scientific socialism, class conflict and international solidarity.[57] The internecine differences intensified and demoralised party ranks. Taking advantage of this, Aref dismissed all the Baathists from his government in November and monopolised power.

An Arab nationalist of Nasserite hue, Aref pursued land reforms initiated by Qassem's Agrarian Reform Law of September 1958 – which fixed ceilings of 1,000 donums (618 acres) for irrigated land and twice as much for unirrigated land – but much less vigorously than his predecessor. For instance, he extended the time limit for the state takeover of excess land from five years to fifteen.[58] Following an agreement with Nasser in May 1964 to unify Iraq with Egypt, he set out to align the economic and political institutions of Iraq with those of Egypt. He nationalised twenty-seven large private companies, including banks and financial institutions, and sections of the import trade.[59]

Aref tried to model the Arab Socialist Union along Egyptian lines, but failed. The basic problem was the differing interpretations of socialism by the groups that had been invited to join. 'To some groups socialism might mean simply social justice, while to others it meant Marxist socialism involving all the forces of production and trade,' explained the minister for unity affairs. 'Under the latter brand of socialism the state must take over all the wealth of the country. Another group of nationalists was prepared to settle for much less than this.'[60] Although the plan for unity with Egypt was not consummated, Aref remained pro-Egypt until his death in April 1966.

His brother, Abdul Rahman, who followed him as president, made little change to state policies. To bolster the strength of the Cairo-led joint military command on the eve of the June 1967 war, he dispatched 12,000 troops to Jordan. He also joined the Arab oil boycott of the West, which only lasted until the end of August. However, when he resumed oil shipments to the West in January, five ministers resigned in protest. As his stock fell, and as popular disenchantment with his rule began to manifest itself in demonstrations for an elected parliament, he resorted to repression and withdrew his earlier promise to hold parliamentary elections by May.

Against this background, former Baathist military officers, led by Bakr, secured the cooperation of Lieutenant-General Ibrahim Daoud, the presidential guard's commander, and Colonel Abdul Razak Nayef, the security chief, in toppling the president. They succeeded in this on 17 July. During the next fortnight the Baathist officers managed to get rid of Daoud and Nayef, and assumed full control of the state.

Conscious of the fact that the majority of Iraqis were dependent on agriculture for their livelihood, the Baathist regime carried out further agrarian reform. Its new law fixed ceilings on irrigated land in the range of 40 to 600 donums – and on unirrigated land from 1,000 to 2,000 donums – depending on several factors. Moreover, it cancelled the compensation due to landlords according to the 1958 act, and empowered the government to take over excess land without compensation and distribute it free to peasants. Another law, promulgated in May 1970, offered incentives to agricultural cooperatives and introduced the concept of collective farming.[61] By the next year, of the 22.9 million donums of cultivated land, 10 million donums had come under government possession since the republican revolution of 1958: of these 3.5 million donums had been distributed to peasants.[62]

Although profound in its socio-economic consequences, land reform could not be presented to the populace at large as a dramatic achievement in order to capture their imagination. Such presentation was the near-monopoly of the Kurdish problem, which had plagued the country since the end of the Second World War, when the Kurds of Iraq and Iran had managed to found an independent republic, with its capital in Mahabad, Iran, and kept it going for a year. The republican coup resulted in peace returning to the Kurdish region; but this did not endure for long, as Qassem proved inflexible on the subject. Led by the Kurdish Democratic Party, the Kurds took up arms against Baghdad in 1961 to press their demand for complete autonomy. It was not until June 1966 that the KDP ceased its operations after signing a twelve-point agreement with Abdul Rahman Bazzaz, a civilian prime minister during the Arefs' rule. However this accord – which included recognition of the Kurdish language and proportional represenation for the Kurds (forming 16 to 25 per cent of the total population)[63] in all state organs – did not hold, as each side accused the other of bad faith.

Now the Baathist regime began implementing part of the twelve-point agreement. Regarding this move as inadequate the KDP launched an armed rebellion in 1969. This went on until March 1970 when a fifteen-point agreement was signed by the two sides. The new accord promised a fair degree of autonomy to the region where the Kurds were in the majority, and the appointment of a Kurd as the republic's vice-president.

A constitutional change, effected in July, recognised the Kurds as one of the two peoples of the republic, and Kurdish as one of the two official languages of the state. But the Baathist Revolutionary Command Council rejected the KDP's nominee for vice-president.

By then the Baath had, through its cells in the military and civil services, consolidated its hold over the state machinery so well that it could easily afford to be unresponsive to the demands of other parties. 'The Baathist units, though meeting in the headquarters of the government department concerned, are presided over not necessarily by the minister or the highest ranking official (who may or may not be a member of the Baath), but by the highest ranking member of the Baath Party in each department,' states Majid Khadduri, an American academic. 'These units meet regularly to weigh the work of each department in the scale of the party principles and guidelines, and submit reports and recommendations to the party's headquarters.'[64]

Party cells were also established in professional syndicates, universities, private businesses, trade unions, and agricultural cooperatives. By the early 1970s party activists amounted to some 20,000,[65] and were organised in a pyramidal structure, moving up from a cell to a circle to a section, with several sections forming a provincial branch – of which there were sixteen – to reach the apex of the national leadership: the party's regional command. The cadre are instructed to keep their party membership secret and be on the lookout for suitable recruits. Once a party member thinks he has found a suitable candidate he informs his cell chief. 'The potential member is then kept under watch from a few months to a few years – for political philosophy, reliability, and moral behaviour,' writes Ralph Joseph. 'When found suitable he is invited to contact the original cell. He then goes through ideological indoctrination which lasts six months to two years. Only then is he accepted as a full member.'[66]

No wonder, over the years, the Iraqi Baath emerged stronger and more cohesive than its counterpart in Syria, with which its relations had been strained since the neo-Baathist coup of February 1966, which had consigned the party's founders – Aflaq and Bitar – to prison or exile. One of the first acts of the Iraqi Baathists after seizing power was to invite Aflaq to Baghdad 'to certify the genuineness of the Iraqi branch as compared to the deviationist-regionalist faction ruling in Syria since 1966'.[67] Relations between the two parties improved somewhat after Assad had displaced the radicals from power in November 1970 and carried out a series of correctionist moves. In fact the Baathists in Baghdad took their cue from Assad, and tried to widen popular support for their rule by inviting other progressive parties to join the government on the basis of the National Action Charter.

By insisting that the Baath should loosen its grip over the state machinery as a precondition for its cooperation, the KDP virtually rejected the Baath's overture. In contrast, the Communists and the Nasserites accepted the four cabinet posts offered to them, in early 1972, after a brief period of hesitation. When Baghdad signed a friendship treaty with Moscow in April, and followed it up with nationalisation of the Western-owned Iraq Petroleum Company two months later, the Communists warmly endorsed these moves. But, in an interview with the *Washington Post* in June 1973, Mustapha Barzani, the KDP leader, stated that if America provided 'political, humanitarian, or military help, open or secret, to the Kurds, they could control the Kirkuk oilfield and give it to an American company to operate'.[68]

Following this interview, and the KDP's refusal to join the Progressive National Front, formally established in July, the Baathists and the Communists refused to accept the KDP as the sole representative of the Kurds. In March the central government enforced the Kurdish autonomy law, stemming from the 1970 accord, as planned, and set the scene for convening the (nominated) legislative council in Erbil, the Kurdish capital. Protesting against the exclusion of such oil-rich areas as Kirkuk, Sinjar and Khanaqin from the Kurdish region, the KDP demanded that enforcement of the autonomy law be postponed until a fresh census revealed the exact distribution of the Kurds in the north-eastern region. When Baghdad ignored the KDP, the latter resumed its armed struggle against the central government. These hostilities claimed 7,600 Kurdish and 9,543 Iraqi military casualties[69] before coming to an end in March 1975 when, with the cessation of aid from the Shah of Iran as a result of the Iraqi–Iranian accord signed in Algiers, the Kurdish rebellion collapsed.

This, and the fivefold increase in revenue from oil exports, provided an unprecedented boost to the morale of the Baathist regime. Its ambitious plan for 1976–80 promised a better future for all. Yet the largest single group in the republic – the Shias – nursed a grievance that they were grossly under-represented in the upper echelons of the police, military, intelligence, and the Baath and the governmental hierarchy. None of the Revolutionary Command Council members was Shia; and of the thirteen members of the Baath regional command only two were.

Sunni dominance of Iraq dates back to the days of the Ottoman Turks, who were of Sunni persuasion. This pattern continued during the Hashemite period, since the Hashemites too were Sunni. Qassem, who ruled the republic for nearly five years, was of mixed parentage; but the Baathist leaders who followed him and who seized power again in 1968 were predominantly Sunni, hailing from the north.

Southern Iraq, which is overwhelmingly Shia, is the heartland of Shiaism: it was here that the Shias' first imam, Ali, and his sons, Hassan and Hussein, lived, fought, and died. Najaf and Karbala, their holiest places, are situated here. And it was in Najaf that Ayatollah Khomeini sought refuge in 1965, after he had been expelled from his native Iran and then Turkey, and was granted asylum on the understanding that he would desist from political activity. This gesture by Baghdad went down well with the Shias in Iraq as well as Iran, most of whom revered Khomeini and considered the Shah an infidel and a pro-Zionist. Khomeini's presence gave a fillip to Al Daawa, a secret religious-political organisation, established in 1960, which drew its support almost exclusively from Shia clergy and laymen.

Baghdad had taken this line in a spirit of pique at the Shah who, it feared, was being heavily armed by the USA and groomed to become the gendarme of the Gulf once the British had left the region by the late 1960s. The accession of the Baathists, and their tilt against the West and towards Moscow, had worsened relations between Tehran and Baghdad. The nadir was reached in 1974 when the Shah openly aided the Iraqi Kurds in their armed rebellion against Baghdad.

In return the Baathist regime began to encourage the Iranian Arabs of Khuzestan to agitate for independence, and generally help the anti-Shah forces. It was this that finally led the Shah to secretly negotiate an accord with Iraq, and sign it at an OPEC summit conference in Algiers. This required each side to stop aiding subversive elements working against the other. It also formalised the border along the Shatt al Arab waterway which the Shah had, through superior military force, imposed on Iraq in 1969–70. In a way what the Shah had done was nothing more than right the wrong forced on Iran by the powerful Ottoman emperor through the treaty of Constantinople of 1897, which allocated all of the waterway to Iraq: an arrangement which ran counter to the convention whereby a waterway demarcating an international boundary is shared equally by neighbouring states.

However, once the Shah and Saddam Hussein of Iraq had signed the accord in Algiers, relations between the two countries began to improve rapidly: a development which went down badly with the exiled Khomeini as well as the bulk of the Iraqi Shias. But the Shias were unable to express their views on this subject or even on those which specifically affected them: the regime's efforts to interfere with some of the characteristically Shia rituals, to weaken the authority of the Shia religious hierarchy, and to impose certain political slogans on them. Resentment became all the stronger during the festival marking the symbolic return of Imam Hussein. 'The fall of Hussein as a martyr in the struggle to regain authority from the Sunni caliph in A.D. 680, is a symbolic event which reminds the Shia community each year that it is still under Sunni rule though the members of the Shia community form the majority of the population in the country,' notes Majid Khadduri.[70]

During the Imam Hussein festival in early February 1977, a convoy of Shia pilgrims was stopped by troops between Najaf and Karbala. This seemingly routine check-up triggered off fighting between the pilgrims and the soldiers, and later snowballed into massive anti-government demonstrations in the two cities. Baghdad rushed large army contingents to restore order there, which they did after fatally shooting dozens of pilgrims and arresting 2,000 Shias, including Hojatalislam Bakr al Hakim, son of the supreme Shia leader, Ayatollah Mohsen al Hakim. Later eight Shia dignitaries, five clergy and three laymen, were sentenced to death and executed.[71]

In October 1978, as the anti-Shah movement, guided by Khomeini, gathered momentum in Iran, the Iraqi government expelled Khomeini: a step which widened the gap existing between the regime and the Shias, especially when it was soon followed by Saddam Hussein's escorting the Shah's wife, Empress Farah Diba, around the Shia holy places. Later, in February, while the Baathists received the news of the Shah's downfall with trepidation, the Shia leader Ayatollah Mohammed Bakr al Sadr stated in his congratulatory message to Khomeini that 'Other tyrants have yet to see their day of reckoning'.[72]

By then a series of events had moved the Iraqi position rightwards, at home and abroad. A wave of unrelenting repression unleashed on the Communists by the government had reduced the Progressive National Front to a paper organisation by the autumn of 1978. The shock of the Camp David accord had jolted the Baathists in Baghdad to discard their hitherto ultra-radical, isolationist position on the Middle East peace process, and stop attacking Syria for accepting UN resolutions 242 (of 1967) and 338 (of 1973), which implied recognition of Israel. In fact, alarmed at the loss of Egypt as Israel's enemy on the western front, the Iraqi rulers invited President Assad to Baghdad, and offered to unite Iraq with Syria in order to create a powerful eastern front against Israel. Through this move, and the hosting of the Arab summit conference in Baghdad against the Camp David agreement, the Iraqi regime improved its standing in the Arab world.

But the dramatic events in Iran caused a miscarriage of the Iraqi–Syrian unity plans. While Assad openly praised the Iranian revolution and immediately recognised the new regime, Baghdad maintained a stony silence. Nervous about the impact of Iran's Islamic revolution on their own Shia majority, the Iraqi Baathists tried to acquire an Islamic image inter alia by cultivating Riyadh – a capital they had so far either shunned or treated gingerly – and signed a limited security pact with it.[73] As Khomeini took to appealing to the Iraqis to overthrow the 'non-Muslim' Baathist regime, Baghdad encouraged the Iranian Arabs in oil-rich Khuzestan to demand autonomy and engage in sabotage of oil installations.

Tehran radio stepped up its anti-Baathist propaganda calling on the faithful to replace 'the gangsters and tyrants of Baghdad' with 'the rule of divine justice'.[74] In mid-June Shias held a series of demonstrations in the southern cities. The government struck back with an iron hand. According to the Islamic Liberation Movement of Iraq, about 200 demonstrators were killed by military firing, and another 3,000 arrested.[75] When Saddam Hussein, then vice-president, moved against many dissident Shia leaders and military officers, and asked President Bakr to sign their execution orders, the president reportedly refused and offered to resign.[76] On 17 July, the eleventh anniversary of the Baathist seizure of power, Saddam Hussein became head of the state as well as the Baath.

Within a fortnight of assuming the highest office, Saddam Hussein discovered a major 'anti-state conspiracy' involving scores of top Baathist and military leaders. Following a summary trial by a specially appointed tribunal of half a dozen of Saddam Hussein's closest allies on the Revolutionary Command Council, twenty-one of them were executed.[77] The list included five of the twenty members of the RCC, including Muhyi Abdul Hussein Mashadi, the general secretary; and Abdul Khaleq Samarrai, who was a senior member of the Baath's national command. Samarrai was known to have proposed political liberalisation,[78] whereas Muhyi Abdul Hussein Mashadi had been bold enough to suggest that the successor to President Bakr ought to be elected through a free vote of the RCC.[79] As one of the three Shias on the RCC, he had also questioned the severity with which the government had dealt with the Shia demonstrations of mid-June. What all the executed RCC members had in common was their enthusiasm for Iraq's union with Syria: a subject on which Saddam Hussein was at best lukewarm. By insisting on an immediate merger of the two Baathist parties at the joint unity meeting, held in June, he had, deliberately or otherwise, taken the steam out of the unification drive.

Having exterminated opposition at the highest level in the party and the armed forces, Saddam Hussein carried out a widespread purge of dissident elements in the trade unions, people's militia, students' unions, and local and provincial governments. He combined these moves with such popular actions as raising the salaries of the military, intelligence, civil service, and judiciary. With oil revenue running at $32 billion a year,[80] his administration could easily afford this extra expenditure which, by raising demand, benefited the economy. In a major reshuffle of the government he appointed his brother, Barzan, as chief of security and intelligence; his cousin, General Adnan Khairallah Talfah, defence minister; and a close relative, Saddoun Shaker, interior minister.

Once Saddam Hussein had consolidated his position in the Baath and the government he concentrated on meeting the challenge posed by the Iranian regime to his rule. By holding a series of referendums and elections on the Islamic republic's constitution, and its representative institutions, in full view of the international mass media, Tehran was inadvertently making Baghdad appear dictatorial. The presidential poll held in Iran in January, followed by elections to parliament, showed the Islamic regime's commitment to a representative system. To overcome the damaging stigma of authoritarianism the Iraqi RCC ratified laws which restored the national parliament that had ceased to exist since the 1958 coup.

Beyond that, the twin-headed policy of portraying the Khomeini regime as representing Iranian imperialism, and suppressing the local Shia hierarchy, was pursued with renewed vigour. In April Iraq demanded that Iran should quit the islands of Lesser and Greater Tumb, and Abu Musa, in the lower Gulf, which had belonged to Ras al Khaima and Sharjah emirates of the UAE before the Shah occupied them on the eve of the British withdrawal from the region in 1971.[81] At the same time Baghdad took to expelling tens of thousands of Shias from the border areas to Iran on the ground that they were not 'real' Iraqi nationals. These steps coincided with reports that the supreme Shia leader, Ayatollah Mohammed Bakr al Sadr, and his sister Bint al Huda, who had been under house arrest in Najaf for many months, had been taken to the capital by the security police and assassinated.[82] Since Ayatollah Sadr was a much revered Shia personality, and a close friend of Khomeini, this action was severely condemned in Iran. Ignoring such protests, Saddam Hussein stepped up his actions against religious as well as secular opposition, making it a capital offence to belong to Al Daawa, which was bitterly opposed to the Baathist regime. Indeed persecution of the government's opponents became so intense that, according to Amnesty International, a London-based human rights organisation, 500 Iraqis had been executed on political grounds in the first six months of 1980 (as against 100 in the whole of the previous year).[83]

It was against this background that elections to the 250-strong Iraqi parliament were held on 20 June. Although all candidates contested as individuals, about 90 per cent of those elected turned out to be Baathists. (The Communists were barred from contesting.) Since the RCC, headed by Saddam Hussein, continued to be the supreme authority, the convening of parliament and the appointment of a new cabinet did not alter the political set-up much. None the less it was a measure of the importance attached to the popularly elected body that President Hussein chose it as the forum to announce, on 17 September, that Iraq was abrogating the 1975 treaty with Iran immediately, and that henceforth all ships entering the Shatt al Arab waterway must fly the Iraqi flag and use Iraqi pilots. As expected, Iran ignored this unilateral declaration.

Five days later on 22 September Iraq launched a fully-fledged attack on Iran at five points along the 720-mile-long border, with the major thrust concentrated along the Shatt al Arab waterway in the south. Baghdad's territorial claims to all of the waterway were widely regarded as a ploy for its political aim of bringing about the overthrow of the Khomeini regime. Reports that Shahpour Bakhtiar and General Ali Ovessi – respectively the last prime minister and the joint chief-of-staff under the Shah – had visited Baghdad in mid-August and conferred with President Hussein on the tactics and timing of the attack on Iran, confirmed the political objective of the Iraqi action.[84]

Baghdad's plans had visualised the Iranian Arabs in Khuzestan welcoming the invading Iraqi forces as liberators, and helping them in their march to the adjoining tribal region in the south-east, where the large Bakhtiar tribe, reportedly loyal to Shahpour Bakhtiar, would join the rebellion against Tehran. These 'liberated areas' would be declared the 'Free Republic of Iran', which would then work for the overthrow of the Khomeini regime.[85] In the event, the Khuzestani Arabs did not rebel; and the Iraqi advance was halted by fierce resistance by the Iranians. Despite the commitment of five of their twelve army divisions to forward positions, the Iraqis failed to gain full control of Khoramshahr port city after seven weeks of fighting – much less Abadan, the refinery city nine miles to the south – in the Shatt al Arab area.

Of the Arab countries only Jordan publicly sided with Iraq. While sympathetic towards Iraq, the Gulf states restrained themselves to aiding it covertly: so too did Syria and Libya in their backing of Iran. President Hussein had hoped to end the war with victory for his country by Eid ul adha (the nearest festival), due on 20 October. Instead, on the eve of the Eid, in his television broadcast he explained to the audience that the Iraqi advance had been slow, because 'the Iranian cannons are greater in number, their tanks more advanced, their navy can reach long-distance targets, and they have better arms', and that the Iranian officers had the benefit of the best American and western training.[86] None the less the general conduct of war – with the commanders relying heavily on artillery and mortar fire and avoiding hand-to-hand combat, thus keeping the casualties low[87] – seemed to be satisfactory to the general public. The war was reported to have unified the populace and enhanced the popular standing of President Hussein.

All along the Iraqi president had tried in his own ways to counter the religious appeal of Khomeini. For instance, in his address to the nation on the eve of the Eid, he urged his soldiers to chop off the heads of their enemies: 'Truly, you are the sword of Allah on earth and the heads you chop off are those of the aggressive . . . backers of Khomeini, the maniac.'[88] The state-controlled mass media, which often described Khomeini as 'a madman' had, since the outbreak of the war, reported that Ayatollah Abol Qassem Khoei, the supreme leader of the Iraqi Shias, had cooperated with Bakhtiar and Ovessi in their plans against Khomeini. They had also reported that Ayatollah Khoei had prayed for the welfare of President Hussein. But the contrary was the case. In an interview with the *Guardian*, Abbas Khoei, the London-based son of the Shia leader, stated that in his telephone conversations from Najaf his father had 'declared himself against the war [with Iran] and against Saddam Hussein'.[89]

Such Shia personages as Ayatollah Khoei oppose President Hussein not because he is a Sunni but because he is an absolute and oppressive ruler, and the Koran enjoins all true Muslims to wage war against such rulers. They cite the Koranic verses of the earlier, Meccan period, which are full of warnings to the rich against neglecting the poor and the needy, to support their case. Moreover, they consider it their religious duty to inspire the weak and the oppressed to fight their oppressors and exploiters.

These views are not the monopoly of the Shias: they are shared inter alia by the Salafiya movement which is predominantly Sunni. The Salafiyans want to conform to the Islam of their salafi, ancestry, at the political level. They stress that since prophet Mohammed was succeeded by the caliph, chosen democratically by the community at large, there can be no place for monarchy in Islam. The movement, originally inspired in the early 1900s by the Egyptian scholar Mohammed Abdu, is now known to exist in the kingdoms of Kuwait, Saudi Arabia, and Jordan.

Outlining the structure of a modern Islamic state along Salafiyan lines, a young leader of the movement in Kuwait envisaged the mujtahids, experts on Islamic law, giving a lead in selecting the caliph, who would then offer himself for selection by the Islamic community. 'The caliph will receive a salary like everybody else, and nothing more,' he added. 'Nobody can overthrow the caliph as long as he conforms to Islam. But if he does not he must go to [Islamic] court. If he refuses he must then be overthrown by the sword. The caliph has no immunity.' The government will consist of a popularly elected advisory council, with ministers appointed by the caliph to carry out his policies. The finance department will have the authority to collect income from natural resources and the compulsory Islamic alms, and distribute them equitably among the citizens. The caliph will command the military, consisting of professionals and volunteers, and appoint governors for the cities. If there are complaints against a governor, and these are proved, he will be changed.[90] In short, the Salafiyans visualise a democratic republican set-up which does not recognise hereditary power at any level.

Not surprisingly their anti-monarchical views led the Kuwaiti Salafiyans to cooperate in the plans to take over the Grand Mosque in Mecca, as a prelude to founding an Islamic republic in Saudi Arabia, and then, hopefully, in the contiguous kingdoms. However, all seven Kuwaiti Salafiyans involved in the operation were either killed or executed.[91] It is not known how many Saudi insurgents belonged to the Salafiyan fraternity.

However, the movement for an Islamic republican Saudi Arabia, with a democratic set-up, has the explicit or implicit support of several important sections of society: Oteiba and Shammar tribes who are not yet reconciled to the Saudi hegemony; the influential merchant families of Hejaz who regard the House of Saud as socially inferior; and, most importantly, the fast increasing population of university-educated

Saudis. As stated earlier, the Hejazi merchant families were involved in the planning of at least one abortive coup against the regime, and the Shammar and Oteiba warriors were prominent in the Mecca uprising.[92]

The process of producing qualified Saudis to man the political-economic system, which had been initiated in the late 1950s, received a boost after the dramatic jump in oil prices following the Yom Kippur war. During the next five years the number of university students more than doubled, with 17,000 studying at home and another 10,000 abroad. By 1980 the figure for those studying abroad, in mainly western countries, had doubled again.[93] 'There is a growing liberal element among Saudis who, returning from Western universities, watch with horror as the scramble for money goes on and vital issues are neglected,' notes Richard Alexander, a British journalist. 'They find themselves powerless to influence the events or play any useful role. There is no political system outside the monarchy and no scope for social development because of the dominant Wahhabi ideology.'[94] Even those being educated at Saudi universities are not immune from republican influences, since most of the teaching staff there are foreign: either Arab or south Asian (i.e. Pakistani, Indian or Bangladeshi), or Western.[95]

This has been happening against a background of an explosion in foreign travel and mass communication, best symbolised by the ubiquitous presence of the transistor radio and television. 'The popularity of television and radio broadcasts has now increased knowledge of outside events,' states James M. Bedore, an expert on Saudi Arabia. 'Tens of thousands of Saudis have travelled outside the kingdom for the first time; urbanisation has taken place on a vast scale; and the impact of non-Saudi Arabs working in the kingdom has been considerable.'[96]

All sections of society are affected by the presence of Arab and non-Arab expatriates. Of the various foreign groups, the Yemenis, unofficially estimated to be one million strong,[97] are the most numerous. Working in predominantly menial jobs on meagre wages, they have contributed a lot to the building up of the Saudi economy. They have also inadvertently transformed North Yemen economically – and therefore politically – particularly after the boom that followed the dramatic oil price increases. Their remittances of over one billion dollars sent each year since the mid-1970s,[98] have fostered a capitalist economy, which has increased the size and prosperity of the small and middle bourgeoisie. For instance, a tenfold rise in imports from $165 million to $1,600 million between 1973 and 1977 left the merchants more prosperous than ever before.[99] Such a development has been conducive to the growth of centrist ideologies and groups. Colonel Ibrahim al Hamdi's seizure of power in mid-1974 happened to coincide with this phase of economic development.

Hamdi's actions accelerated the process of weakening the feudal power of tribal leaders. By replacing many hundreds of the 3,000 army officers – often illiterate tribal leaders – with young trained officers, freshly graduated from the socialist bloc academies,[100] he strengthened the petty bourgeois elements in the military at the expense of the feudal. He struck a blow at the political power of the traditional chiefs by dissolving the consultative assembly, dominated by their nominees, in October 1975. As stated earlier, resentful tribal leaders in the north joined hands and rebelled against the central authority.[101] It was a measure of the military and political strength of the centrist forces, led by Hamdi, that Sanaa was able to defeat the tribal chiefs in July 1977.

Although Hamdi did not lift the ban on political parties he tolerated the clandestine formation of the nationalist-leftist National Democratic Front, consisting of the Revolutionary Democratic Party, the Democratic Party of Popular Unity, the local Baathists, and independent nationalists. He himself favoured the Nasserites, and went as far as presiding over secret meetings of the Nasserite students and staff at Sanaa university.[102] It was the existence of these centrist groups that provided the political ballast for the neutralist policies that Hamdi initiated, and the rapprochement that he reached with Aden, to the apparent consternation of Riyadh.

The assassination of Hamdi, followed by the presidency of Major Ahmed Hussein al Ghashmi, was a setback for the centrist forces. They found themselves on the defensive as Ghashmi, guided by Riyadh, began purging the military and civil services of pro-Hamdi personnel. He reconvened the old consultative assembly and dissolved the supreme Command Council in the spring of 1978, thus neutralising the power of Major Abdullah Abdul-Alem, an erstwhile member, and a loyal supporter of Hamdi's policies.

Major Abdul-Alem left the capital in April with thirty trucks filled with arms and loyal troops for Turbah, his native town, near the border with South Yemen.[103] From there he tried to reach reconciliation with President Ghashmi on the basis of a three-point agreement: a revival of the investigation into Hamdi's assassination; an end to the exclusive dependence on Riyadh; and resumption of talks with Aden on unity. Sanaa responded by despatching troops and fighter aircraft to the south. This led to Abdul-Alem's escaping to South Yemen, and his lieutenants spreading out in the southern region of Hojaira and resorting to guerrilla operations.

In early June the central government undertook counter-insurgency measures against guerrilla activity. Following the assassination of Ghashmi on 24 June, Sanaa pursued the anti-guerrilla campaign with renewed vigour: the new president, Ali Abdullah Saleh, was even more pro-Riyadh than his predecessor.[104] Most of the insurgents belonged to the 13 June Movement (named after the date on which Hamdi assumed power in 1974), formed after Hamdi's murder, to work for the restoration of his policies.

As pressure mounted on the rebels in the south, the leaders of the 13

June Movement, both inside the military and outside, decided to topple President Saleh's regime. On 15 October, while the president was out of Sanaa, his palace was bombed. This was the signal for the coup, in which four army units, stationed in the capital, participated. But they were overpowered by an armoured division loyal to the president. Fighting spread to other parts of the republic, including Saida in the north and Bayda in the south, with Major Mojahed al Kohali directing it in the northern region, and Abdul-Alem in the southern. Skirmishes between rebels and loyalists lasted for a week, and ended with the loyalists emerging victorious. The government capped its victory with the arrest of more than 7,000 military and civilian personnel, and the execution, after a summary trial, of over 100 of them, including cabinet ministers, military officers, and top civil servants.[105] With so many of their supporters lost, the leaders of the centrist 13 June Movement decided to merge their organisation with the nationalist-leftist National Democratic Front.

Thus strengthened, the NDF took up the armed struggle against the pro-Saudi regime. This reached a peak in February when, helped by Aden and led by Abdul-Alem, NDF supporters gained control of the southern border areas of North Yemen and made a bid to capture the strategic Sanaa–Taiz highway. Significantly, the Yemeni Baathists stayed out of this action; and Baghdad, encouraged by Riyadh, successfully pressured the NDF and the Aden government to a cease-fire. As North Yemen's second most important aid-giver, Baghdad had considerable influence in Sanaa too.[106]

However, North Yemen was only one of the three major recipients of Iraqi aid, the other two being Jordan and the Palestinians. Most of the important Jordanian projects in progress in 1980 were being financed by Iraq, whose aid to the Hashemite kingdom was then running at the annual rate of $300 million.[107] The infusion of developmental capital on this scale could only foster a socio-economic environment conducive to the growth of centrist political forces. As it was, the very composition of the Jordanian citizenry favoured such a development: a large majority of the subjects are Palestinians or their descendants, and the petty bourgeoisie is numerically the most dominant class among the Palestinians.

Not surprisingly, therefore, support for such centrist groups as the Baath came chiefly from the West Bank, when it was part of the Hashemite kingdom. A study of the Baath in Jordan of the late 1950s showed that its leaders and an overwhelming majority of its members came from the urban educated class who owned 'little or no property', with teachers and students forming its most active element.[108]

Despite a ban on all political activity in 1957, the Baath continued to exist and was actively helped by the United Arab Republic (1958–61) as an anti-monarchist group. Later the role of aiding the party was taken over by the Syrian Baathists after they had seized power in March 1963. The loss of the West Bank to Israel in the Six Day war resulted in a dramatic weakening of the party in Jordan.

From then on the Baathists in Damascus focused their attention on the Palestinians. They helped establish the Vanguards of the Popular War of Liberation, and its armed wing, Saiqa. The following year Palestinian representatives from the West Bank, Jordan, Syria and Kuwait met to form the United Palestinian Organisation of the Baath Party, with a programme of creating 'revolutionary conditions necessary for the birth of an Arab liberation movement through a popular liberation war'.[109]

Saiqa resorted to launching commando actions against Israel from Jordan; and this brought it many recruits. When fighting broke out between Palestinian commandos and Jordanian troops in September 1970, it was Saiqa which successfully approached the Syrian president, Saleh Jedid, for military aid. Following Assad's ascendancy as the Syrian head of state, two months later, Saiqa underwent 'correction'. Assad purged the organisation of its leftist elements and appointed his protégé, Zuheir Mohsen, as its general secretary. This brought Saiqa closer, ideologically and otherwise, to Fatah, the oldest and largest Palestinian body.

The roots of Fatah can be traced to the Suez war, and the disaffection that the six-month-long Israeli occupation caused in the Gaza strip, particularly among Palestinian students. Among those who had fought the Israelis in the Suez zone was Yasser Arafat who, following his graduation as an engineer from a university in Cairo, had joined the Egyptian army. After the war he went to work in Kuwait, where he and a few other Palestinians founded Fatah as a Palestinian organisation dedicated to liberating Palestine from the Zionists. They set up secret party cells in Kuwait and in the Palestinian refugee camps in Jordan, Syria and Lebanon: a process which was accelerated by the publication of a clandestine monthly, *Falastinuna* (Our Palestine), from Beirut in early 1959. By then the basics of Fatah ideology and tactics had crystallised thus: revolutionary violence, practised by the masses, is the only way to liberate the homeland and liquidate all forms of Zionism.

Fatah remained underground until 1964 when the Arab League established the Palestine Liberation Organisation under the leadership of Ahmed Shukeiri, a traditional Palestinian notable who did not subscribe to the concept of revolutionary action. Of the radical Arab states then, only freshly independent Algeria volunteered to provide military training facilities to Fatah. This was strongly disapproved of by Nasser. While Fatah believed that fighting for the liberation of Palestine would help bring about the liberation of the whole Arab Nation, spread from the Gulf to the Atlantic, Nasser held that various components of the Arab Nation must first liberate themselves, politically and economically, and then form a strong united front to overthrow the Zionist rule in Palestine.

Partly because Nasser opposed Fatah, and partly because Fatah's ranks were liberally sprinkled with Muslim Brethren, King Feisal of Saudi

Arabia supported it. 'In ideology, El Fatah makes no fundamental break with the [conservative] past, while adopting every modern political idea that suits its purpose – except the radical ideology of scientific socialism,' notes Gérard Chaliand, a French author. 'It has spokesmen whose role is to reassure the more conservative elements of the Arab East, but it also has other spokesmen able to win over, to some extent, some sectors of the Western "left".'[110] The party leadership is evenly divided between right and left, with Yasser Arafat (alias Abu Amr) often acting as a mediator between the two sides. Khaled Hassan, a former Muslim Brother who is close to Riyadh, is balanced by Saleh Khalef (alias Abu Iyad), a leftist. Khalil Wazir (alias Abu Jehad), chief of Fatah's military wing, Assifa (Storm) is regarded as being right of centre, whereas Farouk Kadoummi (alias Abu Lutf), head of the foreign affairs department, is considered left of centre.[111] However, the crucial party machine remains in the hands of the triumvirate of Arafat, Hassan and Wazir.[112]

The loss of the West Bank and Gaza to Israel in the Six Day war weakened Shukeiri's position in the PLO, and paved the way for the entry of Fatah and other armed commando groups into the Palestine National Council, which had been established by the PLO in May 1964, and which had hitherto been boycotted by militant Palestinians. Fatah and other armed Palestinian parties attended the fifth PNC session in Cairo in July 1968 which inter alia rejected UN resolution 242.

By the time the next PNC session was called in February, Fatah, with an estimated guerrilla force of 15,000,[113] had emerged as the single largest constituent of the PLO. The PNC elected Arafat president of the PLO's eleven-member executive committee. The new committee consisted of three Fatah members, two Saiqa, and the rest independents.[114] Soon the military wings of the various affiliates to the PLO were put under a joint command: the Palestine Armed Struggle Command.

The direct involvement of Fatah commandos, in conjunction with other mainly leftist forces, in the Palestinian challenge to the Jordanian monarch in September 1970 had the effect of shifting Fatah leftward. This caused a cooling of relations between Fatah and the Saudi rulers. Public evidence of this was provided by the left-wing domination of the Saudi delegation attending the Arab People's Congress in Support of the Palestinian Revolution held in Beirut in November 1972.[115] Not surprisingly, at the Arab summit in Algeria a year later, the Saudi monarch withheld support for the proposal to recognise the PLO as the sole representative of the Palestinians.[116]

In the Lebanese civil war Fatah, along with other Palestinian commando groups, sided with the leftist Lebanese National Movement to fight the right-wing Lebanese Front. Its uncompromising opposition to Sadat's visit to Jerusalem in late 1977, and the Camp David accord of the following year, led Fatah to adopt an openly anti-American position.

That such a stance had the support of the rank and file became clear at the fourth Fatah congress held in Damascus in May 1980. Attended by 450 delegates, many of them young, this congress was the first to be held since the Jordanian civil war. It adopted a radical programme which called for intensifying anti-Zionist activities in the Israeli-occupied territories, and bolstering both the conventional and guerrilla forces and their weaponry.[117]

Fatah's original leaders have been able to retain the loyalty of the party's increasingly young and radical members by moving left. They realise that refusal to do so could only have benefited the rival leftist groups, whose analysis and tactics have, over the decades, been winning increasing acceptance among the Palestinians. As the only Arab people to have been expelled from their homeland, and still lacking an independent state of their own, the Palestinians are instinctively anti-imperialist, and therefore more receptive to leftist views than any other Arab nationality – except, possibly, the South Yemenis.

# 8

# LEFTIST FORCES

The leftist Palestinian spectrum is occupied mainly by the Popular Front for the Liberation of Palestine and the Democratic Front for the Liberation of Palestine, the latter having split away from the former.[1] The PFLP itself evolved out of the Arab Nationalist Movement, which arose out of the merger of two groups, composed chiefly of the students and staff of the American University in Beirut in 1952.

George Habash and Nayef Hawatmeh were among the founders of the ANM whose leading slogan was: 'Unity (of Arabs), Liberation (of Palestine), Revenge (against the Zionist state)'. As a proponent of Arab unity, the ANM applauded the formation of the UAR in 1958, and was disappointed when it broke up three years later. The subsequent failure of attempts to unite any two of the three leading republics – Egypt, Syria, Iraq – left the ANM leaders disenchanted with both Nasserites and Baathists. Emulating the example of Fatah as a purely Palestinian organisation with its own commandos, they set up a Palestinian section, supported by two young Palestinian armed groups, within the ANM.

The Arab defeat in the June 1967 war finally destroyed the ANM's confidence in the Egyptian and Syrian regimes, and led to the pan-Arab body's breaking up into individual sections in different countries. In December the Palestinian section, along with its armed affiliates, combined with the Syria-based Palestine Liberation Front to form the Popular Front for the Liberation of Palestine. Six months later at the PNC session in Cairo the PFLP, in association with Fatah and others, managed to rid the PLO of its traditional, non-revolutionary leadership.

At its first (open) congress in February 1969 the PFLP described 'Israel, the world Zionist movement, world imperialism, and Arab reaction' as the enemies of the Palestinian cause, and stated that the best way to fight them was by mobilising the Palestinian workers and peasants – in alliance with the petty bourgeoisie – through an organisation committed to the concept of scientific socialism, and initiating a guerrilla struggle as a step towards a national liberation war.

To such feudal, reactionary or feudal-capitalistic regimes as those in Saudi Arabia, Jordan and Lebanon, the PFLP offered unqualified opposition. To the petty bourgeois regimes of Egypt, Syria and Iraq, however, it offered intermittent alliance and opposition: because, despite their antagonism towards Israel, imperialism, and Arab reaction, these regimes being incapable of mobilising the masses to confront Zionism, had no option other than to engage in traditional warfare with Israel, or to seek a peaceful settlement with it.

The PFLP congress described Fatah as petty bourgeois, and criticised it for being friendly with reactionary Arab governments. It admitted that the PFLP itself was then a petty bourgeois organisation, and resolved to transform it into a revolutionary party by recruiting peasants and workers into it, imparting appropriate political, organisational and military training to the cadre, and producing a political-tactical programme which met the needs of the Palestinian masses.[2] It adopted an organisational structure which is similar to that of a communist party. The congress, elected by members every four years, and meeting every alternate year, is the highest body. It elects the central committee, which in turn elects the political bureau. It also has the authority directly to elect the general secretary: a position occupied since the party's inception by George Habash.

While pursuing its programme of guerrilla struggle against Israel, the PFLP concentrated on Israeli targets within the occupied territories, where it set up scores of secret cells. It intensified the anti-Zionist campaign there, to the extent that 1970 witnessed 220 armed operations in the occupied territories, including eighty-nine in the tiny Gaza strip.[3] This invited severe Israeli reprisals, particularly in Gaza, which had been placed under emergency regulations since 1968. Following the Palestinian commandos' defeat in Jordan in September, the Israelis succeeded in breaking up the PFLP's clandestine network in the occupied territories. The PFLP, along with other Palestinian bodies, then moved its main operational base to Lebanon.

Since the PFLP made no distinction between Zionist objects in Israel and the occupied territories, or outside, it resorted to attacking Israeli targets abroad – mainly hijacking airliners and making political demands. Between July 1968 and December 1973, when the party congress suspended actions against Israeli targets abroad, the PFLP conducted sixteen foreign operations.[4] The most spectacular of these was the hijacking of three airliners, with 425 passengers, between 7 and 9 September 1970, and taking them to an abandoned airfield near Amman. The dynamiting of the empty planes was the catalyst which set off the ten-day long civil war in Jordan, with adverse consequences for the Palestinians.

When, in the wake of the Yom Kippur war, Arafat made statements which implied recognising Israel, the PFLP left the PLO. It did not end its ultra-rejectionist stance until after Sadat's visit to Jerusalem: it participated in the deliberations of the newly formed Front of Steadfastness and

Confrontation in Tripoli, Libya, in December 1977, and returned to the fold of the PLO. This also marked an improvement in relations with the Democratic Front for the Liberation of Palestine, which had split away from it on the eve of the first open congress nearly eight years before in acrimonious circumstances.

Alleging that the main resolution adopted by the PFLP's clandestine congress in August 1968 – which called for the formation of a broad national front of the Palestinian organisations based on a minimum programme – had not been implemented, the left wing, led by Nayef Hawatmeh[5] and Bilal Hassan, quit to form the Democratic Front for the Liberation of Palestine. The inaugural conference of the DFLP described Fatah as a right-wing body which, by having failed to arouse mass consciousness among the Palestinians, had proved itself incapable of escalating the guerrilla struggle into a fully fledged people's war. It criticised the Jordanian Communists for their reformism, and the PFLP for inter alia its anti-Zionist operations outside Israel and the occupied territories.

By immediately launching guerrilla actions against Israel, the DFLP won the sympathy of militants among the Jordanian Communists as well as the recognition of other Palestinian commando groups. An invitation to join the Palestine Armed Struggle Command, coupled with a modest offer of money and arms from the central pool, helped it to build up its rudimentary militia. Within a year the DFLP's commando force was 1,200 strong,[6] and the fourth largest, after those of Fatah, Saiqa, and the PFLP.

An extraordinary feature of the DFLP was that it paid as much attention to the commandos' political education as it did to their military training. 'Its militant style, its straightforward practice, its political courage and honesty', were described by Gérard Chaliand as 'a radical departure from the petty-bourgeois Arab movements . . . who still hold to conspiracy theories of history and for whom horse-trading is a substitute for strategy'.[7]

Right from its inception the DFLP stressed that the Palestinian and Jordanian struggles were complementary. Unlike Fatah, which called for a government of national unity, including the Palestinians in Jordan, under King Hussein, the DFLP's first open congress, held in August 1970, advocated the overthrow of the Hashemite dynasty and the founding of a national, democratic regime. In this the DFLP had the support of the PFLP. Both Hawatmeh and Habash felt that if the Palestinian–Jordanian progressive forces did not strike at the monarch first, he would launch an offensive against them.

The bitter experience of September 1970 – with Palestinian civilians and commandos suffering heavy losses at the hands of the Jordanian forces – had a salutary effect on the DFLP. Following the complete expulsion of the Palestinian commandos from the Hashemite kingdom in

July 1971, the DFLP moderated its criticism of Fatah, the Syrian and Iraqi Baathists, and the Arab Communist parties.

A chastened DFLP went through a period of soul-searching and came up with the idea, in August 1973, of 'intermediate stages' for the liberation of Palestine, the first step being the establishment of a national, democratic state on both sides of the river Jordan. This plan was initially rejected by all other Palestinian parties. But following the Yom Kippur war, when the Palestinians considered a political solution possible, Fatah endorsed it. A joint document drawn up by the DFLP, Fatah and Saiqa was adopted at the twelfth session of the PNC in June 1974. It envisaged the establishment of a 'national authority' in the West Bank and Gaza as the first stage towards the liberation of 'the whole of Palestine'.[8]

By then the DFLP had shown that the anti-Zionist struggle could be carried out militantly yet flexibly, and that the tactic of 'fight *and* negotiate', which the South Vietnamese Communists were then using against America, was equally valid in the Israeli context. In an interview with *Le Monde* in March, Hawatmeh had expressed the DFLP's willingness to talk to those Israelis who were either anti-Zionist or simply ready to recognise the Palestinians' right to establish 'an independent national authority' in the West Bank and Gaza, and to allow the Palestinian refugees to return to their homes in Israel.[9] The interview had been reprinted in *Yediot Aharonot*, an Israeli paper, the next day. To stress that this did not mark the end of the DFLP's guerrilla struggle, three of its members took over an Israeli school in Maalot on 15 May, Israeli independence day. The subsequent storming of the school by the Israeli authorities resulted in the death of the guerrillas and twenty students.[10]

During the Lebanese civil war the DFLP allied itself as closely with the leftist Lebanese National Movement as did the PFLP. The DFLP's relations with the Lebanese Communists, already good, improved dramatically. While the war helped the Lebanese Communists to expand their base, it diverted the attention of the Jordanian Communists, and interrupted their plan to form an anti-royalist front. Once the DFLP had got over its initial bout of ultra-radicalism, the Jordanian Communist leaders had come to treat it as a fraternal body.

On its part the DFLP had continued to evince special interest in the Hashemite kingdom, manifested partly in its publication of two journals on Jordan and a regular column on the country in *Al Sharara* (the Spark), the party weekly. This was not surprising. After all, the history of the Jordanian leftists is intertwined with that of the Communist Party of Palestine, which came into existence in 1922 and won the formal recognition of the Comintern (Communist International) two years later.

With the dissolution of the Comintern in May 1943 – and thus of an external overseeing organisation – the simmering differences between the Jewish and Arab members came to the surface. Most of the Arab members left the party to form the League of National Liberation. Soon the LNL enlarged its influence by absorbing the existing Arab leftist groups, and setting up the Federation of Arab Trade Unions and Labour Societies.

After the convulsions of partition, war, and absorption of the West Bank into Transjordan, the LNL transformed itself into the Communist Party of Jordan, under the leadership of Fuad Nassar, in June 1951. On the eve of the parliamentary elections in August the party allied itself with the Baath and the Arab Nationalist Movement to form the National Bloc. The Communists, contesting as National Bloc candidates, scored 11 per cent of the popular vote.[11] Upset by this, the monarch arrested the Communist leaders and stiffened the anti-Communist law of 1948 by raising the penalty for propagating Communist doctrine from three years' hard labour to fifteen, and by extending this punishment to cover such misdemeanours as merely carrying a Communist document.

However, once the new constitution of 1952, with its provision for licensed political parties, had been operational for some time, the Communists cooperated with the Baath and the National Socialist Party of Suleiman Nabulsi in establishing the National Front in the spring of 1954. Despite the rigging of the parliamentary elections held in the autumn, two Communist candidates were elected.

The National Front protested against the tampering with the electoral process, and then launched a popular movement to keep Jordan out of the recently inaugurated Baghdad Pact, and to abrogate the Anglo–Jordanian treaty of 1948, which allowed Britain the use of military bases in Jordan for an annual subsidy of £12 million to the king. Massive demonstrations in Amman in December 1955 led the monarch to publicly promise that Jordan would not join the Baghdad Pact. Three months later he dismissed Sir John Bagot Glubb from command of the Arab Legion, which was described by the Communists as 'an instrument of repression against the politically more advanced sections of the Arab population', and 'a defender of the British oil interest in the Arab East'.[12]

Buoyed by these successes, and aided by the anti-Hashemite propaganda of Cairo's press and radio, the National Front pressed for the dissolution of parliament which, it said, had been elected on a rigged vote. The king yielded to popular pressure. He dissolved parliament and ordered fresh elections in October. With no government-sponsored candidates in the field, these elections were free. As a result the nationalist-leftist alliance of the Communist Front, the Baathists and the National Socialists won two fifths of the popular vote and sixteen of the forty seats. The Communist Front secured 13 per cent of the votes cast, and three seats; and the Socialists 18 per cent of the votes, and eleven seats.[13] The coalition government, headed by Suleiman Nabulsi, included a Communist Front member as a minister: the first of his kind in the Arab East.

When the new parliament abrogated the Anglo–Jordanian treaty the monarch did not overrule it. But when the cabinet decided to establish diplomatic relations with Moscow, and allowed the Communist Front to publish a weekly, King Hussein warned it of the dangers of 'Communist infiltration'. Heeding this, the government banned the Communist publication.

As it was, the threat to the monarchy came in April – not from any political party but from the Free Officers, led by the newly appointed Jordanian chief of staff, Ali Abu Nawar. The king overcame the challenge with the support of the bedouin troops personally loyal to him.[14] He then dismissed the Nabulsi government: a step which led to massive pro-Nabulsi demonstrations in the capital on 27 April. The monarch declared martial law, dissolved parliament, and disbanded political parties, trade unions and students' unions.

His repression of the Communist Party was particularly severe, with over 10 per cent of its 2,000 members being thrown into jail during the first eighteen months of martial law, and a ban being imposed on Communist literature, including such works as those of George Bernard Shaw and Maxim Gorky.[15] Communist activity was minimal until 1963, when martial law was lifted. King Hussein's recognition of the USSR in that year, followed by the release of 1,566 political prisoners by the end of 1964,[16] eased the situation somewhat for the Communists.

A chastened party leadership adopted a moderate programme of cooperation with the petty-bourgeois regimes of Egypt, Syria and Algeria abroad, and reform of industry, agriculture and education at home. The period of relative thaw with the royal palace ended in the spring of 1966, when the monarch once again arrested most of the Communist leaders.

The loss of the West Bank to Israel in the Six Day war deprived the party of nearly half of its members. But the subsequent swelling of the Palestinian refugee population in Jordan, and the rise of armed Palestinian commandos in the kingdom, radicalised the rank and file. This was reflected in the division that occurred between the radical central committee and moderate politbureau in early 1969. The politbureau compromised by agreeing to form an armed militia, the Ansars.

Before and during the civil war of September 1970 the Ansars sided with the Palestinian commandos. They were particularly thrilled by the DFLP's claim to have established a 'liberated zone' around Irbid, in the north-west, during the early days of fighting. However, once the Palestinian forces had been finally expelled from Jordan in mid-1971, the politbureau dissolved the Ansars and reverted back to the pre-civil war programme of working for the formation of a national unity government, composed of all national and progressive forces.

This position prevailed until May 1974 when, reflecting the DFLP's switch-over to the demand for a national, democratic state on both sides of the river Jordan, the party called for a 'national liberated authority' on the East Bank, to be achieved through the establishment of a national front of the anti-royalist forces. As stated earlier, this plan was sidetracked by the outbreak of a civil war in Lebanon, which inter alia had the effect of enlarging the Communist influence there.[17]

The seeds of the Lebanese Communist movement were sown in 1922, when a group of intellectuals in Beirut started a journal, *Al Sahafi al Taeh* (The Wandering Journalist), and Fuad Shemali, an expatriate Egyptian Marxist, set up a tobacco workers' union. The two groups were brought together by a delegate of the Third International in 1924, and called the People's Party of Lebanon. It held its first convention the following year, and began organising workers in Beirut and Damascus under the aegis of the Commission for the Organisation of Trade Unions. Later, after it had absorbed the Spartacus Party, a leftist group, it renamed itself the Communist Party of Syria and Lebanon. The party supported the Druze rebellion (1925–7); and this led to its persecution by the French authorities.

It was not until 1928 that the party leaders were released and a successful application made to the Comintern for membership. At the Comintern's behest the party, dominated so far by (Christian) Armenians, began to Arabise itself. This process reached its peak in 1932 when the newly-trained twenty-year-old Khaled Bakdash of Damascus replaced Fuad Shemali, a Copt, as party chief.

A year earlier the parties of Syria–Lebanon and Palestine had examined the Arab national problem and reached a common analysis. 'The gist of the Arab national question consists in the fact that the British, French, Italian and Spanish imperialists have dismembered the living body of the Arab peoples, and hold the Arab countries in a state of feudal fragmentation, deprive each and every one of these countries of the prerequisites of an independent economic and political development, and block the national political unification of the Arab countries,' stated the joint declaration. 'The imperialists had achieved their ends with the support of reactionary monarchical cliques, feudal and semi-feudal landowners and shaikhs, native bourgeois compradors, and higher clergy. Hence the striving of the Arab masses for national unification was inseparable from their endeavours to liberate themselves from the yoke of imperialism and its Arab collaborators.' As the Arab bourgeoisie tended to strike deals with the imperialists 'within the framework of limited pseudo-constitutional concessions' – the joint statement added – it was necessary for the Communists to combat the national reformism of the bourgeoisie. And, since the anti-imperialist struggle had to be coupled with revolutionising workers and peasants, it was a task of the Communists to help form a united front of workers, peasants and petty bourgeoisie, and resort increasingly to mass struggles in order to raise revolutionary consciousness.[18]

The adoption of such a radical line earned the Communist Party of Syria–Lebanon the ire of the French authorities, who refused to recognise the party's Commission for the Organisation of Trade Unions. But the situation changed in 1936, when the leftist Popular Front, backed by the Communists, assumed power in France. Although the Popular Front government in Paris ended two years later, the CPSL's progress was not interrupted until it was banned, along with all other parties, on the eve of the Second World War. During its brief legal existence the party membership in Lebanon jumped from 200 to 2,000.[19]

The CPSL's clandestine period came to an end in July 1941, when the British and Free French forces, having defeated the troops loyal to the Vichy regime, legalised all pro-Allies parties. It participated in the elections for the Syrian and Lebanese parliaments in the summer of 1943. Its first ever congress, held in December, was attended by 190 delegates, representing 7,000 members.[20]

Under the leadership of Farjallah Helou, the Lebanese party rapidly expanded its base, particularly in the trade union field. By resorting to a general strike in May 1946 it successfully pressured the government to pass pro-labour legislation. It cooperated with other anti-imperialist parties in their demand for a total withdrawal of French troops, which finally came about in December. The party was riding a wave of popularity, with its membership at 16,000,[21] when Moscow endorsed a partition plan for Palestine at the United Nations in late 1947. The Communist leaders' decision to support the Soviet stance severely undermined their popular standing. Encouraged by this the government banned the party in January, and then dissolved its trade union organisation. Frequent arrests, accompanied by torture, resulted in the deaths of some party activists in the early 1950s.

By backing the Western-sponsored Baghdad Pact, and refusing to condemn the Anglo–French–Israeli attack on Egypt in late 1956, President Chamoun created a political climate where the Communist Party easily re-established its Arab nationalist credentials by siding with the local Nasserites. Its participation in the 1958 civil war as part of the National Front, dominated by the pan-Arabists, underlined its Arab nationalism. However, its fraternisation with the Nasserites ended when the Nasserite regime in the United Arab Republic dissolved all political parties in Syria, including the Communist Party, and persecuted the Communists. The estrangement from the Nasserites continued until the mid-1960s when President Nasser, having created the Arab Socialist Union at home, began to move leftward.

Analysing the internal situation, in March 1965, the Lebanese Communist leaders stated that the party's aim of securing Lebanon's economic independence could only be achieved by isolating, and confronting, the financial oligarchy which, in league with the capital of the West and the Arab reactionary regimes, dominated the country's economy. To further this objective they joined the Front of the Progressive Parties and Personalities, which consisted among others of the Arab Nationalist

Movement and the Progressive Socialist Party, led by Kemal Jumblatt, a Marxist.

The discrediting of Nasserism, in the wake of the Six Day war, and a slackening of the economic boom of the past decade, created fresh opportunities for the growth of the Communist Party of Lebanon. Aware of this, the second congress, meeting in 1968, decided to launch a recruitment drive: this was helped by the formal lifting of the ban on the CPL two years later. The party's expansion went hand in hand with its radicalisation, caused largely by the presence of the Palestinian commandos, and by their guerrilla actions against Israel. Dropping its earlier criticism of the Palestinian resistance as adventurist, the CPL leadership set up its own armed militia. Not surprisingly the third congress, held in 1972, brought new faces to the fore in the party hierarchy. By resorting to popular forms of agitation and propaganda the CPL widened its base among the students, workers and peasants (mostly on tobacco farms). Its successful call for a general strike in early 1974 paid off. The strike secured concessions for the workers from the government and thus strengthened the party's newly formed National Union of Workers and Employees.

On the eve of the civil war, which broke out in the spring of 1975, the CPL, along with the Progressive Socialist Party and the Organisation of Communist Action in Lebanon,[22] formed the hard core of the National and Progressive Front (later to be called the Lebanese National Movement). Following the leadership's call for an armed overthrow of the existing system, the CPL's militia engaged in fighting against the rightist Lebanese camp. Unlike other Lebanese parties, the Communists combined military action with political education and propaganda. These tactics boosted their strength. By the end of the year the party had acquired 15,000 members – with Shias, the most deprived section of Lebanese society, forming 50 per cent of the total, and Greek Orthodox Christians 30 per cent.[23] The war was then going in favour of the leftist Lebanese–Palestinian alliance whose forces controlled two thirds of the country. As the best organised Lebanese party, the CPL stood to gain by this. 'When the Palestinian forces withdraw, the [Lebanese] Communists will be found to be in their place,' stated Patrick Seale in the *Observer*. 'Already the CPL-inspired "People's Committees", with executive powers, have sprung up in all areas of the country under Palestinian control.'[24]

While the CPL's militancy increased its popularity in Lebanon, it met with disapproval from some of the Arab Communist parties. Following the Syrian intervention in the civil war to help the Lebanese rightists, the CPL's relations with the Communist Party of Syria became strained.[25] As a member of the ruling Progressive National Front in Damascus, the CPS had little choice but to support President Assad's action, or at least to refrain from criticising it in public. It was the first time that the two Communist parties had found themselves on opposite sides of the fence since they had first acquired an independent existence in early 1944.[26]

Like its Lebanese counterpart, the Syrian party, led by Khaled Bakdash, made strides until it was outlawed in the wake of the Soviet vote for the partition of Palestine. During the first four years of its legal existence (1941–5) its membership rose from 1,000 to 10,000.[27] By calling a series of strikes, it played a leading role in frustrating French plans to re-establish their authority over Syria after the Second World War. Later it led a successful campaign for the legal right of Syrian workers to form trade unions.

By dissolving parliament and banning all political parties, in November 1951, Colonel Adib Shishkali engendered an environment where the non-Communists ceased to treat the Communists as political untouchables. In fact the CPS was invited to a clandestine all-party congress in July 1953 to form a united front to overthrow the Shishkali regime, and attended. Following the fall of this regime in February, political activity was restored. The CPS participated in the elections held seven months later. Although it gained only one seat, its popular vote was nearly as large as that of the Baath, which had sixteen seats to its credit.[28] The party cooperated with the Baath and the Democratic Bloc, led by Khaled Azm, who was appointed defence and (acting) foreign minister in early 1955.

Anti-Western feelings aroused by the tripartite aggression against Egypt in October 1956 helped the Communists as well as the Baathists to mobilise popular support for the regime to withstand Western pressure. As described earlier, the discovery of Western-inspired plots in late 1956 and the summer of 1957 had the overall effect of strengthening the nationalist-leftist forces, and helped the rise of Colonel Bizri as commander-in-chief.[29] Both the Communists and the Baathists made impressive gains on the trade union front, with the Communists winning seven of the twelve seats on the executive committee of the General Federation of Trade Unions.[30] The Communists were allowed to join the Popular Resistance Force, a paramilitary body formed to assist the army and the police. The Communist membership of 18,000 was at an all-time high.[31]

This unnerved the Baathists who, as described earlier, opted for an immediate merger with Egypt.[32] The CPS proposed a federal tie. When this was rejected, the top Communist leaders headed by Bakdash, anticipating the dissolution of all political parties in Syria, went into self-exile in Prague, Czechoslovakia.

Emboldened by the Iraqi Communists' success in giving the republican regime's policies a decidedly anti-imperialist thrust during the latter half of 1958, Bakdash attacked Nasser for compromising with imperialism and pampering the national bourgeoisie. This brought the full fury of Nasser against the CPS. Large-scale arrests of Syrian Communists were followed by denunciation of Bakdash's leadership by many of those imprisoned. The CPS leadership responded by openly calling for Syria's secession from the UAR.

However, when this actually happened in September 1961 the new Syrian rulers refused to let Bakdash or any other CPS leader return home. The Baathists, who assumed power eighteen months later, maintained a similar stance towards the Communists. The adoption of a leftist programme by their congress did not alter the situation much. But that did not inhibit the CPS from offering its unqualified backing to nationalisation decrees in 1964, and again in 1965, and to help the regime break down resistance to its policies.[33]

Victory for radical Baathists, in the coup of the following year, led to some changes in the official policy on the CPS. When Bakdash returned to Damascus the regime reluctantly accepted his arrival. Although the CPS's journal remained illegal, its clandestine distribution was allowed to continue. One Communist and two unaffiliated Marxists were appointed to the cabinet, but only in their personal capacity. In any case, whatever acceptance was accorded to the CPS by the government stemmed out of its need to secure some popularity in the urban areas, where the Communists had an organised base. 'Cooperation with the Communists was strictly limited, and did not prevent the [neoBaathist] government from periodically arresting – and sometimes torturing and killing – Communist Party members,' observes Tabitha Petran.[34]

Yet, in early 1967, the Communist Party of the Soviet Union invited a Baath delegation to Moscow; and the two parties issued a joint statement. During the Six Day war the Syrian Communists called for arming the people to fight Israel, but this was rejected by the government. However, severing of ties with Washington by Damascus brought the latter closer to Moscow.

The consequent improvement in relations between the CPS and the Baath caused consternation in some sections of the ruling party. Defence minister Assad undertook a tour of military camps and installations to deny 'rumours that we have turned Communist' and reiterate that the regime adhered to Baathist ideology and none other.[35] Not surprisingly, during the period of power struggle within the Baath, the Communists favoured the anti-Assad forces. They opposed the correctionist coup of Assad. But when Assad promised friendly relations with the Palestinians and the USSR, and followed this up with a plan to form the Progressive National Front, including the CPS, they changed their position, after holding consultations with the international department of the Communist Party of the Soviet Union.[36]

Eight Communists were elected on a common PNF list to the parliament of 1973. Reflecting the cordial ties that grew up between Damascus and Moscow as a result of the Yom Kippur war, relations between the CPS and the Baath improved further. But the trend did not continue. When Assad tried to enlarge the PNF by including business interests the CPS opposed the move, arguing that this would destroy the progressive nature of the PNF. None the less Assad acted to help the capitalists by letting them receive foreign loans, and by removing all restrictions on the movement of private capital into or out of Syria. He also accepted aid from the USA. His dispatch of troops to help the rightist camp in the Lebanese civil war put further strains on relations between the two parties. Reduced Communist representation in the parliament of 1977 was symptomatic of the official lukewarm attitude toward the Communists. In any case the PNF had by then virtually lost whatever power it ever possessed.

It was only when the Muslim Brotherhood's subversion reached a climax in June 1979, with the massacre of cadets at a military academy, that Assad decided to give prominence to the PNF, and induct it into an anti-Brotherhood campaign. The CPS leaders had their reservations about the rough-and-ready methods used by the government to crush the Brethren. But when the Brotherhood not only kept up its practice of murdering Soviet military advisers – at the rate of one a month – but also initiated a programme of assassinating local Communists,[37] the CPS leaders adopted a militantly anti-Brotherhood line.

However, the violence that the Syrian Communists faced from the Brotherhood was nothing compared to that which the Iraqi Communists had been suffering at the government's hands since the spring of 1978. By the end of that year, fifty-four Communists had been executed for attempting to form cells in the military.[38] Persecution had continued since then, and driven most of the Communists either underground or abroad.

This was nothing new for the Communists in Iraq who had suffered a series of persecution drives since they first formed a party in March 1934.[39] The radical section of the progressive Ahali group, formed a few years earlier, was instrumental in the founding of the Communist Party of Iraq. Therefore a successful coup (against the government, not the monarchy) by military officers sympathetic to the Ahali group in October 1936 aroused hopes among the CPI leaders that the new government would carry out their party's programme for socio-economic reform. But it did not. In fact it went on to pass a stiff law against the propagation of communism. An article in the penal code specified that a person found approving or disseminating 'any of the doctrines of Bolshevik socialism (communism), anarchy or the like' among civilians would be imprisoned for seven years, and that anyone doing so among policemen or soldiers would be punished by death or life imprisonment.[40] This drove the party underground.

It was only after the Soviet Union had joined the Allies in fighting the Axis powers in mid-1941 that the Iraq authorities allowed the Communist front organisations to function openly. The party's membership rose from 300 before the war to 3,000 in 1945, when the party (i.e. its main front organisation) held its congress.[41] Particularly active in the trade union field, it also built up a base among teachers, students, and ethnic minorities in towns, and peasants in villages. Its leaders addressed an open letter to the prime minister asking him to legalise the party: nothing came of it. But when they organised a strike of oil workers in July 1946 for higher wages and a right to form a trade union, the government came down heavily on their party.

Despite this, and despite the odium that the CPI earned for endorsing the Soviet position on the Palestine problem in late 1947, it succeeded in spearheading massive demonstrations against the Anglo–Iraqi treaty of 1948. The Iraqi government yielded to popular pressure and rescinded the treaty. It then mounted an anti-Communist drive, which resulted in the arrests of hundreds of Communists and the hanging of four of their leaders. But the Communists were not deterred: they turned jails into educational and recruiting centres. Outside, they concentrated on students, and by late 1954 they became the leading force in the General Association of Iraqi Students, which represented a large majority of high school and university students.

In mid-1956 the CPI joined the United National Front,[42] an umbrella organisation which stood for the abolition of monarchy and feudalism, withdrawal from the Baghdad Pact, the granting of civil liberties and democratic rights to the citizens, and Arab solidarity against Zionism and imperialism. The UNF contacted the central committee of the Free Officers, who were to overthrow the monarchy in July 1958. By then the CPI, a well-knit organisation, had 8,000 activists.[43]

Bolstered by the release of hundreds of Communists in the wake of the revolution, the party expanded its already substantial base among students and workers. It extended its activities to the civil service and the military. It participated actively in the Popular Resistance Force, a paramilitary body formed to protect the fledgling republic against counter-revolution.

Following the promulgation of the Agrarian Reform Law in September, and the appointment of the leftist Ibrahim Kuba as minister of agrarian reform, the Communists took to organising the poor peasants, fellaheen. Aware of the predominantly agrarian nature of society the authors of the party constitution, adopted in 1945, had urged the members to 'recognise and understand feudalism; to explain its oppressive nature and to struggle for its elimination and the confiscation, without compensation, of its lands and properties in Iraq'.[44] But work among the fellaheen had been inhibited by official harassment, made all the more effective by the conspicuousness of an outside 'agitator' in a rural community. Now, however, backed by the new agrarian law, the party cadres set up Peasant Leagues. They in turn called for swift confiscation of landholdings above the legal limit and a further lowering of the ceiling, and demanded a say in the redistribution of the confiscated land and the establishment of agricultural cooperatives. All along the party put primary stress on the wellbeing of the fellaheen. 'The Communists must be given full credit for their declared intention to pin their faith on the destitute fellaheen who were considered non-people in Iraq,' states Rony Gabbay, a specialist on Iraq. 'This attitude was certainly not lost on the fellaheen, and to it one must attribute an important role in the resurrection and eventual legalisation of the Iraqi Communist Party a decade later.'[45]

Rapid progress by the Communists, coupled with an eclipse of the pan-Arabists, created disquiet among feudal lords, tribal chiefs, and a section of military officers. The holding of a conference by the Communist-dominated Partisans for Peace in Mosul, the republic's second largest city, on 6 March 1959, acted as a catalyst to the simmering conflict between the leftists and the pan-Arabists there. Two days later Colonel Abdul Wahhab Shawwaf, commander of the Mosul Force, revolted against Baghdad, alleging that Qassem, the republic's supreme leader, had fallen under Communist influence. But the military and civilian rebels lost control of the city when the pro-Qassem forces and the local Communists, aided by the city's poor, mounted an attack on them.[46]

In order to frustrate any such moves in the future the CPI initiated a programme of forming soldiers' committees in the army, and people's defence committees among workers, throughout the country. At the end of a three-day national congress in Baghdad the Partisans for Peace brought a million people out into the streets in support of the regime, and showed that the Communists had emerged as the leading political force. 'The Communists dominated the whole political and intellectual climate of Iraq [after the revolution]', states Walid W. Kazziha a Lebanese academic. 'The literature they disseminated and the slogans they raised among the lower social classes had a direct impact on the political outlook of [all] the nationalist parties.'[47] On the eve of the first anniversary of the revolution on 14 July, Qassem appointed one more Communist sympathiser to the reshuffled cabinet. In retrospect, however, this was to mark the zenith of Communist influence in the country.

On 14 July riots broke out in Kirkuk, a northern oil centre, inhabited by mutually hostile Kurds, Turkomans, and Arabs. Kurds, who provided cheap labour to the Iraq Petroleum Company and others, were pro-Communist, whereas Turkomans, largely traders and rentiers, were anti-Communist. A celebration of the release of some Turkoman prisoners, as part of the general amnesty on Revolution Day, led to a brawl with Kurds, which escalated into a three-day-long riot, during which seventy-nine people were killed, most of them belonging to the anti-Communist side. In a speech on 19 July Qassem blamed the 'anarchists' (a not-too-subtle reference to Communists) for the 'cruelty and fanaticism' of the events in Kirkuk.[48] The CPI leaders replied that their followers were not involved in mass violence and that they had acted only in self-defence.

Although later evidence indicated that agents provocateurs working for British oil interests, were prominent in instigating and perpetuating the Kirkuk rioting,[49] Qassem used the incident to bring the CPI 'under tighter government control'.[50] The fact that the CPI leadership later blamed the 'adventurism' of their local cadres for the episode played into the hands of Qassem. He appointed military courts to try the accused. They sentenced 112 Communists and pro-Communists to death, and 770 more to various prison terms.[51]

Qassem followed up this action with a systematic, albeit undeclared, policy of clamping down on the CPI. In early 1960 he denied the party an official licence, which went to a splinter group. He then disbanded the Popular Resistance Force and the Partisans for Peace, closed down the party paper, and banned the Communist-dominated General Students Union and Women's League. He encouraged the formation of a rival peasants' organisation. Officially inspired electoral rigging eased the Communists out of leadership positions in the trade unions of teachers, oil workers and dockers. Encouraged by such moves the pan-Arabists increased their attacks on the Communists: by the autumn of 1960 they had killed more than 100 Communists in a campaign of assassination.[52]

The CPI was now clearly put on the defensive, and, having alienated all other parties earlier by its aggressive tactics, it failed to win any sympathy from them. Its leaders thus found that they really had no option but to offer lukewarm support to Qassem whom they still considered anti-imperialist. In fact, as described earlier, the Communists fought on his side when the Baathists launched their coup in February 1963.[53] They lost, and suffered their severest repression yet.

Aided among others by an American espionage agency in the region, armed with the names and whereabouts of individual Communists, the Baathist paramilitary force, the National Guard, meted out summary justice to party members.[54] Those who could fled abroad or took shelter in the Kurdish region, a traditional leftist stronghold. The witch-hunt, which went on for many months, was later legitimised by the revival of the anti-Communist law of the monarchical era. By the time it ended it had claimed the lives of an estimated 3,000 to 5,000 Communists[55] – the worst fate suffered by any political party in the Arab East.

With the fall of the Baathists in November the CPI returned to a 'tolerable state of underground status',[56] with the concomitant risks of 'mass arrests, deportations, raids and occasional executions'.[57] This was so, despite the fact that a chastened leadership moderated both its analysis and its objectives. It substituted its earlier aim of creating a socialist government, led by 'labourers and fellaheen', with participating in a popular front government, based on an alliance of 'all the patriotic forces', working for complete economic and political independence, and social progress.[58] Such a scaling down of party objectives led to splits in the CPI, first in 1965 and then in 1967. On the other hand this enabled the main body, led by the moderate Aziz Mohammed, to achieve a reconciliation with the Baathists – driven underground by the regime of the Aref brothers – on the basis of a call for a return to a multi-party system.

Soon after the Baathists had carried out a successful coup in July 1968, the CPI's central committee demanded a parliamentary system within a constitutional framework embodying democratic principles; a solution to the Kurdish problem on the basis of self-rule; the cancellation of all oil concessions to foreign companies, and an intensification of the struggle against feudalism, imperialism, and Zionism. It also called for the formation of a national front of all progressive forces, and a coalition government.

Though the Baathist rulers did not concede any of the CPI's demands, they let the party express itself freely. The second CPI congress, held in September 1970, combined the earlier party call for a parliamentary system based on free elections with 'freedom to all workers to organise trade unions and cooperative societies', and 'ample opportunity to the military ranks and officers to express their views freely, and a right to participate in political activity'.[59]

In May 1972, *Tareeq al Shaab* (The People's Path), the party's seven-year-old, clandestinely published journal, was allowed to appear as a daily; and two Communists were taken into a cabinet of twenty-eight. This was followed by a formal signing of the National Action Charter by the leaders of the CPI and the Baath on the fifth anniversary of the July 1968 revolution, and the founding of the Progressive National Front.

As a signatory to the National Action Charter, the CPI now became legal. But this also meant that it was required to be loyal to the Baathist revolution, and that it had to refrain from disseminating its ideology among students and members of the armed forces. (In fact the government went on to make it a capital offence to spread a non-Baathist ideology in the military.) The CPI was also required to abstain from labour agitation and help avert strikes. Barring occasional disagreements with the government – such as when it refused to join the Arab oil boycott in the wake of the Yom Kippur war – the Communist leaders managed to get along with the Baathist hierarchy in the PNF for the next four years.

The third CPI congress, convened in May 1976, endorsed the National Action Charter and the party's participation in the PNF: these were seen as steps in 'accomplishing the national democratic revolution and creating prerequisites for transition to socialism in cooperation with the Baathists'. It agreed with the central committee that the present stage of national liberation was to be advanced by an alliance of workers, peasants, urban petty bourgeoisie, and the progressive elements of the middle bourgeoisie.

According to the congress, Iraq had entered the stage of non-capitalist development, and in order to advance in a socialist direction it was necessary to block development of capitalism by enforcing a series of anti-capitalist measures. The task was all the more urgent since private capital, which continued to grow both in town and country, still exercised considerable economic, ideological, and political influence in society and government. While drawing its strength from the vast sphere of small commodity production, and its links with world capital, Iraqi private capital also tried to enrich itself at the expense of the public sector, while at the same time robbing it of its progressive character and thus paving the way for its final abolition. Capitalists were helped in this process by the growing body of contractors, brokers, and top bureaucrats in public-sector undertakings.[60] On the eve of the eighth anniversary of the Baathist revolution, *Tareeq al Shaab*, the party daily, warned of 'the reactionary forces trying to pull the country back to capitalism and make it dependent on imperialism'.[61]

Differences between the Communists and the Baathists, which had existed all along, grew sharper as the regime, determined to achieve fast economic development financed by booming oil revenue, increased its trade links with the West and relaxed controls over private capital at home. The ending of the Kurdish war, in the wake of the Algiers treaty of March 1975, removed the political compulsion which had earlier driven the Baath to court the Communists so as to concentrate on fighting the Kurdish rebels, and use the Communist knowledge of, and popularity in, the Kurdish region against the secessionists.

Once the Kurdish problem had been brought under control the Baathist regime took to curbing Communist influence. Reflecting this, the CPI's annual report of 1977 complained that 'acts of discrimination' against party members had increased dramatically during the year.[62] The party programme, issued in April 1978, criticised the government's non-ideological approach to economic relations with the outside world. A case in point was the fifteenfold increase in trade with America during the decade 1965–75, even though diplomatic ties with Washington, severed after the June 1967 war, had not been restored.[63] The party document also disapproved of the growing collaboration of Iraq with the conservative Arab states within OPEC – the latest manifestation being a series of agreements signed between Baghdad and Kuwait in 1977.[64]

Much worse, in the CPI's view, was the increasing cooperation between the Baathist rulers and the Shah of Iran, dramatically illustrated by the VIP treatment given to the Iranian Empress Farah Diba during her visit to Shia holy places in Iraq in late 1978. The imminence of the Shah's downfall in January drove the Baathist regime to sign an internal security agreement with the House of Saud, whom until a year earlier it had habitually pilloried as the leader of Arab reaction which, along with imperialism and Zionism, was the principal enemy of the Iraqi revolution.

Not surprisingly these developments were accompanied by an increase in the repression of the CPI which had been initiated in early 1977. The party's criticism of the government, published in March and April 1978, followed by a call by its leaders for an end to political repression, the introduction of a parliamentary system, and parity with the Baath in the interim government until elections, were met with a heavy hand by the regime.

This was well conveyed by large-scale arrests in May of party activists in several cities, and the execution of thirty-six Communists on the grounds that they had tried to form cells in the army.[65] To circumvent the fact that many of those sentenced were not members of the military when arrested, the government promulgated a law which made it a capital offence for any soldier retired since 17 July 1968 (the day of the Baathist-led coup), or any conscript no longer in service, to have belonged to a party other than the Baath.[66]

Disturbed by this, the CPI leaders protested – to no avail. They therefore left the PNF but did not publicise their action. They were assured by Saddam Hussein in a secret memo, in September, that their party was still free to work, organise and express its views through its press as long as it remained loyal to the Baathist revolution and its principles and aims.[67] Nevertheless the Communists continued to be purged from the trade unions and professional syndicates, and subjected to frequent arrests and officially inspired assaults. The anti-Communist campaign built up to the point where, in February 1979, there were reports that 1,930 Communists and pro-Communists had 'disappeared'.[68] Two months later the party's paper was closed down.

By the time Saddam Hussein became the state and party chief in July, the CPI was engaged in a clandestine dialogue with other opposition parties with a view to forming a united front based on a common platform. The Baathist regime's hostility to the CPI was well summarised by President Hussein when, in a public speech in early 1980, he described the Iraqi Communists as part of 'the rotten, renegade, atheistic storm that has broken over Iraq'.[69] As expected, the Communists were barred from contesting the parliamentary elections held in June.

President Hussein's military attack on Iran three months later was considered, by the CPI leaders, to be harmful to the overall Arab cause, since it diverted Arab attention and energy away from confronting the main enemy in the region: Israel.[70] This view was shared by dissident Baathists, opposed to Saddam Hussein's leadership, the leftist Popular Union of Kurdistan, and the Nasserites. These parties, and a few smaller groups, met in Damascus in mid-November and announced the formation of the National Democratic and Pan-Arab Front of Iraq, based on the platform of a national coalition government with a programme of a democratic set-up in the republic, and self-rule for the Kurds.[71]

Evidently the future of the Front depended largely on the outcome of the war that the Hussein regime had initiated against Iran, and thus on the performance of the Iranian republic on the battlefield. In other words, post-Shah Iran had emerged as a major factor in the shaping of Iraq's political future. As it happened, the Iran of the Shah's days had played a leading role at a crucial time in the political life of another country in the region: Oman. That was in the mid-1970s, when the rule of Sultan Qaboos was seriously threatened by the leftist guerrillas in Dhofar province.

Guerrilla activity in Oman, which had first erupted in 1965, had grown out of the contacts that the leaders of the Dhofari Liberation Front, composed of Dhofaris working in the Gulf states, had established, in early 1962, with the supporters of the Dhofari branch of the Arab Nationalist Movement, and followers of the anti-Sultan Imam Ghalib ibn Ali. The republican coup in North Yemen in September, followed by the outbreak of an armed rebellion in South Yemen, encouraged the ANM's Dhofari section to merge into the leftist DLF. Aided by President Nasser the enlarged DLF launched its guerrilla struggle in Dhofar soon after its first congress in June 1965.

Two years later, in the wake of the Six Day war which brought about reconciliation between Nasser and the Saudi king, the DLF lost Nasser's backing. But this was more than compensated for by the emergence of South Yemen as an independent Marxist state in November 1967, ready to help the DLF morally and materially. At its second congress in September 1968 the DLF decided to extend its revolutionary activities to the rest of Oman, and other Gulf states, and changed its name to the Popular Front for the Liberation of the Occupied Arab Gulf. Resolved to fight imperialism, neo-colonialism and local oligarchies, the PFLOAG congress stressed the role South Yemen had played in preparing favourable conditions for an armed socialist revolution in Dhofar, and the importance of Dhofar as an intermediate link between South Yemen and the Gulf states.[72]

Having secured large parts of Dhofar the PFLOAG carried out political education and social reform there. It launched campaigns against slavery, illiteracy, tribalism, and the oppression of women; it banned polygamy, and reduced bride-price to a token sum.[73] With most of Dhofar under its control, PFLOAG extended its guerrilla activity to the Oman region of the sultanate in June 1970. This alarmed the British, the dominant political and commercial power in the country, who, as stated earlier, engineered a coup whereby the old, reactionary Sultan Said was replaced by his young son, Qaboos.[74] The new ruler initiated a programme of political and social reform, as well as modernisation and expansion of the armed forces under British aegis.

This led to a modification of tactics by PFLOAG. Its third congress, meeting in July 1971, decided to change the party's main objective from achieving a socialist revolution to accomplishing a national democratic revolution. This opened party membership to non-Marxist nationalists and anti-imperialists. It further widened its base by absorbing the Omani section of the ANM and renaming itself the Popular Front for the Liberation of Oman and the Arab Gulf. The resulting increase in its strength enabled the organisation to withstand three offensives launched against it by the British-led Sultan's Armed Forces, backed by the Special Air Service, the British counter-insurgency force, during the period October 1971 and September 1972. By the time the first offensive ended in late December, the guerrillas had inflicted 136 deaths on the Sultan's troops for their own loss of 31 in 290 skirmishes.[75] The thrust of the last offensive, which was coordinated with the Saudi Arabian/North Yemeni incursions into South Yemen, and which lasted until early December, was also blunted by PFLOAG forces.

However, Sultan Qaboos and his backers redoubled their efforts. By recruiting large numbers of Pakistani mercenaries Qaboos increased his military force fivefold in two years, to 12,500. He also secured the services of nearly a thousand British officers, seconded by Her Majesty's government in London. Saudi Arabia provided money for arms; Jordan trained military and intelligence officers; and Iran lent its helicopters.[76] When all these measures failed to turn the tide in Qaboos's favour, the Shah despatched his troops to Dhofar. This began to hurt the guerrillas.

In mid-1974 PFLOAG leaders decided to narrow their field of action to Oman only, and accordingly renamed their organisation the Popular Front for the Liberation of Oman. These steps proved inadequate as the government forces, backed by the Iranian military and a counter-insurgency campaign, devised and often led by the British, began to make inroads into the PFLO strongholds.[77] In October 1975 the Sultan's forces, working in conjunction with 35,000 Iranian troops and the British SAS, launched a major assault on the PFLO guerrillas, estimated to be 5,000 to 10,000 strong.[78] By the end of the year the authorities claimed to have crushed the revolutionary movement at the expense of less than 400 Omani, British, Jordanian and Iranian troops: a gross underestimate.[79]

'Unmistakably, the SAS – Britain's elite special forces outfit – played a leading role in defeating the Dhofar insurgency,' reported Joseph Fitchett of the *Observer*. 'Operating in enemy-held territory, usually in four-man teams, they gathered intelligence and laid ambushes.'[80] Counter-insurgency measures included driving villagers to the 'strategic hamlets', 'food control', starving guerrillas and encouraging villagers to seek government control, using air power, and waging psychological warfare by combining promises of economic development, as a reward for cooperation, with threats of reprisals as punishment for non-cooperation.[81]

But the PFLO's quiescent period did not last long. During the first half of 1977 it engaged in twenty armed skirmishes with government forces in eastern Dhofar. In June the PFLO's central committee decided to undertake 'ideological, political and military reconstruction', and reorganise its intelligence apparatus. The fact that the government arrested ninety people, including military officers and top civil servants, soon after this meeting showed that it took the PFLO seriously.[82] At the same time, by supporting Sadat's visit to Jerusalem and the Camp David accord,

Sultan Qaboos isolated himself from fellow rulers of the Arabian Peninsula, and thus made himself more vulnerable to attacks by the left. Not surprisingly the PFLO stepped up its actions: in August 1978, for instance, it claimed that in two recent encounters its members had killed twenty-eight Omani soldiers.[83]

It was elated by the Shah's fall and the withdrawal of the last of the Iranian troops in the spring of 1979. The Sultan's subsequent decision to strengthen ties with Washington, culminating in his offering military bases to America, once again showed Qaboos as the only ruler in the Peninsula to totally align with America and thus expose himself to attacks by Omani nationalists as well. It was not until the Iran–Iraq war that Qaboos was able to end his isolation by taking up a pro-Iraqi position along with other monarchs of the Peninsula on the side of Iraq.[84] But that increased the hostility which had existed between Oman and South Yemen, since the latter, as a member of the Front of Steadfastness, favoured Iran.

Insofar as South Yemen won its independence from an imperialist power through a guerrilla war, and has stayed consistently on the left since then, it is the most deviant state in the Arab East. The mass movement against British rule had emerged mainly out of cooperation between the South Yemeni branch of the Arab Nationalist Movement and the Nasserites. It was the local ANM which had first issued a call for armed action, in 1959, to frustrate the British plan to set up a Federation of South Arabia. It was again the ANM which led the move to unite various anti-imperialist groups into the National Liberation Front in 1963.

However, the nationalist ranks were divided when President Nasser, unhappy at the leftward lurch of the NLF, helped to create the Front for the Liberation of Occupied South Yemen in early 1966, as 'the standard-bearer of establishment revolution, with its emphasis on anti-imperialism, ethnic-nationalism, and state socialism, and its denial of the idea of class struggle'.[85] The fact that FLOSY's middle-class leaders concentrated on winning and retaining the support of the urban petty bourgeoisie and better-paid workers, while the NLF leadership concentrated on organising much larger, but hitherto neglected, sections of society – the low-paid workers of Aden and the poor tribals of the hinterland – worked in favour of the latter.

Having armed and educated the most exploited sections of the population, the NLF intensified its attacks on British targets, and went on to initiate a campaign against FLOSY. Nasser's defeat in the June 1967 war had a demoralising effect on FLOSY. The result was that by August the NLF controlled all of the vast Eastern region as well as twelve provinces of the Western region. Its policy of establishing popular committees, a popular guard, and administrative committees composed of old civil servants and local NLF members, encouraged grass-roots participation in governing the liberated areas. This tactic singled out the NLF as an exceptionally revolutionary organisation in the Arab East, and helped it to prevail over FLOSY in the final rounds of fighting, in Aden and elsewhere.

Once the NLF assumed power in November differences between its moderate and radical wings came to the surface. While the radicals offered a programme for accentuating class conflict and establishing dictatorship of the proletariat, the moderates advocated a Nasserite version of socialism, with its disavowal of class conflict. Whereas the moderates wanted merely to reform the existing state machinery, the radicals intended to destroy the colonial administrative and military apparatus, and replace it with popular civilian institutions, a peoples' militia and army, and make the state subservient to the party of the proletariat.

In the clash that occurred between the two sides at the NLF's fourth congress in March 1968, the leftists won. The main resolution described the NLF as 'a revolutionary organisation' representing 'the interests of workers, peasants, soldiers, and revolutionary intellectuals', and adopting 'scientific socialism' as its 'method of analysis and practice', and instructing the government to launch a programme of mass education and cleanse the army and administration of colonial elements.[86]

But the action that President Qahtan al Shaabi initiated two months later amounted to purging the government and the NLF of leftists. The radicals resisted the move; and this led to a series of confrontations between the armed members of the two factions. Had this been allowed to continue, the conflict would have probably escalated into a fully fledged civil war. But the mounting pressures exerted against the new republic by Saudi Arabia, North Yemen and Oman compelled President Shaabi to consolidate the home front by seeking a successful reconciliation with the leftists.

The mobilising of the populace to meet the foreign threat enabled the leftists to tighten their control of the party machine and the popular guards. Finally, in June 1969, they succeeded in displacing President Shaabi: they abolished the office of president, and replaced it with a presidential council of five NLF leaders, including the party's general secretary, Abdul Fatah Ismail. This signalled primacy of the party over the government.

Not surprisingly, the constitution adopted in November 1970 stated that 'the alliance of the people's democratic forces finds its organisational embodiment in the NLF . . . which leads all political activity among the masses, and the mass organisations, in the light of scientific socialism', and that 'the central committee of the NLF is the leading political organ of the country'.[87] As such, the presidential council (reduced to three members by the constitution) is monopolised by NLF leaders, but not so the cabinet.

The mass organisations led by the NLF included those of peasants, workers, soldiers, militia, students and women. What made the land reform carried out by the NLF regime unique in the Arab East was the speed of its execution and the involvement of poor and landless peasants in it. Within a year of independence the government confiscated the lands of all those feudal lords who had cooperated with the British. And, following the political shake-up of June 1969, the government lowered land ceilings from fifty to forty acres for unirrigated land, and from twenty-five to twenty acres for irrigated land, and applied these limits to a family – not an individual, as had been the case hitherto. The peasants' unions, organised by the party, took over lands above the ceiling, and set up popular committees to decide how best to cultivate these. By giving an early and vigorous push to the cooperative and state farming movement, the NLF succeeded in aborting the rise of the kulaks – something which had happened elsewhere in the Arab East.[88]

As a result of encouragement given to trade unionism among workers by the party, the membership of the General Union of Yemeni Workers doubled within five years of independence, to 45,000.[89] Furthermore, many of the workers were drawn into the people's militia and popular defence committees set up after a decision to this effect by the NLF's fifth congress in March 1972. The party won the sympathies of women by launching a successful campaign against the wearing of the veil, and by the passing of a just divorce law by the government. The revolutionary regime expanded educational facilities and the mass media, particularly radio. And it continued the traditional practice of teaching religion at school, as well as the official observance of religious holidays.

Most importantly, the NLF government purged many of the soldiers and officers of the colonial army, and expanded the force by incorporating the politicised guerrilla groups, which had fought the British, into it. A policy of engaging the reconstituted army into such developmental projects as the construction of roads, irrigation facilities, and schools, helped the government to give the force the aura of a people's army. Following its fifth congress the party built up a people's militia: by early 1979 it was nearly 100,000 strong, five times as large as the military.[90]

Such fundamental changes, effected within five years of independence, were inevitably resisted by certain sections of society. President Shaabi was not unresponsive to their woes. But when he fell in mid-1969 it became apparent that the days of moderate reform were over. This led to a migration of tens of thousands of people to East Africa, North Yemen, and Saudi Arabia. Aided by Riyadh and Sanaa, the émigrés set up military camps along the borders of the leftist republic, and carried out pin-prick raids. The regime in Aden reacted to this with more radicalism, not less. It tightened up internal security and mobilised the under-privileged, politically and militarily. These measures enabled it to frustrate the attack against its territory by North Yemen and Saudi Arabia, acting in collusion with South Yemeni expatriates, in the autumn of 1972.

By the time the sixth party congress was held in March 1975 the regime felt secure. It had by then established diplomatic relations with Kuwait, and even accepted a token sum as aid from it; and it was engaged in negotiations with Riyadh. However, accepting the recommendation of the party's general secretary, Abdul Fatah Ismail, the congress turned down a Saudi offer of substantial aid. More importantly, it laid down a political-economic plan for the transitional period of three years between national democracy and socialism. Accordingly the NLF sponsored unification congress, held in October decided to weld the NLF, the Vanguard Party (a Baathist group), and the Popular Democratic Union (a Communist group), to form the United Political Organisation of the NLF, to be reconstituted as the Yemeni Socialist Party three years later.

But before this could actually happen the ruling party went through a violent convulsion in order to resolve the conflict that developed between President Salem Robaye Ali on one hand, and Abdul Fatah Ismail and Prime Minister Ali Nasser Mohammed on the other. The differences centred around the structure of the proposed Yemeni Socialist Party, developmental strategy, and foreign relations, particularly those with Riyadh, which had established diplomatic links with Aden in March 1976 and coupled it with economic aid of $50 million.

By using part of the Saudi aid to bolster the president's budget, over which he had exclusive control,[91] President Ali further strengthened the client system, consisting of party and government functionaries loyal to him, which he had fostered since 1969. His highly personalised mode of operation ran counter to the concept of centralised planning to which the party was theoretically committed. Not surprisingly, he opposed the hierarchical system proposed for the Yemeni Socialist Party. But he was in a minority. The party's central committee decided, in September 1977 and again in January 1978, to divest him of some of his many functions (he was, for instance, the party's assistant general secretary). By the middle of the year it had become clear that the two sides were heading for a showdown.

This was the background against which President Ahmed al Ghashmi was killed on 24 June in his Sanaa office by the explosion of a bomb in a suitcase, allegedly brought by a special emissary of President Ali. At the NLF's central committee meeting, held the next day in Aden, President Ali reportedly agreed to resign. Later, however, he reneged. Fighting broke out between the supporters of the president and those of the rest of the party leadership. It lasted sixteen hours. With 450 of his 600 defenders dead, Ali surrendered and was executed after a summary trial.[92] In a way this was a repetition of what had happened nine years earlier in the case of President Shaabi: personal popularity and the loyalty of a section of the army proved unequal to the strength of the party apparatus and its highly politicised militia.[93]

Once the leadership crisis had been solved, the plan to transform the

United Political Organisation of the NLF into the Yemeni Socialist Party went ahead. Direct elections were held to the Supreme People's Council, the national parliament, which had been established in 1971 with nominated members. Of the 111 deputies elected to the house, only seventy-one belonged to the Yemeni Socialist Party. None the less, the elevation of Abdul Fatah Ismail, the party's general secretary, to the republic's presidency once again underlined primacy of the party.

While South Yemen was going through a period of consolidation and progress, North Yemen was experiencing continued instability. The failure of the attempted coup by the 13 June Movement's supporters in North Yemen in October, and subsequent government repression, weakened the centrist forces there. As stated earlier, the pro-Hamdi movement decided to merge with the National Democratic Front.

The roots of the leftist front went back to the civil war, and the rise of the ANM in North Yemen. During its early years it was pro-Nasser. Later this changed. In fact when the local Nasserites tried to reach a compromise with the royalists, following the reconciliation between the Egyptian president and the Saudi monarch in the wake of the Six Day war, the ANM opposed the move. During the siege of Sanaa by tribal royalists in January 1968 it was the ANM which armed the city's workers, traders and civil servants to defend the capital. The operation was successful: the monarchists lifted the siege in February. But once the royalist threat was overcome the centrist forces within the republican camp consolidated their authority and attacked the leftists. They purged the army of the ANM elements and drove the party's civilian cadre underground.

In June former ANM members re-emerged to form the Revolutionary Democratic Party along the lines of South Yemen's NLF, which was then in power in Aden. Following the NLF's example it began organising peasants' unions in the southern region of the republic, and had some success. Later, when governmental action destroyed its bases among the military and the urban petty bourgeoisie, the party was able to retain its rural base and engage in guerrilla activity. However, after the inter-Yemen war in the autumn of 1972, Sanaa intensified its anti-guerrilla campaign. Between May and October 1973, for instance, the number of subversives who had been officially executed exceeded forty.[94]

The emergence of Colonel Hamdi as president in mid-1974 created an atmosphere where centrist and leftist groups could function semi-clandestinely, if only to help Hamdi to counterbalance the pro-Riyadh conservatives. The revived Revolutionary Democratic Party merged with the Democratic Party of Popular Unity, a Communist group, and the local Baathists in February 1976 to form the National Democratic Front under the leadership of Sultan Ahmed Umar. The NDF decided to work for the consolidation of national independence, which in its view was threatened by 'Saudi reaction'; for the elimination of feudalism; and the democratisation of public life. It offered Hamdi 'critical support', and urged him to pursue progressive policies at home and abroad with conviction and energy.[95]

However, the NDF did not make much headway during Hamdi's rule. It was only after Hamdi's successor, President Ghashmi, began alienating all non-conservative elements with his blatantly pro-Riyadh policies that it acquired importance. It held a secret congress in July 1978 where it called inter alia for unity with South Yemen.[96]

Four months later its ranks were swelled by the members of the 13 June Movement, many of whose leaders, including Major Abdul-Alem, had taken refuge in South Yemen after the failure of their attempted coup against President Ali Abdullah Saleh. Thus strengthened the NDF leadership forged links with military and civilian leaders opposed to President Saleh, most of them being in the southern districts of Ibb, Harib and Bayda. On 22 February 1979 the NDF forces, aided by Aden, secured Harib and Qataba, with local troops offering little or no resistance. From there the leftists fanned out to capture Ibb and Bayda districts. Fighting continued until 2 March, when South Yemen, pressured by Iraq (acting on behalf of Saudi Arabia) and Syria, agreed to a cease-fire. However, the NDF refused to comply; therefore hostilities did not cease altogether for a few more days.[97] Towards the end of the month the presidents of the two Yemens, meeting in Kuwait, agreed on a unification plan, to be executed within a year, with Saleh becoming the head of the united People's Republic of Yemen. This agreement had the backing of the NDF, which was enthusiastic about unity with South Yemen.

However, when no perceptible progress had been made towards a political union by early the following year, the NDF leaders tried to reach a modus vivendi with the government in Sanaa. They entered into negotiations with the president with a set of three demands: freeing of all political prisoners and freedom of action for the NDF; formation of a national unity government with a programme of land reform, unity with South Yemen, and non-alignment in international affairs; and a commitment to holding direct elections to a constituent assembly by June 1981. Sanaa met the demands half way. It released 150 to 200 political prisoners (which still left an unknown number of opposition activists in jail). After the NDF had closed down its radio station operating in South Yemen the government allowed it to publish a weekly, *Al Amal*. The first (uncensored) issue appeared in mid-September. The next month a new cabinet headed by Abdul Karem Iryani, a technocrat, was sworn in. Plans were set in motion by this government to draft a national charter as a prelude to holding elections to a constituent assembly in 1982.[98]

On the other hand, President Saleh's visit to Riyadh in August with a plea for the resumption of Saudi assistance to North Yemen's budget; and the assassinations of Abdul Salam al Dumaini, leader of the military wing of the NDF, and his two brothers, in Sanaa during the same month – probably by pro-Riyadh agents – were fresh reminders that Saudi control over events in North Yemen was still strong.[99]

As before, the Saudi rulers remained deadly opposed to unification of the two Yemens. They dreaded the emergence next door of a united, left-leaning Yemen, populated by seven million people, and supplying over three quarters of a million (much-needed) workers to their own kingdom. After all, it was the rise of republicanism in North Yemen which had caused the longest period of instability experienced by the Saudi kingdom so far. The defection in late 1962 of pilots and crews of the Saudi air force to republican North Yemen, and their declaration that the Movement of Free Officers and Civilians existed in Saudi Arabia,[100] had marked the start of this period.

The anti-royalist forces then consisted of the Nasserite Union of the People of the Arabian Peninsula, the Baathists, and the National Liberation Front, a Marxist group. As stated earlier, opposition reached a peak in 1966, suffered repression, and came up again in 1969 when it attempted two coups.[101] The NLF was the oldest of these organisations, with its roots going back to the Workers' Committees formed in the wake of strikes at oilfields in 1953. They continued underground until the next wave of strikes by oil workers when, as a result of government persecution, they disintegrated. Some of their members allied with local Communists to form the National Reform Front, which renamed itself the National Liberation Front in 1958. The NLF demanded the promulgation of a democratic constitution embodying guarantees of rights to establish political parties, trade unions or other mass organisations, and to demonstrate or strike. It called on the state to dismantle the foreign bases in the country, and to take complete control of oil resources, from prospecting to marketing.[102] In late 1975 it changed its name to the Communist Party of Saudi Arabia.

Although weak, the NLF had supported the coup attempt of June 1969 which was led by the Saudi section of the Arab Nationalist Movement. The latter had begun its existence as a clandestine group in Dhahran in 1964, and had graduated into something bigger in early 1966.[103] During the next three years the party built up a base among military officers, oil workers, civil servants and teachers. Its attempt at a coup in mid-1969 was foiled only a few hours before its scheduled execution. The resulting arrest of 2,000 conspirators, followed by scores of executions, destroyed the party.[104]

During the next year the former members of the ANM and the Marxists outside the NLF joined hands to form the Popular Democratic Party. They believe in Marxism–Leninism, and in the inevitability of an armed struggle to liberate their country from imperialism. For the present, however, they stress the need for forming a broad national front to oppose the royal dictatorship. The party has a special women's section, and draws most of its supporters from students and petty civil servants. Since belonging to the PDP, or the Communist Party, is a capital offence, the membership of these parties inside the country is small. They are predominantly expatriate organisations, active among Saudi students studying abroad and long-term exiles, with no impact on day-to-day events inside the kingdom.

In contrast, the leftists have had an important bearing on the history of Bahrain, the first Arab Gulf territory to witness an industrial strike, in 1938.[105] Since then the workers have been the main supporters of nationalist-leftist causes and parties. For instance, they were the major force behind the anti-British demonstrations of late 1956, an event which resulted in severe reprisals against the popular leaders and a declaration of emergency. Nine years later it was the oil workers' industrial stoppage which escalated into a general strike on the main islands. It assumed political significance and brought the hastily formed Progressive Forces Front to the fore. The Front demanded such political reform as the lifting of the emergency, the granting of civil and trade union rights, and the establishment of an elected assembly.[106] The ruler responded with heavy-handed repression.

But once the British had departed in mid-1971 and the ruler had made half-hearted moves to share power with his ministers, the nationalist-leftist forces – now organised under the Bahrain section of the Popular Front for the Liberation of Oman and the Arab Gulf, and the Bahrain National Liberation Front – began to flex their muscles. In 1972 they twice called a general strike and succeeded. Thus pressured, the monarch agreed to hold elections to a constituent assembly. But because he refused to release all political prisoners and grant the vote to women both the PFLOAG and the NLF boycotted these elections.

However the two parties took different stands on the parliamentary elections of December 1973. The PFLOAG stuck to its earlier policy of boycott, whereas the NLF allied with the Bahrain Nationalist Movement to offer voters a common list of the Popular Bloc, led by Hussein Musa. By winning a large majority of elected seats the Popular Bloc proved itself to be the dominating political force. In parliament Popular Bloc members combined their attacks on the government, on such daily issues as inflation and housing shortage, with demands for political-economic reform – comprising nationalisation of large foreign firms, the institution of income tax, the granting of trade union rights, and the enfranchising of women.[107]

Not surprisingly, while the monarch maintained that the state security law of October 1974 was aimed at 'the Communist elements',[108] the Popular Bloc members regarded it as a move to curtail the already limited civil rights enjoyed by his subjects. Later, in August 1975, the dissolution of parliament by the ruler was coupled with the arrest of thirty leaders of the NLF and PFLOAG.

It was significant that the leaders of the Shia demonstrations of May 1979 should call for a review of the state security law, and that Shia clergy should back the leftist demand that a revived parliament should consist exclusively of elected representatives. In a somewhat similar development in Kuwait the Shia masses were turning away from the ruler, whom they had supported so far, and siding with the opposition, led by Ahmed Khatib, a veteran leftist.[109]

Khatib was one of the founder-leaders of the Arab Nationalist Movement, with headquarters in Beirut. On his return to Kuwait in 1953 he formed the National Cultural Club as a front for the ANM. It performed well in the local elections of 1954, and played a leading role in the democratic movement of Kuwait.[110] In the first parliamentary poll of 1963 four ANM members and eight party sympathisers won. Operating as a fairly cohesive group in parliament, they concentrated on securing redress of the grievances of the 'lower social classes'.[111] Later the ANM was vocal in its protest against the rigging of the 1967 parliamentary poll which, as stated earlier, was unsuccessful.[112]

In the third parliament the nationalist-leftist bloc of six, led by Khatib, concentrated as much on foreign affairs as on domestic. At its behest parliament rejected the deal which gave the government a 25 per cent share in the Western-owned Kuwait Oil Company immediately, rising steadily to 51 per cent in 1981. The radicals won again when, in early 1974, parliament turned down the new participation agreement which stipulated the sale of 60 per cent of the KOC shares to the Kuwaiti government. They reiterated the demand that the state should purchase all the KOC shares immediately.[113]

Even though lacking the organisation and structure of a formal, legal party,[114] the nationalist-leftists have had an important bearing on the country's official policies. It was, for instance, not accidental that Kuwait was the first Gulf state to establish diplomatic links with South Yemen, and was later instrumental in the two Yemens reaching an agreement on unification, after the war of 1979. But the more profound and consistent influence the radicals have exerted has been on Kuwait's stand on Palestinian rights. They are in this case helped by the presence of a large Palestinian community which, while lacking voting rights, is an important factor in the civil service and the privately and publicly owned mass media. The result has been unfaltering generosity by the Kuwaiti rulers in providing financial aid to the PLO. By proposing the discontinuation of Kuwaiti loans and subsidies to Egypt as a reprisal for the Sinai I agreement with Israel in early 1974, the nationalist-leftist parliamentarians laid down a principle which the ruler adopted some years later. They coupled the condemnation of the Camp David accord with a decision to suspend aid to Cairo.

Inside Egypt itself opposition to the Camp David agreement, and to the subsequent peace treaty with Israel, was offered persistently by the leftist Alliance of the Progressive Nationalist Unionists, consisting of Marxists, leftist Nasserites and progressive Islamic elements.[115] But, suffering a systematic curtailment of its freedom of action, the APNU could not do very much to oppose President Sadat's foreign or domestic policies. When the party leaders refused to disband the Alliance in the summer of 1978 – as Sadat publicly advised them to – they became victims of state harassment which drove their party behind closed doors. A police raid in January on the party headquarters in Cairo led to the confiscation of its documents and printing machinery.[116] Widespread electoral malpractices in the parliamentary poll, held in June, deprived the party of any representation in the national legislature.[117] This was the latest in the vicissitudes of the leftist movement dating back to 1921, when a breakaway group of the Socialist Party of Egypt founded the Communist Party of Egypt.

On the eve of the party's admission to the Comintern two years later its programme included demands for Egypt's independence from the British, land reform, the cancellation of peasants' debts, and the right to form trade unions and recognition of existing unions. Its militant policy of calling strikes brought it into conflict with the Wafd government, and led to an official ban in 1924 on the Confederation of Trade Unions, which was dominated by it.

The sixth Comintern congress, meeting in 1928, advised the Egyptian Communists to strengthen the party machine and extend their activities to the countryside, among agricultural labourers. But, in the face of government persecution, the Communist leaders found it difficult to expand the party base; and the movement's growth was slow. The situation changed in 1936 when the Anglo–Egyptian treaty disappointed nationalist aspirations and thus created an environment of militant anti-imperialism. This helped the Communist Party to grow.

Following the Soviet entry into the Second World War in mid-1941, the chances of a freer functioning of the Communists improved. What further aided them was the passing of a law legalising trade unions by the Wafd government, installed into office in early 1942 through the armed intervention of the British embassy in Cairo.[118] (However, this law forbade the formation of peasants' unions or a confederation of trade unions.) This, and the dramatic increase in the size of the working class, caused by the wartime activities of the Allies,[119] enabled the Communists to enlarge their influence among workers. Most of the labour unions were now organised by one of the two Communist groups then active; the Mouvement Egyptien de Libération Nationale, led by Henri Curiel, and the smaller Iskra group, headed by Hillel Schwartz.

By the end of the war the two parties had between them formed 465 unions with 115,000 members.[120] In August 1945 they were all brought together under the umbrella of the Congress of Workers' Unions. Thus strengthened, the trade union leaders organised a series of strikes early next year to secure better working conditions and higher wages for workers. Their action was supported by the leftist National Centre of

Students and Workers, which sponsored demonstrations. A police attempt to break up one such demonstration in Cairo on 9 February led to deaths, by drowning in the Nile, of twenty students. Popular protest at this took the form of a general strike on 21 February. The police action against strikers left three dead and 120 injured. This inflamed feelings against the Wafd government which in turn stepped up its repression of the Communist movement.

Increased persecution by the state brought the two Communist groups together. In May 1947 they merged to form the Mouvement Démocratique de Libération Nationale. Since a large number of the MDLN's 1,500 members were either Christian or Jew,[121] the party's strength was not so adversely affected by the Soviet Union's volte face on Palestine at the United Nations, later in the year, than had been the case elsewhere in the Arab East. None the less the Soviet vote provided the government with a chance to dub the Communists pro-Zionist and put their leaders in jail.

But this did not stop the Communist ranks from organising periodic strikes by workers or students in Cairo. Their big opportunity came in January when policemen went on strike for higher wages and shorter working hours. The Communists led demonstrations of workers and students in support of the policemen's demands. The government had to call in troops to restore order, which by and large they did. However, sporadic demonstrations did not end until May when, on the eve of the Palestine war, martial law was declared.

The defeat of the Egyptian forces in the Palestine war created widespread disaffection against the political establishment headed by King Farouk. Yielding to rising popular pressure the monarch released political prisoners – Communists, Muslim Brethren, and leftist Wafdists – in October 1949, and ordered a general election, to be held three months later.

The Wafd won these elections. As stated earlier, the new government terminated the 1936 Anglo–Egyptian treaty and asked Britain to withdraw its troops, but to no avail.[122] This inflamed nationalist feeling and encouraged such anti-imperialist parties as the Communists, Socialists, and Muslim Brotherhood to forge a united front. When the front launched an armed guerrilla campaign against the British occupation forces in the Suez zone, in October 1951, the Communists participated in it actively. These tactics added to their strength. Not surprisingly, on the eve of the Free Officers' coup in July, the Communist Party, with 5,000 activists,[123] was second in size only to the Muslim Brotherhood.

That the party was involved in the Free Officers' movement became apparent when two of the eighteen members of the ruling Revolutionary Command Council turned out to be Communists: Major Khaled Mohieddin and Lt-Colonel Yusuf Sadeq. But this had no effect on the actions of the RCC, which claimed to be non-ideological. In fact, as described earlier, within weeks of assuming power the RCC summarily crushed a strike near Alexandria.[124] It banned the Communist publication and imprisoned many Communist leaders.

In the power struggle that developed between President Neguib and his deputy, Nasser, the Communists supported the former, since he favoured a return to the parliamentary system. When Neguib lost to Nasser the Communists found themselves in a precarious situation. Not surprisingly, once Nasser had consolidated his hold over the RCC in March 1954, he removed Mohieddin and Sadeq from the ruling body. With this the Communists felt alienated from the regime.

But as Nasser began to pursue an increasingly anti-imperialist line abroad – securing the withdrawal of British troops from Egypt; participating actively in the non-aligned nations' conference in Bandung; and breaking the Western arms embargo by signing an arms deal with Czechoslovakia in September 1955 – the Communists reassessed their policy towards him.

An overt change occurred when Nasser, harassed by an Anglo–French–Israeli attack on Egypt in October 1956, released hundreds of Communist and leftist Wafdist prisoners and let them organise popular resistance to the invaders in the western Suez Canal zone, with government-supplied arms. From then on the Communists were allowed a degree of freedom they had rarely enjoyed before. A simmering feud between the Communist Party of Egypt and the MDLN was resolved, and a unified party forged in January 1958, a few weeks before the inauguration of the United Arab Republic.

However, the Communist unity proved transient. The party leadership failed to evolve a common policy towards the Iraqi Communists who, following the anti-royalist revolution in July, were more interested in establishing a socialist state in Iraq than in working for the merger of Iraq into the UAR. The ideological split hurt the party in more ways than one: it facilitated the arrest of militants by the Egyptian intelligence, and created mutual distrust among the ranks. Later, when Nasser asserted that the anti-imperialist struggle had been won, irrevocably, the moderate Communist faction too turned away from him.

Responding in kind, Nasser followed a twin-headed policy of repressing the Communist movement while incorporating some of the egalitarian ideas of Marxism–Leninism into (what he called) Arab socialism, and executing some of the anti-capitalist measures proposed by the Communists. Arab socialism was enshrined into the National Charter of June 1962, which inter alia expressed belief in scientific socialism and commitment to struggle against exploitation.[125] As such the Charter was received differently by the two Communist factions. The moderates described it as a progressive document, which marked the end of the anti-imperialist revolution and the beginning of the socialist revolution, whereas the radicals regarded it as signifying nothing more than the introduction of state capitalism in Egypt. 'Arab socialism is a mere conglomeration of scientific and utopian socialism, petty bourgeois ideas, narrow nationalism, religious prejudices, and subjective idealism; it does not aim at abolishing exploitation of man by man,' wrote Khaled Bakdash in the *World Marxist Review*.[126]

Nasser formed the Arab Socialist Union in November 1962 as the political organisation to build socialism in Egypt. In order to widen support for his regime, he undertook a policy of gradually releasing political dissidents – mainly Communists and Muslim Brethren – during the summer of 1963. As a result 600 Communists had been set free by the time the Soviet leader Nikita Khrushchev arrived in Egypt on a state visit in May.[127] Later Nasser invited the Communists to join the ASU as individuals. This was received favourably by a joint meeting of the leaders of the Communist parties of Egypt, Syria, Lebanon, Jordan, and Iraq, held in Beirut in September. They tempered their criticism of Arab socialism with the need for 'dispelling mistrust and suspicion between the Communist movement and Nasserism', and for tackling the 'negative features' of Nasserism, such as its dictatorial nature, in a 'friendly and constructive way'.[128]

Adopting the conciliatory tone of the Beirut meeting the Egyptian Communist leaders declared, in April, that since the July 1961 nationalisation decrees Nasser's regime had been following the road of 'non-capitalist development toward socialism', and that the establishment of the ASU had signified a step in the right direction. They dissolved their own party and advised individual members to join the ASU which, they said, would adopt scientific socialism (there being 'only one kind of scientific socialism') and operate democratically, and within which 'new revolutionary forces' would progressively become a majority.[129]

Most members followed the leadership's advice: the dissidents faced either jail or an underground existence. Of those who applied for ASU membership only those whose loyalty to the tenets of the National Charter was found satisfactory were admitted. Less than a hundred were finally given positions in the ASU or state apparatus:[130] the party secretariat, state-run mass media, ministry of education, a public sector undertaking, or an institute of socialist studies.

They were warned by Nasser that any attempt by them to form a bloc within the ASU would be severely punished. None the less, they managed periodically to urge the Egyptian president to fulfil his promise of creating within the ASU a vanguard consisting exclusively of cadres representing the interests of the working class.[131] They also demanded state action to protect peasants from oppression by civil servants, impede the growth of kulaks in the countryside, and broaden the powers of trade unions. Their organisational skills and political convictions were used by Ali Sabri in setting up the Socialist Youth Organisation in 1966. Its anti-feudalist campaign had their enthusiastic backing.[132] On the whole, however, they were treated with circumspection by the regime, and knew it. In the words of Anouar Abdel-Malek, instruction from the top to the management of an institution engaging ex-Communists were: 'Collaborate with them, absorb them, but at all costs keep all decision-making power in your hands'.[133]

Yet the ex-Communists did not waver in their loyalty to Nasser, whom they regarded as anti-imperialist. They were prominent in organising pro-Nasser demonstrations after the June 1967 war. Blaming the military defeat on the preponderance of self-seeking officers in the armed forces, and the continued existence of a chasm between the masses and the civilian leadership, they called for the radicalisation of the revolution by expelling the rightists from the ASU and the government, and strengthening the revolutionary cadres within the ASU. But Nasser reacted differently. As stated earlier, he disbanded the Socialist Youth and changed the ASU's structure to placate traditional elements.[134] His moves disillusioned the former Communists.

There were periodic protests by leftist students and workers against Nasser's rightward drift, including a strike by 27,000 textile workers in Cairo in March 1969.[135] But these were quickly and effectively suppressed by the specially created reserve police force. 'The revolution is still in the hands of the petite bourgeoisie,' said a leftist parliamentarian in September 1970. 'We have failed until now to create real leaders from the working and peasant classes, either in the Arab Socialist Union, or in the national assembly, or anywhere [else] in our society. We are prevented from expressing the radical point of view in the newspapers.'[136]

After Nasser's death the leftists demanded higher representation in the ASU secretariat, the youth section, and the trade unions. Nothing came of it. They were, however, allowed to participate in the debate on the ASU's future role, which was begun in March 1972. But the final report, published a year later, rejected their interpretation of the National Charter.[137] The leftists were now in a bind. They had been reduced to impotency within the ASU; yet, aware of the National Unity Law of September 1972, which specified a stiff penalty for political activity outside the ASU, they dared not leave it.

That Sadat was in no mood to put up with criticism from the left became apparent when, at his behest, the ASU leadership expelled over a hundred leftist intellectuals from the organisation in mid-1973. Since most of them were journalists who, deprived of their ASU membership, could not work, this amounted to condemning them to penury or exile. By dismissing Nasser's long-time confidant, Mohammed Heikal, as editor of *Al Ahram* in January 1974, for criticising Sadat for banking totally on Washington's goodwill, and describing the result of the Yom Kippur war as 'no victory, no defeat', the Egyptian president showed his intolerance even of left-of-centre views.

No wonder the leftist Nasserites allied with the Marxists to form a separate tribune, the Alliance of the Progressive Nationalist Unionists, within the ASU in May 1976. On the eve of the parliamentary poll in October the APNU claimed a membership of 60,000.[138] In its election campaign it called for resistance against attempts being made to weaken the public sector and generally to erode the socialist gains made during Nasser's rule. Aware of the constitutional ambiguity on strikes,[139] it campaigned for a legal right to strike. The subject had become topical due to the Cairo transport workers' strike in September, for higher wages to counter an inflation rate of 40 per cent. Alleging that the Communists had instigated the strike, the government had used force to break it up, and arrested not only the strike leaders but also eleven 'Communists'.[140]

More serious charges and tougher action against the leftists by the government came after widespread riots which flared up, spontaneously, throughout the country, from Alexandria to Aswan, on 18 January 1977. 'The immediate cause of the rioting was the reduction of government price subsidies on such basic commodities as rice, sugar, and cooking gas,' notes Raymond William Baker, an American academic. 'More fundamentally, the disturbances originated with the social strains generated by Sadat's open-door [economic] policy.'[141] Order was restored only after Sadat had personally cancelled price rises on 20 January, and the army firings had, according to the official statement, killed some seventy-nine rioters and injured over 800.[142] Although the most common chant of the demonstrators was 'Nasser, Nasser, Nasser!' the government prosecutor blamed four clandestine Communist groups for the disturbances, with the prime minister publicly indicting the official leftist party, the APNU, for its 'shameful involvement'.[143] Yet, of the 150 APNU members arrested after the riots, only twenty-three were subsequently charged: they were only a small proportion of the total of 1,146 people who were finally put on trial in June.[144]

By then the party's claimed membership had reached 160,000,[145] and was growing. It was being helped by the disaffection created among workers and employees who, threatened with life imprisonment if they struck, had to accept wage increases of about one third of the inflation rate.[146] A dramatic jump in the circulation of the party's weekly, *Al Ahali*, to 100,000 within two months of its launching in February 1978,[147] pleased the party hierarchy as much as it disturbed Sadat. When leftist leaders advised their followers, through the columns of *Al Ahali*, to say 'No' in the referendum on 'guided democracy' in May, the government confiscated the issue.[148] Responding to mounting official pressure to disband the party, its leaders decided to suspend political activity.

Despite continued persecution by the authorities, the APNU has not modified its analysis of the Sadat regime. It has maintained its opposition to the Egyptian president's unilateral actions to secure peace in the Middle East. Harmful to Arab unity, and beneficial primarily to the American interests in the region, it regards these steps as having strengthened American imperialism at the expense of Arab nationalism.

It advocates a peace settlement in the region which involves all Arab states and both the superpowers, and which guarantees the creation of a Palestinian state.

The Egyptian leftists have been among the early proponents of Arab–Israeli peace along these lines. And, like the Marxist Democratic Front for the Liberation of Palestine, they have welcomed contacts with those Israelis who are willing to concede a Palestinian state.[149] Many weeks before Sadat's dramatic announcement that he was ready to visit Jerusalem for the sake of peace, Mohammed Sid-Ahmed, a leader of the APNU, and Issam Sartawi of the PLO secretariat in Beirut, participated in a seminar on 'Peace and the Palestinians' in London, attended among others by Uri Avneri, head of the leftist Israeli Shelli Party, and Mattityahu Peled, an Israeli academic.[150] But the impact of this, or any such subsequent, contact has been minimal, because the Avneris and the Peleds are part of a very weak political trend in their country. One of the salient features of Israel, since its inception in 1948, has been that its political centre has moved steadily rightward.

# PART III

# ISRAEL:
## DOMESTIC POLITICS AND FOREIGN RELATIONS

# 9

# ISRAEL: DOMESTIC POLITICS

Israeli political parties can be broadly labelled as Zionist, non-Zionist, or anti-Zionist. The most prominent anti-Zionist party is Rakah, Reshima Kommunistit Hadash (New Communist List). It is supported in the main by the Arab citizens of Israel, who form about one-sixth of the total population.[1] Not surprisingly, one of its leaders, Emile Touma, is the secretary of the Arab People's Conference in support for the Palestine Revolution whose scheduled congress on 6 December 1980 was banned by the authorities. It was to have endorsed a manifesto, signed six months earlier, by thousands of Israeli Arabs, which called for equality for Arab citizens, and an Israeli–Arab peace on the basis of self-determination for both Israelis and Palestinians, and urged the Israeli government to negotiate with the PLO on the subject of a Palestinian state.[2]

Commitment to the Palestinian cause has been a leading feature of Rakah since its inception fifteen years ago, as the result of a split in Maki, Miflaga Kommunistit Israelit (Israeli Communist Party). The latter came into being in October 1948 as a consequence of the merger of the Communist Party of Palestine and what had remained of the League of National Liberation. The division in the Palestinian Communist movement had occurred five years earlier,[3] with the (Arab) LNL advocating a unified, indivisible, democratic Palestine, and the (Jewish) CPP demanding a binational state in Palestine. Once Moscow came out in favour of partition, in late 1947, the LNL divided into those Arabs who joined the Arab 'preventive war' against Israel, and became exiles, and those who stayed behind in Israel.

In the first parliamentary poll of 1949 Maki secured 3 per cent of the popular vote, with the Arabs – then only 3.5 per cent of the electorate – contributing a third of the total.[4] A rapid increase in the population led to an impressive expansion of the party's base. With 8,000 members on its rolls in 1951, it could claim to be more than three times larger than the CPP and the LNL (of 1946) put together.[5] A split in Mapam – a Marxist but Zionist party – two years later helped Maki further: it brought Mapam's leftist dissidents into its fold. In the parliamentary election of

1955 the party improved its share of seats from four to six (in a house of 120).

Maki took particular interest in the welfare of the Arab minority. It opposed military administration of the Arab-inhabited areas, and fought discrimination against Arab citizens, whether by the military authorities or Histadrut. It was the only party to oppose Israeli aggression in the Suez crisis of 1956, describing it as being 'with the imperialists (and) against the Arab peoples'.[6] This increased its popularity among Arabs, who now joined in greater numbers than Jews. It cooperated with the nationalist elements within the Arab community. But this ended in 1959, when it sided with Iraq's Qassem in his rivalry with Egypt's Nasser. As a result, the party suffered a setback in its Arab constituency. Its parliamentary strength was halved in the elections held in November.

Later, as the Soviet Union patched up its differences with Nasser and began pursuing consistently pro-Arab policies, a cleavage developed in Maki. The pro-Arab faction backed the Soviet line, and called for cooperation with the Arab Communist parties; whereas the pro-Jewish faction opposed Moscow's stance and advocated allying with certain Zionist workers' parties to form a Popular Front, and supporting additional Jewish immigration. The chasm between the two sides widened in late 1963, when Arab–Israeli tension mounted due to Tel Aviv's imminent plans to divert the Jordan river's waters. The pro-Jewish wing proposed joining the national effort to increase security, thus ending the party's isolation from the political mainstream. Arguing that Israeli defences were more than adequate, the pro-Arab wing stated that it was important to help prevent 'declining imperialism from using the rulers of Israel for its aim of provoking conflict [in the region], as it has done in the past'.[7]

During the next year the pro-Jewish wing, led by Moshe Sneh and Shamuel Mikunis, became more critical of Moscow, as the latter refused to change its policy of prohibiting the emigration of Jews, and showed sympathy for the PLO. This in turn accentuated the division within Maki. The international department of the Communist Party of the Soviet Union tried to reconcile the two groups but failed: by June 1965 a split had become inevitable. Two months later Meir Vilner and Tawfiq Toubi, the pro-Arabist leaders, left the parent body, taking with them all the 2,000 Arab members, and a section of the equally numerous Jewish members.[8] The breakaway party offered its own list of candidates in the parliamentary election, held in November, under the name of Rakah. It won three seats; Maki one.

Unwilling to accept the division of the Israeli Communists as permanent, the CPSU international department attempted to unite the two parties. This went on until the June 1967 war, which Maki supported. 'The truth is that Israel has repelled and defeated an aggression which threatened her very existence, and did not attack her neighbours,' said a party statement.[9] In contrast Rakah blamed the Israeli government for 'an aggressive war', with its leader, Vilner, later stating that America had provoked the confrontation in order to prepare the ground for installing a pro-American regime in Damascus.[10] Soon after, the CPSU recognised Rakah as the official Communist party of Israel.

The two parties came out with divergent policies on the post-war situation. Maki's Sneh declared that an unconditional Israeli withdrawal from the occupied territories would be 'tantamount to inviting another war'. Rakah's leaders, on the other hand, opposed annexation of any part of the occupied territories, and endorsed UN resolution 242. Their stand was ratified by the party congress held in early 1969, and attended by 376 delegates, evenly divided among Arabs and Jews.[11] In the autumn elections, their party retained its three seats. (Maki too kept its one seat.)

Israel's performance in the Yom Kippur war made the local Arabs realise that the Zionist state was not invincible. This encouraged more Arabs to vote for Rakah than before, particularly when it was the only party in the December 1973 poll to demand an unconditional Israeli withdrawal from the occupied territories, and recognition of the national rights of the Palestinians. With 37 per cent of the Arabs backing it, Rakah's strength in parliament rose to four. (Maki failed to retain its solitary seat, and finally disintegrated eighteen months later.) In the Arab town of Nazareth, Rakah won 59 per cent of the vote:[12] a performance it repeated in the municipal election held in December 1975 when, in conjunction with a local group of academics, merchants and workers, it secured eleven of the sixteen seats, and mayorship.[13] By spearheading the protest against the government's takeover of 2,000 acres of Arab land in the Galilee district, through a one-day strike on 30 March, named the 'Day of the Land', Rakah consolidated its popularity in the area.[14]

The following month Rakah supporters were gratified when voters on the West Bank elected radical mayors and councillors in all but one of the twenty-four towns.[15] The West Bankers had voted overwhelmingly for the National Bloc candidates, chosen under the aegis of the Palestine National Front – the semi-clandestine arm of the PLO in the occupied territories since 1973 – with which Rakah had fraternal relations.

Not surprisingly, in early May 1977 the Rakah representatives to an international conference in Prague had an official meeting with the PLO delegates: a fact which was publicised by Moscow Radio.[16] The PLO appealed to the Israeli Arabs to vote for the Democratic Front for Peace and Equality, consisting of Rakah and the Black Panther Party, composed of Sephardic Jews.[17] The Front won 50 per cent of all the Arab vote, and five parliamentary seats.[18]

Aside from Rakah and Maki, the only other anti-Zionist party which made any impact on Israeli society, during its decade-long existence, was the Israeli Socialist Organisation, better known by the name of its journal, *Matzpen* (Compass). Formed by a group of former (Jewish) members of Maki in 1962, the ISO made anti-Zionism its primary ideology. It opposed the 1967 war and carried out a dialogue with such Palestinian parties as the DFLP.[19] As such it came to be portrayed as a 'traitor party' by the Zionist establishment. Sustained harassment and the persecution of its members by official agencies led to its disintegration in the early 1970s.

Within the Zionist spectrum, Mapam is the most left-wing. Although formed in 1946 its roots go back to 1919, when about a hundred Zionists from east Europe founded the Hashomer HaTzair (Young Guards). Imbued with Marxism, they envisaged themselves as part of the international proletariat, and established kibbutzim, agricultural settlements. Eight years later they consolidated their collectives under HaKibbutz HaErtzi (National Kibbutz), the largest of the three organisations of its kind.

They joined Mapai, Mifleget Poalei Israel (Israeli Workers' Party, often known as Israeli Labour Party), at the time of its founding in 1930, with the hope that as the Marxist core of the party they would convert the united labour movement to the ideas of class struggle and binational socialist revolution. In 1936 they formed socialist leagues to link up with the Marxists living outside the kibbutzim. Thus strengthened they won a fifth of the seats for the Histadrut conference of 1939.

Opposed to the idea of a Jewish state in Palestine, the Hashomers first joined the League of Jewish–Arab Rapprochement and Cooperation, functioning within the Zionist movement, and then the Ihud (Unity) Association, which was outside the Zionist movement, to promote the idea of a binational state in Palestine. But their efforts failed. In 1945 Hashomer HaTzair transformed itself into a political party, which merged with the leftist LeAhdut HaAvoda (For Labour Unity) in the following year, to form Mapam.

The party was sympathetic towards the USSR, and did not drop its opposition to partition until Moscow had voted for a partition plan at the UN in late 1947. It then rationalised its new stand on the ground that only a divided Palestine offered an opportunity for the realisation of Zionism. Once Israel was founded, Mapam became the leading voice of the left inside parliament and outside. Its nineteen-member bloc in the first Knesset attacked the Mapai-led government for accepting a $100 million loan from the Export-Import Bank of America and a grant from Washington,[20] and endorsing the Tripartite Declaration of May 1950. Internally the party offered a socialist programme for absorbing the large numbers of newly arrived immigrants: to organise them into collective agrarian and industrial units, to nationalise natural resources and large capitalist enterprises, and to rely on internal capital formation for economic development.

Under the leadership of Moshe Sneh its relations with Maki improved, while those with Mapai deteriorated to the point where many kibbutzim began to split along political lines. Such divisions reflected themselves in Mapam's reduced strength in the second Knesset of 1951: down to fifteen. The sentencing of Mordechai Oran, a Mapam leader, during his stay in Prague in late 1952, as a spy, created anti-Soviet bloc feeling in the party, and led to Sneh's expulsion from it. Mapam lost two of its parliamentarians to Mapai, two to Maki (which Sneh joined in 1954), and four to the revived Ahdut HaAvoda (United Labour), a nationalist organisation.

A smaller Mapam contingent in the third Knesset was markedly less leftist and less inclined towards the Soviet bloc. In fact, following the arms deal between Prague and Cairo in September 1955, the party joined the Mapai-led coalition already in office. It formed part of the government which decided to collude with France and Britain to attack Egypt. While it opposed the collusion proposals in the cabinet, it refrained from attacking them publicly.[21] Later, however, Mapam went so far as to demand annexation of Sinai, and led demonstrations against Israeli withdrawal from the peninsula.[22]

For the next three elections it secured eight to nine seats, and coalesced with Mapai in forming the government. When it supported the Six Day war it lost some leftist members, who went on to establish Siah, Smol Israel Hadash (New Israeli Left). It allied itself with Maarach (Alignment) in the 1969 parliamentary poll, and has since then continued this policy. It has refused to merge into the (Labour) Alignment. As a recognised Zionist body, it receives funds from the Jewish Agency, and thus has no financial problem in maintaining the party machine, publishing a daily, *Al Hamishmar* (The Guardian) – with the banner 'To Zionism, Socialism, and Friendship between Nations' – and running a publicity apparatus abroad.

The largest single contribution by the Jewish Agency to a political organisation goes to the Labour Alignment, the biggest political party in Israel. It was formed in 1968 by the amalgamation of a few small parties with Mapai, which was founded nearly four decades earlier. In a wider context, Mapai was part of the Jewish labour movement in Europe, whose roots stretched as far back as September 1897, when Bund (League) was set up in Vilna, Lithuania, as the general Jewish workers' union in Lithuania, Poland, and Russia, a month after the first Zionist congress in Basle, Switzerland.

Three years later Poale Zion (Workers of Zion), the first Zionist workers' party, was established in Minsk, Russia, with a programme of socialism, Zionism, and migration to Palestine. From Russia it spread to Austria and then to America. Its leading ideologue, Don Ber Borochov, a Russian Jew, argued that before Jews could launch a class struggle they had first to achieve nationhood, and for that they had to have a country of their own. He chose Palestine, partly because it was regarded as the historic homeland of Jews, and partly because, being a 'derelict country', it held interest only for small and middle Jewish capitalists – not the big ones – and thus offered revolutionary promise for the Jewish proletariat, which was to be fostered there. He regarded local Arabs as Turkish subjects, lacking national consciousness, and visualised their assimilation, economic and cultural, into the Jewish nation as it developed economically under Jewish initiative and leadership.[23]

Borochov's emphasis on creating a Jewish working class in Palestine seemed to dovetail with the views and actions of Aaron David Gordon, a Ukraine-born Jew, who arrived in Palestine in 1904, and HaPoale HaTzair (Young Workers) who, as followers of the 'conquest of labour' slogan, lived as manual workers. Gordon popularised the 'back to land' slogan of Zionism by taking to physical work on the land. And by resorting to draining marshes and setting up agricultural outposts, HaPoale HaTzair members helped to create Jewish wage labour in agriculture.

When the Borochovists found the established Jewish planters in the coastal plain unwilling to forego cheap Arab labour and hire Jewish immigrants, they went to Galilee, where the WZO's Jewish National Fund had started acquiring land. Here they tried the cooperative principle on land. The first kvutza (collective group) was formed in Degania in 1911, and included Gordon. The next few years witnessed the rise of a dozen kvutzot: a phenomenon which illustrated at this early stage how a link was being forged, through the WZO, between the local socialist Jewish immigrants and bourgeois Jewish capital abroad. As the forerunner of the kibbutzim movement, kvutzot were to have an important socio-economic bearing on Jewish society.

Increasing cooperation between socialist pioneers and the WZO's financial institutions caused a split in Poale Zion, with its leftist section leaving in 1919, and forming Mopsi, Mifleget Poalim Sozialistim (Socialist Workers' Party).[24] Poale Zion's rightist, nationalist faction, led among others by David Ben-Gurion, merged with the 'non-party' followers of Berle Katznelson to establish Ahdut HaAvoda.

Soon Ahdut HaAvodah and HaPoale HaTzair agreed to form an umbrella organisation to encompass all labour-pioneer parties of Zionist persuasion. The result was Histadrut. About three fifths of the 7,000 Jewish workers then in Palestine participated in electing delegates to the founding convention of Histadrut in December 1920. Ahdut HaAvodah emerged as the single largest group in Histadrut, just as it had done in the first Yishuv (Jewish community in Palestine) assembly election held earlier in the year. Both elections were held on the basis of proportional representation – a system which has persisted in these institutions since then.

With successive elections to Histadrut conferences showing Ahdut HaAvoda and HaPoale HaTzair to be the leading parties, pressure grew on their leaders to seek a merger. This resulted in the founding of Mapai in January 1930 under the stewardship of Chaim Arlosoroff. Of the new organisation's 5,650 members about 3,000 came from Ahdut HaAvoda.[25] Following the murder of Arlosoroff in 1933, Ben-Gurion became the head of Mapai.

By then the Yishuv assembly had been given powers – under the British mandate's Religious Communities (Organisation) Ordinance of 1926 – to conduct religious courts, perform such local government functions as education and welfare, and collect taxes on a voluntary basis. The assembly had a national council of twenty-three: of these Mapai held eleven seats. This had a profound effect on the party's ideology and perceptions. 'As Mapai became responsible for national decisions, its concentration on national problems took a toll of [its] socialist commitment, so that in practice the party was increasingly identified in the line of succession to [the nationalist] HaPoale HaTzair,' states Noah Lucas. 'Controversy within the labour movement now shifted from HaPoale HaTzair's nationalist critique of Ahdut HaAvoda to a new socialist critique of Mapai's nationalist policies.'[26]

Over the years the issue of establishing the Jewish state developed as the touchstone to separate socialists from nationalists. The leftists opposed the proposition at the Mapai conference of October 1941. A year later they suffered a setback when the WZO adopted it as its official policy. The crunch came in the autumn of 1944 when Ben-Gurion, as the head of Histadrut, instructed its delegation to an international trade union conference to call for the founding of a Jewish state. By refusing to accept this directive the leftist Histadrut delegates precipitated a split in Mapai. The result was the formation of LeAhdut HaAvoda, which merged with another leftist organisation in 1946 to create Mapam.[27]

Although formed as a non-political trade union federation, Histadrut had functioned as a far more complex body. It had engaged in offering vocational training, building public works, encouraging immigration, settling newcomers, and organising defence. Haganah, its defence organ, grew rapidly during the Arab revolt of 1936–9.[28] With tens of thousands of Jewish settlers joining the Allied forces in the course of the Second World War, the fighting capacity of the Yishuv increased dramatically.

After the war, backed by Jewish Agency funds, Ben-Gurion, in his role of Histadrut chief, began purchasing arms in Europe, particularly France and Czechoslovakia.[29] His appointment as head of the defence department of the WZO in December 1946 enabled him to bring the various Jewish armed organisations in Palestine under a single command. Early the following year, noticing a convergence of the American and Soviet positions on the partition of Palestine, the Yishuv assembly's national council, led once again by Ben-Gurion, began formulating plans to consolidate the Jewish segment, militarily and otherwise. By the time the United Nations adopted the partition plan in late November, the Yishuv had in the Haganah a large, professional fighting force, supported by 79,000 reserves, armed police and home guards.[30]

For the first four months of the Arab–Jewish hostilities, which erupted immediately after the UN resolution, the Zionist forces fought a defensive war. But in April and the first half of May they went on the offensive, and expelled most of the Arab inhabitants from the prospective Jewish state.[31] By then, at the behest of Ben-Gurion, the Jewish Agency (recognised by the British mandate as the official representative of Palestine Jews) had transferred all its executive powers to the people's administrative committee of the Yishuv assembly's national council.

It was this committee of thirteen, headed by Ben-Gurion and functioning as the provisional government, which declared the independence of the state of Israel on 15 May 1948, and which established the Israel Defence Force ten days later. Within two months the IDF emerged as a well-armed and well-trained force of 60,000.

Once it had defeated the Arab armies and consolidated its military positions, negotiations to define Israel's boundaries with its Arab neighbours began, in early January, on the island of Rhodes, Greece. At about the same time Israeli political parties launched their campaigns for elections to the first Knesset. On 25 January 86 per cent of the 506,000 voters participated in the poll, held on the basis of proportional representation.

With forty-six of the 120 parliamentary seats to its credit, Mapai emerged as the leading party. Its share of seats was about the same in the second Knesset, elected in July 1951, when Israel's population was nearly twice as great as at its founding. This did not mean that the recent immigrants, mostly from Arab states, were as social-democratic as those already settled. It simply meant that the newcomers were heavily dependent on help from the bureaucracies of the local and national governments, the Jewish Agency, and Histadrut; and that these were manned by nominees of the various Zionist parties in approximate proportion to their popular standing, as measured by successive elections to the quasi-governmental organs that had grown up since 1920. As 'the most lucid symbol of state power', offering the new immigrant 'the most plausible key to personal participation and assimilation' into Israeli society, Mapai emerged as the most popular party among the newly arrived.[32]

It was during these early years, from 1948 to 1952, that decisions of fundamental importance to the state's future were taken; and by and large they reflected the views of Mapai's leadership. 'The capitalist economy run by labour bureaucracy was chosen rather than socialism; the secular society with a dash of mysticism and sentiment, always making allowances for the minimum proprieties in deference to religious sensibilities, quickly ruled out theocracy; the fully-fledged Western orientation due to pressing need for capital to underpin mass immigration ruled out neutralism; and reliance on force soon superseded the option . . . of conciliation of the Arab world,' states Noah Lucas, a historian of Israel.[33]

Having played a leading role in shaping the basic outline of Israel's internal and external policies, Ben-Gurion, who had dominated the Zionist politics of Palestine since the early 1930s, resigned as prime minister in December 1953. He was followed by Moshe Sharett. His defence minister, Pinchas Lavon, authorised a sabotage campaign in Egypt, which backfired. A Jewish espionage-sabotage cell in Cairo and Alexandria planted bombs in local cinemas, post offices, and railway stations as well as in American consulates, information centres and libraries, in order to create a sense of insecurity, and sour Egypt's relations with the West. Within weeks of these plantings all thirteen Israeli agents were arrested. Lavon resigned on the grounds of an unnamed 'security mishap'. Ben-Gurion was recalled and given the defence portfolio in February 1955, at a time when Israeli leaders and mass media were venomously describing the trial of the accused Jewish saboteurs as 'show trials' being conducted to boost the sagging morale of Nasser's regime. When the two ringleaders were executed by the Egyptian authorities Ben-Gurion retaliated by ordering a massive attack on an Egyptian military camp in Gaza, which resulted in the death of thirty-eight Egyptian soldiers.[34] (This was the trigger which led Nasser to seek arms from the Soviet bloc: a step which culminated in the Suez war.)

As feelings towards Cairo turned more hostile and anger at Moscow more intense – in the wake of the Egyptian–Czech arms deal – the Mapai-led administration secured the cooperation of Mapam (to its left) and Ahdut HaAvoda (to its right) to enlarge popular support for the government. Israel's attack on Egypt in late 1956 thus had the direct backing of all parties, except the right-wing nationalists and the Communists.

The swift occupation of the Sinai peninsula raised the morale of the military, government, and Mapai, as nothing else had done since the founding of the Jewish state. 'After 1956 . . . the frontiers were secure, if not entirely peaceful,' notes V. D. Segre, an Israeli political scientist. 'The Israeli army [consisting mainly of conscripts], which up to 1953 had suffered from problems of organisation and command, had by now established itself as the most efficient military, political, and socially unifying factor in the country. The Sinai campaign had been a crowning achievement of its nationwide efforts at integration. . . . Economically and militarily, it was no longer a question of survival, but of choosing between alternative ways of life.'[35]

Little wonder that Mapai, contesting the November 1959 election under Ben-Gurion, improved its share of seats by seven. But the old controversy about Lavon's 'security mishap' re-surfaced; and this damaged the prestige both of the party and the government. Mapai lost five parliamentary seats in the August 1961 poll, which it fought under the direction of Levi Eshkol.

Simmering controversy erupted within Mapai about ideology and tactics, specially its relations with Ahdut HaAvoda; the Lavon affair; and personality clashes surfaced between Ben-Gurion, the ageing party stalwart, Prime Minister Eshkol, and Lavon – then head of Histadrut: all these combined to produce an atmosphere of crisis in the party. The leadership tried to dissipate it by recommending Mapai's merger with Ahdut HaAvoda.[36] The party's convention, meeting in February 1965, ratified the decision. Disagreeing with this, Ben-Gurion and his followers left the party, and offered their own list, Rafi, Reshima Poale Israel (Israeli Workers' List), in the elections held in November.

Rafi did poorly. It won only ten seats, while Mapai secured forty-five. Ben-Gurion's personal popularity proved woefully unequal to the institutional strength of his former party. But the Mapai leaders found little to rejoice in, as the recession, which had begun earlier in 1966, deepened. It proved to be the first year in Israel's history when it had more emigrants than immigrants. With over 100,000 out of work in early 1967 the country's unemployment rate reached a record 10 per cent.[37]

It was also during this period that Israel became the target of guerrilla attacks by Palestinians operating from Jordan and Syria. The Mapai-led government retaliated with unprecedented harshness. 'The reprisal actions of 1965–66 differed from those which preceded the Sinai campaign,' states *The Paratroopers' Book*, the semi-official history of the IDF's airborne corps. 'The operations were no longer acts of vengeance, savage and nervous, of a small state fighting for its independence. Rather, they were blows struck by a state strong and sure of itself, and which did not fear the army it confronted.'[38]

This was the backdrop against which, on 7 April 1967, the IDF escalated the already tense situation existing on the eastern front by bombing the Syrian Heights, buzzing the outskirts of Damascus, and engaging in dogfights in Syrian airspace.[39] Nationalist fervour rose to such a pitch that even the hitherto untouchable Gahal, Gush Herut-Liberalim (Freedom-Liberal bloc), led by Menachem Begin, became respectable enough to be invited to join the government. It did on 1 June. Four days later the government of national unity launched surprise, pre-emptive attacks on Egypt, Syria and Jordan.

A spectacular victory in the war helped to cement the national unity coalition. It was unanimous in its decision to annex east Jerusalem into Israel. The differences which arose between the coalition partners, and within Mapai, on the future of the rest of the occupied territories were contained by postponing the formulation of a coherent policy on the subject. The consensual climate proved conducive to consummate, in early 1968, the previous decision to amalgamate Mapai with Ahdut HaAvoda (and Rafi as well) to form Maarach, with a resultant parliamentary strength of fifty-five.

These consensual politics were not disturbed by the elections of October 1969. While the Labour Alignment allied with Mapam to offer a joint list of candidates, Gahal offered a manifesto which was not much different from that of the Labour Alignment. The various parties virtually retained their previous strengths in the new Knesset, and the national unity government which followed had the same composition as before. It was not until Prime Minister Golda Meir (who had succeeded Eshkol after his death in February 1969) accepted the William Rogers peace plan in July 1970 that Gahal objected and left the government.

An important consequence of this was that the colonisation of the West Bank, Gaza and Golan Heights, which had been quietly initiated earlier, continued unchecked. The moderates within Maarach were now afraid that any confrontation with the hardliners on the subject would drive them (as well as the National Religious Party in the coalition) into the arms of Gahal, and bring about the downfall of the Alignment-led government. It was thus that the unity of the Labour Alignment was maintained, and the government given a chance to serve its full four-year term.

The attention of all political parties was focused on the impending parliamentary poll, due in late October 1973 – with the newly formed Likud bloc, consisting of Gahal and other small right-wing, nationalist groups, emerging as a serious challenger to the Alignment-Mapam alliance – when the country was attacked by Egypt and Syria on 6 October. The IDF's unpreparedness for war provided additional ammunition to Likud in its attacks on the ruling alliance. The latter tried to counter this by appointing an official committee to investigate the opposition's charges, and by building up the Middle East conference, to be held on 22 December in Geneva, as a major breakthrough to peace and security.

Still, the Alignment-Mapam bloc lost five seats, retaining fifty-one, while Likud gained eight, to score a total of thirty-nine. This encouraged the religious parties to take a hard line in their negotiations with Golda Meir, the Alignment leader, on joining a coalition government. An exasperated Meir formed a minority administration with the support of fifty-eight deputies. It did not last long. The report of the official commission on the Yom Kippur war, published in March, blamed General David Elazar for what went wrong, and cleared Moshe Dayan, the defence minister. However, when Elazar resigned, pressure on Dayan to do the same mounted. He refused. To get around the problem Meir offered the resignation of her full cabinet to the republic's president. In the subsequent election for the party leader, the 600-odd members of the Alignment's central committee favoured Yitzhak Rabin over Shimon Peres by 298 votes to 254.[40]

Since the National Religious Party now agreed to join the coalition headed by Rabin, he managed to form a majority government. However, as the inflation rate soared to 50 per cent a year, and popular discontent grew, the Rabin administration became less and less secure. The year 1976 proved to be one of rising social tensions, and the forerunner of a series of financial scandals. In February the conflict between the government and the trade unions surfaced when union leaders publicly criticised ministers for ignoring resolutions passed by various organs of the Alignment. Three months later, in a milieu of strikes and labour unrest, policemen were subjected to grenade attacks by the slum dwellers of Tel Aviv. In November, following an increase of 20 per cent in food and transport charges, workers staged a series of strikes. Earlier, Asher Yadlin, appointed governor of the Bank of Israel by Rabin, was indicted on charges of bribery and fraud committed during his term as director of Histadrut's sick fund. In December the ruling coalition fell apart and a fresh poll was announced for 17 May.

Events during the run-up to the elections confirmed the Labour Alignment's image as a corrupt and divided party. In January, following a financial scandal, housing minister Avraham Ofer – who had conducted Rabin's successful campaign for party leader in 1974 – committed suicide. Some weeks later Yadlin confessed that he had channelled 'black money' into Alignment funds. Not surprisingly, when Rabin sought re-election as party chief he was challenged by Peres. The fact that he defeated the challenge by a margin of forty-one, in an electoral college of 3,000 delegates, showed that the party was divided right down the middle.[41] In March it was revealed that, while serving as ambassador in Washington, Rabin had maintained an active bank account there, an illegal act. The next month he resigned; and the party delegates elected Peres as leader. This occurred against a background of revelations that organised crime had taken roots in the country. 'We [Labour] allowed crime to flourish, a mafia to establish itself, and the spreading of drugs even in schools,' said David HaCohen, a veteran Labour Alignment leader.[42]

Little wonder that the Alignment-Mapam bloc lost nineteen seats in the May election, and that fifteen of these went to the Democratic Movement for Change, a party formed by Yigael Yadin, an archaeology professor, only seven months earlier. It had contested the parliamentary poll on the platform of reforming the electoral system, improving the lot of the Sephardic Jews, and, above all, cleansing the administrative and political apparatuses, which had been soiled primarily by the corrupt and nepotistic ways of the Labour establishment.[43] 'Israel has been governed [for three decades] by interlocking groups of ministers and senior officials, many of them from an elite of about 250 families who rose to prominence in the pioneering days,' wrote Eric Marsden in the *Sunday Times*. 'Along the way many establishment members, and more particularly their sons, have changed direction. There are many instances of fervent egalitarian socialists from the kibbutzim whose sons have become capitalist entrepreneurs, technocrats or army leaders, with a right-wing outlook, while still paying lip service to the Labour movement.'[44]

As such the emergence of Likud as the largest bloc in the ninth Knesset, ahead of Alignment-Mapam by eleven seats, seemed apt in more ways than one. Headed by Menachem Begin – who had by then won the respect even of his opponents as 'an honest, ascetic patriot and an able and dedicated leader'[45] – Likud had presented itself to the voters as an orderly and principled entity. With the help of the religious parties, which held sixteen seats, and Moshe Dayan, who defected from the Alignment to become foreign minister, Begin formed the government. It had taken him nearly three decades to assume prime executive authority since the formation of Herut, the first political party he had led.

Begin had arrived in Palestine from his native Poland in 1942, and had within a year become the Irgun chief. The origins of Irgun went back to 1931 when a group of Haganah commanders, disagreeing with their organisation's policy of restraint towards their Arab opponents, had led their followers into the camp of the Revisionist Zionists. The latter were so called because they wanted to revise the Labour Zionists' strategy of setting up a Jewish state in Palestine through colonisation, and return to Theodor Herzl's original concept of Jewish statehood through international recognition of Jewish sovereignty over Palestine. Led by Vladimir Jabotinsky, the Revisionists opposed Britain's decision of 1922 to apply the idea of a Jewish homeland only to the Palestine lying west of the river Jordan. They advocated compelling Britain to build a Jewish homeland with all the resources at its disposal. Unlike the Labour Zionists, they were for giving primacy to private capital to develop Palestine, and forbidding the Marxist concept of class struggle.

The International Union of Revisionist Zionists, set up in 1925, steadily improved its standing. At the WZO congress of 1931 one fifth of the delegates supported the Revisionist line. A few years later efforts were made to conciliate the Revisionists with the Labour Zionists in Palestine. These showed promise, but ended in failure. The Revionists left the WZO in 1937 and formed the New Zionist Organisation. In an effort to found institutions parallel to those of Histadrut in Palestine, they turned Irgun into their military wing (just as Haganah was the military arm of Histadrut). During the Arab revolt, Irgun's policy of going on the offensive against the Arabs bolstered its ranks. The restrictions proposed in the British White Paper of 1939 on Jewish immigration further increased the popularity of Irgun, which had resorted to smuggling immigrants into Palestine as early as 1935. Between then and 1942 it brought in 30,000 illegal immigrants.[46] Except for a brief period during the Second World War it pursued a policy of violent opposition to the British mandate.

After the war Irgun members took to sabotaging British military installations and executing soldiers captured during their anti-British raids. Their success in blowing up the King David Hotel in Jerusalem on 22 July 1946 underlined their importance.[47] During the months preceding the founding of Israel they cooperated with Lehy, another armed Zionist body, in carrying out concerted attacks on Arabs – including the massacre of Deir Yassin,[48] and a fully-fledged offensive against the Arabs of Jaffa.

Led by Begin, the Irgun ranks refused to be absorbed into the Israel Defence Force formed by the provisional government on 26 May 1948. They participated in the war against Arab states as a separate entity. In late June, Ben-Gurion, acting as chief executive, brought matters to a head by forbidding Irgun leaders from delivering arms to their troops, scattered along the beaches from Tel Aviv to Haifa, from the ship *Altalena*. When the Irgun commanders tried to steer the ship to the shore, Ben-Gurion ordered the IDF to attack it. Forty Irgun soldiers were killed, and many more injured.[49] This led to the disbandment of Irgun.

Soon Irgun's former ranks and the Revisionists re-emerged as Herut, headed once again by Begin. The party advocated the establishment of Biblical Eretz Israel on both banks of the Jordan, and the separation of trade unions from the various social services and business organisations being managed by Histadrut. 'With its strident nationalist rhetoric and its vehement antipathy towards Histadrut,' states Noah Lucas, 'Herut succeeded in attracting those new immigrants, especially from the countries of the Middle East, who felt dissatisfaction or nursed concrete grievances in the experience of assimilation into their new life.'[50] The importance of Histadrut to the new immigrants lay in the fact that it provided a national health service, and operated mutual aid and pension schemes; and that, over the years, it became the second largest employer, next only to the state, producing over one fifth of the gross national product.[51]

In the 1950s with fourteen to seventeen deputies loyal to it, Herut was often the largest opposition group in parliament. It was not until 1961 that Herut found another group on the opposition benches which matched its strength: the Liberals. During that year the Liberal Party was created by the merger of the General Zionists and the Progressives. Although the term General Zionists (Zionim Klaliyim) was first used at the Zionist congress of 1907 to denote the delegates unattached either to labour Zionism or religious Zionism, the General Zionist party came into being in Palestine only in 1930. Since it had by then come to represent the capitalist strand within Zionism, it drew the support of businessmen, industrialists, planters, and traders. Four years later the party split into the liberal 'A' faction (sympathetic to labour) and the conservative 'B' faction. These factions were reunited in 1944.

Shortly after the founding of Israel the liberal 'A' faction left the parent body to combine with the German-dominated Aliyah Hadash (New Immigrants) Party to form the Progressive Party. Backed by four to six deputies the group joined the various Mapai-dominated governments of the 1950s. During this decade the General Zionists saw their parliamentary strength fall steadily from twenty to eight. Fear of a further, possibly fatal, decline led the General Zionist leaders to seek a merger with the

Progressives on the eve of the 1961 general election. The result was a Liberal Party with a contingent of seventeen deputies in the Knesset.

Sharing the opposition benches in the Knesset, the Liberal and Herut leaders entered negotiations to establish a common bloc – only to find that their differences over equal rights for women, relations between the state and religion, and policies towards their Arab neighbours were insurmountable. But the split in the Labour movement, with Ben-Gurion quitting Mapai, changed the situation. Tempted by the possibility of capturing power in the elections of November 1965, the two opposition parties forged an alliance, Gahal. But Gahal won only twenty-six seats, and trailed well behind Mapai. None the less, its position as the second largest bloc in the new Knesset was secure.

Being invited to join the national unity government on the eve of the June 1967 war made Gahal and particularly its leader, Begin, respectable. Not surprisingly, it retained its previous parliamentary strength in the October 1969 poll. Its exit from the government the next summer helped the hardliners within the Labour Alignment to neutralise the moderates' opposition to the administration's colonisation policies in the occupied territories.[52]

Gahal's electoral chances improved substantially when, following the Yom Kippur war, it combined with two right-wing groups and the Eretz Israel movement – headed by General Ariel Sharon, a hero of the war – to form Likud. The major element which brought these parties together was their commitment to incorporate the occupied territories into Israel. Ideologically, Likud was an alliance of the conservative, capitalist, and ultra-nationalist trends within secular Zionism. The results of the December 1973 election showed that the cumulative strength of these forces, at 30.2 per cent of popular vote, was only 8.5 per cent behind that of the liberal, social democratic forces, as represented by the Alignment–Mapam alliance.[53]

In the subsequent poll of May 1977 Likud, backed by 33.4 per cent of the voters, emerged 7.4 per cent ahead of its rival.[54] This was, in a way, an aggregate measure of the right-wing drift of Israeli society, which had begun soon after the founding of the Jewish state nearly three decades earlier.

That the religious parties responded warmly to Begin's invitation to join the government came as no surprise. After all they had been ideologically more akin to the ultra-nationalism and conservatism preached by Begin than to the liberalism and social democracy advocated by Labour leaders. With an aggregate of 14 per cent of the electorate to its credit, the religious bloc boosted total electoral support for the new administration to over 47 per cent, thus considerably reducing the need for drafting the Democratic Movement for Change into office.

Backed by ten to twelve deputies, Mafdal, Mifleget Datit Leumit (National Religious Party), has been the largest entity of its kind. It was formed in 1956 by the merger of Mizrahi, Merkaz Rouhani (Spiritual Centre), and Poale HaMizrahi (Workers of Mizrahi). Of these two organisations, Mizrahi was the older. In fact, its formation in 1902 by a group of rabbis, in protest against the growing secularisation of the education of Jews in east Europe, marked the rise of religious Zionism as a distinct faction within the overall Zionist movement. The party advocated founding the Jewish national home in Palestine along traditional Judaistic lines.

Since its branch in Palestine had many workers, its younger members formed Poale HaMizrahi in 1921. This, in turn, established a confederation of trade unions, a group of kibbutzim, and a network of religiously oriented schools. It acquired a separate, and a far more important, identity of its own. Both organisations participated in the activities of the Zionist movement, and in the Yishuv's quasi-governmental organs.

In contrast, Agudat Israel (Community of Israel) and Poale Agudat Israel (Workers of the Community of Israel) boycotted these institutions. They did so primarily because the creation of Israel through human endeavour – such as was being undertaken by Zionist pioneers – ran counter to their belief that Israel, as a 'peoplehood', would be redeemed by the Messiah, and secondarily because they were opposed to women's suffrage. Morever, they considered Jews basically to be a religious, not national, entity, and believed that the Jewish problem could only be solved by the Torah, the Jewish law.[55]

On joining Agudat (established in Frankfurt, Germany, in 1911 as an international body), a member had to accept the supremacy of the Torah and regard it as the centrepiece of Jewish life. Agudat developed a major base in Poland: a country where Poale Agudat, formed in 1922, played a significant role in countering the anti-religious tide rising among the Jewish proletariat. In 1934 Poale Agudat in Palestine compromised the parent body's policy of non-cooperation with the World Zionist Organisation – considered non-Judaistic – by accepting money from the Jewish National Fund to set up kibbutzim, as well as a network of Talmudic and theological institutions. This caused a split in the organisation, with the upholders of the parental stance constituting themselves as Neturei Karta (Guardians of the Gate) the following year.[56]

After the founding of Israel, when both Agudat groups decided to participate in the state's affairs, Neturei Karta became the only Jewish body in Israel which refused to recognise the Zionist state.[57] On the eve of the first general election the Agudat parties allied with Mizrahi and Poale HaMizrahi to form the United Religious Front. It won sixteen seats and joined the government, to run inter alia the ministry of religious affairs. This enabled its constituents to determine the financing of religious councils and religious courts, as well as influence the composition and working of the powerful rabbinical council. The Front's disagreement with Prime Minister Ben-Gurion on the degree of control over religious education in schools caused the downfall of the government in mid-1951.

The Mizrahi and the Agudat blocs contested the next election separately, with the former winning ten seats and the latter five. Both were invited to participate in the new administration, and did so. A year later the Agudat parties left in protest against the passing of a law prescribing conscription for women. While maintaining a separate existence, they stayed in opposition throughout the era of the Labour-dominated governments.

Unlike the Agudat organisations, the Mizrahi groups unified to form Mafdal, and joined all the Labour-led administrations. Over the years Mafdal – i.e., the National Religious Party – established a tradition of running the ministries of education, religious affairs, and interior. After the Six Day war the party's commitment to creating Eretz Israel of Biblical times had an important bearing on official policies towards the occupied territories: it favoured hardliners within the Labour movement.

In 1968 some of the younger militant leaders of the NRP set up Gush Emunim (Bloc of the Faithful) within the party, to concentrate on incorporating Judea and Samaria into Israel.[58] Two years later Gush Emunim captured popular imagination by establishing an unauthorised settlement at Kiryat Arba near Hebron. The presence of the NRP inside the cabinet, and the fact that the government had itself initiated a programme of colonisation within months of the Six Day war, saw to it that no action was taken against the Gush settlers.[59] By the time the Labour Alignment lost power in mid-1977, eighty Jewish settlements, most of them authorised, had been set up in the occupied territories, with plans finalised for the building of forty-four more during the next four years; and Gush Emunim had emerged as an independent body.[60]

Installation of the Likud-dominated administration – with General Sharon, as agriculture minister, in charge of the overall settlements policy – boosted the morale of the NRP and Gush, whose views on Judea and Samaria had been endorsed by the powerful Ashkenazim Rabbinical Council.[61] Within three years of this government, Gush had established twenty illegal colonies on the West Bank, and widened its support there to the extent that it could easily muster 30,000 demonstrators on the West Bank.[62] Its settlement at Kiryat Arba, now accommodating 4,000 Jews, was the largest of its kind outside east Jerusalem. It housed not only Rabbi Moshe Levinger, the Gush leader, but also Rabbi Meir Kahane, head of Kach (Thus), which openly advocates the expulsion of all Arabs from Judea and Samaria.[63]

A notable feature of Kach is that its members feel no inhibitions about taking the law into their hands to achieve the party's goals. 'Kach's record in Israel leaves no doubt what it and its clenched fist symbol mean: Kach squads beating up Arabs in their homes, smashing cars and shop windows in Arab towns, insulting Arabs, harassing them, threatening them,' reported Philip Jacobson in October 1980. 'Rabbi Kahane leads by example.'[64] Such activities have brought Kahane sixty-two arrests during his residence in Israel since 1970 – but only two convictions.[65]

What partly explains the aggressiveness of Kach members, numbering 200 to 400, is the fact that most of them are young Jews from the USA who tend to return home after 'a few months of hell-raising on the West Bank'.[66] The ease and frequency with which American Jews travel to and from Israel is not surprising. After all, the Israeli Law of Return of 1950 gives a Jew of the diaspora (i.e. outside Israel[67]) an automatic right of travel to and citizenship of the Jewish state; and the USA and Israel together account for three fifths of world Jewry, with America's share being nearly twice as high as Israel's.[68] The Jewish Agency's estimate that 300,000 to 500,000 Israelis were living in the USA in 1980 illustrates the close ties between the two states.[69]

Almost all Israeli political, religious and social organisations have counterparts in America. Kach, for instance, is the extension of the Jewish Defence League, based in New York, which was headed by Kahane before he migrated to Israel in 1970. The National Religious Party claims the formal loyalty of the Religious Zionists of America; and Agudat Israel maintains close links with Moetzet Gedolei HaTorah (Council of Torah Sages) in the USA. Herut is officially associated with the Zionist Revisionists of America. The same is true of the social democratic spectrum of Israeli politics. The Labour Alignment has formal ties with the Labour Zionists of America, and Mapam with the Americans for Progressive Israel.[70] The American connection is extremely important to the Israeli organisations, particularly in financial terms. Even the non-Zionist Neturei Karta has to depend on the generosity of its patrons in New York to survive.[71]

All the Zionist groups of the USA are affiliated to the World Zionist Organisation, through the American Zionist Federation: so too are the Zionist bodies of Israel, albeit directly. Above and beyond that, the state of Israel has legal links with the WZO as well as the Jewish Agency, which was established in 1929 to concentrate on the 'ingathering' of the Jewish people into Palestine. These ties are spelled out in Israel's Status Law of 1952.[72]

Significantly, a year earlier, the biennial congress of the WZO had met in Israel for the first time, and decided to transfer the WZO headquarters from London to Jerusalem. The move was logical, insofar as at the WZO's founding in 1897 by the first Zionist congress, held in Basle, Theodor Herzl had described it as 'the Jewish state on the way'.[73] The WZO's executive committee emerged as a government of sorts, chosen by a congress elected by the Jews who had paid annual taxes, shekel, to be able to elect a delegate to the congress.[74] The executive's members ran such departments as information, land and development (in Palestine), immigration and absorption, Torah education and culture in the diaspora, and external affairs. This continues: the WZO's departmental heads now work in conjunction with their counterparts in the Israeli civil service.

In 1901 the WZO's land and development section set up the Keren Kayemet LeIsrael (Current Fund for Israel, often known as the Jewish National Fund) to finance the purchase of land in Palestine.[75] JNF leaders worked closely with the Jewish Agency which, soon after its establishment, won the British mandate's recognition as the political representative of the Jews in Palestine. The founding of Israel made little difference to the Jewish Agency's activities. In fact the Status Law specified statutory and covenantal links between the Agency and the Israeli state. By 1977, when the Agency's annual budget stood at $457 million, it had sponsored the immigration and settlement of over 1.5 million Jewish immigrants.[76]

As a result of the major reconstitution, in 1971, of all Jewish fund-raising organisations, the Jewish Agency emerged as the overall collector of contributions to the Zionist cause throughout the world. Although bearing different names – the United Jewish Appeal in America, the Joint Israel Appeal in Britain, and so on – its Keren Kayesod, Foundation Fund, came to operate in seventy countries. The aggregate collection under this heading, during the period 1948–76, amounted to $4,500 million, with two thirds of the sum originating in the USA.[77] This was just one more example of Israel's financial dependence on America, which continues.

The predominance of Americans and Israelis on the executive committees of the Jewish Agency and the WZO[78] underlines the fact that the American link is the single most important factor for Israel, not only financially but also politically. This is not surprising. 'During the course of the Second World War,' notes M. S. Agwani, an Indian specialist on the Middle East, 'the centre of the international Zionist movement had shifted from England to the USA, which housed the largest – and financially and politically the most influential – concentration of Jewish people in the world.'[79] However, the involvement of American administration in Zionist affairs goes as far back as the First World War.

# 10

# ISRAEL AND THE WEST

As an ally of Britain during the First World War, America played a major role, at a crucial moment, in the formulation of the Balfour Declaration, which was the end result of the convergence of Britain's imperial aims with Zionist aspirations. The Turkish offensive against the Allies across the Sinai peninsula, from Palestine, made the British government aware of the importance of Palestine to the defence of the strategic Suez Canal. It therefore resolved to secure exclusive rights over Palestine, after the Ottoman Turks had been defeated. One way to ensure this was to gain the active cooperation of world Jewry.

Yet the pro-Zionists in the government – led by prime minister Lloyd George and foreign minister Balfour – failed to win the approval of the cabinet, at a meeting in early September 1917, for their proposal to give official backing to the Zionist cause. They then sought the advice of Woodrow Wilson, the American president, known to be a pro-Zionist, through a Foreign Office enquiry. Wilson replied that the time was inappropriate for anything more than a statement of general sympathy.[1] But, as Robert W. Stookey, an American researcher and author, points out, 'A month later, under pressure of Zionist urgings and rumours of German courting of the [Zionist] movement, the British reopened the subject with President Wilson who, after some hesitation, approved a draft statement that, with minor editing, was issued by the British foreign minister [Balfour] on 2 November.'[2]

Although America did not join the League of Nations, and thus had nothing to do with the carving up of the former Ottoman empire, its Senate and House of Representatives adopted a joint resolution endorsing the Balfour Declaration soon after Britain had been given the Palestine mandate in 1922.[3] Two years later the American administration signed a treaty with Britain on the basis of the mandate which inter alia guaranteed America's (mainly Jewish) business interests there.

Persecution of Jews in Hitler's Germany of the mid-1930s aroused concern in America. This was officially expressed in the sponsorship of an international conference at Evian in July 1937, on the subject of Jewish refugees, by President Roosevelt. The conference, attended by many

Jewish organisations but not by the WZO, made little overall difference to the policies of the European governments at home.[4] As for the British in Palestine, they had by then allied themselves with the Zionist colonisers to fight the partisans of the Arab revolt: a development which went down well in America. Not surprisingly, the British White Paper of May 1939 was condemned by the House of Representatives foreign affairs committee, and twenty-eight senators, who described the defence of the Jewish settlers in Palestine as 'a moral obligation of the United States'.[5]

Three years later a conference of major American Zionist organisations, meeting at the Biltmore Hotel, New York, set the pace for Zionist goals by demanding that unlimited Jewish immigration be allowed into Palestine, all of which should become the 'Jewish Commonwealth'. These demands were endorsed by the American Jewish Congress, which claimed to represent 2.25 million Jews. By actively pursuing these aims sixteen Zionist bodies, with a membership of nearly half a million,[6] made American Zionism more militant than its British counterpart, or even the WZO. As a result of their efforts the House of Representatives declared in January 1944 that America 'shall . . . take appropriate measures . . . so that the Jewish people may ultimately reconstitute Palestine as a free and democratic Jewish Commonwealth'.[7] Later that year, during his election campaign, President Roosevelt said, 'If elected I shall help to bring about a free and democratic Jewish Commonwealth'.[8]

After Roosevelt's death in April 1945 his successor, Harry Truman, took an unambigiously pro-Zionist position. In August he pressured London immediately to admit all of the 100,000 Jewish refugees encamped in Cyprus. Britain refused, but agreed to the setting up of a joint Anglo–American commission on the Palestine problem. The resolution in favour of an independent Jewish state by the WZO congress in December 1946 strengthened the hands of such western leaders as Truman, who had eight months earlier described the Middle East as 'an area of great economic and strategic importance'.[9]

As Britain prepared to leave Turkey and Greece in early 1947, Truman committed America to protecting these countries against 'Communist aggression', thus inducting the Middle East into America's global strategy. Later in the year America supported the United Nations' plan for the partition of Palestine. 'The [UN] majority proposal met the Zionists' aim of an independent state, if not their concept of its geographic extent, and they mounted a campaign in the United States in its support that has, for pervasiveness, few parallels in our history,' states Robert W. Stookey.[10]

By the spring of 1948 – a presidential election year – the issue of the Jewish state had become entangled in electoral tactics. While Truman's Democratic Party had been weakened by splits, his rival, Thomas Dewey, the successful Republican governor of New York, was making a strong bid for Jewish votes and money. Consequently, contrary to the convention that a new regime is recognised only after it has proved its administrative control of a territory, Truman gave de facto recognition to Israel within ten minutes of its being established on 15 May. A fortnight later he received the president of Israel, Chaim Weizmann, on a state visit to America. During Israel's crucial first year of existence the Truman administration provided it with $200 million in credit and grant-in-aid.[11]

But by far the most significant underwriting of Israel's continued existence came in the form of the Tripartite Declaration by America, Britain and France on 25 May 1950, whereby tl.e signatories pledged 'unalterable opposition to use force or threat of force between any of the States in.the region'.[12] Such a 'guarantee of its frontiers' by the Western powers, coupled with 'the promise to supply it with arms on the basis of a balance of forces between it and the Arab states' pleased Israel immensely.[13] Tel Aviv showed its gratitude to Washington by backing it unconditionally at the United Nations on the issue of the Korean war, which broke out a few weeks later: it supported the later American decision to cross the 38th parallel and overrun North Korea. The following year Israel readily agreed to join the Western-sponsored Middle East Defence Organisation, a body which failed to materialise.

Besides giving financial assistance to Israel, the Truman administration encouraged private contributions to the Jewish state by making donations to the United Jewish Appeal and the purchase of United Israel Bonds tax-exempt.[14] Another country which aided Israel economically in its early years was West Germany. In 1953 Bonn paid Tel Aviv the first of twelve annual instalments to cover a sum of $1,050 million to be paid as reparations for the suffering caused by the Nazi regime to the Jews in Germany, and in the countries it occupied.[15] Since these funds were used by Israel to buy machinery, ships and rolling stock, as well as oil and industrial raw materials, they helped to lay a strong economic foundation for the state. The importance of reparations was highlighted by the fact that in 1954 they accounted for a third of all investment and one eighth of the total state revenue.[16] Additionally, regular restitution payments, amounting to about $130 million a year, received by about half a million Israeli Jews – as heirs to those who had suffered – from the state governments in West Germany provided a boost to the economy for the next many years.[17]

While Bonn established itself as a preeminent aid giver to Israel, Paris took to supplying arms to Tel Aviv, thus contravening an important clause of the Tripartite Declaration. The first shipment probably occurred soon after 1953, when France and Israel agreed to cooperate in nuclear arms research, with Israeli physicists offering France useful data on heavy water production.[18] Nasser's acts of nationalising the Paris-based Universal Suez Maritime Canal Company and confiscating French property in Egypt, combined with aid to the Algerian nationalists against imperial France, resulted in Paris and Tel Aviv tightening their already close bonds. Not surprisingly, France volunteered to supply heavy weaponry, including jet fighters, to Israel, secretly, after the latter tried to balance the effects of the Egyptian–Czech arms agreement of September 1955. Washington turned a blind eye to this, and later endorsed it by relinquishing the North Atlantic Treaty Organisation priority over some sophisticated French weapons in order to permit their 'diversion' to Israel.[19]

Earlier Washington had taken serious note of Tel Aviv's objections to the Baghdad Pact. Arguing that any strengthening of Muslim countries in the Middle East and south-west Asia posed a potential danger to its existence, the Jewish state had objected to the military alliance between Turkey (a member of Nato) and Pakistan signed in the spring of 1954. The flowering of this bilateral agreement, within a year and a half, into a multi-lateral Baghdad Pact – including Iran, Iraq, and Britain, besides the original signatories – alarmed Israel. Deferring to Tel Aviv's apprehension, Washington refused to join the pact as a fully-fledged member, even though it had been the original instigator of the project.

In contrast, France was not offered membership. This left it all the more free to reinforce its ties with Israel. Sharing a common hatred of Nasser, their top leaders conspired in the summer of 1956 to attack Egypt, with the aim of overthrowing Nasser's regime. They later invited their British counterparts to join in the venture; and they did. America was excluded from these plans, and showed its displeasure by opposing the tripartite aggression at the UN and outside. Later, when Israel refused to vacate Sinai, President Dwight Eisenhower suspended American economic and military aid to Tel Aviv.[20] This made Israel's links with France all the stronger, with the latter offering inter alia to erect a 24-megawatt nuclear reactor at Dimona in the Negev desert. The project received a boost when Israel agreed to withdraw only after the Eisenhower administration had promised its clandestine cooperation in developing its nuclear programme plans.[21]

At the same time Tel Aviv became the beneficiary of increased military and diplomatic assistance from Bonn. In December 1957 *HaBoker*, an Israeli paper, openly advocated linking Israel with Nato 'through the intermediary of the German Federal Republic'.[22] When this idea failed to materialise Bonn agreed secretly to pay 20 per cent of its reparations to Tel Aviv in weapons.[23] Soon after, it was revealed that fifty Israeli officers were undergoing training in West Germany, and that German experts were involved in constructing rocket launching sites in Israel.[24]

The pace of building armament factories in Israel – many of them erected by West Germans as part of reparations – had been such that, by the late 1950s, the country was looking for export outlets for its arms. It ended up as a supplier of small arms to the member-states of Nato, particularly West Germany. In June 1959, for instance, it contracted to supply West Germany with 250,000 locally designed and manufactured sub-machineguns. Early next year there were reports of Tel Aviv contracting to sell a quarter million mines to Bonn.[25]

By then Israel had proved itself to be a reliable member of the Western bloc. It had endorsed the Eisenhower doctrine in June 1958,[26] and allowed Britain to use its airspace to land paratroopers in Jordan to forestall any attempt to overthrow the monarch following an anti-royalist coup in Iraq in July. The arrival of John F. Kennedy, a Democrat, at the White House in January 1961 pleased the Israeli leaders. They were aware of the traditional Jewish support for the Democratic candidate, and equally aware that, having won by a margin of 112,000 out of 68 million votes, Kennedy was all the more grateful for Jewish political and financial backing. No wonder they publicly called for an American–Israeli mutual defence pact. Kennedy rejected this proposal, because it would have undermined America's oil and other interests in the Arab world.

However, in March, at the behest of the Kennedy administration, the West German chancellor and the Israeli prime minister met in New York. They announced that Bonn would give a soft loan of $500 million for developing the Negev desert,[27] and agreed privately that the West German government would supply heavy weapons worth $100 million to Israel. As a party to the secret arms deal, America arranged for its tanks, combat planes, and torpedo boats to be sold to West Germany, for (nominal) delivery to Portugal – a member of Nato – to be shipped directly to Israel.[28]

Soon after Nasser had provided military aid to the republican forces in North Yemen's civil war, which broke out in late September 1962, Kennedy adopted a more pro-Israeli stance. The next month he took the unprecedented step of openly approving the sale of Hawk anti-aircraft missiles, termed 'defensive' weapons, to Israel.[29] During the visit of the Israeli foreign minister to Washington in 1963 he declared that America regarded Israel as an ally even though this was not backed by any formal treaty.

Kennedy's assassination in November made no difference to American–Israeli relations. If anything his successor, Lyndon B. Johnson, was even more pro-Israeli. 'Johnson's personal sentiments toward Israel seemed warm and admiring,' notes William B. Quandt, an American specialist on the Middle East. 'Many of his closest advisers were well-known friends of Israel, and his own contacts with the American Jewish community had been close throughout his political career.'[30]

Not surprisingly it was President Johnson who took the leap from supplying defensive weapons to the Israelis to selling them such offensive weapons as tanks and fighter bombers. He did so after he had won the presidential election of November 1964, and after revelations in the Egyptian press, a month later, of the secret West Germany–Israeli arms deal had led to its termination.[31] In February 1966 the American state department publicly confirmed that the USA had sold tanks and missiles to Israel.

Later the White House's acceptance of a special report on the Middle East by Julius Holmes, a career diplomat, put American–Israeli relations into a global military-strategic context. 'The president and the White House staff concluded from the [Julius Holmes] study that, without Soviet aid and support, the Arab states would long since have been forced to make peace with Israel,' states Robert W. Stookey. 'The Egyptian president was assumed to have unlimited expansionist ambitions in the Arab world as well as against Israel, and it seemed probable that when Nasserist regimes were in power in all the countries adjoining Israel, a full-scale Arab attack would occur. . . . Since the United States could not permit the destruction of Israel, it would be obliged to intervene, at the risk of precipitating a . . . general war.'[32] It was therefore considered essential for America to keep Israel strong: only then could it help to protect Western interests, curb Soviet expansion, and underwrite the resolve of the moderate, pro-West regimes in the region to counter internal radical forces.

By carrying out a successful blitzkrieg against its Arab neighbours in June 1967, on its own, Israel proved the thesis of the pro-Israeli lobby in Washington that the stronger the Jewish state was the less need there was for direct American intervention in the Middle East in order to roll back the Soviet advance or fight Arab radicalism: an important consideration for an American administration which had by then despatched tens of thousands of its armed forces to South Vietnam. This encouraged Washington to withhold its consent to any UN Security Council resolution which included a call for Israeli withdrawal to the 4 June 1967 positions. 'It is clear . . . that a return to the situation of 4 June 1967 will not bring peace,' President Johnson said at a meeting of Bnai Brith, a Jewish fraternity, in Washington on 10 September. 'No one wishes to see the Holy City again divided by barbed wire and by machine guns.'[33]

Both Israel and America were intent on using the occupied Arab territories as a lever to gain Arab recognition of the Jewish state, followed by peace treaties. They succeeded when this principle was incorporated in resolution 242 of the UN Security Council, passed unanimously on 22 November. Its operative clause balanced a call for 'Withdrawal of Israeli armed forces from territories occupied in the recent conflict' with another for 'Termination of all claims or states of belligerency, and respect for and acknowledgement of the sovereignty, territorial integrity, and political independence of every state in the area, and their right to live in peace within secure and recognised boundaries free from threats or acts of force.'[34]

Among those who voted for resolution 242 at the UN was France: a country whose president, Charles de Gaulle, had imposed an embargo on arms sales to Israel in line with his earlier threat to take suitable action against the party which committed aggression against the other. Since Paris had until then been Tel Aviv's prime purveyor of heavy weaponry, specially military aircraft, Israel lost an important source of arms supplies. But this gap was soon filled when Johnson announced, in January 1968, the lifting of the embargo on weapons' shipments to the region. This was, however, a formality. Three months earlier his administration had announced that it had allowed the sale of forty-eight A4 Skyhawk planes to go through in early 1966.[35] Following the public statement of a policy change, Johnson sanctioned the supply of fifty F-4 Phantom bombers and other weapons to Israel. 'The size of the transaction and the quality of planes involved were dramatic, but no less important was the fact that the transaction represented the first move by the United States to support by military means, not just diplomatic action, the thesis that Israel should hold on to the conquered territories until the Arabs were prepared to make peace,' states Nadav Safran. 'Second, even as Israel proceeded to protect its military edge to retain its bargaining counters, it began to tilt increasingly toward a "tougher" conception of an acceptable bargain.'[36]

It was against this background that President Nasser launched a 'war of attrition' against the Jewish state, in the spring of 1969, to ensure that the world did not come to accept Israel's new boundaries as permanent, or semi-permanent. The rising tempo of hostilities worried the Nixon administration in Washington. It initiated consultations with the Kremlin on the subject, and prepared a peace plan. The American proposals visualised Israeli withdrawal to the 1967 borders, except in Gaza (where boundaries were to be negotiated by the parties) – and the Palestinian 'refugees' either repatriated to Israel at an agreed annual quota, or resettled outside Israel and given compensation. Washington submitted its peace package to the various parties to the dispute. Israel rejected it outright; and so did Egypt. Nasser was particularly angered by the decision of the US Congress in October to allow American citizens to serve in the IDF.[37] Denouncing America as 'the number one enemy of the Arabs', he tried to rally the heads of Arab states at a summit conference in Rabat, on 20 December, behind a policy of military confrontation with Israel. He failed.

Early next month Israel resorted to 'systematic bombing' of targets deep in Egyptian territory. The reason for escalating the conflict was more political than military. 'The Israelis sought to topple Nasser by showing him to be incapable of protecting his people, or at least to compel him to renounce war and to cease fire, thus terminating the situation that, in their judgement, had brought about the undesirable development in America's policy [towards Israel],' observes Nadav Safran.[38] This led Nasser to seek increased Soviet aid in defending the republic. As soon as the Soviet agreement to supply Egypt with missiles and supersonic jets, enabling it to counter Israel's deep penetration bombing, became known (in March), Washington announced that it was shipping arms and offering $100 million in credits to Tel Aviv.[39]

At the same time American efforts to end the war of attrition continued, mainly through the secretary of state, William Rogers. Success came in early August when Egypt, Jordan, and Israel agreed to a cease-fire for ninety days.[40] This period was meant to be utilised by Rogers to persuade Israel to move its troops back from the Suez Canal, and thus facilitate its reopening, as a step toward the implementation of UN resolution 242. But Israel refused to oblige. Rogers suggested using American arms delivery terms as a means to bring Tel Aviv into line, but was overruled by President Nixon.[41]

The PLO and the Syrian regime considered the acceptance of the Rogers plan a betrayal of the basic Arab position as agreed at the Khartoum summit three years earlier. The consequent souring of relations between the PLO and the Jordanian monarch was to culminate in a civil war in Jordan. While the crisis was maturing in Jordan, President Nixon announced (on 18 September) military aid of $500 million and an early delivery of eighteen Phantom bombers to Israel.[42] The next day King Hussein sent an urgent message to the White House to ask Israel to attack the Syrian troops massed along the northern Jordanian border. Nixon then directed the head of the National Security Council, Henry Kissinger, to prepare joint intervention plans in conjunction with the Israeli ambassador, Yitzhak Rabin. They did so. In the event, it was not necessary to execute these plans. None the less, Nixon sent a message of thanks to Rabin. 'The President will never forget the role which Israel played in foiling the attempt to bring about a change of rule in Jordan,' it read. 'The United States is lucky to have an ally like Israel in the Middle East.'[43] These events were of course not publicly known at the time. However, as Robert W. Stookey observes: 'The American–Israeli exercise in joint planning for military action against Arabs . . . had significant consequence. It resulted at once in a new spiral in the regional arms race.'[44]

It was a dramatic illustration of the close bond between Washington and Tel Aviv that on the very day, in November 1971, the American senate sanctioned, by eighty-one votes to fourteen, $500 million as credit to Israel for the purchase of Phantoms and other weapons, the state department announced that William Rogers would cease his peacemaking efforts forthwith.[45] During the same month the USA signed a 'memorandum of understanding' with Israel to help the latter increase its military self-sufficiency. This meant inter alia that the USA would supply engines for the military planes which Israel, having clandestinely obtained the blueprints of the French Mirage jet fighter, was planning to manufacture.[46] The pace and size of American military and economic assistance to Israel increased to the extent that by 1972 the three-year-old

Nixon administration had given more aid to Israel than all of the previous administrations since 1948 put together.[47]

Given such a strong American backing, Israel stiffened its position regarding a peace settlement with the Arabs. Following the Soviet military advisers' expulsion from Egypt in July 1972, the Israeli defence minister offered a bilateral interim peace agreement to Egypt which would have restored half of Sinai to Cairo in exchange for recognising Israel. President Sadat ignored the proposal. More seriously, Tel Aviv suggested 'proximity talks' with Cairo, with Washington acting as the intermediary. However, this proposal fell victim to the shock wave which swept Israel in the wake of the murder of eleven Israeli athletes at the Munich Olympics in early September.

With a presidential election campaign hotting up in America, the subject of Israeli–Arab negotiations became quiescent. Nixon had so thoroughly established his bonafides as a partisan of Israel that the Israeli ambassador, Rabin, came 'very close' to endorsing Nixon against his Democratic rival, Senator George McGovern.[48] Once Nixon had begun his second term as president, in January 1973, his national security adviser, Henry Kissinger, offered President Sadat a package of 'proximity talks' with Israel in public, and serious secret negotiations through him. The Egyptian leader rejected the proposal.

This led Moshe Dayan – a hawk in the Israeli government – to launch a campaign in early April for the annexation of the West Bank, parts of Sinai, and Golan. 'In his usual style,' states Nadav Safran, 'Dayan not only forcefully advocated his ideas verbally, but also stretched the considerable authority of his office to create facts (such as settlements and resettlements) and generate concrete plans (such as the proposal to establish a port city to be called Yammit astride the former Egyptian–Israeli border) that practically began the application of his ideas.'[49] Four months later the ruling Alignment backed the Galili Document, which proposed that both individuals and public organisations be allowed to purchase land in the occupied territories, and that privately established colonies be supplemented by government-aided settlements.

Since this marked a departure from the commonly agreed policy that Israel was merely to retain its Arab territories until the Arab states were prepared to negotiate with it directly, Washington disapproved of the Galili Document. But that affected neither the Israeli stance nor America's relationship with the Jewish state. Yet a subtle change was taking place: there were signs that America was beginning to realise its growing dependence on Arab oil. The nationalisation of the American oil companies in Libya had brought the point home – as had the Saudi threat not to increase its oil output, in order to meet the rising American demand, if Washington did not modify its uncritical support of Israel. The extent of America's growing commitment to Israel could be gauged from the fact that Washington's aid to Tel Aviv during the period between the Jordanian civil war and the Yom Kippur war amounted to nine times the sum provided in the previous three years.[50]

Moreover, the American decision to help Israel in its nuclear weapons programme, initiated by President Eisenhower, had by then borne fruit. The nuclear reactor at Dimona had been commissioned in 1963 as a 'textile plant'. Two years later Senator Robert Kennedy stated that Israel had stockpiled 'weapons grade fissionable material' and 'could fabricate an atomic device within a few months'.[51] Israel's stock of nuclear fuel increased dramatically when, in 1968, Israeli agents hijacked a ship carrying 200 tons of uranium on its way from Antwerp, Holland, to Genoa, Italy.[52] In July 1970 American officials were quoted as saying that they believed Israel had either assembled an atomic bomb or had all the necessary components for it.[53] Evidence collected since then, by different sources, indicates that during the early days of the Yom Kippur war, fearing the worst, Israeli Prime Minister Meir ordered that the entire stock of about ten atomic bombs (each one equivalent to 20,000 tons of TNT) be taken out of bunkers and mounted on specially adopted bombers. It was partly because the Israeli position on the ground improved, and partly because Tel Aviv was warned by Washington that a Soviet ship carrying a nuclear bomb was on its way to Egypt that the Israeli atomic bombs remained in their racks.[54]

The Pentagon's plans to assist Israel were delayed by a few days when Turkey – which had diplomatic relations with Israel – refused to let its planes use American bases on Turkish soil. However, once Portugal had offered refuelling facilities to the American planes on the Azores, the USA established a direct air link with Israel. It used its own military aircraft as well as Israeli airline El Al's planes to transport arms – on a massive scale. Between 14 and 25 October it sent not only 11,000 tons of weapons, but also forty Phantoms, forty-eight A4 Skyhawk jets, and twelve C-130 transporters to Israel.[55] The American government's commitment to Israel was superseded only by that of its Jewish citizens. During the first week of the war they contributed $100 million to the United Jewish Appeal.[56]

As such, Israel lacked neither weapons nor funds to fight the war effectively. Yet the military result of the war could only be described as 'no victory, no defeat'. In non-military terms, Israel was the loser, because the conflagration transformed 'almost entirely' Israel's diplomatic-strategic position, and the change was 'completely for the worse'.[57] Since Moscow had backed Cairo and Damascus, and played a leading part in the diplomatic manoeuvres at the UN and elsewhere, America and Israel had to concede an important role to the Soviet Union in future Middle East talks. In that sense the convening of the Middle East peace conference in Geneva, under UN auspices, with America and Russia acting as co-chairman, was a climb-down for Washington and Tel Aviv. On the other hand, the presence of the Egyptians and the Jordanians at the conference on 21 December enabled the Israelis to claim that they had after all succeeded in having Arabs engage in face-to-face talks with them. Due to impending elections in Israel the conference did little more than 'instruct' Israel and Egypt to negotiate the disengagement of their forces, and adjourn.

But, to the chagrin of the radical Arab capitals and Moscow, having won the election on 31 December, Israel's Labour Alignment government did not return to Geneva on 7 January, as scheduled, for talks with Egypt. Instead it approached the American secretary of state, Henry Kissinger, to undertake personal diplomacy to bring about an agreement with Egypt. President Sadat went along with this. The result was the Sinai I agreement between Cairo and Tel Aviv on 18 January 1974.

This helped Kissinger to persuade the Arab oil states to lift the oil embargo imposed during the Yom Kippur war. They did so in March. Having thus weakened the hand of President Assad of Syria, Kissinger tried to induct Assad into his step-by-step approach to peace. Assad cooperated, but unlike Sadat he kept the Kremlin informed of his moves. It was not until after the Soviet foreign minister had visited Damascus at a crucial stage of the negotiations that Syria finally signed an accord with Israel, on the disengagement of their troops, on 31 May in Geneva.

Once Israel had solved the pressing problems of demarcating boundaries with Egypt and Syria, and the disengagement of troops, it lost interest in any further talks with its Arab adversaries. It rebuffed Kissinger's efforts to draw it into negotiations with Jordan.[58] Nixon's resignation in early August, as the result of the Watergate scandal,[59] had the effect of dimming Kissinger's prestige. Not surprisingly, Israel refused to consider President Sadat's proposal for withdrawal beyond the Mitla and Gidi passes in Sinai, and thus caused the failure of Kissinger's third round of personal diplomacy on 22 March.

On Kissinger's recommendation, President Gerald Ford ordered 'a reassessment' of USA policy in the Middle East, and suspended military and economic aid to Israel in the meanwhile.[60] This, and the cordiality of the meeting between President Ford and President Sadat in Salzburg, Austria, in June made Israel re-think its position. It resumed negotiations with Egypt through Kissinger. These were successful and led to the signing of the Sinai II accord in early September. Aid from America began to flow immediately.

What Israel gained by reaching this agreement was far more than resumption of massive American aid. It had made Egypt subscribe to the mutual promise of not resorting to 'the threat, or use, of force or military blockade against each other', as well as committing itself (formally) to let non-military cargoes for Israel through the Suez Canal, and (informally) to reduce its anti-Israeli propaganda and relax the boycott of American companies trading with Israel.[61]

More importantly, Israel secured from the USA a long list of undertakings, commitments, and assurances, contained in two Memorandums of Agreement and a document entitled 'Assurances from US Administration to Israel'. While the First Memorandum, comprising sixteen articles, covered a wide spectrum of subjects, the second dealt exclusively with the prospect of a future peace conference in Geneva. These articles bound America to help Israel meet its long-term military, economic and energy needs, as well as to prepare contingency plans to provide it with military assistance in an emergency. Reaffirming its earlier commitment to uphold the 'survival and security' of Israel, the USA administration promised to view 'with particular gravity threats to Israel's security or sovereignty by a world power', and to lend assistance, 'diplomatic or otherwise', to Israel in the event of such threat. It also agreed to underwrite Israel's right of navigation through the straits of Bab al Mandeb and Gibraltar. In the Second Memorandum the USA government promised to refuse to recognise the PLO, or to deal with it, until and unless it had accepted Israel's right to exist, and to oppose any attempt to modify UN Security Council resolutions 242 and 338. It pledged to work in conjunction with Israel regarding the reconvening of the Geneva peace conference, and the strategy to be followed there. 'The package as a whole was quite impressive,' observes Nadav Safran. 'But for the fact that it bore the label of Executive Agreements, it exceeded in many ways a formal treaty signed by the United States.'[62]

The signing of the Sinai II agreement brought Israel other rewards. The accord caused an open break between Cairo and Damascus – which denounced it as a step towards an eventual bilateral peace treaty between Egypt and Israel – and created discord among the Arab states. The result was an intensification of the Lebanese civil war. This suited both Israel and America. However, having blunted the offensive of the rightist Christian forces against them, in early January, with the help of Syria, the alliance of the Lebanese left and the Palestinians began to gain the upper hand in the conflict. An apprehensive Israeli prime minister warned Syria in early April not to cross the 'definite red line' in its involvement in the Lebanese war, and was backed by Kissinger. The need for overt Israeli intervention in Lebanon became urgent when the leftist forces mounted a successful offensive in late May. But Israel was denied the opportunity, because President Assad, intent on keeping Israel out of Lebanon at all costs, sent regular Syrian troops to aid the hard-pressed Christian forces.[63] Israel was still on the lookout for an advantage, and secured it. As the PLO commandos left their bases in the south of Lebanon in order to resist the Syrian troops in the north, the Israelis aided their rightist Lebanese Christian allies to occupy the strategic south: a situation which persists.

Evidence made public since then shows that America played the leading role in worsening the Lebanese conflict. 'Only a few days ago former President Nixon admitted that American policy after the October

1973 war was aimed at shattering Arab ranks,' President Assad told the Paris-based *Al Mustaqabal* in June 1977. 'When America's policy [of making Arabs incapable of fighting] failed, it turned to Lebanon to bring about a massacre there. America was behind what happened in Lebanon, so that all Arabs would drown in the Lebanese civil war.'[64] A year earlier Winslow Peck, a former analyst at the American National Security Agency, had revealed that the Central Intelligence Agency station in Athens, Greece, had activated the Phalange members and right-wing Palestinians in Lebanon, and that it had used American banks in Athens to finance these forces.[65] 'The clandestine supply of arms to the Christian right by Israel, with US blessing, has been confirmed by the Lebanese,' said Wilbur Crane Eveland, author of *Ropes of Sand*, and once the CIA's chief representative in the Middle East, in October 1980. 'There are indications of CIA involvement [in the Lebanese civil war], and that Greece was the CIA staging post. I don't have positive proof of this, but I have talked to people who should know, and I believe them.'[66]

The CIA's coordination of its activities with those of Mossad, Israel's intelligence service, during the Lebanese civil war was the culmination of the relationship established between the two bodies in 1957. James Angleton of the CIA was the founder of this bond. 'Angleton was the man with Mossad,' stated Wilber Crane Eveland. 'I was told in 1959 by Allen Dulles [the CIA chief] that it [cooperation between the CIA and Mossad] was going to be expanded.'[67] And it was. Over the years, according to the American columnists Rowland Evans and Robert Novak, the CIA paid 'tens of millions of dollars' to the Israeli secret service for copies of its intelligence reports on the personalities and organisations of the Middle East and Africa.[68] Following the Yom Kippur war this link became tighter as Israel began supplying America with secret reports on Soviet weapons captured from its Arab opponents.[69]

In any case, besides helping Israel lodge its Christian protagonists in southern Lebanon, the strategy on the Lebanese civil war served another important purpose. 'The absorption of the Arabs into the Lebanese conflict and the divisions in their ranks removed all pressure from the United States to even pretend to keep the momentum of Middle East diplomacy alive, and allowed it to turn its attention fully to the [presidential] election campaign,' notes Nadav Safran.[70]

As in the past, the electoral contest worked in favour of Israel. Being the incumbent who had, on 1 July, signed a bill providing grants and loans of $4.3 billion to Israel for the period of June 1975 to September 1977, President Ford had a head start in projecting himself as a partisan of Israel.[71] When James Carter, the Democratic candidate, pointed out that it was Kennedy, a Democrat, who had first authorised the shipping of heavy American weapons to Israel, Ford proclaimed: 'Since I've been president we've sold the Israelis over $4 billion [worth] in military hardware.'[72] During the last weeks of the campaign it was announced in

Washington (unofficially) that the USA government had agreed to sell 'concussion' bombs to Israel,[73] and (officially) that joint production of F-16 fighter bombers with Israel was being considered.[74]

Such concern about Israel by the leading contenders could not be explained adequately by their need to attract the Jewish vote, a mere 3 per cent of the 140 million electors. A more convincing reason lay in the fact that the party candidates at all levels find that the Jews are the single most important source of funds for their election campaigns. Quoting a reliable estimate the New York correspondent of the *Guardian*, Jane Rosen, stated that, until 1974, Jews provided 60 per cent of all campaign funds for the Democratic candidates and 40 per cent for the Republicans.[75] This was not surprising: after all 'the vast majority' of the Democratic Party members who earned over $25,000 a year were Jewish.[76] According to the editor of a well-informed Washington newsletter, 40–50 per cent of the large individual (as against corporate) contributors to Carter's campaign were Jews. Of the twenty major individual financiers of Nixon's campaign (of 1972), five or six were Jewish.[77]

Jewish influence goes beyond election finances. It extends to branches of the government. The American–Israeli Public Affairs Committee, with a budget of over a million dollars a year,[78] is a powerful Zionist lobby in Washington. It has forty-eight canvassers, and can count on uncritical support for Israel from about twenty-five (of the 100) senators and seventy-five (of the 438) congressmen.[79] The AIPAC is intermeshed with the community at large through some 5,000 largely wealthy personalities who lead hundreds of religious, cultural and Zionist organisations of Jews. ' "The 5,000", who control American–Jewish community life, also finance the AIPAC, under the political tutorship of the pro-consuls in the Israeli embassy and consulates, and through the Jewish Agency and the World Zionist Organisation's shlihim (envoys),' states Maxim Ghilan, a French Jewish author. 'They are also the most active in mobilising help for Israel, and contribute much to the United Jewish Appeal and the United Israel Bonds campaign.'[80] What gives additional power to the voice of the Jewish community is the existence of a single central body: the Conference of Presidents of Major American Jewish Organisations. In 1978 this had thirty-three constituents, including the American Zionist Federation, which coordinates the activities of fourteen Zionist organisations, with an estimated membership of 893,000.[81]

Not surprisingly, in September 1977 the AIPAC could list the following in its impressive catalogue of successes, achieved during the previous few years: 'A trade law making US trade benefits conditional on free emigration for the Soviet Jews; a letter to President Ford from seventy-six senators calling for strong financial aid to Israel . . . ; a halt to American aid to UNESCO (United Nations Educational, Scientific, and Cultural Organisation) because of its anti-Israel actions; a law limiting American companies' compliance with the Arab boycott of Israel; approval of billions of dollars in military and economic aid to Israel; and cuts and modifications in proposed military aid to Arab nations'.[82]

The next month American Zionists proved their effectiveness by causing a virtual reversal of the government's stand on the Middle East peace process within days. On 1 October, following President Carter's statement favouring 'some form of PLO representation at the peace talks',[83] and a series of meetings between the American secretary of state and the Soviet foreign minister, a joint American–Soviet communiqué was issued. It referred inter alia to 'the resolution of the Palestinian question including insuring the legitimate rights of the Palestinian people', and the participation in the Geneva peace conference of 'the representatives of all the parties involved in the conflict including those of the Palestinian people'.[84] The Zionist lobby was upset by the mention of the Palestinians' 'legitimate rights' in the official document because, in the words of *Time*, 'This implicitly recognises that the solution to the Palestinian issue requires political measures in addition to the humanitarian task of finding homes for [Palestinian] refugees'.[85] The result was a barrage of 827 telephone calls and 7,268 telegrams of protest to the White House during the next four days.[86]

This put Carter on the defensive. 'I would rather commit political suicide than hurt Israel,' he reassured a delegation of American Jewish leaders.[87] He instructed his secretary of state to confer with the Israeli foreign minister, Moshe Dayan. On 5 October they produced an American–Israeli 'working paper', which 'seemed to back away from the freshly minted US–Soviet declaration in many ways'.[88] Confirmation of this came eight days later when Moshe Dayan told the Israeli parliament that the procedures agreed with America in the 'working paper' would bar the PLO, and any discussion on a Palestinian state, from the peace conference, and would not automatically compel Israel to withdraw from all of the occupied territories.[89]

Both the official documents were, however, overtaken by President Sadat's visit to Jerusalem, and his address to the Knesset on 20 November, in which he said, 'In all sincerity, I tell you, we welcome you among us, with full security and safety'.[90] Yet a formal accord between Israel and Egypt was not reached until ten months later – and that too only after Carter had spent thirteen days in intense negotiations with Sadat and the Israeli prime minister, Begin, at the Camp David presidential retreat in the Maryland mountains. By publicly declaring that he had rejected twenty-three earlier drafts, Begin confirmed that the final agreement had been reached basically on his terms. This was not surprising. After all, Israel was negotiating from a position of strength, which had been bolstered, in the main, by public and private aid from the USA after the Yom Kippur war.

Of the \$3.8 billion financial assistance received by Israel in 1977, nearly \$1.8 billion had come from the USA treasury, and most of the rest from private American sources.[91] Assured of continued arms supplies from Washington, the Israeli leaders confidently announced that by the end of the following year their country would be in a position to defeat *any* combination of the Arab states.[92] That there was to be no slackening in the pace of arming Israel was underlined by the fact that 43 per cent of the total American aid of $4.14 billion (to forty-nine countries) for the fiscal year, starting October 1978, was earmarked for Israel.[93]

Tel Aviv received a promise of further financial aid the following February. This happened when Begin and Sadat failed to sign a peace treaty by the previously agreed deadline of 31 December 1978. Once again Carter intervened, directly, by visiting Egypt and Israel. His participation in Israeli cabinet meetings (a most extraordinary event to occur between any two sovereign states, however friendly) highlighted the closeness of bonds between America and Israel. It was revealed later that one of the pledges Carter made to the Israeli government was that the USA would protect the Jewish state against any possible violation of the treaty by Egypt.[94] Not surprisingly Washington was the venue for the formal signing, on 26 March, of the Israeli–Egyptian treaty: an event which had been made possible at the cost of an American commitment of 'at least $10 billion' in military and economic aid to the two signatories.[95]

Given this, Tel Aviv could easily afford to ignore periodic American protests against Israel's continuing colonisation of the occupied territories or its repeated attacks on targets in Lebanon. In August Israel was heartened by the American Zionist lobby's success in bringing about the resignation of the American ambassador to the UN, Andrew Young, a black Democrat leader considered to be pro-PLO.[96] When, in mid-September, the Israeli government decided to let its citizens purchase land in the West Bank, the American state department described the step as 'contrary to the spirit and the intent of the peace process'.[97] But that changed nothing. Some weeks later, to the relief of the Israeli leaders, official and public attention in the USA was diverted to the fate of the American diplomats taken hostage in Tehran, Iran, and stayed there for many months.

As the American presidential contest got under way the following summer, each of the two leading candidates tried to present himself as more pro-Israel than the other. Carter stressed the fact that, by giving $11 billion in aid to Israel, his administration had achieved as much as previous presidents had done in all the twenty-eight years of Israel's existence.[98] Two weeks before polling day the Carter administration signed an agreement with Israel which brought the latter under American protection in the International Energy Authority's plans for sharing oil in an emergency.[99] This amounted to the IEA, consisting of twenty-one industrialised nations, conferring its privileges on a non-member state.

But Carter was outflanked on this front by his Republican rival, Ronald Reagan. 'I believe in the right of Israeli settlements in the West Bank,'

Reagan stated during his election campaign. 'Israel is the [American] military offset to the Soviet Union in the Middle East.'[100] The power of the American 'offset' in the region can be gauged by the fact that Israel possesses more combat aircraft, tanks, and armoured vehicles than Britain, an advanced European state with fifteen times more people than Israel; and that, at $1,000 per capita, Israel is spending four times as much on defence as any country of Nato, or five times as much as any member of the Warsaw Pact.[101]

Israel welcomed Reagan's victory. 'Israeli policymakers noted during the campaign, with intense but unvoiced satisfaction, Mr Reagan's frequent references to Israel as a strategic asset and ally of the US,' reported David Landau in the *Guardian*.[102] Soon after assuming office President Reagan stated that the USA had 'a moral commitment to preserving Israel's right to continue as a nation': a reiteration of previous American policy. He then expressed his disagreement with the Carter administration's description of the Jewish settlements in the West Bank as illegal. 'They are not illegal, not under the UN resolution that leaves the West Bank open to all people – Arab and Israeli alike, Christian alike,' he said.[103] Such a statement indicated to Israeli leaders and others that in the Reagan administration Israel had found an uncritical ally.

The single strongest bond between Reagan and his advisers and the Israeli leaders – whether they be of Likud, Labour Alignment or NRP persuasion – is their hostility towards the Soviet Union. Whereas the attitude of the American leaders – engaged as they are in a global contest with the Soviets for supremacy – is understandable, that of the Israeli leaders is far less so. After all, the USSR played a crucial role in the founding of Israel.

While the antipathy of America towards the USSR stems from the rivalry that exists between the two superpowers, Israeli hostility is rooted mainly in the Soviet Union's severing of ties with the Jewish state in the wake of the Six Day war, its pro-Arab stance, and certain restrictions (allegedly) imposed on Soviet Jews. To be sure, Moscow had cut its links with Tel Aviv before – in the early 1950s – but the estrangement had lasted only a year and a half. Before that break, however, the USSR had emerged as the first major country to accord de jure recognition to Israel. This had happened at a time when Soviet Jewry was the second largest in the world, and had only recently lost the first place it had held for one and a half centuries.

# 11

# ISRAEL AND THE SOVIET BLOC

Having thrice annexed parts of Poland with large Jewish populations, between 1772 and 1795, Czarist Russia emerged as a country with more Jews than the rest of Europe combined.[1] But that made no difference to the status of Jews there. They were confined to the ghettos and villages of the 'pale of settlement' as before, and denied citizenship. The situation changed during the rule of Alexander II, which began in 1855. Due to his liberal policies Jews became active in law, banking, medicine, industry and architecture. His assassination in 1881 resulted in a reign of terror being unleashed by his successor, Alexander III. An officially inspired pogrom in 1882 caused immense suffering. Jews started migrating in large numbers. They all went westwards, except for a small proportion who headed for Palestine.[2]

During that year Leo Pinsker, a Jew from Odessa, argued in his pamphlet, *Auto-emancipation: A Warning of A Russian Jew to His Brethren*, that Jews would be able to solve their problem not by securing emancipation in a non-Jewish state but by establishing a state of their own, thus ending their existence as a 'ghost nation'. He considered Palestine as one of the possibilities, the other being 'any part of America'.[3] He attracted the attention of the Lovers of Zion groups, which had until then drawn their inspiration from Moses Hess's *Rome and Jerusalem*.[4] Once Pinsker had narrowed his choice to Zion as the Jewish homeland, he was adopted as the leader of the Lovers of Zion, who held their first national congress in Kattowitz in 1887.[5]

Not surprisingly, Russian Jewry provided sixty-six of the 199 delegates to the founding congress of the World Zionist Organisation in 1897.[6] Despite an official ban by Czar Nicholas II the Zionist movement spread rapidly. By 1903 – a year which saw yet another pogrom – Zionism, political and religious, had secured the loyalty of 1,572 groups throughout the country.[7] In the process it had aroused the hostility of the Marxist revolutionaries. 'The idea of a Jewish "nationality" is manifestly reactionary,' wrote Vladimir I. Lenin in 1903. 'It is in conflict with the interests of the Jewish proletariat, for it engenders in its ranks a sword hostile to assimilation – a "ghetto" mood.'[8] Echoing similar sentiments

Joseph V. Stalin, in his *Marxism and the National Question*, written a decade later, described Zionism as 'a reactionary and nationalist movement recruiting its followers from among the Jewish petty and middle bourgeois,' which aimed to 'organise a Jewish bourgeois state in Palestine', and endeavoured to 'isolate the Jewish working class mass from the general struggle of the proletariat'.[9]

Anxious to win the sympathies of Jewry in central and eastern Europe and America, the British and French governments pressured Nicholas II to end discrimination against Jews. He responded slowly but positively. Following his abdication, in March 1917, the Russian government removed restrictions on the Zionist movement. Eight months later the Czarist regime collapsed under the offensive of the Bolsheviks, who promised self-determination, cultural and political, to the major nationalities in the country. The result was the creation, in January, of the commissariat for Jewish affairs, attached to the people's commissariat for nationality affairs.

A clear distinction was now made between Zionism as a cultural movement and as a political creed. 'Since the cultural and educational activities of the Zionist organisation do not contradict the decisions of the Communist Party, the Presidium of the All Russian Central Executive Committee of the Soviets instructs all Soviet organisations not to hamper the Zionist party in its activities,' stated the directive issued by the Presidium of ARCECS in July 1919.[10] In contrast, political Zionism was described as a reactionary ideology used by Jewish capitalists to exploit Jewish workers, and the concept of founding a national home for Jews in Palestine labelled regressive, running counter to the movement for proletarian internationalism. Such an analysis fitted the economic needs of the state. 'We cannot allow emigration as we ourselves need manpower,' said Georgi V. Chicherin, foreign minister, in February 1921.[11]

As part of the First Five Year Plan (1928–32) – which laid special stress on the development of Central Asia, the Urals, and Siberia – the Soviet government demarcated the Birobidzhan area in south-east Siberia, contiguous to the Chinese border, for colonisation by Jews. Three years later it designated Birobidzhan as a Jewish district and finally, in May 1934, upgraded it as an autonomous Jewish region within the Russian Soviet Federated Socialist Republic. Expressing the official hope, President Mikhail Kalinin said: 'The Jews will become socialist colonisers with strong fists and sharp teeth, a strong national group within the Soviet family of nations.'[12] Evidently the government's intention was to combine the development of a distant region with the consummation of a Jewish desire to have a territory of their own within the USSR.

On Palestine the Communist Party of the Soviet Union subscribed to the position adopted by the sixth Communist International congress held in 1928. 'Zionism is the expression of the exploiting and great power strivings of the Jewish bourgeoisie, which makes use of the persecution of the Jewish national minorities in eastern Europe for the purpose of imperialistic policy to insure its domination,' stated the Communist International's resolution. 'To achieve this goal, Zionism has allied itself via the (British) mandate and the Balfour Declaration with British imperialism. In return for the support extended to it by the British imperialists, Zionism has turned itself into a tool of British imperialism to suppress the national liberation movement of the Arab masses.'[13] As such the party, headed by Stalin, sided with the Arabs in the Arab–Jewish riots of 1929 as well as the far more serious Arab revolt of 1936–9.

In line with the decision of the 1935 congress of the Communist International the CPSU supported anti-Fascist organisations in the Middle East, whether led by Arabs or Jews, or both. When the Zionists turned against the British, in the wake of the White Paper of May 1939, the party applauded the development. Following Hitler's attack on the USSR in June 1941, and Stalin's assumption of prime ministership, the Soviet Union began to temper its opposition to Zionism. As an integral part of the Allies' front in the war, the Soviet embassies in London, Washington, Tehran and Ankara received Zionist and Jewish delegations to be briefed on Zionist aims in Palestine. In mid-1942 two Soviet diplomats in Ankara travelled to Palestine to attend the inaugural meeting of the (Jewish) League of Friendly Relations with the USSR. During his visit to Palestine in August 1943, Ivan Mikhailovich Maisky, Soviet deputy foreign minister, met David Ben-Gurion. A year later Stalin – by then well-informed on Nazi atrocities against Jews – told Emile Somerstein, a member of the provisional government of Poland, that once the war had ended the USSR would back an 'international solution' to the Jewish problem.[14]

However, since Britain refused to place the Palestine issue before the United Nations' founding conference in April 1945, the Soviet Union had no opportunity to participate in solving the Jewish problem, or even to express an official opinion on the subject. Indications of the Kremlin's thinking came only indirectly. In *Countries of the Arab League* and *Palestine Problem*, both published in 1946, Vladimir B. Lutsky, a Soviet expert on the Middle East, expressed opposition to Zionism. During the same year Meir Vilner of the Palestine Communist Party opposed partition, and called for an independent, unified Arab–Jewish state in Palestine.

It was only after Britain had referred the Palestine problem to the UN in early 1947, and the General Assembly had taken it up for debate, that Moscow got a chance to take a public stand. On 14 May the Soviet foreign minister stated that the USSR favoured a federated union of Arabs and Jews in Palestine, and that only if such a plan proved impossible to realise would his country consider the other viable alternative: partition. Despite the big 'if' in the statement, the Zionists welcomed it warmly.

The report of the UN Special Commission on Palestine, submitted in early September, was unanimous on terminating the British mandate, but divided on what to do next. While a majority of the commission's members recommended partition, a minority favoured a federal state. Later that month the General Assembly began a debate on the report which lasted two months. On 13 October the USSR declared its support for the partition plan, something America had done two days earlier. The Soviet action was acclaimed rapturously by the Zionists, and attacked bitterly by the Arabs.

What made the USSR subordinate its historic opposition to Zionism was its immediate objective of getting the British out of the Middle East – particularly strategically situated Palestine. It was quite uncertain whether the British mandate in Palestine would be ended as recommended by UNSCOP. Britain had in fact expected that since neither of UNSCOP's plans for a post-mandate Palestine would win the required two thirds majority in the UN General Assembly, it would be asked to continue its mandate. In anticipation, it had already started moving its military personnel and weapons from the Suez Canal and Nile delta of Egypt to Al Arish, near the border with Palestine.[15] As it happened, but for the support of the eight-strong Soviet bloc, the partition plan would not have been passed, by thirty-three votes to thirteen, at the General Assembly on 29 November.

Stalin was responsible for this switch in Soviet policy. His move seemed to have stemmed from his continuing disappointment with the pan-Arabists, and the Arab rulers. Many of the Arab nationalists had shown pro-Axis sympathies during the Second World War, while the major figures among the rulers had joined the British-sponsored Arab League in March 1945. In contrast, Stalin had been impressed by the consistently anti-imperialist line followed by such militant Zionist groups as Lehy. 'We do not fight the British mandate,' Nathan Yalin-Mor of Lehy often stated. 'We fight imperialism which is directed equally against all the peoples of the Middle East.'[16]

Having supported the partition plan, the USSR tried to neutralise Western influence in the prospective Jewish state by quickly building up goodwill for itself. The best way to do this was by supplying arms to the Zionists. But this needed to be done surreptitiously. Given the existence of Lehy's branches in Czechoslovakia, Hungary, and Rumania,[17] this did not present much of a problem. The first consignment of arms from Czechoslovakia reached the Yishuv in March 1948,[18] two months before the formal establishment of Israel, which was accorded de jure recognition by Moscow.[19]

But the Soviet–Israeli honeymoon proved to be shortlived. The opening of an Israeli legation in Moscow in October led to a series of (unauthorised) demonstrations by local Jews in honour of the Israeli envoy, and reports of Jewish citizens establishing direct links with the legation. This displeased the Kremlin. The Soviet hope that Israel would emerge as a progressive state was disappointed in January, when the leftist Mapam was excluded from the coalition government formed after the first general election.

The subsequent opening of Israel to Western capital, the raising of private and governmental loans and grants from America, and the withdrawal of the Histadrut from the Prague-based World Federation of Trade Unions: all these indicated to Moscow that Tel Aviv was drifting to the right. The Tripartite Declaration of May 1950 widened the distance between Israel and the USSR. While the Israeli Prime Minister Ben-Gurion welcomed it, the *New Times*, an authoritative Soviet weekly, described it as 'a deliberate effort [by the signatories] to prolong the strained situation artificially . . . to set one state against another, and thus to keep control of all the Near Eastern countries'.[20] Tel Aviv's unqualified support for Washington in the Korean war led Moscow to conclude that Israel had joined the Western bloc.

The signing of an American–Israeli treaty of friendship, commerce, and navigation in October 1951 drew sharp words from Moscow – as did Israeli eagerness to join the Western-sponsored Middle East Defence Organisation. The trial of Rudolf Slansky, the (Jewish) secretary of the Czechoslovak Communist Party, in November 1952, for maintaining subversive links with Israel and the WZO, soured relations between the Soviet bloc and the Jewish state. During the following January nine prominent Moscow doctors, four of them Jewish, were tried for conspiring with the Joint Distribution Committee, an American espionage agency, to liquidate top Soviet military and civilian leaders. This had a deleterious effect on Tel Aviv–Moscow ties. In February the Soviet legation in Tel Aviv was bombed. The USSR responded angrily, and severed relations with Israel altogether.

It was not until July 1953 – four months after Stalin's death – that Moscow decided to restore diplomatic links with Tel Aviv. However, the actual reopening of legations occurred in December, after Israel had reassured the USSR that it would not join any anti-Soviet military alliance.[21] In return Moscow signed a trade agreement with Tel Aviv which allowed the Jewish state to import oil from the USSR, and thus circumvent the most damaging aspect of the Arab boycott. The following year, when the legations were raised to embassy level in both capitals, Israeli imports from the Soviet Union amounted to ten times the figure for 1950–1.[22]

Yet the political and military interests of the two states remained as incompatible as before. While Israel viewed the departure of the British troops from the Suez Canal zone during the autumn of 1954 as having removed the brake on Egypt's aggressive ambitions against it, the USSR welcomed the event, and hoped that something similar would happen in Jordan and Iraq. Within a year there was an open clash of interests between the two sides. The occasion was the announcement of an arms-for-cotton deal between Czechoslovakia and Egypt in September. Since the agreement included such offensive weapons as tanks and jet fighters, Israel was alarmed.[23] It protested vehemently, but in vain. It then did to Syria what it had done to Egypt earlier in the year. In a single raid on the Syrian positions along Lake Tiberias, on 11 December, its forces killed fifty-six Syrians.[24] This drew from Moscow the most blistering attack on Israel yet. 'From the first days of its existence the state of Israel has taken a hostile and threatening position towards its neighbours,' Nikita Khrushchev, the CPSU chief, said on 29 December in his speech to the Supreme Soviet. 'Imperialists are seeking to use Israel as their tool against the Arab people with a view to ruthlessly exploiting the natural wealth of that area.'[25]

Ignoring the Soviet strictures, Israel responded to periodic Arab guerrilla actions with 'massive murderous raids against Arab positions'.[26] It resorted to criticising the Soviet bloc not only for selling arms to the Arabs but also for mistreating its Jewish minority. Emboldened by the delivery of the first instalment of French Mystère jet fighters in mid-April,[27] Prime minister Ben-Gurion publicly called on the USSR to allow its Jewish citizens to migrate to Israel.

In the dispute that developed between Nasser and the West about the financing of the Aswan Dam, and Nasser's subsequent nationalisation of the Suez Canal, Israel kept its distance in the early stages. But as the USSR lined up with Nasser, declaring that any threat to Egypt was a threat to all Arab states, and as the Western countries combined against Egypt, Israel openly backed the West. Its leaders felt that if the West succeeded in forcing Nasser to retrace his steps, their country would be that much more secure. The Israeli–Western alignment led *Izvestia*, the Soviet government's paper, to predict as early as 21 September that, 'Any military action by the Western powers against Egypt is inconceivable without the direct or indirect participation of Israel.'[28] As it happened, Israel was the first to move against Egypt, on 29 October, providing an excuse for its collaborators – France and Britain – to intervene with an ultimatum to Egypt and Israel to cease fire.

Moscow was quick to cooperate with Washington (which was not privy to the Anglo–French–Israeli plans) in sponsoring a resolution condemning aggression against Egypt at the UN General Assembly.[29] This happened on 2 November. Three days later the Soviet prime minister, Nikolai Bulganin, addressed a letter to David Ben-Gurion which read: 'It [the aggression] is sowing a hatred of the state of Israel among the peoples of the East such as cannot but make itself felt with regard to the future of Israel, and which puts in jeopardy the very existence of Israel as a state.'[30]

When Israel refused to vacate the conquered Arab territories Moscow advocated imposing economic sanctions against it through the UN, and insisted that an Israeli withdrawal must be unconditional. On 7 February the USSR unilaterally cancelled its oil supply agreement with Israel in order to compel it to implement the UN resolution on the Suez war.[31] This, and other pressures, led to the final Israeli withdrawal which began on 4 March.

Later that month the American Congress adopted the Eisenhower doctrine. By endorsing the doctrine, Tel Aviv alienated itself further from Moscow. Not surprisingly, Israel figured prominently in the Soviet press as one of the pro-West states plotting aggression against Syria during the crisis that built up between Damascus and Washington in the summer. On 10 September the Soviet army's paper, *Krasnaya Zvezda*, went so far as to state that Israel and Turkey were planning to attack Syria at the bidding of the West.[32] However, a series of moves made by the Saudi monarch and President Nasser – coupled with some internal changes within Syria – helped to defuse the situation.[33]

The republican coup of July 1958 in Iraq accentuated the differences between Tel Aviv and Moscow. In a note to the Israeli government the Kremlin stated that by allowing overflights by British military planes, Israel had become a 'direct accomplice' in Britain's plans for Jordan.[34] Tel Aviv replied that the arrangement was temporary, and terminated it on 5 August. Dismissing Western claims that the British paratroopers had arrived in Jordan to forestall a possible Israeli attack on the country, Moscow Radio stated that Tel Aviv would take such an action only in collusion with London and Washington, and that it would do so to provide its Western allies with an excuse to maintain a military presence in Jordan.[35] The growing importance of Israel to the West was expressed by *Sovietski Flot*, the Soviet navy's journal, thus: 'With the Nuri al Said bulwark of the colonisers in the Arab East having been destroyed by the revolution in Iraq, the imperialists pitch an even larger stake in Israel.'[36]

Aware of the emotional attachment many of its Jewish citizens felt towards Israel, the Kremlin allowed nine prominent Jews to visit Israel as official guests in the autumn of 1958. On their return home they painted a bleak picture of life in Israel, with a pointed reference to the discrimination suffered by Sephardic Jews there.[37] The Soviet press often debunked claims that a socialist society had been established in the Jewish state. Khrushchev summed up the official view when, during his state visit to America in September 1959, he described the government of Israel as a 'pure and simple bourgeois government run by capitalists'.[38]

Next July, in an interview with an Israeli newsagency, Khrushchev stated: 'The portfolio of our ministry of internal affairs contains no requests of persons of Jewish nationality wishing to go to Israel.'[39] This was hotly disputed by the Israeli and Zionist leaders, who had earlier decided to give top priority to the fate of Soviet Jewry. At the WZO congress in January 1961 Ben-Gurion reiterated his concern for the welfare of the USSR's Jews. In an apparent response to this, the Soviet authorities allowed Jews greater cultural freedom, including publication of a magazine in Yiddish, *Sovietish Heimland*.

But the basic Soviet policy toward Tel Aviv remained unchanged. When, for instance, Israel launched a research rocket in July, *Krasnaya Zvezda* described the event as part of 'a campaign of intimidation against the Arab states'.[40] The USSR condemned President Kennedy's decision, announced on 2 October 1962, to supply American missiles to Israel. Replying to the Soviet stricture the Israeli prime minister said, 'As long as Arab belligerency continues – since the Soviet Union gives them arms – Israel will take all necessary measures to be capable of protecting itself'.[41] Three weeks later Kennedy compelled Khrushchev to withdraw offensive missiles that the USSR had by then supplied to the Communist regime of Cuba. This enhanced American prestige and pleased the Western bloc, including Israel.

On 6 May the *Jerusalem Post* reported that Israel had approached America for a mutual defence treaty. A fortnight later the USSR (which had in January signed a nuclear test ban treaty with the USA) offered a proposal to Israel whereby the Mediterranean and the Middle East would be declared a 'nuclear free zone' and treated as an 'out of bounds [region] for atomic weapons' in case of war.[42] While Washington rejected Tel Aviv's initiative, Tel Aviv rejected Moscow's. Israeli–Soviet relations remained where they had been for the past many years.

However, the following year witnessed a steady deterioration in Moscow–Tel Aviv relations, a trend which culminated in the termination of links between the two capitals in June 1967. When the heads of Arab states decided in early January to confront Israel on the issue of its plan to divert the waters of the river Jordan, the USSR welcomed the Arab stance, with *Pravda*, the CPSU's paper, describing the summit as 'the most representative conference of Arab leaders in history'.[43] During his visit to Egypt in May, Khrushchev attacked Israel and its backers thus: 'Imperialism, with all its strength, strives to increase the threat of aggression by facilitating the emigration of Jews to Israel, giving it financial aid, and encouraging its expansionist ambitions, as we see from the example of the Jordan waters'.[44]

Pursuing their decision of 1961, Israeli and Zionist leaders kept up pressure on the Soviet government to allow its Jewish citizens to emigrate. In a speech before the Knesset, in March 1965, the Israeli foreign minister called on the USSR to let its Jews either lead their 'national' life or leave the country to reunite with their families living abroad. In response a group of eminent Soviet Jews attacked Israel for forging friendly relations with the West German government and buying arms from 'the former Nazis whose hands are soaked in the blood of Jews and other people';[45] and the Kremlin accused the Israeli ambassador to the USSR of establishing clandestine contacts with Jews in several Soviet towns and cities. Later, when Zionist bodies began orchestrating well-planned anti-Soviet campaigns among the Jews of America and other

Western countries, Moscow protested vehemently. On 14 October the USSR proposed at the United Nations that Zionism be added to Nazism and neo-Nazism as doctrines which lead to racial crimes; but failed.[46]

The following year, yielding to persistent Israeli–Zionist pressure, the Soviet government accepted the principle of letting its Jewish citizens reunite with their families settled abroad. Those who applied to leave amounted to 'a few thousands'. Of these, 2,700 were allowed to migrate to Israel.[47] The Soviet decision was welcomed by the Israeli leaders, particularly since it came at a time when immigration into the Jewish state was running at half the level of the previous year (at 30,736),[48] and their country was experiencing a new outflow of Jews.[49]

But this failed to reverse the downward trend in Israeli–Soviet relationships. The main reason was the neo-Baathist seizure of power in Syria, which in turn led to increased Palestinian guerrilla activity. On 14 July Israeli jets bombed the Banias river diversion site inside Syria: an action which *Izvestia* described as 'a piratical act'.[50] A month later, when Israeli planes, exercising 'the right to pursuit', shot down two Syrian MiGs inside the Arab republic's boundaries, Soviet condemnation followed. In early September an attempted coup by Major Salem Hatum, inspired by pro-West Arab states, failed.[51] With this – the Soviet analysts surmised – the onus for toppling the radical Syrian regime fell squarely on Israel. Soon after, in an interview with *BaMahane*, the IDF's official journal, the Israeli chief-of-staff, General Rabin, said as much.[52] Despite the massive Israeli raid on the Jordanian town of Al Samu on 9 November, in which eighteen people were killed and fifty-four injured, the Soviets stood by their assessment of the chief Israeli objective. 'Although the first blow has been delivered against the territory of Jordan, the true target of the Israeli militarists is certainly Syria,' wrote *Pravda*. 'As far back as September, the chief-of-staff of the Israeli army, General Rabin, stated that his government's aim was "change of the Syrian regime".'[53]

In February Israel witnessed a week-long programme of activities highlighting the plight of Soviet Jews. Although these were sponsored by the WZO, Israeli officials participated actively in the events, with the foreign minister playing a leading role. Moscow Radio described the 'Week of Soviet Jewry' as an expression of the Israeli ruling circles' desire to 'participate in an anti-Soviet cold war led by the United States'.[54] In early April, within a few days of the Israeli Prime Minister's statement to an American news magazine that if necessary the USA Sixth Fleet, stationed in the Mediterranean, would protect Israel (which was not rebutted by Washington),[55] Israeli planes penetrated Syrian airspace and shot down six Syrian MiGs.[56] Noting that the Israeli action had to do with a border dispute, General Rabin warned that the same 'rules of military operations' could be applied to other areas of friction between the two states.[57] 'Israel is given the part of starting conflicts in the Near East . . .

which Washington can [then] use as pretext for direct intervention,' commented Moscow Radio on 14 April.[58]

On 11 May General Rabin gave a clear hint of Israeli intentions when he said on Israel Radio: 'The moment is coming when we will march on Damascus to overthrow the Syrian government, because it seems that only military operations can discourage the plans for a people's war with which they threaten us'.[59] Two days later the Israeli Prime Minister, Levi Eshkol, referred to Syria as 'the focal point of [Palestinian] terrorists', and added, 'We have laid down the principle that we shall choose the time, the place, and the means to counter the aggressor.'[60] *Izvestia* referred to these statements as typical of the voices being heard in military and political circles of Israel 'which increasingly talk about the necessity of demonstrating strength again'.[61]

When Eshkol termed Egypt's closing of the straits of Tiran to Israeli shipping on 23 May 'aggression against Israel',[62] Tass, the Soviet news-agency, accused Israel of creating tension in the region, and warned that 'He who will try aggression in the Middle East will be met not only by the united forces of the Arab countries but also with an energetic restraint from the Soviet Union'.[63] Three days later the Soviet prime minister addressed a note to his Israeli counterpart in which he stated: 'We want you to use all means to avoid the outbreak of an armed conflict which would have serious consequences for international peace and security.'[64] On 29 May, at the UN security council, the Soviet representative called Israel 'the real culprit in the dangerous aggravation of tensions'.[65] Later, on 3 June, he condemned America for its 'policies and actions', including 'its complicity with the extremist circles in Israel which are perpetrating aggression against neighbouring Arab states'.[66]

The day after the Israeli attack on its Arab neighbours on 5 June, the Soviet representative at the UN called on the Security Council to condemn the Israeli aggression, and demanded that Israel pull back its troops 'beyond the truce lines (of 1957)'.[67] Tel Aviv disregarded the Soviet call as well as the Security Council's demand for an immediate cease-fire. On 8 June the USSR formally introduced a motion at the Security Council in line with its earlier demands. But since Israel was making lightning progress on the battlefield, and since America was against the call for an unconditional Israeli withdrawal, the USSR compromised the next day by agreeing to the idea of an immediate cease-fire in situ: a proposal which secured the necessary support of the Security Council. As Israel had by then (9 June) conquered all of Sinai, the West Bank and Gaza, it ceased fire on the Egyptian and Jordanian fronts.

But, ignoring Syria's acceptance of the UN cease-fire call, Israel launched a major offensive on the Syrian front, with a pointed thrust towards Damascus. On that day the leaders of the Communist parties of the Soviet bloc, except Rumania, issued a joint statement warning Israel that if it did not halt its offensive immediately, they would do 'everything necessary to help the peoples of the Arab countries administer a resolute rebuff to the aggressor'.[68] Israel ignored the statement. Next day the Kremlin severed relations with Israel and warned it of further action if it persisted in its aggression.[69] The Soviet prime minister, Alexei Kosygin, sent a message to President Johnson on the 'hot line' stating that the USSR would take all 'necessary action, including military', if Israel continued its march into Syria. It was 9 a.m. (local time) when the White House received the Soviet note.[70] At noon Israel ceased fire. Within the next three days all members of the Soviet bloc, except Rumania, broke off diplomatic ties with Tel Aviv.

Moscow persisted in its efforts to secure the unconditional withdrawal of Israeli forces from the occupied territories by introducing a resolution to that effect at the UN General Assembly on 19 June, but it did not win the required two thirds majority. The same fate befell a pro-Israeli motion by America. Then the Soviet Union backed a pro-Arab resolution introduced by Yugoslavia, and the USA a pro-Israel resolution offered by a group of Latin American states. Since neither of these secured the necessary support at the UN the issue remained unresolved. The special emergency session of the General Assembly, called on 18 September, failed to break the deadlock.

On 21 October Egypt sank the Israeli destroyer *Eilat*, and Israel retaliated by bombing the port of Suez three days later. This led to the Arab–Israeli conflict being referred back once again to the Security Council. After three resolutions submitted respectively by America, the USSR, and a group of non-aligned nations had failed to satisfy the various parties, Britain introduced a motion on 16 November which specifically called for an Israeli withdrawal from the territories occupied during 'the recent conflict': a point which the American proposal had lacked. Titled Resolution 242, it won the unanimous support of the Security Council, including the Soviet Union, which interpreted it to mean 'all the territories' occupied by Israel.[71]

The severing of ties between Moscow and Tel Aviv led to a decline in the Jewish emigration from the Soviet Union. Israeli and Zionist leaders now relied on Washington to pressure Moscow on this subject. When the Nixon administration took to briefing (even sometimes consulting) the Kremlin on its peace-seeking moves on the basis of Resolution 242 – with a major success in July 1970 with the acceptance of the Rogers plan – the latter eased up on the emigration procedures for Jewish citizens. The situation changed further as Moscow signed a record wheat purchase deal with Washington in the spring of 1972, and as the American Congress insisted on a liberalisation of the Soviet policy on Jewish migration before according the USSR 'most favoured nation' status in trading matters.[72] The result was that during 1970–4 some 110,000 Soviet Jews migrated to Israel: an outflow which amounted to half of the total Jewish inflow into

Israel in that period. This had the effect of reducing the size of Soviet Jewry to third largest in the world, with Israel emerging as the number two.[73]

While the October 1973 war had an adverse effect on the Soviet Jews' desire to migrate to Israel,[74] it established the USSR as a leading factor in the Middle East equation. During the Geneva peace conference, held in late December, the American secretary of state, Kissinger, arranged a private meeting between Abba Eban and Andrei Gromyko, the respective foreign ministers of Israel and the USSR. Gromyko reportedly 'indicated' to Eban that once the Arab–Israeli negotiations had shown 'meaningful progress', the Soviet Union would restore diplomatic links with Israel.[75] However, as stated earlier, Israel abandoned the Geneva conference route to peace, and instead opted for negotiations with the Arabs under the exclusive aegis of America.[76]

'Mr Gromyko proffered [an olive branch] . . . by stating that Israel could, if it so desired, obtain "the very strictest guarantees" from the Soviet Union, provided it withdrew from the occupied territories,' reported Edmund Stevens, the Moscow correspondent of *The Times*, in April 1975.[77] Tel Aviv's response came a few months later, when it was revealed that the series of assurances and guarantees which Israel had obtained from America, on the eve of signing the Sinai II agreement, included a pointed reference to threats to Israel's security or sovereignty from 'a world power' (i.e. the USSR).[78]

Oddly enough Rumania – the only member of the Soviet bloc which did not sever ties with Israel in the wake of the Six Day war – improved its relations with the Jewish state. It arranged to have Iranian crude oil delivered to its tankers through the Israeli pipeline running from Eilat (in the Gulf of Aqaba) to the Mediterranean.[79] The diplomatic value of President Nicolae Ceausescu of Rumania to Israel was underlined by the fact that, after the May 1977 Israeli elections, President Sadat used him as a sounding board for his chances of reaching a peace settlement with Prime Minister Begin. Ceausescu thus played an important part in preparing the ground for Sadat's visit to Jerusalem in November.

By then, to the pleasure of Sadat and the Israeli leaders, the joint Soviet–American declaration of 1 October, on the peace process, had been effectively torpedoed. That the Israeli government had been actively involved in this operation was apparent from the statement made by the Israeli housing minister, Gideon Patt, later in the month. 'Israel has laboured very hard in the last ten years to keep the Soviet Union out of the Middle East,' he said in an interview with the *Guardian*. 'Israel has succeeded in diminishing the Soviet influence [in the region] and in replacing it by that of the United States.'[80]

But whatever the state of play between the superpowers at any given time, certain physical realities cannot be altered. 'It is a fact of geography that the Soviet Union is a Middle East power in a way that the United

States is not,' states R. D. McLaurin, an American academic researcher. 'The borders of the USSR are very close to the Mediterranean; the Black Sea coast of the USSR is vulnerable to naval operations from the Mediterranean; more geographically, the oilfields of Baku are closer to Iraq's, the Persian Gulf's, and far closer to Iran's oilfields than Cairo is; and Cairo is closer to Soviet territory than it is to the capitals of Sudan, Saudi Arabia, either of the Yemens, Oman, the Union of Arab Emirates, Qatar, Bahrain, or Iran, not to mention Libya or the rest of the Maghreb.'[81]

# PART IV

# THE ARABS AND THE SUPERPOWER BLOCS

# 12

# THE ARABS AND THE SOVIET BLOC

As the result of victories in a series of wars with the Ottoman Turks during the eighteenth century, Russia became an integral part of Middle Eastern politics. The Russian rulers were, however, unhappy to see the Ottoman empire decline during the first half of the nineteenth century, through a steady loss of territories in the Balkans and an increasing economic dependence on England and Prussia. The reason was spelled out by Karl Nesselrode, the architect of Russian foreign policy, in his memorandum of 1844: the Ottoman empire's disintegration would bring the powerful west European nations to the southern frontiers of Russia.[1]

Russia's Middle Eastern connection was underlined by the Crimean war (1854–6) which was triggered off by a dispute between Russian-backed Orthodox Christians and French-backed Catholics over the guardianship of holy places in Palestine.[2] Following its defeat in the Crimean war, Russia had to deal directly with such powerful west European nations as Britain, France and Prussia. The same thing happened again when the treaty of San Stefano, which it had signed with the Ottomans in March 1878, was revised at a congress in Berlin later in the year. Nearly three decades later, Russia even reached a modus vivendi with Britain in Iran. Together they divided up the country into northern (Russian) and southern (British) zones, with a neutral region in between.

In the First World War, Czarist Russia sided with Britain and France to fight Germany and Ottoman Turkey. According to the secret (Anglo-French) Sykes–Picot pact of 1916, the Czar was promised Constantinople, small territories on both sides of the Bosphorus, and large parts of the four Turkish provinces contiguous to Russia, as part of the spoils of war.[3] But nothing came of this; the Bolsheviks overthrew the Czarist regime in November 1917, withdrew from the war, and having published the Sykes–Picot pact, to the deep embarrassment of Britain and France,[4] repudiated it. In fact following the civil war, which broke out in the wake of the revolution, the Bolsheviks ceded the provinces of Kars and Ardahan to Turkey in 1921. These actions created goodwill for the Bolshevik regime among Turks as well as Arabs.

Bolshevik interest in the fate of colonised people in general, and

Middle East Arabs in particular, was apparent from the fact that they had, in September 1920, sponsored the first Congress of the Eastern People in the Azerbaijani city of Baku. The consensus of the congress was that nationalist movements in the colonies were struggling against foreign imperialists as well as local landlords and capitalists who were in league with the former; and that only after national independence had been achieved could the Communists concentrate on attacking the indigenous exploiters. Over the years analysis along these lines was sharpened at the congresses of the Communist International. The end result was the publication of the document 'The Tasks of the Communists in the All Arab National Movement' in 1928. 'The Communists are duty bound to wage a struggle for national independence and national unity, not only within the narrow and artificial boundaries created by imperialism and the dynastic interests of certain Arab countries, but on an all-Arab scale, for the national unification of the entire East, it stated. 'The Communist parties must try to attract to the side of the anti-imperialist struggle, not only the workers and peasants, but also the broad strata of urban petite bourgeoisie.'[5]

By then the Soviet government had established diplomatic relations with Saudi Arabia and Yemen – the only Arab states then free to conduct their own external affairs. Although many Arab countries declared themselves independent and took up seats at the League of Nations over the next two decades, their foreign policies were controlled by Britain or France. As such, Moscow's overtures to them for formal links fell flat. It was not until mid-1941, when the USSR joined the Allies, that the situation began to change. During the next three years the Kremlin forged diplomatic ties with Egypt, Iraq, Syria and Lebanon. Following this it lost no time in supporting Syria and Lebanon in their demand, at the newly formed United Nations, for a total withdrawal of French troops from their territories.

As stated earlier, the USSR supported the partition of Palestine at the UN in 1947: a step which cost it dearly. Its standing in the Arab world, at both official and popular levels, fell dramatically. But as Moscow began distancing itself from Tel Aviv – particularly after the latter's backing of American action in the Korean war in June 1950 – and as Arab states joined the neutralist camp on the Korean conflict issue, relations between Arabs and the Soviet Union began to improve. Indeed a few months earlier – following a call by the Islamic Socialist Front of Syria for an Arab rapprochement with the Soviet Union to counter Anglo–American pressures – the Syrian minister for the national economy, Maruf Dawalibi, had suggested a non-aggression pact with the USSR, and initiated trade talks with Moscow.[6]

When Egypt turned down an invitation to become a founder member of the Middle East Defence Organisation along with America, Britain, France, and Turkey, in October 1951, the Kremlin praised its decision publicly.[7] The following July the USSR was taken by surprise by the Free Officers' coup: an event in which it saw the hand of the American CIA, a judgement not totally without foundation.[8] The military regime's persecution of local Communists strengthened Soviet suspicions; and Moscow–Cairo relations remained cool for many months.

Matters improved after the death of Stalin in March, when Soviet foreign policy was liberalised in general: a move which dovetailed with the Kremlin's earlier decision to increase trade with the Afro–Asian countries, signalled by the holding of an International Economic Conference in the Soviet capital in 1952. Moscow invited an Egyptian trade delegation to the USSR in January 1954. The economic agreement, concluded two months later, allowed Egypt to import wheat and oil from the Soviet Union. At the same time the legations in Moscow and Cairo were promoted to embassy status.

Events over the next year brought the two countries closer. With the departure of British troops from the Suez Canal zone in the autumn, Egypt became free to determine its foreign policy completely on its own. Jealous of Arabs' newly won independence, President Nasser lost no time in attacking the decision of royalist Iraq – taken in December at the behest of America and Britain – to sign a military pact with Turkey, a member of Nato. As a pan-Arabist, Nasser was against the idea of an Arab state joining either of the international blocs.[9] Israel was upset about the British withdrawal from Egypt and Iraq's indirect linkage with Nato – developments which occurred against a background of the arrest and trial of a group of Egyptian Jews accused of being Israeli agent-saboteurs. As stated earlier, Israeli forces attacked Egyptian military positions in Gaza in February to avenge the execution of the leaders of the Egyptian Jewish ring.[10] Nasser felt humiliated. In order to strengthen the Egyptian military he approached America for arms. Aware of the lack of hard currency in Egypt's treasury, the Eisenhower administration insisted on cash payment and thus snubbed Nasser's approach.[11]

This was the state of play between Nasser and America when the Egyptian leader flew to Bandung, Indonesia, in April to attend the first conference of the non-aligned nations. His discussions there with Yugoslavia's President Josip Tito and India's Premier Jawaharlal Nehru made him an active proponent of 'positive neutrality', a concept which Moscow came to approve. As for his need for military hardware, the Chinese Premier Chou En-lai, attending the conference, reportedly advised him to approach the USSR. He did. Moscow responded positively. At its behest Prague signed an arms-for-cotton deal, worth $90 to $200 million, with Cairo in May. The agreement was made public four months later.[12]

'Despite the varying accounts of the origins and size of the deal, its impact was enormous and irrefutable,' notes Karen Dawisha, a British academic. 'Egypt's own centrality in the Arab and Afro–Asian world was reasserted and strengthened; Iraq's position was undermined; and in the months following the deal, the armed forces of Egypt, Syria, Saudi Arabia and the Yemen were placed under a joint Egyptian-dominated command. On the Soviet side . . . similar, if less substantial, agreements [were] signed with Syria and the Yemen.'[13]

Moscow went one step further to help Cairo. Aware of the slump in the price of cotton (which then formed 85 per cent of Egypt's exports), the USSR offered to buy Egyptian cotton and advised its allies to do the same.[14] On the diplomatic front, during his visit to Britain in April 1956, Khrushchev declared a Soviet readiness to join the arms embargo to the Middle East under the aegis of 'the United Nations or otherwise'.[15] Britain turned down the proposal, if only because it would have deprived Iraq – a leading member of the Baghdad Pact – of sophisticated weapons. This enabled Egypt and the USSR to show that the Western outcry at the Cairo–Prague arms deal was hypocritical.

Three months later the Kremlin supported Nasser's nationalisation of the Suez Canal company, carried out in retaliation for the withdrawal of an offer by America, Britain, and the World Bank to finance construction of the Aswan Dam. In its notes to America, Britain, France and Israel, it described the Suez nationalisation as well within Egypt's legal rights, and warned against military plans (by Britain and France) to seize the Suez Canal.

When Egypt was attacked on 29 October the USSR moved swiftly to rally support for it at the United Nations. The result was the UN General Assembly resolution of 2 November which demanded an immediate cease-fire and the withdrawal of the attacking nations to their pre-war positions. When Israel, France, and Britain ignored the call, the Soviet prime minister Nikolai Bulganin sent a letter to President Eisenhower suggesting a joint American–Soviet military action to stop the aggression. Eisenhower rejected the proposal. On 5 November Bulganin addressed letters to the British and French prime ministers which contained a Soviet threat to use force 'to destroy the aggressors', including missile attacks on the capitals of the aggressor nations.[16] Simultaneously the Kremlin promised to send 'volunteers' to defend Egypt. The next day Cairo asked for Soviet volunteers.[17] Neither the threat nor the promise were carried out, because the cease-fire went into effect on 6 November. 'Nevertheless Soviet diplomatic activity did secure additional prestige for the Soviet Union in the Arab world, where the population seemed to be impressed with the style, if not the substance, of the Soviet stand,' states Karen Dawisha. 'In the immediate postwar period, supplies of food, medicine and arms replacements to both Egypt and Syria contributed to Soviet popularity.'[18]

The events preceding and following the Suez war helped sustain the tolerant policy which Nasser had adopted towards the Egyptian Communists in the wake of the promulgation of the republican constitution in January 1956. As described earlier, hundreds of Communists released during the war were allowed to function freely, and this enabled the two leading Marxist groups to form a united Communist party in early 1958. By then the USSR had agreed to finance the first stage of the Aswan Dam, and provide $175 million in soft loans to Egypt.[19]

Moscow had its reservations about the merger of Egypt and Syria into the United Arab Republic, and would have preferred a loose federation. But once the UAR was formed, *Pravda* welcomed it.[20] During his state visit to the USSR in April, Nasser was warmly received by the Soviet leadership. Three months later he flew to Moscow, on his own initiative, to appraise himself of intended Soviet response to the landing of American and British forces into Lebanon and Jordan in the wake of the republican coup in Iraq. He found the Soviet leaders cautious. Despite his espousal of decisive action, they committed themselves to nothing more dramatic than military manoeuvres along the Bulgarian–Turkish border.[21]

With the emergence of Iraq as a progressive republic, Moscow began to divide its attentions between Cairo and Baghdad. As the Iraqi regime became increasingly reformist at home and anti-imperialist abroad – with the Communists coming to the fore at the expense of the pan-Arabists – Moscow became solicitous of Baghdad. Nasser resented this. He resented too the attack made on him by Khaled Bakdash, the Syrian Communist leader, for compromising with imperialism and pampering the national bourgeoisie.[22] He responded by launching an anti-Communist campaign in early 1959, and entering into a bitter correspondence with Khrushchev. The failure of the pan-Arabist revolt in Mosul, Iraq, in early March, partly due to diligent action by the local Communists,[23] angered and disappointed Nasser further. Giving vent to his feelings in a public speech later that month, he accused the Soviets of working towards the objective of establishing a 'Red Fertile Crescent'.[24] *Pravda* responded by criticising 'a leading figure in the Arab world' for his sweeping policy of immediate unification of all the Arab countries, and his propensity to dub all those who disagreed with his ideas as 'Communists, Zionists, and enemies of the Arab people'.[25]

However, by late April differences between the two sides were patched up, after Khrushchev had reassured Nasser that the UAR's policy towards the local Communists was a domestic matter,[26] and that the Soviet Union had no intention of interfering, directly or indirectly, in the internal affairs of another country. How far the USSR stood by its promise of non-interference was made public by Nasser in an interview with *Al Ahram*, the semi-official paper of Egypt, a year later. 'In spite of the divergence of opinions, Moscow never put pressure on us, never threatened to stop her aid,' he said.[27]

Moscow–Cairo relations improved further when Qassem, the Iraqi ruler, began curtailing Communist influence soon after the celebration of the first anniversary of the revolution in July 1959, thus dimming the

USSR's earlier hopes of a firm Communist ascendancy in Iraqi politics. By the end of the year the Soviets were engaged in building the first stage of the Aswan Dam, and discussing plans for the second stage. When completed, the dam was expected to add 1.3 million acres of arable land to the existing 6 million acres, and provide perennial irrigation to another 700,000 acres in the Nile delta then dependent on basin irrigation.[28] It was apparent that state-to-state relations between Egypt and the USSR were growing friendlier. But that did not affect the evaluation of Egyptian society and government by the Communist Party of the Soviet Union – more specifically its central committee's international department.

The year 1960 was particularly active for the international department of the CPSU, which played host to eighty foreign Communist and Workers' parties at an international congress in November. One of the achievements of the congress, held in Moscow, was the formulation and adoption of the concept of national democracy and the national democratic state. National democracy was defined as a transient stage between bourgeois democracy and proletarian (or people's) democracy. 'In those liberated countries where the people are still without democratic liberties,' wrote Boris Ponomaryev, secretary of the international department of the CPSU's central committee, in *Kommunist*, the party's theoretical journal, 'the struggle for the creation of a national democratic state gives the progressive forces the opportunity to remove the remnants of the colonial administration, to seize power from the national traitors who serve imperialism, and take the fate of the country into their hands.'[29]

While welcoming the nationalisation decrees of July 1961 – promulgated by Nasser to protect 'the revolutionary regime from feudalism, monopolies, and exploiting capitalism' – Victor Mayevsky, the Cairo correspondent of *Pravda*, pointed out that these measures only partly altered property relations in the countryside, where the majority of the people lived.[30] As stated earlier, these decrees paved the way for Syria's secession from the UAR: a development which in turn led Nasser to accelerate the process of radical change in Egypt.[31] The result was the adoption of the National Charter, which combined a commitment to 'scientific socialism' – defined as 'the suitable style for finding the right method leading to progress'[32] – with the aim of achieving unity of 'all the working forces of the people'.[33]

Not surprisingly, the Egyptian National Charter became part of the debate then in progress among the CPSU ideologist on the nature of national liberation struggles, national democracy, and socialism of a national type. Such radicals as B. Abasov criticised the Charter for accepting 'non-exploitative private property, its stress on religion, and its permitting of private land ownership'.[34] This view was endorsed by Boris Ponomaryev. Criticising the Charter for rejecting the concepts of class conflict and the abolition of private property, he expressed doubt about the ability of Egypt's regime to enact genuinely socialist measures while denying the necessity for proletarian hegemony.[35] The moderates, on the other hand, agreed with Georgi Mirsky. Appreciative of what had been accomplished in Egypt so far, Mirsky argued that judging by the evolution in the international outlook which the 'revolutionary democrats', leading the Egyptian nation, had undergone, they were quite capable of achieving 'scientific socialism' at home.[36] Among those who subscribed to this view was Khrushchev.

What weakened the Soviet moderates' argument was the fact that Nasser continued to hold most of the Egyptian Communists in such dreaded places as the Abu Zaabal and Kharga prison/concentration camps. The publication, in mid-1963, of an appeal by Egypt's Communists – entitled 'Save Our Lives' – in the *World Marxist Review*, a theoretical journal sympathetic to the CPSU's international department, showed that the situation was indeed serious.[37]

In June 1963 Khrushchev sent Alexei Adzhubei, editor of *Izvestia*, to Cairo for top-level discussions, which included the fate of the Communist prisoners. Two months later Nasser followed up his decree nationalising a new category of private companies[38] with a decision to enlarge the base of the fledgling ASU by gradually releasing political prisoners, of both left and right, and inviting them to join the ASU.

By the time Khrushchev arrived in Egypt in May to inaugurate the first stage of the Aswan Dam – a project to which the Soviet commitment was to amount to $130 million in soft loans and the services of 5,000 technicians[39] – nearly 600 Communists had been released.[40] During this visit Khrushchev conferred the title of 'Hero of the Soviet Union' on Nasser and the Egyptian defence minister, Field-Marshal Abdul Hakim Amr, and raised the level of promised Soviet aid for the next year to a record $277 million.[41] Commending the progressive nature of the regime's reforms at home, he stated that Egypt was 'embarking on the path of socialist construction'.[42] He promised more arms to the republic if 'it became necessary to repel the schemes of the [Israeli] aggressor'.[43] On his return to Moscow he said that in Egypt the question of Arab unity was undergoing change, with greater stress being laid on 'the unity of the Arab working people'.[44]

Khruschev lost his position in the government and the party in mid-October. But that made no difference to the USSR's policy towards Egypt and its president. The formal signing of the Soviet–Egyptian military agreement, scheduled for November, took place in Moscow. During the first half of 1965 the two states exchanged a series of delegations. President Nasser visited Moscow in August with the main objective of acquainting himself with the post-Khrushchev leadership.

By then the Egyptian Communist leaders had dissolved their party and advised members to join the Arab Socialist Union:[45] a step which encouraged Soviet ideologist to regard the ASU as a national democratic front engaged in carrying out a national democratic revolution. The favourable view of the ASU was summarised by I. I. Garshin, a theoretician, thus: 'It is a particular feature of the situation that [while] those who lead the Egyptian revolution are not Marxists, they are putting into practice measures which in many respects are similar to the measures taken by Communists at a certain stage of a social revolution.'[46]

The popularity of Nasser among the Arab masses, and his involvement in North Yemen's civil war on the republican side and in South Yemen against British imperialism, were much appreciated by Soviet leaders as well as theoreticians. Conversely, the overthrow of President Sukarno's national democratic regime by military leaders – acting in league with the American CIA – was received with shock and gloom in Moscow, particularly when the coup was followed by the massacre of up to half a million Communists. In the Middle East the Saudi monarch hit back at Nasser with announcements, in December, that Saudi Arabia had concluded an arms deal worth $360 million with Britain and America,[47] and that he was actively exploring the possibility of launching an Islamic Alliance to counter Nasserite socialism. In an interview with *Izvestia* in February, Nasser summed up the international situation thus: 'The forces of colonialism and reaction inside and outside the Arab world are launching a new offensive and, therefore, all progressive forces inside and outside the Arab world should close their ranks, solidify their unity, and redouble their vigilance and thus become effective.'[48]

Soviet Prime Minister Kosygin took up this theme during his visit to Egypt in May: he called for a united front of the progressive Arab states of Egypt, Algeria, Syria and Iraq in order to 'confront imperialism and reaction'.[49] He was particularly keen to see Egypt form a united front with Syria where the radical Baathist regime, which had assumed power in February, was under mortal threat from Israel. This came about six months later, with the two states signing a joint defence pact: a step facilitated by the fact that both military forces were equipped with Soviet weapons.

By then Moscow had supplied an estimated one billion dollars worth of arms to Cairo. Its economic aid, given largely for building up Egypt's infrastructure in irrigation, power plants, heavy industry, and transport, amounted to $780 million.[50] In addition Soviet allies in East Europe had provided Egypt with a further $540 million.[51] Despite these injections of foreign aid the Egyptian economy was in an unhealthy state. Soviet analysts were aware of this. Writing in *Pravda*, Igor Belyayev and Yevgeny Primakov blamed the poor performance of Egypt's agriculture on the inadequate and improperly implemented land reform, which had led to the rise of a kulak class and a capitalist mode of production. In industry, they noted, the mixed economy was allowing the private sector to use public funds to increase its profits.[52]

The root cause of economic sluggishness lay in the absence of a revolutionary party. The ASU, with its membership running into millions, was a dull instrument to effect revolutionary change in society. The proper course lay in creating an active, ideologically committed cadre within the party, and getting the working masses involved in running the organisation. This was the gist of contributions made by Soviet and Egyptian Marxists attending a seminar on 'National and Social Revolution in Africa' in Cairo in October 1966.[53] By then the ASU had made a start of a kind along these lines, and its ancillary, the Socialist Youth Organisation, had launched an anti-feudal campaign during the summer. As stated earlier, the ASU was in the process of transforming itself into a popular mobilisation agency when the Six Day war broke out.[54]

During the weeks preceding the war the Soviet Union tried to restrain Egypt and Syria, once Nasser's action in closing the straits of Tiran on 23 May had gone unchallenged. Kosygin reportedly told the visiting Egyptian defence minister: 'You have won a political victory. So it is time now to compromise, to work politically.'[55] To restrain its Arab allies, the Kremlin told the Egyptian and Syrian leaders that the USSR would not support them if they attacked Israel, thus risking confrontation with America as well, and that in case they were attacked by Israel alone, the USSR would not back them militarily.[56] The Soviet leaders were in constant touch with the White House in Washington over the 'hot line'. Acting on an Israeli message that its intelligence reports predicted an Egyptian attack on Israel on 27 May, the White House contacted the Kremlin. This in turn led to the Soviet ambassador in Cairo waking Nasser at 3 a.m. on 27 May to ask whether Egyptian action was imminent. It was not. He stressed the need for restraint, and reiterated the adverse political consequences of being an aggressor.[57]

Under the circumstances the USSR was all the more angry and embarrassed when Israel launched a surprise blitzkrieg against Egypt, Syria and Jordan on 5 June. It did its best to bring about a cease-fire.[58] Once that was accomplished, it hastened to repair the damage done to the military machines of Egypt and Syria. With the first shipment of Soviet weapons arriving in Egypt on 23 June, the arms build-up proceeded at a fast pace. In early November the Soviet chief-of-staff, M. V. Zakharov, said to Nasser, 'Mr President, I think Egypt can now stand up to anything Israel can deliver. . . . The [Egyptian] defences are perfectly all right.'[59] For doing all this the USSR had charged Egypt nothing.

'We have so far paid not one penny for the arms we obtained from the Soviet Union to equip our armed forces,' Nasser told the ASU national congress on 23 July 1968. 'The Soviet Union has never tried, not even in the time of our greatest trials, to dictate conditions to us or ask anything of us. . . . Even when I told them [in Moscow] that I felt ashamed that we were making so many demands while they had asked nothing from us . . . they told us: "We take this stand on the basis of our ideology".'[60]

Not surprisingly, Soviet experts on the Middle East were quick to analyse the war, and offer solutions to the problems it had highlighted. The reasons for the Egyptian defeat, they wrote, were: the predominance of self-seeking officers, concerned more with their privileges and lifestyle than the country's defences; poorly educated, overwhelmingly peasant, ranks; and improper and insufficient use of Soviet weapons. In the political sphere, they stated, insufficient contact between the leadership and the masses was the main weakness of the regime. The solution lay in purging the right-wing elements from the military and the ASU, and reforming political life so as to draw the working masses into the running of the country.[61]

Nasser reacted differently to advice in the military and political fields. He followed up the immediate dismissal of fifty top army and air force officers with more purges – which together affected 600 officers – and attached 1,500 Soviet military advisers to the Egyptian armed forces. In the political sphere, however, he not only ignored the counsel offered by Soviet analysts (as well as the Marxists within the ASU) but acted contrary to it. As stated earlier, he disbanded the Socialist Youth Organisation and the Leadership Groups within the ASU.[62] In September 1969 he demoted (left-leaning) Ali Sabri and his cohorts in the ASU hierarchy; and three months later appointed (rightist) Anwar Sadat as a vice-president of the republic.

But this had no adverse effect on his growing friendship with and dependence on the Kremlin. Unable to bear the continued humiliation of Israel's air raids deep into Egyptian territory, Nasser flew to Moscow in January. There he threatened to resign unless the Soviet leaders agreed to increase their involvement in Egypt's defences, and actively help safeguard Egyptian territory. This led to a day-long meeting of the CPSU politbureau and top Soviet military leaders. At the end the CPSU chief, Leonid Brezhnev, told Nasser that they had agreed to his request, reluctantly, and that, in view of their decision being 'fraught with grave consequences', the Egyptians would have to behave with restraint.[63] This was enough to please Nasser. 'Our relations with the Russians are unique,' he told Eric Rouleau of *Le Monde* in February. 'They have written off half the debts we contracted and they have extended facilities for repaying the rest.'[64]

In order to emphasise to America (and Israel) the limited nature of its commitment to Egypt's defences, the Kremlin made no secret either of its shipment of advanced ground-to-air missiles (driven through city streets in daylight) or its deployment of Soviet pilots (conversing freely in Russian on their intercoms) in intercepting Israeli jets violating Egyptian airspace. The Egyptian–Soviet purpose was served when, following the loss of a few jet fighters in the air, Israel stopped deep penetration bombing of Egypt in mid-April. This helped to revive peace efforts by the American secretary of state, William Rogers. Soon after his return from a three-week-long visit to Moscow, Nasser accepted the Rogers plan on 24

July. *Pravda* described Nasser's decision as signifying 'great political courage'.[65]

But there was to be no slackening in Egypt's military preparedness. 'Soviet arms supplies [to Egypt] increased quantitatively and qualitatively to include the latest and most sophisticated weaponry,' states Karen Dawisha. 'It was, nevertheless, an important feature of this build-up that however massive it may have appeared to the Western observer, it was first of all the product of Nasser's own demands and secondly it always fell short of these demands.'[66]

Nasser's sudden death in late September 1970 caused anxiety in Moscow, but seemed to have no immediate effect on Soviet–Egyptian relations. As planned earlier, a CPSU delegation led by Boris Ponomaryev arrived in Egypt in December to strengthen ties between the CPSU and the Egyptian ASU. During its visit to the recently opened Institute of Socialist Studies in Cairo, Diauddin Daoud, an ASU leader, said, 'The CPSU's experience in the selection, ideological education, and training of personnel is of tremendous importance for the cause of our revolution.'[67] The significance of the CPSU delegation's Egyptian trip was underlined by Ponomaryev when he wrote in the *World Marxist Review*: 'Ties of this kind . . . actually represent a fundamentally new form of solidarity between the world Communist movement and the forces of national liberation.'[68]

Moscow went through another period of trepidation when President Sadat arrested Ali Sabri and other left-leaning leaders on 15 May. One of those arrested was Sami Sharif who, as minister for presidential affairs, had visited Moscow earlier to negotiate terms for a proposed treaty of friendship and cooperation between the two states. However, Sadat showed no indication of reneging on the plans to sign the treaty. The fall of the Ali Sabri group made the Kremlin leaders all the more eager to place their country's relations with Egypt within a more binding framework: a decision taken earlier to meet the rising criticism within CPSU portals for continued large-scale military and economic aid to Egypt. The treaty, valid for fifteen years, was signed in Cairo on 27 May. In the operative articles, numbers 7 and 8, the signatories agreed to enter into immediate consultation in the event of any threat to peace, and to continue cooperation in the development of Egypt's military potential.

The treaty failed to paper over fundamental differences that existed between the political outlooks of Sadat and the Soviet leaders. This was illustrated in their divergent reactions to the military coup in Sudan on 19 July, when the leftist Major Hashem Atta overthrew President Jaafar Numeiri. Moscow recognised the Atta regime immediately. But Sadat actively helped Numeiri to launch a counter-coup, which was successful. 'We Arabs will never be Marxists,' Sadat said. 'That is why we cannot allow a Communist regime to exist in the Arab world.'[69] The Kremlin showed its displeasure with Sadat by slowing down arms deliveries to Egypt.[70]

Despite two visits to Moscow during the first half of 1972 Sadat failed to obtain advanced Soviet fighter bombers (similar to the American Phantoms) and ground-to-ground missiles. He was dismayed by the apparent decision of Leonid Brezhnev and President Nixon, during the latter's visit to the Soviet capital in May–June (primarily to sign the Strategic Arms Limitation Treaty I), to set aside all regional disputes from their bilateral relations. He made one more attempt to secure a Soviet promise to supply Egypt with sophisticated military hardware, but failed.

In a dramatic move, Sadat asked the Kremlin on 7 July either to place in Egyptian hands or remove the advanced Soviet weaponry already in Egypt, and that all the Soviet advisers who had arrived after the Six Day war should leave within the next ten days. As a result, some 15,000 Soviet military personnel left Egypt, taking with them such Soviet weaponry as MiG-25s, SU-11 interceptors, and advanced SAM missile batteries.[71] Although shocked and angered, the Kremlin, which had by then provided Egypt with total military aid of $5 billion,[72] limited its protest to recalling its ambassador from Cairo. Sadat did the same with the Egyptian ambassador in Moscow.

Soviet theoreticians reflected the coolness now existing between Cairo and Moscow in their writings. 'In many villages, richer peasants, who profited from the agrarian reforms, and who hold the village elders and other local chiefs in the hollow of their hands, call the tune,' wrote Georgi Mirsky, a moderate theorist, on the eve of the twentieth anniversary of Egypt's republican revolution. 'In urban areas, even though the state controls 85 per cent of the industrial production, there is a strong private sector which incoporates not only shopkeepers and artisans, but also growing numbers of middlemen, profiteers, building contractors and other such bourgeois elements. The higher paid bureaucrats display a tendency to link up with the private sector.'[73]

The downward slide in Soviet–Egyptian relations was interrupted by the killing of Israeli athletes in Munich in early September, which in turn led to the death of 200 to 500 Arabs in Israeli air raids over Lebanon and Syria:[74] events which, due to their emotional impact, brought about a clear-cut division between Israel on one side and all the Arab states on the other. Against this background the ambassadors of Egypt and the USSR returned to their posts in October, and the Soviet and Egyptian leaders resumed their dialogue. Soviet arms began arriving in Egypt at such a pace that Sadat declared publicly in the spring that he was satisfied with arms shipments. The military build-up continued throughout the summer, with Sadat having complete control over both the Soviet-supplied weapons as well as the necessary Soviet experts needed for the upkeep of the sophisticated military hardware.

Two days before the planned Egyptian attack on the Israeli-occupied

Arab territories, Sadat informed Brezhnev of his plans. In reply Brezhnev repeated his earlier warning to Sadat not to attack Israel within its pre-1967 borders, and stated that while Arabs could count on Soviet backing, the decision to fight must rest solely on them.[75]

Once the war started Brezhnev reached an understanding with President Nixon over the 'hot line' that it was not to be allowed to rise above the regional level. Within that framework the two superpowers began airlifting arms to their protagonists. However, the rate of arms supplies from the USSR to Egypt and Syria was a fraction of the daily shipment of about 1,500 tons of weapons that America airlifted to Israel in its own and El Al's planes.[76] At the United Nations the USSR refused to endorse cease-fire calls as long as Arabs were winning on the battlefield. When, on 15 October, Israel established a bridgehead over the Suez Canal, to the north of the Great Bitter Lake, Prime Minister Kosygin flew into Cairo. He did not leave until four days later when Sadat agreed to let the USSR try for a cease-fire in situ. This came about on 22 October.

When Israel violated the cease-fire immediately, with a view to encircling Egypt's Third Army, deployed to the south of the Great Bitter Lake, the Kremlin issued a statement warning Israel of 'the gravest consequences' if it did not return to the lines of 22 October and honour the cease-fire. The next day Brezhnev sent a message to Nixon to the effect that if he did not agree to Sadat's earlier proposal for a joint American–Soviet contingent to enforce the cease-fire, under UN auspices, the USSR would urgently consider 'the question of taking appropriate steps unilaterally'.[77]

To back up its words with action, the Soviet Union added twenty-five ships, including some troop carriers, to its Mediterranean fleet of sixty, increased the number of its airborne divisions on a high state of alert from three (on 7 October) to seven, and requested Yugoslavia for permission to fly military aircraft carrying troops through its airspace.[78] On 25 October the Kremlin sent a group of seventy Soviet personnel to Cairo to form part of the proposed UN joint force. That day 'several' Soviet combat ships, including two amphibious landing crafts, detached themselves from the Soviet squadron stationed near Crete, and started sailing towards the Egyptian coast.[79] It was only after Israel had agreed, under American pressure, to respect the cease-fire, and provide food and water to the surrounded Egyptian Third Army that, later in the day, the Soviet ships changed direction. With this the USSR accomplished its immediate objective of saving the Egyptian troops from decimation by the Israelis.

However, this had come about after a day of heightened tension with a global dimension. Nixon had reacted to the Soviet statement about unilateral action if Israel persisted in its cease-fire violations by putting American forces throughout the world on 'defence condition three' – stage three alert – on 25 October. Although the alert lasted only a day, it aroused considerable consternation among America's allies who were not consulted, and condemnation in the Kremlin. Reflecting the official view, a Tass statement of 27 October referred to the adverse effects of the American alert on the superpower détente, since it was ordered 'in an attempt to intimidate the Soviet Union'.[80]

On the whole Moscow had good reason to be pleased with the outcome of the war. It had shown that America and its European allies were divided in their policy towards the Middle East, and had led the Arab states to impose an oil embargo against the Western supporters of Israel. In territorial terms, while the Syrians had lost Mount Hermon, the Egyptians had lodged themselves firmly on the eastern side of the Suez Canal.

Summing up the overall impact of the October war, Georgi Mirsky wrote in the *New Times* that it had dispelled four myths: Israeli military force is invincible; Arab weaponry is inferior to that of Israel; the Arabs can never act in unison; and détente is insufficient to prevent the outbreak of wars or bring about an early cease-fire. The effectiveness of Soviet-made anti-tank rockets and anti-aircraft missiles had destroyed the second myth. 'The third myth dispelled [by the war] related to the alleged fragility and illusoriness of Arab solidarity,' he wrote. 'Today this solidarity, founded on the sense of Arab brotherhood and an awareness of facing a common enemy . . . was confirmed in the course of the October fighting. Iraqi, Moroccan, Jordanian and Saudi troops fought side by side with the Syrian army; the Palestinians and the Kuwaitis also saw action, and Algerian aircraft took part in the air war. But perhaps even more important is the solidarity of the oil-producing Arab states. . . . Even such countries as Saudi Arabia and Kuwait announced an oil boycott of the countries supporting Israel.'[81]

Soviet praise for Arab unity was evidently well received at the Arab League summit held in Algiers in late November. 'The participants in the [summit] conference expressed profound satisfaction with the political and military assistance that the Soviet Union and other socialist states have rendered the Arab countries,' reported *Pravda*.[82] The USSR's prestige in the Arab world rose when its foreign minister acted as a co-chairman – on a par with his American counterpart – at the Geneva peace conference a few weeks later. In retrospect, however, this was to prove to be the pinnacle of Soviet diplomatic achievements in the Middle East. For, as stated earlier, Sadat cooperated with the Israeli leaders in not returning to Geneva for talks, and instead used the American secretary of state as a go-between.[83]

The first result of this effort was the Sinai I agreement on troop disengagement between Cairo and Tel Aviv. Referring to this agreement, *Pravda* warned that it could be a positive step only if it was followed up by 'the withdrawal of Israeli troops from all Arab occupied territories and guaranteeing the legitimate rights of the Arab people of Palestine'.[84]

As Sadat and the Saudi king sought an end to the Arab oil embargo, the

Soviet mass media expressed disapproval of their efforts. 'If today some Arab leaders are ready to surrender in the face of American pressure and lift the ban on oil before the demands [for complete Israeli withdrawal and recognition of the Palestinians' legitimate rights] are fulfilled, they are challenging the whole Arab world and progressive forces of the world which insist on the continued use of the oil weapon,' said a commentator on Moscow Radio on 12 March.[85] Such statements went unheeded by the Arab oil states: they lifted the embargo within a week.

Hopeful of securing the financial backing of the rich oil states, particularly Saudi Arabia, to buy weapons in the West, Sadat declared in mid-April that he wished to end Egypt's exclusive reliance on the USSR for arms.[86] Moscow tried to placate him by resuming arms shipments to Egypt. Despite Kissinger's statement, on the eve of President Nixon's extensive tour of the Middle East in June, that America had 'no intention of trying to eliminate Soviet influence in the Middle East',[87] Soviet leaders viewed the elaborate American exercise with apprehension. Their fears were fulfilled when Sadat signed a number of Egyptian–American agreements of a non-military nature, during Nixon's visit, and followed this up with guarantees for American investment in Egypt and permission to major American banks to open branches in the republic. All this was part of the 'open door' economic policy that Sadat was pursuing with vigour. Criticising this, Lev Tolkunov, editor of *Izvestia*, wrote that encouragement to foreign and indigenous private capital held no long-term advantage for the Egyptian masses. '[This policy] may in time, as the experience of history teaches, turn into a bitter hangover for Egypt, and especially for its people.'[88] A special article on the Egyptian economy, published in *Pravda* in late December, issued a similar warning. 'The strengthening of private enterprise trends which one notes in the country, given the fairly complex class structure of Egyptian society, can complicate the struggle for the continuation of progressive transformation,' it said.[89]

It was obvious from the mildness of these criticisms of Sadat that Moscow hoped to regain his friendship. Its chance came when Kissinger's shuttle diplomacy reached a dead end in March 1975. Soviet leaders now tried, with Sadat's aid, to revive the Geneva peace conference. They did not get very far, because the Arabs lacked unity, and because their own attention was soon engaged by more pressing problems at home and abroad. The dismissal from the politbureau (in April) of Alexei Shelepin – a radical who had all along questioned the policies of providing massive aid to Egypt and the CPSU's fraternising with such bodies as the Egyptian ASU and the Syrian Baath – created intra-party problems, which needed to be tackled immediately. Then the Soviet leadership became preoccupied with the crowning achievement of the Conference of Security and Cooperation in Europe: a summit meeting of European leaders in Helsinki, Finland, in August, to sign the final document.

Sadat coupled the signing of the Sinai II agreement between Egypt and Israel in early September with an announcement of his plan to visit the USA the next month. The Kremlin was upset on both counts. Not surprisingly, therefore, when Sadat later aired his periodic complaint about Soviet arms being either withheld or supplied slowly, it reacted sharply, 'Since the October war of 1973, the Soviet Union has been consistently continuing the policy of furthering friendly cooperation with Egypt in the military field in accordance with the existing agreements,' wrote *Pravda*. 'But cooperation, of course, is a two-sided matter. It cannot develop if one of the sides is pursuing a policy of undermining it.'[90]

Faced with the prospect of Egypt's payments deficit rising to $5 billion (from the current year's $3 billion), Sadat approached Soviet leaders for a ten-year moratorium on debt repayments.[91] They rejected the suggestion. Displeased, Sadat refused to sign the (annual) Egyptian–Soviet trade agreement for the coming year. When he finally climbed down, in early February, and expressed his willingness to conclude the protocol, the Kremlin asked for a postponement. Sadat retaliated by unilaterally abrogating the Egyptian–Soviet treaty of friendship and cooperation on 14 March, ten years before its expiry date. The Kremlin was not surprised. A statement issued by Tass described the abrogation as 'a new manifestation of the unfriendly policy with regard to the Soviet Union which President Sadat has been pursuing in practice for a long time'.[92] Moscow finally signed the trade protocol with Cairo in late April.

With the supply of Soviet arms now down to a trickle, Sadat felt freer to express his views on Soviet–Egyptian relations. In his memoirs, published in early February, he alleged inter alia, that the Soviet weapons shipped to Egypt before the Yom Kippur war were insufficient and obsolete. Soviet response was curt and sharp. Accusing Sadat of indulging in 'political libel' and 'historical falsification', an editorial in *Pravda* stated that the Egyptian leader had gone 'far beyond the limits of elementary propriety and generally accepted norms of relations between states'.[93]

Yet, aware of the strategic and political importance of Egypt in the Middle East, the Kremlin kept Cairo informed of its diplomatic moves to secure a comprehensive peace in the region. Following his talks with the American secretary of state Cyrus Vance, in May, the Soviet foreign minister Gromyko held consultations with his Egyptian counterpart, Ismail Fahmi, in Moscow in June. But any goodwill generated by this gesture was dissipated when a six-day-long border conflict broke out between Egypt and Libya on 21 July. Sadat alleged that by jamming Egyptian radio communication the Soviet navy, stationed just outside Egypt's territorial waters, had aided Libya.[94]

During the period between this conflict and his trip to Jerusalem four months later, Sadat suspended cotton exports to the USSR, recalled all Egyptian students and military personnel engaged in studies or training in the Soviet bloc, and finally imposed a unilateral moratorium on debt repayments to Moscow. Soviet credits to Egypt then amounted to at least $11 billion: $7 billion for military supplies, and $4 billion for non-military goods and services.[95] The economic aid provided by the USSR had not only helped construct the Aswan Dam (whose hydroelectric plant had trebled Egypt's electricity output), and increased the Helwan iron and steel plant's production capacity fivefold, but also built most of the thousand new factories in the country.[96]

When the leaders of the PLO and five Arab states friendly with the USSR gathered in the Libyan capital to form the Front of Steadfastness in early December, Sadat reacted by severing diplomatic relations with the Front's members – and closing down all Soviet consulates outside Cairo as well as the Soviet cultural centre in Cairo.[97] With this, relations between Egypt and the USSR reverted back to the days preceding the sensational arms deal between Cairo and Prague for Soviet arms twenty-three years before.

As stated earlier, the Cairo–Prague agreement proved to be the forerunner of similar deals between Syria and the Soviet bloc.[98] The possibility of the Soviet Union supplying arms to Syria arose in March when the latter, threatened by troop concentrations from Turkey and (monarchist) Iraq along its borders, found itself unable to procure arms from France – its traditional supplier – due to French anger at Syrian support for the Algerian nationalists. Damascus reached an agreement in principle with Moscow regarding the supply of Soviet arms in June.[99] But no action was taken until December when, following a massive Israeli raid on Syrian posts near Lake Tiberias, which caused scores of deaths,[100] the matter acquired urgency. The Damascus–Prague deal was signed in February 1956.[101] By then Syria had established substantial commercial links with the Soviet bloc, whose members had participated in the Damascus international fair in September 1954, and received a Syrian trade delegation in their capitals during the following summer. The commercial and military pacts concluded between the two sides brought the number of Soviet bloc experts present in Syria in May 1956 to about 300.[102]

Between then and the Suez war Damascus signed a new trade and cultural agreement with Moscow. The USSR's support for Egypt in the Suez conflict led to greater cooperation between Syria and the Soviet Union. This increased further when Damascus proclaimed its opposition to the Eisenhower doctrine, thus earning the anger of America and the pro-West governments in Turkey, Iraq, Lebanon, Jordan and Israel. The conclusion of an extensive Syrian–Soviet economic agreement in July – covering dams and power plants, railroads, fertiliser factories, and oil and mineral prospecting – increased anti-Damascus feeling in the neighbouring capitals. Hostility towards Syria reached a point where, in the words of President Eisenhower, a consensus emerged at a meeting of the representatives of America and Syria's moderate Arab neighbours that 'the present regime in Syria had to go'.[103]

Aware of the grave threat to the Syrian regime, the USSR stepped in to protect it. As stated earlier, the Soviet army newspaper specifically named Turkey and Israel as the countries planning aggression against Syria.[104] Of the two Turkey, with 50,000 troops amassed along its borders with Syria,[105] was regarded as the more menacing. Warning Turkey that any action against Syria would not remain 'localised',[106] the Kremlin dispatched a naval squadron to the Syrian port of Latakia. A series of anti-American demonstrations held during September in the Arab states bordering Syria had the effect of dissipating the threat to Damascus. But the Turkish troops were withdrawn from their forward positions only after the USSR had ordered joint navy and army exercises along the Soviet–Turkish border, and Marshal Georgi Zhukov, the Soviet defence minister, had declared on 24 October on Albanian radio, that the USSR was ready to 'strike at any military adventure organised by the United States near our southern borders'.[107]

Thus aided by Moscow, the National Front government, composed of anti-imperialist forces, succeeded in safeguarding the territorial integrity of the republic. But, as stated earlier, once the external threat had receded, the Baathists parted company with the Communists within the Front – and joined the move for an immediate merger of Syria with Egypt, which was consummated in early 1958.[108] During the United Arab Republic's three and a half years of existence, Syrian Communist leaders living in exile in Prague criticised Nasser for a series of undemocratic actions, the subordination of Syria to Egypt, and the persecution of the Communists. Their views were generally shared by Soviet theoreticians writing in such journals as the *World Marxist Review*. No wonder that the USSR recognised Syria as an independent entity within a fortnight of the separatist coup on 28 September 1961. Addressing the twenty-second congress of the CPSU in October, Khaled Bakdash described the UAR's break-up as signifying 'the bankruptcy of the policy of anti-Communism'.[109]

Yet the Communists in Syria were not released until January. They were then denied the right to participate in political or trade union activity. Moscow–Damascus relations, therefore, remained cool and correct. The Baathist seizure of power in March 1963, and the new regime's expression of friendship with the USSR, made little difference. Moscow chose to judge the Baathist rulers by their deeds, and found them censurable. *Izvestia* criticised the Baathists for indulging in adventurism, terrorism, and anti-Communist propaganda, and for professing sham socialism.[110]

Moscow took note of the victory of the leftist faction over its opponents at the regional and national congresses of the Baath party in September and October. In a general sense, the newly adopted programme gave priority to socialism over Arab unity. This development was described by a commentator in *Pravda* as marking the defeat of 'the treacherous, discredited clique of old style politicians' (such as Aflaq and Bitar) at the hands of 'healthy, honest, energetic, patriotic elements' (led by Nureddin Attasi and Amin Hafez).[111]

When the radicalised regime in Damascus undertook a programme of economic reform during 1964 and early 1965, and made use of the recently released Communists, among others, to overcome resistance to the new measures, the Soviet press and radio expressed approval. In Georgi Mirsky's view, the Syrian government's actions were the end result of the declining influence of the right-wing Baathists, 'the objective necessity of economic advancement', and the example set by Egypt.[112]

Although on the decline, the right-wing Baathists attempted a come-back. As described earlier, they failed.[113] The radicals consolidated their power in the wake of the February 1966 coup. From then on relations between Damascus and Moscow improved rapidly. Writing in the *New Times*, Pavel Demchenko, a Soviet analyst, stated that the policies of the new regime, led by leftist Baathists and other progressives, were in accord with 'the interests of the working people'.[114] While the Kremlin found the Syrian government resolved to 'apply socialist principles in industry and agriculture', Prime Minister Yusuf Zayen described support of the USSR as 'a vital necessity for Syria'.[115] During Zayen's visit to Moscow in April, the Kremlin promised Syria economic aid of $133 million, mainly for building the Euphrates Dam, meant to irrigate 1.5 million acres of land,[116] and for developing oilfields. It also warned Syria's neighbours against attempts to overthrow the radical regime in Damascus.

Seven months later the USSR played an important role in bringing about the mutual defence pact between Syria and Egypt.[117] In January a Baath delegation went to Moscow at the invitation of the CPSU, thus heralding a new chapter – fraternisation with a radical, but non-Communist, foreign party – in the life of the CPSU. The Soviet party representatives praised the progressive policies of the Baath which, they said, opened up prospects for a socialist transformation of society.

Having forged such close and varied ties with Syria, the USSR was determined to protect the radical regime in Damascus from external threats. During the spring, as tension along the Syrian–Israeli border mounted, Moscow spelled out its commitment to Damascus. On 18 May *Krasnaya Zvezda* coupled its condemnation of Israel, America and Britain for escalating tension in the region with a warning: 'Syria has reliable friends who will not leave her in need.'[118] At the same time, as stated earlier, the Kremlin privately urged both Syria and Egypt not to commit aggression against Israel.[119]

During the Six Day war, when Israel launched its offensive against Syria on 9 June (the day Nasser, accepting blame for Egypt's defeat, offered to resign) in order to achieve its long-held objective of toppling the regime in Damascus, the Kremlin acted decisively. It backed up its threat of military action against Israel (contained in its message to the White House) by putting its paratroop divisions on alert.[120]

Following the cease-fire, the USSR replaced Syria's military losses, including two thirds of its air force planes. As in the case of Egypt, Syrian and Soviet theorists combined the reasons for Arab defeat with a list of tasks to be performed. *Za Rubezhom*, a Soviet journal, published an article by Khaled Bakdash in which he stated that the Arab states should combine rearming with forging stronger links with the socialist bloc, and that progressive Arab regimes should form a united front of all progressive forces at home in order to successfully tackle major problems.[121] In March a Baathist delegation visited Moscow for ideological discussions with the CPSU. According to the joint communiqué issued at the end, the two delegations held 'similar or identical views' on world affairs.

However, with the rise of factionalism in the Baath – one group led by General Saleh Jedid and Yusuf Zayen, and the other by the defence minister, Hafez Assad – the Soviets faced a dilemma. They disapproved of the Jedid–Zayen faction's continued stress on launching people's wars to liberate Palestine from Zionism and the Arab world from imperialism, and its refusal to accept UN Security Council resolution 242. At the same time they were unhappy about Assad's tactics of accusing Zayen of 'behaving like a Soviet agent' who 'continuously informed the Russian ambassador about the country's affairs without consulting the cabinet',[122] and purging military and party leadership of Marxists and pro-Marxists.[123]

Later, during 1969, when the conflict between the two groups sharpened, with the Assad wing steadily emerging stronger, the Soviets kept out of the intra-party dispute. While they liked Assad's espousal of policies aimed at ending Syria's isolation in the Arab world, they resented his continued persecution of the Communists. In July 1970 *Trud* ('Labour'), the Soviet trade union newspaper, published an article which protested at the imprisonment and assassination of a number of Communists in Syria.[124]

The civil war in Jordan found the Soviets sharing their overall assessment of the situation with Assad. Both parties wished to see the hostilities contained. And both were aware that the prospect of King Hussein's downfall would draw Israel/America directly into the arena, and thus enlarge the conflict. As such, Assad's refusal to provide air cover to the Palestinian–Syrian forces, deployed in northern Jordan to fight the royalists, could only have been received with relief and approval in Moscow.

Not surprisingly Assad promised to strengthen Syria's ties with the USSR, once he had gained total power in the wake of a bloodless coup in November. He flew to Moscow three months later to establish working relations with the Soviet leaders. On the eve of the Baath party congress in May, the Damascus correspondent of *Pravda* upheld the 'progressive measures' taken so far by the Baath which, he stated, 'are welcomed by the Soviet people who are helping Syria to solve its economic problems'.[125]

Among other things the congress decided to work for the establishment of a progressive national front: an idea first aired nearly three years before in the columns of *Za Rubezhom* by Khaled Bakdash.[126] The Communist party was the most important of the four non-Baathist parties invited to join the front, which came into being ten months later. Welcoming its formation, Pavel Demchenko described it as 'a broad alliance of forces taking anti-imperialist positions' which would eventuaally transform society along 'socialist lines'.[127]

Expressing similar sentiments during President Assad's visit to Moscow in early July, President Nikolai Podgorny congratulated Syria, as well as Iraq, for the recent nationalisation of the assets of the Western-owned Iraq Petroleum Company. The degree of rapprochement between Syria and the USSR was illustrated by the fact that Assad volunteered to persuade President Sadat to reverse his decision to expel Soviet military advisers from Egypt. He flew from Moscow to Cairo for this purpose, but was disappointed. Back in Damascus, he reaffirmed the need for Soviet military and economic personnel in Syria. 'I believe it is now in the Syrian people's interest to continue to benefit from the Russian experts,' he said.[128]

This statement was all the more pertinent because, during his stay in Moscow, Assad had signed agreements for the supply of Soviet arms, the expansion of existing Syrian ports and the construction of new airbases with Soviet help. When the Israelis mounted massive air raids on targets inside Syria, in retaliation for the killing of the Israeli athletes in early September, Assad called on the Kremlin to expedite the despatch of weapons. The latter responded by airlifting arms.

A year later Syria received the same advice from Moscow as did Egypt: not to attack Israel within its pre-1967 frontiers. As such the Syrian offensive, launched on 6 October 1973, limited itself to recovering the Golan Heights, which had been lost to Israel in the Six Day war. The initial success achieved by the Syrian forces on the ground – and the heavy toll of Israeli planes which their Soviet-made rockets and missiles took – compelled the Israelis to resort to deep penetration bombing of Syria. Israeli planes hit not only the refinery in Homs and the defence ministry building in Damascus, but also the Soviet cultural centre in the Syrian capital.[129] When the Golan Heights battle began to go against the Syrians, the Kremlin rushed arms to Damascus by air.[130] More significantly, within days of the final cease-fire on 25 October, the Syrian defence minister, Mustapha Tlas, stated publicly that during the war the Kremlin had made 55,000 Soviet troops ready to fight alongside the Syrian forces to defend Syria.[131]

Despite its close relations with Moscow, Damascus refused to yield to Soviet pressure to attend the Geneva peace conference, or endorse UN

Security Council resolution 242. The failure of the Geneva conference vindicated the Syrian stand. By refusing to join in ending the Arab oil embargo against America in March, Syria (as well as Libya) underlined its anti-imperialist credentials. During Assad's visit to Moscow in mid-April, the Kremlin agreed to supply Syria with such advanced weapons as MiG-23s, and put a twelve-year moratorium on Syrian repayments of its military debts.[132] In turn Assad re-stressed the need for Soviet involvement in all stages of the Middle East peace process. This strategy apparently helped Assad secure more favourable terms on troop disengagement with Israel, arranged through Kissinger, than Sadat had. In the words of Brezhnev, the better deal for Damascus was the result of 'a unified position' shared by Syria and the USSR.[133]

An appreciative Kremlin signed an arms deal worth $2 billion with Syria during Assad's visit to the Soviet capital in late September.[134] The overall purpose was to make Syria militarily strong, and enable it to forge a robust 'eastern front' against Israel with the active cooperation of Jordan, Lebanon, and the PLO. The need for pursuing such a strategy became all the more urgent a year later, when Sadat's conclusion of the Sinai II agreement with Israel indicated to Damascus and Moscow that Sadat was heading for unilateral peace with Israel.

During the first half of the Lebanese civil war, Damascus and Moscow followed identical policies of supporting the alliance of the leftist Lebanese and the Palestinians, and opposing the partition of Lebanon. But, as described earlier, when this alliance seemed to be on the verge of total victory over its enemy, in late May 1976, Assad sent Syrian troops into Lebanon to fight it.[135] This strained relations between Syria and the USSR. In July Brezhnev addressed two letters to Assad on the subject. 'You can play a great part in ending the conflict by withdrawing your forces,' wrote Brezhnev in his letter of 11 July. 'If Syria is going to persist in the course she has taken, she will make it possible for the imperialists and their collaborators to bring the Arab people, the region's progressive movements, and the Arab states with progressive regimes under their control.'[136] To add weight to his message he slowed down Soviet arms deliveries to Syria.

However, as the Lebanese conflict came to an end in October, Damascus–Moscow relations regained their old cordiality. While the pre-eminent role assigned to Syria, in the Arab Deterrent Force, of maintaining peace in Lebanon pleased Moscow, the emergence of Saudi Arabia as the chief mediator and paymaster did not. The USSR wished to see Syria help forge a front of the progressive Arab states, and act as a counterpoint to Egypt, which was allying itself increasingly with America.

Sadat's visit to Jerusalem in November 1977 provided the Kremlin with a dramatic opportunity. Condemning the Egyptian president's overture, the USSR called on all progressive forces in the Arab world to form a united front 'against the aggressor [Israel] and against those who are willing to bargain with him'.[137] Not surprisingly, as the only member-state sharing borders with Israel, Syria emerged as the leader of the Front of Steadfastness and Confrontation formed in Tripoli. This added to the stature of Assad, who was greeted warmly by Soviet leaders during his visit to Moscow in February.

Once the Camp David accord had destroyed the last trace of hope among Arab leaders of bringing Sadat back into their fold, Libya offered $1 billion to finance the purchase of Soviet weapons by members of the Steadfastness Front.[138] The country which felt the greatest need for arming itself was Syria. With the conclusion of the Egyptian–Israeli peace treaty in March 1979 finally removing Egypt as a potential combatant against the Jewish state, and the failure of unity plans with Iraq robbing Syria of a committed ally to its east, Syria's need for arms became urgent. Aware of this, the Kremlin granted all of the Syrian requests for sophisticated weapons during Assad's visit to Moscow in October. 'The Soviet Union does not want to be held responsible for a Syrian collapse in the face of Israeli military pressure,' reported Dev Murarka from Moscow. 'President Assad has not shown any willingness to contemplate a treaty of friendship with the Soviet Union, and until recently, Moscow has lived with this ambivalence.'[139]

Over the next twelve months the situation changed. Assad found himself at odds with the Jordanian monarch, who in league with the Iraqi president was (allegedly) aiding his political opponents. Tempted to take advantage of Syria's isolation, Israel and its rightist Lebanese allies stepped up their attacks on south Lebanon in the hope of engaging the Syrian forces stationed in Lebanon, and using that conflict to deliver a mortal blow to the regime in Damascus. In May the number of Israeli or Israeli-aided raids on southern Lebanon rose to ten.[140] The cumulative pressure of these problems made Assad amenable to signing a treaty of friendship with the USSR. The outbreak of the Iraq–Iran war in late September, and the polarisation it caused in the Arab world, added urgency to the matter. On 8 October during Assad's visit to Moscow, Assad and Brezhnev signed a twenty-year treaty of friendship and cooperation between their countries. Like similar treaties in the past it stipulated consultation 'in the event of a situation jeopardising the peace and security of either party'.[141]

Later it was revealed that the treaty contained a secret clause dealing with the use of atomic weapons by a potential attacker. 'The Soviet Union has promised to take all necessary steps – including the threat of nuclear reprisal – to prevent Israel using atomic weapons against Syria,' reported Patrick Seale in the *Observer*.[142] Whether true or not, the treaty had the effect of boosting Syria's confidence. Describing it as strengthening 'forces confronting aggression, conspiracy, and the violation of UN resolutions', Ahmed Iskander, the influential Syrian minister of information, said that any attempt by Israel to annex the occupied Golan Heights or move into southern Lebanon would lead Syria to take 'any step or measure to secure our rights'.[143]

A confident Syria argued that due to the Iraq–Iran war the proposed Arab summit, to be held in Amman in late November, be postponed. When it failed to sway the majority of the Arab League's steering committee, it lobbied individual states to boycott the summit. In this it received the backing not only of its fellow-members of the Steadfastness Front but also of Lebanon. Such an achievement in diplomacy could only have pleased the Soviet Union whose relations with Lebanon had in general been quite unremarkable.

For a whole decade, following the exchange of envoys in 1944, the USSR and Lebanon had limited their relations to diplomacy. It was not until April 1954 that the first Soviet–Lebanese trade agreement was signed. Two years later a Soviet delegation arrived in Beirut to strengthen economic and industrial ties. However, the prospect of further improvement was dimmed by the outbreak of a civil war in Lebanon in May 1958, and the overthrow of the monarchy in Iraq: events which in turn brought American forces into Lebanon.

The Soviet Union raised the issue of American troops in Lebanon (and the British in Jordan) at the UN Security Council. Demanding their immediate withdrawal, the Soviet representative at the UN, Arkady Sobolev, warned that the USSR could not remain indifferent to 'the events creating danger in this region adjacent to her borders', and reserved 'the [Soviet] right to take necessary measures to preserve peace and security'.[144] In order to bypass the Great Power veto, the USSR referred the matter to the UN General Assembly. The overall tone of the debate there was so overwhelmingly against the presence of Western armed forces in Lebanon and Jordan that on 18 August America and Britain notified the Assembly that they would withdraw their troops when so requested by the appropriate authorities. The American forces departed from Lebanon on 25 October, and the British from Jordan on 2 November.

Although this development was a major setback for the pro-West forces in Lebanon, it did not pave the way for an uncontested ascendancy of nationalist-leftist elements, advocating neutralism in foreign affairs. Certainly these forces were not strong enough in 1966 to successfully pressure the government to join the Egyptian–Syrian defence pact. The consequent non-involvement of Lebanon in the Six Day war meant that it was left unmolested by Israel. However, as described earlier, a large influx of Palestinian refugees into the republic, caused by the war, changed its political landscape.[145] When friction between the Palestinian commandos and the Lebanese security forces took the form of armed skirmishes in 1969, Soviet diplomats in Beirut tried to mediate between the two sides, with some success. By then the USSR's consistently pro-Arab bias, combined with its (free of charge) re-equipment of the

Egyptian and Syrian armed forces, had enhanced its prestige among the Lebanese population, particularly its Muslim section. This was reflected in such governmental actions as the legalisation of the Lebanese Communist party in August 1970, and the signing of an arms deal worth $8 million with the USSR a little over a year later.[146]

Moscow's involvement in the October war on the side of the Arabs added to its stature in the eyes of both the people and the government of Lebanon. Intent on frustrating American designs to intensify the civil war in Lebanon, Soviet diplomats in Beirut tried many times to bring about a lasting cease-fire. They failed. When hostilities finally ended in October 1976 the Kremlin upheld the development.[147]

It was quick to denounce the Israeli invasion of south Lebanon in March 1978. An official statement placed the responsibility for 'the sequel to the Israeli aggression' on the Israeli government, and demanded an immediate withdrawal of Israeli forces.[148] Following the UN Security Council's resolution, on 19 March, calling for an Israeli withdrawal, *Izvestia* condemned 'the veritable genocide' committed by the invading forces in south Lebanon.[149]

Despite the stationing of UN peace-keeping force in south Lebanon, the Kremlin did not rule out the possibility of another large-scale aggression against Lebanon by Israel. On 4 February 1980, Moscow Radio warned that such a move was imminent.[150] In the event, no such attack materialised. If it had, it would have been justified on the grounds of protecting Lebanon's Christian minority.[151] The March 1978 invasion was mounted by Israel to 'eliminate the [Palestinian] fedayeen bases along the border as well as the special training installations from which they launched their attacks on Israel'.[152] Since their expulsion from Jordan in 1970–1, the PLO and other Palestinian organisations had moved to Lebanon and set up their headquarters in the Lebanese capital. Beirut had thus become the virtual capital of the Palestinians living outside the (Israeli) occupied territories; and foreign governments had come to treat it as such.

Although the Palestinian resistance movement came into existence in 1959 (in the form of Fatah), no mention of it was made in the party or government circles of Moscow for eight years. The first public reference to it came in the text of the joint communiqué issued by the CPSU and the visiting Syrian Baath delegation in January 1967.[153] The Six Day war made little difference to the Soviet stance.

A subtle change began in July 1968 after Yasser Arafat had visited Moscow secretly, as a member of the Egyptian delegation led by Nasser. This was reflected in an article by a group of Soviet jurists published in the January 1969 issue of *Mezhdunarodnaya Zhizn* (International Life). 'The guerrilla activities are a lawful expression of the Arab people's right of self-defence in the conditions of continued aggression,' they wrote. 'In this case, the situation is similar to the one which existed during the

Second World War when the resistance movement was active in the Nazi-occupied territory.'[154]

With Arafat replacing Ahmed Shukeiri as the PLO's head the following month, Soviet interest in Palestinian resistance increased. Reports of Palestinian guerrilla activities began appearing in the Soviet mass media. In October Moscow Radio broadcast a statement made by Alexei Shelepin, a politbureau member, in his address to the congress of the World Federation of Trade Unions in Budapest: 'We consider the Palestinian patriots' struggle to eliminate the consequences of Israeli aggression a just anti-imperialist struggle for national liberation, and we'll support it.'[155] On 10 December Prime Minister Kosygin promised support to Palestinian organisations by 'the Soviet people'.[156] In February the semi-official Soviet Committee for Afro–Asian Solidarity played host to Arafat in Moscow.

Soon after the civil war in Jordan, Brezhnev referred to the Palestinian commandos as 'the troops of the Palestinian resistance'.[157] Yet these forces had fought the Jordanian royalists with weapons supplied mainly by the People's Republic of China, which had been arming them for the past five years. The Kremlin had limited its role to supplying arms 'timidly and secretly' to just one group: Saiqa, attached to the (Syrian) Baath.[158] Despite a systematic expulsion of Palestinian commandos from Jordan during the first half of 1971, carried out by royalist troops with the aid and advice of America, the Kremlin persisted in its cautious policy towards Palestinian resistance.

It was not until September 1972 that the Soviet leaders changed their stance. They did so because expulsion of Soviet military advisers from Egypt compelled them to diversify their interests in the region.[159] Secondly, they could not help responding positively to the urgent call for aid by the PLO – sent in the wake of hundreds of deaths caused by large-scale Israeli raids on nine Palestinian targets in Syria and Lebanon, which had been mounted to avenge the killings of the Israeli athletes in Munich. They ordered an airlift of medical supplies – and possibly weapons – to the Palestinians in Lebanon.[160]

But there was no change in Soviet opposition to hijackings and assassinations. Writing in *Pravda*, Pavel Demchenko criticised such 'acts of desperation' as hijacking passenger aircraft and blowing up civilian targets.[161] In the political sphere, citing Faiq Warrad, a member of the Palestine National Council, Demchenko advised 'the unification of the ranks of the Palestinian movement within the framework, for instance, of a national front with a political programme that will take into account the diversity of the situation and of the forms of struggle, and will help to begin work among the Palestinians in occupied territory and among the refugees, especially in Jordan'.[162]

The fact that the Arab People's Congress for Support of the Palestine Revolution was convened in Beirut in November, and that all the Arab

Communist parties attended it, showed that Soviet political advice was being taken seriously. Significantly, the eleventh session of the PNC, held in January 1973, dropped rightist Khaled Hassan from the executive committee. Seven months later came the formation of the Palestine National Front in the occupied territories, which included not only the Communists, Baathists, socialists, and trade unionists but also non-political professionals. Earlier, on 25 June, Brezhnev had succeeded in having a reference to the 'legitimate interests of the Palestinian people' inserted in the joint Soviet–American communiqué issued after his meeting with Nixon in San Clemente, California. This marked a change in the American attitude to the Palestinians.

Soviet–Palestinian relations improved rapidly in the wake of the Yom Kippur war. Within days of the cease-fire the USSR addressed memorandums to Arafat, Habash, and Hawatmeh recognising the 'Palestinian resistance' as 'the sole legitimate authority representing the Palestinian people', and advising them to be realistic and constructive in their demand for the return of territories lost in 1967.[163] In mid-November a Palestinian delegation, including the above leaders, had a series of meetings with Soviet officials, including some members of the politbureau, in Moscow. The joint statement issued by the two sides reasserted the right to self-determination of the Palestinian people in the West Bank and Gaza.[164] The twelfth PNC session, held in June, opted for the establishment of a 'national authority' in the West Bank and Gaza, and adopted a ten-point programme which included strengthening 'the PLO's solidarity with the socialist countries and the world forces of liberation and progress, to foil all Zionist, reactionary and imperialist schemes'.[165]

In order to aid the Palestinians defend their camps in Lebanon against Israeli air raids, the USSR began supplying them with SAM-7 missiles. During the PLO delegation's visit to Moscow in July – sponsored this time by the Supreme Soviet – the Kremlin agreed to let the PLO open an office in Moscow, and called for the PLO's participation at a future Geneva conference on an equal basis with other participants. The PLO in return thanked the USSR for its 'unvarying support and assistance'.[166]

Moscow welcomed the decision of the Arab summit, held in Rabat in late October, to recognise the PLO as 'the sole and legitimate representative of the Palestinian people', and its right 'to establish the independent Palestinian authority on any liberated Palestinian territory'. Analysis of the event followed shortly. 'The process of Arab consolidation is gaining headway,' wrote Dmitri Volsky in *New Times*. 'It is gaining headway, moreover, on an anti-imperialist platform and with the support of all progressive forces, primarily the USSR which, as the Soviet leaders emphasised in their message to the Rabat summit, will continue to "do everything to secure a genuinely just Middle East settlement".'[167]

The PLO was buoyed by UN General Assembly resolution 3236,

passed by eighty-nine votes to eight (on 22 November), which recognised the Palestinians' right to 'national independence and sovereignty' and the PLO as their sole representative.[168] In the course of his visit to Moscow in April, Arafat stated that the Geneva conference should be convened on the basis of the new resolution which, in his opinion, had superseded the earlier UN Security Council resolution 242. But it was not until his subsequent visit to the Soviet capital in November that the Kremlin concurred with this view.[169]

As stated earlier, Soviet leaders were deeply disturbed by President Assad's military move against the PLO (and the leftist Lebanese) in the Lebanese civil war in June 1976.[170] Explaining this, Hella Pick, a specialist on Soviet affairs, wrote, 'The Soviet Union's commitment to the PLO is deep, overriding its other allegiances in the Arab world, and is the key factor in its Middle East policies.'[171] This was borne out further when the Kremlin sent a cable to the American state department asking it to intervene and help break the naval blockade of Lebanon imposed by Israel.[172] But taking such steps did not stop the Soviets from being openly critical of their protagonists when the situation demanded it. In early September, for instance, *Pravda* criticised 'some leftist elements within the Palestinian resistance and the [Lebanese] patriotic forces' for rejecting 'out of hand any peaceful proposals'.[173]

Opposed to the 'all or nothing' approach of Palestinian radicals, Moscow was pleased to see the thirteenth PNC session, held in March 1977, adopt a resolution which stressed the 'need to start a dialogue and establish relations between the PLO and Jewish democratic and progressive forces struggling against Zionism' inside and outside Israel. The CPSU played an active role in arranging an 'official' meeting between the PLO and the (Israeli) Rakah representatives in Prague in May, under the auspices of the Czech Communist party.[174]

Moscow's wish to deal with all the Palestinian organisations through the PLO was consummated in late 1977 when, following Sadat's defection from Arab ranks, the PFLP and the (Iraq-backed) Arab Liberation Front ended their boycott of the PLO. The Israeli invasion of south Lebanon had the effect of further unifying the Palestinians. Equipped with Soviet weapons, some 3,500 Palestinian commandos offered spirited resistance to the invading force, causing (in their estimation) 450 Israeli casualties.[175] Soviet officials were reportedly pleased by the Palestinian performance, which they attributed to the right combination of military expertise with ideological commitment.

Within a year of the Israeli withdrawal from south Lebanon in June 1978, about a third of the PLO's 23,000 commandos found their way to posts south of the river Litani.[176] Israel tried to discourage this by frequent bombing of targets in Lebanon (the period of 22 April to 30 June witnessing eleven such attacks), and in the process causing hundreds of civilian casualties.[177] Extensive reporting of these Israeli acts in the Soviet mass media was accompanied by strong condemnation. The overall result of the Israeli strategy was to reinforce Soviet–PLO bonds, particularly in military affairs.

With its annual budget running at $500 million,[178] the PLO had enough resources to not only arm its commando force but also equip its (regular) Palestine Liberation Army with tanks and aircraft. In early 1980, when the threat of a fully fledged Israeli invasion of Lebanon seemed real, the PLO requested Moscow to supply thirty to forty advanced T-62 tanks. The Kremlin agreed.[179]

All along the Soviets have continued to impart advanced guerrilla training to select PLO recruits. Details of this were given by Adnan Jaber, one of the Palestinians accused of machine gunning six Jews in Hebron in May 1980. He was a member of a PLO guerrilla unit that underwent six months of training in 1974 in Skhodnya, a town near Moscow. The training consisted of 'instructions in the use of Kalashnikov assault rifles and other light arms, explosives, command techniques, and topography'. Despite their diverse political affiliations – to Fatah, Saiqa, the PFLP, the DFLP et al – the twenty-one guerrillas worked together as a team and, significantly, detected no partiality being shown by their Soviet instructors towards any particular political sub-group among them.[180]

Just as Soviet military instructors are particular to be impartial to members of different parties within the overall context of the Palestinian national liberation movement, so the top Soviet leaders, in the post-Stalin era, have been keen to have good relations with all independent Arab states, irrespective of their political inclinations. Jordan is a good example. Despite periodic criticism of the Hashemite kingdom as feudal and reactionary in the Soviet press, in the mid-1950s, Soviet leaders wished to have diplomatic relations with it. They were disappointed when, in early 1957, the monarch overruled his popularly elected government's decision to exchange envoys with the USSR.

It was only after King Hussein had successfully withstood a popular upsurge against the West and pressures to join the United Arab Republic (which broke up in September 1961), that he began to soften his militantly anti-Soviet stance. He established diplomatic relations with the USSR in August 1963, but declared that this signified no change in his foreign policy. His refusal to join the Soviet-backed Egyptian–Syrian defence pact, formed in November 1966, provided convincing proof.

However, since Hussein joined this pact at the last moment, in a fit of impetuosity, Jordan became the target of Israeli aggression in June 1967. His allegations during the war, that the USA had intervened on the Israeli side, led to the suspension of American arms to the Hashemite kingdom. It was against this background that he undertook his first visit to Moscow in October. There, Soviet leaders offered to re-equip the Jordanian military just as they had done the Egyptian and Syrian ones. He spurned the Soviet overture.

Although he re-established working relations with Washington early in the next year, his open support for Palestinian guerrilla activity against Israel, from Jordan, led Soviet analysts to think that he was gradually becoming anti-imperialist. The Kremlin therefore repeated (in August) its earlier offer to re-equip the kingdom's armed forces. His response was once again negative.

The USSR's endorsement of the Rogers peace plan, which Jordan accepted in July 1970, convinced Amman that Moscow's overall strategy in the Middle East was basically pragmatic. Further evidence of this came when the Kremlin behaved with restraint during the Jordanian civil war. It sympathised with moderate elements in Damascus. And, once the Syrian–Palestinian forces had withdrawn from northern Jordan, its official communiqué on 23 September stated: 'Firm confidence has been expressed from the Soviet side that everything should be done to end as soon as possible the fratricidal fighting in Jordan. Permanent contact is being maintained with President Nasser on all questions linked with the developments in Jordan.'[181]

Such Soviet behaviour laid the foundation for cooperation between Amman and Moscow in non-military fields. Following lengthy negotiations between their representatives, the two governments signed agreements on economic and technical cooperation in November 1971. The USSR provided experts to Jordan to assist it in exploiting its minerals, mainly phosphates, which are its major source of foreign earnings.[182] The acceptance of the PLO as the sole representative of the Palestinians by Jordan, three years later, helped to improve political relations between Amman and Moscow. The process was aided by growing cordiality between King Hussein and President Assad, who decided in the wake of the Sinai II agreement to work for an economic union of their countries.

The next spring, when Jordan's deal with American corporations for the building of its air defence system, at the cost of $792 million, ran into financial and other problems, Assad encouraged Hussein to seek Moscow's advice. He did so. A Soviet team, led by the country's air force commander, arrived in Amman in May. Hussein went to Moscow the following month to discuss the plan. He was tempted to accept the Soviet missile system, since Soviet missiles were considered to be superior to American; top Jordanian military officers were already cooperating with their Syrian counterparts who were inter alia operating a Soviet system; and a joint Syrian–Jordanian air defence umbrella had much to recommend itself (not least because the Israelis, equipped with an American missile system, were unfamiliar with it). But the Saudi monarch, who had agreed to finance the project, refused to pay for the Soviet missile system.[183] In the end, therefore, Hussein opted for the American plan.

In December Hussein and Assad agreed to enlarge the scope of their states' unification by including educational, legal, telecommunication, and customs systems into it. This commitment was one of the reasons why

Hussein successfully resisted Washington's pressure to join the Egyptian–Israeli peace talks in 1978. Jordan's stance pleased the USSR. Later Amman joined in the denunciation of the Camp David accord, described by Moscow as 'a plot against the Arabs'.[184] Such unanimity on the diplomatic front paved the way for Amman to place orders for certain Soviet weapons, including anti-aircraft guns.

By early 1980 the USSR had delivered the weapons ordered by Jordan. In August the two countries signed a cultural cooperation agreement.[185] More importantly, during his visit to Moscow the following May, King Hussein endorsed President Brezhnev's call for an international conference on the Middle East crisis (first made at the CPSU congress in February), and expressed Jordan's gratitude for 'Soviet support for the Arabs'.[186]

It was significant that King Hussein had visited Baghdad and Riyadh before flying to Moscow. With Iraq emerging as an important benefactor, and Assad's backing for Iran's Islamic revolution clashing with the Hashemite monarch's condemnation of it, Jordan had begun drifting away from Syria in early 1980. When Iraq attacked Iran in September, the Jordanian king sided with Iraq, thus openly offending Syria's Assad. By then, despite its friendship treaty with Moscow, Iraq had turned cool towards the USSR.

This was the latest turn in the chequered history of Iraqi–Soviet relations first established during the Second World War, in 1944. When the USSR became too critical of the Baghdad Pact the Iraqi government, led by Nuri al Said, severed its ties with Moscow. It was not until after the anti-monarchical coup of July 1958 that diplomatic links were restored. Committed to follow a neutralist line in foreign affairs, the republican regime, headed by Abdul Karem Qassem, improved its relations with the Soviet Union. Before the end of the year the two states signed trade pacts, and the USSR agreed to supply Iraq with 100 to 150 tanks.[187] In March Moscow promised Baghdad economic and technical aid worth $137 million for fourteen major industrial projects, and improvement of railway and navigation facilities.[188]

Aware of the view then prevalent in Western capitals that Iraq was 'going Communist', Khrushchev told a visiting Iraqi delegation that, in the Soviet government's view, Iraq was neither a Communist state nor moving in that direction. However, he added, 'In Iraq a more advanced (social) system is being established than in the neighbouring countries of the Arab East.'[189] He implied by this that the USSR preferred Baghdad to Cairo: a point borne out by the Soviet cooperation agreement with Iraq on peaceful uses of atomic energy.[190]

Later, as Qassem began curtailing and then repressing Communist activity in the republic, his actions were criticised by the Soviet press. But this left state-to-state relations intact.[191] There was no cessation, or even slowing down, of the flow of Soviet arms to Iraq. By May 1960, according to the *New York Times* correspondent, Moscow had provided military aid of $120 million to Baghdad.[192] But, as Qassem intensified the persecution of Communists, the CPSU and its organs became vocal in their protests. At the twenty-second congress of the CPSU, in October 1961, Khrushchev (as the party's first secretary) attacked 'forces within the ruling circles' of former colonies for refusing to cooperate with 'the broad strata of working people' as well as 'considerable part of the national bourgeoisie interested in the accomplishment of the basic tasks of the anti-imperialist, anti-feudal revolution'.[193] That the criticism was aimed at such regimes as the one led by Qassem was apparent. Not surprisingly, Khrushchev's speech was banned in Iraq. Four days later, addressing the CPSU congress, Salem Adil, the Iraqi Communist leader, described the extent of the persecution that the Communists had suffered in the two years after the Kirkuk riots.[194]

Although Soviet–Iraqi trade reached a record level in 1962, and Moscow continued to supply weapons to Baghdad, relations between the two states cooled considerably. This was manifested inter alia by the failure of *Izvestia* to even mention the fourth anniversary of the Iraqi revolution on 14 July.[195] The overthrow of Qassem by the Baathists did not reverse the trend: indeed it only accelerated it. This had to do with the large-scale massacre of Communists that the Baathists carried out. Within a week of the Kremlin's recognition of the new regime on 11 February 1963, the central committee of the CPSU condemned the 'bloody terror' against the Iraqi Communists which, it said, was 'in conflict with . . . the policy of national unity, freedom and democracy and social justice' proclaimed by the Baath.[196] Another protest by the CPSU's central committee a month later was followed by a mass demonstration outside the Iraqi embassy in Moscow: a rare occurrence.

When the Baathist government initiated armed action against the Kurds (who contributed substantially to Communist ranks) in June, the USSR tried to raise the issue at international forums, but failed. This soured relations between the two capitals even further, and led to increased persecution of the Iraqi Communists during the next few months. Protesting that the official list of the 120 executed Communists and pro-Communists was incomplete, *Pravda* of 6 October 1963 stated that hundreds more had been executed secretly, and hundreds had perished in prisons and concentration camps as a result of barbaric torture.[197]

The downfall of the Baathists in November was welcomed in Moscow: so too was the dissolution of the National Guard, as ordered by the new ruler, Abdul Salam Aref, since, in *Pravda*'s view, it had been formed by the Baathists with the sole purpose of annihilating the Communists and pro-Communists.[198] But the Communists were still under a shadow. The situation changed somewhat after hostilities against the Kurds ceased in July 1964, and shipment of Soviet arms was resumed.[199]

Aref's nationalisation decrees on the eve of the sixth anniversary of the revolution were praised by the Kremlin. With the appointment of Abdul Rahman Bazzaz as prime minister, serious efforts were made by the government in Baghdad to bring about an enduring peace in the Kurdish region. These succeeded in June 1966. Appreciative of this, the joint Soviet–Iraqi communiqué issued at the end of Bazzaz's visit to Moscow in August made a reference to the 'peaceful settlement of the conflict in northern Iraq on the basis of recognising their equal rights and obligations'.[200] Economic ties, already strong between the two countries, were reinforced when, in December 1967 (during the presidency of Abdul Rahman Aref), the USSR agreed in principle to provide credit and equipment for the development of the northern Rumeila oilfields, with Iraqi repayments to be made in oil.

Moscow expressed no regrets when Abdul Rahmam Aref was overthrown by Baathist military officers acting in league with two of his closest aides. 'The Aref regime fell because it had no solid base and no definite ideological orientation,' stated Georgi Mirsky. 'Only democratisation of public life, renunciation of the old methods of government, and an anti-imperialist foreign policy can win the new government mass support.'[201]

Soviet leaders were unperturbed by the return of the Baathists to power, because the latter had reached a modus operandi with the Communists during their years of underground existence under the Arefs' regime.[202] The Baathist Revolutionary Command Council released hundreds of Communists, and appointed one, Aziz Sharif, a cabinet minister in his personal capacity; but did not lift the ban on the party. These measures, coupled with the launching of an anti-imperialist, anti-Zionist campaign by the new regime led to an increased flow of aid from Moscow. The USSR finally signed the long-term agreement for developing the northern Rumeila oilfields in exchange for Iraqi oil: a move which strengthened the hands of Baghdad in its dispute with Iraq Petroleum Company.

In March 1970, Baghdad succeeded in reaching a settlement with the Kurds. This removed a problem which had for long been a point of friction between Iraq and the USSR. But there was as yet no sign of an end to the Baathist practice of periodic arrests and killings of Communists. Protesting at the murder of two Communists in a Baghdad prison in February, *Trud* asked, 'How much longer will the criminal reactionary elements in Iraq enjoy the freedom to carry out their black deeds and thus besmirch the name of their country in the eyes of progressive and democratic people?'.[203]

On the whole, however, the CPSU considered the Baath, as well as the Kurdish Democratic Party, as 'revolutionary democratic'. In pursuance of its policy of fraternisation with such parties, the CPSU invited the Baath and the KDP to send delegations to its twenty-fourth congress in

Moscow in late March. They did. 'The participation of national democratic parties in the work of the 24th congress reflects the growth of our mutual ties,' wrote Boris Ponomaryev in the *World Marxist Review*. 'In recent years this has been one of the specific directions in the alliance between the CPSU and the national liberation forces. . . . The participation of revolutionary democracies in the CPSU congresses, our party hopes, will not only stimulate their greater cooperation with our party and the world Communist movement, but will also facilitate allied relations between them and the Communists in their own countries.'[204]

At the time of the CPSU congress such hopes had still to be realised in the case of the Iraqi Baath. Addressing the assembly, Aziz Mohammed, the Iraqi Communist leader, criticised the Baathists for persecuting the Communists and monopolising political power.[205] (Oddly enough, this speech came a day after the Kremlin had signed an agreement offering Iraq $224 million in credit for a project involving an oil refinery and two pipelines.[206]) The CPSU's efforts to reconcile differences between the two parties were only partially successful. In May Aziz Mohammed flew to Moscow for consultations with the CPSU's international department. Together they blamed 'the intrigues of imperialist agents and reaction' and 'the persecution of the Communist Party' for any lack of implementation of the programme 'of the unity of the progressive patriotic forces'.[207] Only then did the Baathist government relax restrictions on the Communists.

Early in July a delegation led by Soviet Vice-Prime Minister, Vladimir Novikov, signed an Iraqi–Soviet protocol of cooperation in Baghdad. On the anniversary of Iraq's republican revolution *Pravda* published an article by R. Petrov, a specialist on the Middle East. While welcoming the Baathists' decision to form a national front that would combine 'all progressive anti-imperialist organisations, including the Communist Party of Iraq', he pointed out that there were still 'remnants of anti-Communism and mistrust of Iraqi Communists in the Baath party and in the military'.[208] Following the leftist coup in Sudan by Major Atta on 19 July, Iraq became the only major Arab state to recognise the new regime immediately: a step which pleased the Kremlin.

During his visit to Moscow in February, Saddam Hussein, then deputy head of the RCC and assistant general-secretary of the Baath, called for 'qualitative progress in the nature of relations between us', and declared that 'the firm strategic alliance between our peoples, parties, and governments is the foundation on which [our] economic, technical, cultural and other relations are being built and will continue to be built'.[209] He stressed ideological concurrence – opposition to Western imperialism, Zionism, and American designs for peace in the Middle East – as the common ground for mutual friendship.[210] This led to the conclusion of a fifteen-year-long Iraqi–Soviet treaty of friendship and cooperation on 9 April. Alexei Kosygin – visiting Iraq primarily to inaugurate the northern

Rumeila oilfields – signed it on behalf of the USSR. The signatories agreed to contact each other in case of 'danger to the peace of either party or . . . danger to peace', and to refrain from joining an alliance (with another country or group of countries) aimed against the other. They also resolved to 'develop cooperation in the strengthening of their defence capacity'.[211]

Soviet success in developing the Rumeila oilfields showed the Iraqis that they need not be totally dependent on Western capital or enterprise for the progress of their oil industry. 'The recent commissioning of oilfields in north Rumeila, which were opened with the USSR's assistance, has created new opportunities for the Iraqi people in their struggle against domination by foreign monopolies,' wrote Irina Pogodina in *Pravda* on 24 May. 'Iraq's fruitful cooperation with the socialist states, which is developing successfully, has created auspicious conditions for the country's achievement of full economic independence.'[212]

As it happened, Iraq was then in the middle of a serious dispute with the IPC concerning the application of Law 80 (of 1961), which expropriated almost all of the unexploited concessionary areas originally allotted to them – as a result of which the IPC had reduced output at its Kirkuk oilfields by half in March. The Iraqi oil minister's warning to the IPC representatives on 17 May that negotiations would be terminated if the government's demands were not met in two weeks were not taken seriously. Consequently the government nationalised the IPC oilfields on 1 June.[213] The next day the Iraqi oil minister flew to Moscow. Within a week he had signed an agreement with the USSR whereby the latter undertook to transport Iraqi oil, build an oil refinery with an annual capacity of 1.5 million tons, and assist in oil prospecting in the south.[214]

While economic and military cooperation between the two states was being continually increased, little progress was being made towards the formation of an alliance of the Baathists and the Communists under the aegis of a progressive national front. The Baathists were unwilling to share power, and the Communists were reluctant to go too far in compromising their ideological principles. Writing in *Izvestia* in early June, Viktor Kudryavtsev, a political analyst, coupled his criticism of the Baathists for not going beyond 'talks' in the creation of a progressive front (agreed in principle two years earlier), with some ideological-tactical advice to the Iraqi Communists. He referred to Lenin's recognition of the need for the proletarian vanguard's link with the non-proletarian masses, and added, 'Obviously, if we are to apply this to Iraq, the national front . . . will help the vanguard to merge with the broadest masses of the Iraqi working people, while the national democrats [i.e. Baathists] will gradually master the theory and practice of scientific socialism.'[215]

Nothing came of this. In mid-September President Ahmed Bakr flew to Moscow to hold talks with Soviet leaders in the wake of large-scale Israeli raids on Lebanon and Syria, and the Shah of Iran's threats to Iraq.

President Podgorny stated that the unity of Arab states on the basis of anti-imperialism and the unity of all progressive forces within an Arab state were interrelated.[216] Elaborating on this theme, Rotislav Ulyanovsky, deputy head of the CPSU's international department, urged the Iraqi Baathists to put their promise about the progressive front into practice.[217] Yet the final decision to formally establish the Progressive National Front was not taken by the Baath RCC until after a traumatic experience on 30 June 1973, when Nasim Kazar, the powerful security chief, attempted an unsuccessful coup.[218]

While Iraq welcomed the USSR's material and moral aid to the Arabs in the October 1973 war, and sent its troops to Syria to fight the Israelis, it did not join the Arab oil boycott of Israeli's supporters. It turned down Soviet advice to accept UN Security Council resolutions 242 and 338. It also rejected the Soviet suggestion that it attend the Arab summit in Algiers in November on coordinating Arab strategy against Israel. And, like Syria, it stayed away from the Geneva peace conference.

In March, when the KDP leader Mustapha Barzani refused to participate in the implementation of the Kurdish autonomy plan, agreed four years earlier, the USSR sided with the Baathist rulers. 'Foreign agents are still interfering in the Kurdish affairs,' wrote Pavel Demchenko in *Pravda* on 14 March. 'The activity of the rightist elements which have penetrated the Kurdish Democratic Party as a result of its class heterogeneity, and which are trying to arouse separatist sentiments, is becoming more evident.'[219] As such, the Kremlin was ready to concur with whatever action Baghdad decided to take against the Kurdish separatists. The seriousness of the problem, and Soviet involvement in it, were underlined by the report in *Pravda* later in the month that Marshal Andrei Grechko, Soviet defence minister, had visited Iraq for two days for a detailed discussion on 'the present state and future developments of Soviet–Iraqi cooperation in the military and other spheres'.[221]

As Baghdad prepared to launch an offensive against the KDP, Soviet support became stronger. 'Reports indicate that in making this decision [to reject the autonomy plan], the Kurdish leaders were not free from interference by imperialist and other reactionary forces who are trying to sow discord between the Arab and Kurdish populations of Iraq, and weaken the progressive regime in that country,' stated *Pravda*. 'For these purposes they are supplying the Kurdish extremists with weapons and ammunition and considerable financial support.'[221]

Evidence in support of such statements appeared five years later, after the death of Mustapha Barzani at a clinic in Minnesota, USA. 'The final phase of Barzani's guerrilla career . . . dragged on for eleven years [from 1961] when the Shah [of Iran], who was having troubles with neighbouring Iraq, decided it would be useful to back the Kurds in their struggle,' stated the obituary of Barzani by the Associated Press from Washington. 'According to Barzani, the Shah arranged for his American allies to receive a Kurdish delegation secretly in Washington in 1972. There, the CIA promised to supply arms to the Kurds. With these weapons, the struggle grew.'[222] However, long before that, the collapse of the KDP's armed insurgency, in the wake of the treaty concluded by the Shah with Iraq in March 1975, had provided circumstantial evidence of the KDP's total reliance on Iran for weapons and money.[223]

At the height of its offensive against the Kurdish insurgents, in the winter of 1974–5, the Baathist government agreed to provide naval facilities to Soviet ships at Fao and Umm Qasr.[224] This was in accordance with the clause in the Iraqi–Soviet friendship treaty which called for mutual cooperation in strengthening the defence capacities of the signatories. A year later events in Lebanon – where Iraq lined up with Libya and Syria (as well as the USSR) in backing the leftist Lebanese–Palestinian alliance – revived Soviet hopes for the emergence of a front of progressive Arab states. As such, Syria's turnabout in June 1976 came as a rude shock to Moscow. It was significant that Brezhnev sent copies of his letters to President Assad, protesting at the Syrian action, to the Iraqi president among others.[225]

Although Iraq expressed outrage at Sadat's visit to Jerusalem, it did not join the Front of Steadfastness and Confrontation on the ground that the front refused to disavow a peaceful solution to the Middle East conflict. Moscow was disappointed by Baghdad's continued ultra-rejectionism, which it considered unrealistic. But the Camp David accord changed the situation dramatically. Iraq seized the opportunity to end its isolation in the Arab world: it sent out invitations to members of the Arab League (except Egypt) for a summit conference in early November. At the same time it declared its readiness to station troops in Syria 'to ensure an Arab force capable of confronting the [Zionist] enemy'.[226] Given this, Soviet leaders encouraged Assad to respond positively to the Iraqi gesture: a process which was helped by the Syrian president's visit to Moscow in mid-October. The decision of Iraq and Syria to form a joint military command, taken later in the month in Baghdad, pleased the Kremlin which had been equipping their armed forces for many years. Furthermore, the Iraqi leaders' success in conciliating differences between moderates and radicals at the ninth Arab summit, held in Baghdad, convinced Moscow that Iraq had finally shed its ultra-rejectionism.

As described earlier, Iraqi–Syrian unification plans began to go awry, particularly after the success of the Iranian revolution – an event which took the Iraqi rulers' attention away from fighting the Zionist entity to countering an ideological-political challenge from the (Iranian) east. The accession of Saddam Hussein to the presidency in July, and his discovery, within a fortnight, of a plot against him (allegedly instigated by Syria) destroyed the last shred of hope for unity.[227] By then, to Moscow's regret, the Progressive National Front in Iraq had broken up, and Communists were once again being hounded on a large scale.[228] This was accompanied by open criticism of the USSR by President Hussein. Such actions seemed to remind the Kremlin of President Sadat's behaviour in the mid-1970s. Soviet exasperation at this was summarised by Dev Murarka thus: 'Moscow is still prepared to maintain close bilateral relations with many Arab states, but this will now be on a strictly reciprocal basis. The point is above all intended for the Iraqis. President Saddam Hussein will no longer be able to take for granted Iraq's alliance with the Soviet Union while vilifying Moscow in public.'[229]

Disregarding these hints, the Baathist government criticised the USSR vociferously for its intervention in Afghanistan in late December. At the Islamic foreign ministers' conference, held in Islamabad, Pakistan, in January, Iraq combined with Saudi Arabia to lead a diplomatic attack on Moscow on the issue of Afghanistan. This caused a strain in Soviet–Iraqi relations. On the other hand, in early February, Saddam Hussein unveiled an eight-point Arab National Charter, which stressed neutrality in international conflicts and 'a unified Arab economic structure', and rejected the presence on Arab soil of 'any foreign troops or military forces' or the granting of 'facilities . . . to them in any form or under any pretext or cover':[230] principles which have in general been endorsed by the Soviets in the past.

However, as relations between Iraq and Iran began to deteriorate in the spring, with their forces engaging in frequent border clashes, the USSR became apprehensive of the prospect of war between these states: one having a friendship treaty with it, and the other going through a phase of militant anti-imperialism. When this finally happened, with Iraq attacking Iran on 22 September, the Kremlin was 'embarrassed and alarmed'.[231] *Pravda* accused America of 'setting Iraq and Iran against each other'.[232] The Soviet appeal to both sides to show 'restraint and common sense'[233] was followed a few days later by an authorised article by Tass, which told Iraq and Iran that their war 'was undermining the national liberation movement in the Middle East in its struggle against imperialism and Zionism'.[234]

The USSR observed strict neutrality between the warring parties. It stopped supplying weapons, or even spare parts, to Iraq in order to help bring about a cessation of hostilities. 'In the Soviet view the [Gulf] war is against Iraqi, Arab and Soviet interests,' reported the Moscow correspondent of *The Middle East*. 'The signal is being relayed [to Iraq] indirectly, at lower levels, to make it less offensive.'[235] An article published in *Krasnaya Zvezda* in late October gave a strong hint of where Soviet sympathies lay. 'The declared aims of the [Iraqi] military actions are being changed,' said the article. 'At first Iraq claimed the comparatively small area of 508 square kilometres . . . but now the Iraqi press is publishing maps in which the whole province of Khuzestan, called Arabistan in Baghdad, is marked as Iraqi territory.'[236] Iraq had compounded its culpability by combining its expansionist intention with cooperation with Washington. 'The Soviets . . . accept that Saddam Hussein wanted to emerge as a powerful leader in the Gulf and to protect himself from the instigated resentment of the Shia majority in Iraq,' stated the Moscow correspondent of *The Middle East*. 'But they maintain that he acted in concert with the Americans and with their help and guidance.'[237]

Such a development ran counter to the hopes of CPSU theoreticians and tacticians in the early 1970s that daily contact with the Communists, under the aegis of a progressive front, would encourage the revolutionary democrats (leading the Iraqi Baathists) to gradually adopt scientific socialism, initiate the socialist transformation of society at home, and reinforce their ties with the socialist bloc abroad. But if Iraq had disappointed these theorists and others in Moscow, South Yemen has had a contrary impact. There the hopes that revolutionary democrats could emerge as Marxist-Leninists had been realised less than a decade after the country's independence.

During the mid-1960s, when the South Yemenis were engaged in guerrilla warfare against the British, the USSR regarded both FLOSY (backed by Nasser) and the NLF as patriotic organisations. A few weeks before the British departure from the colony, a commentary by the Prague-based Peace and Progress Radio described the NLF's programme as 'promising', because it stood inter alia for the expropriation of vast lands owned by the local feudal lords.[238] On South Yemen's independence day, *Pravda* carried an article which referred to the strategic significance of Aden, an important port on the oil tanker route from the (Arabian/Persian) Gulf to Europe.[239]

Moscow recognised the People's Republic of South Yemen immediately, and sent an ambassador to Aden in February. The CPSU noted with satisfaction that the NLF congress, held in early March, declared the NLF 'a revolutionary organisation' which represented 'the interests of workers, peasants, soldiers and revolutionary intellectuals'.[240] Analysing the NLF congress and its programme A. Shvakov, a Soviet political commentator, stated that South Yemeni socialism was a mixture of elements of scientific socialism and concepts of 'revolutionary democracy' and 'religious, petit bourgeois and other ideas'.[241]

Once President Qahtan al Shaabi had signed economic and technical cooperation agreements with the USSR during his visit to Moscow in February 1969, the flow of Soviet aid increased. Shaabi's overthrow by the leftists within the NLF four months later led to a radicalisation of the government: a process which was accelerated after March 1970 when a Saudi-backed coup attempt was foiled.[242] The fast pace of change caused concern among Soviet theorists. Writing in the *New Times*, Alexei Vasilyev criticised those leaders of the 'leftist trend' who wanted to telescope all the stages of a socialist revolution into one. The desire to nationalise everything and place everything on a cooperative basis with the objective of 'smashing production relations formed over the centuries' could, he cautioned, ruin the economy totally, and 'undermine the faith of the people in socialist principles'.[243]

Warnings such as this had no effect on the flow of Soviet economic and military aid to South Yemen: by 1971 it amounted to $27.5 million.[244] During his visit to Moscow in September, South Yemen's prime minister thanked the USSR for its material aid as well as its assistance in frustrating imperialist conspiracies against the socialist regime in Aden.[245] Soviet military aid enabled the South Yemeni government to enlarge the army from its pre-independence strength of 6,000 to 14,000 in 1972.[246] Its armed forces were strong enough to thwart an invasion mounted by South Yemeni exiles and North Yemeni tribesmen in September. When this raised the possibility of overt aggression by Saudi Arabia and/or North Yemen, Prime Minister Ali Nasser Mohammed warned, 'The Soviet Union will not stand by with folded arms in the event of an invasion of South Yemen.'[247] This had a salutary effect on Aden's adversaries.

The conflict ended with a cease-fire agreement on 28 October, and an astonishing announcement that the two Yemens had agreed to unite. But before details could be finalised, President Salem Robaye Ali went to Moscow for consultations. On 21 November Tass referred to 'further deepening of Soviet–Yemeni state relations', and referred to fraternal links between the NLF and the CPSU.[248] Five days later a joint Soviet–South Yemen communiqué welcomed Aden's efforts to normalise relations with Sanaa.[249] The presidents of the two Yemens signed a unity pact on 28 November. But, as described earlier, nothing came of it.[250] South Yemen continued the policy of strengthening its ties with the Soviet bloc. During his tour of Hungary, Czechoslovakia, and Poland in the following spring, Prime Minister Mohammed secured a total aid commitment of $37 million from these countries.[251]

South Yemen participated in the fourth Arab–Israeli war (in October) by barring Israeli ships from the Bab al Mandeb: it did so by reinforcing its artillery on Perim island at the mouth of the straits. This stopped the flow of oil – then running at the rate of about a million barrels a day – from Iran to Eilat, for the Israeli pipeline connecting Eilat to a port on the Mediterranean.[252]

Encouraged by the atmosphere of Arab unity, caused by the war and a successful imposition of an Arab oil embargo, Saudi Arabia and Egypt tried to wean Aden away from Moscow by offering it aid which amounted to one fifth of South Yemen's gross national product.[253] But, following the lead of the party's general secretary, Abdul Fatah Ismail, the fifth NLF congress, meeting in March 1975, rejected the overture – and thus opted for continued close links with the Soviet Union.[254] Saudi Arabia persisted. Soon after it had exchanged ambassadors with South Yemen a year later, it reportedly offered $300 million in aid to Aden as an incentive to end its ties with Moscow.[255] Aden refused again. The result was a reduction of

$250 million in the Saudi assistance actually given.

In the autumn of 1977 South Yemen agreed to provide the USSR with transit and other facilities for its arms airlift to Ethiopia, undertaken to help Ethiopia fight its adversaries, including (Saudi-backed) Somalia. This angered Riyadh, which cancelled all promises of future economic assistance. In contrast, a gratified Moscow offered MiG-21s and long-range rockets to Aden mainly to enable it to withstand threats from Riyadh.[256] These became real when Saudi Arabia blamed the South Yemeni government for the assassination of North Yemen's president in late June. 'The world's largest oil exporting country cannot tolerate the presence of Communism on its southern borders,' warned Riyadh Radio.[257]

This time, because of its membership of the Steadfastness Front, South Yemen could count on allies in the Arab world to withstand threats from its powerful neighbour. Responding to its call for support, the Steadfastness Front summit, meeting in Damascus on 20 September, opposed the economic boycott of South Yemen decided on two months earlier by a majority of Arab League members at Saudi Arabia's behest. Moscow was pleased by this: it meant that the Steadfastness Front was gradually transcending its original (limited) objective of resisting Israeli gains, and emerging as a cohesive progressive front of Arab states. The cancellation of the resolution for a boycott of South Yemen by the ninth Arab summit in Baghdad was welcomed by Moscow.

Early the following year, during hostilities between the two Yemens, the USSR helped the South clandestinely. It could do so because it had military advisers attached to North Yemen's military, which had been using Soviet weapons since the mid-1950s. 'We cannot do a thing without the other side [South Yemen] knowing about it,' said a North Yemeni official. 'The Russians are with our forces as well, and they simply pass on [to South Yemen] all our secrets.'[258] Not surprisingly, the South (and its allies from the North) did well on the battlefield. As described earlier, the cease-fire agreement between the warring sides led once more to a pact for unifying the two countries within a year.[259]

Such a commitment inhibited Aden from signing a friendship treaty with Moscow, which the latter wanted. However, the chances for political unity receded rapidly as the size and content of the American weapons shipments to Sanaa became known, and the North Yemeni government increased the size of its armed forces dramatically by introducing conscription, while Saudi Arabia showed no sign of softening its opposition to Yemeni unity. Under the circumstances South Yemen reconsidered its position as regards entering into a long-term relationship with the Soviet Union. During his visit to Moscow in October, President Abdul Fatah Ismail signed a twenty-year friendship and cooperation treaty with the USSR.[260] 'The overriding aim of the People's Democratic Republic of Yemen [i.e. South Yemen] government is survival,' notes Fred Halliday, a British specialist on the Middle East. 'Only the Soviet Union has the military power to guarantee that, both in providing arms and training, and in giving a general guarantee of support via its air and naval power.'[261]

Interestingly, the first Arab state with which the Soviet Union signed a friendship treaty was North Yemen. It did so in 1929, a year after it had recognised Imam Yahya as the monarch, in order to help him safeguard the independence and territorial integrity of his kingdom (then known simply as Yemen), which were threatened by Britain. Under this treaty, valid for ten years, Moscow sent doctors to North Yemen, and built the first electricity generating plant in the country. Although the treaty was renewed for another ten years,[262] relations between Sanaa and Moscow soured when Imam Yahya refused to modify his policy of neutrality between the opposing sides in the Second World War.

A liberalisation in Soviet foreign policy after Stalin's death, and the influence of the progressive-minded crown prince, Mohammed al Badr, on his father, Imam Ahmed, led to the conclusion of a Soviet–Yemeni treaty of friendship and trade in 1955. As stated earlier, the Egyptian–Czech arms deal of that year encouraged North Yemen to seek a similar arrangement through Moscow.[263] The Kremlin was willing, because Imam Ahmed was pursuing a policy of arming nationalists in South Yemen to drive out the British, and bring about the unification of the two Yemens under his rule. Prince Badr signed the deal during his visit to Moscow in 1956. By the time he went to Moscow again, five years later the Soviets had supplied North Yemen with such weapons as tanks, jet planes, and anti-aircraft guns – and built inter alia the port of Hodeida.

Following the anti-royalist coup of September 1962 the USSR recognised the regime of Brigadier-General Abdullah Sallal. In conjunction with Egypt it aided the republicans in their fight against the royalists. In a radio broadcast in November 1963 a Soviet commentator stated that the presence of Egyptian troops and the supply of Soviet weapons had played 'an important role' in strengthening the republicans against the reactionaries.[264] Periodic claims by the royalists to have shot down Soviet planes confirmed the veracity of such statements. The Soviets were also known to be maintaining the republicans' tanks and fighter planes, and building an airfield near Sanaa. At the same time attention was being paid to economic aid. During his visit to Moscow in March, President Sallal signed an economic and technical cooperation agreement with the USSR.

Moscow was disappointed by the lack of a decisive victory by the republicans in the civil war. Yevgeny Primakov and Dmitri Volsky, specialists on the Middle East, attributed this to the predominance of rich merchants in the republican camp, the paucity of patriotic military officers, a lack of political consciousness among the masses, and the absence of political parties.[265] But there was no slackening of Soviet assistance to the republicans. When the Egyptian troops began withdrawing in late 1967, Soviet transport planes brought 10,000 tons of weapons to North Yemen within four weeks.[266] It was this move – combined with the use of Soviet ground crews and instructors, and Algerian and Syrian pilots – which enabled the republicans to frustrate the royalist offensive launched against Sanaa after the Egyptian military withdrawal in December.[267]

However, as North Yemen, now ruled by the 'Third Force' leaders, began drifting rightwards in the late 1960s,[268] and as the Kremlin grew more interested in the recently independent South Yemen, the Soviet commitment to Sanaa waned. When North Yemen became embroiled in designs to overthrow the regime in Aden, Moscow stopped its supply of weapons and spare parts to Sanaa towards the end of 1969.[269] But Soviet economic aid continued, and was the major theme of talks between Soviet leaders and the North Yemeni president during the latter's visit to Moscow in December 1971. Not surprisingly, the USSR condemned the inter-Yemeni hostilities in the autumn of 1972, with the *New Times* describing them as 'imperialist inspired'.[270]

In the wake of a general easing of intra-Arab tensions after the October 1973 war, the USSR relaxed its ban on arms shipments to North Yemen. The lackadaisical relations existing between the two states were not altered by the accession to power of Colonel Hamdi in mid-1974. He set out to diversify his sources of weapons' supplies; and in this he was helped by Riyadh with funds. But as Saudi Arabia tried to channel all the economic and military aid offered to North Yemen by the West and the Gulf states through itself,[271] President Hamdi reacted against this. In 1977 he began implementing a two-pronged policy of courting South Yemen on the platform of unity, and cultivating friendly relations with the USSR. Moscow responded positively. As a result, the number of Soviet civilian and military experts in the republic grew steadily.[272] The USSR, therefore, regretted his assassination in October in more ways than one.

Despite his pro-Riyadh leanings, and an awareness of his government's financial dependence on Saudi Arabia, President Ghashmi felt the need to make a gesture that would prove Yemeni independence. Conscious of this, and the paucity of foreign exchange in Sanaa's treasury, the Soviets offered to sell North Yemen weapons cheaply. Thus encouraged, Ghashmi ordered 100 Soviet T-55 tanks.[273] With the tanks came Soviet military experts. As a result there were as described earlier, Soviet military advisers posted in the country when inter-Yemeni hostilities broke out in early 1979.[274]

Among other things, this war led to the arrival in North Yemen of twelve American F-5E jet fighters and sixty-four M-60 tanks, paid for by Riyadh.[275] But with the introduction of conscription in September, the size of the military grew abruptly – and with it the need for weapons. Since the government lacked funds, particularly in foreign currencies, and since it was keen not to be reminded once again of its humiliating dependence on Riyadh, the president found the Soviet offer of heavy weapons at give-away prices too tempting to reject. The result was a Soviet–Yemeni arms deal involving thirty-six MiG-21s, fourteen SU-22s, and 300 T-55 tanks.[276]

When Soviet instructors began arriving with the weapons later in the year, the Saudi rulers became angry. They cut off their budgetary assistance, running at $300 million a year, to Sanaa, and suspended all economic aid. Following President Saleh's visit to Riyadh in August, Saudi subsidies were resumed partially. Yet, by early 1981, the Saudi wish to see all Soviet advisers depart from North Yemen had still to be fulfilled, for there were then 120–150 military, and 250–300 civilian, Soviet experts in the republic.[277]

It is obvious that the USSR and Saudi Arabia have been acting as adversaries in North Yemen since the republican coup. What partly explains this behaviour is the fact that Moscow and Riyadh maintain no diplomatic or trade links. This has been the case for more than four decades. Yet the Soviet Union was the first country to recognise Abdul Aziz ibn Abdul Rahman al Saud and his domain. It did so in 1926, a year earlier than Britain. The decision was based on the view held, among others, by A. I. Pershits, a Soviet academic, that the rise of a monarchy in Arabia from among competing feudatories was a 'progressive historical development'.[278] Five years later the Kremlin gave credits to the king to help him overcome the financial crisis he faced.[279] Relations improved further when Prince Feisal ibn Abdul Aziz visited Moscow in 1932 and received a warm welcome.

But the trend did not continue. The Saudi king showed scant interest or aptitude for encouraging those fellow-Arabs living under British tutelage in the adjoining territories to rebel against their colonial masters. This disappointed Moscow, which had earlier visualised King Abdul Aziz emerging as a powerful nationalist figure, and coming into conflict with imperial Britain. The result was a suspension of Soviet–Saudi links in 1939, initiated by Moscow.

Although Saudi Arabia declared war on the Axis powers in the Second World War, it did so only in March 1945, and after having forged strong economic and military links with America and Britain. As such, Soviet comment on Saudi Arabia in the post-war period was in general caustic. Soviet analysts often described the Saudi king as an agent of Anglo–American imperialism, and Wahhabism as the reactionary ideology of a feudal regime which was opposed to the national liberation movement of the Arab world.[280]

The Soviet press gave prominence to reports of oilworkers' strikes in 1953 and 1956, and the formation of the National Liberation Front in March 1958.[281] These were presented as symptoms of a rising tide of anti-imperialist struggle in the kingdom. In the Soviet view, the Saudi state had become a tool of the feudatories and the trading bourgeoisie, and was using Wahhabism as a means to divert the attention of the emerging working class from its socio-economic problems to religion.[282] While the Kremlin attacked Riyadh for renewing its five-year lease with America on maintaining a military base in Dhahran in 1956, it praised the Saudi rulers for opposing the landing of American and British troops in Lebanon and Jordan in July 1958.

In the eight-year-long battle for supremacy between King Saud and Crown Prince Feisal, the Soviet press took no sides. However, when Feisal was installed as the monarch in November, *Pravda* pointed out that he had earlier implemented such financial reforms as controlling the (extravagant) royal expenses.[283] Feisal's policies at home and abroad quickly dissipated whatever goodwill existed for him in Moscow. His ruthless repression of opposition and active cooperation with America, culminating in the launching of the anti-Nasserist Islamic Alliance in late 1965, won him the epithet of 'the avowed henchman of imperialism and Arab reaction' from *Pravda*.[284]

When the defeat in the Six Day war left Nasser weakened, and thus led him to withdraw Egyptian troops from North Yemen,[285] the USSR found itself the chief external supporter of the republicans in North Yemen, fighting the royalists backed by Saudi Arabia. This accentuated Moscow–Riyadh hostility. 'It is not just a matter of threatening . . . South Yemen and Aden; he [King Feisal] also wants to drive through to the Indian Ocean,' wrote K. Ivanov, a Soviet commentator, in *International Life*. 'Those who reduce Feisal's role to that of a lackey of the Americans are mistaken, for he has his own policy for the South Arabian peninsula.'[286]

King Feisal made no secret of his hatred of Communism and his intention to eliminate Soviet influence in the Arab world. His own power was bolstered by the death of Nasser and fast rising oil revenue. The Kremlin believed that it was Feisal (working in league with America) who instigated President Sadat to demand the expulsion of Soviet military advisers from Egypt, and then rewarded him with large financial subsidies. It also believed that success in his Egyptian endeavour in July 1972 led Feisal to encourage South Yemeni émigrés and North Yemeni tribesmen to attack South Yemen. Apprehensive that an advance here would lead Feisal to strike somewhere else at their position in the Middle East, Soviet leaders decided to act resolutely. They encouraged the South Yemeni government to play the card of Soviet intervention in case of overt aggression against it by any of its neighbours. Aden did so; and the plan worked.[287]

Although the Kremlin succeeded in checkmating Riyadh in this instance, it detected no sign of weakening in the Saudi offensive against the socialist bloc. 'Year after year it [the Saudi monarchy] spends dozens, even hundreds, of millions of dollars on what it calls "Arab Policy", the aim of which is to thwart social and economic reforms in other Arab states, and subvert their cooperation with the socialist countries,' stated

Dmitri Volsky. 'Saudi "dollar diplomacy" is out to rally the Arab nations not for struggle against imperialism and Israeli aggression . . . but on purely religious foundations. Riyadh endlessly thumps the drum of the "jihad" or "holy war" that King Feisal has declared against "Communism–Zionism", that fantastic invention of present day obscurantists.'[288]

The October 1973 war and its aftermath helped to lessen tensions between the USSR and Saudi Arabia. Moscow was surprised and pleased by the decision of King Feisal to join the Arab oil embargo against the Western supporters of Israel, and said so.[289] The king noted the change and reciprocated. He sent a congratulatory message to Soviet leaders on the fifty-sixth anniversary of the Bolshevik revolution.[290] However, the thaw in Riyadh–Moscow relations proved temporary. The Saudi monarch ignored Soviet advice, offered publicly, not to yield to pressures by Washington to end the oil boycott before the original conditions for its lifting were met.[291]

The accession of Khaled ibn Abdul Aziz to the throne in March 1975 made little difference to Saudi policy towards the USSR. By refusing to pay the cost of an air defence system for Jordan if King Hussein signed the deal with the Soviet Union, King Khaled succeeded in destroying Moscow's chances of forging military ties with Amman.[292] Soviet dismay at this was compounded by the emergence of Saudi Arabia as the principal peacemaker and paymaster in the Lebanese civil war in the autumn of 1976.[293]

Later, oddly enough, it was the actions of President Sadat (who had originally been encouraged by the Saudis to cut Egypt's ties with the USSR), which had the inadvertent effect of lessening antagonism between Moscow and Riyadh. The consistent refusal of the Saudi rulers to give in to American pressures and join the Egyptian–Israeli talks pleased Moscow. Informal Soviet–Saudi relations, maintained through their envoys in Sanaa, improved – only to be soured by the bloody events of June 1978 in the two Yemens.

But the Camp David accord changed the situation almost overnight. Three days later, on the Saudi national day, Moscow Radio said, 'The Saudi Arabian people are an indivisible part of the Arab nation; with those peoples the Soviet Union is successfully developing friendly cooperation, despite their different political and social systems'.[294] Riyadh responded positively by letting the USSR resume its Moscow-to-Sanaa passenger flights, through Saudi airspace, early the following year.[295] 'The absence of diplomatic relations does not mean that we do not recognise the Soviet Union, or that we do not recognise the important role it plays in world politics,' said Prince Saud ibn Feisal, Saudi foreign minister, in March. 'We have always expressed our gratitude to the positive stand adopted by the Soviet Union regarding Arab problems.'[296] A few weeks later Riyadh granted permission to the USSR to operate a weekly passenger flight from Sanaa to Kuwait by using Saudi airspace.[297]

These were pointers towards the establishment of formal relations between the two states. In late December, Crown Prince Fahd stated in an interview with a leftist Beirut daily, *Al Safir*, that the USSR was beginning to understand Saudi policies, and that Saudi Arabia was satisfied with the development of its relations with Moscow. Referring to the possibility of diplomatic ties with the Soviet Union, he said, 'We first have to prepare our people, but we are satisfied that this will be accomplished at the right time'.[298] But, following Soviet intervention in Afghanistan on 27 December, Saudi Arabia took a leading role in rallying opposition to the Soviet move at the Islamic foreign ministers' conference.[299] Riyadh kept up its campaign. In July, Prince Saud said that Saudi Arabia could not open diplomatic relations with the USSR while 'it kept its troops in Afghanistan'.[300]

As for the Soviets, they seemed more concerned with the general direction of Saudi foreign policy than establishing formal ties with Riyadh. In their view the events of the late 1970s had made the Saudi leaders distance themselves from the American camp, and show an increasing independence in conducting their foreign affairs. 'Since the fall of the Shah [say the Russian analysts], the Saudis have been keeping their distance from the US alliance-building moves,' reported the Moscow correspondent of *Events*. 'By now Moscow has learned . . . that Saudi Arabia has a unique position in the Arab world, and [shares] goals in common with those of the Soviet Union: containment of Israel, establishment of a Palestinian homeland, and exclusion of Jerusalem from Israeli control.'[301]

In the late 1970s the other prominent state in the Arabian Peninsula which actively shared these objectives with the USSR was Kuwait. Soviet relations with Kuwait had grown with a remarkable evenness. When, on recognising the independent state of Kuwait in mid-1961, Moscow offered to exchange envoys, the Kuwaiti ruler agreed in principle, if only to bolster the international status of his kingdom, then under threat from Iraq. This was done in March 1962. The Soviet press reported the holding of the first parliamentary election in Kuwait in January 1963 as an unprecedented, and welcome, event in the history of the Arabian Peninsula.

Nikita Khrushchev's jibe at the 'little ruler' of Kuwait as being corrupt, during his tour of Egypt in May 1964,[302] had little effect on the general wish of the two governments to diversify and strengthen their ties. As a result of the Kuwait industry ministry's visit to Moscow later in the year, the USSR and Kuwait signed a sixteen-year economic and technical cooperation agreement. Reviewing Kuwait's foreign policy, soon after the accession of Shaikh Sabah in late 1965, an editorial in the *New Times* lauded Kuwait for following a neutralist line in external affairs, and praised Crown Prince Jaber al Sabah for his interest in developing good relations with Moscow.[303]

The presence of a small but vocal leftist opposition in parliament in the early 1970s helped to make Kuwait's external stance the least pro-West among the Gulf states. And the presence of a large Palestinian community in the country meant that, as the Soviet bloc became more supportive of the PLO, the Kuwaiti government improved its relations with the socialist states. In 1976 it followed up a modest arms deal with Moscow with trade pacts with east European countries.[304]

The suspension of parliament by the ruler later that year made no difference to the government's foreign policy. In March 1977 it finalised a $1.25 billion agreement with Rumania to build a petrochemical complex on the Black Sea, to refine Kuwaiti crude oil, with Kuwait contributing 49 per cent of the cost.[305] Nearly three years later the Kuwaiti defence minister surprised the world by revealing that the Kuwaiti army had tested Soviet-made ground-to-ground Lunar missiles as part of military exercises conducted 'in a desert region', and by expressing the hope that these [Soviet] missiles would be available 'on the expected day of liberation of the Arab land under Israeli occupation'.[306]

Some weeks after the newly elected parliament had been convened in March 1981, Kuwait's deputy premier and foreign minister, Shaikh Sabah al Ahmed al Sabah, visited Moscow for a meeting with Soviet foreign minister Gromyko. A joint communiqué issued by the two leaders expressed opposition to the Camp David peace process and backed President Brezhnev's proposal for an international conference on the Middle East, which would include not only the USSR, the USA, and Israel, but also the PLO.[307] 'There have been reports that Shaikh Sabah's visit had the tacit backing of the Saudis, not just to test the water on Soviet reinvolvement in the Middle East but also to show Arab independence of Washington,' wrote Michel Szwed-Cousins of *8 Days*.[308]

Thus, among the Gulf states, while Kuwait has shown much interest in developing relations with the Soviet bloc, Oman has shown none. As a state which is most closely attached to the Western bloc, Oman has been a prime target of verbal attacks by Moscow. Yet, when the rule of Sultan Said ibn Taimur was challenged by Dhofari rebels in the mid-1960s, the USSR evinced little interest. In fact, as in the case of the PLO (of that time), Moscow was somewhat wary of the Dhofari Liberation Front, and its successor, the Popular Front for the Liberation of the Occupied Arab Gulf – not least because of the aid they were then receiving from Peking.

It was only after the South Yemeni government (the main supporter of PFLOAG) had arranged for Soviet journalists to tour the liberated zone in Dhofar in 1970 that Moscow revised its stance. Just as in the case of the PLO, favourable reports of PFLOAG's activities against the repressive regime of Sultan Qaboos in the Soviet press during the summer of 1971 were followed by an invitation to a PFLOAG delegation to visit Moscow by the Soviet section of the Afro–Asian Solidarity Committee.[309] Within a year the USSR had begun supplying arms to PFLOAG and training its cadres.[310] The importance of Soviet assistance grew as China first reduced its aid to PFLOAG and its successor (in Oman), the Popular Front for the Liberation of Oman, and then stopped it altogether in 1976.

Moscow attacked the Sultan for using 'Iranian and British mercenaries' in his drive against the 'Omani patriots' during the winter of 1975–6, and bemoaned the PFLO's loss of the liberated zone on Dhofar. When the PFLO revived guerrilla activity on a limited scale in 1977, and then stepped it up next year, the Soviet press reported this prominently, and presented it as growing signs of popular discontent against the Sultan's internal and external policies. Following the Shah's downfall, and the signing of the Egyptian–Israeli peace treaty in March 1979, the CPSU's international department invited the PFLO head, Abdul Aziz Qadi, to Moscow for talks.[311]

Later in the year, when tension between revolutionary Iran and the USA increased sharply – in the wake of occupation of the American embassy in Tehran and the taking of sixty-seven diplomats hostage by militant Iranian students – the Straits of Hormuz became the focus of attention of the Soviet Union and the Western bloc. Scores of warships from both sides assembled in the international waters of the north Arabian Sea at the mouth of the straits, underlining the strategic significance of Oman. This stems from the fact that sixteen million barrels of Gulf oil, amounting to one third of the total oil consumption of the non-Communist world,[312] pass daily through the Hormuz Straits. But Oman was strategically important in the pre-oil era too, to the leading power of the West: Britain. Its southern coastline, as well as Iran's, lay along the shortest route between Britain and its most prized colony, India. In fact it was the military and commercial need to protect this sea lane that led Britain to establish political control over the countries that lay en route, and in the process become the supreme imperialist power in the Arab East for a century.

# 13

# THE ARABS AND THE WEST

Starting with Robert Clive's victory at Plassey in 1757, it took the British about a century to extend their rule to the whole of the Indian subcontinent. Throughout this period, and long after, Britain fought hard to keep open its shortest communication line to India via the Middle East. When Napoleon Bonaparte's conquest of Egypt in 1798 disrupted this (sea-land-sea) route, the British allied with the Ottoman Turks to attack the French fleet off the Egyptian coast. France suffered defeat; and the Ottomans reclaimed Egypt. But the French continued to exercise political influence in Cairo. Rivalry between France and Britain – which persisted throughout the construction of the Suez Canal (1859–69) – was not resolved until 1882, when the British conquered Egypt.

The revival of French political interest in Egypt, in the wake of France's alliance with Britain to frustrate German designs on Egypt in the late 1890s, proved temporary. In 1904 the French finally renounced political ambition in Egypt, and agreed to confine themselves to maintaining the cultural influence which they, as the harbingers of secular education in Egypt in 1869, had come to exercise. Egyptian intellectuals were thus greatly influenced by France. This was also true of the intellectuals in the Levant and Greater Syria, where France's religious-educational interest in local Catholics was officially recognised by the Ottomans in 1649.[1]

The Americans were the other Western nationals to limit themselves to education and religion in the Arab East. They opened institutes of higher education in Cairo and Beirut in 1863 – thirty-two years after Washington had signed a treaty of amity and commerce with Constantinople. This treaty remained technically unaffected by the American entry into the First World War in April 1917: for, the USA did not declare war against Turkey. As such Woodrow Wilson, the American president, evinced little interest in the fate of Turkey's Arab empire, except for offering advice on Palestine and the Jews (when so asked by British leaders),[2] and appointing in May 1919 a committee headed by Henry King and Charles Crane to assess the political desires of the people of the Middle East.[3] America's withdrawal from the Paris peace conference in December, and its failure to join the subsequent League of Nations, meant that Washington had nothing to do with the terms of the Anglo–French mandates in the Middle East.

As leaders of the League of Nations, Britain and France defined the mandates in such a way as to secure the best possible terms for themselves. Between the two, Britain emerged as by far the stronger party. Its writ now ran not only in Egypt, Palestine, Transjordan, and Iraq but also in southern Arabia, Oman, and the Gulf principalities. When its authority was seriously challenged by the populace, Britain managed to retain hegemony over a territory by tying up the local ruler in a restrictive treaty. 'First came military occupation [by Britain]; and then the . . . disorder that followed [mainly as a reaction to foreign domination] was used to justify continued occupation,' notes P. Edward Haley, an American academic. 'Finally, the British sought to achieve the benefits of occupation without its expense. . . . In all the Arab countries, the British sought to protect their empire to the east by a network of bilateral Anglo–Arab alliances that guaranteed them the widest possible rights of transit, storage, and communications, and exclusive access to the local armed forces.'[4]

Egypt was a good example. The Anglo–Egyptian treaty of 1936 bound the two states in a military alliance. It gave Britain the exclusive right to equip and train the Egyptian military. While it required Egypt to expand its transport and communications facilities, and make them available to the British forces, it entitled Britain to build as many new airbases as it wished. British troops were to be stationed specifically to guard the Suez Canal until such time that the two signatories agreed that Egypt could do the job alone. As described earlier, the popularly elected Egyptian government unilaterally abrogated the treaty in October 1951, five years before its expiry date.[5] The subsequent tussle between London and Cairo paved the way for the overthrow of the monarchy in less than a year.

By then America had emerged as the leader of the Western bloc, and its president, Harry Truman, had declared the Middle East to be strategically important, and drawn it into America's overall global strategy.[6] Since, unlike Britain and France, America did not have a history of imperialism in the region, it had a much better chance of getting along with such Arab nationalist republicans as the Free Officers of Egypt. Not surprisingly – according to Miles Copeland, an American CIA official posted in the Middle East in the 1950s – the CIA knew as early as March 1952 that a 'secret military society' was 'plotting a coup'. Before the coup the CIA's Cairo station, headed by Kermit Roosevelt, had three meetings with some of the officers of the group. 'The large area of agreement reached by Roosevelt and this [Egyptian] officer, speaking for Nasser himself, is noteworthy,' writes Copeland.[7]

Egypt's military rulers were anxious to make the republic truly independent by securing the withdrawal of 70,000 British troops stationed in the Suez zone,[8] and occupying 300 square miles of Egyptian territory.

America played an important mediatory role in bringing this about. Significantly, the Anglo–Egyptian agreement on the withdrawal of British troops, initialled in July 1954, entitled Britain to reoccupy the Suez zone 'with Egypt's agreement' in the case of an attack on Egypt by 'any outside power'.[9] 'In return for its agreeing that the British would be able to return in the event of war, President Eisenhower made an unprecedented decision to grant military aid to the Egyptian army,' states Wilbur Crane Eveland. 'This was a courageous act because the Israeli lobby was very much against it, but it was top secret.'[10] The Anglo–Egyptian agreement was signed in October. The following month America decided to give Egypt $40 million in economic aid.[11]

But when, following a large-scale Israeli attack on Egyptian military posts in Gaza in early 1955, Nasser approached the White House for arms worth $20 million (as per the secret agreement), the latter demanded cash payment in hard currency. Since Egypt's total foreign reserves then amounted to $20 million, Nasser was in no position to meet this condition.[12] His subsequent decision to procure Soviet arms through Czechoslovakia on a barter basis shocked and angered the Western capitals. Yet, not wishing to alienate the charismatic leader of Egypt, a most strategic country in the region, Washington and London continued discussions with Cairo on financing the Aswan Dam – with the International Bank for Reconstruction and Development (known as the World Bank) offering credits of $200 million, and America and Britain together another $70 million, in hard currencies – matching $900 million to be provided by Egypt in local services and goods. An agreement was signed in February. Three months later Nasser recognised the People's Republic of China, a step which the American secretary of state, John Foster Dulles, described as 'regrettable'.[13] On 19 July the USA withdrew its offer of financial assistance for the Aswan Dam, and a day later Britain followed suit. 'The US and Britain believed that even if he did not fall from power, Nasser would become more pliable,' states the author of the section 'Egypt' in *The Middle East*. 'Instead he retaliated by announcing a week later (on the fourth anniversary of the Revolution) the nationalisation of the Suez Canal Company.'[14]

As described earlier, Britain and France colluded with Israel to attack Egypt.[15] Two days after Israel had attacked the Sinai peninsula on 29 October, Britain and France went into action claiming to 'separate' the two sides. Britain bombed Cairo, Alexandria, Port Said, and Ismailia, and destroyed most of the Egyptian air force. Egypt retaliated by sinking ships in the Suez Canal and blocking it. Syria stopped the flow of Arab oil to West Europe by blowing up the oil pipeline from Iraq to the Mediterranean: this led to petrol rationing in Britain, and a steep fall in the value of the British pound in foreign exchange markets. Within a fortnight of the cease-fire on 6 November, Britain and France agreed to a phased withdrawal from Egypt.[16]

America won considerable goodwill in Egypt and elsewhere in the Arab world by opposing the tripartite aggression, and later pressuring Israel into withdrawing from Sinai. But most of it was dissipated when Washington refused to supply urgently needed food and medicines to Egypt, or to let its government purchase these in America with the funds frozen by the White House after the Suez nationalisation. The promulgation, in early 1957, of the Eisenhower doctrine – which promised American aid to any Middle East state seeking protection against 'overt armed aggression from any nation controlled by international Communism' – soured relations between Washington and Cairo.[17] Egypt described the doctrine as a 'form of imperialist pressure'.[18] Later events vindicated the Egyptian description. 'It is true that the doctrine spoke of providing protection only against overt aggression, and only hinted at the Nasser[ite] threat by speaking of aggression on the part of "any nation controlled by international Communism",' notes Nadav Safran. 'But these, as events were to prove, were merely diplomatic phrasings designed to facilitate the aim of openly rallying friendly governments behind the doctrine; they did not restrict the freedom of action of the American government, which was, after all, free to interpret as it wished the meaning of its own doctrine.'[19]

The Eisenhower doctrine marked a deliberate American entry into the Middle East to fill what Eisenhower called a 'vacuum' left by the eclipse of British and French power (as illustrated by the failure of their attack on Egypt). During the next year and a half the doctrine was applied three times: to solve the internal crisis of Jordan in April 1957, to pressure the nationalist-leftist regime of Syria during the summer, and to provide troops to Lebanon in July 1958. Since, in the cases of Jordan and Lebanon, the American move was made to check the rise of the Nasserite forces there, Egypt felt hostile towards the USA. On its part the Eisenhower administration, aware of the geographical and political importance of Egypt, tried not to alienate Nasser totally. Therefore, after the Egyptian government had settled its dispute with the Suez Canal company regarding compensation, Washington offered food to Cairo under Public Law 480, which allowed the administration to sell American surplus food abroad in local currencies.

Cairo–Washington relations improved when, soon after assuming office, President Kennedy initiated a correspondence with Nasser to exchange views. During the first year of his presidency, food aid to Egypt amounted to $220 million.[20] At the time of the Soviet–American confrontation on the issue of Soviet missiles in Cuba, in October 1962, Nasser kept a low profile, and desisted from supporting Moscow publicly or privately. Kennedy appreciated this. However, both the American president and Congress became critical of Nasser as he increased the Egyptian commitment to the republicans in North Yemen's civil war. In 1963 congressional leaders were reluctant to provide surplus food to Egypt, but Kennedy managed to overcome the hurdle.

Two years later, during Johnson's presidency, Congress amended Public Law 480 to exclude Egypt, unless the president deemed otherwise. Johnson, who showed 'little sympathy for the radical brand of Arab nationalism expounded by Egypt's President Nasser',[21] made an exception: once. Thus food aid to Egypt ended in January 1966. By then Cairo had severed its diplomatic ties with Bonn for supplying arms clandestinely to Israel,[22] and with London for failing to crush the minority rebel government of Ian Smith in Rhodesia (now Zimbabwe).

From then on until the Six Day war, relations between Egypt and America deteriorated steadily. Confirmation by the state department in February 1966 that America had supplied tanks to Israel and Jordan, and missiles to Israel and Saudi Arabia, provided evidence to Nasser that America was intent on destroying the progressive regimes in the Arab world.[23] On the other hand the Johnson administration interpreted Nasser's decision to form a joint defence command with the radical Baathist regime in Damascus as further evidence of his drift into the Soviet orbit. Nasser had signed the pact with Syria in the hope that this would deter 'a large scale Israeli attack and thus stave off a war for which the Arabs were as yet unprepared'.[24] But events took a different turn.

As described earlier, tension between Syria and Israel rose sharply in April.[25] Following threatening statements by Israeli leaders against the Syrian regime, Cairo and Damascus feared an Israeli invasion on 17 May.[26] Nasser began moving Egyptian troops from the Suez Canal to forward positions on 14 May. Two days later Egypt asked the UN general secretary to withdraw the United Nations Emergency Force from certain posts along the Israeli–Egyptian border. The general secretary replied that a demand for withdrawal had to apply to the whole force or none at all. His consultations with the advisory committee at the UN showed that, while members were divided on the issue of the legality of Egypt's demand, they were unanimous in their view that it was impracticable to station the UNEF if the host country objected. The UNEF therefore withdrew on 18 May. Egyptian troops took up all the vacated posts, including the one at Sharm al Shaikh, overlooking the Straits of Tiran. Nasser made no further move for three days. Late on 22 May, in a speech at an airbase in Sinai, he declared that since America and Britain were arming Israel in order to overthrow the progressive Arab regimes, the Straits of Tiran were to be immediately closed to ships flying the Israeli flag, or carrying strategic materials to the Israeli port of Eilat.[27]

The next day President Johnson stated that the Gulf of Aqaba was an international waterwar, and that 'a blockade of Israeli shipping is illegal and potentially dangerous to the cause of peace'.[28] Urgent consultation between American and Israeli leaders ensued in Washington. On 26 May, after a top-level meeting of Israeli and American officials, Johnson told his aides at the White House, 'Israel is going to hit them [the Arabs]'.[29]

But to keep the Arab states off guard, Johnson responded positively to a Soviet appeal the next day for restraint, and cautioned the Israeli prime minister against initiating hostilities.[30]

Alarmed at the prospect of an Israeli invasion, King Hussein rushed to see his erstwhile adversary, President Nasser, in Cairo on 30 May, and immediately joined the Egyptian–Syrian defence pact. The following day, in reply to a journalist's question, the American secretary of state, Dean Rusk, replied, 'I don't think it's our business to restrain anybody.'[31] On 1 June the Israeli president swore in a government of national unity. The next day the Israeli ambassador in Washington sought 'further confirmation' that America would not object 'too strenuously if Israel acted on its own'.[32]

At the same time the White House was in touch with Cairo. On 3 June the Egyptian government announced that Vice-President Zakaria Mohieddin would visit Washington on 7 June, ostensibly to seek a peaceful solution to the Straits of Tiran problem. Aware that such a visit could 'only work to their disadvantage',[33] Israeli leaders got ready to act. Once they had a 'diplomatic formulation of the go-ahead' from President Johnson on 4 June, they acted immediately.[34]

The scale and speed of Israeli attacks on Egyptian military airfields, and then on Syrian and Jordanian air bases, led President Nasser (and King Hussein) to accuse America and Britain of direct participation in the war. The Arab oil ministers, meeting in Baghdad, decided to cut off oil supplies to America and Britain. Egypt, Syria and Iraq severed diplomatic links with these countries.

After the cease-fire President Johnson felt that military defeat would drive the Arab states to the negotiating table with Israel. He was to be disappointed. The fourth Arab summit in Khartoum in late August combined the three Noes – no recognition (of Israel), no negotiations, no peace treaty – with a reiteration of the Palestinian people's rights in 'their own country'. Bolstered by Soviet weapons and the recall of Egyptian troops from North Yemen, Nasser went through the stages of 'standing firm' (i.e. resisting Israeli diplomatic and military pressures), and 'active deterrence' (i.e. keeping the conflict alive, thus preventing the status quo from congealing),[35] to reach the final stage – 'war of attrition' – in March 1969.

Despite the heavy losses suffered by Egypt in the renewed conflict with Israel, Nasser rejected the overtures made in July by the American secretary of state, William Rogers, for a cease-fire, to be followed by the implementation of UN Security Council resolution 242. It was a year later – and only after Nasser had proved to the Egyptians that, aided by the Soviets, the Egyptian military could protect the republic against deep penetration bombing by Israel – that he finally accepted the Rogers plan. This in turn lessened the hostility that had existed between Egypt and America since the Six Day war.

Sadat's accession to the presidency, on Nasser's death, brought about a noticeable improvement in Washington–Cairo relations. Within three months America had resumed shipments of wheat and edible oil to Egypt, and pressured the World Bank into giving loans to the republic.[36] These actions were accompanied by strong hints by the Nixon administration that it wished to see the presence of Soviet military advisers in Egypt ended. Sadat replied that he would be willing to do as a quid pro quo for the first stage of an Israeli withdrawal from the occupied territories. America tried to persuade Israel to move its troops some distance from the Suez Canal as the first step in the implementation of UN resolution 242, but failed. Sadat was disappointed: he signed a friendship treaty with the USSR.

America then turned to the Saudi monarch, Feisal (with whom Sadat had close relations), to help loosen the links between Cairo and Moscow. Feisal succeeded, in July 1972.[37] He showed his appreciation of Sadat's action by increasing aid to Egypt. In contrast, President Nixon did nothing: a lapse which Sadat attributed to the vagaries of the American presidential election campaign then gathering momentum.

Nixon was re-elected president and began his second term of office in January. Late in February, he and his national security chief, Kissinger, had meetings with Sadat's security chief, Hafez Ismail, in America.[38] They offered a negotiating formula of public 'proximity talks' between Israel and Egypt, with the American state department participating, and secret, serious negotiations between the parties through Kissinger.[39] On the substance of the negotiations, according to Egyptian sources, Nixon told Ismail that the USA would pressure Israel only if Egypt made concessions in public which went beyond the Rogers plan.[40] A few weeks later the White House announced that it had authorised a sale of forty-eight more Phantom fighter aircraft to Israel. Not surprisingly, by the time Kissinger had another secret meeting with Ismail, outside Paris on 20 May, 'the promising tone of the February talks' was missing.[41]

About a month earlier, Arnaud de Borchgrave of *Newsweek* had quoted a 'top-level American official' (later identified as Kissinger) as saying, 'It is a sad fact of Middle Eastern life today that a political settlement does not seem possible without a major crisis first.' Commenting on the possibility of Kissinger, then engaged in delicate negotiations aimed at ending the war in Vietnam, undertaking a similar task in the Middle East, de Borchgrave added: 'Kissinger is not a man to undertake a diplomatic mission that does not have a reasonable chance of success. In the current Middle East situation, there is no such chance. Cairo insists that it will not concede an inch of Arab land to the Israelis. And the Israelis are satisfied with the present status quo – as are many Americans. The next move is Sadat's.'[42]

Yet when Sadat made his move on 6 October, both America and Israel were caught by surprise. Having started the war, Sadat made an immediate and frequent use of the 'back channel' with Washington that he had established nearly two years earlier. Straightaway he made it clear to the White House that he did not want a confrontation with America.[43] His political intention to retain American goodwill was severely strained when President Nixon ordered a massive airlift of weapons and ammunition to Israel on 9 October, and escalated it sharply four days later. The Soviet Union's arms supplies to Egypt (and Syria) were no match for what America was delivering to Israel, often straight to the battle airfields in Sinai.[44] Later revelations showed that Sadat twice overruled his chief of staff, General Saad al Din Shazli, when he proposed bombing Israel supply lines in Sinai – once before and once after the Israelis had established a bridgehead over the Suez Canal on 15 October.[45] Sadat did so in order to avoid antagonising the American administration, with whom he maintained regular contact through the 'back channel',[46] that is, the CIA, in all probability.

Given this, it was not surprising that once a cease-fire had been enforced on 25 October, relations between the Egyptian and American governments improved rapidly. As stated earlier, Sadat collaborated with Israeli leaders in not returning to Geneva for negotiations in early January, as previously agreed, and instead using Kissinger as the intermediary.[47] Since then every major move made by Sadat to align Egypt with the Western bloc – diplomatically, militarily and economically – or encourage private enterprise in Egypt, has been rewarded by one or more of the Western nations.

President Sadat resumed diplomatic relations with the USA in March. He combined a warm welcome to Nixon and Kissinger during their visit to Cairo in June with the signing of a series of Egyptian–American agreements, including one guaranteeing American investments in Egypt.[48] Following this, West Germany offered Egypt a loan of $200 million.[49] With Kissinger staying on as secretary of state – after Nixon's resignation in August – friendship between the two countries continued to grow.

In early 1976, as Kissinger prepared to undertake the next round of 'shuttle diplomacy' to implement a step-by-step peace in the Middle East, Sadat declared that America held 'virtually all the trump cards' for bringing about peace in the region.[50] Kissinger failed to get Israel to withdraw from the Mitla and Gidi passes and the oilfields in Sinai in return for Sadat's promise of 'non-use of force' against Israel. His shuttle ground to a halt on 22 March. Sadat tried to help revive the process by announcing, on the eve of his meeting with President Gerald Ford in Salzburg on 1 June, that the Suez Canal would be reopened on 5 June. Two months later he gave a secret promise to American leaders 'not to join the fighting if Syria attacked Israel'.[51] It was on the basis of such promises, and a series of American undertakings to Israel, that Kissinger brought about the Sinai II agreement in September.[52] The pact involved an Israeli withdrawal from the passes in Sinai, with the proviso that the early warning system there was to be supervised by a contingent of American civilians.

During his visit to Washington in October, Sadat requested a fourfold increase in American economic aid, then running at $250 million a year, and the lifting of the twenty-year-old arms embargo. The administration responded positively. Sadat's decision soon after, to open the Suez Canal to Israeli shipping helped to create goodwill for him in the American Congress. Early in March Kissinger recommended to Congress the sale of six C-130 Hercules transport aircraft on the ground that such an action was 'in the interests of Israel'. 'Egypt has courageously committed itself to pursuing peace, and ending its long-time close dependence on the Soviet Union, while moving towards closer relations with the West,' he stated. 'It is clearly in our interest to demonstrate that countries which pursue such policies can obtain the support of the United States.'[53] The sale was sanctioned. Ten days later Sadat unilaterally abrogated the friendship treaty with the USSR. Towards the end of the year, guided by Washington, Sadat took a secret, but highly significant, step in his policy towards Israel. He agreed to cooperation between the intelligence services of Egypt and Israel in monitoring the Soviet arms build-up in Libya.[54]

Food riots in Cairo and elsewhere in January underlined the extent of internal problems facing Sadat's regime. These helped to secure Egypt economic aid worth one billion dollars (including $250 million in food grains), in the current fiscal year, that its president had earlier asked of America.[55] As such, during his second visit to Washington in March, undertaken mainly to establish a working relationship with the new president, James Carter, Sadat concentrated on securing American tanks and aircraft. (Aware of the strength of the Israeli lobby in Congress, the previous administration had tried to help Egypt by encouraging Britain and France to sell it heavy weapons; and both countries had in principle agreed to do so.) Sadat made some headway. Later, as he distanced himself further from the USSR, after the Egyptian–Libyan conflict in July,[56] his chances of procuring heavy American weapons improved.

Sadat was at the same time cooperating with the Carter administration in designing a framework for reconvening the Geneva peace conference. Ismail Fahmi, the Egyptian foreign minister, acted as an intermediary between the American administration and the PLO to devise a formula which would enable American officials to sit with the PLO at a peace conference. According to Fahmi, the 'working paper' agreed between America and Israel on 5 October was a 'bilateral thing', which left the American–Soviet joint statement of 1 October 'intact', to be 'respected by the Americans and the Russians'.[57]

Suddenly, on 9 November, in his speech to the Egyptian parliament, Sadat said that he was ready to go anywhere 'including the Israeli parliament itself' to discuss peace. This seemingly surprised President

Carter and his advisers, who behaved as if they did not know how to respond to Sadat's move. 'They waited a little to watch things, but when they examined the pros and cons they had no choice but to support it [Sadat's initiative],' stated Ismail Fahmi. 'Here is the biggest Arab country in the area offering a separate peace with Israel, so why the hell shouldn't the Americans profit from this, bearing in mind their own internal problems with the Jewish community and the Jewish lobby?'[58]

President Sadat's forty-four hours in Israel were carried live by the Western television companies, and had direct impact on viewers in the West, particularly in America. It established him as a 'man of courage' and a 'man of peace'. This in turn diminished Congressional opposition to selling offensive weapons to Egypt. Early next year the Carter administration recommended to Congress a $2.4 billion arms deal, involving sixty F-15 fighter aircraft to Saudi Arabia and fifty F-5Es to Egypt.[59] In May the Senate passed the appropriate legislation by fifty-four votes to forty-four.[60] During that fiscal year the pace of American arms sales to Egypt picked up so fast that by the time President Carter had assembled President Sadat and the Israeli prime minister, Begin, and their advisers at Camp David on 5 September – to make a final, determined attempt to reach a peace accord – Egypt's purchases of American weapons amounted to $937 million.[61]

The direction of the talks at Camp David was dictated by the stark reality of the imbalance of power existing between the negotiating countries. Egypt, on its own, faced Israel, which was militarily far superior to it, and was also in actual possession of Arab land. At the outset Begin wanted to make a clear distinction between Israeli–Egyptian relations, and the future of the West Bank and Gaza. This was agreed. According to Begin, for the first eight days of the negotiations, he was under pressure from the Americans to sign a document conceding the 'inadmissability of territories acquired by war'. He flatly refused. When Carter warned him that unless Israel relinquished the occupied territories there could be no peace settlement, Begin replied, 'Let my right hand forget its cunning before I sign such a document.' Carter and Begin then searched for a compromise on the West Bank and Gaza. Begin suggested that the question of Palestinian sovereignty be left 'open'. 'Let us give the Palestinian people autonomy and the Israelis security,' he said. This was agreed in principle. Later, according to Begin, the Americans (and the Egyptians) demanded a commitment from him to leave the Golan Heights. He refused. The point was dropped. On the tenth day of talks the question of Arab Jerusalem was raised by the Americans. Begin told them bluntly that 'the Arab flag . . . in Jerusalem' was 'out of the question'.[62] The subject was left unresolved, with Begin stating that east Jerusalem belonged to Israel, with Carter (and later Sadat) taking a contrary view. The next day, a Saturday, after sunset, Begin and Carter thrashed out details of American compensation to Israel for vacating Sinai, including the oilfields and the air bases, and the terms of Palestinian autonomy.[63]

Carter spent the next day with Sadat, and secured his consent after making a number of verbal promises, including the one which said in effect, 'Any Arab aid to Egypt that is reduced or cut off in retaliation for the Camp David accords will be replaced by a consortium of Western nations organised by the US.'[64] Begin insisted that the agreement was to be a bilateral affair, with President Carter signing as a 'witness', and the three governments then exchanging letters.[65] Sadat agreed. When he informed his foreign minister, Mohammed Ibrahim Kemal, that he was going to give his consent to the document, the latter reportedly said, 'This is the very agreement we've refused for twelve days,' and resigned.[66] The Camp David accord was signed at the White House in Washington on the night of 18 September 1978.

'Egypt, coming to Camp David without the Arab world supporting it explicitly, had been reduced to a minor power – important, but still minor,' explained Eric Rouleau, Middle East editor of *Le Monde*. 'Carter was having these two people facing each other, and one of them was giving in to the other. Carter could not be more royalist than Sadat. . . . And Carter maybe thought that for his own good – because his image in the US would improve, and because he couldn't exercise any more pressure on Begin anyway, and maybe he thought why not, let's try it, even a separate peace might lead to a comprehensive settlement – for these reasons we have had Camp David.'[67]

Later these reasons – and the downfall of the Shah of Iran, America's trusted ally for nearly four decades, and Sadat's close friend – compelled Carter to intervene directly, and bring about a peace treaty between Egypt and Israel. Once again the document was signed, on 26 March, by Sadat and Begin in the White House.[68] With this, the Arab League decided to treat Egypt as an outcast. It moved its headquarters from Cairo to Tunis. Aid from the governments and banks of the Arab states to Egypt – which, during the period of October 1973 to December 1977 had amounted to $17.2 billion – ceased forthwith.[69] The Saudi monarch withdrew the pledge he had made in 1977 to finance 'the development of Egypt's armed forces' for the next five years.[70] Consequently the Saudi contract to supply Egypt with fifty American F-5E combat aircraft, for $575 million, had to be scrapped.

Under the circumstances all the secret, verbal agreements reached between Sadat and Carter at Camp David needed to be implemented. These included not only compensating Egypt for losses resulting from the Arab economic boycott, but also re-equipping the Egyptian military with 'large numbers of US armoured personnel carriers, self-propelled artillery, anti-aircraft missiles, advanced combat aircraft, and ground-to-ground missiles', with deliveries of weapons linked to 'progress in carrying out the Camp David accords'.[71] Within weeks of the peace treaty Cairo and Washington signed a comprehensive military agreement which provided for the delivery of $2 billion worth of American weapons to Egypt to help it deter 'the threat from Libya', for coproduction of American arms in Egypt, and the use of military 'facilities' in Egypt by American armed forces.[72] The supply of American weapons to Egypt was facilitated by the fact that with effect from 1 October 1978, the beginning of American fiscal year 1979, Egypt had been placed on the list of countries entitled to 'grant aid' (i.e. free) weapons.[73]

Thus, in less than a decade, Sadat had pulled Egypt out of the Soviet orbit and integrated it firmly into the competing orbit of America. His government celebrated the first anniversary of the Camp David accord by taking delivery of seven Phantom F-4 jets and fifty armoured personnel carriers, supplied by Washington, as part of a deal involving thirty-five Phantom F-4s and 800 personnel carriers.[74] The Pentagon made use of the Egyptian 'facilities' in April when, during its abortive mission to free the hostages in Tehran, its planes used an airbase near Cairo for refuelling. By then Egypt and Israel had exchanged ambassadors and signed a trade agreement, following Israel's return of nearly half of occupied Sinai to Egypt, as stipulated in the Camp David accord.

President Carter's decision to set up a Rapid Deployment Force, mainly to secure the Gulf oilfields and oil routes in case of a major conflict in the area, gave additional weight to America's military ties with Cairo. During the autumn and winter of 1980, contingents of the Egyptian military and the American RDF carried out a series of military exercises in the Egyptian desert, using scores of Egyptian and American warplanes and two American aircraft carriers. Cairo had by then provided 'permanent facilities' to American forces at Ras Banas on the Red Sea (about 175 miles from the holy city of Medina), and the Pentagon had announced plans for modernising the base at the cost of $1 billion.[75]

Despite the failure of Egypt and Israel to agree on a plan for Palestinian autonomy by 26 May – as required by the Camp David accords – Cairo–Tel Aviv relations improved rapidly, with mutual cooperation extending to 'tourism, culture, science, trade, agriculture, land reclamation, and communications';[76] and with the existing cooperation between their intelligence services being expanded.[77]

Carter's defeat in the presidential election in November meant that the planned summit with Sadat and Begin in December, to produce a blueprint for Palestinian autonomy, had to be cancelled. But the visit of the Egyptian vice-president, Hosni Mubarak, to Washington in early December proved highly successful: the Pentagon agreed to advance deliveries of M-60 tanks, anti-armour Tow missiles, and air-to-air missiles from the end of 1981 to January 1981.[78] This was significant, because it apparently had the approval of the transition team of the president-elect Ronald Reagan. President Reagan's subsequent statement in support of the Camp David accords showed that his administration planned to pursue the policies initiated by Carter.

The death of the Egyptian defence minister and nine generals in a helicopter crash in early March, during an inspection tour of the western front[79] indicated that large numbers of Egyptian forces had been moved to the border with Libya, and that military activity in the area was being stepped up. Cairo's decision to transfer the bulk of its forces from the Egyptian–Israeli lines to the Libyan border, in the wake of the peace treaty, had led Israel to focus its attention on the eastern front, mainly Syria. In addition to meeting increased military pressure from Israel, the regime in Damascus had to plan support for Libya, in case of an attack on it by Egypt, as part of the political-military unity plans for Syria and Libya announced in September 1980. Since Damascus considered Washington to be the prime mover behind the Cairo–Tel Aviv rapprochement as well as Cairo's increasingly belligerent stance towards Tripoli, it felt more hostile towards Washington than it had done for many years. Leaving aside brief periods of mutual understanding, even sympathy – such as when, during the spring and summer of 1976, America expressed approval of Syria's anti-leftist actions in the Lebanese civil war – Damascus–Washington relations have in general been correct at best, and belligerent at worst.

America had the distinction of aiding the overthrow of the parliamentary system in Syria, which had preceded by a year its independence and international recognition in 1944. In March 1949 the army chief of staff, Colonel Hosni Zaim, working in league with the American embassy in Damascus,[80] arrested President Quwatli, dissolved parliament, and imposed military rule. But his overtly pro-USA policies – supporting the American proposal for a Middle East military pact, expressing solidarity with Turkey, which had recently joined Nato, and signing an armistice agreement with Israel – made him unpopular with the civilian population as well as with military officers, and paved the way for his fall. Five months later he was displaced (and executed) by Colonel Sami Hinnawi, who then withdrew the military from politics. He in turn was overthrown by Colonel Adib Shishakli in December.

The quick succession of coups did not discourage America and Britain from applying pressure on Syria's rulers to reach a peace settlement with Israel. This proved counter-productive; the bulk of politicians and military officers hated Israel, and held America and Britain primarily responsible for its creation. Reflecting the popular mood, the Syrian prime minister rejected an offer of American aid under the Point IV (technical aid) programme in February. 'Even pro-West politicians insisted on satisfaction on the Palestine question as a condition for alignment with the West,' notes Tabitha Petran. 'At the United Nations, growing Syrian and Egyptian abstention on cold war resolutions contributed to the formation of the Afro–Asian bloc.'[81]

After two years Shishakli established a dictatorship, which continued until early 1954. Aware of the dangers of alignment with America or Britain, and hostile towards the USSR, President Shishakli opted for active cooperation with France. But this did not last long. Following his downfall, and the accession of a popularly elected government in September, France was soon to lose favour with the Syrians. This was due to the increasingly repressive policy pursued by French authorities against the Algerian nationalist movement, launched in late 1954. Damascus expressed its displeasure by inter alia imposing an embargo on wheat sales to France. When in June 1956 Syrian authorities lifted the ban, the students rioted and brought down the government. Four months later a successful general strike in support of Algerian nationalists showed the degree of anti-French feeling then prevalent in the country. This reached a peak when France, in league with Britain and Israel, attacked Egypt. Damascus severed diplomatic relations with Paris and London, and did not resume them until Israel had withdrawn from the occupied territories the following March.

During that month a hotly contested contract for the construction of an oil refinery in Homs went to a Czech state agency, and not an American company. Washington retaliated by dumping wheat in Greece and Italy, the 'customary markets' for hard Syrian wheat, and refusing to supply spare parts for Syrian civilian aircraft.[82] These events set the scene for an American-led campaign against the 'Communist menace' rising in Syria. It reached a peak in August, with the American embassy once again plotting a coup against the elected Syrian government. 'Convinced that Syria was "going Communist", the United States had been exploring ways of reversing the trend,' states Patrick Seale. 'Its officials had had clandestine contacts with members of Syrian armed forces with a view to organising the overthrow of the government. This, at least, is what emerges from the evidence.'[83] The attempt failed, because some of the Syrian officers, when approached by American officials, reported back to their superiors. The Syrian government expelled three American diplomats and recalled its ambassador to Washington.[84] The USA reciprocated.

As stated earlier, pressure against Syria built up, with its neighbours, particularly Israel and Turkey, amassing troops along their Syrian borders.[85] The Saudi monarch intervened to lessen tension between Damascus and Washington. In early November Saleh Bitar, the Baathist foreign minister of Syria, had a meeting with Henry Cabot Lodge, the American ambassador to the United Nations, in New York. Soon after the ambassadors of the two countries returned to their posts. Later in the month, as Turkish troops withdrew from the Syrian frontier, Bitar returned to Damascus along with Norman Thomas, leader of the American Socialist Party. In a series of lectures, given under the aegis of the Baath, Thomas expressed the American government's sympathy for 'anti-Communist Arab socialist movements'.[86] Baath leaders feared the possibility that Khaled Azm, the pro-Soviet leader of the National Front, might emerge as a serious candidate in the 1958 presidential election. Unable to alter the course of the government through normal procedures, they encouraged their followers in the army – a primary target of American pressures – to act.

Exhausted by the climate of continued tension over the past year between Syria and its neighbours, the officers were particularly receptive to Baathist appeals. Not surprisingly, leading a delegation of top officers, Syrian chief-of-staff Bizri flew secretly to Cairo in mid-January to seek a union of the two armies.[87] This set the scene for the merger of Syria and Egypt into the UAR on 1 February. 'Without the crisis atmosphere manufactured by the year-long American campaign against Syria, the stampede into unity [with Egypt] would not have been possible,' notes Tabitha Petran. 'By this time, the union suited American purposes. Since August 1957, at least, Cairo had shared Washington's concern about "Communism" in Syria.'[88]

In 1960 the USSR submitted a feasibility study on the Euphrates Dam in Syria, which it had begun a few years earlier. But President Nasser ignored the Soviet Union as a potential financier and builder of the dam, and approached West Germany for the purpose. The following year he reached an agreement with Bonn on the project. However, no action could be taken, since Syria seceded from the UAR in September. Later Bonn agreed to build the dam only if Damascus were to give oil exploration rights in the Jezira area to a West German company, Concordia. The Syrian decree on oil resources, issued in December 1964, destroyed any such possibility, because it restricted oil exploration, extraction, and marketing rights to indigenous firms. A few weeks later came the revelation that, in collusion with Washington, Bonn had been supplying American arms to Israel clandestinely since 1961.[89] Protesting against this, Damascus severed links with Bonn. The discovery of the secret arms deal with Tel Aviv also had a deleterious effect on Syria's relations with the USA. Following the takeover of power by radical Baathists in early 1966, Syrian–American relations deteriorated rapidly. Just as it had in 1957, Damascus considered America to be the final source of active hostility shown towards it by Amman, Riyadh, and Tel Aviv.

Within days of Nasser's statement on 5 June 1967 that America and Britain were actively aiding Israel in the war, Damascus broke its links with Washington and London and shut off its oil pipelines. It joined the Arab oil embargo on America, Britain and West Germany. In contrast its relations with France improved, since President de Gaulle condemned Israeli aggression. Yet the Syrian government had no compunction in nationalising the assets of the Iraq Petroleum Company, partially owned by the French, in June 1972, in order to complement a similar move made by Baghdad.[90]

Unlike Cairo, Damascus was adamant in its rejection of UN resolution 242. In July 1970 it turned down the Rogers peace plan. Two months later the Baathist government came under heavy pressure from America to pull back the Syrian–Palestinian forces it had sent to northern Jordan during the fighting between Jordanian troops and Palestinian commandos. It did so. This destroyed any chance of a rapprochement with the USA. However, its hostility towards Britain subsided steadily; and it resumed diplomatic ties with London in September 1973.

Following Henry Kissinger's success in securing a troop disengagement agreement between Egypt and Israel, President Assad cooperated with Kissinger in working out a similar arrangement between Syria and Israel. The result was a Syrian–Israeli accord which was signed on 30 May. Within a fortnight Assad welcomed President Nixon in the Syrian capital. The assumption of diplomatic links between Damascus and Washington was soon followed by American economic aid of $60 million to Syria.[91] But if American officials saw this as an opening likely to lead to a Syrian–American collaboration of the kind they were then achieving with Sadat, they were to be sorely disappointed. Assad saw the Sinai II agreement of September 1975 as paving the way for a separate peace treaty between Egypt and Israel, and condemned it vehemently. 'Syria will never accept American offers to mediate a new agreement on the Golan Heights like the one reached on Sinai,' he declared.[92] A basic principle of Syrian foreign policy was summed up by an aide to Assad thus: 'We want good relations with the US, but not at the expense of our relations with the Soviet Union.'[93]

In early April Assad supported President Franjieh of Lebanon in his refusal to accede to the leftists' demand for his resignation five months before the end of his term – and sent Syrian forces three miles inside Lebanon as a further sign of his displeasure with the alliance of the Lebanese left and the Palestinians. This pleased Washington. 'President Ford has dropped his total opposition to outside military intervention in Lebanon, and approves of Syrian actions there,' said a White House spokesman. 'Syria has been playing a constructive role.'[94] Washington's overt backing for his moves in Lebanon embarrassed Assad. Significantly, therefore, the American administration refrained from making any statement when Assad ordered a full Syrian military intervention in Lebanon on 1 June. The convergence of Syrian and American interests in Lebanon ended with the Lebanese cease-fire in October.

However, the departure of Kissinger from the American state department – in the wake of James Carter's accession to the presidency in January 1977 – augured well for an improvement in Damascus–Washington relations. These hopes were consummated when, following a cordial meeting in Geneva in May, Carter and Assad backed the idea of reconvening the Geneva peace conference. But, as described earlier, this plan was subverted by Sadat's visit to Jerusalem and the events thereafter.[95] The resulting polarisation in the Arab world found Syria leading an anti-Sadat campaign. By mid-1979 relations between Damascus and Washington had deteriorated to the extent that the Syrian foreign minister warned his American counterpart, during a meeting in New York, that if the USA continued to bludgeon Arab states into the 'Camp David alliance', then Syria would be forced to redress the balance by aligning with the USSR.[96] This had no effect on the direction of American policy in the region. The Syrian disappointment turned into anger. In March, writing in *Al Mustaqabal*, a Paris-based weekly, Syrian defence minister Mustapha Tlas stated that President Carter, in whom President Assad had once put his trust, had turned out to be 'the worst enemy of the Arabs and Islam'.[97]

Earlier, President Assad, reacting to the rising terrorism of the Muslim Brotherhood in the republic, had been even harsher towards the Carter administration. In a public speech he accused it of masterminding the campaign of 'explosions and assassinations' by Muslim Brethren against his regime. 'He who activates them is the big boss sitting there on a distant continent – there in the United States of America,' he said.[98]

Such a statement by the Syrian president had come a few weeks after reports that the Lebanese rightists were 'harbouring and training' some of the Muslim Brethren of Syria.[99] The fact that these very Lebanese rightists were also at the same time in (semi-clandestine) contact with the Israeli authorities meant that the Muslim Brethren had inadvertently pitted themselves on the same side as Israel: a truly bizarre situation. What had made these disparate elements cooperate with one another was their deep hatred of Assad's regime because of its pro-Soviet bias.

While the foreign policy of independent Syria has been generally tilted in favour of the USSR, the contrary has been the case with its neighbour, Lebanon. The determining factors here have been the political and economic dominance of the Maronite Christians – and their historical ties with the West, particularly the Vatican and France – and the emergence of Beirut after the Second World War as the leading financial and banking centre of the Middle East, linked tightly to the financial institutions of the West.

What made Lebanon doubly attractive to the Western nations, particularly America, was the laissez faire economic policies followed by President Khouri from 1943 to 1952. His successor, Camille Chamoun, assumed the presidency at a time when the underprivileged Muslim community lacked a leader of the standing of Riad al Solh (assassinated in the summer of 1951) who, as prime minister, had provided a strong counterpoint to Khouri. Chamoun was therefore able to exercise power unchallenged, and pursued his pro-capital and pro-West policies with an increasing audacity. This endeared him to the American embassy in Beirut. He was well disposed to taking Lebanon into the Baghdad Pact, but in the end did not do so for the practical reason that Lebanon did not share borders with any of the existing or potential members of the Pact. When Egypt became a victim of the tripartite aggression in October 1956, Chamoun rejected the repeated advice of his prime minister, Abdullah Yafi, and foreign minister, Saab Salam, to sever links with Britain and France.

He became the first Arab head of state to endorse the Eisenhower doctrine in early 1957, and did so unreservedly. In return the CIA financed the election campaign of his followers in the parliamentary poll held in June. 'Throughout the elections I travelled regularly to the presidential palace with a briefcase full of Lebanese pounds, then returned late at night to the embassy with an empty twin case I'd carried away for Harvey Armado's CIA finance people to replenish,' writes Wilbur Crane Eveland. 'Soon my gold DeSoto with its stark white top was a common sight outside the palace, and I proposed to Chamoun that he use an intermediary and a more remote spot.'[100] The election result was so overwhelmingly pro-Chamounist that such leading Muslim personalities as Abdullah Yafi, Saab Salam, and Kemal Jumblatt were defeated. This set the scene for the civil war which broke out the next May.

Lebanon was in the midst of civil strife when a group of military officers overthrew the monarchy in Iraq: an event which Western capitals attributed to the machinations of Nasser. An alarmed Chamoun urged Washington to help his regime with its armed forces. President Eisenhower complied immediately, and ordered the Sixth Fleet, stationed in the Mediterranean, to land marines in Lebanon. Within two days Lebanon had more American marines (numbering 10,000) than soldiers and officers in its own army.[101] Eisenhower sent Robert Murphy, under-secretary of state, to Beirut to help in ending the civil war. After consultations with various parties he recommended General Fuad Chehab, the chief of staff, as presidential nominee. On 31 July the Lebanese deputies acted accordingly and elected Chehab president. He took office after Chamoun had resigned on 22 September. Meanwhile, yielding to intense UN pressure, America had agreed to withdraw its forces if and when so requested by the Lebanese president.[102] Chehab made the request, and the USA marines left on 25 October.

Chehab corrected the excesses of Chamoun's pro-American policy by pursuing a course which lay midway between those being followed by pro-West Arab monarchs and the neutralist Arab presidents. In the absence of an effective leftist opposition, Chehab (enjoying the total loyalty of his military officers) managed to stay on this path throughout his presidency. This was not the case with his successor, Charles Helou, who assumed power in 1964. With the establishment of the Front of the Progressive Parties and Personalities later that year, he came under increasing pressure to adopt a neutralist stance in world affairs. During the Six Day war popular feelings against America and Britain ran high. Despite this Helou refused to cut diplomatic links with Washington and

London. Instead he advised the American and British ambassadors to leave (temporarily).

By the time Suleiman Franjieh took office in September 1970, the Palestinian presence in the country had begun to affect both the internal and external policies of the government. When Israel responded to Palestinian pinpricks with massive raids on Lebanon, condemnation of Israel at the UN security council was often vetoed by the USA. This contributed greatly to making America unpopular, especially among Lebanese Muslims. During Franjieh's presidency Lebanon witnessed a growing involvement of the Western nations, primarily the USA, in clandestinely supporting and arming the right-wing militias, which had begun modestly in the late 1960s. The fact that nearly a million (mostly Christian) Lebanese immigrants were then settled in America facilitated the process.[103] This, and the traditionally weak government in Lebanon, made the republic an ideal country for bloody strife. It was significant that the civil war broke out three weeks after Kissinger's shuttle diplomacy had ground to a halt (on 22 March 1975), and that Camille Chamoun was interior minister in the government then in office. In his book *Uncertain Greatness*, Roger Morris, a former assistant to Kissinger at the National Security Council, states that 'the special Israeli bureau of the CIA' played a key role in fostering the civil strife in Lebanon so as to keep the Arabs engaged in a debilitating war.[104] 'In its relations with Lebanon, the United States violated its professed standards of morality in its international undertakings, that is, refraining from intervention in the internal affairs of other nations,' notes Wilbur Crane Eveland. 'By using Lebanon as a base for the CIA's covert operations, America undermined that country's stability and precipitated attempts by its neighbours to bring down the Lebanese government.'[105]

However, when the leftists emerged as the stronger party in the Lebanese conflict in early 1976, the American administration became alarmed. On 31 March the state department sent a former American ambassador to Jordan, Dean Brown, to Beirut to promote a political settlement. A few weeks later at the intercession of the Jordanian king – then on cordial terms with President Assad, and committed to a step-by-step union of Jordan and Syria – the White House publicly dropped its opposition to 'outside military intervention'. This allowed Syria to become the dominant Arab power in Lebanon. On 8 May the Lebanese deputies chose Elias Sarkis, a nominee of Syria (with the tacit support of America), as president. Four days later the new American ambassador, Francis Meloy, arrived in Beirut. He presented his credentials not to the existing president, Franjieh, but to Sarkis, the president-elect. On 16 June, while Meloy was on his way from the embassy in west Beirut, a Muslim area, to the residence of Sarkis in the Maronite-controlled Hazmieh district, he was kidnapped and assassinated. Following this America reduced its Beirut embassy staff drastically, and evacuated them by sea. It was once again significant that the final, effective cease-fire in the Lebanese war occurred two weeks before the American presidential election on 2 November.

Soon after the Carter administration had settled in it announced economic aid of $50 million to Lebanon, and then increased it by another $20 million.[106] When the rightist Lebanese Front pressed for the concept of 'decentralised unity' to be applied to the republic's internal composition, the American government considered it prudent to refrain from backing the demand, publicly. In March 1978 it condemned both the PLO's terroristic action in Israel, and the latter's full-scale invasion of south Lebanon. 'We expect Israel to withdraw [from south Lebanon],' said a White House statement.[107] America took the initiative at the UN security council to bring about a cease-fire in south Lebanon, and the formation of a UN peacekeeping force to be posted there. Among the countries which contributed a contingent to the United Nations Interim Force in Lebanon was France. In November President Sarkis visited Paris to meet President Giscard d'Estaing. In a joint communiqué the two presidents expressed their opposition to the division of Lebanon into 'cantons on religious or other lines'. France agreed to train Lebanese military officers and sell $350 million worth of arms, including heavy tanks and missiles, to Lebanon.[108]

Next spring, as Israel stepped up its attacks on southern Lebanon, President Sarkis appealed to Washington to try to curb Israel. In order to convince the Carter administration of the gravity of the situation, the Lebanese foreign ministry submitted to the American state department, in late August, a detailed survey of the extensive destruction of human life and property caused by Israeli shelling and air raids, including the deaths of ninety-six Lebanese civilians, fifty-one of them women and children.[109] This led to a lull in Israeli attacks; but it did not last long.

During President Carter's term of office the Lebanese Front, increasingly dominated by the Kataeb–Phalange, consolidated the Christian mini-state it had carved out earlier and successfully kept out the Lebanese army and the Syrian peacekeeping force from the territory. Buoyed by the American voters' decision in November 1980 to opt for Ronald Reagan – who had repeatedly labelled the PLO as a terrorist organisation – the Kataeb–Phalange leaders published a 'historical document' on 23 December. It demanded that the Palestinians must leave Lebanon before any reconstitution of the Lebanese state, involving a redistribution of power, could be discussed. Such a demand was unrealistic, and was rejected by the others. This reportedly led the Phalange leaders – now in near-total control of the Lebanese Front – to give the 'final touches' to a plan, designed to be implemented in collusion with Israel, to 'liberate' Lebanon from the PLO and the Syrians. The plan, known to be recommended by the CIA but opposed by the state department, envisaged Phalangist forces expelling the Palestinian militias from west Beirut while the Israelis engaged the Syrian troops in Bekaa valley.[110]

As described earlier, the execution of this plan began in early 1981, and led to a confrontation between Israel and Syria on the question of the deployment of Syrian missiles in Lebanon.[111] In early May President Reagan sent a personal envoy, Philip Habib, to the region to try and defuse the situation. While the Reagan administration attempted to play a moderating role in the Syrian–Israeli crisis – with an American spokesman in Beirut stating that Syria had an important part to play in the future Middle East negotiations – it showed no sign of softening its view of the PLO as a terrorist organisation, unworthy of official or quasi-official contact.

For many years the American administration derived its stand on the Palestinians and the PLO from UN security council resolution 242 of November 1967, which affirmed the necessity of achieving a 'just solution to the refugee problem'.[112] The fact that, starting July 1968, some Palestinian groups resorted to hijacking civilian aircraft made the Palestinians and their organisations highly unpopular with the American people and their government. None the less, by assisting King Hussein, diplomatically and militarily, to defeat the Palestinian commandos in Jordan, in September 1970, the Nixon administration inadvertently recognised the existence of the Palestinians as a separate, collectivist entity. The rise of the Black September Organisation, in the wake of the Palestinian debacle in Jordan, underlined the point. The most sensational of the BSO's acts was the taking hostage of Israeli athletes at the Olympic village near Munich in September 1972. Whatever the moral arguments against this act, its tactical value in highlighting the existence of the Palestinians as a people with a deeply felt grievance could not be disputed. When a Palestinian spokesman later described the operation like 'painting the name of Palestine on top of a mountain that can be seen from the four corners of the earth',[113] he was hardly exaggerating: the Olympics were being covered by 6,000 newsmen, and the largest set-up of television equipment ever assembled anywhere.[114]

Among those who seemed to have noticed the (symbolic) sign were top American officials, including the president. For, the following June a joint American–Soviet communiqué issued after the Nixon–Brezhnev summit in San Clemente, California, stated that the Middle East peace settlement should 'take into account the legitimate interests of the Palestinian people'.[115] A year later Nixon repeated the view in a statement, issued after his talks with President Sadat in Cairo, referring to 'the legitimate interests of all the peoples of the Middle East, including the Palestinian people'.[116]

A few months later the PLO announced its opposition to hijackings and similar actions outside Israel, and added that it would punish those Palestinians who undertook such operations.[117] In October it sentenced five Palestinians to jail sentences of ten to fifteen years for attempting a hijacking.[118] It was against this background that the PLO was accorded the status of being the Palestinians' sole and legitimate representative by the Arab summit held in Rabat in late October. Yasser Arafat's address to the UN general assembly in mid-November, and the assembly's decision to accord the PLO an observer status, showed that the PLO was winning widespread diplomatic acceptance. This improved its chance of opening an official dialogue with Washington.

Determined to abort such a development, Israel introduced the subject as part of preconditions to be met by America before it resumed negotiations on part withdrawal from Sinai. As stated earlier, according to the Second Memorandum of Agreement, the United States government promised not to recognise or negotiate with the PLO so long as it refused to accept Israel's right to existence and UN security council resolution 242.[119]

Yet, since the PLO was an important party in the civil war then raging in Lebanon, the American administration found itself in practical need of establishing a channel of communication with it. Not surprisingly, therefore, there were reports in January 1976 that Professor Norton Mezvinsky of the Central Connecticut College had carried 'two or three' messages between American officials and the PLO headquarters in Beirut.[120] Following the assassination of the American ambassador in Beirut, in mid-June, embassy officials dealt with the PLO authorities (then controlling west Beirut) to arrange evacuation of staff members and their families. In November three American senators visiting Cairo had a meeting with the PLO representative in Egypt.[121]

During the early period of the Carter administration, America showed distinct signs of reducing its antipathy towards Palestinian aspirations. Within two months of taking office Carter said in a public speech, 'There has to be a homeland provided for the Palestinian refugees who have suffered for many, many years.'[122] In early May the PLO sent a message to Washington through Soviet diplomatic channels that it would recognise Israel if the latter would simultaneously recognise the Palestinian people's right to a national homeland.[123] Two months later Carter said that the Palestinian 'homeland', to be created out of the occupied territories, should be 'linked' to Jordan 'later'.[124] The PLO rejected the idea – only to reverse its stand the next month. 'We are in favour of a link between that [Palestinian] state and Jordan,' said Farouk Kaddoumi, the virtual 'foreign minister' of the PLO. 'But . . . before the nature of such a relationship can be determined, we must have the West Bank and Gaza in our hands, as an independent Palestinian state.'[125] But when, in late August, America insisted on the PLO accepting UN resolution 242, the PLO rejected this outright: taking such a step implied unilateral recognition of Israel.[126]

Yet this did not interrupt, or reverse, a rapprochement between the

USA and the PLO. Two days before the joint American–Soviet statement of 1 October (on the Geneva conference), Carter stated that the United States was 'committed to some form of PLO representation at the peace talks'.[127] And, despite the furore created by the Zionist lobby against the communiqué, Carter stated at the UN general assembly on 4 October that 'the legitimate rights of the Palestinian people must be recognised'.[128]

But once President Sadat had broken away from the Geneva conference approach to peace, and received the backing of the American administration, the tone of Carter's statements on the Palestinians changed. 'I have never favoured an independent Palestinian state; I still don't favour one, and I have no intention of deviating from that position,' he declared in April. 'We will have no contact with the PLO until it takes action to recognise the right of Israel to exist.'[129] His national security adviser, Zbigniew Brzezinski, summed up the American policy on the PLO thus: 'Bye, bye, PLO!'. The freeze in American–PLO relations continued for more than a year.

In early August the PLO representative in Amman revealed that the USA and the PLO had started 'indirect negotiations' through other parties, 'particularly the West European countries'.[130] He seemed unaware that the American ambassador to Austria, Milton Wolf, had already had one 'non-substantive' and two 'chance' meetings with Issam Sartawi, a PLO leader – or that the United States ambassador to the UN, Andrew Young, had had a meeting with Zehdi Terzi, the PLO representative at the UN, at the apartment of the Kuwaiti ambassador to the UN on 26 July. However, when Young's meeting with Terzi became public – through Israeli intelligence, operating in New York, passing on the information to *Newsweek* – Young was reprimanded by the secretary of state, Cyrus Vance. The subsequent resignation of Young, a popular black leader, led to a ground-swell of support for the PLO by American blacks.[131] A nationwide poll conducted by the *Los Angeles Times* in mid-September showed two to one support for USA–PLO talks.[132] Soon after American diplomats were taken hostage in Tehran in early November, Yasser Arafat offered to mediate between the USA and Iran, but was rebuffed by Washington.

While America continued to be unresponsive to Palestinian aspirations, the European countries reacted otherwise. During his tour of the Gulf states in March, President Giscard d'Estaing called for self-determination for the Palestinian people. Ten days later the Austrian vice-chancellor, Bruno Kreisky, a non-Zionist Jew, granted official status to the PLO, which had so far won the recognition of 115 states.[133] In June a joint communiqué issued by the chief executives of the nine-member European Economic Community stated that the PLO 'would have to be associated' with negotiations for the Middle East peace settlement.[134] A special emissary was appointed to tour the Middle East, and make recommendations for launching a European peace initiative in the region. But progress along these lines was slowed down by the impending presidential elections in America.

With Ronald Reagan's accession to the White House, the existing differences between America and its European allies on the subject solidified. 'We must not become exclusively concerned, for example, with oil diplomacy, or with Arab–Israeli differences in isolation,' said Alexander Haig, the American secretary of state. 'These must be viewed against a backdrop of increasing Soviet intervention in the area.'[135] In contrast the British Foreign Office was just then circulating a memorandum concerning 'the scope and character of Palestinian self-determination in the event of an Israeli withdrawal from the occupied West Bank and Gaza strip', among fellow-members of the EEC.[136] Lord Carrington, the British foreign minister, was reported to be planning a formal meeting with Yasser Arafat (after he had assumed the chairmanship of the EEC's council of ministers on 1 July),[137] and thus give impetus to the European peace initiative in the Middle East.

By then King Hussein of Jordan had reaffirmed his stand to the effect that the PLO was the sole representative of the Palestinian people at the third Islamic summit at Taif, Saudi Arabia . 'There can be no solution [to the Middle East problem] without the PLO,' he said. 'There can be no alternative to the PLO.'[138] As a corollary he had also rejected the idea of the 'Jordanian option', floated by Washington and Israel's Labour Alignment, whereby he would be given control of the West Bank in exchange for signing a separate peace treaty with Israel.[139] Such a stance distanced the Jordanian monarch politically from America, and brought him nearer to Britain, the European power which had created Transjordan, the predecessor to Jordan, and had dominated the kingdom until the mid-1950s.

As stated earlier, the Anglo–Jordanian treaty of March 1948 entitled Britain to maintain bases in Jordan. One of the first acts of the Jordanian parliament, elected in October 1956, was to call for the abrogation of this treaty.[140] In January, Egypt, Syria and Saudi Arabia together offered to replace the annual British subsidy of £12 million to Jordan for at least ten years. Backed by these moves, King Hussein approached the British government to end the treaty. This was done on 13 March, eleven years before the original expiry date. Soon after, the Jordanian government spurned an offer of aid by Washington under the Eisenhower doctrine.[141] These developments were noted in London and Washington with grave concern.

A few weeks later, when the king's authority was challenged by the Free Officers, led by the chief-of-staff, General Ali Abu Nawar, the American president declared that the integrity of Jordan was 'vital' to the United States. The British government, with its troops stationed in Jordan,[142] made a similar statement. President Eisenhower ordered the

(American) Sixth Fleet into the eastern Mediterranean, and authorised emergency aid of $10 million for Jordan. Thus backed by America and Britain, King Hussein dismissed the popularly elected government, dissolved parliament, disbanded political and other organisations, and imposed martial law. 'The Eisenhower doctrine thus appeared to be working effectively as a prop for an Arab regime that sought American help for its survival, although involvement of "international Communism" in the situation was remote or non-existent, aside from Hussein's public stand against it,' notes Robert W. Stookey.[143]

King Hussein's successful military coup against his own government marked the emergence of America as the dominant Western power in Jordan. And, as was to be revealed twenty years later, it enabled the CIA to make direct subventions to the Jordanian ruler as part of its super-secret operations. 'One of the most closely held and sensitive of all CIA covert activities, the payments to Hussein (made under the codeword project name of "No Beef") were usually made by the CIA station chief in Amman,' reported Bob Woodward of the *Washington Post*. 'The CIA claimed . . . [that] Hussein himself provided intelligence to the CIA, and forwarded money from the payments to other government officials who provided intelligence or cooperated with the CIA. . . . The "No Beef" project has been considered in the CIA as one of its most successful operations, giving the US great leverage and unusual access to the leader of a sovereign state. . . . The initial payments [the first having been made in 1957] ran to millions of dollars, but they were sharply curtailed to the $750,000 level last year [1976].'[144] Not surprisingly, King Hussein's regime figured prominently in the American plans to destabilise the parliamentary government in Syria in the summer of 1957.[145]

When King Hussein felt threatened again, in the wake of the republican coup in July 1958, he called on London for military assistance, and received it immediately. He approached Britain, not America, simply because British troops were familiar with Jordan, having spent nearly thirty-five years in the kingdom before their final departure in the previous July. On its part, Washington stepped up economic and military assistance to Amman. Between 1958 and 1965 American aid to Jordan amounted to an average of $64 million a year.[146]

In 1966, as tension mounted between Israel and the Palestinian guerrillas, operating mainly from Syria, Jordan became a target of Israeli raids. In November a particularly heavy attack by Israel, involving tanks and aircraft, on Al Samu had important national, regional and international repercussions. While the inhabitants of the area bordering Israel demanded to be armed to protect themselves, Egypt and Syria offered their troops for deployment along the Israeli border. Washington feared that Hussein's regime would not survive the stationing of Egyptian and Syrian forces inside Jordan. President Johnson therefore strengthened American naval forces in the eastern Mediterranean and airlifted arms to

Jordan 'as a caution to Hussein's Arab adversaries and as a rebuke to Israel.'[147]

Having resisted pressures to join the joint Cairo–Damascus military command for seven months, King Hussein finally did so on 30 May, making Jordan a legitimate target for Israeli war planners. The extent and speed of Israeli air attacks on the military airfields of Egypt, Syria, Jordan and Iraq convinced President Nasser that American planes from the Sixth Fleet's aircraft carriers and British planes from Britain's airbases in Cyprus had participated in the Israeli air raids. Although King Hussein concurred with this view, publicly, he did not sever relations with London or Washington.

But since Hussein's claim turned out to be false, both the American and British governments were angry with him. Their mood was not tempered by the fact that the king lost all the territory west of the river Jordan, including the old city of Jerusalem, with a third of the kingdom's population. However, the consequent loss of the American subsidy to the Jordanian budget, which had been a feature of the country's economy for a decade, was more than compensated for by the promise of Saudi Arabia, Kuwait, and Libya to provide Jordan with $100 million a year 'until the effects of war had been removed'.[148]

There was still the problem of re-equipping the military after its shattering defeat by the Israelis. For six months diplomatic relations between Amman and Washington were strained (possibly with little effect on the clandestine contacts between the king and the CIA) as the monarch weighed the prospect of equipping his armed forces with Soviet weapons – as advised by Egypt and Syria. In the end he decided against the proposition. This regained him the special position that Washington had carved out for him since 1957. The American arms shipments, resumed in early 1968, continued at a pace which enabled the king to finish re-equipping the military by March of the following year. During the summer he launched a diplomatic offensive to secure a peace settlement with Israel, by visiting Washington, London and Paris. He also resumed clandestine face-to-face contacts with Israeli leaders which he had initiated just before the Six Day war, with a secret meeting in London with Yigael Allon, the then Israeli deputy prime minister.[149] Nothing concrete came of these talks with Western or Israeli leaders.

At home relations between the Jordanian army and the Palestinian commandos grew worse, with outbreaks of violence occurring in the spring of 1970. The truce between the two sides, secured by the Arab League mediation team in June, became precarious when the monarch accepted the Rogers peace plan (regarded by the Palestinians as running counter to the decisions of the Khartoum summit) in early August. With the arrival from Europe of three hijacked planes (one British, one American, one Swiss) between 7 and 9 September at an airfield near Amman, tension mounted in the country. The planes were blown up on

12 September when the hijackers' demand for the release of Palestinian prisoners held in West Germany, Switzerland, and Israel was not met. Of the forty-four passengers retained by the hijackers as hostages, thirty-four were American. Two days earlier President Nixon had ordered the Sixth Fleet to the eastern Mediterranean, and a squadron of ten transport planes and twenty-five Phantom jets to fly to an airbase in Turkey, to be ready ostensibly to evacuate American citizens from Jordan. Thus encouraged, King Hussein formed a military government on 15 September, and moved his army against the Palestinian commandos.[150]

The next day, in an off-the-record briefing to a group of editors in Chicago, President Nixon stated that America was 'prepared to intervene directly in the Jordanian war should Syria and Iraq enter the conflict and tip the military balance against government forces loyal to Hussein'.[151] By 17 September fighting between the Jordanian troops and the Palestinian commandos had become widespread, with Amman and north Jordan emerging as the main centres of hostilities. The following day Nixon announced military aid of half a billion dollars to Israel, after a meeting with the Israeli prime minister, Golda Meir.[152] On 19 September tank units of the Palestine Liberation/Syrian army crossed into north Jordan from Syria. Nixon reinforced the sixth fleet with a third aircraft carrier, put American airborne troops stationed in West Germany on high alert, and asked the USSR to restrain Syria. King Hussein ordered his trusted aide, Zaid Rifai, to request the US ambassador in Amman, Dean Brown, by radio 'for intervention by air and land from any quarter against the Syrian tanks'.[153]

On 20 September the Palestinian/Syrian tanks captured Irbid in northern Jordan. Nixon responded by instructing his national security adviser, Henry Kissinger, to work with Israeli officials in Washington on plans to aid the Jordanian monarch. King Hussein repeated his call for help, stating that he preferred that 'the United States or Great Britain be involved, not just the Israelis'.[154] The White House was reluctant to involve America directly. By ordering an American military intervention (unauthorised by Congress) in Cambodia in May, it had alienated public opinion, and virtually foreclosed the possibility of dispatching American troops to a foreign country. Moreover, top American officials felt that direct American action on his behalf would probably discredit King Hussein 'so irretrievably within the Arab world at large that his future would be highly problematical'.[155] Nixon therefore opted for a joint Israeli–American plan – envisaging initial moves by Israel alone – which had been prepared within twenty-four hours. By then the Jordanian armoured unit had managed to check the advance of the Palestinian/Syrian tanks, and the Soviet envoy in Washington had informed the White House that the USSR had urged restraint on Syria, and suggested that the USA should do the same to Israel.

The following day, assured of American and Israeli backing, Hussein ordered his air force to attack the enemy's armoured forces in the Irbid area. Since General Hafez Assad, the commander of the Syrian air force, refused to commit Syrian warplanes to help the tank units, and since the 12,000 Iraqi troops, stationed in Jordan (since the Six Day war), too refused to aid the Palestinians, the Jordanian forces gained the upper hand. In the afternoon the Palestinian/Syrian tanks began to withdraw. Yet King Hussein sent a message to Washington that an Israeli air attack on the enemy's armoured units would still be welcome, but that any Israeli intervention on land must be limited to Syrian territory.[156] Since Israel was unwilling to take ground action in Syria only (due to possible Soviet reaction), it did not mount any operation at all. In any case, as the Palestinian/Syrian withdrawal continued throughout the evening, and was completed by the next day, there was no need for Israeli or American intervention. The conflict ended on 25 September when, responding to the appeals of an inter-Arab mission, the two sides agreed to an immediate cease-fire.

Nixon presented the Jordan crisis as 'the greatest threat to world peace since this administration came to office', and compared it to the Cuban missile crisis of eight years before: a confrontation between the two superpowers which ended with an American victory. Such an assessment was misconceived. As stated earlier, the USSR played a moderating role with respect to both the Syrian regime and the PLO; and so did the commander of the Syrian air force, Assad.[157] 'The United States' decision to treat the situation as a conflict between American and Soviet interests appears to have been based on a mechanistic analysis of the Middle East problem in terms of a single variable of power,' notes Robert W. Stookey. 'The assumption that both the Palestinians and the Syrians were acting at the behest, and in the interest of, the Soviet Union in their attempt to overthrow the Jordanian regime was based on dubious evidence in both cases and ignored the long historical background of inter-Arab and Arab–Israel animosities, which had little or nothing to do with Soviet ambitions.'[158]

Encouraged by its success in solving the crisis, the Nixon administration airlifted weapons to Jordan and increased its financial aid to the Hashemite kingdom. Thus fortified, Hussein kept up pressure against the Palestinian commandos and finally expelled the last of them in July: an achievement which endeared him further to Washington. Yet the White House was aware that the Jordanian monarch's military victory over the PLO was not enough, and that the Palestinian problem demanded a political solution. Nixon therefore covertly endorsed King Hussein's plan for a United Arab Kingdom, composed of the provinces of Jordan and Palestine (the name to be given to the West Bank once Israel had vacated it), with east Jerusalem as its capital, which the monarch launched the following March.[159] But the Palestine National Council rejected the idea summarily,[160] and the matter rested there.

During the October 1973 war King Hussein rejected calls by Egypt, Syria and Saudi Arabia to open a third front against Israel, and accepted Washington's advice to stay out of the conflict. He was rewarded for this. American economic aid for the next fiscal year (starting 1 October 1975) was, at $100 million, double the previous year's level; and military assistance was raised to an unprecedented $107 million.[161] Hussein now felt confident enough to resume face-to-face negotiations with Israeli leaders: he often did so by flying his own helicopter to a meeting-place inside Israel.[162] But neither these talks nor those with American leaders in the summer of 1974 yielded anything concrete. The result was the Arab summit's decision, in late October, to deprive him of the right to speak for the residents of the occupied West Bank, and confer it upon the PLO. This disappointed him as much as it did Kissinger, who had so far been 'trying to strengthen King Hussein at the expense of the PLO'.[163]

Hussein now became the proponent of a comprehensive peace settlement through a Geneva conference. Since the Sinai II agreement, a brainchild of Kissinger, detracted from this, he condemned it. His opposition to it was so strong as to lead him to team up with President Assad. This went down badly in Washington; but it did not deter the Ford administration from agreeing to sell the Hawk missile system to Jordan for $343 million, to be paid by Riyadh. However, during his visit to the American capital next March, King Hussein was told that in view of the extras he had demanded, the revised cost of the air defence umbrella would be $792 million. The monarch protested; and the talks broke down. He then considered buying the Soviet SAM missile system. But, as described earlier, the idea had to be scrapped because the Saudi ruler refused to finance arms purchase from the USSR.[164] Finally, in early August, when the Americans lopped off $250 million from the previous figure, and Riyadh agreed to pay, the missile deal was signed.[165] By then Hussein had proved himself to be a useful intermediary between the Assad regime and the American administration, both of whom were then deeply involved in the Lebanese civil war.

The departure of Kissinger from the American administration, in the wake of James Carter's election to the presidency, augured well for an improvement in Amman–Washington relations. By receiving a four-man PLO committee in Amman in February 1977, Hussein enhanced his standing in the Arab world.[166] His visit to Washington two months later was greeted by an official announcement of $64 million in technical military aid to Jordan, as part of the building of the Hawk missile system and the training of Jordanians in its use.[167] President Carter listened sympathetically to Hussein's suggestion that Israeli objection to the presence of the PLO at the Geneva conference could be overcome by including Palestinians in a single Arab delegation to the conference.[168] Later this idea gained wide support, and was to have been implemented if the peace conference had been held in late December.

But such plans were subverted by Sadat's dramatic gesture of visiting Jerusalem. Hussein now came under contrary pressures, with Washington urging him to join the Egyptian–Israeli talks, and Damascus to join the Steadfastness Front. He stayed away from both. The Carter administration was displeased, and curtailed economic aid to Amman to $40 million for the fiscal year.[169] As, guided and goaded by Carter, Sadat and Begin pursued the path to a separate peace treaty, Hussein repeatedly voiced his opposition to the process. During his visit to Washington in June 1980 he said that the Camp David process was 'limited' and 'doomed to failure', and that Israeli occupation forces must withdraw from the West Bank and Gaza before he could join 'any talks'.[170] But differences on tactics for securing peace in the Middle East had no adverse effect on military ties between Amman and Washington. The United States agreed to bolster Jordan's stock of 300 M-47 tanks by selling it 200 M-60 tanks, a hundred of them to be shipped immediately.[171]

When, in early December, tension between Jordan and Syria mounted – with two army divisions deployed on each side of the border – America publicly backed the Hashemite kingdom. 'Jordan is a friend whose security is important to us, and with whom we have a long-standing military supply relationship,' said a state department spokesman.[172] Although successful Saudi mediation brought about a cooling of tempers on both sides, Washington announced that it would airlift weapons to Jordan immediately.[173]

Following a wave of anti-American demonstrations in the Muslim world in the wake of the Islamic revolution in Iran, Washington had come to value King Hussein's friendship all the more. He had been critical of the Khomeini regime in Tehran; and, since he was a direct descendant of the prophet Mohammed, his stance had carried much weight in Islamic circles throughout the world. He had, inadvertently, rendered further service to the United States by vociferously backing Iraq in its war with Iran, whose regime was then engaged in a crusade against America, described by it as the Great Satan.

As it was, the Hashemite monarch had enjoyed friendly relations with Saddam Hussein since the early 1970s. These had been useful in persuading the Iraqi leader during the mid-1970s to reach a rapprochement with the Shah of Iran. While he had interceded with Saddam Hussein, President Sadat had done so with the Shah; and together they had laid the foundation for the Iraq–Iran treaty of March 1975. They had worked in conjunction with Henry Kissinger, who had visited Baghdad clandestinely during one of his frequent rounds of 'shuttle diplomacy' in the Middle East after the October war. Such contacts aside, diplomatic relations between America and republican Iraq have been either cool or non-existent. Unlike Jordan, the United States did not establish itself as the dominant Western power in Iraq, leaving it to Britain, the one-time mandate authority in the country, to continue to play that role.[174]

The British mandate in Iraq ended in October 1932 as a result of the Anglo–Iraqi treaty signed two years earlier. America recognised Iraq soon after, and posted a consul-general in Baghdad. However, since the Anglo–Iraqi treaty entitled London to formulate Baghdad's foreign policy and station British troops in the country, Iraqi independence was incomplete. A major upheaval in the country during the Second World War confirmed the supremacy of Britain over Iraqi nationalist forces.[175] After the war Britain tried to meet the widespread Iraqi desire for full independence by renegotiating the terms of the 1930 treaty, and presenting the new document as signifying an alliance between two equals. But because it did not include the withdrawal of British troops from Iraq it was received with popular hostility in the Arab kingdom. Large-scale demonstrations against the treaty in Baghdad brought the Iraqi government down, and led finally to its annulment.

Increasingly apprehensive that the 1930 treaty would not be renewed by Baghdad beyond its twenty-five-year term, London began devising other means of maintaining a military presence in Iraq. Besides its strategic location, the Arab kingdom was a leading producer of oil, on which Britain was heavily dependent. London worked closely with Washington in planning a suitable strategy for Iraq. In 1953 America initiated talks with Iraq for the supply of weapons as grant-aid (i.e. free of charge). These were successful. In April 1954 Washington agreed to give the Iraqi government arms worth $30 million over a three-year period, provided it allowed the stationing of American military advisers in the country.[176] Within a year of this Iraq – led by its pro-West prime minister Nuri al Said – shared its membership of the Middle East Treaty Organisation (popularly known as the Baghdad Pact) with Britain.

Nuri al Said proved so loyal to the Baghdad Pact that he refused to condemn the Anglo–French–Israeli aggression against Egypt in October 1956 so as not to offend Britain, a fellow-member of the pact. In contrast he endorsed the Eisenhower doctrine wholeheartedly. Bolstered by speedy deliveries of American weapons he cooperated actively with pro-West neighbours in implementing the American plan, in the summer of 1957, to harass the Syrian regime. The British government collaborated with the American administration: it had wished all along to see Syria become part of Greater Iraq under a Hashemite king.

The overthrow of the monarchy – accompanied by the assassinations of the royal family and Nuri al Said – by the Free Officers headed by Brigadier Abdul Karem Qassem, in July 1958, came as a shock to London and Washington. Their hostile reaction to the coup, coupled with military moves in Lebanon and Jordan, did not surprise the new rulers. Yet the republic's leaders were unable to return Western hostility by, say, severing diplomatic ties with the Western capitals; for Iraq was much too tightly linked with Britain and America, militarily and economically. Although the Free Officers were committed to withdrawing Iraq from the

Baghdad Pact, Qassem waited eight months before doing so.

By then the British and American embassies in Baghdad had registered alarm at the growing friendship of the new regime with the USSR, and the rising influence of the Communists in Iraqi politics. At the same time they were aware of the sharp divisions arising between the leftists, the (pan-Arab) Nasserites, and the followers of Qassem. As described earlier, the conflict between the Communists and the pan-Arabists turned violent in Mosul on 8 March after the local military commander had alleged that Qassem had come under Communist influence. More serious rioting broke out on 14 July in Kirkuk, the major centre of operations by the Western-owned Iraq Petroleum Company. The event provided Qassem with a reason to attack the 'anarchists', a thinly-disguised reference to the Communists.[177] On both occasions British involvement was suspected. 'An eminent Egyptian journalist, who must remain anonymous, told this writer two years later [in 1961] that the Mosul and Kirkuk incidents were not entirely the work of the Communists, and that the British agents, who had infiltrated the demonstrators on both occasions, did most of the dirty job [of murdering anti-Communists],' states M. S. Agwani. 'It enabled the British to undermine the position of the Baathists, the Nasserites, and the Communists, their real foes, and to safeguard their vital oil interests.'[178]

While the Western governments approved of Qassem's efforts to curtail Communist influence, they were unhappy to see him host a conference of Kuwait, Saudi Arabia, Iran and Venezuela, in September 1960, to form the Organisation of Petroleum Exporting Countries to serve a 'a collective bargaining agency'.[179] They were openly critical of his promulgation of Law 80 in the following year. This decree deprived the IPC of 99.5 per cent of the 160,000 square miles originally allocated to it for prospecting, and which covered all of Iraq (excepting the Basrah region in the south) including the oil-rich area of north Rumeila. The IPC challenged the law and demanded international arbitration. The subsequent talks between the government and the IPC dragged on for six years.[180] Not surprisingly, the Western bloc was pleased to see Qassem overthrown in February 1963, particularly when this was done by the Baathist military leaders who were, in the main, militantly anti-Communist.

As described earlier, the Baathist National Guard carried out a systematic liquidation of the Communists.[181] They were aided in this by at least one Western agency. Mohammed Heikal, the then editor of *Al Ahram*, stated, on the authority of King Hussein, that 'an American espionage service', which had been in touch with the Iraqi Baath, conveyed to the latter on a secret broadcasting service the names and addresses of the Iraqi Communists.[182]

Since the Aref brothers' regimes were in general close to President Nasser, and since Nasser was frequently at odds with the West, particularly America, during the mid-1960s, Baghdad's relations with London and Washington were on the whole uneasy. In early 1965 Iraq followed Egypt's lead in cutting off diplomatic relations with Bonn in protest against West Germany's supply of weapons to Israel. It did the same during the June 1967 war, and severed links with America and Britain.

Although Iraq resumed relations with Britain the following May, any chance of rapprochement with the USA was destroyed by the seizure of power by the Baathists in July, and their energetic drive against imperialism and Zionism. America responded in kind. It instigated the Shah of Iran to follow an increasingly aggressive policy toward Iraq. He did so. In January 1970 the Baathist regime aborted an attempted coup which, it said, had been planned by the Shah and the American administration.[183] Towards the end of 1971 Baghdad alleged that the British government had encouraged the Shah to occupy three islands near the Straits of Hormuz, belonging to the rulers of Ras al Khaima and Sharjah, and severed diplomatic relations with London.[184] However this had no effect on commercial links with Britain.

The following June the Baathist government nationalised the Iraq Petroleum Company. This marked the end of an era which had begun in 1912, with the Ottoman emperor giving an oil concession in his easternmost province to the Turkish Petroleum Company, consisting of British, French and German interests. The composition of the TPC changed after the First World War when the British government-controlled company acquired 75 per cent of its shares. Working in conjunction with the French, the British tried to keep the American oil companies out of Iraq. Washington argued that it was entitled to a share, because it had supplied 80 per cent of the oil needs of the Allies during the war.[185] Years of complicated and protracted negotiations followed. The result was the creation, in 1931, of the Iraq Petroleum Company, with its shares divided evenly between Britain, France, Holland, and America (represented by two oil companies Standard Oil of New Jersey, and Standard Oil of New York).[186] Oil production, commenced in 1927 in the Kirkuk district, reached such proportions by the Second World War that Britain found it essential to intervene militarily to overthrow the anti-British government of Rashed Ali Gailani in 1941. More than three decades later Iraqi authorities had to seek Soviet help to ensure that the nationalisation of the IPC held. It did.[187] Thus encouraged, they took over the American and Dutch interests in the Basrah Petroleum Company, operating in the south, during the October 1973 war.

While this left commercial links with America (and Holland) unaffected, political relations between Baghdad and Washington deteriorated further. The statement by Mustapha Barzani, the KDP leader, four months earlier, that the Kurds would secure the Kirkuk oilfield and hand it over to an American company to operate if the USA government provided aid to his followers, openly or secretly,[188] had provided circumstantial evidence of Barzani's complicity with the CIA. Not surprisingly, the Iraqi authorities now routinely described Barzani as a CIA agent.[189] His refusal, in the spring of 1974, to cooperate in implementing the Kurdish autonomy law of 1970 made Baghdad more hostile to him and the American administration.

The end to the armed conflict with Kurdish secessionists, which followed the conclusion of the Iraq–Iran treaty in March 1975, opened up the possibility of a resumption of diplomatic ties between Baghdad and Washington; but nothing tangible happened. However, commercial ties with America improved, mainly because a fivefold jump in oil revenue, in the wake of the October 1973 war, led to a corresponding rise in foreign trade.

In 1976 trade between Iraq and America amounted to $500 million, up from $20 million three years earlier.[190] During that year imports from West Germany totalled $860 million, and those from France $316 million.[191] The single most important commodity that Iraq exported to these countries was, of course, oil. To win Iraqi goodwill the French government agreed in 1974 to sell heavy weapons to Iraq and sign a nuclear cooperation treaty with it. A year later France contracted to supply Iraq with two nuclear reactors – one of forty megawatt capacity, and the other of 500 kilowatt – to be operated on enriched uranium. But before the bigger nuclear reactor could be commissioned (some time during the latter half of 1981), it was bombed by Israel on 7 June on the ground that it was designed to produce atomic bombs. Reiterating the French Atomic Energy Commission's conclusion that the Iraqi nuclear plant had presented 'no possibility of physical danger to Israel', mainly because it would have been under effective control of French engineers until 1989, President François Mitterrand stated that France would reconstruct the Iraqi nuclear centre destroyed by Israel if Iraq would agree to 'the new, strict safeguards against possible military use that will apply to all future French nuclear sales'.[192] Meanwhile Italy, another consumer of Iraqi oil, had sold Iraq a 'hot cell' laboratory capable of reprocessing, on a limited scale, irradiated uranium for extracting plutonium: the material used for making a plutonium (atomic) bomb.[193] In the field of conventional weapons, Iraq's policy of diversifying its sources of supply led to the situation where half of its military purchases in the late 1970s were from the West, including Spain and Brazil.[194]

With the steep reduction in oil supplies from Iran, after the revolution in February 1979, France and West Germany became even more solicitous of Iraq. Also their common hatred of the revolutionary regime in Tehran brought Baghdad and Washington diplomatically nearer. Given the presence of a large contingent of American 'commercial' diplomats in Baghdad, operating from the embassy of Belgium (officially representing the interests of the United States), communications between the Iraqi and American governments were fairly easy. In December the Iraqi foreign minister met the American secretary of state at the United Nations in New York with a view to reaching 'limited cooperation on matters of mutual interest'.[195] Evidently one such matter concerned devising a means of countering the political-ideological threat posed by Iran's Islamic government to the Gulf states. In early May, at the time of the seizure of the Iranian embassy in London by five armed Arab–Iranians from Khuzestan (who had arrived in London under an Iraqi mentor from Baghdad), there were reports that 'back channel' communications between Baghdad and Washington had been 'active', and that Hamilton Jordan, the White House chief of staff, had visited the Iraqi capital in March/April.[196] As stated earlier, American military experts were among those who were consulted by Iraqi officials in Paris before Iraq's plans for an attack on Iran were finalised.[197] It was significant that Iraq attacked Iran six weeks before the American presidential election.[198]

One result of the Iraq–Iran war was that the OPEC conference scheduled for later in the year in Baghdad, to mark the twentieth anniversary of the organisation, was cancelled. During those years OPEC's membership had increased to thirteen, with proven reserves of 420 billion barrels, amounting to two thirds of the world total.[199] The Gulf region, known to contain 55 per cent of global oil reserves, now contributed six members to OPEC. Iran was the first country in the area to yield oil in commercial quantities. This happened in 1908, seven years after a British prospector, William Knox D'Arcy, had won an oil concession covering nearly all the 628,000 square miles of Iran. His firm expanded to become the Anglo–Persian Oil Company (Anglo–Iranian, after Persia was renamed Iran in 1933, then British Petroleum). With the British admiralty's decision in 1913 to switch from coal to oil, the importance of oil increased. To ensure supplies the British government acquired a controlling interest (40 per cent of the shares) in APOC. It also imposed a series of agreements on the rulers of Kuwait (1913), Bahrain (1914), Qatar (1916), and the lower Gulf principalities and Oman (mid-1920s), whereby they were barred from giving oil concessions to non-British companies without London's prior permission. After the First World War British-owned APOC became the dominant partner in the TPC in Iraq.[200]

As described earlier, Britain and France tried to keep American companies out of the region on the ground that they had ample opportunities to exploit vast reserves at home.[201] But they yielded to pressures by the US government, and accepted two American corporations as partners in their operations in Iraq, which proved successful in 1927. Among the small companies then active in the Gulf was the Eastern and General Syndicate, owned by Frank Holmes, a New Zealander. Although the company had acquired many concessions, it lacked enough capital to undertake large-scale exploration. Having failed to interest either the Anglo–Persian or the Royal Dutch-Shell to take up his option in Bahrain,

Holmes began approaching American corporations. One of them, Standard Oil of California (Socal, later Chevron), agreed to this in 1929 – on the basis of successful work done earlier by another American company. Socal then combined with Texas Company (Texaco) to form Bahrain Petroleum Company (Bapco). In order to get around the restrictions of the Anglo–Bahraini treaty of 1914 they registered Bapco in Canada, a British dominion. Bapco commenced commercial production in 1932.

Its success in Bahrain encouraged Socal to bid for an oil concession in Saudi Arabia. By offering ten times more money, as advance against future royalties, it beat its rival, the IPC.[202] It secured (in May 1933) exploration rights in the eastern province of Hasa, and preferential rights elsewhere in the kingdom. Three years later, repeating its performance in Bahrain, it invited Texaco to form a joint company: Caltex (later Arabian American Oil Company, Aramco). By then the Anglo–Iranian Oil Company had obtained concessions in Qatar and Oman (in 1935) on its own – and had formed the Kuwait Oil Company, in partnership with the (American) Gulf Oil Company, and secured rights in all of Kuwait (in 1934). Bapco built an oil refinery in Bahrain in 1937. The next year oilfields in Saudi Arabia and Kuwait yielded petroleum in commercial quantities, with Kuwait's Burgan field proving to be a gigantic reserve of oil. During 1939 – when oil was discovered in Qatar – the Abu Dhabi Petroleum Company, an IPC subsidiary, obtained exploration rights in Abu Dhabi. Thus, on the eve of the Second World War, virtually all of the oil-bearing areas in the Gulf region had been acquired by eight giant Western companies: Socal (later Chevron); Texaco; Gulf Oil; Standard Oil Company of New Jersey (later Esso, then Exxon); Standard Oil Company of New York (later Socony-Vacuum, then Mobil); Anglo–Iranian Oil Company (later British Petroleum); Royal Dutch-Shell; and Compagnie Française des Pétroles.

'The terms of the concessions [to oil companies] fell into a common pattern – long duration, vast areas, exemption from local taxes and modest royalties to the host countries,' states M. S. Agwani. 'The tenure of the various concessions ranged from sixty to ninety-five years. . . . The leased area of the Iraq Petroleum Company and its sister companies in Iraq covered 171,000 square miles, and that of the Arabian American Oil Company in Saudi Arabia considerably more than 500,000 square miles. . . . The fiscal provisions of the original concessions debarred the governments [of the host countries] from taxing the concession throughout the life of the agreement. . . . Finally, the royalty payable to the host country was treated as a rental which varied not with the price of the product but with the yield of the land.'[203] Royalty was paltry, varying from two to five British shillings per ton of oil, or three to eight British pennies (i.e. eight to twenty American cents) per barrel of thirty-five imperial gallons.[204]

Since the Second World War interrupted oil production, royalties accruing to the host governments were insignificant. After the war, however, output picked up rapidly, and boosted company earnings. The profits of the Arabian American Oil Company, for instance, jumped from $2.8 million in 1944 to $115 million five years later.[205] This encouraged the Saudi monarch to follow the example of the Venezuelan government, which had passed a law in 1947 requiring oil firms to pay half of their profits as tax. Soon Iraq and Kuwait did the same.

Once tax on profits was introduced, the host countries' interest went beyond the volume of production (which determined royalties) to the price of oil, which determined profits. As it happened, the major oil companies had created a cartel and rigged prices since 1928, and got away with it. The controversy aroused by the nationalisation of the AIOC in Iran in 1951 focused public attention on the workings of the giant oil corporations, the majority of whom were American. In the United States the Senate select sub-committee on small business conducted an inquiry into the operations of the oil majors. Its report *The International Petroleum Cartel*, published in 1952, established that a huge international combine was enriching itself at their countries' expense.[206] The sub-committee named seven companies as members of the cartel, five of them being American (Esso, Gulf, Socal, Socony, and Texaco), one British (British Petroleum), and the remaining one Anglo–Dutch (Royal Dutch-Shell).

However, a series of developments in the 1950s caused a breakdown of the elaborately built up pricing system of the oil cartel: the disruption of oil supplies from Iran (1951 to 1954); the closure of the Suez Canal in 1956; the emergence of strong, independent (i.e. not tied to the oil majors) companies in the oil industry; determined bids made by the government-backed oil agencies of France and Italy to break into the lucrative world oil market; and, finally, the entry of the USSR into the market with offers of prices below the 'posted prices' of the oil cartel, combined with easy terms or barter deals.

The only way the oil giants could meet the challenge was by reducing prices. Starting in early 1959 they introduced a series of price reductions, which aggregated to twenty-eight American cents a barrel, or nearly a third of the original price. The Arab oil countries protested. They held the first Arab Petroleum Congress in Cairo in the spring to devise a common line of action against the oil majors. Later they contacted such non-Arab oil producing countries as Iran and Venezuela. In September of the following year representatives of Iraq, Iran, Kuwait, Saudi Arabia and Venezuela met in Baghdad to form the Organisation of Petroleum Exporting Countries.[207]

Throughout the 1960s the oil majors paid scant attention to OPEC. But events in the Gulf and elsewhere were running against them. Many independent American oil corporations, as well as Japanese and Italian companies, offered unprecedently favourable terms to the producing countries, and acquired an increasingly important role in the industry, thus undermining the hitherto monopolistic hold of the oil majors. In 1960 the Kuwaiti government established the Kuwait National Petroleum Company, mainly to undertake oil prospecting in the neutral zone (between Kuwait and Saudi Arabia) which had not been allocated to any foreign firm. Kuwait's example was soon followed by Saudi Arabia and Iraq: they respectively set up the Petroleum and Minerals Organisation (Petromin) and the Iraq National Oil Company. Besides exploring the unallocated areas, these companies undertook oil refining and distribution for the domestic market, which had hitherto been the monopoly of foreign firms. The oil giants received a major blow when, in 1961, Iraq's republican regime took over all but 0.5 per cent of the concession area originally allocated to the IPC. As described earlier, the IPC (owned by four oil majors and CFDP) challenged the move.[208]

Ironically, while the oil majors operated more or less as a cartel, they were determined not to enter into 'collective bargaining' with producer countries through OPEC, or the Organisation of Arab Petroleum Exporting Countries (formed in January 1968, in the wake of the Six Day war). They were opposed to OPEC's aims and policies, spelled out first in June 1962, and reiterated six years later – the ultimate objective being the direct development of a member state's hydrocarbon resources by its government.[209] They were particularly resistant to OPEC's demand that oil companies must maintain accounts as stipulated by the local government, and make them available at all times for governmental inspection. The most they would concede was to stop subtracting royalties from profits – thus reducing profit tax to be paid to the government – and instead treat them as part of production expenses.

It was widely known that the oil companies were making astronomical profits. During the period 1948–60 the average rate of return on capital of the oil corporations operating in the Gulf was 111 per cent.[210] Reflecting fast growth in production, actual business turnovers and profits of these companies rose sharply. By the late 1960s oil output in the Gulf amounted to 30 per cent of the world total – up from 5 per cent three decades ago. The main beneficiaries of this development were the five American oil giants. They had entered the Middle East oil industry as junior partners during the inter-war years, but were now handling two thirds of total Middle East oil exports.[211] Most of their shipments went to West Europe and Japan, where demand for oil had risen dramatically.

Between 1945 and 1967 consumption of oil and oil products increased tenfold in West Europe, providing about half of its total energy needs.[212] The switch from coal to oil was motivated as much by health considerations as by economics. A heat unit obtained from oil cost only 30 to 40 per cent as much as that obtained from locally mined coal.[213] The changeover from coal to oil during the 1950s and 1960s saved West Europe $3.5 billion a year.[214] America too registered a dramatic increase in the use of petroleum and petroleum products. Unlike West Europe, however, the United States had substantial oil reserves. But, because the cost of production of oil in America was many times that in the Gulf or Venezuela,[215] President Eisenhower tried to safeguard the local oil industry by imposing an import quota on petroleum in 1959. He fixed the quota at 12.8 per cent of the domestic output, or 11.3 per cent of the total consumption. (The import quota did not apply to Canada). But as consumption rose sharply – resulting in America, with 5 per cent of the world's population, using 33 per cent of global oil output – and as oil drillers at home encountered more and more dry holes, pressure built up on the administration to relax the quota system. Responding to this President Nixon did so, in 1970.

Conscious of the rising demand for oil in the West, and the relaxing of the import quota for America, the republican regime in Libya imposed production cuts on oil companies, as a pressure tactic to secure higher taxes and royalties.[216] The oil companies dreaded the idea of the governments in the Gulf region emulating Libya. They therefore agreed to negotiate with Iraq, Iran, and Saudi Arabia as representatives of all the Gulf oil states, and reached an accord with them in Tehran in February 1971. The agreement, valid for five years, required the oil companies to pay 55 per cent of their profits as tax, and raise the oil price immediately by 21 per cent (from $1.79 a barrel to $2.17), with subsequent annual increases of five cents, plus 2.5 per cent to compensate for inflation. (Libya managed to secure even better terms in its agreement with the oil corporations signed in Tripoli the following month.)[217] OPEC members then began pressing for a share in the running of the local oil industry. They reached an agreement with the major oil corporations in October 1972, whereby the national oil companies of Abu Dhabi, Kuwait, Qatar, and Saudi Arabia immediately acquired 25 per cent of the shares of the foreign concessionaires, with a provision for a further 2.5 per cent increase in shareholding until they reached the 51 per cent level (in 1982).

By then OPEC members had also won a compensatory addition of 8.5 per cent to the oil price for 1972, so as to neutralise the effect of the August 1971 devaluation of the American dollar, the currency for oil payments. The need to do something similar arose again when the American dollar was devalued in March 1973: a step which coincided with a growing realisation in the Western states that they were facing an energy crisis. The dollar devaluation prompted the Saudi oil minister, Shaikh Ahmed Zaki Yamani, to declare that the Tehran agreement of 1971 was 'dead or dying'. Aware of the energy crisis facing their main customer countries, and their own near-monopoly over oil supplies[218] – and intent on securing compensation for the latest dollar devaluation – the OPEC members, meeting in Vienna in September, decided to double the price, from $2.55 to $5.09 a barrel. But before their decision could be implemented they had to have talks with the major oil companies. This was arranged for October, but was postponed due to the outbreak of the Yom Kippur war.

The war gave extraordinary significance to the meeting of OAPEC's oil ministers in Kuwait on 16 October – since OAPEC, unlike OPEC, had always regarded itself as a facet of Arab nationalism.[219] Reacting to President Nixon's order to airlift weapons to Israel on a massive scale, OAPEC members decided on 17 October that 'all Arab oil exporting countries shall forthwith cut production by no less than five per cent of the September production, and maintain the same rate of reduction each month until the Israeli forces are fully withdrawn from all Arab territories occupied during the 1967 war, and the legitimate rights of the Palestinian people are restored'.[220] In order to apply economic pressure they categorised the consumer countries as friendly, neutral, or hostile to the Arab cause, with the friendly nations to be supplied at the September level, the neutrals at a reduced level, and the hostile ones not at all. They also confirmed the price rise decided earlier by OPEC members.

These decisions did not surprise the West European governments, who remembered the twelve-week-long oil embargo imposed by the Arab oil states during the June 1967 war. They had managed to withstand it by increasing their imports from North America and Venezuela, and by persuading the Shah of Iran to raise oil output and exports substantially. Between the two Arab–Israeli wars their oil consumption had risen from 9.3 million to 16.4 million bpd, amounting to a third of the world output.[221] On the eve of the Yom Kippur war they were importing 80 per cent of their oil needs, with two thirds of the imports coming from the Middle East.[222] Aware of their dependence on Arab oil, the West European governments refused to cooperate with the USA in its actions to assist Israel in the war, particularly as regards airlifting of arms. Bonn went so far as to protest publicly against the Pentagon's airlifting of its weapons from the American bases in West Germany for destinations in Israel. When Washington urged West European leaders to help as American allies, the latter replied that as members of Nato their responsibilities were limited to the Nato region, not beyond. Only the Dutch government chose to aid Israel and cooperate with the USA, thus making Holland a target of the Arab oil embargo.[223]

Later, at their summit conference in Algiers on 28 November, the Arab leaders put Portugal on the embargo list, because it had provided refuelling facilities to the American and Israeli planes carrying weapons to Israel during the war.[224] On 30 November the Algerian government raised the price of its 'sweet' crude from $4.80 to $9.25 a barrel.[225] Three weeks later the oil ministers of the Gulf states raised the tax reference price of oil to $11.65 a barrel, effective from 1 January. Thus, within three months the price of oil jumped from $2.55 to $11.65 per barrel, with the host government's average takings per barrel rising fivefold, from $1.38 to $7.[226] Consequently the oil income of OAPEC members, running at the annual rate of $11 billion in early 1973, shot up to a total of $63 billion the following year.[227]

Moreover, the Middle East war created a climate in which the governments of Abu Dhabi, Kuwait, Qatar, and Saudi Arabia acquired majority holdings in the equity of the foreign concessionaires operating in their countries, thus unilaterally telescoping a provision in the October 1972 agreement. They did so after compensating the foreign companies adequately, and guaranteeing them oil supplies. The cumulative effect of these moves was that the 'availability and destination of Arab oil as well as its cost-price' were now dependent on the 'sovereign will' of the Arab governments.[228] At the same time, emulating the example of Iraq and Libya, the Arab oil states in the Gulf withdrew many of the old concessions given to the oil majors and reallocated them to either Japanese firms or such American independents as Getty, Occidental, Sinclair, and Sun.

Unlike the Arab oil boycott imposed in the wake of the Six Day war, the 1973 embargo had a deleterious effect on America. This was so partly because it was applied during autumn and winter, when demand for heating oil is high, and partly because America was then more dependent on Arab oil than six years earlier. On the eve of the October war the United States was (directly or indirectly) importing two million bpd, amounting to one seventh of its total oil consumption.[229] The five-month-long Arab oil embargo thus had the effect of reducing American gross national product by $10 billion to $20 billion.[230] 'The Arab embargo closed factories, increased unemployment, chilled homes, reduced the citizen's traditional easy mobility, lengthened lines at service stations, and raised a threat of rationing of fuel of all types,' states Robert W. Stookey. 'The notion that the United States needed Arab oil was a novel one.'[231]

America managed to partially cushion the effect of the Arab embargo by increasing oil imports from Canada. At the same time it combined threats (such as the possible occupation of Abu Dhabi's oilfields[232]) with blandishments to get the embargo lifted. It succeeded in March 1974. But that did not lead to a cessation of American attempts to mobilise the Western nations against OPEC to effect a reduction in oil prices. It failed.[233] America persisted in giving hints about the use of force to secure oil supplies. 'I am not saying that there's no circumstance where we would not use force,' said Henry Kissinger in January 1975. 'But it is one thing to use it in the case of a dispute over price, it's another where there is some actual strangulation of the industrialised world.'[234] This statement was promptly endorsed by President Ford.[235]

The United States participated in the conference of oil producing and consuming nations in Paris in April 1975 with a view to organising the consumer countries as a bloc to confront OPEC and destroy its solidarity. But this strategy failed, because it ran counter to the basic law of demand and supply. Global demand for oil was buoyant; and OPEC leaders were in a position summarised by Kuwait's under-secretary for oil, Abdul

Wahhab Mohammed, thus: 'A barrel of oil in the ground is worth much more to us than a barrel on the market now.'[236] America itself was a case in point. At eighteen million bpd, its oil consumption in 1975 was running at an all-time high, with a quarter of it being imported from the Arab states.[237] The next year Saudi Arabia overtook Nigeria and became the largest supplier of oil to the USA.[238] American consumption stabilised around seventeen million bpd in 1977 and after, with half of it being imported.[239]

Attempting to counterbalance the effect of inflation in the West and the concomitant diminution in the value of the American dollar, OPEC members raised oil prices three times in five years – in October 1975, December 1976 and July 1977 – to about $14 a barrel.[240] The comparative stability of oil prices and supplies was shaken by the political turmoil in Iran in late 1978. Responding to a call by their exiled leader, Ayatollah Khomeini, the petroleum workers of Iran went on strike, bringing Iranian oil exports, then running at 5.5 million bpd, to a halt. The disruption of supplies in the middle of winter pushed up the oil price to $28 a barrel. Saudi Arabia stepped in to fill the gap left by Iran. It raised its production by 1.5 to 2 million bpd, to reach a daily output of 10 million bpd.[241] This made Saudi Arabia the second largest oil producer in the world, behind the USSR (at 11.4 million bdp), but well ahead of the USA (at 8.5 million bpd): its income from oil exports in 1979 was expected to exceed $66 billion.[242] With its imports running around 8 million bpd, America was expected to pay a record sum of $61 billion for its oil imports in 1979.[243] With the loss of Iran as an important and reliable supplier of oil, America became even more dependent on Saudi Arabia.

By then the crucial importance of Saudi Arabia to the United States had been grasped by Americans of all classes and ages. According to a study conducted (in late 1978) by the Chicago Council of Foreign Affairs – in collaboration with the Gallup Poll Organisation – Saudi Arabia was given the top rating among America's foreign policy interests, with 80 per cent of the general public (and 96 per cent of 'a carefully chosen leadership group') naming Saudi Arabia as 'important to the United States for political, economic, and security reasons'.[244]

Given this, President Carter had no difficulty in rallying support for his policy statement, made in the aftermath of Soviet intervention in Afghanistan – and contained in his 'state of the Union' message to Congress in January 1980 – that America would act militarily to defend 'the Persian Gulf region' if it became a target of external aggression. 'Carter's objective is to convince Moscow that America – with or without allies – will respond militarily to any aggression that might threaten the Gulf or Arabian oilfields,' wrote Henry Brandon, the Washington correspondent of the *Sunday Times*.[245] Since the Gulf states were then supplying 60 per cent of the oil needs of the West and Japan,[246] and since Saudi Arabia produced three quarters as much oil as all the other Gulf states combined,[247] Saudi Arabia was at the centre of American concern for the Gulf region.

Historically, Washington's interest in Saudi Arabia has been related to its significance as an oil producing country. It rejected King Abdul Aziz's request for recognition as an independent monarch in 1928, and did not reconsider the decision for three years. A formal recognition then was followed by talks on a basic treaty of friendship and navigation. This was signed in November 1933, six months after the Saudi king had awarded an oil concession to the Standard Oil Company of California. Seven years lapsed before Washington named its non-resident consul to Saudi Arabia, and two more years before it opened an embassy in Jeddah, the diplomatic capital of the kingdom. Part of the reason for this lack of interest lay in the fact that the state department was 'generally prepared to leave the handling of the West's political interests in the Arab world to Britain'.[248]

Britain was the first Western nation to recognise King Abdul Aziz. It did so as part of the Treaty of Jeddah, signed in May 1927, whereby Abdul Aziz accepted Britain as the 'protector' of the Arab principalities in the Gulf and Oman. When Abdul Aziz's decision to disband the Ikhwan – his erstwhile armed followers – led to a rebellion by a majority of them, the British aided the monarch by providing him with motorised weapons. This enabled Abdul Aziz to defeat the Ikhwan in 1929 and consolidate his power.[249] But later, when he tried to enlarge his domain by attacking North Yemen in 1934, the British opposed him. In general, Britain was determined to curb the ambition of Abdul Aziz who wanted to bring all of the Arabian Peninsula under his control.

What put an additional brake on Abdul Aziz's aspirations was lack of funds. His financial problem was made worse by the outbreak of World War II which interrupted both the arrival of Muslim pilgrims and oil production. Caltex, the American oil combine, helped the monarch by paying him advances against future royalties which were running at an annual rate of $2 million before the war. It also appealed to President Roosevelt to help solve Abdul Aziz's financial crisis. Lacking any legal authority to aid the Saudi king directly, Roosevelt instructed the official then negotiating a large American loan to Britain, to stipulate increased financial assistance to the Saudi king by the British as one of the conditions for Washington's credits to London. Consequently Britain's payments to Saudi Arabia rose fortyfold in three years: from $403,000 in 1940 to $16.6 million in 1943.[250]

This in turn created a new problem. The Caltex officials feared that an increased indebtedness to Britain might lead the king to partially or totally cancel the oil concession given to them. Sharing their fears, Roosevelt took steps to include Saudi Arabia in the American lend-lease assistance programme, which had been launched soon after the USA joined the Second World War in December 1941. Following this, an American military mission arrived in the kingdom to assist the Saudi army. In February 1945 Roosevelt had an amicable meeting with King Abdul Aziz aboard an American warship at Suez.[251] The next month the Saudi monarch declared war against the Axis powers. By then American military engineers had begun constructing a vast airbase at Dhahran near the oilfields. Once completed, it proved to be a crucially important airlink in America's global logistics, particularly during the cold war years. Washington was now generous in its aid to King Abdul Aziz, who received an estimated $100 million from 1944 to 1947.[252]

While economic, military, and diplomatic ties between Saudi Arabia and America grew tighter, those between Saudi Arabia and Britain came under strain. In 1946, when Abdul Aziz laid claim to the Buraimi oasis, the rulers of Abu Dhabi and Oman contested it, and received the active backing of Britain, their 'protector'. The ensuing dispute dragged on for three years, and was eventually suspended. Meanwhile, the Arabian American Oil Company spent $200 million on constructing a 1,000 mile pipeline from the oilfields to the Lebanese port of Sidon – and put it in operation in 1950. Intent on securing a long lease on the Dhahran military airbase, the American administration exempted Aramco from the bulk of US income tax to enable it to raise its royalties to the Saudi king. This, combined with an increase in oil production, caused a rise in Aramco's royalty payments from $44 million to $110 million the following year.[253] In 1951, when Abdul Aziz's relations with Britain deteriorated once again due to a renewed dispute over the Buraimi oasis, he signed an agreement with America which entitled the latter to a five-year lease on the Dhahran airbase. In return America assumed responsibility for training the officers of the National Guard (then called the White Guard) as well as the regular army – a task until then performed by Egypt and Britain – and helping to establish the Saudi navy and air force. Abdul Aziz died two years later.

His successor, King Saud, proved erratic in his loyalty to America. In August 1954 he asked Washington to discontinue its technical aid, under the 1951 agreement, then running at $4.6 million a year. Following the establishment of the Western-sponsored Baghdad Pact in early 1955, he allied himself with the Egyptian and Syrian presidents to form a rival defence pact: a step which puzzled and disturbed both Washington and London. He let the 1951 agreement with the USA expire in 1956, and resorted to renewing it on a monthly basis. He supported Nasser's nationalisation of the Suez Canal. Later he condemned the Anglo–French–Israeli attack on Egypt, and severed diplomatic ties with Britain and France. But, since America too opposed the tripartite aggression, Saud's relations with the American administration improved. President Eisenhower went out of his way to accord a warm welcome to King Saud during his state visit to the USA in February 1957. A new agreement signed between Saudi Arabia and the United States renewed the American lease on the Dhahran airbase, and committed the USA to help expand the Saudi army (to twice its strength of 15,000), navy and air force, and equip them with American weapons. Later, after the American Congress had passed the Eisenhower doctrine on 9 March, King Saud endorsed it, with reservations. He then became the recipient of personal subventions by the CIA to help him fight 'international Communism'.[254]

The following year he received $25 million as aid from America. Yet he was perpetually short of funds. He was a compulsive spender, and his kingdom lacked even the rudiments of a state budget. American officials, therefore, covertly backed the crown prince, Feisal, in his protracted bid for the crown. The power struggle at the top was not finally settled until November 1964; but Saud's authority had been undermined earlier when, following a republican coup in North Yemen in September 1962, he failed to provide firm and consistent leadership. When, in January 1963, Egyptian planes bombed Saudi border positions – from where arms were being supplied to the royalists in North Yemen – America dispatched eight jet fighters and a destroyer to Saudi Arabia to show its support for Riyadh.[255]

One of the first acts of Feisal as king was to resume diplomatic relations with Britain. His government soon opened negotiations with Britain and America for the supply of an air defence umbrella for the kingdom. In December 1965 arms deals worth £140 million – involving (American) Hawk anti-aircraft missiles, sixty-five (British) jet aircraft, and (British) Thunderbolt air-to-air missiles – were signed.[256] Following the American company's inability to expedite deliveries of Hawk missiles, Saudi Arabia ordered more aircraft and air-to-air missiles from Britain. Given this, Feisal considered it unwise to follow Nasser's lead in severing diplomatic links with Washington and London during the June 1967 war. Instead he allied with the Kuwaiti and Libyan rulers to impose an oil embargo against Israel's leading friends: America and Britain. During the summit in Khartoum in late August, Feisal won the approval of Arab leaders to lift the oil embargo with a promise that he (and the Kuwaiti and Libyan monarchs) would give annual subsidies to Egypt and Jordan to compensate them for 'war losses'.[257]

Although Feisal's rapprochement with Nasser at the Khartoum summit led to a de-escalation of the civil war in North Yemen, there was no slowing down in Saudi Arabia's military build-up. Between 1969 and 1971, Riyadh signed deals with Britain and America for the supply of three squadrons of jet fighters,[258] and with France for amphibious tanks. All told, in the first seven years of his rule, Feisal spent a third of the total oil revenue of $7.33 billion on buying weapons.[259]

With the United States importing Saudi oil for the first time in 1970,[260] the American administration became directly interested in the production plans of Aramco. During his visit to Washington in May 1970, King Feisal reportedly reached an understanding with American officials on oil production targets for the future in his kingdom. Aramco's plans, announced next year, to raise output from the current six million bpd to twenty million bpd showed the extent of the planned increase.[261] At the same time Feisal pursued foreign policies in the region which were in line with those of Washington. He gave financial assistance to Sultan Qaboos to bolster his fight against the leftist insurgents in Dhofar, kept up pressure against the radical regime in South Yemen, and successfully persuaded Sadat to expel Soviet military advisers from Egypt.

But, while Feisal was an avowed anti-Communist, he was also an anti-Zionist, committed to achieving the evacuation of the occupied Arab territories, including Arab Jerusalem, by Israel. When the pro-Israeli American Senate tried to stop the sale of Phantom jets to Saudi Arabia in June 1973, Feisal retaliated by suspending talks with Aramco on its plans to increase oil output. The American administration, particularly Henry Kissinger, responded with statements to the effect that it would not let the 'oil factor' dictate its Middle East policy, and that dependence of America and the Arab oil states was mutual, not one-sided.

The fourth Arab–Israeli war, which broke out in October, provided a chance to test the validity or otherwise of these statements. King Feisal immediately dispatched 'several thousands of infantrymen' to Jordan and Syria,[262] and (unsuccessfully) urged King Hussein to enter the war. He then agreed to the Arab oil ministers' decision to impose an oil embargo against Israel's backers, and ordered a 25 per cent cut in production, then running at eight million bpd.[263] This gave the oil weapon a kind of force which nobody had thought possible before.

Although Britain was not included in the boycott list, its prime minister, Edward Heath, sent a personal emissary to King Feisal in December to 'use the argument, which is certain to appeal to the king, that any prolonged oil squeeze will, by weakening the West, strengthen Communism'.[264] Feisal responded positively, and agreed inter alia not to withdraw Saudi deposits at the Bank of England and thus weaken the British pound. Some weeks later, expressing his concern for 'the economy of the whole world', Saudi oil minister, Shaikh Yamani, said, 'We don't want in any way to destroy it.'[265] Given this, it did not take long for Sadat, who had by then become a personal friend of Kissinger, to convince Feisal to lift the oil embargo. Feisal and Sadat then prevailed upon the other members of OAPEC to do so, in mid-March, as 'a token of Arab goodwill' to the West.

In any case, the oil boycott had left diplomatic, military, and (non-oil) economic relations between Riyadh and Washington virtually unaffected. Following the dramatic rise in its oil revenue, the Saudi government went on a buying spree, which benefited Japan and the West, particularly America. During the period of less than three years after the Yom Kippur war, Saudi purchases of American weapons soared to $12.1 billion: more than twenty times the sum spent by Riyadh on American arms during the period 1950–73.[266] Saudi Arabia aided the American economy in other ways. By purchasing US Treasury certificates on a large scale it helped to bolster the sagging American dollar – and simultaneously acquired a vested interest in the future health of America's domestic economy. Its example was followed by other Arab oil states: by late 1976 their total investments in America exceeded $40 billion.[267]

At the same time Riyadh and Washington reinforced the ties that had existed between their intelligence services for many years. Raymond Close, CIA station head in Saudi Arabia (from 1971 to 1977) worked closely with the Saudi security chief, Kemal Adham (brother of King Feisal's only wife), to develop a special intelligence service to 'protect the monarchy'.[268] In his step-by-step approach to Middle East peace, Kissinger accorded as much importance to Riyadh as he did to Cairo or Tel Aviv. He reportedly secured Feisal's backing for a plan meant to replace the January 1974 Egyptian–Israeli disengagement agreement on 20 March 1975, in Riyadh, before leaving for Israel. His shuttle diplomacy ended on 22 March, and three days later came Feisal's assassination – an event which clearly shook Kissinger.

But the accession of the crown prince, Khaled, to the Saudi throne went smoothly enough to reassure the American administration. Later in the year his government launched an American-engineered development plan which envisaged an expenditure of $30,000 per Saudi citizen over the next five years. Saudi contacts with the West had now grown to the extent that the number of Saudi students at universities in the West, particularly America, was far higher than the 14,500 at home.[269] The emergence, in 1976, of Saudi Arabia as the top oil supplier to the USA, with 1.13 million bpd, underlined the growing importance of the kingdom.[270] In December, Patrick Seale of the *Observer* reported that Riyadh and Washington had reached a secret deal under which America was assured of Saudi oil in exchange for 'far-reaching protection of the Saudi regime'.[271]

The vigorous implementation of ambitious economic and military plans – including the building of three military cities at Hafar al Batin, Tabuk, and Khamis Mushait[272] – led inter alia to a rapid increase in the size of the American community in the kingdom. In early 1977 the number of civilian and military American personnel was estimated at 30,000, or five times the figure in 1971.[273] In their day-to-day business they often dealt with Saudi ministers and top civil servants who were themselves American-educated, and enamoured of the American 'lifestyle'.[274]

Given this, the acquisition in 1978 of the remaining 40 per cent of Aramco's shares by the Saudi government at $1.5 billion presented no problem. The erstwhile minority owners of Aramco – Exxon, Mobil, Socal and Texaco – were reassured by the government's promise to provide them with 6.5 to 7 million bpd for worldwide marketing.[275] With oil production then running in the region of 8.5 million bpd, there was enough oil left to meet the home demand of half a million bpd as well as provide more than a million bpd to such non-American oil majors as British Petroleum and Royal Dutch-Shell. The proven Saudi oil reserves were so vast that at that rate they were expected to last five decades or more. (In contrast, the life of proven American reserves, extracted at the same rate, was put at one decade.) In fact, by the late 1970s Saudi Arabia emerged as one of the few countries in the world where each year more oil was being discovered than extracted. The estimate of Saudi oil reserves at 113 billion barrels in 1976 was raised to 150 billion in 1978, and then to 180 billion the next year, thus making Saudi Arabia the owner of a quarter of the world's total oil reserves.[276] Not surprisingly, in 1979 fifteen of Aramco's thirty-eight oilfields were (voluntarily) sealed.[277]

With oil prices doubling in early 1979, the Saudi authorities could have curtailed output by half without jeopardising the country's economic growth. 'The Saudis insist that they need to sell just five million to six million barrels daily to finance their enormous internal development programme,' reported the Riyadh correspondent of Associated Press-Dow Jones.[278] Instead, as described earlier, they raised oil production to meet the shortfall caused by the loss of Iranian exports.[279] Furthermore, for many months they continued to charge $18 a barrel, instead of the going rate of $30, thus subsidising their mainly Western customers to the tune of $125 million a day. 'Crown Prince Fahd says plainly that it is in Saudi Arabia's interest to keep the Western world afloat,' said a Western diplomat in Jeddah.[280] By increasing its oil output, and charging less than market price for it, Saudi Arabia frustrated the wish of other OPEC members to raise oil prices further.

All along, the Western nations, especially America, benefited enormously from Saudi contracts for supplies of weapons as well as the building up of its military infrastructure. In 1977 the US army corps of engineers was engaged in fulfilling contracts worth $16 billion for building roads, ports, and other military facilities.[281] The next year the Saudi defence ministry ordered sixty (American) F-15 advanced jet fighters at the cost of $2.4 billion, amounting to a quarter of its annual budget, then rated as the highest per capita defence budget in the world.[282] Not surprisingly, the arms manufacturers in America experienced a boom, expecting to raise their exports (largely to the Middle East) from $9.3 billion in 1977 to $13.2 in 1978, a 42 per cent increase in a year.[283]

When, in the wake of the Shah's downfall in early 1979, Saudi rulers became nervous about their own future, the Carter administration reassured them by inter alia dispatching a squadron of F-15s to the oil-rich eastern province of the kingdom. (Saudi Arabia's own F-15s were not due for delivery until 1982.) But Carter lost much of the goodwill so gained when he prevailed upon Sadat and Begin to sign a peace treaty in March. Saudi rulers were disturbed by the desertion of Egypt from the Arab ranks, and the change in American policy from working for a comprehensive peace settlement in the region to backing a separate peace treaty between Egypt and Israel. Beyond that, however, they were divided. While Crown Prince Fahd, and defence minister Prince Sultan, proposed continued close alignment with America, King Khaled and National Guard commander Prince Abdullah advocated distancing the kingdom from America, militarily and diplomatically. The departure of Fahd, along with his large entourage, on 22 March, for a 'holiday' in Spain indicated that he had lost the argument – and that the Carter administration's offer to increase the American military presence in the kingdom if the Saudi regime backed the Egyptian–Israeli peace treaty, and agreed to raise oil output to seventeen million bpd and buy US treasury certificates to offset America's balance of payments problem, had been rejected.[284]

The resulting ill-feeling between Riyadh and Washington was highlighted by the vehemence with which Sadat (reflecting the feeling prevalent at the White House) began attacking the Saudi royal family publicly. Matters were eased only after Fahd had a secret meeting with Hermann Eilts, a former American ambassador to Saudi Arabia and Egypt, in Rome in May. At this meeting it was reportedly agreed that the United States would come to the aid of Saudi Arabia in the event of a direct threat to the kingdom, that the American military presence in the Gulf region would be increased 'without publicity', and that the White House would pressure Israel in the autumn, and wring concessions from it on the Palestinian issue.[285]

But the Fahd–Eilts meeting failed to restore the rapport which had existed between Riyadh and Washington for many years before. In any case, by successfully branding the USA the number one enemy of Islam, the Khomeini regime in Tehran had made close ties with America by an Islamic state, such as Saudi Arabia, less than desirable. The Saudi rulers therefore seemed to have decided to concentrate on broadening and deepening ties with West Europe. Given their growing dependence on Saudi oil, and the chances of securing lucrative military and non-military contracts in the kingdom, the West Europeans, particularly the French and the Germans, were only too glad to reciprocate.

It was significant that King Khaled approached President Giscard d'Estaing for the dispatch of specialists from the French National Gendarmerie's Intervention Group to assist Saudi forces in regaining control of Mecca's Grand Mosque from armed rebels in late November. The final assault against the rebels was made only after a French government plane had flown special anti-terrorist equipment, including explosives and gas, to Mecca.[286] A month after the successful operation in Mecca the Saudi monarch reportedly assured the French president that France's supplies of oil from the kingdom were confirmed for another three years.[287] During his tour of the Gulf states next March, the French president told Saudi leaders that the French government would welcome an arrangement under which a French company, Dassault, could be expected to receive aid of up to $1.5 billion to develop and produce Mirage 4000: a jet fighter billed to 'outclass all military aircraft'.[288]

A report about a week before King Khaled's visit to Bonn in mid-June that the West German government had 'recently' secured a loan of $1.7 billion from Saudi Arabia re-stressed the importance of Saudi oil supplies to West Germany, then running at 670,000 bpd.[289] The disruption of Iraqi oil exports, caused by the outbreak of the Gulf war in September, made West Germany as well as France look elsewhere for most of the 560,000 bpd they had until then been receiving from Iraq. Since Saudi Arabia (and Kuwait) volunteered to fill the gap left by Iraq, West Germany and France became even more dependent on Riyadh for oil.

Next April, on the eve of West German Chancellor Helmut Schmidt's visit to Riyadh, it was reported that Saudi Arabia had in fact lent more than half of the $13.5 billion that West Germany had borrowed abroad in 1980.[290] One of the subjects of discussion between Schmidt and the Saudi monarch was West Germany's borrowing needs for 1981. Soon after, Schmidt confirmed that the training of a Saudi anti-terrorist squad by the West German anti-terrorist unit, GSG-9, was 'one of the many examples of Saudi–German friendship'.[291]

Earlier, France was reported to have joined West Germany in negotiating a joint loan from Saudi Arabia. Growing cooperation between Paris and Riyadh was underlined by the fact that six months earlier French firms had signed a deal with Riyadh, worth $3.5 billion, for the supply of 'an entire navy', including frigates, oil tankers, patrol boats, and helicopters.[292] By the time François Mitterrand was elected president of France in May 1981, France was importing 53 per cent of its oil needs from Saudi Arabia.[293] Little wonder that Mitterand decided to pay his first official presidential visit overseas to Saudi Arabia.

By increasing its oil output to 10.3 million bpd, amounting to 40 per cent of total OPEC production,[294] Saudi Arabia had made itself even more indispensable to the West. Not surprisingly, within ten days of the outbreak of the Gulf war, the Pentagon dispatched four radar surveillance aircraft (known as Awacs, Airborne Warning and Control System) to Saudi Arabia, along with 400 military personnel to fly them and operate the ground control systems. In addition America and its allies – Britain, France, and Australia – built up their naval strength around the mouth of the Gulf to the extent that by December there were 'at least sixty' Western warships in the area.[295] Although the US Awacs were under nominal Saudi control, and were not known to have been in contact with the American navy stationed around the Hormuz Straits, it would have been a fairly simple operation to feed Awacs' surveillance information to the American warships, if the situation demanded it.[296]

As it was, after joint American–British war exercises had been conducted in the Gulf around the middle of October, unpublicised,[297] the Western allies chose to assume an even lower profile. 'We don't want a high profile,' said a Western diplomat in the region. 'We have the reality of coordination [in the Gulf] without giving the impression that Nato and some client states in the Gulf are ganging up on anybody.'[298]

However, once the threat of Iranian airstrikes against Saudi oilfields, or an Iraqi attack on the Iranian-occupied islands near the Hormuz Straits, had passed, and the US presidential election had removed political uncertainty, American intentions were reiterated publicly. This was done first by Henry Kissinger. As a potential adviser to the incoming Reagan administration on the Middle East, he said, 'We must put a visible American presence into the perimeter of the facilities that have already been negotiated by the Carter administration.'[299] The reference was to the military facilities secured by America in Oman, Somalia, Kenya, and Egypt since early 1979, when the administration decided to form a joint task force to meet any emergency arising in the Gulf.

Six years earlier it was Kissinger who, as secretary of state, had stated publicly that the use of force by America to secure oil supplies from the Gulf could not be ruled out. The succeeding administration, led by Carter, took a less hawkish line on the issue. During its tenure the Congressional Research Service of the US Library of Congress commissioned John M. Collins and Clyde R. Mark, foreign and defence affairs specialists, to study the subject. Their report, *Petroleum Imports from the Persian Gulf: Use of US Armed Forces to Ensure Supplies*, published in April 1979, discussed two possibilities of American involvement in the region: the US seizing selected oilfields if 'embargoes or unbearable price-gouging' created 'chaos . . . in the US or elsewhere in the industrial world'; or the US assisting a government in the Gulf which faces the risk of losing oil resources as a result of 'internal turmoil or attacks by a hostile power'. They concluded that it was doubtful that the US would be able to seize and operate selected oilfields in the face of non-cooperation by the local people/government. As for aiding a friendly government which sought assistance, the US could help effectively only if it had a joint task force – consisting of infantry, marine, navy and airforce personnel – which was either stationed in or around the region, or was highly mobile.[300]

Two months before the publication of the report (and almost coinciding with the downfall of the Shah), the Carter administration decided to establish a joint task force of 50,000 for safeguarding Gulf oil supplies, and to build up the American fifth fleet, operating from the island of Diego Garcia, near Mauritius, in the Indian Ocean.[301] Soviet intervention in Afghanistan, and the proclamation of the Carter doctrine, added urgency to the newly-formed force, now called the Rapid Deployment Force. Plans were laid to make it 300,000 strong by the mid-1980s;[302] and increased efforts were made to secure American military bases in and around the Gulf.

The Reagan administration went a step beyond Kissinger's public recommendations: it tried to involve its allies in its military plans for the Gulf. Addressing a conference of military experts in Munich, in late February 1981, American deputy defence secretary, Frank Carlucci, asked Nato allies to 'station troops in the Gulf'. He secured the immediate support of the British under-secretary for defence.[303] Early next month, during her visit to Washington, British prime minister Margaret Thatcher backed the idea of a multinational RDF. 'There is an urgent need for a new defence policy beyond the North Atlantic,' she said. 'As a loyal ally, Britain will help [the American RDF] to the very maximum of her ability.' Her statement coincided with a report that the Reagan administration was seriously considering placing the RDF under its European Command, with its headquarters in Brussels, Belgium, which is also the headquarters of Nato.[304] A few days later the US secretary of defence publicly called for permanent American military bases in Egypt and Saudi Arabia.

Riyadh reacted quickly and sharply. 'The Gulf region is not in need of tutelage,' said the Saudi minister of information, Shaikh Mohammed Abdo Yamani. ('This is a usual Arabic phrase for rejecting what are seen as "neo-colonialist designs",' explained John Bulloch of the *Daily Telegraph*.)[305] Some weeks earlier, addressing the third Islamic summit in Taif, Saudi Arabia, King Khaled had favoured non-alignment in international affairs. 'Our loyalty must be neither to an Eastern bloc nor a Western bloc,' he said. 'The security of the Islamic nation will not be assured by joining a military alliance, nor by taking refuge under the umbrella of a superpower.'[306] Repeating the theme in a different context, Saudi leaders told the visiting American secretary of state, Alexander Haig, in April that the deployment of the American RDF in or around the Gulf would sharpen superpower rivalries in the region, and raise tensions.[307]

While Saudi leaders were steadfast in their refusal to lease military bases to America, they were receptive to the informal advice given to them by Britain and France to create a supra-national body of the Gulf states, which could call on the West for military assistance in the event of serious internal or external threat to one or more of its members. Part of the reason why they accepted this advice was that it seemed to be an extension of the idea they themselves had been canvassing among their neighbours ever since the Mecca uprising: namely, an internal security pact covering Saudi Arabia, Kuwait, Bahrain, Qatar, the UAE, and Oman. The outbreak of the Iran–Iraq war in September 1980 gave additional urgency to their proposition. Prince Nayef, the Saudi interior minister, toured the Gulf states later in the year to win support for the plan, and discuss the structure of the proposed Gulf organisation. The third Islamic summit, held under the auspices of the Organisation of the Islamic Conference in Saudi Arabia in late January, provided a chance for the heads of the six Gulf states to meet. The result was a decision to form the Gulf Cooperation Council.[308] A meeting of the Gulf foreign ministers, held a week later in Riyadh, decided inter alia to establish a coordination committee to unify 'the military potential of the Gulf region' by recommending ways of rationalising arms procurement, and developing inter-Gulf cooperation in 'training and the use of weapons'.[309]

Though it would be some time before the coordination committee submitted its report, and still more before some or all of its recommendations were implemented by the member states, differences on the basic approach to the Gulf's external security was quick to emerge among the GCC's constituents. Kuwait seemed to be advocating the creation of a joint military command for the Gulf which would be self-reliant; whereas Oman proposed the establishment of a joint Arab Gulf force for the purpose of defending the Hormuz Straits, (preferably) under a Western umbrella. Indeed, the Omani foreign minister reportedly suggested at the GCC's preliminary meeting in Riyadh that the GCC should invite the Western allies to station their forces in the region 'to protect the Hormuz Straits and maintain stability in the area' until such time as the joint Arab Gulf force was formed to work in conjunction with the Western RDF.[310]

Oman's blatantly pro-West stance is not surprising. It is the one state in the Arabian Peninsula whose armed forces are still led by the nationals of a Western state, Britain. There are more British officers (308) than non-British (299) in the Omani army, which is commanded by a British general. The ratio of British officers to non-British (that is, Omani and Pakistani) in the air force is even higher: 224 to 126. All the senior officers in the Omani navy are British.[311] Furthermore, Oman's internal security chief is British.[312] This was the case sixteen years after the UN general assembly had condemned the colonial presence of Britain in Oman, and called for an end to British domination 'in any form'.[313]

Britain's domination of Oman, dating back to 1871,[314] had remained unchallenged by other Western nations – including America, which had signed a treaty of commerce and friendship with Oman in 1834. In fact, lacking any trade between the two countries, the US state department closed its legation in Muscat in 1915. However, it dispatched its consul in Baghdad to Muscat in 1934 to celebrate the first centenary of the American–Omani treaty. Four years later Sultan Said (who had succeeded his father, Sultan Taimur, deposed by the British in 1932[315]) visited Washington as a state guest. Yet America did not open an embassy in Muscat until July 1972, many months after Britain's formal renunciation of its imperial role in the region.

As Oman's 'protector', Britain sided with the Sultan in his dispute with the Saudi monarch over the Buraimi oasis in 1951.[316] Later, in 1954 and 1957, it helped him to quell an internal rebellion by Imam Ghalib ibn Ali.[317] Once the Sultan had withdrawn, in 1958, to his palace in the port town of Salalah, six hundred miles to the south-west of Muscat, administrative control of the sultanate passed almost totally into the hands of his British civil servants. Whitehall provided funds for all development projects, while Petroleum Development (Oman) – 85 per cent of it owned by Royal Dutch-Shell – accelerated its exploration of oil, and achieved commercial success in 1962.[318] The overthrow of Sultan Said on 23 July 1970, in favour of Qaboos, his only son – masterminded by Whitehall – confirmed British hold over the sultanate.

Although party to the British plans, Qaboos seemed to face a dilemma after he had occupied the throne. He wished to make himself immune from the treatment accorded to his father and grandfather by the British, but did not know how. He therefore welcomed the American administration's offer to channel CIA subventions to him, through the Saudi monarch (since America then lacked an embassy in Muscat), to finance the creation and upkeep of an intelligence service, personally loyal to him. Not surprisingly, the members of this service kept a watchful eye on senior British officers in the sultanate.[319]

During the next five years, as Sultan Qaboos intensified the war against leftist guerrillas, British involvement in Omani affairs increased.[320] In contrast, despite the opening of an embassy in Muscat, America maintained a fairly low profile. The Nixon administration was aware that public opinion at home, recoiling against American involvement in Indo–China, would not have tolerated direct American involvement in Oman. In any case, it felt, Britain was doing a good job and so was Iran.

None the less, as described earlier, America made headway in strengthening its intelligence and military ties with the sultan.[321] Once the ruler had defeated leftist insurgents, and Britain and Iran had reduced their overwhelming presence in the sultanate in 1976, he provided naval and air facilities to the US military in Masirah island.[322] American–Omani links became stronger after the Shah's downfall and the Carter administration's decision to form a joint task force for the Gulf. Oman purchased American weapons, something it had not done before.[323] In April 1980 the Pentagon used Masirah island as 'the staging area' for its incursion into Iran to secure, and fly out, the American diplomats held hostage in Tehran.[324] Two months later America and Oman concluded a military accord, under which Oman agreed to let the USA use its harbours and airports, and stockpile military supplies there, in exchange for an American commitment to defend Oman in case of an attack by the USSR. This was followed by an economic agreement, whereby the American government undertook to encourage private companies to invest in Oman.[325]

When the Iraq–Iran war broke out in late September, the United States activated its military accord with Oman. American warplanes began refuelling regularly at the Masirah airbase; and naval ships of the American RDF, steaming about a hundred miles from the Omani capital, began using Muscat at their refuelling and supplies base.[326] Determined to abort any chance of the conflict spreading to other Gulf states, and thus severely disrupting oil supplies to the West and Japan, both America and Britain pressured Sultan Qaboos to withdraw his consent to Iraq to use its territory for launching an attack on the Iranian-held islands near Hormuz Straits.[327] Next February 250 US military personnel arrived in Masirah island to set up a communications centre; and the following month Oman and America carried out joint military exercises.[328] By then America had earmarked $78.5 million for 'developing' harbour and airport facilities in Oman – as part of its $418.8 million programme to develop RDF bases in Oman, Somalia, Kenya, and Egypt – during the next fiscal year.[329]

At the same time, aware of the strategic advantages that Bahrain offers – proximity to the oilfields of Saudi Arabia, Qatar, and the UAE, and an ideal naval base from where to conduct reconnaissance missions in the Gulf – the Pentagon maintained its interest in Bahrain, which went as far back as 1949. Since Bahrain was then a protectorate of Britain, a close ally of America, the US navy had no problem maintaining a presence there. On the eve of British military withdrawal from Bahrain in December 1971, America signed a secret agreement with the ruler, Shaikh Issa al Khalifa. It included leasing naval facilities, previously used by the British, to America for an annual rental of £300,000.[330] Bahrain now became the headquarters of America's Middle East Force. American–Bahraini relations soured during the October 1973 war when, angered at American support for Israel, the ruler stated that he had abrogated the agreement. But what he had actually done was to cancel the provision about providing fuelling facilities to the US navy, and raise the annual rental to £2 million.[331]

Later the Bahraini–American military agreement, specifying naval and air facilities to the US armed forces, was clandestinely renewed beyond its expiry date of June 1977.[332] The upsurge in US naval activity in Bahrain – following the Iranian takeover of the American embassy and its staff in November 1979 – offered circumstantial evidence of continuing military cooperation between Washington and Manamah. In late December, there were reports of American planes landing regularly at Muharraq airport.[333] The American–Bahraini link was confirmed when, following their unsuccessful attempt to free American hostages in Tehran, American military planes refuelled in Bahrain before taking off for Turkey.

The Bahraini ruler maintained military ties with Washington without loosening those with London. Britain continued to provide weapons for Bahrain's defence forces as well as training for its officers. Nearly a decade after independence, the islands' internal security department was still in the hands of two British officers, who had acquired considerable experience in counter-insurgency operations elsewhere in the British empire.[334] This was also true of the financial institutions in both public and private sectors. The Bahrain Monetary Agency, the country's central bank, established in 1973, was headed by a Briton. The Agency's decision to open an offshore banking centre in Bahrain in 1975 led to a fuller integration of Bahrain into the financial infrastructure of the West. The Citibank (of America) alone accounted for more than half of the offshore banking centre's total business of $6 billion in 1976.[335]

Forty per cent of the funds deposited in Bahrain's offshore banks came from such Gulf oil states as the UAE.[336] The UAE's oil income rose so dramatically in the mid-1970s as to make it one of the richest states in the world by the end of the decade.[337] The rulers of its oil-bearing principalities (chiefly Abu Dhabi and Dubai) knew that the bonanza would not last, and that oil revenue surpluses ought to be invested wisely for the good of future generations. This led to the creation inter alia of the Abu Dhabi Investment Authority in 1976. Within two years it had invested $5 billion to $6 billion, mostly in the equities listed on the stock exchanges of New York, London, Zurich, and Tokyo.[338] Most of the orders for the supply of consumer, capital and military goods – required to execute the federation's economic and military development plans and to meet the fast rising demands of the population – went to the West and Japan. The extent and speed of the development was indicated by the sixfold increase in the UAE's imports in the five-year period 1973–7: from $608 million to $3,844 million.[339]

These imports included military hardware. Britain's departure in 1971 had made the UAE leaders accelerate the military build-up which the British government had initiated in the principalities, in the wake of its earlier exit from South Yemen. The result was that within eight years of independence the strength of the UAE's armed forces rose from 20,000 to 37,000.[340] The main beneficiary of the expansion and modernisation of the UAE's army was Britain; and that of its air force was France, which supplied thirty-two Mirage V jet fighters.[341]

Earlier, France had signed a deal with Kuwait for the supply of a squadron of Mirage F1 jet fighters.[342] It was part of a $1.4 billion armament plan launched by the Kuwaiti government in the wake of border clashes with Iraq in the spring of 1972, when Iraq laid claim to the Kuwaiti offshore islands of Warbah and Bubiyan.[343] In its attempt to update its armed forces, Kuwait also ordered Skyhawk warplanes, Hawk anti-aircraft missiles, and Sidewinder air-to-air missiles from America: transactions for which the Nixon administration had to work hard to secure Congressional approval. These purchases signalled a move away from Britain, which had so far been the only supplier of military hardware to Kuwait.

On the whole independent Kuwait had been exceptionally loyal to Britain. As in pre-independence days, its government and citizens continued to invest their savings in London. With steadily rising oil income, these investments became large in both relative and absolute terms: in mid-1967 they amounted to £979 million, the share of Kuwaiti citizens being £430 million.[344] Moreover, the Kuwait government was then the largest single depositor of American dollars (received for oil sales) at Britain's central bank, the Bank of England, accounting for nearly a quarter of the total deposits of about £1,000 million in gold and foreign currencies at the Bank. A wholesale withdrawal of its funds from the Bank of England by Kuwait would have caused a major financial crisis in

Britain. As it was, facing a large trade deficit, the British government devalued the pound sterling in November 1967. This adversely affected all those with deposits at the Bank of England. Yet Kuwait continued to direct its oil revenue surplus to London. As a result the sterling balances of the Middle East countries, primarily Kuwait and Saudi Arabia, rose to £534 million in 1971.[345]

With a dramatic upsurge in oil prices in late 1973, the impact of Kuwait on the financial institutions of London, as well as New York and Zurich, grew. In 1975, when Kuwaiti oil production was running at two thirds of the 1973 level of three million bpd, the government's oil revenue soared to $7.2 billion. Since the state budget could only absorb $2.9 billion, the rest was available as aid and investment abroad.[346] 'Total Kuwaiti government investment is estimated at around $16 billion,' stated the *Middle East Economic Digest* in August 1977. 'Such sums are a force in the international monetary system, and can no longer be ignored.'[347] However, this could not be said of the impact made on world trade by the rise in Kuwaiti imports, from $1.1 billion in 1973 to $2.43 billion in 1975.[348] Yet, given its population of only about a million, Kuwait soon became the richest country in the world in terms of per capita income.[349] It is likely to retain that position for a long time to come. Although smaller in area than the American state of Massachusetts, Kuwait possesses more than twice as much oil as the whole of the USA: seventy billion barrels versus thirty-one billion.[350] At a steady output of two million bpd Kuwaiti reserves will last until 2072.

Even though America was not importing Kuwaiti oil, Kuwait was generous in investing its oil surplus funds in the United States, particularly its treasury certificates.[351] In late 1979, when Kuwaiti investments abroad amounted to $30 billion,[352] Washington took an action which shook Kuwait's confidence in the USA. Retaliating against the taking hostage of American diplomats in Tehran, President Carter froze all Iranian assets (estimated at $13 billion) held by American banks in the United States and abroad: an unprecedented step to take against a country which was not at war with America. 'Kuwaiti oil minister Ali Khalifa al Sabah explained that such action [of seizure of assets] gave no incentive for any [oil] country to produce more than it needed,' reported Judith Perera, political editor of *The Middle East*. Another Arab oil official commented, "The US threatens to confiscate our assets if we produce enough oil to satisfy Western demand thus producing a financial surplus. It threatens to invade us if we don't produce as much oil as the West wants. We can't win." '[353] Significantly, in February Kuwait carried out military exercises, simulating takeover of its oilfields by the enemy, which involved using Soviet-made ground-to-ground missiles.[354]

In some ways Kuwait's foreign policy stance is nearer to Iraq's than to Saudi Arabia's. Alone among the Gulf Cooperation Council members, Kuwait reportedly suggested expanding the Council by inviting Iraq and

North Yemen to join.[355] Part of the reason for this was that Kuwait wished to offset Saudi dominance of the GCC.

At about the same time, Sanaa accused Riyadh of making its president, Ali Abdullah Saleh, a target of Saudi espionage. The arrest and trial in April 1981 of Abdullah al Asnaj – adviser to President Saleh, and a former foreign minister – on charges of spying for Saudi intelligence and the CIA,[356] indicated North Yemen's increasing exasperation with Saudi and American interference in its internal affairs. Whereas Saudi Arabia had a long history of involvement in North Yemeni politics, America was a comparative newcomer to the field.

When Imam Yahya approached Washington for recognition after he had expanded and consolidated his domain, in the wake of the Ottoman defeat in October 1918, his request was ignored. America did nothing more than maintain informal, intermittent contacts with North Yemen through its resident consul in the British colony of Aden. Even Britain, which signed a forty-year treaty of friendship and cooperation with North Yemen in 1934, dealt with Imam Yahya through the governor of Aden.

America recognised North Yemen formally in 1945, but did not appoint a resident (or non-resident) envoy to Sanaa. Britain established an embassy in Sanaa in 1950, when Imam Ahmed was the ruler. After signing a series of friendship treaties with members of the Soviet bloc, Imam Ahmed decided to develop relations with Washington. As a result, America opened an embassy in Sanaa in 1959, and initiated a programme of technical cooperation in the kingdom, comprising road construction, water supply, and agriculture.

With the overthrow of monarchy in September 1962, and subsequent civil war, the Western governments agonised over the question of recognising the republican regime. Wishing to bring about a de-escalation of the civil war, President Kennedy worked for simultaneous withdrawal of Egyptian troops from North Yemen and cessation of Saudi and Jordanian aid to the royalists. His recognition of the Yemen Arab Republic on 19 December coincided with statements by Sanaa that it would live in peace with its neighbours, and by Cairo that it would withdraw its troops when so requested by the republican authorities.[357]

In the event, Egyptian troops were not withdrawn until five years later; and Saudi involvement in North Yemeni politics never ceased. Indeed, following Moscow's disenchantment with the 'Third Force' leaders who gained power in Sanaa in the late 1960s, and its subsequent cessation of arms and spare parts supplies in October 1969, Saudi Arabia helped to re-equip North Yemen's military with American weapons, and encouraged Sanaa to send its military cadets for training to West Germany and America.[358] Riyadh did all this openly, after recognising the Yemen Arab Republic in July 1970 (a step which was then emulated by Britain and France).

Riyadh's increasing control of North Yemen paved the way for a corresponding rise in Western influence there. Following the seizure of power in mid-1974, Colonel Hamdi tried to diversify sources of weapons supplies and military training. He worked in conjunction with Riyadh, which held the purse-strings. He bought French arms. He was allowed (by Riyadh) to order American weapons for the infantry; but his wish to purchase American F-5 warplanes was overruled.[359] From 1976 to early 1979, Sanaa spent $170 million on American arms.[360] North Yemen's stress on armament and rapid economic development, combined with lack of sufficient internal sources of revenue, made it increasingly dependent on foreign aid. In order to balance its budget in 1978–9, for instance, it had to secure subsidies amounting to an unprecedented $1.1 billion.[361] These came in the main from a group of Arab oil states (Saudi Arabia, Iraq, Kuwait and the UAE) – and West Germany, France, Italy, and Japan.

When Sanaa fared badly in its clashes with North Yemeni rebels (who were aided by South Yemen) in early 1979, Riyadh stepped in to pay $387 million to finance an arms deal with Washington, which included F-5E jet warplanes, M-60 tanks, and M-113 armoured personnel carriers. Responding to the urgent Sanaa–Riyadh call for military assistance, President Carter invoked the waiver provision in the Arms Export Control Act to make these weapons immediately available to North Yemen without waiting for Congressional approval.[362]

As such, Riyadh was alarmed to find Soviet MiGs arriving in North Yemen later in the year;[363] and so was Washington. When rebuked by Riyadh, Sanaa promised to distance itself from Moscow. But this did not happen. For, in the final analysis, the state of Sanaa–Moscow links was determined by relations between Sanaa and Aden, and the latter had been improving uninterruptedly. By early 1981 two points had become manifest: there was no chance of North Yemen regaining its three provinces from Saudi Arabia in the near future; and popular pressure was slowly, but surely, pushing the regimes in North Yemen and South Yemen towards greater cooperation – and unification. The major barrier to Yemeni unity remained Saudi Arabia. North Yemeni leaders tried to reassure Riyadh that since northerners outnumbered southerners by three to one, a united Yemen would reflect more the north than the south. But neither Riyadh nor Washington was convinced.

While the southerners are less numerous than the northerners they have in the past displayed an exceptional degree of ideological and organisational coherence. It was the militancy of the southern masses in the mid-1960s which frustrated the British plan to form a federation of South Arabia, grant it independence within the British Commonwealth, and retain (through a negotiated treaty) control over 'the most important Western military installation east of Suez',[364] which supported Anglo-American presence in the Gulf. Not surprisingly, Whitehall reduced its offer of aid to the prospective independent state from £60 million to £12 million, and finally gave the radical regime of South Yemen only £3 million.[365]

The question of economic aid by America did not seriously arise, for American diplomatic presence in independent Aden lasted less than two years. In October 1969, protesting against the passing of an American law which allowed a United States citizen to join the Israel Defence Force, Aden broke off relations with Washington.[366] Four months later, during the fighting between President Qahtan al Shaabi, supported by the army (of pre-independence days) and the left-wingers, the military attaché at the American embassy had allegedly acted as an adviser to the army.[367]

It was significant that President Carter's special envoy, Congressman Paul Findlay, was in Aden to hold discussions with President Salem Robaye Ali on 'the possibility of improving US–South Yemen relations', when armed clashes erupted in late June 1978 between the followers of President Ali and those loyal to the National Liberation Front and its leadership. There were reports of President Ali having been 'in secret contact with the US'. These were given credence by the fact that the American administration had originally planned to send a delegation to Aden to follow up Findlay's talks on improving ties between the two countries.[368] The ousting and execution of Ali destroyed whatever chances then existed of normalising relations between Aden and Washington.

With Ronald Reagan in the White House, there was no prospect of Washington and Aden resuming even unofficial contacts, much less diplomatic links. In the superpower context, this meant that a certain balance had been struck along the southern coastline of the Arabian Peninsula. Oman lacked diplomatic relations with the USSR; and South Yemen with the USA.

# PART V

# THE MIDDLE EAST:

## AN ANALYSIS, AND FUTURE TRENDS

14

# THE MIDDLE EAST: AN ANALYSIS

Long before they lost their empire in the First World War, the Ottomans had learnt to tailor their actions to suit the ambitions of Russia and the West European nations. Yielding to Western pressures, Sultan Midhat Pasha promulgated in 1876 a constitution which, modelled along French lines, included a bill of rights, and stipulated an elected chamber. But two years later, following a disastrous war with the Czar of Russia, Sultan Abdul Hamid II suspended the constitution and prorogued the chamber. By then Constantinople, heavily indebted to Paris and London, had already mortgaged its economic independence to West Europe in a series of commercial treaties, known as Capitulations, which exempted European imports from any tariffs. The French had secured economic concessions in Greater Syria and taken to building ports, railways, and roads to help foreign trade.

Its military victory in Egypt in 1882 gave Britain virtual sovereignty over that country, still nominally part of the Ottoman empire. This accelerated the process whereby Egypt was being transformed into a cotton-producing country for the benefit of the textile mills in Britain, whose products were entitled to duty-free entry into Egyptian markets. European, mainly British, capitalists and merchants established banks and commercial companies. 'They provided financial facilities and controlled the sophisticated organisation of the cotton trade, including the futures market in Alexandria,' notes Robert Mabro, a British economist. 'Foreign private enterprise found opportunities in public utilities, mortgage and land companies, and in construction.'[1]

By securing mandates over different parts of the Fertile Crescent in the wake of the First World War, Britain and France tightened their already considerable grip over the region. France acquired political control over Greater Syria (i.e. Syria and Lebanon), where tribal chiefs and town notables had, since the land laws of 1858, gradually transformed their hold over agricultural land into de facto ownership. In Iraq, a semi-arid country, the British mandate distributed 90 per cent of the (hitherto state-owned) land to about a thousand tribal chiefs.[2] These landlords soon clustered around the king who ruled in collaboration with the

British. When a constitution introduced a representative form of government, these landlords and their propertied allies in towns had no difficulty in monopolising seats in parliament. A similar situation existed in Egypt, where agricultural land, as well as the population, was concentrated in the Nile delta and along the banks of the Nile. Here the Wafd was primarily the representative of the propertied classes. The economic interests of local landlords (who wanted higher price for cotton) and commercial classes (who were unable to compete with powerful British commercial and financial institutions) came into increasing conflict with British capital. The situation could only be resolved satisfactorily by the British giving up part of their political-military control of Egypt. They did so; and this was enshrined in the Anglo–Egyptian treaty of 1936.

Since Syria and Lebanon lacked Arab kings, the French mandate found itself facing a popular movement for independence, which was led largely by feudal lords and urban aristocrats. However, once France had conceded a degree of independence to these countries, the landlord-aristocrat coalition cooperated with Paris.

The net result of this development was that the most politically conscious sections of society – salaried middle and upper-middle classes in towns, and middle-sized farmers in villages – were excluded from the portals of power. This proved to be a fatal drawback in the system, particularly since these segments of society provided the bulk of the military officer corps. For instance, a study of the social background of Egyptian officers killed in the Palestine war of 1948–9 showed that most of them came from the families of middle-grade civil servants, professionals, army officers, and village notables. On the other hand there were no officers from aristocratic families; and none from the ranks of poor peasants, industrial workers, artisans, urban labourers, and small shopkeepers, who together accounted for 80 per cent of the Egyptian population then.[3]

By failing to defeat Israel in the Palestine war, the Arab regimes rapidly lost prestige at home. The ease with which Hosni Zaim, a military officer, was able to overthrow Syria's parliamentary government in 1949 showed the extent to which defeat in the first Arab–Israeli war had eroded the government's popularity. But the event which properly heralded the transfer of power from the feudal-bourgeois coalition to the petty bourgeoisie, in the guise of military officers, was the Egyptian Free Officers' coup in July 1952. Efforts by military officers with similar social background to seize power succeeded in Iraq in 1956, but failed in Jordan a year later. Another success came in North Yemen in 1962.

Since the Free Officers and their immediate followers had no ties with Egypt's feudal lords, they lost little time in carrying out land reform. This won them popularity in the countryside, where 79 per cent of the peasants were either landless or owned less than an acre of land, and where another 15 per cent of the population was categorised as petty bourgeoisie.[4] In towns and cities, while the petty bourgeoisie accounted for 31 per cent of the population, the 'popular masses' – the unemployed, house servants, and lumpenproletariat – amounted to 51 per cent, and the proletariat to 10 per cent.[5] Small wonder that the only way the military regime could consolidate and expand its popularity was by assuming a socialist stance. 'Nasser was driven to socialism by the developing climate of opinion among Egyptian intellectuals and workers,' notes Elieze Be'eri. 'Whether he wanted to or not, he has had to meet some of the socialist demands of the people, and the best method was to take the lead.'[6]

However, Nasser relied exclusively on state bureaucracy, an important part of the petty bourgeoisie, to carry out socio-economic reform in rural and urban areas. It was not until mid-1966 that he used a section of the state-sponsored Arab Socialist Union, and its youth wing, to launch an anti-feudal campaign in the countryside. But, as described earlier, this process was cut short by the June 1967 war, and the rightward drift it induced.[7]

The Free Officers in Iraq had basically the same class background as those in Egypt. Lacking connection with 'any feudal or property-owning elements',[8] they too immediately initiated economic reforms in agriculture and industry. In this they were aided by the well-knit Communist Party. It galvanised popular support for, and participation in, effecting government's progressive decrees. In the process the Communists aroused the hostility of the supporters of Nasser and the Baath. While both the Nasserites and the Baathists drew their main support from the petty bourgeoisie, there was an important historical difference between them: the military officers led by Nasser had developed an ideology and a political organisation after they had seized state power, whereas the Baathists were a party with an ideology and cadre long before they acquired power.

Initially the Baath's (civilian) leaders were determined to keep army officers out of the party ranks. It was only after Syria's secession from the United Arab Republic in September 1961, carried out by military leaders, that they relented. They found many officers receptive to their leftist ideas. The main reason was that once the Syrian government had opened the only military academy at Homs to all social classes in 1946, on the departure of the French, the desire of the sons of the poor and middle peasants to gain 'social promotion' through the only means open to them – the officer corps – had made the social base of the Syrian officer corps 'progressively more rural'.[9]

Not surprisingly, when the nationalisation decrees of 1964 and 1965 were opposed by the merchants and industrialists of the cities, the military officers (assisted by the leftist Baathists and the Communists) were only too willing to crush the opposition.[10] The neo-Baathist victory in early 1966 signified the ascendancy of these forces within the ruling party. It was the neo-Baathist policy of accelerating the socio-economic change, and intensifying the struggle against Zionism and reactionary Arab regimes, which alarmed Syria's neighbours – and finally led to Israeli aggression in June 1967.

While the Arab defeat paved the way inter alia for Assad's seizure of power in Syria in late 1970, the cumulative effect of the radical Baathist policies during the 1960s had been to bring about considerable changes in property ownership. During that decade the size of the commercial and industrial bourgeoisie was reduced by two thirds in cities, and by seven eighths in villages.[11] In contrast, the proportion of small peasantry in the total population rose by a half: from 27.4 to 41.5 per cent. These changes were achieved without altering the substantial size of the petty bourgeoisie: up slightly from 27.5 per cent in 1960 to 30.7 per cent in 1970.[12]

Since Palestine exiles, often living in refugee camps in or near cities, are removed from agricultural pursuits, the size of the petty bourgeoisie among them is even higher than among Syrians. This is also the case with Jordanian society, two thirds of whose members are of Palestinian origin. The victory of the nationalist-leftist front, led by Suleiman Nabulsi, in the only free election held in Jordan (in 1956) illustrated the importance of this class.[13] But since a majority of military officers were bedouin – and therefore loyal to the monarch – the attempt at a coup in 1957 by the Free Officers, drawn mainly from petty bourgeois families, failed. Since then economic prosperity, fuelled partly by foreign subsidies to the Jordanian government and partly by the remittances of Jordanian–Palestinians working in Arab oil states, has enlarged and strengthened this section of society. However, assisted by extraordinarily efficient military and civilian intelligence, the continued loyalty of the bedouin majority in the military officer corps, and firm backing from Washington as well as Riyadh, the king has survived various attempts at subverting or overthrowing the system, and maintained his monopoly over power.

North Yemen provides a contrasting case. Here the Nasserite officers, representing petty bourgeois interests and aspirations, succeeded (in 1962) in overthrowing the monarchy where, due to an extremely underdeveloped economy, the size of the educated middle classes was very small. The outbreak of a civil war, and its inordinate length, were as much symptoms of this socio-economic fact as they were of the geopolitical reality that North Yemen is contiguous to Saudi Arabia. No wonder that a resolution to the conflict was achieved only after the traditional tribal chiefs had been given important positions of power.

In a larger context, the compromise in North Yemen was a result of the decline in Nasser's popularity due to Egypt's defeat in the June 1967 war. Israel's victory had a varied impact on the Arab East. It induced a rightward drift in Egypt and Syria, whereas it had a contrary effect in Jordan. Having lost a third of his subjects to Israel as a result of the war, the Jordanian monarch allowed the Palestinian guerrillas to attack Israel from the rest of his kingdom. This coincided with a dramatic radicalisation of the Palestinians who, determined to act independently of any Arab government, now frequently talked of waging a 'people's war' against both the Zionist entity and Arab reaction. Their armed presence in the kingdom encouraged those Jordanians who were opposed to the authoritarian monarchy. The growing alliance between Palestinian commandos and progressive Jordanians became such a powerful force that the king had either to challenge and crush the alliance, or allow his regime to collapse, gradually or suddenly. In the confrontation that came in September 1970 the Palestinians lost, partly because the Palestinian segment of Jordan's military did not defect en masse as the Palestinian leaders had hoped, and partly because fully fledged military support from Syria did not materialise.

Nasser's defeat also weakened the pro-Egypt regime in Baghdad. But the Baathist military leaders who seized power in 1968 were by and large free of the virulent anti-Communism which had been the hallmark of their predecessors of 1963. At the same time, being essentially the representatives of the petty bourgeoisie, the Baathists were far from being friendly with the Communists whose major support came from peasants, workers, and Kurds. While the Baathists were willing to cooperate with the Communists in their propaganda against Zionism and imperialism, they were reluctant to give the Communists free rein to organise workers and peasants. There was of course no question of letting the Communists propagate their views among military officers or ranks.[14] The Baathists took five years to fulfil their promise to coopt the Communists into a progressive national front, nominally charged with running the administration. Not surprisingly, the front lasted only about five years. By the late 1970s the Communists were being hounded and persecuted by the Baathist government. Iraqi Baathist behaviour towards the Communists had a parallel in Nasser's treatment of the Egyptian Communists during the decade of 1954–64: persecution; friendly tolerance following the Suez war; persecution; restricted freedom; and finally the party's dissolution by its leaders (induced by Nasser).

Nasser's diminished status in the Arab East in the wake of the Six Day war had an adverse effect on the pro-Nasser Front for the Liberation of South Yemen. Its more radical rival, the National Liberation Front, emerged as the victor, and took over power from the departing British in November 1967. Later, in mid-1969, the NLF split – with the rightist faction, led by President Qahtan al Shaabi, advocating Nasserite socialism, and the leftist faction opting for Marxism–Leninism. In the conflict that developed the leftists won. They did so chiefly because, from the start, they had concentrated on organising and arming the most exploited sections of society – the landless peasants in rural areas and the unskilled workers in Aden's industries – who had numerical superiority over others. They then consolidated their victory by breaking up the colonial army, based on tribal loyalties, and initiating a programme of social reform through campaigns against tribalism, illiteracy, and the oppression of women. They were inadvertently helped by the persistent hostility of the rulers of Saudi Arabia, North Yemen, and Oman, who encouraged border raids. This enabled the NLF cadre to mobilise the masses on a patriotic basis, and accelerate socialist transformation of society in economic and social spheres.

At the same time the South Yemeni government aided the leftist Dhofari insurgents in neighbouring Oman, who succeeded in setting up liberated zones. This in turn led Saudi Arabia and (monarchical) Iran to increase their financial and military assistance to Sultan Qaboos of Oman. In the end an effective counter-insurgency campaign devised and led by British mercenaries, and the induction of large numbers of Iranian troops into Dhofar, enabled the sultan to defeat the insurgents. The leftist insurgency in Dhofar was a departure from previous conflicts in the country. These had stemmed either from tensions between the sultan and Dhofari nationalists (who, feeling alienated and exploited, sought independence), or between the sultan as the secular ruler, operating from the capital on the coast, and the imam as the religious leader with his base in the interior. The oil income, although comparatively modest in the context of Gulf oil states, has helped to build up an infrastructure of communications and electric power, and has financed a programme of educational and health facilities in a society which until 1970 had lived in medieval times, and was divided broadly into bedouins and townsfolk.

But the country which has shown the most extensive and impressive progress in the fields of power, communications, and social services is Saudi Arabia. The rapid change has created new socio-political tensions in a milieu where traditional tensions and rivalries dating back to the days of the founding of the kingdom have persisted unresolved. Since practically all menial and unskilled tasks are performed by foreigners (who form three quarters of the total workforce in the kingdom), the size of the working class in Saudi society is small. In contrast, with the (tertiary) service sector accounting for more than half of the total non-oil gross domestic product,[15] the petty bourgeois section of society is larger here than even in the Hashemite kingdom of Jordan. Also, because the House of Saud numbers more than 4,000 princes, and the wealth of the traditional merchant class has increased manyfold due to a boom in imports,[16] the comparative size and importance of the royals and the mercantile bourgeoisie are greater here than anywhere else in the Arab East, except Qatar.

While all classes have benefited by the spurt in oil prices, the distribution of oil wealth has been extremely uneven. Moreover, despite repeated promises made since 1960 to share power, the House of Saud continues to monopolise political power. The result is a society permeated with tensions – between the royals and (commoner) technocrats, the royals and rich merchant families (who place the Sauds low on the social scale), and the royals and the religious establishment – in addition to traditional rivalries between, say, the Shammar and Oteiba tribes and the Sauds.

However, since the technocrats are not a cohesive group, in a tribal, regional or trade union sense, and are thus unable to act in unison, they do not present a serious threat to the status quo. As for the rich merchant families, chiefly from Hejaz, at least once they tried to induce a military coup, which failed.[17] The religious establishment at the top is propitiated through generous subsidies by the ruler; and so are the leaders of various tribes. It is the lower and middle ranks of the religious hierarchy who present a danger to the monarchy. Their disgust at the corruption rampant among the royals, and their opposition to close ties with the Americans – whom they regard as morally and spiritually degenerate – are shared by many in the kingdom, particularly in the officer corps of the military and the National Guard. It was significant that a return to the true values of Islam, and the severing of links with the Americans, were the salient points of the document adopted by the military officers who attempted an unsuccessful coup in July 1977.[18]

It was equally significant that the next serious challenge to the monarchy – in the form of an armed uprising in Mecca in November 1979 – was led by a young Oteiba and a former student of the Islamic university of Riyadh, and whose followers had won the sympathies of the garrison stationed in Mecca; and that the rebels' demands included declaration of Saudi Arabia as an Islamic republic, an immediate cessation of oil exports to the West, and severing of all ties with the West, particularly America.[19] Although the timing of the uprising coincided with the beginning of Islam's fifteenth century, its occurrence within a year of the Islamic revolution in Iran gave it added importance.

The impact of the Iranian revolution on the Arab East has been so widespread as to earn it a place alongside the 1952 anti-royalist coup in Egypt, and the rise of the radical Palestinian resistance movement in the late 1960s. The Egyptian revolution heralded an era of militant Arab nationalism which was intensely hostile to European imperialism. It caught the imagination of the masses, particularly after the coordinated British and French attempt to regain their old glory was foiled in late 1956. It reached a peak in 1962 when the Algerians overthrew French imperialism by waging an armed struggle. It was feared and opposed not only by imperialist powers, but also by Arab monarchs. King Feisal was one of them. Using ruthless methods he blunted its edge in his kingdom, and went on to strengthen his ties with the West. The second wave of radicalism, caused by the emergence of the Palestinian resistance movement after the Six Day war, left the Saudi kingdom unaffected: its impact was limited to Jordan and Lebanon. In contrast, the Iranian revolution caused deep alarm in Saudi Arabia and the other kingdoms of the Gulf.

By basing their anti-monarchical and anti-imperialist actions on the teachings of the Koran, the Iranian revolutionaries undermined the unchallenged monopoly over the interpretation of the Koran which the Saudi rulers and their loyal religious establishment had hitherto enjoyed. Beyond the Koran, the Iranian revolutionaries articulated feelings about the ostentatious and wasteful life styles of the Saudi and other Gulf rulers, which touched a popular chord in the region. By branding America the number one exploiter of the resources of the Muslim and other oppressed people of the world, the Iranian revolutionaries made the Saudis' action in stepping up oil output to 10.3 million bpd seem un-Islamic. Their zealous campaign against Zionism helped create a political climate in the Arab East which made it unwise for both Saudi Arabia and Jordan to join the Camp David peace process. (The Jordanian monarch was made freshly aware that, given the predominance of the Palestinians in his kingdom, any move towards an alignment with the American–Israeli–Egyptian axis would create such turmoil in his country as to threaten the very future of the Hashemite monarchy.)

For various reasons Bahrain remains most vulnerable to the revolutionary winds from Tehran: Shias form the majority in a population which has a very high literacy rate; most people remember that the nationalist-leftist bloc of deputies was the dominant force in the freely elected parliament of 1973–5; and the country has a substantial industrial working class which has in the past staged strikes. But should the monarchy appear in imminent danger of collapse, or should a coup or an armed uprising or a general strike (or a combination of all three) succeed in overthrowing the monarchy, Saudi Arabia – acting within or outside the Gulf Cooperation Council – would immediately step in to quell the anti-royalist forces or overthrow the young republic. Given its military strength Saudi Arabia would have no difficulty in achieving its objective swiftly.

The dramatic military build-up in Saudi Arabia – as well as in Kuwait, Qatar, and the UAE – was financed by the rise in oil prices in 1973 and later: as was the impressive economic development of the 1970s in these countries. Yet the oil wealth was so immense that large sums were channelled by these regimes into the governmental and private institutions of the confrontation states. Being the largest confrontation state, Egypt was the main beneficiary of this policy. The Gulf's super-rich used their investments mainly for financing the purchase or construction of expensive real estate in Cairo and other cities, and (liberalised) imports of consumer goods from the West. This development, coupled with the return of the (pre-revolutionary) Egyptian bourgeoisie from exile, led to the revival of the old bourgeoisie and the emergence of a new class of middlemen and profiteers.[20]

A creature of Sadat's rightward drift in economic and political policies, this coalition of rich classes acted as a catalyst for Egypt's economic and political integration into the international capitalist system. For such a process to be completed it was necessary to have Western companies invest in Egypt. This could only happen after the Western corporations had been reassured that Egypt was no longer a war-ridden country, and that it was at peace with its long-time enemy, Israel. Hence Sadat's eagerness to conclude a peace treaty with Israel: a political step so blatantly pro-West, and detrimental to Arab unity that even his monarchical backers refused to endorse it.

Although unwilling to openly join the newly forged Washington–Cairo–Tel Aviv axis, the Gulf monarchies, particularly Saudi Arabia and Oman, strengthened their military and intelligence links with America. On its part, America continued its traditional method of dealing with the countries of the Arab East: cooperation with and manipulation of top political and military leaders, with little regard for the opinion or mood of the masses. The sponsoring of a military coup in Syria in early 1949 inaugurated this style of operation. However, many of the successes which America scored in the region proved temporary. For instance, a well-orchestrated campaign against the neutralist regime in Damascus in 1957 paved the way for Syria's merger with Egypt. But the Syria which broke away from the United Arab Republic in 1961 later went in for more profound socio-economic change than had been envisaged in the late 1950s.

With a rapid decline in its own petroleum reserves, and an abrupt rise in oil price, America now attaches more importance to Saudi Arabia and other oil-bearing Gulf monarchies than ever before. This has manifested itself in the tightening of military and intelligence links between Washington and Riyadh.[21] Through the mechanism of the recently established Gulf Cooperation Council, the Washington connection will be automatically transferred to all other Gulf monarchies. However, being armed with the latest intelligence-gathering devices and techniques cannot be a substitute for solving the deeply embedded religious and political problems of the Arabian Peninsula. The question of the unification of the two Yemens is an example.

As the emergent urban petty bourgeoisie becomes the politically dominant class, at the expense of the traditional tribal power structure, the drive for unity with South Yemen is likely to gather momentum. But a united Yemen could only materialise on the basis of a common political-economic ground between present-day Yemens: something less than the proletarian democracy of South Yemen, but more than the semi-authoritarian, feudal set-up of North Yemen. The new, enlarged state may well be a 'national democracy',[22] committed to moderate socio-economic reform at home and non-alignment abroad. Such a state would claim the nominal loyalty of its three quarter million nationals working in

Saudi Arabia: a nightmarish prospect for Saudi rulers. More specifically, a united Yemen is bound to demand the return of the three Yemeni provinces from Riyadh, something which should have happened in 1973. But all that is in the future.

At present the overriding problem facing the pro-West Gulf monarchies is this: in spite of acquiring huge arsenals of Western-manufactured weapons and assuring an uninterrupted flow of oil to the West, the Arab territories of the West Bank and Gaza continue to be occupied by Israel's military administration, which daily confiscates more and more Arab land and humiliates and harasses Palestinian Arabs. The subjugation of about 30 per cent of the Palestinians, and the continued exile of the remaining in a dozen Arab countries,[23] are the most telling and hurtful signs of the impotence of the Arab monarchs; and they know it. They also know that the persistence of the Palestinian problem, made real by the presence of hundreds of thousands of Palestinians in their countries, is steadily eroding the legitimacy of their rule.

Since these rulers are friends of the West, the Palestinian problem also poses a dilemma for the Western leaders. By chance or design the Western nations are divided on the issue: America, steadfast to Israel, is opposed to having any dealings with the PLO; and America's European allies who, while committed to the survival and welfare of Israel, are prepared to bring the PLO into a framework of multilateral negotiations with a view to reaching an agreement on the establishment of an independent Palestinian entity. America's attachment to Israel is as much a result of the presence of a strong Zionist lobby in the USA as it is of the deep hatred for the Soviet Union and Communism that the two countries share.

In the early stages of the Zionist movement, however, the Zionists were more interested in winning over the British and French governments than the American. They argued that the colonisation of Palestine by European Jews would create a Western outpost in the Middle East which would be immensely beneficial to the West. This was a convincing enough argument, as the Balfour Declaration amply showed. The discovery of commercial quantities of oil in Iraq in 1927 increased the strategic and economic value of Palestine, since it provided a gateway to the Iraqi oilfields through the British protectorate of Transjordan. With this the chance of the British quitting Palestine disappeared.

The familiar argument of an occupying power that if it departed the local people, divided into hostile groups, would drag the country down into a bloody confrontation, had little chance of being accepted: at 8 per cent of the population Jews were hardly in a position to initiate or sustain a civil strife. The only way to make the Jewish community a viable opponent of the Arabs was by letting it enlarge itself dramatically. And this is what the British actively encouraged in the late 1920s and thereafter. Once the Jews had become about a third of the population, and thus large enough to sustain a civil war, they provided the British with an excuse for staying on. The fact that, fearing expulsion from the Suez Canal zone after the Second World War, the British moved their troops and weapons to Al Arish,[24] showed that they were determined to hold on to Palestine as a gateway to the Iraqi oilfields. It was only when the fear of a forced withdrawal from the Suez had passed,[25] that London finally decided that Palestine had become 'ungovernable', and referred the problem to the United Nations.

By then the centre of Zionist activity had shifted to America, which had emerged as the uncontested leader of the West. A brief concurrence in the short-term objectives of the USA and the USSR in 1947 laid the foundation for the state of Israel. Once Israel had materialised, its links with America increased rapidly. These became all the more important as the Suez war in 1956 sounded the death-knell for British and French imperialism in the region.

Over the next decade American commitment to the survival and strengthening of Israel became so strong that by the time of the 1967 crisis, 'the American intelligence effort in Egypt . . . had been geared to Israeli needs'.[26] Israel's total alignment with America in the international arena had its parallel in domestic politics: the centre of gravity of Israeli politics moved steadily rightwards. A milestone was reached in mid-1967 when ultranationalist groups, hitherto considered untouchable by the Labour establishment, were invited by it to join a government of national unity.

In a global context the Israeli aggression of June 1967 fitted in well with a series of counter-revolutionary developments in various parts of the world in the wake of Washington's success in its confrontation with Moscow in the Cuban missile crisis of October 1962. American military intervention in South Vietnam in 1963 was followed by the CIA-inspired coups in Brazil (1964), Indonesia (1965), and Ghana (1966), which respectively overthrew the regimes of João Goulart, Sukarno, and Kwame Nkrumah.

While the 1967 victory generated an overconfidence in Tel Aviv which translated itself inter alia into an immediate programme for the colonisation of the occupied Arab territories, Israel's military, economic and intelligence links with America became tighter than ever before. Israel was now 'a valued military proxy' of the United States in the Middle East.[27] As such, the USA simply could not allow Israel to suffer even a limited setback in the October 1973 war. Its immediate dispatch of seventy-six military aircraft, followed by an airlift of over 33,000 tons of weapons[28] showed the extent to which it was prepared to back its proxy. The end result of the 1973 war – in which the Arabs presented the most united and effective military and economic fronts so far – was a belated diplomatic gain for Israel. Within five years, aided by America, it had laid the foundation for a separate peace treaty with Egypt, which had been the objective of its leaders since 1967.[29]

A salient point about the Camp David accord, and the subsequent peace treaty, is that while the political gains accruing to the Carter administration (such as an impressive jump in the president's popularity rating, etc.) were immediate and dramatic, the political and diplomatic price which America has paid since then, for its moment of glory in September 1978 (in terms of loss of cordiality with its erstwhile allies in the Arab East), has been considerable. By May 1981 Alexander Haig, the US secretary of state, was referring to the possibility of 'American incompetence and mismanagement' as factors which had contributed to Riyadh's disenchantment with the Camp David peace process.[30]

But this did not mean that the Reagan administration was planning any drastic change in America's Middle East policy. After all, twenty-nine of its thirty-four nominees to the National Security Council, the state department, and the Pentagon were pro-Israel. Within weeks of taking office the new administration had shown its preoccupation with East–West confrontation. This was illustrated by the way Richard Burt, director for the bureau of politico-military affairs at the state department, ranked American objectives in the region: to show an American ability to counter Soviet influence; to ensure continued Western access to oil 'in adequate quantities and at a reasonable price'; to ensure 'the continued survival and strength of America's friends' in the Middle East; and to continue to work for peace between Israel and its neighbours. The last objective is to be achieved within 'a strategic framework that recognises and is responsive to the larger threat of Soviet expansionism'. As such the American strategy will consist of providing 'security assistance to friendly states in the region, maintaining a direct military presence in the area, building up a reinforcement capability to deploy the necessary additional forces in a crisis, encouraging a role for the regional states, and winning support from America's European and Asian allies'.[31]

Since this strategy is based on American guarantees of Israel's qualitative military superiority in the Middle East, it was opposed among others by Clovis Maqsoud, the Arab League's ambassador to the United Nations. 'Any Arab country that joins this [American] consensus has to accept the pivotal role of Israel in this strategy,' he said. 'It reduces any Arab member to a satellite [of America] and reduces the central issue in the Middle East, namely the Arab–Israeli conflict and Palestinian rights, to a marginal one.'[32]

The minimum demand of even the most pro-American Arab regime is that a Palestinian state be established on the West Bank and Gaza, which must be vacated by Israel. On the other hand even Lord Carrington, the British foreign minister widely regarded as sympathetic to the Arabs, has declared that an independent Palestine can be founded only with the consent of Israel. There is no sign at present that Israel, whether ruled by Likud or the Labour Alignment, is prepared to agree. However, there is always a chance that the situation may change.

15

# THE FUTURE: PROSPECTS AND POSSIBILITIES

According to the Camp David agreement, Israel is required to negotiate with Egypt the terms for Palestinian autonomy: a concept which explicitly invests Israel with sovereignty over the land and waters of the West Bank and Gaza, and the right to protect them. This means that an accord on the Palestinian issue is expected to spell out how the people living in the West Bank and Gaza are to run their internal affairs, once Israeli military administration is ended and Israeli troops withdrawn to specified garrisons in the territories. Even if Israel and Egypt were to reach such an agreement it seems unlikely that the West Bankers and Gazans would execute a plan in whose creation they have had no role at all.[1] As such, this avenue of progress must be considered closed.

In that case the EEC's Middle East initiative is likely to acquire importance. Aware of the aversion that most Israeli leaders have towards the PLO, a tentative EEC plan is known to specify a referendum of all the Palestinians living in various countries to determine their political loyalty,[2] as a preliminary to starting negotiations on the establishment of a Palestinian state: the European hope is that a referendum would reveal that the PLO is not the sole representative of the Palestinians. However, no referendum can be held among the Palestinians unless the PLO cooperates; and it is hard to visualise this happening. Thus the idea of a referendum is a non-starter.

Moreover, EEC leaders continue to insist that the PLO must recognise the right of Israel to exist within secure borders as a precondition for being invited to formal negotiations. Leaving aside the fact that this runs counter to an article in the PLO's charter, its leaders regard Israel's recognition as an important bargaining point to be exchanged for some major concessions by Israel.[3] Thus the chances of the EEC initiative succeeding do not seem promising – unless Israel, which is opposed to the EEC move, shows an unexpected flexibility and understanding, or undergoes a sudden change of heart.

There is however another way of solving the Palestinian issue. Since two thirds of the people living in Jordan today are of Palestinian origin, Jordan may well be renamed Palestine – and enlarged a bit, with Israeli help, by attaching parts of the West Bank to it. Such an idea has been seriously considered in the past by both America and Israel. It was not pursued mainly because Washington and Tel Aviv realised that in order to win Palestinian acceptance they would have to remove the Hashemite dynasty from the throne. Not surprisingly, the concept was fiercely opposed by King Hussein, whose fears that the plan may be resurrected in the future have not been allayed totally. However, any revival of the idea would also be bitterly opposed by the Saudi monarch. He would regard the precedent of replacing an Arab monarchy with a republic as a threat to the future of his own dynasty. Besides, the founding of a radical, or even a progressive, republic of Palestine along Saudi Arabia's northern border is the last thing that the Saudi royals wish to see happening.

However, pressure on the West by friendly Arab regimes to help solve the Palestine question will grow, if only because the unresolved Palestinian problem has already created a severe Lebanese crisis – and the latter cannot be tackled until and unless the former is. The Israeli answer to this is quite different: the problem can be solved by offering the Palestinian Arabs in the West Bank and Gaza internal autonomy, and by destroying the PLO as a fighting force. Israel seems set to pursue the policy of allying with the Lebanese Maronites in order to expel the Palestinians from Lebanon, and crush the PLO politically and militarily. Having secured its western frontier with Egypt through a peace treaty, and its north-eastern border by occupying and colonising the Golan Heights; and having effectively neutralised Jordan to its east; Israel is in a position to concentrate its forces and firepower along its northern frontier with Lebanon, where the PLO forces are now active. There is therefore a likelihood of Israel invading southern Lebanon – and/or attacking Syria either through the (Lebanese) Bekaa valley or the Christian enclave in the north (in alliance with the local Maronite forces). This would lead to a fully fledged war with Syria.

No matter how an Israeli–Syrian conflict starts, and no matter what the state of relations is between Syria and the Arab states outside the Steadfastness Front, it is most likely that, once hostilities have commenced, all the members of the Arab League (excepting Egypt, whose membership remains suspended) will side with Syria.[4] The Arabs would once again use their oil weapon. If America threatened to take over the oilfields of the Gulf, this might well drive Iraq, which still has a formal friendship treaty with Moscow – or even Iran, which regards the USA as the Great Satan – to invite the USSR into the region. In addition, this would also encourage the oil workers, who by and large dislike their rulers' Western connections, to sabotage the oilfields. The Arab states might also threaten to withdraw their enormous investments in the West. Although oil stockpiles would help the West to withstand an Arab oil embargo for a few months, even a hint of the withdrawal of Arab funds would create chaos in Western financial markets.[5] The overall effect of these (actual or potential) developments would be a diminution of popular support for Israel in the West.

On the battlefront the Arab states' combined strength would be substantially higher than that of Israel; but lack of a single joint command, with previous experience of coordination of various armed forces, would be a serious handicap for the Arab side. If Syria found itself losing, it would most likely call on the USSR for military assistance according to the friendship treaty of October 1980. The Soviets are reported to have stockpiled heavy weaponry in Syria for such a contingency.[6] Even when such a treaty did not exist, Moscow had alerted its airborne troops for an airlift to the Syrian front during the October 1973 war.[7]

If, on the other hand, Israel seemed to be losing, Washington would actively help Tel Aviv, but stop short of airlifting its own troops to Israel – a step precluded by the widespread opposition it would arouse in Congress and among the American public. Thus constrained, Israel might be tempted to use one or more of its about twenty 'nuclear weapons'.[8] In that case Israel might, in turn, become the target of a nuclear attack: according to a secret clause in the friendship treaty, the USSR is required to protect Syria against such an eventuality.[9] After all, when the threat of nuclear attack became real during the early days of the October 1973 war, the Soviet Union sent nuclear weapons to Egypt.[10] If Israel were to be the first to drop an atomic bomb on an Arab target, it would lose a lot of public sympathy in the West, which, in the final analysis, remains the surest guarantee of its continued survival. A steep decline in popular support for Israel in the West could only cause an erosion of the Israeli leaders' intransigence on the issue of negotiating with the PLO.

But if the region were to be spared a full-scale war, it is likely that mounting pressures to resolve the Lebanese problem would lead to the convening of an international conference. At such a gathering both the PLO and the USSR would play important roles. They might successfully bargain with the Lebanese Maronites that the PLO would offer the Maronites its cooperation in restoring the status quo ante in Lebanon if they persuaded their political and military backers – Israeli leaders[11] – to join direct or indirect talks about the establishment of an independent Palestine.

The main thrust of the Israeli argument against the founding of an independent Palestine is that it would become a Soviet satellite, and pose an intolerable security threat to the Jewish state. Since Israel is only nine miles wide at its narrowest (about ten miles north of Tel Aviv), it would be vulnerable to artillery and rocket attacks by the hostile residents of Palestine. To quell such Israeli fears the Palestinian leaders would be required to agree to having demilitarised zones along the Israeli–Palestinian border, backed by UN peacekeeping forces on the Palestinian side.[12]

In addition, Israel, tacitly backed by conservative Arab regimes, would insist on the new state forming a federation or co-federation with

Jordan – as a precondition for its founding – thus agreeing in advance to curtailing its freedom of action, primarily in its diplomatic relations, particularly with the Soviet bloc. This would be a sticky point. For no matter how much the conservative and moderate Palestinian leaders might wish to forge a formal link with Jordan, radical Palestinians would not concede this as a precondition. The most the Palestinian leaders could unanimously agree on would be to give a promise to seriously consider a tie-up with Jordan after the establishment of Palestine. Even then the Palestinian–Jordanian link would be problematical, since Palestine would be a democratic republic, and Jordan an authoritarian monarchy.

The other thorny problem would be the future of the Jewish settlements in the West Bank and Gaza. The PLO would insist on following the precedent set by the Camp David accord regarding the Jewish colonies in Sinai: all of these were removed. The Israeli negotiators would resist this on the grounds that unlike the Jewish settlements in Sinai, those on the West Bank are part of a military plan to ensure Israel's security. When pressured on this point, they might suggest exchanging Arab citizens of Israel for Jewish settlers in Palestine. The idea that more than 600,000 Israeli Arabs be exchanged for about 100,000 Jewish settlers in Palestine would most likely be rejected by the PLO. A compromise might then be found by agreeing to a one-to-one exchange. Intertwined with this is the issue of the future of Arab Jerusalem and the custody of the Muslim shrines there. This will tax the ingenuity of the middlemen, since the PLO would regard Palestine as headless without Jerusalem as its capital, while Israel's insistence on keeping Jerusalem as an undivided city would preclude such a possibility.

With the creation of Palestine, the Arab citizens of Israel would come under increasing pressure to migrate to the new state. The pursuit of such a policy would be beneficial to the Israeli authorities in more ways than one: it would help them to get rid of a troublesome section of the population; and by decreasing the non-Jewish section of society it would compensate for a falling rate of Jewish immigration into Israel as well as a rising rate of Jewish emigration from it.[13] Thus the establishment of Palestine, while solving certain problems, will create others.

Any forcible expulsion of Arabs from Israel into Palestine will help those forces within Palestine who had earlier visualised the founding of an 'independent entity' in an area comprising only 40 per cent of what had been offered to Arabs by the UN in 1947, as an intermediate step towards liberating the rest of (original) Palestine from the forces of Zionism and imperialism. There is an even chance that this would become the main dynamic of the internal politics of a mini-Palestine. The current example of Northern Ireland shows that certain problems are so deeprooted that they defy satisfactory solution for many generations.

It is ironic that while Israel is committed to upholding and expanding Western interests in the Middle East, and countering Communist and

Soviet influence there, it has, by conquering and colonising the West Bank and Gaza, created conditions to the contrary. Growing up under Israeli military rule since 1967 has converted tens of thousands of young Palestinians to radical Marxism. They are the up-and-coming generation of Palestine; and as time goes by, others would have to recognise its leftist inclinations. At the very least these Palestinians would work for the de-Zionification of Israel.

As the power currently in possession of Arab territories, Israel wishes to use these as bargaining ploys to secure separate peace treaties with Arab countries: the Golan Heights in its negotiations with Syria; the West Bank in its talks with Jordan; and the status of Jerusalem's Muslim shrines with Saudi Arabia. The grand strategy of Israel (backed by America) consists of the negative aspect of isolating and neutralising Syria, and the positive feature of extending the current Tel Aviv–Cairo axis to include Amman and Riyadh with the main purpose of eradicating Soviet influence from the region, and making it safe for Western interests.

The Egyptian regime is already cooperating with the Israeli government on this front. (It is also working actively on its own to counter Soviet influence in North Africa and elsewhere in the continent.) The Jordanian monarch would be quite willing to join the anti-Soviet axis, provided the future of his dynasty were guaranteed by its members and the West, and a solution to the Palestinian problem secured without any cost to the Hashemite kingdom. The House of Saud too would be ready to join the axis, provided the Palestinian issue were solved, and eastern Jerusalem, with its Islamic shrines, returned to Arab control.

As leaders of the Islamic community of nations, the Saudi rulers would welcome a special role in the guardianship of the Islamic shrines in Jerusalem. Their enormous oil wealth, and the absence of checks and balances in their governmental system, have provided them with unprecedented financial power, which fuels their ambition. What tempers it is the realisation that their kingdom, with long land and sea frontiers, is thinly populated and difficult to defend, and that they lack a large body of armed followers who are truly loyal to them and their way of life. Their efforts to overcome this fundamental weakness by hiring large numbers of mercenaries[14] and expanding their intelligence services are not likely to produce long-lasting success: they may even prove counter-productive.

The Saudi rulers regret the loss of Egypt from the ranks of the Arab League and the Organisation of the Islamic Conference, and wish to reclaim it and its president. For this they are willing to offer tempting subsidies to Egypt, to help it lessen its economic dependence on America and its allies, and regain a semblance of independence and dignity in international affairs. Equally, they wish to wrest Assad's Syria from the embrace of the Soviet Union by using a combination of tactics: financial assistance, and a threat to encourage the Muslim Brotherhood to revive its subversive activities. At the same time they want to contain Syria's ambitions for controlling Lebanon's destiny by maintaining a strong military presence there, and being big brother to the PLO. Since they know that as long as the Lebanese crisis exists Syria will be militarily present there, they wish to see the crisis resolved: this is of course not possible until and unless the Palestine problem is solved. Meanwhile they will continue to provide generous subsidies to the PLO in order to be able to exert influence over it and contain its leftist tendencies.

Determined to blunt the thrust of Iran's Islamic revolution, the Saudi royals are committed to aiding Iraq fully in its war with Iran. They are aware that a defeat on the battlefield would seriously jeopardise the future of Saddam Hussein's regime. Its possible overthrow by a group of military leaders, and/or a popular insurrection in the Shia south of the country, would cause a political earthquake in the whole region. By encouraging populist, republican Islamic forces, it would threaten the future of all of the Gulf monarchies.

At the same time the House of Saud does not really wish to see Iraq emerge as a clear victor in the Gulf war. That would enhance the prestige of President Hussein, who has all along been intent on making Iraq the leader of the Arab Gulf states. An unbeaten, but weakened, Iraq would best suit the Saudi royals, who have already assumed the leadership of the Arab Gulf, through the recently constituted Gulf Cooperation Council.

The creation of the GCC had the encouragement and blessing of the West, particularly its European section. Thoughtful leaders of West Europe would ideally like to see the present autocracies in the Gulf evolve into constitutional monarchies through a series of reforms, designed to coopt increasing numbers of citizens into the decision-making processes at various levels, and introduced at a measured pace. That would be the best scenario for the Arabian Peninsula that the future could offer the West.

A contrasting scenario for the West would be the violent overthrow of the Saudi monarchy by military and/or National Guard officers, who would then set out to eradicate Western influence from the country's military, economic and cultural spheres.[15] Such an event would be all the more damaging to the West if the new (republican) regime were to emulate revolutionary Iran's example of attacking *both* superpowers with equal vehemence. That would deprive the Western leaders and mass media of a chance to arouse popular anger by raising the cry of Soviet conspiracy and expansionism – as a prelude to justifying Western military intervention to crush the Islamic republic of Arabia. As for Moscow, it would most probably consider the new regime's verbal attacks on it as minor irritants. The mere fact of the world's largest oil exporter, and a hitherto staunch anti-Communist state, breaking away from the Western orbit would in itself be regarded as a positive development of crucial importance.

Moscow would be quite content to see the military regime in Riyadh evolve into a civilian one representing all classes – excepting the ex-royals and the super-rich – and committed to a programme of democratic reform at home and anti-imperialism and anti-Zionism abroad. Such a situation would not be too different from that which has been prevalent in Tehran since the revolution. Going by Soviet behaviour in the case of post-Shah Iran, the chances are that Moscow would limit itself to offering advice to the Islamic republic, publicly, to guard against counter-revolution, and to consolidate the political and economic gains of the anti-royalist revolution by organising mass education and encouraging popular participation in the running of the country's institutions, both old and new.

For the present, Soviet leaders and theorists may well be quietly expectant about the prospects of a sudden change in the Arabian Peninsula. The political climate currently prevalent in the Middle East – as summarised by Hisham Shirabi, an academic of Georgetown University, Washington, DC – seems to favour them, if only inadvertently. 'The United States is seen today by more and more people in the Arab world as cynical, manipulative, and coercive,' Shirabi told the Centre for Contemporary Arab Studies in April 1981. 'The main reason for this is that the US government treats the region only in terms of its own interests and in terms of its anti-Soviet crusade. . . . Arab frustration with the US has reached its highest point since World War II.'[16]

Two months later, Iraq's reaction to the American threat to veto a resolution at the UN Security Council, which called for economic sanctions against Israel for its unprovoked attack on Iraq's nuclear installation on 7 June, illustrated the point. Addressing an emergency meeting of the Arab Parliamentary Federation in Beirut, Naim Haddad, the speaker of the Iraqi parliament, recommended that the Arab countries should impose sanctions, including an oil boycott, against America.[17]

Beyond and above the political realities of today lie more fundamental factors which seem to favour the USSR and the socialist bloc: geography, and the socio-economic evolution of the societies of the Middle East. In purely geographical terms the USSR is a Middle Eastern state in a way no Western country is. This fact cannot be altered. Socialist theorists believe that the maturing of capitalism in the Middle East, particularly the Arabian Peninsula, will create well-defined classes in society,[18] and set the scene for a popular struggle for democratic reform at the expense of the royal prerogative. Although long and protracted, the resulting conflict will finally be resolved in favour of the masses. Time, they feel, is against the ruling hierarchies of the Gulf allied to the capitalist West.

# POSTSCRIPT

A five-month-long election campaign gave enough time to Likud to outbid its rival, Labour Alignment, in popularity. The Likud-led government slashed taxes on such consumer goods as television sets and cars, a step particularly welcomed by the poorer Sephardic community, the traditional mainstay of Likud. By sponsoring guided tours of the Jewish settlements in the occupied Arab territories, engaging in a war of nerves with Syria on the issue of the deployment of missiles in Lebanon, and knocking out the nuclear plant near Baghdad, Likud leaders whipped up nationalist fervour – to their electoral advantage. The result was that Likud, which was expected, in early 1981, to lose half of its forty-three seats, improved its strength by five. Aided by the religious parties, commanding a total of thirteen seats in the tenth Knesset, it formed the new government.[1]

Within days of the official announcement of the election results on 9 July, the Israeli administration ordered air raids on four targets in south Lebanon. The PLO retaliated with rocket fire aimed at Kriyat Shimona in north Israel. After minor air raids for the next few days the Israelis attacked twelve targets in Lebanon and shot down a Syrian MiG.[2] On 15 July the PLO rocket attacks on Nahariya coastal town left three Israelis dead and twenty-five injured. The next day the Israelis launched air raids on the bridges and roads being used by the PLO commandos, an unprecedented step.

On 17 July, a Friday, Israeli planes bombed central Beirut with the aim of destroying the command headquarters of the PLO's major constituents. In the event, however, of the ten buildings hit by Israeli bombs, only two were partially occupied by the DFLP and the AFL. The Israeli action left 300 people dead and over 800 injured, most of them civilian and Lebanese. Of the 200 corpses recovered, 175 were civilian; and so were 700 of the injured, including 197 children.[3]

The event aroused widespread condemnation of Israel. 'The kind of blanket bombing that Israelis have engaged over the past five days is tantamount to terror bombing,' wrote *The Times* on 21 July. 'There can be no excuse for wreaking such havoc in the centre of Beirut. The indiscriminate killing of women and children is appalling.' Similar sentiments were also expressed in America at official and popular levels. An opinion poll showed 89 per cent of all Americans (and 59 per cent of Jewish Americans) favouring suspension of arms shipments to Israel.[4]

President Reagan, as well as his secretaries of state and defence, was reported to have criticised Begin, who was described by one top US official as the 'Mad Bomber'.[5] At the same time the US administration, aided by the Saudis, continued its efforts to bring about a ceasefire between Israel and the PLO.

On 20 and 21 July the Israelis and the PLO exchanged heavy rocket and artillery fire. The next day Israeli planes bombed civilian traffic in south Lebanon, killing forty people with direct hits. On 23 July the Israelis bombed Sidon and Tyre. That night the Arab League's Joint Defence Council, meeting in Tunis, threatened to take 'global measures' against 'all countries' still continuing to help Israel.[6] The following day the PLO and its leftist Lebanese allies foiled Israel's attempt to land its forces at Jiyeh, twelve miles south of Beirut. On 25 July a ceasefire went into effect at 13:30 hours. The final casualty figures of the fortnight-long Israel-PLO fighting were: 5 Israelis dead, 100 injured; and 386 Lebanese and Palestinians dead, and 1,100 wounded.[7]

Israel suffered little in human life; but its image in the West was badly tarnished. 'Dramatic film of Israeli jets bombing civilians struggling to get out of burning vehicles on the road to Sidon has been flashed across America, severely damaging the Israeli image with every frame,' reported John Shirley of the *Sunday Times*.[8] Contrary was the case with the PLO. The fighting showed the Arab states that the PLO could sustain an intensive and extended military campaign against Israel. It compelled the US administration to negotiate with the PLO (albeit indirectly) the terms of a ceasefire. It created such an anti-Israeli feeling in Lebanon that the Kataeb-Phalange leader stated publicly that they would sever links with Tel Aviv.[9]

While the Israel-PLO conflict rallied even such moderate states as Saudi Arabia and Qatar on the Palestinian-Lebanese side, it strained the peace process between Israel and Egypt. 'We see Israel returning to the mentality prevailing before peace [with Egypt], and denying the spirit of historic reconciliation,' said Hosni Mubarak, Egypt's vice-president. 'It is resorting to reckless activities in an Arab country, seeking temporary gains that will evaporate at the first test.'[10]

But beyond voicing public disapproval of Israel, and letting some Egyptian doctors fly to Beirut to tend the wounded, Cairo did nothing. This severely undermined Sadat's popular standing. On Eid ul fitr (on 1 August), encouraged by the Islamic Committees, over 100,000 faithful gathered in Abdin Square, outside the presidential palace in Cairo, for prayers, and shouted anti-Sadat slogans.[11]

It was against this background that Sadat visited Washington mainly to acquaint himself with President Reagan and his top aides. There he was reported to have been briefed by American intelligence experts on the activities of radical Islamic and pro-Libya groups within the Egyptian military.[12] He was also reported to have given a 'written promise' to the

Reagan administration that Egypt would provide the US with 'every facility' in any future emergency.[13] It was probably the signing of this (secret) document which led Sadat to declare, on his return home, that a 'special arrangement' had been achieved between Cairo and Washington.

A fortnight later, during the Egyptian-Israeli summit in Alexandria in late August, Begin reportedly pointed out that by tolerating Egyptian forces opposed to normalisation with Israel, Sadat was breaking that clause of the Camp David accord which states that any propaganda against Israel is tantamount to propaganda against the accord. If this continued, Begin warned, Israel would not withdraw from the rest of Sinai in April 1982.[14] Faced with this stark choice, Sadat decided to act against *all* those opposed to full normalisation with Israel.

In the early hours of 3 September Egyptian security forces arrested 1,539 dissidents: 1,300 Islamic and 150 Coptic militants, and the rest, politicians and professionals holding neoWafdist to Marxist views.[15] The government banned ten Islamic and four Coptic societies, six Muslim and Coptic publications (as well as the 'official' opposition Socialist Labour Party's weekly), took over 40,000 privately-owned mosques, and imposed compulsory licensing of all Muslim preachers by the waqfs ministry.

Sadat's sweeping action shocked some of the resident Western journalists: they began to lace their reports with a critical assessment of Sadat, a new development. 'Mr Sadat has always been a paternalist who doesn't like anyone to answer back, and in his experiments with democracy he has tried to prevent any of the opposition groups from actually opposing him,' reported Bob Jobbins, the Cairo correspondent of the BBC. 'Referendum results have to show close to 100 per cent support, political opponents have to lose elections, professional organisations which criticise his policies are disciplined.'[16]

Not surprisingly the referendum held on 10 September on the question, 'Do you agree to the procedures and principles of national unity and social peace?' produced 99.45 per cent backing for Sadat. A few days later Sadat declared that fresh measures, to be enforced from 1 October, would deal with 'a lack of discipline . . . in the street, in the government, at the universities, in factories, in the public sector, and in the private sector'.[17] Soon new disciplinary councils for students and civil servants were set up.

At the same time sporadic attempts at protest, made mainly by the supporters of Islamic militants, were swiftly squashed, and the military was purged of 200 officers considered to be too sympathetic to Islamic elements. All this happened at a time when the vast majority of Muslims held Sadat's regime in low esteem. 'The new Egyptian ruling class is said to be out of touch with Islamic values, and the television service is blamed for allowing programmes which show drinking and sexuality,' reported Philip Finnegan. 'The moral decay led a writer in *Al Daawa* magazine to ask: "Who is protecting corruption in Egypt, the heart of Arabism and the lighthouse of Islam? Things have gone too far. The stench is spreading and an explosion is feared.'' '[18]

The explosion occurred on 6 October. Four soldiers, armed with automatic weapons and hand grenades, attacked the review stand at the military parade in a Cairo suburb to celebrate the Egyptian performance in the fourth Arab-Israeli war. They killed Sadat and seven others, and injured thirty-eight more. They were led by Lt Khaled Ahmed Shawki Islambouli whose brother was one of the 469 members of the Takfir wal Hijra organisation arrested on 3 September.[19]

While the Egyptian people by and large went about their business as usual, a clandestine Islamic group staged an uprising in Asyut by taking over the police headquarters and holding it for a day and a half. By the time the army had restored order in the city, 118 people, including fifty-four policemen, had been killed, and 200 injured.[20] A highlight of Sadat's funeral on 10 October was the absence of local mourners and Arab dignitaries. 'All Egypt . . . remained as steadfastly indifferent to Sadat's internment as it had to his passing last Tuesday,' reported Simon Winchester of the *Sunday Times*. 'The only mourners at the noon funeral, aside from Sadat's family and government, were the (Western) foreigners whose admiration and adoration he had so assiduously courted and won.'[21] In general, the people in the Fertile Crescent were openly jubilant at Sadat's assassination. The prevalent mood there was captured by the headline in the Damascus-based daily *Tishrin*: 'Traitor Falls; Egypt Remains'.[22]

For the next few weeks the government-controlled press in Egypt was full of stories of confrontations between armed Islamic groups and the security forces. On 25 October *Al Ahram* reported that Islamic groups had planned 'a bloody terrorist plot to impose a Khomeini-style regime in Egypt', and that this was to have been carried out on 13 October – the day the presidential election was held.[23]

In the referendum Hosni Mubarak secured 98.46 per cent of the votes cast. Mubarak differentiated between secular and religious sections of opposition. While he entered into dialogue with secular opposition leaders he repressed the Islamic organisations responsible for Sadat's murder. By the end of October, 700 more Islamic militants, including 427 members of the Takfir wal Hijra were imprisoned, and over 200 military officers either arrested or transferred to civilian jobs.[24] Significantly, the purge of the officer corps was carried out by the Central Security Forces, a quarter-million-strong force run by the interior ministry.[25]

As Mubarak had been vice-president since 1975 he was widely known in Western capitals, particularly Washington. The US administration was quick to offer its support to post-Sadat government, and put its Sixth Fleet and RDF on 'increased readiness'. It coupled its warning to Libya not to attack Egypt with an increase in military aid to Sudan, Egypt's ally to the south.

However, this did not imply any modification in the Reagan administration's basic policy of treating the Middle East more in global terms – as an important piece in American confrontation with the Soviet Union – rather than purely regional terms of securing Arab-Israeli peace. This stance, coupled with the Reagan administration's commitment to ensure Western access to oil 'in adequate quantities and at a reasonable price',[26] had promoted Saudi Arabia to the status of America's strategic ally in the Arab world (at the expense of Egypt). Not surprisingly, Reagan and his aides went to extraordinary lengths to secure the Senate's sanction of the sale to Riyadh of five Awacs and other military equipment. In this they were successful. On 28 October the Senate decided by 52 votes to 48 not to block the $8.5 billion worth arms sale.

While the Saudi leaders were publicly and profusely thankful to Reagan for the Awacs sale, they were privately pleased by the state department's earlier statement that it welcomed 'some aspects' of the Saudi peace plan. The eight-point plan, launched by Crown Prince Fahd on 7 August, consisted of: withdrawal of Israel from all Arab territories occupied in 1967, including east Jerusalem; removal of all settlements established by Israel in Arab lands after 1967; guarantee of freedom of worship and religious rights for all religions in the holy places; confirmation of the right of the Palestinian people to return, and compensation for those who choose not to do so; United Nations trusteeship in the West Bank and Gaza during a transition period not exceeding several months; the establishment of an independent Palestinian state with east Jerusalem as its capital; guarantee of 'the right of the states in the region to live in peace'; and the guarantee of the implementation of these principles by the United Nations or some of its members.

Riyadh and Washington seemed to have reached a tacit understanding that while the former would strive to secure Arab consensus on recognising Israel the latter would induce Israel to withdraw from the occupied territories and recognise Palestinian right to an independent state. A hint of this came in a Reagan interview published in the Beruit-based *Al Nahar* on 24 October. 'I think this [US-PLO] dialogue is at stake here,' Reagan said. 'I think Saudi Arabia could be an element in this.' When asked if this meant bringing in the PLO, he replied, 'Yes.'[27] In early November, Secretary Haig twice described the PLO as being an 'umbrella' which contained 'some terrorists and some moderates'.[28] This was a shift from the earlier statements of the PLO being a terrorist organisation.

The US-Saudi peace strategy did not get very far. Fahd failed to secure backing for his peace plan at the Arab League summit in Fez, Morocco, on 25 November. Only seven members were ready to back the plan unambiguously; an equal number were opposed to it mainly due to its point about implied Israeli recognition; and the rest were lukewarm in their support.[29]

But this had no effect on the American commitment to uphold the

House of Saud as spelled out by Reagan on 1 October. 'There is no way we could stand by and see that [country] taken over by anyone [internal or external] that would shut off that oil [to the West],' said President Reagan. 'Saudi Arabia, we will not permit to be an Iran . . . I am not going to talk about the specifics of how we would do it.'[30]

Obviously, present political, religious and demographic conditions of Saudi Arabia are different from those prevailing in the Shah's Iran. Saudi Arabia, for instance, lacks a conurbation of the magnitude of Greater Tehran which, with one-fifth of the national population of thirty-five million, became the seething centre of Iranian revolution. Any upheaval in Saudi Arabia would most likely follow the pattern of the events in North Yemen in September 1962 and after. That is, a group of military and/or National Guard officers would launch a successful coup against the House of Saud, and this would lead to a protracted civil war between republicans and monarchists. The royalists would set up a government in a part of the vast (former) kingdom, or in one of the adjoining states: Qatar, the UAE, or Oman. More importantly, with or without the consent of the (deposed) Saudi king, the US forces would immediately take over the oilfields.

Significantly, following the approval of the Awacs sale, the *Washington Post* quoted a (secret) Pentagon issue paper stating that the Awacs deal set 'the stage for the development, with US backing, of a regional air defence system for the entire Gulf region,' at the cost of $35 billion to $60 billion to the Saudis. The overall plan visualises the Saudis building a network of command, naval and air defence facilities (to US military specifications) large enough to store more than 90 days' supply of equipment, munitions and supplies for the US forces.[31] Such facilities would be as useful to American military in countering attacks on the oilfields by the republican forces of Arabia as they would be in fighting the USSR, which would most likely recognise, and side with, the republic of Arabia.

But American actions would not remain merely defensive. According to the secret US plan, codenamed Tripwire, America would invade southern Iran and other Middle East countries in case of conflict with the USSR.[32] It was significant that among the American forces participating in the joint US-Egyptian-Somali-Omani military exercise – codenamed Bright Star 82 – in late November was the US 24th Infantry Division. 'The Californian and west Texas deserts, where the US 24th Infantry Division has been training, resemble the rugged deserts and mountainous terrain of Iraq and Iran rather than Egypt, Sudan, Somali or the Gulf states,' reported Robert Fisk of *The Times*.[33]

Such American plans were somewhat counterbalanced by the Soviet Union's entry into the defence system of Jordan. King Hussein chose his visit to America to reveal that he had signed a $200 million deal for a mobile SAM-7 system with Moscow. Since the equivalent American equipment would have cost $450 million, he justified his decision on economic grounds.[34] But US officials were not convinced. After all, the previous month Jordan had contracted to buy a nuclear accelerator from East Germany.[35] Before that, during his visit to Moscow in the spring, Hussein had endorsed the Soviet idea for convening an international peace conference on the Middle East: a proposal which has since then been backed not only by the PLO's Arafat but also North Yemen's president, Saleh.

Moscow was gratified to note that, following his twelve-day long visit to Romania, Hungary and Bulgaria in September, the Kuwaiti ruler said publicly that he would advise other Gulf rulers to establish diplomatic and economic links with the Soviet bloc. The UAE's Zaid, who had earlier agreed to let Moscow open a trade mission and Aeroflot office in Abu Dhabi, seemed receptive to the idea.[36] Even Saudi Arabia's Fahd went so far as to reveal that Saudi and Soviet diplomats had been meeting in 'various capitals'.

This was a convoluted way in which the conservative Arab rulers chose to show their public disapproval of the agreement on US-Israeli strategic co-operation which had been agreed in principle during Begin's visit to Washington in early September. The agreement was known to allow America the use of Israeli airbases in Negev, and provide for joint naval and air exercises and sharing of military intelligence. After it was signed on 30 November, it was rightly described by Begin as the first *written* military agreement between Israel and America, and the first to name the USSR as the common enemy. 'United States-Israeli strategic co-operation . . . is designed against the threat to peace and security of the region caused by the Soviet Union or Soviet-controlled forces from outside the region introduced into the region,' stated the joint memorandum.[37]

In a way the Israeli-American agreement was a counterpoint to the Syrian-Soviet friendship treaty signed a year earlier. When relations between Syria and Israel became tense in the wake of the Syrian deployment of missiles in Bekaa valley in the spring of 1981, Moscow and Damascus decided to hold joint naval exercises in order to warn Israel against any precipitate action against Syria. These exercises were conducted in early July, with Soviet troops landing on Syrian beaches between Banias and Tartus.[38] Their purpose was served. Five months later the Syrian missiles were still in Lebanon, unharmed.

But Tel Aviv found a way to get even with Damascus. On 14 December the Begin government decided to extend Israeli law to the occupied Golan Heights. By passing the necessary bill (by 63 votes to 21) within a few hours, the Knesset achieved an 'instant annexation' of the Golan Heights. This was in contrast to the process of 'creeping annexation' which was put into train on 1 December in the West Bank and Gaza.

On that day the two areas were placed under civilian administrators, thus ending the military occupation which had existed since June 1967.

The West Bankers and Gazans protested through large-scale strikes and demonstrations. The Gazans went on an indefinite commercial strike on 1 December. It was only after Israeli troops had welded over 200 shops, including food stores and pharmacies, that the strikers relented after nine days.[39] Such Israeli actions were accompanied by officially inspired stories that one million Jews were to be settled by 2010 in the West Bank and Gaza, which were routinely described as part of the historical land promised to the Jews by God. Begin used the historical argument to justify the annexation of the Golan Heights as well.[40]

Syria announced that by annexing the Golan Heights, Tel Aviv had nullified the armistice agreement of May 1974, and that this amounted to declaring war against Damascus. If Israel were to knock out the Syrian missiles in Bekaa valley – a distinct possibility – this may well trigger off a real war between the two states. The PLO would then immediately join Syria, and its lead would be followed by all the Arab states, except Egypt. If the main adversaries were to reach the kind of stalemate on the battlefield that Israel and Egypt did in the October 1973 war, it may lead to serious negotiations between Israel and Syria-PLO. But if one side were to win decisively over the other, it may sow the seeds of a future confrontation.

Syria's diplomatic standing in the Arab world rose when Iran regained Khoramshahr from Iraq on 24 May. Assad had all along condemned Saddam Hussein for his large scale aggression against Iran merely to settle minor border disputes. It was significant that on the same day Saudi foreign minister, Prince Saud ibn Faisal, had a six-hour meeting with Assad in Damascus.

Meanwhile the foreign ministers of the Steadfastness Front met in Algiers and announced that they would strengthen ties with Tehran and try to stop any Arab involvement in the Gulf war.[41] The ministers also declared that Egypt would not be re-admitted to the Arab League as long as it adhered to the Camp David accord. In contrast, a desperate Saddam Hussein stated that if the Egyptian troops came to Baghdad 'We would . . . open all doors to them'.[42]

President Mubarak showed no sign of increasing his support for Iraq beyond selling it arms and ammunition. He repeated that he intended to abide by the Camp David accord. By handing over the last third of Sinai to Egypt on 26 April, the Begin administration had met its obligation under the Israeli–Egyptian peace treaty. Washington had played an active role in getting Israel to do so.

The three governments were agreed that Iran's success on the battlefield established it as the region's dominant military power. This development worried them as much as it did the Gulf monarchies, especially since Iran insisted on Saddam Hussein's removal as a precondition for ceasefire. The overthrow of Hussein's regime will have far-reaching consequences in the region. Thus the Middle East seems set to enter a period of extraordinary turbulence.

# NOTES

## Chapter 1 Introduction

1 Michael C. Hudson, *Arab Politics: The Search for Legitimacy*, Yale University Press, New Haven, Com. and London, 1977, p. 34.
2 David Holden, *Farewell to Arabia*, Faber, London, 1966, p. 242.
3 Literally, recitation. The Koran is regarded as the literal Word of Allah conveyed through the archangel Gabriel to the prophet Mohammed.
4 Umma is a derivative of um, meaning mother or source.
5 Literally, an old man; figuratively, a title of respect accorded to a wise person.
6 Bernard Lewis, *The Arabs in History*, Hutchinson, London, 5th edn, 1970, pp. 43–4.
7 Hudson, op. cit., p. 48.
8 Ibid., p. 52.
9 The Twelvers' imams are: Ali, Hassan, Hussein, Ali II, Mohammed al Bakr, Jafar al Sadeq, Abu al Hassan Musa, Ali III, Abu Jafar Mohammed, Ali IV, Abu Mohammed al Hassan, and Mohammed al Mahdi. The last imam is believed to have disappeared, and is expected to reappear on the eve of the Day of Judgment. Zaid, a son of Ali II, and Ismail, a son of Jafar al Sadeq, are not accepted as imams by the Twelvers.
10 Interestingly, the Arabic term for both the Ismailis and the Alawis is 'al bataniya': a derivative of the root meaning 'hidden or secret'.
11 Hudson, op. cit., p. 68.
12 The founding conference was attended by observers from Palestine, then still under a British mandate. Peter Mansfield (ed.), *The Middle East: A Political and Economic Survey*, Oxford University Press, London and New York, 4th edn, 1973, p. 2.
13 The eleventh Arab League summit conference, held in Amman in November 1980, endorsed an 'Arab economic solidarity plan', which envisages investments of $19 billion in infrastructure and social development schemes, $8 billion in scientific research and technology transfers, and $10 billion in joint industrial ventures. *Economic and Political Weekly*, 29 November 1980, p. 1996.
14 *The Middle East*, May 1979, p. 12. Following Egypt's unilateral peace treaty with Israel in March 1979, Egypt was suspended from the Arab League, and their headquarters moved from Cairo to Tunis. The remaining twenty-one members of the Arab League (in chronological order) were: Iraq (1945), Jordan (1945), Lebanon (1945), North Yemen (1945), Saudi Arabia (1945), Syria (1945), Libya (1953), Sudan (1956), Morocco (1958), Tunisia (1958), Kuwait (1961), Algeria (1962), South Yemen (1967), Bahrain (1971), Oman

(1971), Qatar (1971), United Arab Emirates (1971), Mauritania (1971), Somalia (1974), the Palestine Liberation Organisation (1974), and Djibouti (1977).

Chapter 2 Arab monarchies

1 Literally, commanders.
2 Michael C. Hudson, *Arab Politics*, pp. 165–6.
3 Literally, kingdom.
4 Literally, outgoers or seceders.
5 He was sent into exile to London, where he died three years later.
6 Hudson, op. cit., p. 270.
7 Fred Halliday, *Arabia Without Sultans*, Penguin Books, Harmondsworth, 1974, p. 276. In 1970 Oman's foreign reserves stood at £80 million.
8 *Arab World File*, no. 640, 11 May 1974; Hudson, op. cit., p. 208.
9 Financial mismanagement was so acute that, despite rising oil royalties, the Saudi Arabian government needed an American grant of $25 million in 1958. Halliday, op. cit., p. 55.
10 *Arab World File*, no. 100, 16 October 1974.
11 Literally, the one who delivers a fatwa, a legal deduction. His task is to give opinion on matters of religious-legal import referred to him by a secular or religious authority.
12 Ramon Knauerhase, *The Saudi Arabian Economy*, Fredrick Praeger, New York and London, 1975, p. 52; Emile A. Nakhleh, *The United States and Saudi Arabia: A Policy Study*, American Enterprise Institute for Public Policy Research, Washington, DC, 1975, pp. 36–7.
13 The Sharia, the Islamic law, is a complex and comprehensive set of obligations, rulings, and restrictions based on the Koran, the hadith (recorded sayings and acts of prophet Mohammed), and the sunna (tradition). By mastering the art of qiyas – logical deduction and analogy – a scholar of the Sharia, an alem, should be able to relate present-day conditions to the past, and help formulate laws and judgments which have contemporary relevance.
14 *Time*, 29 May 1978, p. 20.
15 *Guardian*, 20 March 1980.
16 According to unofficial estimates three quarters of the Saudi workforce is foreign, reported John Andrews of the *Guardian*, 8 May 1980. Earlier, correspondents of *The Middle East* had stated that 2.1 million foreign residents of Saudi Arabia formed 75 per cent of the total labour force. February 1978, p. 29; May 1978, p. 54.
17 In the late 1970s there were an estimated half a million bedouin. *The Times*, 23 November 1979. The results of the official census conducted in 1974 – which reportedly put the total Saudi population at 4.3 million – were not made public. The figure of 4.5 million, published by Paul Martin in *The Times* of 16 February 1977, remains the most reliable. The official statements of 6.5 to 7 million Saudi nationals are widely regarded as exaggerated.
18 *The Middle East*, May 1978, p. 54.
19 Of the four codes of the Sharia – Hanifi (founded by Abu Hanifa, died 767); Maliki (by Malik ibn Anas, died 795); Shafei (by Idris al Shafei, died 820); and Hanbali (by Ahmed ibn Hanbal, died 855) – the last, Hanbali, is the strictest.
20 *The Times*, 3 September 1976.
21 In the absence of such an agreement Qatar would have certainly been absorbed into the Saudi kingdom later.
22 *Arab World File*, no. 364, 27 August 1975.
23 *The Times*, 3 September 1976.

24 'Survey of Arabia' in *The Economist*, 10 December 1977, p. 14.
25 *Daily Telegraph Magazine*, 15 February 1974, p. 30.
26 Ras al Khaima, the seventh emirate, joined the federation in February 1972.
27 'Survey of Arabia' in *The Economist*, 10 December 1977, p. 14.
28 *The Middle East*, June 1980, p. 31.
29 *Guardian*, 20 May 1980. Two decades earlier the population was only about 50,000. Halliday, op. cit., p. 450.
30 *The Middle East*, February 1978, p. 54.
31 *Newsweek*, 3 March 1980, p. 20.
32 *The Middle East*, September 1979, p. 18.
33 *Newsweek*, 3 March 1980, p. 20.
34 *The Middle East*, July 1980, p. 32.
35 Halliday, op. cit., p. 429.
36 Ralph Shaw, *Kuwait*, Macmillan, London, 1976, p. 26.
37 The franchise is limited to those Kuwaiti males, aged twenty or above, who can trace their ancestry in the state to 1920 or before. Of the 440,000 Kuwaiti nationals in 1975, less than 50,000 were eligible to vote. Five years later the total electorate amounted to 41,700. *The Middle East*, July 1980, p. 32; *8 Days*, 28 February 1981, p. 15; Shaw, op. cit., p. 48.
38 The national assembly was primarily concerned with approving legislation; the cabinet's policy drafts on foreign affairs, oil, defence, finance, and other subjects; and the ruler's ministerial appointments.
39 Hudson, op. cit., p. 186.
40 According to the 1980 census, Kuwaiti nationals were 41 per cent of the total population of 1.3 million. *8 Days*, 28 February 1981, p. 15.
41 *Guardian*, 30 August 1976.
42 *The Middle East*, July 1980, p. 30.
43 Ibid., January 1980, p. 55, citing the World Bank's *World Development Report, 1979*.
44 See p. 12.
45 Martial law was imposed during 1957–63, 1966–7, and 1967–73. Hudson, op. cit., p. 216.
46 *Arab World File*, no. 171, 8 January 1975. As stated earlier (p. 22), King Hussein resurrected the lower house as a fully nominated consultative council with a tenure of one year, in the wake of the Iranian revolution. The second consultative council met in late April 1980. *Daily Telegraph*, 28 April 1980.
47 Hudson, op. cit., p. 216.

Chapter 3 Arab republics and the Palestinians

1 According to article 76 of the 1971 constitution, a presidential nominee needs at least one third of the national assembly members to propose his name, and a two thirds majority for adoption by the assembly. He is then 'referred to the people for a plebiscite', where he must secure an absolute majority of the votes cast to be elected president. *The Constitution of the Arab Republic of Egypt*, Ministry of Information, Cairo, September 1971, pp. 28–9.
2 W. F. Abboushi, *Political Systems of the Middle East in the Twentieth Century*, Dodd Mead, New York, 1970, p. 159.
3 *The Constitution of the Arab Republic of Egypt*, pp. 5–6.
4 *Guardian*, 11 June 1979.
5 *Daily Telegraph*, 24 May 1980. This was one of the many points offered, as a package, for a single Yes/No vote. See pp. 126–8.
6 The coup by army officers was in protest against the government's failure to

support the Syrian people's struggle against the French mandate, and the Arab rebellion against the British mandate in Palestine. Robert W. Stookey, *America and the Arab States: An Uneasy Encounter*, John Wiley, New York and London, 1975, p. 51.

7 *Arab World File*, no. 495, 5 May 1976; and Majid Khadduri, *Republican Iraq: a Study in Iraqi Politics since the Revolution of 1958*, Oxford University Press, London and New York, 1969, p. 17. According to Rony Gabbay, an Israeli specialist on Iraq, the Free Officers had been in existence since 1952. *Communism and Agrarian Reform in Iraq*, Croom Helm, London, 1978, p. 108.

8 Elections were held to the 250-member national assembly on 20 June 1980. But whether this signalled the beginning of 'a genuine parliamentary democracy' remains debatable.

9 Khadduri, op. cit., p. 227.

10 In the Baath party's view, Arabs from the Gulf to the Atlantic form a single nation, and the present Arab state boundaries signify regions of the Arab Nation.

11 Majid Khadduri, *Socialist Iraq: a Study in Iraqi Politics since 1968*, The Middle East Institute, Washington, DC, 1978, pp. 34–5.

12 Ibid., p. 35.

13 *Guardian*, 18 July 1979. Saddam Hussein was made an 'honorary' major-general in March 1975. Ibid., 6 April 1977.

14 The Shafeis are the followers of Idris al Shafei, a leading authority on the Sharia, who died in 820. See earlier note 19, ch. 2.

15 Fred Halliday, *Arabia Without Sultans*, p. 147. The forty-year period ended in 1973; Saudi Arabia still continues to hold these provinces.

16 The military officer corps was then about 400 strong. Halliday, op. cit., p. 102.

17 Peter Mansfield (ed.), *The Middle East*, p. 162.

18 Halliday, op. cit., p. 106; *Sunday Times*, 16 October 1977.

19 *The Times*, 26 June 1978.

20 *The Middle East*, January 1980, p. 34.

21 *Guardian*, 7 May 1980.

22 Originally consisting of eleven members, the general command of the NLF was expanded to twenty-one members, and then to forty-one, before being disbanded in 1971 as a result of the new constitution.

23 *Arab World File*, no. 195, 5 February 1975; Michael C. Hudson, *Arab Politics*, p. 356.

24 Hudson, op. cit., p. 360.

25 Tabitha Petran, *Syria: A Modern History*, Ernest Benn, London, p. 63.

26 Ibid., pp. 59, 107.

27 *Arab World File*, no. 7, 3 July 1974.

28 *Guardian*, 5 February 1980.

29 *Arab World File*, no. 393, 26 November 1975; Hudson, op. cit., p. 285. The ninety-nine seats in parliament are divided as follows: Christian, 54 (Maronite, 30; Greek Orthodox, 11; Greek Catholic, 6; Armenian Orthodox, 4; and minorities, 3); and non-Christian, 45 (Sunni, 20; Shia, 19; and Druze, 6).

30 Maronites are the followers of Saint Maron, a fourth-century hermit, who lived in north-east Syria. See p. 114.

31 The elections due in 1976 and 1980 were not called due to the civil war of 1975–6 and its aftermath.

32 *Arab World File*, no. 393, 26 November 1975. This was one of the original articles of the 1926 constitution which had been left untouched. It runs counter to article 12, which states that individual merit is the 'only' criterion to be considered in appointing someone to a public-sector job.

33 *The Times*, 15 May 1976; *Arab World File*, no. 411, 10 December 1976.
34 Phalange is a derivative of phalanx (or battalion), the literal translation of the Arabic word Kataeb.
35 *The Times*, 15 March 1976. Also see p. 45.
36 President Assad's unpublicised argument was that if the Syrian troops had not intervened on behalf of the right-wing Maronites, Israel would have done so, and decimated the Lebanese–Palestinian forces in the process.
37 *New York Times*, 15 February 1976; *The Middle East*, January 1977, p. 18; *Egyptian Gazette*, 7 January 1978.
38 *Newsweek*, 27 March 1978, p. 19; *Egyptian Gazette*, 11 April 1978.
39 *International Herald Tribune*, 21 March 1978.
40 *Washington Post*, 31 August 1979.
41 *The Middle East*, August 1980, p. 21.
42 *Guardian*, 11 July 1980. Massive Israeli strikes against Palestinian positions in southern Lebanon some weeks later confirmed Palestinian suspicions. Ibid., 20 August 1980.
43 Cited in J. C. Hurewitz, *Diplomacy in the Near and Middle East: a Documentary Record*, vol. 2: 1914–56, Princeton University Press, Princeton, NJ, 1957, p. 18.
44 The pact was named after Sir Mark Sykes, a British diplomat with speciali. : knowledge of the Middle East, and François Georges Picot, a former French consul in Beirut.
45 The British–French domination of the League of Nations was underlined by none other than Lord Curzon, the British foreign minister, in 1920. 'It is quite a mistake to suppose . . . that under the Covenant of the League, or any other instrument, the gift of the mandate rests with the League of Nations,' he told the House of Lords on 25 June 1920. 'It does not do so. It rests with the powers who conquered the territories, which it then falls to them to distribute, and it was in these circumstances that the mandate for Palestine and Mesopotamia [i.e. Iraq] was conferred upon and accepted by us, and the mandate for Syria was conferred upon and accepted by France.' *Parliamentary Debates (Hansard), House of Lords*, 5th series, XL (1920), col. 877.
46 232 Arabs and 339 Jews were wounded. *Guardian*, 1 April 1976.
47 Whereas the ratio of the injured to the killed was about 3:1 among Britons, and approximately 5:2 among Jews, it was nearly 1:2 among Arabs. The actual figures for the wounded were: 386 Britons, 857 Jews, and 1,775 Arabs. In addition, 5,679 Arabs were arrested. Maxim Ghilan, *How Israel Lost Its Soul*, Penguin Books, Harmondsworth, 1974, p. 78.
48 Peter Mansfield, *The Arabs*, Penguin Books, Harmondsworth, 1978, p. 280.
49 Maxime Rodinson, *Israel and the Arabs*, Penguin Books, Harmondsworth, 1968, p. 39.
50 Mansfield, *The Arabs*, p. 280.
51 Fatah is the reverse of the acronym Hataf, which in Arabic stands for Harakat al Tehrir al Falastini: that is, the Movement for the Liberation of Palestine.
52 Cited in *Arab World File*, no. 134, 20 November 1974. Interestingly, the idea of a Palestine 'entity', whereby the Palestinian refugees would form a government-in-exile and raise an army to liberate Palestine from Zionism, was first aired publicly in 1959, in neighbouring Iraq, by its leader, Abdul Karem Qassem. Stookey, op. cit., p. 194.
53 Hudson, op. cit., p. 302.
54 Mansfield, *The Middle East*, p. 388.
55 Although originally drafted in 1964, the Palestine National Charter became significant only in July 1968, when the fourth PNC assembly inserted in it inter

alia the article: 'Armed struggle is the only way to liberate Palestine'. The Charter, consisting of thirty-three articles, makes four major points: Israel was established with force, and is therefore illegal; the Palestine Arabs are the true inhabitants of Palestine; the Palestinians are committed to liberating by force what was taken from them by force; and they expect support from other Arabs in their struggle. *The Middle East*, January 1980, p. 16.

56 Ibid., p. 18.

57 UN General Assembly resolution 3236 of 22 November 1974. *The Times*, 23 November 1974.

58 *Guardian*, 16 October 1977.

59 The first such conference was held in Geneva, Switzerland, in December 1973, and was co-chaired by America and the Soviet Union.

60 *Daily Telegraph*, 30 July 1980. Only seven countries voted against the resolution while twenty-four abstained. Ever since America vetoed a similar resolution at the UN Security Council in January 1976, the Arab states had been urging an emergency session of the UN General Assembly as a follow-up of the General Assembly's resolution 3236 in November 1974.

61 *Guardian*, 31 July 1980.

## Chapter 4 Israel

1 Literally, prevailing with God.

2 Hebrew is the English version of the Biblical term *Ivriim*, meaning those 'who crossed over' – the river Euphrates, in this case.

3 Jehovah is a derivative of JHVH in Hebrew. Since uttering God's name was forbidden until the second century B.C., and since Hebrew vowel points were not invented until many centuries later, the original pronunciation of the Word (for God) is unknown.

4 Genesis, Old Testament, xii, 1.

5 Ibid., xii, 7.

6 Literally, people of the sea.

7 Jew is the English version of Jeu (old French), which is a derivative of the Latin word, Judaeus: from or of Judea.

8 Palestina is a derivative of Philistia, the land of the Philistines. Significantly, the Arabic term for the Palestinians is Filistines/Falastines.

9 On the eve of the First World War there were thirteen million Jews in the world, of which six million were in Czarist Russia, and three million in Poland. Arnold Krammer, *The Forgotten Friendship: Israel and the Soviet Bloc, 1947–53*, University of Illinois Press, Urbana and London, 1974, p. 5; Nadav Safran, *Israel: The Embattled Ally*, The Belknap Press of Harvard University Press, Cambridge, Mass., and London, 1978, p. 21.

10 Plural of aliyah: literally, ascent (to Palestine); figuratively, immigration wave.

11 Sephardim, plural of Sephardi, meaning 'from Spain'. Sephardic Jews are Ladino-speaking. Ashkenazim, plural of Ashkenazi, meaning 'from Central Europe'. Ashkenazi Jews are Yiddish-speaking.

12 Histadrut is the short form of Histadrut HaKelalit Shel HaOvdim HaIrviim BeEretz Israel: General Federation of Hebrew Workers in Eretz Israel.

13 Safran, op. cit., pp. 84, 88.

14 Don Peretz, *The Government and Politics of Israel*, Westview Press, Boulder, 1979, p. 42.

15 The number of Jewish settlements went up from 47 in 1922 to 200 in 1939. Peter Mansfield, *The Arabs*, p. 252.

16 Peretz, op. cit., p. 42.
17 Maxim Ghilan, *How Israel Lost Its Soul*, p. 72.
18 The actual figures were: Arabs, 509,780; Jews, 499,020. Irene L. Gendzier (ed.), *The Middle East Reader*, Pegasus, New York, 1969, p. 338.
19 Lehy is the acronym of Lohamey Herut Y'Israel: Fighters for the Freedom of Israel. It was led by Abraham Stern.
20 David Hirst, *The Gun and the Olive Branch: The Roots of Violence in the Middle East*, Futura Publications, London, 1978, p. 125. When their dynamite ran out, the attackers worked through the remaining buildings with grenades and Sten guns. Ibid.
21 Menachim Begin, *The Revolt*, W. H. Allen, London, 1951, p. 164.
22 Hirst, op. cit., p. 134.
23 The Israelis call it the War of Independence (from Britain); and the Arabs the Palestine War.
24 Safran, op. cit., pp. 62–3. At the ratio of two dead to five injured, the Israelis probably suffered about 8,000 deaths. 'No accurate figure is available for Arab deaths, but the Israelis admit to 6,000 dead,' writes Colin Smith. *The Palestinians*, Minority Rights Group, London, 1975, p. 6.
25 Part of the reason for this postponement lay with the Israelis' reluctance to define their country's constitutional boundaries. The statement by David Ben-Gurion, the state's first prime minister, that Israel's borders extended 'as far as our army can reach' summed up the national mood. Cited in *The Middle East*, January 1980, p. 19.
26 *The Times*, 8 October 1976; *Guardian*, 19 June 1980.
27 See p. 217.
28 V. D. Segre, *Israel: A Society in Transition*, Oxford University Press, London and New York, 1971, p. 179; and Mansfield, op. cit., p. 302. Israel's material losses were more than offset by its capture of Egyptian weapons and military supplies.
29 *Statistical Abstract Of Israel, 1978*, Central Bureau of Statistics, Government of Israel, Jerusalem, 1978, p. 162.
30 *The Times*, 15 April 1968; *New York Times*, 22 October 1968.
31 Tabitha Petran, *Syria*, p. 199; Peter Mansfield (ed.), *The Middle East*, pp. 239, 356; and Safran, op. cit., p. 246.
32 Herut, meaning freedom, is the short form of Tenua Herut: Freedom Movement.
33 Mapam is the acronym of Mifleget Poalim Meuhedet: United Workers' Party.
34 Mansfield, *The Arabs*, p. 362; and Safran, op. cit., p. 311.
35 Literally, unity.
36 The breakdown of the Jewish colonies was: sixty-six in the West Bank, twenty-one in Gaza, and thirty in the Golan Heights. *Daily Telegraph*, 5 June 1980. By the middle of 1980 the Israeli government had acquired 26 per cent of the land of the West Bank through expropriation or compulsory purchase orders. *Guardian*, 8 January 1981. During the run-up to the parliamentary election of 30 June 1981 the Israeli government accelerated the process of expansion of the sixty-six West Bank settlements, with the enlargement of the Kiryat Arba colony, overlooking Hebron, along entailing confiscation of 4,000 acres of Arab land. *Sunday Times*, 22 March 1981.
37 Literally, the festival of 'breaking the fast'.
38 *Daily Telegraph*, 14 August 1980. The religious importance of Jerusalem to Muslim Arabs can be gauged by the fact that it is called Al Quds (The Holy) in Arabic. 'While Mecca is the historic and traditional focus of the Islamic faith, the first shrine of Islam is Jerusalem,' wrote Mohamed Heikal, an Egyptian journalist and author. *Sunday Times*, 18 January 1981.

## Chapter 5 Socio-economic context: an outline

1 Article 31 of the South Yemeni constitution expressly calls on the state to 'liberate society from backward tribalism'. Michael C. Hudson, *Arab Politics*, pp. 356–7.
2 *Arab World File*, no. 936, 19 April 1978.
3 Ibid., no. 509, 4 August 1976; no. 721, 10 August 1977.
4 The actual figure was 53.4 per cent in 1975. *Arab World File*, no. 721, 10 August 1977.
5 Ibid., no. 425, 31 December 1975; no. 887, 22 February 1978.
6 Until the creation of the Yemeni Socialist Party in October 1978, the South Yemeni regime allowed the existence of more than one party of the working classes. See p. 179.
7 For instance, the (tertiary) service sector in Saudi Arabia amounted to 45 per cent of the non-oil gross domestic product in 1976. *Arab World File*, no. 832, 21 December 1977.

## Chapter 6 Conservative forces

1 Helen Lackner, *A House Built on Sand: A Political Economy of Saudi Arabia*, Ithaca Press, London, 1978, p. 74.
2 *Time*, 29 May 1978, p. 21; *Newsweek*, 3 March 1980, p. 21.
3 Oil production rose from 50,000 bpd in 1945 to 500,000 in 1949. Michael C. Hudson, *Arab Politics*, p. 174.
4 The 'Free Princes' were so sure of the impending change that shortly after Saud was reinstated as the supreme executive, they announced on Mecca radio in December 1960 that Saudi Arabia would soon be declared a constitutional monarchy. Lackner, op. cit., p. 63.
5 Saud was sent into exile. He died in Athens in 1969.
6 This point promised 'the promulgation of a Basic Law for the government of the country, drawn from the Koran and the Tradition of the Prophet (i.e. Hadith) and the acts of the Orthodox Caliphs, that will set forth explicitly the fundamental principles of government and the relationship between the governor and the governed, organise the various powers of the state and the relationship among these powers, and provide for the basic rights of the citizen, including the right to freely express his opinion within the limit of the Islamic belief and public policy'. Cited in Lackner, op. cit., p. 65.
7 Ibid., p. 101.
8 *New York Times*, 29 March 1967.
9 *Le Monde*, 6, 7, 8, 26 September 1969.
10 As a progeny of Tarfah al Shaikh, Feisal belonged to the Shaikh clan related to the founder of Wahhabism.
11 *Newsweek*, 3 March 1980, p. 22. Huge fortunes have been made by the princes, acting as 'agents' for foreign companies anxious to secure orders. One such deal involved $200 million in agent's fees. The other familiar tack is for the royal family to grant land – secretly earmarked for residential or industrial development – to a prince, who then sells it to the government at a grossly inflated price. Ibid.
12 Lackner, op. cit., p. 76; *Guardian*, 28 May 1979.
13 *The Middle East*, May 1978, p. 31.
14 Lackner, op. cit., pp. 77–8.
15 'Report on Saudi Arabia' in *Mainstream*, 10 May 1980, pp. 15–28 (a reprint

of the *Middle East Currency Reports*, March, 1980, published by International Currency Review, London), p. 16.

16 *Time*, 29 May 1978, p. 17.

17 Interview with a Saudi journalist in London on 12 November 1978.

18 'Report on Saudi Arabia' in *Mainstream*, 10 May 1980, p. 17.

19 Ibid., p. 21.

20 In the late 1970s, military and quasi-military American personnel engaged in training the Saudi forces, as well as building three vast military cities in the kingdom, amounted to 20–25,000. Interview with a former Saudi Arabia correspondent of a British daily in London on 13 May 1980. The corresponding figure in 1975 was 10,000. Lackner, op. cit., p. 77.

21 'Report on Saudi Arabia' in *Mainstream*, 10 May 1980, p. 25.

22 *International Herald Tribune*, 18 December 1979; interview with a Saudi journalist in London on 24 June 1980; *Guardian*, 8 September 1980.

23 Of those executed, forty-one were Saudis, ten Egyptians, six South Yemenis, three Kuwaitis, one North Yemeni, one Sudanese, and one Iraqi. *Guardian*, 10 January 1980.

24 'Report on Saudi Arabia' in *Mainstream*, 10 May 1980, p. 27. According to *Le Point*, a Paris-based French magazine: 'The Grand Mosque occupation appeared to be part of a much wider revolt with sympathy from inside the Saudi army, as there were other incidents, including a bomb explosion in the royal palace.' Cited in *Guardian*, 29 January 1980.

25 *The Times*, 5 December 1979. The other political organisation which claimed to have played a part in the uprising was the Islamic Revolutionary Movement in the Arabian Peninsula. *Newsweek*, 17 December 1979, p. 17.

26 *Newsweek*, 17 December 1979, p. 17.

27 *International Herald Tribune*, 4 December 1979.

28 Interview with a Saudi journalist in London on 24 June 1980.

29 *Observer*, 12 August 1979. 'Custodian of Islam's holy places, Saudi Arabia has no intention of being upstaged in religious rectitude by Ayatollah Khomeini,' wrote a correspondent recently returned from Riyadh.

30 *Guardian*, 21 June 1977.

31 'The Saudi royal family . . . apparently distrusts its own army,' reported Della Denman from Islamabad. *Guardian*, 8 September 1980. 'The first two brigades of the Pakistani force have already left for Riyadh,' reported Bruce Loudon from Islamabad. 'The Pakistanis, who will wear Saudi uniforms and practically be integrated into the Saudi army, will be paid Saudi rates, which are consistently higher than in Pakistan. The arrangement was settled last week when Crown Prince Fahd held talks with General Mohammed Zia-ul-Haq, Pakistan's military ruler. The Pakistani force will include infantry, armoured, and anti-aircraft units.' *Daily Telegraph*, 20 December 1980.

32 *8 Days*, 8 March 1980, p. 16.

33 See p. 36.

34 *The Middle East*, November 1977, p. 10.

35 'There are rival theories about who actually pulled the trigger [to kill Hamdi], but the consensus is that Ghashmi and the army officers who succeeded Hamdi were the ones who killed him; and – no one fails to add – they did so in league with Saudi Arabia,' reported David Hirst. *Guardian*, 31 August 1978.

36 Ibid., 31 August 1978. The Saudi subsidies to the North Yemeni budget were running at $700 million a year. Ibid., 30 August 1978. Sanaa uses most of these funds to pay the military and the civil service. When Riyadh reduced its subsidy (paid monthly) in December 1979, Sanaa could not pay its civil servants. *The Middle East*, April 1980, p. 25.

37 'The Saudis maintain the tribal buffer zone along their own border with North Yemen by keeping the tribals supplied with arms and money; and use the Islamic Front of the tribes sometimes to put pressure on Sanaa, and sometimes farther south to fight the National Democratic Front,' reported John Bulloch. *Daily Telegraph*, 26 November 1980.
38 *New Statesman*, 2 January 1976, p. 6.
39 Hudson, op. cit., p. 208; and *Arab World File*, no. 667, 8 June 1977.
40 *Oman: A Nation Builds its Future*, Ministry of Information and Culture, Muscat, 1979, p. 34.
41 *The Times*, 18 October 1975; *Middle East Economic Digest*, 18 November 1977, p. 4. Of the five infantry battalions, for instance, three consisted of Pakistanis. Ibid.
42 Hudson, op. cit., pp. 208–9.
43 The other member was Sudan.
44 *Observer*, 11 March 1979; *Time*, 10 December 1979, p. 29. 'There have been persistent reports of up to 8,000 Egyptian troops being active in Oman.' *The Middle East*, June 1979, p. 20.
45 *Newsweek*, 3 March 1980, p. 23.
46 At 297,000 bpd in 1979, the oil production was a quarter down on the figure for 1976. *8 Days*, 5 January 1980, p. 17.
47 *Newsweek*, 3 March 1980, p. 20. Oil output had declined steadily from 70,000 bpd in 1972 to 59,000 in 1976. *The Times*, 16 December 1976.
48 Of the 739 policemen in 1959, 73 per cent were non-Bahraini; and of the twenty-nine officers, 59 per cent were British. Fred Halliday, *Arabia Without Sultans*, pp. 445–6.
49 Hudson, op. cit., p. 196.
50 Cited in *Arab World File*, no. 453, 17 March 1976.
51 Ibid.
52 Peter Mansfield (ed.), *The Middle East*, p. 196; Hudson, op. cit., p. 194.
53 Halliday, op. cit., p. 449.
54 In the 1950s and 1960s Dubai became known for its import and export of gold. In 1970 as much as 250 tons of gold passed through Dubai on its way to the Indian subcontinent from the West. Halliday, op. cit., p. 453.
55 Michael Tomkinson, *The United Arab Emirates*, Tomkinson, London, 1975, p. 37.
56 Hudson, op. cit., p. 202.
57 Cited in *The Middle East*, June 1980, p. 31.
58 See p. 20.
59 During the period 1952–60 the percentage of school-age children enrolled at school rose from 17 to 72. Hudson, op. cit., p. 148.
60 Kuwaiti nationals were only 30 per cent of the total labour force in 1976. *The Times*, 12 July 1977.
61 Ibid. Taking into account their investments in Kuwait, the total may well have exceeded $10,000 million.
62 Cited in *The Middle East*, July 1980, p. 30.
63 Ibid., p. 31.
64 *Sunday Times*, 30 December 1979.
65 *Guardian*, 26 July 1979.
66 See p. 22.
67 *Newsweek*, 3 March 1980, p. 20; *The Middle East*, July 1980, p. 32.
68 *Sunday Times*, 30 December 1979.
69 *World Report, August 1980*, published by The First National Bank of Chicago, cited in *The Middle East*, September 1980, p. 67.
70 Charles L. Taylor and Michael C. Hudson, *World Handbook of Political and*

*Social Indicators*, Yale University Press, New Haven, Conn., and London, 1972, p. 207.
71 *Arab World File*, no. 793, 2 November 1977. Actual figures in Jordanian dinars were: Saudi Arabia–Kuwait, 20 million; America, 15 million.
72 *UN Statistical Yearbook*, 1972, table 196; ibid., 1974, table 197. The actual increase was 620 per cent.
73 Hudson, op. cit., p. 215.
74 Interview in Amman in February 1978.
75 Elieze Be'eri, *Army Officers in Arab Politics and Society*, Pall Mall, London, 1970, p. 342.
76 *The Middle East*, January 1979, p. 23.
77 Hudson, op. cit., p. 218.
78 Moshe Ma'oz (ed.), *Palestinian Arab Politics*, Jerusalem Academic Press, Jerusalem, 1975, p. 33.
79 The Liberation Party was thus advocating ideas which were to become the prime movers of the Islamic revolution in Iran in 1978–9.
80 Ma'oz, op. cit., pp. 37, 39, 41.
81 The Muslim Brotherhood's active membership was about 700. Ma'oz, op. cit., p. 41.
82 Ibid., p. 25.
83 Interview with Tasleem in Amman in February 1978.
84 *Guardian*, 9 August 1980; *Daily Telegraph*, 25 August 1980.
85 Tabitha Petran, *Syria*, p. 153.
86 *Arab World File*, no. 801, 16 November 1977.
87 Cited in Petran, op. cit., p. 197.
88 The article was entitled: 'The Means of Creating the New Arab Man'. In the offending sentence the author urged that 'God, religion, feudalism, capitalism, and colonialism, and all the values that prevailed under the old society' be consigned to 'the museum of history', and that 'absolute belief in man's ability' be treated as the only new value. Cited in ibid., p. 197.
89 *Arab World File*, no. 825, 14 December 1977.
90 Moshe Ma'oz, *Syria Under Hafiz al-Asad*, Hebrew University of Jerusalem, Jerusalem, 1975, p. 10.
91 *Arab World File*, no. 838, 28 December 1977.
92 President Assad's speeches of 6 and 21 October 1973 on Damascus radio. Cited in Moshe Ma'oz, *Syria Under Hafiz al-Asad*, p. 11.
93 *Sunday Times*, 16 April 1978.
94 *Guardian*, 25 June and 4 September 1979. Ibrahim Yusuf managed to escape after the Aleppo incident, but was killed about a year later by the Syrian security forces. Ibid., 18 August 1980.
95 Ibid., 4 and 7 September 1979; *Observer*, 9 September 1979.
96 *The Middle East*, November 1979, p. 14.
97 *Guardian*, 12 March 1980.
98 *Sunday Times*, 30 March 1980.
99 *Guardian*, 28 June 1980.
100 *Daily Telegraph*, 8 July 1980. That the government's measures had taken 'a heavy toll of the organisation's members' was conceded by Adnan Saad al Din, the Brotherhood's Syrian leader, in an interview to the *Daily Telegraph* in London (20 January 1981). By then the Brotherhood had split, with one wing being led by Adnan Saad al Din, and the other by Issam Attar, living in exile in Aachen, West Germany. *The Middle East*, June 1981, p. 9.
101 *Guardian*, 3 September 1980. However, a complete merger of Syria and Libya was ruled out by President Assad, who reportedly told Yasser Arafat that only the foreign, economic and military policies of the two countries

would be 'merged'. *The Middle East*, November 1980, p. 19.

102 Cited in W. F. Abboushi, *Political Systems of the Middle East*, p. 143.

103 Peter Mansfield, *The Middle East*, p. 74.

104 Ibid., p. 74.

105 One Egyptian feddan equals 1.038 acres.

106 *Arab World File*, no. 120, 5 February 1975.

107 Raymond William Baker, *Egypt's Uncertain Revolution under Nasser and Sadat*, Harvard University Press, Cambridge, Mass., and London, 1978, p. 241.

108 Its circulation was about 80,000. *Arab World File*, no. 771, 12 October 1977.

109 Before the official crackdown the Repentance and Flight sect was about 3,000 to 4,000 strong. *Arab World File*, no. 771, 12 October 1977.

110 The fact that many names are common to both Copts and Egyptian Muslims means that a Christian convert to Islam does not even have to change his name, and vice versa.

111 *The Times*, 16 November 1978.

112 Ibid.

113 A law passed soon after the January 1977 riots made a participant in a strike or demonstration, which 'may harm public interest or damage the national economy', liable to life imprisonment with hard labour. *Arab World File*, no. 636, 4 May 1977.

114 The students were reported to be enrolling members to their movement outside the campuses. *Observer*, 18 March 1979.

115 *Guardian*, 21 February, 1979.

116 Ibid., 24 June 1980.

117 Cited in *Guardian*, 24 June 1980.

118 Significantly, Pierre Gamayel and Camille Chamoun, the leading figures of the Lebanese Front, had visited Israel in May. *The Middle East*, September 1978, p. 18. Within the next two years relations between Israel and the Lebanese Front had become so established that the Israeli chief of staff visited Jounieh, the capital of the Christian enclave in the north, three times during March–April 1981. *Daily Telegraph*, 11 April 1981.

119 The full name of the organisation is The Lebanese Kataeb Social Democratic Party. See earlier note 34, chapter 3.

120 Roger Owen, 'Crisis in the Lebanon', *New Society*, 23 October 1975, p. 209.

121 Harald Vocke, *The Lebanese War: Its Origins and Political Dimensions*, Hurst, London, 1978, p. 25.

122 *The Times*, 19 September 1974.

123 *Economic and Political Weekly*, 24 June 1976, p. 1109; *The Times*, 27 October 1976; *Guardian*, 16 August 1977.

124 *Guardian*, 16 September 1978.

125 Interview with Maroun Helou of the National Liberal Party in Beirut on 6 March 1978.

126 Interview with Bashir Gamayel in Beirut on 4 March 1978.

127 *Guardian*, 4 July 1977.

128 Ibid., 31 July 1979; *The Times*, 24 November 1979.

129 *The Middle East*, September 1978, pp. 14, 23.

130 Ibid., May 1978, p. 34.

131 *Sunday Times*, 15 October 1978.

132 These ports were the chief source of smuggled goods into Lebanon, and thus very lucrative to control. The Kataeb alleged that the NLP was involved in exporting hashish to Europe. *Guardian*, 10 July 1980.

133 Ibid.

134 In early 1976 only 40 per cent of the 2.7 million Lebanese were Christian.

*New York Times*, 15 February 1976. Allowing for the exodus of Christians during the rest of the civil war, and the presence of Christians outside their main area, the Christian population of the mini-state could only be under one million.

135 'Villagers in the region [of Zahle] say that Israeli troops are operating alongside the Phalangists in this area', reported David Butter of Inter Press Service. *8 Days*, 2 May 1981, p. 16.

136 *Sunday Times*, 12 April 1981. Also see pp. 315–16.

137 *Guardian*, 15 April 1981. Earlier John Bulloch of the *Daily Telegraph* had reported that General Eitan had visited Jounieh three times during March–April. 11 April 1981.

138 *Guardian*, 25 May 1981.

Chapter 7 Centrist forces: secular and religious

1 Cited in *Arab World File*, no. 147, 11 December 1974.

2 Peter Mansfield (ed.), *The Middle East*, p. 224.

3 Mahmoud Hussein, *Class Conflict in Egypt: 1945–70*, Monthly Review Press, New York and London, 1973, p. 125.

4 *Arab World File*, no. 147, 11 December 1974.

5 Cited in ibid.

6 Iliya Harik, 'The single party as a subordinate movement', in *World Politics*, October 1973, p. 87.

7 The Second Agrarian Reform Law of June 1961 lowered the land ceiling for a family holding from 300 to 100 feddans.

8 *Arab World File*, no. 153, 16 December 1974.

9 The official definition of a worker was very wide: anybody employed by a company who was not a university postgraduate or member of a professional syndicate. Interview with Salaama Ahmed Salaama of *Al Ahram* in Cairo on 12 April 1978.

10 This scheme was launched independently of the organisational reform of the ASU that followed, and resulted in the creation of the 'secret' or 'special' apparatus operating at universities, schools, clubs, government offices, and factories. The task was assigned to two presidential aides, Sharawi Juma and Sami Sharaf, who later worked in conjunction with Ali Sabri. Iliya Harik, op. cit., pp. 97–8; Shimon Shamir, 'The Marxists in Egypt: The "Licensed Infiltration" in practice', in Michael Confino and Shimon Shamir (eds), *The USSR and the Middle East*, Israel Universities Press, Jerusalem, 1973, p. 310.

11 Raymond William Baker, *Egypt's Uncertain Revolution under Nasser and Sadat*, p. 100.

12 Cited in Iliya Harik, op. cit., p. 93.

13 Lafif Lakhdar, 'The development of class struggle in Egypt', in *Khamsin 5*, 1978, p. 68.

14 During the last four years of Nasser's rule exports by the private sector increased eight-fold. *Egyptian Gazette*, 26 February 1971.

15 All the remaining eight seats, to be nominated by the president, went to the Copts: the minority which often found itself totally unrepresented in the list of the ASU – and of the subsequent parties/tribunes.

16 At the same time President Sadat retained the authority to appoint the chairman and half of the directors of these publishing companies. Following the establishment of an elected Consultative Council of 210 members in May 1980, the ASU was formally dissolved and its press powers transferred to the

Consultative Council. Since the Council was dominated by Sadat's National Democratic Party (with 205 members), the press was in effect controlled by the ruling party. 'Now every chief editor [appointed by the Consultative Council] is a censor because he is chosen by the government,' said Ihsan Abdul Kaddous, an Egyptian writer. 'Every night he gets a telephone call telling him what not to publish.' *8 Days*, 7 February 1981, p. 14.

17 Interview with Jamal Utifi, deputy speaker of the Egyptian parliament, in Cairo on 9 April 1978.

18 *Events*, 16 June 1978, p. 21.

19 Ibid.

20 *International Herald Tribune*, 22 May 1978; *Guardian*, 23 May 1978.

21 *Middle East International*, July 1978, p. 12.

22 *Events*, 22 September 1978, p. 24.

23 When Mustapha Amin, an ardent supporter of Sadat, said in his column in *Al Akhbar* that the Arab Socialist parliamentarians should have waited to study the new party's programme before joining, he was immediately deprived of his daily column. *Guardian*, 21 August 1978.

24 *The Middle East*, October 1978, p. 39.

25 For instance, the February 1977 referendum on punishing strikers and unauthorised demonstrators included inter alia a provision for abolishing income tax for low income groups. *Arab World File*, no. 636, 4 May 1977.

26 A list of complaints about electoral irregularities by an opposition party ran into seven foolscap pages. *Guardian*, 11 June 1979.

27 Ibid., 10 July 1979.

28 *New Left Review*, no. 98, July–August 1976, p. 90.

29 Raymond William Baker puts the number of the super-rich families, who lost their properties during Nasser's regime, as 'at least 600'. Op. cit., p. 156.

30 *New York Times*, 10 February 1976.

31 *Guardian*, 25 May 1978.

32 'The revolution aims at creating socialist society without class distinction,' said Nasser in a public speech. Cited in Elieze Be'eri, *Army Officers in Arab Politics and Society*, p. 392.

33 Cited in *The Middle East*, March 1977, p. 42.

34 Tabitha Petran, *Syria*, p. 92. 'The great majority of recruits to the Baath belonged to the middle and small bourgeoisie,' states Eric Rouleau, a French journalist and author. 'Baathist ideology seemed equally attractive to the middle classes, who were sincerely nationalist but hostile both to the traditional political formations in Syria, dominated by the large landowning and merchant bourgeoisie, and to the Communist Party.' 'What is Baath?', in Irene L. Gendzier, *The Middle East Reader*, p. 162.

35 'Arab Political Movements', in Peter Mansfield, op. cit., p. 84.

36 Petran, op. cit., p. 111.

37 Between 1948 and 1956 the Syrian army's strength rose from 10,000 to 42,000. Petran, op. cit., p. 97; Walter Laqueur, 'Syria on the Move: Ascendancy of the Left Wing', in Gendzier, op. cit., p. 151.

38 Petran, op. cit., p. 122.

39 Ibid., p. 125.

40 Eric Rouleau, 'What is Baath?', in Gendzier, op. cit., pp. 169–70. The concentration of landownership could be gauged by the fact that four families in Hama province owned eighty villages, and forty families in the Jezira region possessed 90 per cent of all land. *Arab World File*, no. 133, 20 November 1974.

41 Ibid.

42 Cited in George Lenczowski (ed.), *The Political Awakening in the Middle*

*East*, Prentice Hall, Englewood Cliffs, NJ, 1970, p. 136.

43 Rouleau, op. cit., p. 169.

44 Interview with Nassur Sachour of the General Union of Peasants in Damascus on 23 March 1978. The Union's claimed membership then stood at 265,036.

45 *Arab World File*, no. 144, 4 December 1974; Petran, op. cit., p. 207.

46 See p. 104.

47 Petran, op. cit., pp. 182–3.

48 *Arab World*, 20 July 1966.

49 Rouleau, op. cit., p. 170.

50 Ibid., pp. 170–1; *Al Hayat*, 4 December 1971.

51 Article 7 of the Covenant of the National Progressive Front states: 'All forms of strife and conflict in the ranks of the army and armed forces should be eliminated and shunned altogether. Therefore the non-Baathist parties in the Front commit themselves not to found any organisation or pursue any party activity within the ranks of the armed forces.' Article 9, pertaining to the students, states: 'The non-Baathist parties commit themselves to work hard on ending their organisational activities in this particular sector.' *Covenant of the National Progressive Front*, The Baath Arab Socialist Party National Leadership, Damascus, March 1972, pp. 13–14.

52 See p. 105.

53 Excepting the General Federation of Trade Unions (established in 1936), all other mass organisations were founded by the Baath. In 1969, of the 300,000 industrial workers, 145,337 were members of the 165 unions affiliated to the General Federation. The non-Baathists were tolerated at various levels of the trade union hierarchy. Petran, op. cit., pp. 230–2.

54 Moshe Ma'oz, *Syria Under Hafiz al-Asad*, p. 8.

55 *The Middle East*, February 1980, p. 17.

56 Ibid., September 1979, pp. 13–14.

57 See p. 134.

58 Roný Gabbay, *Communism and Agrarian Reform in Iraq*, p. 117.

59 Phoebe A. Marr, 'The Political Elite in Iraq', in George Lenczowski (ed.), *Political Elites in the Middle East Arab World*, American Enterprise Institute for Public Policy Research, Washington, DC, 1975, p. 132.

60 Cited in Malcolm H. Kerr, *The Arab Cold War*, Oxford University Press, London and New York, 3rd edn, 1975, p. 123.

61 By early 1978 seventy-seven collective farms and forty state farms covered a total of two million donums. *Arab World File*, no. 954, 10 May 1978.

62 Gabbay, op. cit., pp. 118, 120.

63 The exact proportion of Kurds to the Iraqi population is not reliably known yet.

64 Majid Khadduri, *Socialist Iraq*, Middle East Institute, Washington, DC, 1978, p. 38.

65 Michael C. Hudson, *Arab Politics*, p. 275.

66 *The Middle East*, August 1976, p. 11.

67 Hudson, op. cit., p. 275.

68 Cited in Mansfield (ed.), op. cit., p. 430.

69 Of the 9,543 Iraqi casualties, 1,640 were killed and the rest wounded. *Guardian*, 24 October 1975.

70 Khadduri, op. cit., p. 68.

71 *The Middle East*, March 1977, p. 44; *Guardian*, 6 April 1977.

72 Cited in *Guardian*, 28 February 1979.

73 Ibid.

74 *Observer*, 24 June 1979.

75 *Daily Telegraph*, 10 July 1979. Persecution escalated: Al Daawa members in

exile in Iran claimed a thousand 'martyrs' during 1979 and 1980 'in combat, under torture, or on the gallows'. *Guardian*, 29 December 1980.

76 Ibid., 30 July 1979.

77 Thirty-three of the accused were sentenced to various prison terms, and thirteen were acquitted. Ibid., 9 August 1979.

78 *The Middle East*, September 1979, p. 13.

79 *Observer*, 5 August 1979.

80 Ibid., 20 May 1979. In 1980 oil revenue was running at $45.7 billion a year before the outbreak of war with Iran. *8 Days*, 18 October 1980, p. 5.

81 While Lesser and Greater Tumb were occupied exclusively by Iran, Abu Musa was shared by Iran with the UAE. In November 1971 the emir of Sharjah allowed the Shah to occupy part of Abu Musa on the understanding that the Shah would pay him an annual subsidy of £1.5 million until his oil income reached £3 million a year. Fred Halliday, *Arabia Without Sultans*, p. 459. In contrast, Shaikh Sakr ibn Mohammed al Qassemi, the ruler of Ras al Khaima, refused to cooperate with the Shah: he also refused to join the British-backed United Arab Emirates. Acting in connivance with the (departing) British, the Shah occupied the two Tumbs by using force.

82 *Guardian*, 15 April and 31 October 1980.

83 *Sunday Times*, 27 July 1980.

84 Significantly, in one of their frequent broadcasts from Baghdad, both Bakhtiar and Ovessi had reportedly appealed to schoolchildren to stay away from classes on 22 September. *Daily Telegraph*, 26 September 1980.

85 *Sunday Times*, 26 October 1980.

86 Cited in *Guardian*, 20 October 1980.

87 By the end of October, Iraqi forces had suffered 1,800 deaths. The total military strength of Iraq was 242,250. *Sunday Times*, 28 September 1980; *Guardian*, 30 October 1980. But as the war continued, combat deaths mounted. Iraq was reported to have suffered 5,000 casualties in capturing Khoramshahr alone, in early 1981. *Sunday Times*, 24 May 1981.

88 Cited in *Guardian*, 20 October 1980. On the eve of the Islamic new year, Saddam Hussein called for Muslim support for Iraq's 'holy war' against the descendants of the Persian empire, which was 'destroyed by Islam' fourteen centuries ago. Ibid., 10 November 1980.

89 *Guardian*, 31 October 1980. By the following spring, Shia resistance had grown from occasional shoot-outs in Baghdad between Al Daawa gunmen, operating from the back of pick-up trucks, and the Baathist militia, to the blowing up of the Baghdad–Basra railway ninety miles south of the capital. Taking advantage of the daily blackout, necessitated by the war, Al Daawa activists had intensified their campaign of sabotage and assassinations. Ibid., 24 December 1980; *Sunday Times*, 24 May 1981.

90 *The Middle East*, July 1980, p. 33.

91 *Guardian*, 10 January 1980; *The Middle East*, July 1980, p. 32. Also see note 23, chapter 6.

92 See pp. 82, 85.

93 *8 Days*, 20 September 1980, p. 19.

94 *New Statesman*, 21 July 1978, p. 82.

95 *8 Days*, 20 September 1980, p. 19

96 *Middle East International*, January 1978, p. 15.

97 This figure is probably made up of three quarter million North Yemenis (about 600,000 workers plus the families of a section of them), and a quarter million South Yemeni refugees. Interview with a former Saudi Arabia correspondent of a British daily in London on 13 May 1980; and *8 Days*, September 1980, p. 4. No official statistics are available.

98 Estimated remittances to North Yemen in 1978 and 1979 were respectively $1.2 billion and $1.5 billion. *Observer*, 11 February 1979; *8 Days*, 2 May 1981, p. 8.
99 *Guardian*, 31 August 1978.
100 *Events*, 1 October 1976, p. 26.
101 See p. 90.
102 *Times Higher Education Supplement*, 14 July 1978, p. 8.
103 *The Middle East*, July 1978, p. 33.
104 The rebels alleged that Lt-Colonel Ali Abdullah Saleh had killed President Hamdi at Ghashmi's residence in October 1977. *Middle East Research and Information Project*, no. 81 (October 1979), p. 22.
105 Ibid.; *The Middle East*, December 1978, p. 12.
106 Baghdad promised Sanaa $300 million in aid in 1980. *The Middle East*, February 1980, p. 18.
107 Ibid., November 1980, p. 15.
108 Moshe Ma'oz, *Palestinian Arab Politics*, p. 36.
109 Riad N. El Rayyes and Duniya Nahas (eds), *Guerrillas for Palestine*, An Nahar Press Services SARL, Beirut, 1974, pp. 49–50.
110 Gérard Chaliand, *The Palestinian Resistance*, Penguin Books, Harmondsworth, 1972, p. 70.
111 Interview with Anis Sayegh, former head of the PLO research department, in Beirut on 14 March 1978.
112 Chaliand, op. cit., p. 70.
113 Hudson, op. cit., p. 302. In 1965 Fatah's membership was about 200. Interview with Rashed Khalidi of the *Journal of Palestine Studies* in Beirut on 1 March 1978.
114 The following political-military organisations were affiliated to the PLO at the end of the fifteenth assembly of the PNC in April 1981: Fatah, Saiqa, the PFLP, the DFLP, the PFLP-General Command, Arab Liberation Front, and Palestine Liberation Front. *Guardian*, 20 April 1981. In addition, such popular organisations as the General Union of Palestinian Workers were affiliated to the PLO.
115 Rayyes and Nahas, op. cit., p. 148.
116 Ibid., pp. 149–50.
117 *Daily Telegraph*, 27 May 1980.

## Chapter 8 Leftist forces

1 During its early years the breakaway organisation called itself the Popular Democratic Front for the Liberation of Palestine. But for the sake of uniformity, only the latter name, the Democratic Front for the Liberation of Palestine, has been used throughout the text.
2 By 1971 the PFLP was known to have 2,000 to 3,000 members, together with a commando force of 2,000. Gérard Chaliand, *The Palestinian Resistance*, p. 83.
3 *Arab World File*, no. 622, 6 October 1976.
4 The first PFLP hijacking, directed by Wadi Haddad, a colleague of George Habash, occurred in July 1968. It involved taking an El Al (Israeli) airline plane to Algiers, and securing the release of sixteen Palestinian prisoners in Israel. *Kuwait Times*, 2 April 1978.
5 Nayef Hawatmeh's first exposure to communism and Arab Communists occurred in late 1958, when he was sent to Baghdad as an emissary of the

Beirut-based Arab Nationalist Movement. Walid W. Kazziha, *Revolutionary Transformation in the Arab World*, Charles Knight, London, 1975, pp. 37–9.

6 Chaliand, op. cit., p. 90.
7 Ibid., p. 92.
8 *Arab World File*, no. 95, 9 October 1974.
9 *Le Monde*, 23 March 1974.
10 David Hirst, *The Gun and the Olive Branch*, pp. 329–30.
11 M. S. Agwani, *Communism in the Arab East*, Asia Publishing House, New Delhi and London, 1969, p. 72.
12 Ibid., p. 74.
13 Ibid., p. 151.
14 See pp. 100–1.
15 *Arab World File*, no. 736, 31 August 1977. The party membership of 2,000 – divided evenly between the West Bank and East Bank – consisted primarily of workers, white-collar employees, and professionals. Moshe Ma'oz, *Palestinian Arab Politics*, p. 41.
16 Agwani, op. cit., p. 157.
17 See p. 159.
18 Cited in Agwani, op. cit., pp. 15–16.
19 Walter Z. Laqueur, *The Soviet Union and the Middle East*, Routledge & Kegan Paul, London, 1959, pp. 142, 145.
20 Agwani, op. cit., p. 25; *Arab World File*, no. 449, 10 March 1976.
21 *Labour Monthly*, February 1946, p. 45.
22 The Organisation of Communist Action in Lebanon emerged in May 1971 as the result of the merger of the Socialist Lebanon, a leftist group, and the Organisation of Lebanese Socialists, an offshoot of the Arab Nationalist Movement in Lebanon, Tareq Y. Ismael, *The Arab Left*, Syracuse University Press, Syracuse, NY, 1976, pp. 62, 69.
23 *Arab World File*, no. 502, 12 May 1976.
24 *Observer*, 2 November 1975.
25 *Events*, 15 October 1976, p. 10.
26 In order to withstand the repression unleashed against them, the Communist parties of Syria and Lebanon united in 1950. This continued until 1958 when, following the formation of the United Arab Republic of Egypt and Syria, the two parties separated.
27 *Labour Monthly*, February 1946, pp. 45–6.
28 Tabitha Petran, *Syria*, p. 108.
29 See pp. 43, 131–2.
30 Petran, op. cit., p. 120.
31 Gordon S. Torrey, *Syrian Politics and the Military*, Ohio State University Press, Columbus, 1964, p. 295.
32 See pp. 43, 132.
33 See pp. 104–5, 135.
34 Petran, op. cit., p. 184.
35 Jean Pennar, *The USSR and the Arabs: The Ideological Dimension*, Hurst, London, 1973, p. 108.
36 See pp. 266–7.
37 During May–June 1980 three Communists were assassinated by the Brotherhood. From mid-1979 to mid-1980, more than a dozen Soviet military advisers were killed by the Brotherhood. *The Times*, 23 June 1980; *Daily Telegraph*, 26 June 1980.
38 *Daily American*, 4 January 1979; *Guardian*, 27 February 1979.
39 The party was informally established in 1927, three years after the first

Marxist study circle had been formed in the country. Jean Pennar, op. cit., pp. 37–8.
40 Rony Gabbay, *Communism and Agrarian Reform in Iraq*, p. 52.
41 Ibid., pp. 52, 73.
42 For the remaining constituents, see p. 139.
43 Gabbay, op. cit., p. 63.
44 Cited in *The Iraqi Communist Party and the Agrarian Problem* (in Arabic), Pamphlet 14, Iraqi Communist Party, Baghdad, 1974, p. 49.
45 Gabbay, op. cit., p. 168.
46 Majid Khadduri, *Republican Iraq*, pp. 109–10.
47 Kazziha, op. cit., p. 80.
48 Uriel Dann, *Iraq Under Qassem: A Political History, 1958–1963*, Pall Mall, London, 1969, pp. 223–4; Khadduri, op. cit., pp. 124–5.
49 See p. 327.
50 Oleg M. Smolansky, *The Soviet Union and the Arab East under Khrushchev*, Bucknell University Press, Lewisburg, Pa, 1974, p. 161.
51 *Pravda*, 25 October 1961. However, many of the death sentences were later commuted.
52 *New Age*, 12 February 1961.
53 See p. 140.
54 See p. 327.
55 *Economic and Political Weekly*, 10 June 1978, p. 932; Eric Rouleau, 'What is the Baath?', in Irene L. Gendzier (ed.), *The Middle East Reader*, p. 169.
56 Gabbay, op. cit., p. 174.
57 Dann, op. cit., p. 379.
58 *Al Nida* (The Call), 11 June 1965.
59 Cited in Majid Khadduri, *Socialist Iraq*, pp. 86–7.
60 *Tareeq al Shaab*, 8 and 16 May 1976.
61 Ibid., 13 July 1976.
62 *Events*, 14 July 1978, p. 21.
63 Iraqi–American trade rose from $20 million in 1965 to $300 million in 1975. *The Middle East*, February 1976, p. 30. The trend continued: American exports to Iraq were expected to exceed $1,000 million in 1980, according to the estimates made before the outbreak of the Gulf war. *8 Days*, 11 October 1980, p. 57.
64 *Events*, 14 July 1978, p. 21.
65 *Guardian*, 8 June 1978; *Economic and Political Weekly*, 10 June 1978, p. 932.
66 *Guardian*, 27 February. The new law also made the following a capital offence: failure to name the party/parties to which a recruit to the Baath had belonged in the past; leaving the Baath to join any other party; and encouraging Baathists to leave the organisation. *The Middle East*, April 1979, p. 12.
67 *Guardian*, 27 February 1979.
68 *The Middle East*, April 1979, p. 12.
69 *Guardian*, 12 February 1980.
70 More specifically, the Iraqi opposition argued, there was no justification for the Hussein regime to attack Iran, with air raids on its capital, merely to solve a border demarcation problem.
71 *Guardian*, 18 November 1980. A fortnight later there were reports that the Communists had (also) formed an alliance with the Kurdish Democratic Party, and that their guerrillas had killed fifty-two Iraqi soldiers in an armed encounter with the government forces in the Kurdish region. *Daily Telegraph*, 3 December 1980.
72 Fred Halliday, *Arabia Without Sultans*, p. 367.

73 Ibid., pp. 374, 380–1.
74 See p. 10.
75 Halliday, op. cit., p. 337.
76 Ibid., p. 348.
77 As against the official figure of 600 British Military personnel in Oman then, the real figure was more than 2,000 including over 100 SAS men. They worked as combat officers and pilots, training operatives, and servicing and communications experts at the Royal Air Force bases at Salala in Dhofar and on Masira island. *New Statesman*, 2 January 1976, p. 6.
78 Ibid.; *Arab World File*, no. 922, 5 April 1978.
79 While the official figures for the deaths of British SAS men was eleven, the real number was seventy-three, reported Joseph Fitchett. *Observer*, 11 January 1976. 'It was a war that the press was never allowed to see, in which the British casualties are still an official secret,' wrote Max Hastings. *New Standard*, 17 November 1980.
80 *Observer*, 11 January 1980.
81 *New Statesman*, 2 January 1976, p. 7.
82 *Arab World File*, no. 922, 5 April 1978.
83 *Events*, 11 August 1978, pp. 4–5.
84 Significantly, Oman was not listed among the Gulf states which purportedly signed secret agreements with Iraq before the outbreak of the Gulf war. 'Two days before the start of the Iraqi war against Iran, Iraq signed an agreement with Saudi Arabia, Kuwait, the United Arab Emirates, Qatar and Bahrain under which these countries agreed to supply Iraq with all necessary military and non-military requirements,' said an official statement of Iran. *Daily Telegraph*, 4 February 1981.
85 Michael C. Hudson, *Arab Politics*, p. 356.
86 Cited in Halliday, op. cit., p. 234.
87 *Arab World File*, no. 351, 13 August 1975.
88 In less than five years of independence South Yemen had established twenty-one agricultural cooperatives and twenty-four state farms. Halliday, op. cit., p. 249.
89 Ibid., p. 241. By 1979 trade union membership had reached 84,000. *Middle East Research and Information Project*, no. 81 (October 1979), p. 12.
90 Peasants made up 60 per cent of the ranks of the people's militia, and workers 30 per cent. *Middle East Research and Information Project*, no. 81, p. 10.
91 It was alleged that President Ali had maintained a secret link with Saudi Arabia through the South Yemeni ambassador in Riyadh, who was related to him. Ibid., p. 19.
92 Including the casualties caused by the fighting outside Aden, more than 600 people were killed. *Guardian*, 29 August 1978.
93 Significantly, Hussein Komateh, chief of the people's militia, had been appointed the head of the committee for reorganisation of the army before the June showdown. Ibid.
94 Halliday, op. cit., p. 147.
95 *Middle East Research and Information Project*, no. 81 (October 1979), p. 21.
96 *The Middle East*, August 1978, p. 7.
97 *Guardian*, 1, 3, and 13 March 1979.
98 *The Middle East*, April 1980, p. 25; January 1981, p. 25; *8 Days*, 2 May 1981, p. 8.
99 *Guardian*, 9 September 1980; *The Middle East*, January 1981, p. 26.
100 Helen Lackner, *A House Built on Sand*, p. 99; and see p. 81.
101 See p. 82.

102 Cited in *Peace, Freedom, and Socialism*, November 1974.
103 Kazziha, op. cit., pp. 35–6.
104 Lackner, op. cit., p. 101; and see p. 82.
105 See p. 18.
106 See p. 93.
107 See p. 19.
108 *The Middle East*, August 1980, p. 34; and see p. 19.
109 'We have won the Shias to our side, and they no longer support the government,' Ahmed Khatib told *The Middle East*. July 1980, p. 32. However, his pro-Iran sympathies in the Gulf war, and the government's gerrymandering of the constituencies, paved the way for Khatib's defeat in the February 1981 parliamentary election by less than 100 votes. *8 Days*, 7 March 1981, p. 3.
110 See p. 21.
111 Kazziha, op. cit., p. 35. Kuwait was the venue of the regional conference of the ANM in 1964, where it was decided inter alia to form branches in Saudi Arabia and Bahrain. The attempt succeeded in Saudi Arabia, but failed in Bahrain. Ibid., pp. 35–6.
112 See p. 97. Among those who joined the ANM in protesting against 'gross interference in the elections' by the government were 'two outgoing ministers, the Kuwaiti Newspaper Owners Association, and various student and professional associations'. Peter Mansfield (ed.), *The Middle East*, p. 189.
113 *The Times*, 11 March 1974.
114 As elsewhere in the Arabian Peninsula, excepting South Yemen, political parties are banned in Kuwait.
115 During its brief life the APNU's weekly, *Al Ahali*, carried a regular column on Islam.
116 *Guardian*, 24 January 1979.
117 See pp. 128.
118 See p. 27.
119 British and American armies alone engaged 300,000 Egyptians. Agwani, op. cit., p. 44.
120 *United States Congress House Committee of Foreign Affairs, Report of Sub-Committee number 5*, Washington, DC, pp. 20–1.
121 Agwani, op. cit., p. 45; Pennar, op. cit., p. 52.
122 See p. 27.
123 Agwani, op. cit., p. 47.
124 See p. 120.
125 See pp. 122.
126 *World Marxist Review*, July 1964, p. 17. Khaled Bakdash, the Syrian Communist leader, was then in exile in Prague.
127 Pennar, op. cit., p. 53.
128 *Peace, Freedom, and Socialism*, September 1964.
129 Shimon Shamir, 'The Marxists in Egypt: The "Licensed Infiltration" in Practice', in Michael Confino and Shimon Shamir, *The USSR and the Middle East*, p. 295.
130 Ibid., p. 298.
131 Unknown to the ex-Communists, a vanguard of sorts was created. But it lacked any class orientation or ideology. See p. 124, note 10.
132 See p. 124.
133 Anouar Abdel-Malek, *Egypt: Military Society*, Vintage Books, New York, 1968, p. 297.
134 See p. 124.
135 *Khamsin 5*, 1978, p. 69.

136 *New York Times Magazine*, 20 September 1970.
137 Shamir, op. cit., pp. 313–14.
138 *Events*, 15 October 1976, p. 35.
139 According to Jalal Emam of the Federation of Egyptian Trade Unions, the Egyptian constitution is neutral on the subject of strikes: it says nothing about them. Interview in Cairo on 4 April 1978.
140 *Events*, 15 October 1976, p. 35.
141 Raymond William Baker, *Egypt's Uncertain Revolution under Nasser and Sadat*, p. 165.
142 *The Times*, 27 January 1977. According to David Hirst these riots were worse than those on 26 January 1952 which presaged the overthrow of King Farouk. *Guardian*, 23 July 1977.
143 *New York Times*, 30 January 1977.
144 *Arab Dawn*, June 1977, p. 6; *Guardian*, 28 June 1977.
145 *The Times*, 27 January 1977.
146 See p. 129.
147 *Sunday Times*, 30 April 1978.
148 Following the seizure of the APNU's printing facilities at its headquarters in Cairo in January 1979, the publication of the party journal ceased altogether. See p. 185.
149 See p. 159.
150 The seminar was organised by the British section of the Parliamentary Association for Euro–Arab Cooperation. *Guardian*, 1 October 1977.

## Chapter 9 Israel: domestic politics

1 In 1979 the Israeli population consisted of about 3,000,000 Jews and 600,000 Arabs. *The Times*, 2 December 1980.
2 Ibid.; *Guardian*, 2 December 1980.
3 See p. 159.
4 Duniya Nahas, *Israeli Communist Party*, Croom Helm, London, 1976, p. 35.
5 Ibid., p. 28. In 1946 the CPP had 1,500 members, and the LNL about 1,000. M. S. Agwani, *Communism in the Arab East*, p. 40.
6 Maki Central Committee, Foreign Relations Department, *Information Bulletin*, October 1965, Tel Aviv, p. 16.
7 Ibid., p. 50.
8 Nahas, op. cit., p. 28. In early 1965 Maki's membership amounted to 4,000–5,000. Walter Z. Laqueur, *Communism and Nationalism in the Middle East*, Routledge & Kegan Paul, London, 1961, p. 118.
9 Cited in Nahas, op. cit., p. 78.
10 Cited in ibid., pp. 78–9.
11 Ibid., p. 82.
12 Ibid., p. 85.
13 *The Times*, 11 December 1975.
14 *Sunday Times*, 4 April 1976. Since then, 30 March is celebrated as the 'Day of the Land' by all the Arabs of Palestine.
15 'Apart from Bethlehem, all the major communities of the West Bank have elected radical mayors and councillors, often displacing pliant notables who had run the Arab towns since the Israeli occupation began in 1967,' reported Eric Silver in the *Observer* of 25 April 1976. An estimated three quarters of the 200 councillors elected were 'new and radical'. *Guardian*, 13 April 1976.
16 Moscow Radio, 5 and 7 May 1977.

17 Baruch Gurevitz, 'Soviets and Israeli Arabs' in Yaacov Ro'i (ed.), *The Limits to Power: Soviet Policy in the Middle East*, Croom Helm, London, 1979, p. 274.
18 Don Peretz, *The Government and Politics of Israel*, p. 103. The rest of the Arabs voted for the Arab list attached to the Labour Alignment.
19 *New Left Review*, no. 65, January–February 1971, p. 25.
20 Noah Lucas, *The Modern History of Israel*, Weidenfeld & Nicolson, London, 1975, p. 275.
21 Nadav Safran, *Israel: The Embattled Ally*, p. 166.
22 Arie Bober (ed.), *The Other Israel*, Doubleday, New York, 1972, p. 105.
23 V. D. Segre, *Israel: A Society in Transition*, p. 42; Safran, op. cit., p. 37.
24 Mopsi was later to foster the Communist Party of Palestine.
25 Lucas, op. cit., p. 129.
26 Ibid., p. 130.
27 See p. 198.
28 See p. 60.
29 Lucas, op. cit., p. 245. These were mainly German surplus weapons, and were purchased through Haganah's network in Europe. Arnold Krammer, *The Forgotten Friendship*, p. 31.
30 See p. 62.
31 See p. 62.
32 Lucas, op. cit., p. 309.
33 Ibid., p. 310.
34 Two of the Israeli agents committed suicide in jail, and the rest, given long prison sentences, were handed over to Israel as part of the prisoners-of-war exchange after the June 1967 hostilities. These and other facts about Lavon's 'security mishap' affair became available to the Israelis only in 1979, when Hagai Eshed, an Israeli, published a well-researched (but censored) book on the subject. *Guardian*, 17 July 1979.
35 Segre, op. cit., p. 175.
36 In 1965, Mapai had over 200,000 members. Peretz, op. cit., p. 90.
37 Segre, op. cit., p. 205.
38 *The Paratroopers' Book* (Hebrew), Tel Aviv, 1969, pp. 157–8, cited in Bober, op. cit., p. 74.
39 Bober, op. cit., p. 216.
40 Safran, op. cit., p. 187.
41 1,445 delegates voted for Rabin, and 1,404 for Peres. Ibid.
42 Cited in the *Sunday Times*, 22 May 1977.
43 Within a few years the Democratic Movement for Change split into factions and lost its importance.
44 *Sunday Times*, 22 May 1977.
45 Safran, op. cit., p. 197.
46 After the 1939 White Paper the official Zionist bodies too organised illegal immigration. Peretz, op. cit., p. 109.
47 See p. 61.
48 See p. 62.
49 *The Times*, 19 May 1977.
50 Lucas, op. cit., pp. 282–3.
51 Histadrut is an 'economic empire', consisting of 'holding corporations, companies, banks, industrial concerns, and agro-industries'. According to the *Encyclopaedia Judaica*, Histadrut-controlled industries employed 23.3 per cent of the total labour force, and produced 20.8 per cent of the gross national product, in 1968–9. Although three quarters of all Israeli workers and employees belong to Histadrut, its department of labour unions is only one of

its many specialised sections. Uri Davis, *Israel: Utopia Incorporated*, Zed Press, London, 1977, p. 49.

52 See p. 205.

53 Peretz, op. cit., p. 80.

54 Ibid., p. 81.

55 Israel T. Naamani, *Israel: A Profile*, Pall Mall, London, 1972, p. 114; Peretz, op. cit., p. 115.

56 Literally, Guardians of the Gate – in Aramaic language.

57 During the Palestine war of 1948–9 many of the Neturei Karta members tried to remain in Arab Jerusalem, but failed. In 1980 the sect had 6,000 members: they lived mainly in Jerusalem and a suburb of Tel Aviv. *Sunday Times*, 28 December 1980; Peretz, op. cit., p. 115.

58 Peretz, op. cit., p. 137.

59 The first Jewish colonisation in the occupied territories occurred on 15 June 1967. The settlement, built by private citizens, at Merom HaGolan on the Golan Heights was later sanctioned by the government. *The Times*, 25 June 1976.

60 *Financial Times*, 2 July 1977. Gush Emunim became an independent entity in early 1974. *Sunday Times*, 7 May 1978.

61 Safran, op cit., p. 212.

62 *Guardian*, 9 June 1980.

63 *Sunday Times Magazine*, 5 October 1980, p. 52. 'Our final goal is to expel all Arabs from the Land of Israel,' Meir Kahane said in mid-1980. 'We want the [Israeli] government to make the Arabs as miserable as possible by cutting off social benefits . . . [If that fails] we're calling on the government to organise a Jewish terrorist group that would throw bombs and grenades and kill Arabs.' Cited in *Newsweek*, 16 June 1980, p. 18.

64 *Sunday Times Magazine*, 5 October 1980, p. 50.

65 *Newsweek*, 16 June 1980, p. 18. Kahane was released six months before the end of his second prison sentence. *Guardian*, 13 December 1980.

66 *Guardian*, 9 June 1980; *Newsweek*, 16 June 1980, p. 19; *Sunday Times Magazine*, 5 October 1980, pp. 50–1.

67 Literally, dispersion; idomatically, Jewish settlements in all countries other than Israel.

68 According to the *American Jewish Yearbook*, 1977, of the 14.3 million Jews in the world, 5.8 million were in America, and nearly 3 million in Israel. Cited in *Kuwait Times*, 5 February 1978. 'Eighty per cent of all Jews still live outside Israel's borders,' noted an editorial of the *Sunday Times*, 10 May 1981.

69 *Guardian*, 2 January 1981.

70 Naamani, op. cit., p. 114; Peretz, op. cit., p. 132.

71 *Sunday Times*, 28 December 1980.

72 The Status Law openly discriminates against non-Jews living in Israel. Lucas, op. cit., pp. 277–8.

73 Cited in Safran, op. cit., p. 147.

74 Bober, op. cit., p. 55. The principle of proportional representation saw to it that the numerous trends within the Zionist movement were all reflected at the WZO congress.

75 During the next four decades the Jewish National Fund purchased 250,000 acres of land in Palestine. *New York Times*, 17 September 1979.

76 Hanan Sher (ed.), *Facts About Israel*, Israel Information Centre, Jerusalem, 1978, pp. 119–20.

77 Ibid., p. 119. Such contributions have been tax-exempt in America since 1948.

78 Peretz, op. cit., p. 130.

79 Agwani, op. cit., p. 36.

Chapter 10 Israel and the West

1 It is worth noting that since America had not declared war against Turkey, it was in general disinterested in the fate of its empire.
2 Robert W. Stookey, *America and the Arab States*, p. 44.
3 The US Congress resolution stated that 'The United States of America favours the establishment in Palestine of a national home for the Jewish people, it being clearly understood that nothing shall be done which may prejudice the civil and religious rights of Christians and all other non-Jewish communities in Palestine, and that the holy places and religious buildings and sites in Palestine shall be adequately protected.' Cited in Ralph M. Magnus (ed.), *Documents on the Middle East*, American Enterprise Institute for Public Policy Research, Washington, DC, 1969, p. 40.
4 Opposed to separating the issues of Jewish refugees and Palestine, the WZO argued that absorption of refugees elsewhere would be a setback to Zionism. 'If we allow a separation between the refugee problem and the Palestine problem, we are risking the existence of Zionism,' wrote David Ben-Gurion. Cited in Arie Bober (ed.), *The Other Israel*, 171. Also see p. 60.
5 Cited in Nadav Safran, *Israel: The Embattled Ally*, p. 36.
6 Stookey, op. cit., p. 108.
7 Cited in Richard P. Stevens, *American Zionism and US Foreign Policy*, Pageant Press, New York, 1962, p. 38.
8 Cited in George Kent, 'Congress and American Middle East Policy', in Willard A. Belling (ed.), *The Middle East: Quest for an American Policy*, State University of New York Press, Albany, NY, 1973, p. 287.
9 Harry N. Howard, 'The United States and the Middle East', in Tareq Y. Ismael et al., *The Middle East in World Politics*, Syracuse University Press, NY, 1974, p. 123.
10 Stookey, op. cit., p. 112.
11 Safran, op. cit., p. 573; and see p. 198.
12 Cited in Michla Pomerance, *American Guarantees to Israel and the Law of American Foreign Relations*, The Hebrew University of Jerusalem, Jerusalem, 1976, p. 8.
13 Safran, op. cit., p. 339.
14 *Sunday Times*, 2 December 1973. This continues.
15 Reparation continued to be paid after 1965. They amounted to $125 million a year until 1967, and $210 million a year thereafter, with 80–90 per cent in grants, and the rest in loans. Safran, op. cit., p. 123.
16 Tadeusz Walichnowski, *The Tel Aviv–Bonn Axis and Poland*, Interpress, Warsaw, 1968, p. 58.
17 By 1962 the restitutions given to individuals had already exceeded the reparations paid to the state of Israel. Dan Avni-Segre, 'Israel: A Society in Transition', in Irene L. Gendzier (ed.), *The Middle East Reader*, p. 228. Altogether the state governments of West Germany paid a total of $800 million in restitutions to Israeli Jews of central European origin. *The Times*, 4 June 1981.
18 Nasser H. Aruri and Natalie K. Hevener, 'France and the Middle East', in Ismael, op. cit., p. 67.
19 Safran, op. cit., p. 353.
20 Walichnowski, op. cit., p. 63.
21 According to the article of Ted Szulc, a former foreign and diplomatic correspondent of the *New York Times*, published in the September 1975 issue of *Penthouse*, the Eisenhower administration decided, after the Suez war of 1956, to help Israel develop an atomic weapon. James Angleton, the

CIA's counter-intelligence chief, was put in charge of the project. As a result, several American nuclear scientists were secretly sent to work at Dimona nuclear research centre. *The Times*, 21 August 1975. Five years later this version of events was confirmed by Wilbur Crane Eveland, former CIA chief in the Middle East in the 1950s, in his book as well as an interview with *The Middle East*, October 1980, p. 46. See note 66 below.

22 *HaBoker*, 18 December 1957.
23 Walichnowski, op. cit., p. 67.
24 *Neues Deutschland*, 31 January 1958.
25 Surendra Bhutani, *Israeli Soviet Cold War*, Atul Prakashan, Delhi, 1975, p. 128; *Münchner Illustrierte*, 16 January 1960.
26 The doctrine was summed up aptly by President Eisenhower when he said on 1 January 1957, 'The existing vacuum in the Middle East must be filled by the United States before it is filled by Russia'. Cited in Fred Halliday, *Arabia Without Sultans*, p. 54. In the American view, 'the existing vacuum' had been caused by the expulsion of British and French influence from the region in the wake of the Suez war fiasco of October–November 1956.
27 Safran, op. cit., p. 376.
28 Walichnowski, op. cit., p. 87.
29 *Izvestia*, 3 October 1962.
30 William B. Quandt, *Decade of Decisions: American Policy Toward the Arab–Israeli Conflict, 1967–1976*, University of California Press, Berkeley and London, 1977, p. 37.
31 In order to pacify the Arab protest, Bonn stopped shipping arms to Tel Aviv. Israel was outraged. It was not until West Germany promised additional economic aid of $820 million that Tel Aviv ceased its denunciation of Bonn. Walichnowski, op. cit., p. 92; and see note 15 above. Bonn continued to aid Tel Aviv militarily in other ways. During the period 1964–75 West Germany trained 4,000 Israeli officers, while 500 West German experts worked in the Israeli arms industry, and over 100 West German nuclear physicists at Dimona research centre. *Economic and Political Weekly*, 4 September 1976, p. 1443.
32 Stookey, op. cit., p. 215.
33 *US Department of State Bulletin*, 7 October 1968, Washington, DC, p. 347.
34 Cited in Quandt, op. cit., p. 65. See p. 67.
35 Later the number of aircraft was increased to 100. Quandt, op. cit., p. 66, note 55.
36 Safran, op. cit., p. 431.
37 Halliday, op. cit., p. 253.
38 Safran, op. cit., p. 436.
39 Harry N. Howard, 'The United States and the Middle East', in Tareq Y. Ismael et al., op. cit., p. 131.
40 Israel accepted the Rogers plan only after President Nixon had assured it inter alia that its borders would not be those of 4 June 1967, and that the USA would continue to provide Israel with arms as well as large-scale economic aid. Safran, op. cit., p. 446.
41 'Israel's ambassador to Washington, General Yitzhak Rabin, led an extraordinarily undiplomatic campaign to mobilise American public opinion against Secretary [of State] Rogers and his views,' states Robert W. Stookey, op. cit., p. 223.
42 Quandt, op. cit., p. 114.
43 Cited in an excerpt of Yitzhak Rabin's memoirs, published in *Maariv*, an Israeli daily. *Guardian*, 11 August 1979.
44 Stookey, op. cit., p. 232.

45 Safran, op. cit., p. 346. The date was 21 November 1971, exactly four years after the USA had voted for resolution 242 at the UN Security Council.
46 *New York Times*, 30 August 1976.
47 Harry N. Howard, 'The United States and the Middle East', in Ismael, op. cit., p. 135.
48 Quandt, op. cit., p. 147.
49 Safran, op. cit., p. 473.
50 The actual figures were $1,153 million and $135 million. Quandt, op. cit., p. 163.
51 *The Middle East*, June 1980, p. 11.
52 *The Times*, 30 April 1977. Next January there were reports that 'a few years earlier' 206 pounds of enriched uranium had 'disappeared' from a private nuclear fuel fabricating plant in Apollo, Pennsylvania, USA. *Guardian*, 28 January 1978.
53 *New York Times*, 17 July 1970.
54 In 1976, *Wehrtechnik*, a West German military journal, stated that Israel had thirteen atomic bombs. Cited in the *Economic and Political Weekly*, 4 September 1976, p. 1443. Later, Erich Follath of *Der Spiegel*, a West German weekly, reported that, based on five months of research, he had concluded that Israel had had atomic bombs since the early 1970s. Referring to the first days of the Yom Kippur war, the magazine wrote that 'the world was [then] on the brink of a nuclear war'. Cited in the *Guardian*, 12 March 1980. (It is worth noting that during the period 1964–75 more than 100 West German nuclear scientists worked at Dimona nuclear plant. See note 31 above.) According to a special American Broadcasting Company's television documentary, *Near Armageddon: The Spread of Nuclear Weapons in the Middle East*, the CIA sighted a Soviet vessel giving off neutron emissions attributed to a nuclear bomb on board, passing through the Bosphorus on its way to Egypt. *8 Days*, 9 May 1981, p. 3.
55 Before the airlift ended on 15 November (on the eve of the arrival of armament ships at Israeli ports), over 33,500 tons of American weapons, as well as seventy-six military aircraft, had been transported to Israel. *Aviation Week and Space Technology*, 10 December 1973, pp. 16–19.
56 The United Jewish Appeal's target of $750 million for 1974 was three times the figure for 1972. *Sunday Times*, 2 December 1973.
57 Safran, op. cit., p. 495.
58 Israel's intransigence apparently hurt its long-term interests. Had Kissinger succeeded in improving King Hussein's position vis-à-vis Israel, through negotiations, it is probable that the Jordanian monarch would not have lost his position as the recognised representative of the Palestinians to the PLO at the Arab summit in October.
59 The political scandal was named after the apartment block in Washington DC, where the offices of the Democratic Party were broken into by the agents of President Nixon's campaign managers in the summer of 1972.
60 *New York Times*, 7 April 1975. Later Kissinger promised increased aid to Israel if it agreed to a revival of the negotiations. *New York Times Magazine*, 1 June 1975.
61 Safran, op. cit., p. 555.
62 Ibid., p. 557. 'Some of these [undertakings, commitments, assurances], as Secretary Kissinger was to point out before Congress, were legally binding while others were in the nature of assurances about American political intentions; some were entirely within the purview of the authority of the President of the United States while others depended on existing or prior authorisation and appropriation by Congress; some were formal reaffirma-

tions of existing American policy while others referred to contingencies that might never arise,' states Safran.

63 See pp. 45, 138.
64 Cited in the *Guardian*, 28 June 1977.
65 Interview with *Anti*, an Athens-based magazine, cited in the *Guardian*, 19 April 1976.
66 *The Middle East*, October 1980, p. 46. 'The CIA station in Greece supplied some support for the Christian-led militias; when this wasn't enough the United States had Israel ship them large quantities of supplies and captured weapons,' writes Wilbur Crane Eveland. *Ropes of Sand: America's Failure in the Middle East*, W. W. Norton, New York, 1980, p. 341.
67 *The Middle East*, October 1980, p. 46.
68 *The Times*, 25 February 1977.
69 *Sunday Times*, 24 July 1977.
70 Safran, op. cit., p. 564.
71 Ibid.
72 *Guardian*, 12 October 1976. See p. 218.
73 *The Times*, 14 October 1976.
74 Safran, op. cit., p. 564. This was undertaken later.
75 *Guardian*, 19 September 1977.
76 *The Middle East*, June 1978, p. 40.
77 Ibid.
78 In 1981 the AIPAC's budget was $1.3 million. *New York Times*, 2 October 1981. It originated in the American Zionist Council, and acquired its present name in 1954. Don Peretz, *The Government and Politics of Israel*, p. 132.
79 *Guardian*, 19 September 1977.
80 *The Middle East*, July 1978, p. 40. As all fund-raising in the local Jewish communities is carried out jointly for Zionist and local welfare purposes through the United Jewish Appeal under the aegis of the Jewish Agency's Keren Hayesod – there is no way a protesting American Jew can dissociate himself from any of the internal or external policies of Israel without, in the process, hurting the welfare programme for local Jews. See p. 213.
81 Peretz, op. cit., p. 132. Of these, 200,000 participated in electing delegates to the 1978 congress of the WZO. *The Middle East*, June 1978, p. 39.
82 *Guardian*, 19 September 1977.
83 Ibid., 30 September 1977.
84 *Middle East International*, November 1977, p. 34.
85 *Time*, 17 October 1977, p. 26.
86 Ibid.
87 Cited in *Palestine*, January 1978, p. 78.
88 *Time*, 17 October 1977, pp. 25–6.
89 *Guardian*, 14 October 1977.
90 *Jerusalem Post*, 21 November 1977.
91 *The Middle East*, February 1978, p. 33.
92 *Middle East Economic Digest*, 11 November 1977, p. 41.
93 *Jordan Times*, 24 February 1978.
94 *Guardian*, 30 March 1979.
95 Ibid.
96 There were unconfirmed reports that the Israeli secret service, Mossad, had bugged Andrew Young's meeting on 26 July with Zehdi Terzi, the PLO observer at the UN, at the New York apartment of the Kuwaiti ambassador to the UN. *Guardian*, 17 August 1979; *Observer*, 19 August 1979.
97 *New York Times*, 19 September 1979. This amounted to implementing one of the recommendations contained in the Galili Document, which was adopted

by the ruling Labour Alignment in August 1973. See p. 222.

98 *Daily Telegraph*, 19 July 1980.

99 *Guardian*, 22 October 1980.

100 Cited in *The Middle East*, December 1980, p. 36.

101 *Financial Times*, 23 December 1980. Israel spends 26 per cent of its GNP on defence: 15 per cent at home and 11 per cent on imported weaponry. *Guardian*, 19 June 1980.

102 Ibid., 6 November 1980.

103 Ibid., 4 February 1981. Alone among Western leaders, President Reagan was inclined to accept Israel's reason for bombing the Iraqi nuclear centre near Baghdad on 7 June. 'In conducting that mission, Israel might have sincerely believed it was a defensive more,' he said. *The Times*, 19 June 1981.

Chapter 11 Israel and the Soviet bloc

1 Max I. Dimont, *Jews, God And History*, New American Library, New York, 1962, pp. 241–2.

2 See p. 59.

3 Nadav Safran, *Israel: The Embattled Ally*, p. 17.

4 See p. 59.

5 At that time there were about eighty Lovers of Zion groups in fifty Russian towns and cities. Lionel Kochan (ed.), *The Jews in Soviet Russia since 1917*, Oxford University Press, London and New York, 1970, p. 1.

6 Ibid., p. 99.

7 Surendra Bhutani, *Israeli Soviet Cold War*, p. 3.

8 V. I. Lenin, *Collected Works: Volume 7*, Foreign Languages Publishing House, Moscow, 1952, p. 83.

9 J. V. Stalin, *Collected Works: Volume 2*, Foreign Languages Publishing House, Moscow, 1952, p. 335.

10 Cited in Arnold Krammer, *The Forgotten Friendship*, p. 7.

11 Cited in Greger Aronson et al. (eds), *Russian Jewry*, Thomas Yoseloff, New York and London, 1969, p. 416.

12 Cited in Walter Zander, *Soviet Jewry, Palestine and the West*, Victor Gollancz, London, 1947, p. 29. Earlier, reflecting Moscow's view, the Communist International Congress of 1920 had condemned Zionist policies in Palestine.

13 Cited in Ivar Spector, *The Soviet Union and the Muslim World, 1917–1958*, University of Washington Press, Seattle, 1959, p. 132.

14 Yaacov Ro'i, 'Soviet–Israeli Relations, 1947–1954', in Michael Confino and Shimon Shamir (eds), *The USSR and the Middle East*, p. 123.

15 Ibid., p. 126.

16 Cited in Maxim Ghilan, *How Israel Lost Its Soul*, p. 103.

17 Ibid., p. 101.

18 Ro'i, op. cit., p. 128.

19 While Vyacheslav M. Molotov, the Soviet foreign minister, explicitly recognised 'the state of Israel and its provisional government', President Truman limited his recognition to 'the provisional government as the *de facto* authority of the new state of Israel'. Cited in the *American Journal of International Law*, July 1948, p. 621.

20 *New Times*, 5 July 1980.

21 Safran, op. cit., p. 347.

22 Walter Z. Laqueur, *The Soviet Union and the Middle East*, p. 204.

23 Prague acted as a proxy fc: Moscow which – having reached an agreement with the Western powers (in the summer) to inaugurate an independent,

neutral Austria by ending the four-power occupating of that country – did not wish to spoil its as yet tenuous rapprochement with the West.

24 Since Syria and Saudi Arabia had, in March, allied with Egypt to form a joint economic and defence organisation, as a potential rival to the Baghdad Pact, Israel wished to prove to Syria that Egypt was in no position to help it defend its territory. Peter Mansfield (ed.), *The Middle East*, p. 467; *Jerusalem Post*, 19 January 1956.

25 Cited in *New Times*, 26 January 1956.

26 Safran, op. cit., p. 353.

27 Enver M. Koury, *The Super-Powers and the Balance of Power in the Arab World*, Catholic Press, Beirut, 1970, p. 184.

28 Cited in Bhutani, op. cit., p. 65.

29 The superpowers had to use the General Assembly, because the Security Council had been paralysed by the vetoes of Britain and France, two of the five permanent members invested with powers of veto.

30 *Izvestia*, 6 November 1956.

31 *Pravda*, 8 February 1957.

32 Cited in Bhutani, op. cit., p. 80.

33 Tabitha Petran, *Syria*, pp. 123–4; and see p. 132.

34 *Pravda*, 4 August 1958; and see p. 218.

35 *BBC Summary of World Broadcasts, Part I*, 25 August 1958, p. 20.

36 *Sovietski Flot*, 27 October 1958.

37 This was also one of the themes of the book (*The State of Israel, Its Position and Po!icy*, in Russian), by I. Ivanov and Z. Sheinis, published in Moscow in the autumn of 1958. Cited in Bhutani, op. cit., p. 84, note 39.

38 *New York Times*, 22 September 1959.

39 *Pravda*, 9 July 1960.

40 *Krasnaya Zvezda*, 27 July 1961.

41 *New York Times*, 10 October 1962.

42 *Pravda*, 21 May 1963.

43 Ibid., 6 January 1964.

44 Ibid., 10 May 1964.

45 *Izvestia*, 11 April 1965.

46 Bhutani, op. cit., p. 121. Ten years later the UN General Assembly passed, by seventy-two votes to thirty-five, a resolution which described Zionism as 'a form of racism and racial discrimination'. *The Times*, 11 November 1975.

47 Aranson et al., op. cit., p. 439.

48 The figures for 1965 and 1966 were 30,736 and 15,730. *Statistical Abstract of Israel, 1978*, p. 137.

49 See p. 204.

50 *Izvestia*, 16 July 1966.

51 'Major Hatum attempted a coup by luring government and party leaders to the Jebel Druze, where he seized them as hostages,' writes Tabith Petran. 'During these tense days Amman Radio repeatedly interrupted its programmes to call on Syrians to revolt.' Op. cit., p. 185.

52 Cited in *Le Monde*, 13 September 1966.

53 *Pravda*, 17 November 1966.

54 Cited in Bhutani, op. cit., p. 137.

55 *US News and World Report*, 6 April 1967.

56 See p. 204.

57 *Jerusalem Post*, 9 April 1967.

58 *BBC Summary of World Broadcasts, Part I*, 14 April 1967, p. 10.

59 Cited in Godfrey Jansen, 'New Light on the 1967 War', in *Daily Star*, Beirut, 15 November 1973.

60 *Jerusalem Post*, 14 May 1967.
61 *Izvestia*, 16 May 1967.
62 *Jerusalem Post*, 24 May 1967.
63 Cited in *Pravda*, 24 May 1967.
64 Cited in Avigdor Dagan, *Moscow and Jerusalem: Twenty Years of Relations between Israel and the Soviet Union*, Abelard-Schumann, London and New York, 1970, p. 217. A similar note was handed to President Nasser.
65 *Security Council Official Records*, Meeting 1343, p. 19.
66 Ibid., Meeting 1346, p. 15.
67 *Pravda*, 7 June 1967.
68 Ibid., 10 June 1967.
69 Ibid., 11 June 1967.
70 Lyndon Baines Johnson, *The Vantage Point*, Holt, Rinehart & Winston, New York, 1971, p. 302.
71 Ibid., p. 175.
72 See p. 227.
73 221,333 immigrants arrived into Israel during 1970–4. *Statistical Abstract of Israel, 1978*, p. 137. At the end of 1974, there were 2.9 million Jews in Israel. Ibid., p. 3. Based on the estimates of three million Jews in the USSR in 1972, and 2.5 million six years later, Soviet Jewry probably amounted to 2.8 million in late 1974. *Sunday Times*, 7 May 1973, *Observer*, 1 July 1979.
74 Between 1973 and 1974 the inflow of Soviet Jews into Israel was halved, from 34,000 to 17,000. *The Times*, 23 April 1975. The downward trend continued: in 1977 the USSR contributed only 8,348 immigrants to Israel. *Statistical Abstract of Israel, 1978*, p. 138. Soviet Jews arrived at transit points in Austria, and then chose where to go. By the late 1970s America had emerged as the most popular destination, with Israel well down the list: a repetition of what had happened during 1882–1914, when an estimated 2.5 million Jews left Czarist Russia. Safran, op. cit., p. 86.
75 Safran, op. cit., p. 520.
76 See p. 224.
77 *The Times*, 30 April 1975.
78 See p. 225.
79 P. M. Dadant, 'American and Soviet Defence Systems vis-à-vis the Middle East', in Willard A. Beling (ed.), *The Middle East*, p. 178.
80 *Guardian*, 26 October 1977.
81 R. D. McLaurin, *The Middle East in Soviet Policy*, Lexington Books, Lexington and London, 1975, p. 15.

Chapter 12 The Arabs and the Soviet bloc

1 Ben-Cion Pinchuk, 'Soviet Penetration into the Middle East in Historical Perspective', in Michael Confino and Shimon Shamir (eds), *The USSR and the Middle East*, p. 63.
2 The major reason for the Crimean war was the Russian demand, made in 1853, that it be recognised as the official protector of the Orthodox Christians in the Ottoman empire just as France had been of the Maronite Catholics since 1649. Naseer H. Aruri and Natalie K. Hevener, 'France and the Middle East', in Tareq Y. Ismael et al., *The Middle East in World Politics*, p. 60. In the final line-up Russia fought an alliance of Turkey, France, Britain and Sardinia.
3 Peter Mansfield (ed.), *The Middle East*, p. 13.
4 The provisions of the Sykes–Picot pact regarding the Arab section of the Ottoman empire ran counter to the promises made by the British to Sharif

Hussein to secure his support against the Ottomans. See p. 50.

5 Cited in Arnold Krammer, *The Forgotten Friendship*, pp. 4–5.
6 Tabitha Petran, *Syria*, p. 101; and *Al Misri*, 9 April 1950.
7 *Izvestia*, 23 November 1951.
8 See p. 297.
9 Since Iraq had not repudiated its membership of the Arab Collective Security Pact, formed in 1950 under the aegis of the Arab League, to provide protection against Israeli aggression, Nasser felt that by signing a military pact with Turkey, Iraq had (in theory) tied the Arab League to Nato. For details of the Arab Collective Security Pact, see Petran, op. cit., pp. 108, 127.
10 See p. 203.
11 P. Edward Haley, 'Britain and the Middle East', in Tareq Y. Ismael et al., op. cit., p. 44.
12 This is based on the account of events given by Mohammed Heikal, a confidant of Nasser, published after Nasser's death. *Sunday Telegraph*, 12 September 1971. Due to large fluctuations in world cotton prices during the period the exact value of the deal could not be established.
13 Karen Dawisha, *Soviet Foreign Policy Towards Egypt*, Macmillan, London, 1979, pp. 11–12.
14 Tarun Chandra Bose, *The Superpowers and the Middle East*, Asia Publishing House, New Delhi and London, 1972, pp. 20–1.
15 *Observer*, 27 April 1956.
16 *Izvestia*, 6 November 1956.
17 *The Times*, 7 November 1956.
18 Dawisha, op. cit., p. 15.
19 Walter Z. Laqueur, *The Struggle for the Middle East: The Soviet Union and the Middle East, 1958–68*, Routledge & Kegan Paul, London, 1969, p. 64.
20 *Pravda*, 15 February 1958.
21 Mohamed Heikal, *Nasser: The Cairo Documents*, New English Library, London, 1972, pp. 131–2.
22 See p. 165.
23 See p. 169.
24 Cited in Laqueur, op. cit., p. 65.
25 *Pravda*, 30 March 1959.
26 *New York Times*, 22 February 1959.
27 *Al Ahram*, 9 May 1960.
28 Laqueur, op. cit., p. 66; Mansfield (ed.), op. cit., p. 256.
29 *Kommunist*, no. 8, 1961, p. 41.
30 *Pravda*, 24 August 1961.
31 See p. 122.
32 United Arab Republic, Department of Information, *The Charter*, Cairo, 1961, p. 50.
33 See p. 122.
34 Cited in *Mizan Newsletter*, July–August 1962, p. 8.
35 *Pravda*, 18 November 1962.
36 *New Times*, no. 4, 1962, pp. 12–15; *Mirovaya Ekonomika i Mezhdunarodnie Otnosheniya* (World Economics and International Relations), no. 2, 1964, p. 22.
37 *World Marxist Review*, no. 6, 1963, pp. 93–5. 'From 1959 to 1964 the left suffered horribly in Egypt's concentration camps,' writes Raymond William Baker. 'The brutally murdered included Shohdi Atia al Shafei, a brilliant Marxist historian and theoretician.' *Egypt's Uncertain Revolution under Nasser and Sadat*, p. 99.

38 See p. 123.
39 *New York Times*, 13 February 1966; *Le Monde*, 18 February 1970.
40 See p. 188.
41 Jaan Pennar, *The USSR and the Arabs*, p. 70.
42 *Mizan Newsletter*, no. 5, 1964, p. 65.
43 Moscow Radio, 19 May 1964.
44 *Pravda*, 24 May 1964.
45 See p. 188.
46 Y. M. Zhukov (ed.), *Contemporary Socialist Theories* (in Russian), Moscow, 1967, p. 148.
47 The deal concerned building up a Saudi air defence system. Britain was the major recipient of military orders, worth £140 million in total. *The Arms Trade with the Third World*, Stockholm International Peace Research Institute, Stockholm, 1971, p. 563.
48 United Arab Republic, Department of Information, *Collected Letters, Interviews and Statements of President Gamal Abdul Nasser, Vol. 5*, (in Arabic), Cairo, no date, p. 488.
49 *New York Times*, 18 May 1966.
50 Soviet aid was provided as a loan at 2.5 per cent interest. The figure for the total sum for the period 1954–66 varied between $780 million (Soviet sources) and $1,011 million (Western sources). Vassil Vassilev, *Policy in the Soviet Bloc on Aid to Developing Countries*, Development Centre of the Organisation for Economic Cooperation and Development, Paris, 1969, p. 63.
51 Laqueur, op. cit., p. 74.
52 *Pravda*, 23 July, 8 August and 29 October 1966.
53 *Problems of Peace and Socialism*, December 1966.
54 See p. 124.
55 Mohamed Heikal, op. cit., p. 219.
56 Robert Stephens, *Nasser: A Political Biography*, Allen Lane: The Penguin Press, London, 1971, p. 484.
57 Mohamed Heikal, op. cit., p. 220.
58 See p. 240.
59 Cited in Mohamed Heikal, *The Road to Ramadan*, Fontana, London, 1976, p. 49.
60 Cairo Radio, 23 July 1968. Within a year of the Six Day war the Arab states (mainly Egypt and Syria) had received $1.7 billion in military aid and another $1 billion in economic assistance from the USSR. Harry N. Howard, 'The Soviet Union in Lebanon, Syria, and Jordan', in Ivo J. Lederer and Wayne S. Vucinich (eds), *The Soviet Union and the Middle East: The Post World War II Era*, Hoover Institution Press, Stanford, Cal., 1974, p. 154.
61 *New Times*, no. 26, 1967, p. 7; *Za Rubezhom* (Abroad), no. 27, 1967, pp. 7–8; *Pravda*, 31 July 1967; *Literaturnaya Gazeta* (Literary Gazette), 9 August 1967, pp. 31–6.
62 See p. 124.
63 Mohamed Heikal, *The Road to Ramadan*, pp. 81–7.
64 *Le Monde*, 18 February 1970.
65 *Pravda*, 30 July 1970.
66 Dawisha, op. cit., p. 47.
67 Tass, 20 December 1970.
68 *World Marxist Review*, no. 6, 1971, p. 3.
69 Cited in *Le Monde*, 28 August 1971.
70 This happened also because, following the signing of a friendship treaty with India in August, the USSR began shipping arms to India, which was at the

time planning a military intervention in what was then East Pakistan.

71 Of various estimates of the expelled Soviet military personnel, the figure of 15,000 given by President Sadat in his memoirs, *In Search of Identity* (Collins, London, 1978) is probably the most reliable. *Observer*, 19 March 1978.

72 *Economic and Political Weekly*, 25 December 1976, p. 1989.

73 *New Times*, no. 30, 1972, p. 23.

74 *L'Orient-Le Jour*, 10 September 1972; *Al Nahar Arab Report*, 18 September 1972.

75 Dawisha, op. cit., p. 66.

76 See p. 223. According to William B. Quandt, the first Soviet airlift to Syria on 10 October amounted to 200 tons of military equipment. *Decade of Decisions*, pp. 178–9.

77 The Soviet warning to Israel was issued publicly. Tass, 23 October 1973. However, the text of the Soviet message to President Nixon was not revealed until the following April. *New York Times*, 10 April 1974.

78 Galia Golan, *The Soviet Union and the Arab–Israel War of October 1973*, The Hebrew University of Jerusalem, Jerusalem, 1974, p. 20; and William B. Quandt, 'Soviet Policy in the October Middle Ease War–II', *International Affairs*, October 1977, pp. 590, 598. According to Galia Golan, the Soviet airborne divisions consisted of about 45,000 'operational troops' and 100,000 'logistic and support troops'.

79 Quandt, *Decade of Decisions*, pp. 197–8.

80 *Pravda*, 28 October 1973.

81 Fourthly, Mirsky stressed the positive achievement of détente in containing the conflict. 'Who knows what might have happened were the cold war still at its height, had there been no relaxation of world tension in the past year-and-a-half or two?' he wrote. *New Times*, no. 48, 1973, pp. 18–19.

82 *Pravda*, 4 December 1973.

83 See p. 223.

84 *Pravda*, 30 January 1974.

85 Cited in *New York Times*, 13 March 1974.

86 *New York Times*, 19 April 1974.

87 Ibid., 7 June 1974.

88 *Izvestia*, 25 July 1974.

89 *Pravda*, 28 December 1974.

90 *Pravda*, 25 October 1975. Such criticisms had little effect on Soviet military supplies to Egypt. Between January 1975 and March 1976 (when Sadat unilaterally abrogated the friendship treaty with the USSR), these amounted to $1.5 billion. *Economic and Political Weekly*, 25 December 1976, p. 1989.

91 Baker, op. cit., p. 139.

92 Tass, 15 March 1976.

93 *Pravda*, 19 February 1977.

94 *New York Times*, 25 July 1977. The war soon ended, because President Houari Boumedienne of Algeria warned that if the Egyptian troops did not withdraw immediately, Algerian troops would enter Libya from their end to fight the Egyptian forces. *Guardian*, 10 January 1981.

95 *Kessing's Contemporary Archives*, Vol. XXII, p. 27810. These figures excluded the value of the Soviet weapons shipped to Egypt in the wake of the Six Day war, and half of the Soviet credits outstanding in early 1970. See pp. 255–6. Soviet military hardware supplied to Egypt, to replenish its Six Day war losses, included 300 jet fighters, 50 bombers, and 450 tanks. *The Times*, 25 April 1968.

96 *The Times*, 6 April 1976; Mansfield (ed.), op. cit., pp. 254, 257. The Helwan plant's annual production capacity rose from 300,000 tons to 1.5 million tons. Ibid., p. 254.
97 Following the Soviet intervention in Afghanistan in December 1979, Sadat asked the Soviet ambassador in Cairo to reduce the embassy staff from fifty to seven, and withdraw the remaining 200 Soviet civilian technicians from Egypt. *New York Times*, 29 January 1980.
98 See p. 250.
99 Petran, op. cit., p. 110.
100 See p. 236.
101 As in the case of the Egyptian arms deal, Czechoslovakia acted as a proxy for the USSR.
102 Harry N. Howard, op. cit., p. 140.
103 Dwight D. Eisenhower, *The White House Years: Volume II*, Doubleday, New York, 1965, p. 197.
104 See p. 237.
105 Eisenhower, op. cit., p. 203.
106 *Soviet News*, 16 September 1957.
107 Cited in M. J. Mackintosh, *Strategy and Tactics of Soviet Foreign Policy*, Oxford University Press, London and New York, 1962, p. 229.
108 See p. 132.
109 *BBC Summary of World Broadcasts, Part I*, 27 October 1961.
110 *Izvestia*, 7 June and 20 July 1963.
111 *Pravda*, 14 November 1963.
112 George Mirsky, *Arab Peoples Continue the Struggle* (in Russian), Mezhdunarodnya Otnosheniya, Moscow, 1965, pp. 86–7.
113 See p. 135.
114 *New Times*, no. 16, 1966, p. 24.
115 Cited in Petran, op. cit., p. 184.
116 Dawisha, op. cit., p. 38; and Laqueur, op. cit., p. 89.
117 See p. 254.
118 Cited in Dawisha, op. cit., p. 40.
119 See p. 255.
120 Dawisha, op. cit., p. 42. Also see p. 259.
121 *Za Rubezhom*, 29 September 1967, pp. 11–12.
122 *Süddeutsche Zeitung*, 30 October 1968.
123 Pennar, op. cit., p. 110.
124 *Trud*, 18 July 1970.
125 *Pravda*, 22 May 1971.
126 See p. 266.
127 *Pravda*, 11 March 1972.
128 Middle East News Agency, 10 August 1972.
129 Quandt, *Decade of Decisions*, pp. 174–5, 177.
130 See p. 259.
131 *Al Rai al Aam*, 28 October 1973.
132 Iraqi News Agency, 26 May 1974.
133 Moscow Radio, 30 May 1974, cited in Moshe Ma'oz, *Syria Under Hafiz al-Asad*, p. 25. According to this agreement, Israel returned to Syria 'all the land it had lost in the 1973 war as well as the city of Kuneitra lost in the 1967 war'. Robert O. Freedman, *Soviet Policy Toward the Middle East since 1970*, Frederick Praeger, New York and London, 1975, p. 149. Also see p. 224.
134 United Press International, 1 October 1974.
135 See pp. 45, 138, 164.

136 Cited in *Events*, 1 October 1976, p. 23.
137 *BBC Summary of World Broadcasts, Part I*, 30 November 1977.
138 *The Middle East*, December 1980, p. 22.
139 Ibid., December 1979, p. 32. The Soviet weapons delivered to Syria by the following summer included MiG-25s, MiG-27s, and T-72 tanks. The number of Soviet military personnel then present in Syria was put at 2,000. *Guardian*, 23 August 1980.
140 *The Middle East*, February 1981, p. 14.
141 *Guardian*, 10 October 1980.
142 *Observer*, 9 November 1980. Soviet commitment to Syria was underlined during the May 1981 Syria–Israel crisis over the deployment of Syrian anti-aircraft missiles in Lebanon. Following a three-day visit to Damascus by Georgy Korniyenko, the Soviet first deputy foreign minister, the Syrian defence ministry stated that air defences, including missiles, were part of the Syrian armed forces, and would exist 'anywhere Syrian troops are present, to be ready for use whenever they need them'. *The Times*, 6 May 1981; *Guardian*, 9 May 1981.
143 *Daily Telegraph*, 10 November 1980. Earlier Guela Cohen (the initiator of Arab Jerusalem's annexation) had made an unsuccessful move for the Golan Heights' annexation. *Financial Times*, 18 and 23 September 1980.
144 Cited in Harry N. Howard, op. cit., p. 146. But the Kremlin had done little to back up its threat – as President Nasser was to discover during his visit to Moscow. See pp. 251.
145 See pp. 48, 115–16.
146 *Al Nahar* (The Day), 4 November 1971.
147 *Soviet News*, 2 November 1976.
148 Tass, 16 March 1978.
149 *Izvestia*, 21 March 1978.
150 Cited in *Guardian*, 6 February 1980.
151 'If the [Lebanese] Christian minority, either in the south or the north, is being attacked, Israel will not be passive,' said Prime Minister Begin. *Guardian*, 8 February 1980.
152 Cited in *Arab World File*, no. 945, 3 May 1978.
153 During his visit to Cairo in May 1966, Soviet Prime Minister Kosygin had a meeting with Ahmed Shukeiri, head of the PLO, 'later on denounced by the Russians as a nationalist hothead whom no one had ever taken seriously'. Laqueur, op. cit., pp. 73–4.
154 *Mezhdunariodnaya Zhizn*, January 1969, p. 42.
155 Moscow Radio, 21 October 1969.
156 Cited in John K. Cooley, *Green March, Black September: The Story of the Palestinian Arabs*, Frank Cass, London, 1973, p. 168.
157 *Pravda*, 3 October 1970.
158 Cooley, op. cit., p. 166. In addition, the USSR had pressured its east European allies to let the Palestinians buy weapons there. Ibid.
159 On the very day Sadat announced the expulsion of Soviet advisers from Egypt – 17 July 1972 – a Palestinian delegation had a meeting with Soviet officials led by Boris Ponomaryev, head of the CPSU's international department. *Arab World File*, no. 25, 24 July 1974.
160 Palestinian sources in Beirut were quoted as saying that the USSR had started shipping them arms directly. *New York Times*, 22 September 1972.
161 *Pravda*, 29 August 1972. A few months later *Al Hadaf*, a radical Palestinian journal, reported that in their conversations with Soviet leaders a group of Palestinian leaders pointed out that 'the Munich operation struck a blow to those Arab circles which called for the severing of relations with the socialist

camp, spurred Egypt into improving relations with the USSR, forced America and Israel to recognise the Palestinian entity, and raised the morale of the Palestinians in the Arab countries'. 16 December 1972.

162 *Pravda*, 29 August 1972.
163 Cited in *Le Monde*, 6 November 1973.
164 *Arab World File*, no. 25, 24 July 1974.
165 Cited in *Middle East Monitor*, 30 June 1974, p. 4.
166 *Pravda*, 4 August 1974.
167 *New Times*, no. 45, 1974, p. 11.
168 See p. 55.
169 Tass, 9 November 1975.
170 See pp. 268.
171 *Guardian*, 3 June 1976.
172 Israel had imposed the blockade with the prime objective of intercepting arms supplies to the PLO and the Lebanese left from the USSR and Libya. *New York Times*, 16 August 1976.
173 *Pravda*, 8 September 1976.
174 Rakah had two Jews and two Arabs in its delegation. *Guardian*, 6 May 1977. Three years later four Rakah members of the Knesset met Yasser Arafat at the conference of the Council of World Peace in Sofia, Bulgaria. Ibid., 26 September 1980.
175 *Arab World File*, no. 946, 3 May 1978.
176 *Guardian*, 31 August 1979.
177 *Observer*, 8 July 1979. Intensified Israeli air strikes and shellings, from 1 April to the end of July, caused 315 Lebanese civilian casualties (ninety-one dead, the rest wounded) as well as (unspecified) Palestinian civilian and guerrilla casualties, and displaced 175,000 Lebanese and 50,000 Palestinian civilians. *Washington Post*, 31 August 1979.
178 Of this, $350 million were provided as grants by various Arab governments, and the rest was 'Palestine tax' often collected as a surcharge on certain public services rendered in their countries. *BBC World Service*, 14 November 1979.
179 *Sunday Times*, 2 March 1980.
180 *Washington Post*, 18 November 1980.
181 *Keesing's Contemporary Archives: Vol. XVII*, p. 24230.
182 Within five years the Soviet bloc had become a major buyer of Jordanian phosphates. *The Middle East*, May 1977, pp. 34–5.
183 *The Times*, 2 August 1976.
184 *Guardian*, 19 September 1978.
185 *Daily Telegraph*, 21 June and 21 August 1980.
186 *The Times*, 27 May 1981.
187 *New York Times*, 10 February 1959.
188 *Middle East Journal*, Summer 1959, p. 290.
189 *Pravda*, 17 March 1959.
190 *Iraqi Times*, 21 August 1959.
191 Earlier, in his correspondence with Nasser, Khrushchev had stated that a government's policy towards the local Communists was its own, internal affair. See p. 251.
192 *New York Times*, 8 May 1960.
193 *Pravda*, 21 October 1961.
194 See p. 170, note 51 (chapter 8).
195 Oleg M. Smolansky, *The Soviet Union and the Arab East under Khrushchev*, p. 185.
196 *Pravda*, 17 February 1963.

197 See p. 170.
198 *Pravda*, 17 February 1963.
199 See p. 170.
200 *Izvestia*, 5 August 1966.
201 *New Times*, no. 34, 1968, p. 13.
202 See p. 170.
203 *Trud*, 11 February 1971.
204 *World Marxist Review*, no. 6, 1971, p. 13.
205 *Pravda*, 9 April 1971.
206 Freedman, op. cit., p. 47.
207 *Pravda*, 7 May 1971.
208 Ibid., 14 July 1971.
209 Ibid., 12 February 1972.
210 Majid Khadduri, *Socialist Iraq*, p. 145.
211 *New Times*, no. 16, 1972, pp. 4–5.
212 Cited in Freedman, op. cit., p. 72. According to the barter agreement between the two sides, the state-owned Iraq National Oil Company contracted to pay for the Soviet goods and services used for developing the oilfield in petroleum extracted from that oilfield: fifty million barrels, to be shipped over a period of four years. Peter Mansfield (ed.), op. cit., pp. 335–6.
213 Khadduri, op. cit., pp. 123, 126–7. At the same time the Syrian government nationalised the IPC pipeline complex passing through its territory to the Mediterranean. See p. 267.
214 Freedman, op. cit., p. 72.
215 *Izvestia*, 8 June 1972.
216 *Pravda*, 15 September 1972.
217 *New Times*, no. 41, 1972, p. 19.
218 See p. 171.
219 Cited in Freedman, op. cit., p. 145.
220 *Pravda*, 27 March 1974.
221 Ibid., 26 April 1974.
222 *Guardian*, 3 March 1979. 'Russia still recalls how [Iranian] Savak, the CIA and [Israeli] Mossad conspired to supply the Iraqi Kurds with Soviet weapons, via Iran, in order to create a rift between Moscow and Baghdad,' reported the Moscow correspondent of *Events*. 'Moscow is still so bitter about it that the death of Mustapha Barzani was simply noted here, without comment or eulogy.' 23 March 1979, p. 13.
223 See p. 143.
224 According to American sources, these arrangements came into effect in December 1974. *The Middle East*, April 1977, p. 26. Since no naval facilities were available to the Soviets in Iraq on the eve of the Iraq–Iran war in September 1980, they must have ended some time in the late 1970s.
225 Among those who received the copies of Brezhnev's letters were the heads of Libya, the PLO, and the Lebanese National Movement. *Events*, 1 October 1976, p. 23.
226 Cited in *The Middle East*, January 1979, p. 23.
227 See pp. 139, 146.
228 See p. 173.
229 *The Middle East*, December 1979, p. 32.
230 The Arab National Charter was published on 8 February. *Guardian*, 12 February 1980. The full text was carried by *The Middle East*, April 1980, p. 20.
231 *Guardian*, 22 September 1980.

232 *Pravda*, 23 September 1980.
233 *Daily Telegraph*, 25 September 1980.
234 Tass, 28 September 1980.
235 *The Middle East*, December 1980, p. 12.
236 *Krasnaya Zvezda*, 26 October 1980.
237 *The Middle East*, December 1980, p. 13. In an interview with Eric Rouleau of *Le Monde* on 7 October the Iranian president, Abol Hassan Bani-Sadr, said: 'At the beginning of August we already had in our hands outlines of Saddam Hussein's [war] plans as well as a detailed account of the conversations which had taken place in France among the Iranian counter-revolutionaries, the Iraqi representatives, Americans, and Israeli military experts. We had to pay dearly for these documents which were bought in Paris. They have proved to be surprisingly accurate.' Cited in *Guardian*, 9 October 1980.
238 Peace and Progress Radio, 14 November 1967.
239 *Pravda*, 29 November 1967.
240 See p. 177.
241 *Aziya i Afrika Segodnya* (Asia and Africa Today), no. 6, 1968, p. 8.
242 Peter Mansfield, op. cit., p. 175.
243 *New Times*, no. 30, 1970, p. 29.
244 A. Yodfat and M. Abir, *In the Direction of the Persian Gulf: The Soviet Union and the Persian Gulf*, Frank Cass, London, 1977, p. 111.
245 Tass, 30 September 1971.
246 Fred Halliday, *Arabia Without Sultans*, pp. 254–5.
247 *L'Orient-Le Jour*, 6 October 1972.
248 Cited in Yodfat and Abir, op. cit., p. 112.
249 *Pravda*, 26 November 1972.
250 See pp. 36, 89.
251 Yodfat and Abir, op. cit., p. 113.
252 This pipeline was commissioned in 1970. Most of the oil was carried from Iran to Israel semi-clandestinely. *Sunday Times*, 13 December 1970; Fred Halliday, op. cit., p. 262.
253 Michael C. Hudson, *Arab Politics*, p. 363.
254 See p. 179.
255 *The Middle East*, March 1978, p. 23.
256 *Guardian*, 27 June 1978.
257 Cited in ibid., 30 June 1978.
258 *Middle East Economic Digest*, 9 March 1979, pp. 13, 23.
259 See p. 181.
260 The next month South Yemen signed similar treaties with East Germany and Czechoslovakia. *International Herald Tribune*, 3 December 1979.
261 *Middle East Research and Information Project*, no. 81 (October 1979), p. 16. In late 1980 Moscow promised $750 million worth of military aid to Aden. In return South Yemen agreed to 'a Soviet request to use an airfield near Aden, and to have anchorage facilities in South Yemeni ports'. *Arabia: The Islamic World Review*, February 1981, p. 55.
262 Wayne S. Vucinich, 'Soviet Studies on the Middle East', in Lederer and Vucinich, op. cit., p. 214.
263 See p. 250.
264 Baku Radio, 1 November 1963.
265 *Pravda*, 2 February 1966; *Novoe Vremia* (New Times), 12 May 1967.
266 *New York Times*, 15 December 1967.
267 See pp. 35, 36.
268 See pp. 35, 89.
269 Halliday, op. cit., pp. 143–4.

270 *New Times*, no. 48, 1972, p. 15.
271 *The Middle East*, September 1977, p. 16.
272 Ibid., November 1977, p. 10.
273 According to a Western diplomat in Sanaa, the Soviets had sold weapons to the North Yemenis at one tenth of the normal price. Cited in *The Middle East*, January 1981, p. 26.
274 See p. 287.
275 To fly the American military jets Riyadh used Taiwanese pilots. *International Herald Tribune*, 3 December 1979.
276 *The Middle East*, January 1981, p. 26.
277 Ibid. Tony Hall of the news magazine *8 Days* put the number of Soviet military advisers at 250–300. 2 May 1981, p. 8.
278 *The Economy and the Social and Political Order in Northern Arabia in the Nineteenth and the First Third of the Twentieth Century* (in Russian), Moscow, 1961, p. 221.
279 Wayne S. Vucinich, op. cit., p. 211. Riyadh used part of the credits to buy Soviet wheat.
280 Stephen Page, *The USSR and Arabia*, Central Asian Research Centre, London, 1971, p. 20.
281 See pp. 80, 182.
282 Vucinich, op. cit., p. 212.
283 *Pravda*, 4 November 1964.
284 Ibid., 27 May 1966.
285 See p. 82.
286 *International Life*, March 1968, p. 44.
287 See p. 286.
288 *New Times*, no. 5, 1973, pp. 26–7.
289 See p. 260, note 81 (chapter 12).
290 *The Times*, 10 November 1973.
291 See p. 261.
292 See p. 276.
293 See p. 268.
294 Cited in *The Middle East*, November 1978, p. 46.
295 *Guardian*, 7 February 1979.
296 *Events*, 9 March 1979, p. 19.
297 This flight started on 20 March 1979. *Guardian*, 1 June 1979.
298 Cited in *The Middle East*, February 1980, p. 10; March 1980, p. 13.
299 *Guardian*, 29 January 1980.
300 *Monday Morning*, 31 July 1980.
301 *Events*, 23 March 1979, p. 4.
302 Cairo Radio, 20 May 1964.
303 *New Times*, no. 1, 1966, p. 11.
304 *Guardian*, 30 December 1976; *The Middle East*, June 1978, p. 32.
305 Interestingly, led by the radical deputies, the Kuwaiti parliament had blocked this trade agreement with Rumania for almost a year, in 1975, on the grounds that, because of its existing diplomatic relations with Tel Aviv, Rumania was 'sympathetic' to Israel. *Middle East Economic Digest*, August 1977 (Special Report on Kuwait), p. 40.
306 *8 Days*, 23 February 1980, p. 3.
307 *Daily Telegraph*, 24 April 1981.
308 *8 Days*, 9 May 1981, p. 2.
309 Freedman, op. cit., p. 61. Also see p. 272.
310 Halliday, op. cit., p. 389; Freedman, op. cit., p. 105.
311 *The Middle East*, June 1977, p. 20.

312 About three quarters of this oil is bound for ports in the West and Japan. *Daily Telegraph*, 25 September 1980; *Guardian*, 25 September 1980.

Chapter 13 The Arabs and the West

1 See p. 247, note 2 (chapter 12).
2 See p. 214.
3 Naseer H. Aruri and Natalie K. Hevener, 'France and the Middle East', in Tareq Y. Ismael et al., *The Middle East in World Politics*, p. 67. The King–Crane commission recommended that 'the desire of the overwhelming majority for Syrian unity be respected', and that a single mandate for Greater Syria be awarded, preferably to America. It also recommended that a programme for a Jewish Commonwealth in Palestine be abandoned. But nothing came of the report (submitted in late August), as President Wilson fell gravely ill in the autumn. The document was not officially published until 1947. Robert W. Stookey, *America and the Arab States*, pp. 37–8.
4 P. Edward Haley, 'Britain and the Middle East', in Ismael et al., op. cit., p. 24.
5 See pp. 27–8.
6 See p. 215.
7 Miles Copeland, *The Game of Nations: The Amorality of Power Politics*, Weidenfeld & Nicolson, London, 1969, p. 53.
8 At 70,000, the British troops posted in the Suez zone were seven times the figure specified by the Anglo–Egyptian treaty of 1936. Peter Mansfield, *The Arabs*, p. 275.
9 Peter Mansfield (ed.), *The Middle East*, p. 227.
10 *The Middle East*, October 1980, p. 45.
11 Mansfield (ed.), *The Middle East*, p. 227.
12 Kennett Love, *Suez: the Twice-Fought War*, McGraw-Hill, New York, 1969, p. 88. Also see p. 249.
13 Enver M. Koury, *The Super-Powers and the Balance of Power in the Arab World*, p. 184.
14 Mansfield (ed.), *The Middle East*, p. 228.
15 See pp. 64, 217, 236, 250.
16 During the Suez crisis the British government instigated plans to assassinate Nasser. 'The MI6 [Military Intelligence 6] in charge of the operation described how the assistance of some young Egyptian officers, who were strongly opposed to Nasser, had been secured and how special weapons had been buried at a convenient spot near Cairo,' states Chapman Pincher, a British journalist and author. 'They were never used because certain circumstances essential to the operation did not materialise. . . . Eden, then prime minister . . . had vetoed an all-British effort to kill or capture Nasser using Special Air Service troops, but agreed, or turned a blind eye, to the MI6 operation in which the killing would have been accomplished by Egyptian officers who were eventually dealt with by their president when he learned of their treachery.' *Inside Story: A Documentary of the Pursuit of Power*, Sidgwick & Jackson, London, 1978, p. 90. Efforts by the British government to achieve this end continued after the Suez war. Describing a top-level meeting of American and British intelligence services in Beirut in April 1957, Wilbur Crane Eveland refers to the British Secret Intelligence Service officer, sent from London, thus: 'Teams had been fielded to assassinate Nasser, he informed us, and then rumbled on about the bloody Egyptians, who'd planned to turn the Middle East over to the Commies.' *Ropes of Sand*, p. 247. On the American side, 'these activities emanated from a

triumvirate consisting of the secretary of state, John Foster Dulles, Allen Dulles (the CIA director), and Kermit Roosevelt,' states Eveland. 'As the hero of the Iran coup [in 1953], Kermit Roosevelt had been charged by the Dulles brothers to work with the British to bring down Nasser without further delay.' Op. cit., p. 248.

17 See p. 65.
18 Peter Mansfield (ed.), *The Middle East*, p. 230.
19 Nadav Safran, *Israel: The Embattled Ally*, pp. 360–1.
20 Two years earlier American food aid to Egypt had amounted to $125 million. Tarun Chandra Bose, *The Superpowers and the Middle East*, p. 70.
21 William B. Quandt, *Decade of Decisions*, p. 38.
22 See p. 218.
23 Nasser made a statement to this effect in an interview with *Izvestia*. See p. 254.
24 Stookey, op. cit., p. 201.
25 See pp. 239–40, 265.
26 Stookey, op. cit., p. 204.
27 Ibid.
28 *US Department of State Bulletin*, 12 June 1967, p. 870.
29 Cited in Quandt, op. cit., p. 54, note 33.
30 On their part the Soviet leaders had cautioned the Egyptian and Syrian presidents against an attack on Israel. See p. 255.
31 Cited in Michel Bar Zohar, *Embassies in Crisis*, Prentice Hall, Englewood Cliffs, NJ, 1970, p. 157.
32 Quandt, op. cit., p. 58.
33 Ibid., p. 59.
34 *Maariv*, 3 May 1968.
35 Safran, op. cit., pp. 262–3.
36 Stookey, op. cit., p. 241.
37 *Sunday Times*, 25 November 1973. See pp. 258, 291.
38 'Ismail was the first high-level Egyptian official to meet with Nixon in some time,' writes William B. Quandt. 'The visit had been arranged through the "back channel". The state department was not informed until the last moment.' Op. cit., p. 154.
39 See p. 222.
40 Stookey, op. cit., p. 243.
41 Quandt, op. cit., p. 159.
42 *Newsweek*, 23 April 1973, cited in Mohamed Sid-Ahmed, *After the Guns Fall Silent*, Croom Helm, London, 1976, pp. 22–3.
43 'Kissinger subsequently told Egyptian officials that he was very impressed when they began to send messages through the "back channel" shortly after the war began,' states William B. Quandt. 'Nixon and Kissinger attached considerable importance to the possibility of improving US–Arab relations after the war was over.' Op. cit., p. 173, note 16.
44 See p. 223.
45 These revelations were made by General Shazli after he had resigned his post as Egyptian ambassador to Portugal in June 1978. The authenticity of his statements was not challenged either by President Sadat or Hafez Ismail, the then defence minister. *Guardian*, 20 and 21 June 1978; *Observer*, 7 October 1979.
46 William B. Quandt refers to 'the encouraging tone of US–Egyptian exchanges' through the 'back channel' during the period of 6 to 20 October. Op. cit. p. 191.
47 See pp. 242, 260.

48 See p. 261.
49 Karen Dawisha, *Soviet Foreign Policy Towards Egypt*, p. 73.
50 *Le Monde*, 21 January 1975.
51 This revelation was made by Edward F. R. Sheehan, an American specialist on the Middle East, in an article in the magazine *Foreign Policy*. Cited in *The Times*, 8 March 1976.
52 See pp. 224–51.
53 *The Times*, 27 March 1976.
54 In his article 'Secrets of Camp David', Arnaud de Borchgrave listed one of 'the secret verbal understandings reached at Camp David between Sadat and Jimmy Carter' as: 'The secret cooperation between Egyptian and Israeli intelligence services, started at the time of the Libyan–Soviet buildup against Egypt at the end of 1976 will be expanded'. *Newsweek*, 23 October 1978, p. 20.
55 This means that Egypt received more economic aid from the USA than the rest of Africa and all of Latin America combined. Raymond William Baker, *Egypt's Uncertain Revolution under Nasser and Sadat*, p. 141.
56 See pp. 262.
57 Ismail Fahmi's interview with Mark Bruzonsky. *The Middle East*, July 1979, p. 54. Fahmi resigned in protest over Sadat's visit to Jerusalem. President Sadat was at the same time engaged in clandestine contacts with top Israeli leaders. On 16 September 1977 Hassan Touhami, one of Sadat's closest aides (later to be appointed a deputy prime minister), had a secret meeting with Israeli defence minister, Moshe Dayan, in Tangier, Morocco, to convey Sadat's positive response to Begin's suggestion for a secret meeting between him and Sadat. Moshe Dayan's memoirs, cited in *Guardian*, 10 March 1981. Nine months earlier Wilbur Crane Eveland had mentioned this. *Ropes of Sand*, p. 99n.
58 *The Middle East*, July 1979, p. 53. However, it is difficult to believe that the surprise and the indecision displayed briefly by Carter and his aides were genuine. Given that Hassan Touhami had been a CIA contact since the early days of the anti-royalist coup in 1953, and that he was very close to Sadat, it is reasonable to assume that the CIA had established direct or indirect contacts with Sadat soon after he became president in September 1970. Given this, and the role played by the CIA in arranging cooperation between the Egyptian and Israeli intelligence services in late 1976, it is equally reasonable to assume that President Carter was kept informed of the clandestine moves being made to bring about a face-to-face meeting between Sadat and Begin. See notes 38, 46, and 57 above; and Eveland, op. cit., pp. 98–9.
59 *Time*, 29 May 1978, p. 23.
60 *The Times*, 15 May 1978.
61 US defence department figures for the fiscal year 1 October 1977 to 30 September 1978, cited in *Events*, 20 October 1978, p. 5.
62 Begin's press conference in New York on 20 September 1978. *Guardian*, 21 September 1978.
63 *Events*, 6 October 1978, p. 6.
64 Arnaud de Borchgrave, 'Secrets of Camp David', in *Newsweek*, 23 October 1978, p. 20.
65 With this Begin realised the long-cherished hope of many Israeli leaders. 'Since 1967 I've heard from many Israelis that a separate peace with Egypt was . . . their objective, their dream,' said Eric Rouleau of *Le Monde*. 'Just after the October 1973 war General Chaim Bar-Lev told me that Israel had very strong indications that there was a good chance for a separate peace

with Egypt. And I just could not believe him.' *The Middle East*, November 1978, p. 61.

66 Ibid., p. 64.

67 Ibid., p. 62.

68 See p. 229. The peace treaty came into effect two months later, after it had been ratified by the parliaments of Egypt and Israel.

69 *The Middle East*, July 1981, p. 12.

70 *Sunday Times*, 17 July 1977.

71 Arnaud de Borchgrave, 'Secrets of Camp David', in *Newsweek*, 23 October 1978, p. 20.

72 *Events*, 6 April 1979, p. 9; *Guardian*, 12 December 1980.

73 *Events*, 20 October 1978, p. 5.

74 *New York Times*, 19 September 1979.

75 *Guardian*, 10 November and 23 December 1980; 12 March 1981.

76 Ibid., 10 December 1980. This development destroyed any lingering notion of 'linkage' between progress in Egyptian–Israeli relations and Palestinian autonomy.

77 See note 54 above.

78 *Daily Telegraph*, 8 December 1980.

79 Ibid., 4 March 1981.

80 Miles Copeland, op. cit., pp. 50, 186. Copeland was a member of the American embassy in Damascus in 1949.

81 Tabitha Petran, *Syria*, pp. 201–2.

82 Ibid., p. 102.

83 Patrick Seale, *The Struggle for Syria: A Study of Post-War Arab Politics, 1945–1958*, Oxford University Press, London and New York, 1965, p. 293.

84 'Syrian army officers assigned major roles [in the planned coup] simply walked into the G-2 offices of Colonel Abdul Hamid Sarraj [Syrian military intelligence chief], turned in their money, and named the CIA officers who'd paid them,' writes Wilbur Crane Eveland. Of the three American diplomats expelled two were 'career' CIA officers ('caught red-handed') and the third was the army attaché. Op. cit., p. 254.

85 See pp. 132, 237.

86 Petran, op. cit., p. 124.

87 See p. 132.

88 Petran, op. cit., p. 126. Also see Miles Copeland, op. cit., pp. 176, 186.

89 See pp. 218.

90 See pp. 267, 281.

91 *The Times*, 6 August 1974.

92 Ibid., 20 October 1975.

93 *Guardian*, 7 November 1975.

94 Ibid., 20 April 1976.

95 See pp. 263, 305.

96 *Guardian*, 18 March 1980.

97 Cited in ibid.

98 *Guardian*, 10 March 1980.

99 'The [privately run] Phalange radio is always quick to report these acts [of terrorism by the Muslim Brotherhood in Syria] for the benefit of the Syrian troops stationed in Lebanon,' reported David Hirst. Ibid., 19 February 1980.

100 Eveland, op. cit., p. 252. Soon after the elections Washington announced economic aid of $15 million to Beirut. Ibid. Eveland had direct access to the CIA director Allen Dulles, whose brother, John Foster Dulles, was the secretary of state.

101 Stookey, op. cit., p. 155.
102 See p. 270.
103 The totals up to 1977 were 1.22 million in America and 80,000 in Canada. Statistics published on the reverse of the official map of Lebanon, Ministry of Information, Government of Lebanon, Beirut, 1978.
104 'As Lebanon plunged into a bloody civil war, the CIA, with the connivance of the intrepid if short-sighted Israeli intelligence service, was accused by some officials of supporting covertly the fighting that inflicted an awful, temporarily crippling attrition on the PLO,' writes Roger Morris. 'Allegedly conducted by the special Israeli bureau of the CIA, the Lebanese operation proceeded, according to these sources, while unknowing American diplomats (like Korry in Chile) tried to arrange a ceasefire, and while Congressional and executive oversight groups were consistently misled on the scope and purpose of our covert involvement in Lebanon.' *Uncertain Greatness: Henry Kissinger and American Foreign Policy*, Quartet, London, 1978, p. 261.
105 Eveland, op. cit., p. 342.
106 *The Times*, 4 July 1977.
107 *Newsweek*, 27 March 1978, p. 15.
108 *Guardian*, 30 November 1978. The joint statement on Lebanese unity was significant insofar as it was France which had created the Lebanon of today. Equally significantly, France, which had for centuries acted as the official protector of Maronites under the Ottoman empire, now openly criticised the right-wing Christian militias for 'acting [against the state] with Israeli encouragement'. Ibid.
109 *Washington Post*, 31 August 1979.
110 *The Middle East*, March 1981, p. 11.
111 See p. 118.
112 Cited in Safran, op. cit., p. 430.
113 *Al Sayyed*, 13 September 1972.
114 David Hirst, *The Gun and the Olive Branch*, p. 311.
115 *New York Times*, 26 June 1973. Also see p. 273.
116 *Observer*, 16 June 1974.
117 The PLO was helped in this by the fact that the PFLP, the originator of this tactic, had decided in December 1973 to 'suspend' such actions outside of Israel. See p. 157.
118 *The Times*, 30 January 1975. Following an unsuccessful attempt to hijack a British Airways plane in late November, the PLO arrested twenty-eight Palestinians. *Observer*, 30 November 1974.
119 See p. 225. In accordance with this undertaking, in January 1976 America vetoed a UN Security Council resolution which combined the essence of UN General Assembly resolution 3236 (of November 1974) regarding the Palestinian right to establish an independent state in Palestine, with a proviso about the right of all states in the region to exist in peace, territorial integrity and independence (thus underwriting Israel's right to an independent existence). Edward W. Said, *The Question of Palestine*, Routledge & Kegan Paul, London, 1980, pp. 225–6.
120 *Financial Times*, 16 January 1978.
121 *Guardian*, 17 November 1976.
122 Ibid., 18 March 1977. 'It [homeland] is a word as charged with emotional significance for Palestinians now as it was for Jews then [in 1917],' stated an editorial in *The Times* on 26 March 1977.
123 *The Times*, 10 May 1977.
124 Ibid., 8 July 1977.

125 *Guardian*, 15 August 1977.
126 *Sunday Times*, 28 August 1977.
127 *Guardian*, 30 September 1977. As stated earlier, Ismail Fahmi, the Egyptian foreign minister, acted as an intermediary between the US administration and the PLO. See note 57 above.
128 *Guardian*, 5 October 1977.
129 *Sunday Times*, 30 April 1978. Recognition of the right of Israel to exist runs counter inter alia to article twenty of the Palestine National Charter, adopted by the PLO in 1964. 'The Balfour declaration, the mandate of Palestine, and everything that has been based upon them, are deemed null and void,' states the article. Cited in *The Middle East*, January 1980, p. 17. See also p. 55.
130 *Guardian*, 3 August 1979.
131 Ibid., 16, 18 and 20 August 1979; *Observer*, 19 August 1979. See p. 229.
132 Cited in *The Middle East*, November 1979, p. 42.
133 *Guardian*, 14 March 1980. In contrast Israel enjoyed the recognition of about fifty nations.
134 *The Times*, 14 June 1980.
135 *Guardian*, 25 February 1981.
136 Ibid.
137 *Newsweek*, 2 March 1981, p. 16. It is worth noting that the British government of (the Conservative) Edward Heath had allowed the PLO to open an office in London in late 1973.
138 *Guardian*, 28 January 1981.
139 *Sunday Times*, 15 February 1981; *Daily Telegraph*, 16 February 1981.
140 See p. 160. Anti-British feelings were running particularly high due to Anglo–French–Israeli aggression against Egypt.
141 Washington had recognised the Hashemite Kingdom of Jordan in January 1949.
142 Although the Anglo–Jordanian treaty was ended on 13 March, the British troops did not finally leave Jordan until 6 July. Mansfield (ed.), *The Middle East*, p. 379.
143 Stookey, op. cit., p. 151.
144 Bob Woodward was one of the two reporters of the *Washington Post* who investigated the Watergate scandal which led to the resignation of President Nixon in August 1974. According to Woodward, the 'No Beef' project was so secret that even President Carter was not informed of it. 19 February 1977. 'As far as I am concerned, anything I get for Jordan and its people is proper,' said King Hussein. 'To us the CIA is part of the [US] government.' Cited in *The Middle East*, April 1977, p. 95.
145 See pp. 309–10.
146 See p. 100, note 70 (chapter 6).
147 Stookey, op. cit., p. 202.
148 The decision was taken at the Arab summit conference in Khartoum in late August 1967. Stookey, op. cit., p. 213.
149 King Hussein resumed personal contacts with Israeli leaders in September 1967. Talks between the two sides continued intermittently for about three years, often in foreign capitals. During this period Yigael Allon met the monarch fourteen times; and Abba Eban, the Israeli foreign minister, twelve times. Later the venue of talks changed to boats in the Gulf of Aqaba, and then to a tent in the Negev desert. *The Times*, 5 December 1974; *Guardian*, 18 April 1980. Since the second set of revelations of these clandestine meetings, a secret rendezvous occurred between Prince Mohammed of Jordan and Shimon Peres, the Israeli Labour Alignment leader, in

London in March 1981. *Guardian*, 20 and 21 March 1981.

150 King Hussein launched an offensive against the Palestinian commandos only after the hostages had been found in a Palestinian refugee camp in Amman and moved to safety. Safran, op. cit., p. 451.

151 However, the *Chicago Sun-Times* published the Nixon statement in the evening edition of 17 September 1970.

152 See p. 221, note 42 (chapter 10).

153 'Communications in Amman between the American embassy and the royal palace were extremely difficult,' writes William B. Waundt. 'Radio and walkie-talkie were used, and the fedayeen [i.e. Palestinian commandos] often eavesdropped on sensitive conversations.' Op. cit., p. 116, note 15.

154 Ibid.

155 Stookey, op. cit., p. 231.

156 Qaundt, op. cit., p. 118.

157 See pp. 266, 272, 276. According to Mohamed Heikal, the Soviets urged 'utmost restraint' on President Nasser during the Jordanian crisis. *The Road to Ramadan*, pp. 98–9.

158 Stookey, op. cit., p. 232.

159 Eveland, op. cit., p. 330.

160 See p. 54.

161 Quandt, op. cit., p. 235. Yet the total amounted to only about half of the Jordanian budget deficit of $400 million in 1975. *Guardian*, 6 December 1975. American budget proposals for the fiscal year, starting on 1 October, are normally made by the president in January, and passed by Congress in spring.

162 *Guardian*, 18 April 1980.

163 Quandt, op. cit., p. 257.

164 See p. 276.

165 *The Times*, 2 August 1976.

166 *Guardian*, 23 February 1977.

167 *The Times*, 27 April 1977.

168 Ibid.

169 *Arab News*, 24 December 1977.

170 *Daily Telegraph*, 19 June and 4 December 1980.

171 *Guardian*, 20 June 1980; *Daily Telegraph*, 29 June and 3 December 1980.

172 *Guardian*, 2 December 1980.

173 *Daily Telegraph*, 6 December 1980.

174 This was a deliberate policy. 'In his reply [to the American ambassador in Baghdad in August 1953], secretary of state Dulles, said that the United States considered Iraq to be entirely within Britain's political sphere, and that in spite of the ambassador's pleas the US would deal with Iraq only in a manner consistent with British objectives,' writes Wilbur Crane Eveland. Op. cit., p. 67.

175 See pp. 30–1.

176 Wilbur Crane Eveland, op. cit., pp. 82, 85. Since this was the first arms deal between the USA and an Arab state, American officials worked closely with the British in their negotiations with the Iraqis.

177 See pp. 169–70.

178 M. S. Agwani, *Communism in the Arab East*, p. 129.

179 The condition for OPEC's membership is that the country must be exporting a minimum of twenty million tons of oil (i.e. about 150 million barrels) a year.

180 Even then only a partial agreement was reached between the IPC and the Iraqi government. See p. 281.

181 See p. 170.
182 8 November 1963; cited in Agwani, op. cit., p. 143. Almost certainly the American agency referred to was the CIA. See p. 320. France's Service de Documentation Extérieure et de Contre-Espionnage too helped to overthrow Qassem and repress the Communists. *The Middle East*, August 1981, p. 33.
183 Mansfield (ed.), *The Middle East*, p. 328.
184 Ironically, a decade later the possession of these islands by the Islamic regime in Iran became a matter of apprehension in Western capitals.
185 Harry N. Howard, *The King–Crane Commission*, Khayats, Beirut, 1963, p. 59.
186 Whereas Britain, France and Holland were each represented by a government-controlled company, America was represented by two private corporations. The share of the four countries involved was 23.75 per cent each, with the remaining 5 per cent going to C. S. Gulbenkian, who had been the middleman in the original TPC concession granted by the Ottoman ruler. Stookey, op. cit., p. 62.
187 See p. 281.
188 See p. 143.
189 Majid Khadduri, *Socialist Iraq*, p. 174.
190 Ibid., p. 173. Also see p. 172, note 63 (chapter 8).
191 *Statistical Pocket Book, 1976*. Republic of Iraq Ministry of Planning, Baghdad, 1977, p. 55. In contrast, non-military imports from the Soviet bloc in 1976 amounted to $340 million. Ibid., p. 56.
192 *Washington Post*, 18 June 1981; *Guardian*, 22 June 1981. Iraq secured its first nuclear reactor (capacity, two megawatts) from the USSR in 1967. It has since then been producing isotopes for research in agriculture, science and industry. *8 Days*, 20 June 1981, p. 8.
193 *Sunday Times*, 14 June 1981. Iraq was reportedly negotiating the purchase of a small plutonium reprocessing plant from an Italian company. *The Times*, 20 June 1981.
194 *Sunday Times*, 5 November 1978.
195 *The Middle East*, May 1980, p. 31. Earlier, only strong opposition by Congressional leaders had made the Carter administration reverse its decision to sanction a sale of Boeing jets, worth $200 million, to Iraq. *Guardian*, 7 and 30 August 1980.
196 *Observer*, 4 May 1980.
197 See p. 285, note 237. (chapter 12).
198 President Carter's aides seemed to have reckoned that within two to three weeks, unable to withstand the Iraqi onslaught, Iranian leaders would approach the White House for spare parts for their American-made warplanes and tanks. Carter would agree to this request in exchange for the release of the American hostages. Since these negotiations would take one to two weeks to finish successfully, the hostages would be expected to arrive in America about a week before polling day – in time to ensure Carter's re-election. In the event it did not happen that way.
199 In the late 1970s the proven world reserves of oil were estimated to be 650 billion barrels. *Now!*, 7 December 1979, p. 70. OPEC's members then were: Algeria, Ecuador, Gabon (associate), Indonesia, Iran, Iraq, Kuwait, Libya, Nigeria, Qatar, Saudi Arabia, the United Arab Emirates, and Venezuela.
200 See p. 328.
201 Lord Curzon, the British foreign minister, countered the American argument for supplementing America's depleted oil reserves by stating that the USA produced 70 per cent of the world's petroleum, and its nationals

another 12 per cent in Mexico, whereas the British share of world oil production was only 4.5 per cent. Stookey, op. cit., p. 60.

202 The IPC offered £5,000 as advance. Mansfield, *The Arabs*, p. 241. While the Saudi ruler received £50,000 as advance against future royalties, the Iraqi king had received £400,000 as advance in 1927. See p. 12; and Halliday, *Arabia Without Sultans*, p. 405.

203 M. S. Agwani, *Politics in the Gulf*, Vikas, New Delhi, 1978, pp. 36–7.

204 At that time one British Pound, divided into 20 shillings or 240 pennies, was equal to $4.75.

205 Stookey, op. cit., p. 72. In order to finance the construction of the 1,000 mile long Trans-Arabian Pipeline from the oilfields in the Gulf to Sidon, Lebanon, the parent companies of Aramco coopted the Standard Oil Company of New Jersey and the Standard Oil Company of New York in 1946. The final distribution of Aramco's shares was: Socal, Texaco, and Esso (later Exxon), 30 per cent each; and Socony (later Mobil), 10 per cent. Mansfield (ed.), *The Middle East*, p. 148.

206 Stookey, op. cit., p. 75. When, in July 1952, the American justice department instituted a grand jury investigation for criminal indictment of the five American major oil corporations for conspiring illegally to restrain international oil trade, the secretary of state, Dean Acheson, opposed the move. Later, in 1954, President Truman instructed the justice department to abandon criminal action against the oil majors and institute a civil complaint instead. Ibid., pp. 83, 85.

207 Lack of political independence and/or failure to meet the minimum export requirement kept the following Arab oil-producing countries out of OPEC's founding membership: Bahrain, Qatar, Oman, Syria and Egypt.

208 See pp. 281, 327.

209 Until the ultimate goal is achieved, the OPEC document stated, the government of a member state should see to it that the contracted arrangements with the concessionaires provide for maximum governmental participation and control over all aspects of their operations. Also, the government should set a 'tax reference' price, and should progressively and expeditiously reduce the area of existing concessions. Cited in Sam H. Schurr, Paul T. Homan et al., *Middle Eastern Oil and the Western World: Prospects and Problems*, American Elsevier, New York, 1971, pp. 124–6.

210 Halliday, op. cit., p. 411.

211 Stookey, op. cit., p. 76. In 1968 the five American oil majors (Exxon, Gulf, Mobil, Socal and Texaco), and British Petroleum and Royal Dutch-Shell together controlled 77.9 per cent of world oil production, 60.9 per cent of refining, and 55.6 per cent of marketing facilities. Halliday, op. cit., p. 396.

212 Walter Z. Laqueur, *The Struggle for the Middle East*, p. 125.

213 At $10 to $12 a metric ton, oil cost about half as much as locally-mined coal in West Europe, selling at $16 a metric ton (plus a subsidy of $5); and it provided one and a half times as much heat as did coal. Ibid., p. 126. The remarkable degree of industrial expansion in the US, Japan and West Europe was made possible 'partly by a copious and dependable supply of inexpensive energy' in the form of oil imported from the Middle East. Stookey, op. cit., p. 256.

214 Laqueur, op. cit., p. 126.

215 In the late 1960s the cost price of an oil barrel varied in the Gulf from six American cents in Kuwait to thirty-five cents for Dubai's off-shore oilwells. The corresponding figure for Venezuela was fifty cents to a dollar; and for America, three dollars or more. Halliday, op. cit., p. 411.

216 The monarchy was overthrown in Libya on 1 September 1969. The republi-

can regime was also aware of the disruption in oil supplies from Saudi Arabia through the Trans-Arabian Pipeline, which became virtually inoperable in late 1969 due to repeated breakdowns caused by the Palestinian commandos operating in Lebanon. Halliday, op. cit., p. 77, note 24.

217 While Libya was assured of takings of $2.20 a barrel (versus $1 in 1969), the Gulf states received only $1.30 a barrel. Tareq Y. Ismael, 'Oil: The New Diplomacy', in Ismael et al., op. cit., p. 232. The main reason for the difference was that whereas Libya negotiated with the (comparatively small) American independent oil companies, the Gulf states had to deal with the American oil giants.

218 In 1973 OPEC members possessed 90 per cent of the world's proven oil reserves. *The Times*, 12 June 1973.

219 The Organisation of Arab Petroleum Exporting Countries was formed by Kuwait, Libya and Saudi Arabia in January 1968, with its membership limited to those Arab states which had oil 'as the principal and basic source of national income'. Three years later, when this requirement was dropped, its membership increased to ten – including Algeria, Bahrain, Egypt, Iraq, Qatar, Syria, and the UAE. Agwani, *Politics in the Gulf*, p. 43.

220 *The Times*, 18 October and 17 November 1973. Iraq did not accept this resolution, or the one on the Arab oil boycott. Stating that 'We [Arabs] must not punish the whole world', the Iraqi oil minister argued for total nationalisation of all American and Dutch interests in the Arab world, and withdrawal of all Arab funds from American banks. Cited in Agwani, *Politics in the Gulf*, p. 45.

221 *Economist*, 7 July 1973; Halliday, op. cit., p. 395.

222 Walter Z. Laqueur, op. cit., p. 125; Halliday, op. cit., p. 45.

223 OAPEC's embargo against Holland lasted until 10 July 1974, nearly eight weeks longer than that against America. *The Times*, 11 July 1974.

224 Joseph Churba, *The Politics of Defeat: America's Decline in the Middle East*, Cyrco Press, New York and London, 1977, p. 159.

225 Stookey, op. cit., p. 258.

226 Agwani, *Politics in the Gulf*, p. 258.

227 *Time*, 2 April 1973, p. 21; *Middle East Economic Digest*, 27 December 1974, p. 1589.

228 Stookey, op. cit., p. 261.

229 American imports consisted of one million bpd of Arab crude oil and one million bpd of 'products refined from [crude] oil originating in Arab states'. Ibid., p. 57. As in West Europe, oil provided half the total energy needs of America.

230 *Ike*, 8 March 1978.

231 Stookey, op. cit., p. 57.

232 Agwani, *Politics in the Gulf*, p. 46.

233 OPEC members stuck to the agreed price of $11.65 a barrel. But due to economic recession and restraints imposed on oil usage in the West and Japan in 1974, they received an average of 93 per cent of the tax reference price of $11.65 a barrel. Stookey, op. cit., p. 259.

234 *Business Week*, 13 January 1975, p. 69.

235 Stookey, op. cit., p. 275.

236 *International Herald Tribune*, 7 April 1973.

237 *Observer*, 27 July 1975.

238 Churba, op. cit., p. 157.

239 *Guardian*, 1 November 1979.

240 According to Herman Kahn of the Hoover Institute of California, oil prices had fallen by 20 to 50 per cent during the period of 1974–9: that is, it had

lagged behind the inflation rate by that much in different countries of the West. *Daily Telegraph*, 23 July 1980.

241 *Daily American*, 4 January 1979.

242 *International Herald Tribune*, 21 December 1979; *8 Days*, 5 January 1980, p. 17.

243 *Time*, 26 November 1979, p. 25.

244 With 78 per cent of the general public mentioning it, Japan tied with Israel as the second most important foreign country to America. *Guardian*, 14 March 1980.

245 *Sunday Times*, 27 January 1980.

246 Gulf oil imports accounted for 90 per cent of Japan's oil needs, 65 per cent of West Europe's, and 30 per cent of America's. *Guardian*, 25 September 1980.

247 The actual production figures for the first ten months of 1979 were: Saudi Arabia, 9.2 million bpd; and all other Gulf states, 12.1 million bpd. *8 Days*, 5 January 1980, p. 17.

248 Mansfield, *The Arabs*, p. 273.

249 Ramon Knauerhase, *The Saudi Arabian Economy*, p. 45.

250 George W. Stocking, *Middle East Oil: A Study in Political and Economic Controversy*, Vanderbilt University Press, Nashville, Tenn., 1970, pp. 92–5.

251 'The [Saudi] king took the occasion to express Arab apprehension at Jewish immigration into Palestine,' write Robert W. Stookey. 'The [American] president, who had reassured him on this score a few years before, repeated, and shortly afterward confirmed in writing, that the United States would make no basic change in its policy in Palestine without full and prior consultation with both Jews and Arabs.' Op. cit., pp. 88–9. Some months earlier President Roosevelt had given an election pledge which ran contrary to this statement. See p. 215.

252 Halliday, op. cit., p. 51.

253 At the same time the US income tax liability of Aramco fell from $30 million to $5 million. Ibid.

254 Eveland, op. cit., p. 245.

255 Halliday, op. cit., pp. 58, 141. Earlier, on 25 October 1962, President Kennedy had written a letter to Crown Prince Feisal (then attending a UN session) assuring him that America would defend Saudi Arabia. Stookey, op. cit., p. 184.

256 Of this, orders for British weapons amounted to £120 million. This was the largest single military deal that Britain had concluded so far. See p. 254, note 47 (chapter 12).

257 Mansfield (ed.), *The Middle East*, p. 145. Syria was absent from this summit. and did not receive any subsidies from the Arab monarchs.

258 *The Times*, 8 July 1970; *Daily Telegraph*, 13 July 1971.

259 Halliday, op. cit., pp. 61, 63.

260 American oil imports from Saudi Arabia in 1970 amounted to 40,000 bpd. *The Middle East*, February 1977, p. 40.

261 *Observer*, 17 November 1973.

262 However, Saudi troops did not engage in combat action. *International Herald Tribune*, 13 January 1978.

263 *The Times*, 18 October and 27 December 1973.

264 Ibid., 12 December 1973.

265 *Financial Times*, 28 January 1974.

266 The actual sum for the period 1950–73 was $600 million; and the exact period after the Yom Kippur war was November 1973 to July 1976. *The Middle East*, February 1977, p. 40. The Saudi purchases from America included 110 F-5E jet warplanes and 2,500 missiles. *New York Times*, 30 September 1979.

267 Between 1973 and 1976 the total current account surplus of OPEC members was $144 billion. *The Middle East*, August 1979, p. 26.

268 Eveland, op. cit., p. 332. In early 1980 there were three intelligence services in Saudi Arabia: one under Prince Nayef, the interior minister; and two under Prince Turki (a son of King Feisal), the security chief. *Guardian*, 6 February 1980. In the spring of 1981 there were 'thousands of US ex-military personnel training Saudis under the auspices of the Vinnel Corporation, a CIA-organised enterprise'. *New Statesman*, 1 May 1981, p. 12. For details of the Vinnel Corporation, see Eveland, op. cit., pp. 310–13, 317–18, 338. Eveland was at one time a director of the Vinnel Corporation.

269 *The Times*, 15 September 1975. The trend continued. In March 1979 American universities alone had 15,000 Saudi students on their rolls. *The Middle East*, May 1979, p. 31.

270 *The Middle East*, February 1977, p. 40.

271 *Observer*, 19 December 1976.

272 Hafar al Batin, Tabuk and Khamis Mushait are respectively near (land or sea) borders with Iraq, Israel and South Yemen.

273 *Le Monde*, 29 January 1977. Also see p. 86.

274 'Many Saudis in top government jobs are American-educated, and the US lifestyle has captured their imagination,' wrote David Shirreff. *Middle East Economic Digest*, 11 November 1977, p. 5. In 1979 more than half of Saudi cabinet ministers had advanced American university degrees. *The Middle East*, May 1979, p. 31.

275 *Guardian*, 1 October 1977; *The Middle East*, February 1978, p. 75.

276 *Time*, 29 May 1978, p. 16, and 31 December 1979, p. 28; *International Herald Tribune*, 14 December 1979.

277 *The Middle East*, May 1979, p. 28.

278 *International Herald Tribune*, 14 December 1979.

279 See p. 337.

280 *Newsweek*, 3 March 1980, p. 23.

281 *The Middle East*, June 1977, p. 80.

282 *Time*, 29 May 1978, pp. 22–3; *Observer*, 17 September 1978. In 1980 defence spending per capita in the Gulf states was: Saudi Arabia, $2,400; the UAE, $2,100; Qatar, $1,700; Kuwait, $1,200; and Oman, $1,060. The corresponding figure for Israel was $1,000, and for America, $600. *Financial Times*, 23 December 1980; *The Middle East*, April 1981, pp. 9–10.

283 This happened despite the Carter administration's decision not to let arms exports rise above $11 billion in 1978. *Emirates News*, 15 January 1978.

284 *Guardian*, 2 April and 5 May 1979.

285 *Observer*, 15 July 1979. Significantly, following the Fahd-Eilts meetings, Sadat's attacks on Saudi rulers ceased.

286 A detailed account of the French assistance to Saudi forces in Mecca was published in *Le Point*, a Paris-based magazine, and summarised by the *Guardian* on 29 January 1980.

287 Ibid.

288 *Observer*, 23 March 1980.

289 *Daily Telegraph*, 7 June 1980; *Guardian*, 25 September 1980. Before the year's end, when Saudi oil supplies amounted to a quarter of West German needs, the Saudi loan increased to $2.7 billion. *Daily Telegraph*, 21 February and 4 April 1981.

290 *Daily Telegraph*, 27 April 1981.

291 Ibid., 2 May 1981.

292 *Sunday Times*, 19 October 1980. Earlier the French had sold military equipment worth $2.3 billion to the Saudi army. Ibid.

293 *The Times*, 15 June 1981. On the eve of the Gulf war French oil imports from Saudi Arabia, at 900,000 bpd, were twice those from Iraq. *Guardian*, 25 September 1980.
294 In late 1980 total OPEC output was around twenty-six million bpd; and the non-Communist world's oil consumption was forty-seven million bpd. *Guardian*, 15 December 1980.
295 *The Middle East*, December 1980, p. 11.
296 Next March the Reagan administration announced its decision to recommend sale of these Awacs to Saudi Arabia to Congress. Saudi diplomats claimed that the previous administration had agreed to the sale. In October the Senate decided not to block the sale. *Guardian*, 22 April 1981; *Daily Telegraph*, 23 April 1981; *Financial Times*, 29 October 1981.
297 Public knowledge of these exercises came only after the USSR had denounced them.
298 Cited in *The Middle East*, December 1980, p. 11.
299 *Guardian*, 7 January 1981.
300 A summary of the publication appeared in *The Middle East*. June 1979, pp. 32–3.
301 *Observer*, 11 March 1975. Diego Garcia was brought by Britain from Mauritius for £3 million. Later it became part of the group of islands known as the British Indian Ocean Territory, established by Britain in November 1965. As a result of an Anglo–American agreement signed in December 1966, these islands became available to the American and British governments for 'defence activities' for fifty years. *Mainstream*, 3 January 1981, pp. 9–10.
302 *The Middle East*, December 1980, p. 11. The first RDF military exercise – named Red Flag – was held in June 1980 at the Nellis airbase in Nevada, USA. *Arabia: The Islamic World Review*, February 1981, p. 35.
303 *Guardian*, 23 February 1981.
304 Ibid., 2 and 3 March 1981. The remaining commands of American armed forces are: Pacific, and Continental US. *The Middle East*, June 1979, p. 33.
305 *Daily Telegraph*, 10 March 1981.
306 *Guardian*, 26 January 1981.
307 To underline its point that refusal to join the American camp overtly did not signify any diminution in its opposition to Communism, the Saudi government broke off diplomatic relations with the leftist regime in Afghanistan on the day the American secretary of state arrived in Riyadh. *Guardian*, 8 April 1981.
308 *Sunday Times*, 1 February 1981. The Gulf Cooperation Council was formally established on 26 May 1981 after a meeting of the heads of six Gulf states in Abu Dhabi. Abdullah Bishra, a veteran Kuwaiti diplomat, was appointed the secretary-general of the GCC with its secretariat in Riyadh. *The Times*, 27 May 1981.
309 *Guardian*, 5 and 21 February 1981.
310 Ibid., 21 February 1981; *The Middle East*, April 1981, p. 4.
311 *Daily Telegraph*, 28 March 1981. British officers led forces which were more Pakistani than Omani. See p. 91, note 41 (chapter 6). 'There are 700 British servicemen in Oman, and the British prime minister [Mrs Thatcher] announced before she left [Oman] that there will be more,' reported Stephen Fay. 'In addition to the Sultan's army and air force, his police force, royal guard and his secret service are led by British officers.' *Sunday Times*, 26 April 1981.
312 *Nation*, 23 February 1980, p. 211.
313 Mansfield (ed.), *The Middle East*, p. 210.

314 See p. 10.
315 See ibid.
316 See p. 339.
317 See p. 10.
318 Mansfield (ed.), *The Middle East*, p. 207, 210.
319 *The Economist Foreign Report*, 3 February 1972, p. 3.
320 See pp. 91, 176.
321 See p. 91.
322 *Palestine*, January 1978, p. 79; *International Herald Tribune*, 20 December 1980.
323 Omani purchases included American anti-tank missiles and artillery. *Nation*, 23 February 1980, p. 211.
324 *Guardian*, 21 February 1981.
325 Ibid., 11 April and 20 August 1980; *Daily Telegraph*, 28 March 1981. Saudi leaders encouraged Sultan Qaboos to conclude these agreements with America. See p. 92.
326 *Guardian*, 4 October 1980.
327 *Daily Telegraph*, 6 October 1980.
328 *Guardian*, 28 February 1981; *The Middle East*, April 1981, p. 9.
329 *Daily Telegraph*, 28 March 1981; *The Middle East*, April 1981, p. 9.
330 *The Times*, 17 October 1975.
331 Ibid.; and Halliday, op. cit., p. 79.
332 *Palestine*, January 1978, p. 79.
333 *Sunday Times*, 30 December 1979.
334 *Nation*, 23 February 1980, p. 211.
335 *The Times*, 16 December 1976.
336 Ibid.
337 The World Bank's *World Development Report, 1979*, put the per capita income of the UAE (in 1977) at $14,420, Kuwait at $12,270, and Qatar at $11,670. Cited in *The Middle East*, January 1980, p. 55. The figures for the following year, published by the World Bank, were: Kuwait, $15,970; Qatar, $15,050; and the UAE, $15,020. *Guardian*, 11 April 1981.
338 *Financial Times*, 26 June 1978.
339 Ibid.
340 Eighty per cent of the ranks, and many of the officers, were Omani or Pakistani. *Guardian*, 20 May 1980.
341 *The Times*, 21 June 1977.
342 *Middle East Economic Digest*, August 1977, p. 40.
343 *Guardian*, 25 February 1976. Since June 1967, when Paris condemned Israeli aggression against the Arab states, France's political stock had been rising steadily in the Arab world. This gave an advantage to French arms exporters over their American and British rivals. Not surprisingly, France sold a 'mini-navy' to Qatar for $360 million in 1980. *Sunday Times*, 19 October 1980.
344 *The Times*, 7 June 1967.
345 In 1962 the Middle East countries' sterling balances amounted to £286 million. Halliday, op. cit., p. 414.
346 *Middle East Economic Digest*, August 1977, 'Special Report on Kuwait', p. 43.
347 Ibid., p. 3.
348 Ibid., p. 43.
349 See earlier note 337.
350 *The Times*, 12 July 1977. The respective areas of Kuwait and Massachusetts are 7,400 and 7,907 sq. miles.

351 A reliable breakdown of Kuwaiti investments abroad was unavailable. However, of the $60 billion invested abroad by OPEC members (mainly Saudi Arabia, Kuwait, and the UAE) during 1974–8, the US received $42 billion. *The Middle East*, August 1979, p. 26. According to David Mizrahi, editor of the *Mideast Report*, total OPEC investments in the US until 1980 amounted to $200 billion (versus the official figure of $51.3 billion): Saudi Arabia, $100 billion; Kuwait, $55 billion; and the UAE, $40 to $45 billion. *International Herald Tribune*, 24 September 1981.
352 *Guardian*, 23 May 1980.
353 March 1980, p. 12. To insure itself against a future American freeze of its assets, Kuwait resorted to banking its oil money with the Moscow Narodny Bank in London. In April 1981 three Arab oil states, including Kuwait, deposited $1.2 billion with the Soviet bank. *New Statesman*, 24 April 1981, p. 15.
354 See p. 294.
355 *8 Days*, 7 March 1981, p. 21.
356 *Daily Telegraph*, 13 and 16 April 1981.
357 Stookey, op. cit., p. 184. America was the fifty-first state to recognise the Yemen Arab Republic. Mansfield (ed.), *The Middle East*, p. 161.
358 Halliday, op. cit. pp. 143–4.
359 *The Middle East*, July 1977, p. 20, and September 1977, p. 35.
360 *International Herald Tribune*, 3 December 1979.
361 *The Middle East*, October 1980, p. 25.
362 This was the first (and the last) time President Carter invoked this provision of the Arms Export Control Act. *The Middle East*, May 1979, p. 19. Also see p. 289.
363 See p. 290.
364 Stookey, op. cit., p. 180. There was a precedent in Cyprus, where Britain secured sovereign rights over two airbases on the island during the negotiations leading to Cyprus's independence in 1960.
365 Halliday, op. cit., p. 250.
366 Ibid., p. 253.
367 Ibid., p. 235.
368 *Guardian*, 1 July 1978. Paul Findlay first visited South Yemen in 1974. *The Middle East*, December 1979, p. 51. Also see p. 179.

## Chapter 14 The Middle East: an analysis

1 Robert Mabro, *The Egyptian Economy: 1952–1972*, Clarendon Press, Oxford, 1974, pp. 10–11.
2 Samir Amin, *The Arab Nation: Nationalism and Class Struggle*, Zed Press, London, 1978, p. 41.
3 Elieze Be'eri, *Army Officers in Arab Politics and Society*, pp. 316–17.
4 Seventy-three per cent of all peasants were landless, and 6 per cent owned less than an acre of land. Mahmoud Hussein, *Class Conflict in Egypt*, p. 45.
5 The breakdown of the urban petty bourgeoisie was: subordinate office employees, 14 per cent; regularly self-employed, 9 per cent; and middle-level managers, 8 per cent. Egypt's urban population was then put at 8 million, and rural population at 18.95 million. Ibid.
6 Be'eri, op. cit., pp. 394–5.
7 See pp. 124. 'Two of Nasser's closest associates, Ali Sabri and Zakariya Mohieddin, became associated with the left and right alternatives [in 1965–6],' states Raymond William Baker. 'Nasser's own uncertainties about the

most fruitful direction for Egypt are reflected in his alternation of the two men as prime ministers.' *Egypt's Uncertain Revolution under Nasser and Sadat*, p. 90.

8 Be'eri, op. cit., p. 331.
9 Tabitha Petran, *Syria*, p. 89.
10 See pp. 134–5.
11 The actual figures for the urban bourgeoisie were 2.2 and 0.7 per cent; and those for the rural bourgeoisie, 4.5 and 0.6 per cent. *Middle East Research and Information Project*, no. 77 (May 1979), p. 4.
12 Ibid.
13 See p. 160.
14 In fact such an act was declared a capital offence. See p. 171.
15 See p. 77, note 7 (chapter 5); and p. 150.
16 Between 1974 and 1978 Saudi imports rose by 510 per cent. *Guardian*, 7 April 1981.
17 See p. 82.
18 See pp. 85, 150.
19 See p. 86.
20 See p. 129. Referring to the situation existing in 1975, Raymond William Baker states: 'These new elements have made the interstices between the public and the private sectors the domain of their operations, notably in subcontracting and the black market.' Op. cit., p. 150.
21 See p. 86, note 20 (chapter 6); and p. 342, note 268 (chapter 13). It was widely acknowledged that in an emergency America could take over the network of airfields being built by the US corps of engineers. *New Statesman*, 1 May 1981, p. 12. Furthermore, as the most important part of the peacekeeping force (to be composed of a few Western nations under the command of an American) to police Egyptian–Israeli borders in Sinai from April 1982, the American government would have access to two modern airbases in Sinai for 'emergency aid' to the Gulf states. *The Times*, 26 June 1981.
22 For a definition of 'national democracy', see p. 252.
23 Of the estimated 4.25 million Palestinians in early 1980, 1.14 million were living in the West Bank and Gaza. In 1946 Palestinian Arabs amounted to 1.2 million. *Sunday Times*, 6 July 1980.
24 See p. 234.
25 By controlling Suez, Aden, and Oman and other Gulf territories, Britain secured its oil lifeline from Iraq.
26 Peter Mangold, *Superpower Intervention in the Middle East*, Croom Helm, London, 1977, p. 145. The author is a former member of the research department of the British Foreign and Commonwealth Office in London.
27 Ibid., p. 142.
28 See p. 223, note 55 (chapter 10).
29 See p. 306, note 65 (chapter 13).
30 *The Middle East*, May 1981, p. 20.
31 Ibid., p. 19.
32 Ibid., pp. 19–20.

## Chapter 15 The future: prospects and possibilities

1 The main reason for their boycott of the Israeli–Egyptian talks, which led to the Camp David accord, was that Israel refuses to have any dealings with the PLO, and Egyptian and Israeli efforts to draw non-PLO representatives of the West Bankers and Gazans into the negotiations failed.

2 *8 Days*, 28 February 1981, p. 13.
3 'Recognition is the only thing the Israelis cannot win by force,' stated an editorial of the *Guardian* on 22 June 1981. 'It is the only token the Arabs have to exchange for the creation of a Palestinian state.'
4 Despite their differences with Syria, Arab monarchies as well as Iraq volunteered to support it in its confrontation with Israel on the issue of the deployment of anti-aircraft missiles in Lebanon in May 1981. 'All Arabs will fight alongside Syria if it were attacked by Israel,' said Crown Prince Fahd of Saudi Arabia. *Guardian*, 21 May 1981. A few days later this was confirmed by the Arab League foreign ministers meeting in Tunis. *BBC World Service*, 24 May 1981.
5 The extent of the West's financial dependence on Arab oil states can be gauged by the fact that by 1980 Saudi Arabia, Kuwait and the UAE had invested $200 billion in US government and private financial institutions alone. *International Herald Tribune*, 24 September 1981. See note 351 (chapter 14).
6 The Soviet heavy weaponry stored in Syria for possible use by Soviet forces include 1,000 Soviet tanks. (The number of tanks possessed by the Syrian military totalled 2,600.) *Daily Telegraph*, 8 May 1981.
7 See p. 267.
8 In April 1976 a well-informed CIA official estimated that Israel already had 'between ten to twenty nuclear weapons ready for use'. *Guardian*, 23 February 1980.
9 See p. 269.
10 See p. 223. Moreover, there is a probability of Saudi Arabia gaining access to a Pakistani hydrogen bomb. Pakistan is expected to detonate a fission bomb by the end of 1982: a project which during its later stages reportedly received a Saudi subsidy of $800 million. According to Indian sources, by 1990 Pakistan would have acquired an arsenal of nuclear warheads as well as suitable aircraft and missiles to deliver them. *Sunday Times*, 18 January 1981; *The Middle East*, June 1981, p. 32. With Iraqi potential (however remote) for making an atomic bomb destroyed by the Israeli raid of 7 June 1981, the Pakistani project acquired greater importance and urgency for the Arabs.
11 According to Suleiman Franjieh, a former president of Lebanon, the Phalange's military council was commanded by an Israeli military officer. *The Times*, 8 June 1981.
12 Going by its past behaviour, Israel is unlikely to agree to the presence of United Nations or any other foreign troops (except possibly American) within its boundaries.
13 The seriousness of the problem can be judged by the following figures: in 1980 the net outflow of Jews from Israel was 31,000; for the fourth month in a row, during late 1980–early 1981, the number of Jewish immigrants into Israel fell below 1,000; and at 1.9 per cent a year the Jewish birthrate was about half that of the Arabs (at 3.4 per cent). *Guardian*, 18 March 1981.
14 See p. 88, note 31 (chapter 6).
15 A succesful coup against any other monarchy in the Gulf would not last: the new regime would be overthrown by a direct or indirect intervention of Saudi Arabia.
16 *The Middle East*, May 1981, p. 20.
17 *The Times*, 23 June 1981.
18 This is already the case in Bahrain.

POSTSCRIPT

1 The breakdown was: NRP, 6; Agudat Israel, 4; and Tami, a breakaway of the NRP, 3. The Labour Alignment returned to its pre-1977 strength of 47. 2 In a television interview Lt-General Rafael Eitan, Israeli chief of staff, said, 'We are simply continuing the same policy which we have followed in the past: to attack the terrorists at our initiative, and not in reaction'. *The Times*, 15 July 1981. 3 *The Economist*, 25 July 1981, p. 44. Even in south Lebanon, where Israeli targets are 'military', the ratio of civilian casualties to military were 5 to 6: 1, reported the Levant correspondent of *The Economist*. Ibid. 4 Cited in *8 Days*, 1 August 1981, p. 8. 5 *The Times*, 20 July 1981. 6 The 'global measures' were reported to include the oil weapon and the use of Arab money and investments. Ibid. 24 July 1981. 7 *Sunday Times*, 26 July 1981. Israel was believed to have expended as many shells in its bombardment of Lebanon as it had done during the June 1967 war. *8 Days*, 8 August 1981, p. 13. 8 26 July 1981. 9 *The Economist*, 1 August 1981, p. 36. 10 *The Times*, 23 July 1981. 11 *Sunday Times*, 11 October 1981. 12 With 600 US intelligence advisers and technicians affixed to the Egyptian military, Washington was able to monitor the situation. These experts were part of the 12,000 US military advisers attached to Egypt's 376,000 troops. *8 Days*, 17 October 1981, pp. 8, 58–9. 13 *The Times*, 9 September 1981. 14 Interview with Mohammed Sid-Ahmed, former deputy editor of *Al Ahram*, in London on 3 December 1981. 15 *International Herald Tribune*, 12–13 September 1981; *Financial Times*, 6 October 1981. 16 *Listener*, 24 September 1981, p. 324. 17 *The Times*, 19 September 1981. 18 *Sunday Times*, 30 August 1981. 19 Ibid., 11 October 1981. 20 *The Times*, 12 October 1981. 21 11 October 1981. 22 Cited in *New York Times*, 8 October 1981. 23 *The Times*, 26 October 1981. 24 Ibid., 28 October 1981; *Guardian*, 13 November 1981. 25 *New Statesman*, 13 November 1981, p. 13. 26 See earlier p. 370. 27 Cited in *The Times*, 26 October 1981. 28 *Sunday Times*, 8 November 1981. 29 *New Statesman*, 27 November 1981, p. 4. 30 *New York Times*, 2 October 1981. 31 1 November 1981. 32 *Sunday Times*, 13 December 1981. 33 26 November 1981. 34 *The Times*, 9 November 1981. 35 *New York Times*, 4 October 1981. 36 *The Middle East*, August 1981, p. 13; *Financial Times*, 18 September 1981. 37 *The Times*, 19 November and 4 December 1981. 38 *8 Days*, 25 July 1981, p. 20. 39 *The Times*, 11 December 1981. 40 Ibid., 15 December 1981. 41 *Guardian*, 25 May 1982. 42 *Al Siyassa*, 24 May 1982.

# SELECT BIBLIOGRAPHY

*For a name starting with Al, El or Ul, see its second part.*

BOOKS


Abboushi, W. F., *Political Systems of the Middle East in the Twentieth Century*, Dodd Mead, New York, 1970.

Abdel-Malek, Anouar, *Egypt: Military Society*, Vintage Books, New York, 1968.

Agwani, M. S., *Communism in the Arab East*, Asia Publishing House, New Delhi and London, 1969.

Agwani, M. S., *Politics in the Gulf*, Vikas, New Delhi, 1978.

Amin, Samir, *The Arab Nation: Nationalism and Class Struggles*, Zed Press, London, 1978.

Baker, Raymond William, *Egypt's Uncertain Revolution under Nasser and Sadat*, Harvard University Press, Cambridge and London, 1978.

Be'eri, Elieze, *Army Officers in Arab Politics and Society*, Pall Mall, London, 1970.

Begin, Menachem, *The Revolt*, W. H. Allen, London, 1951.

Beling, Willard A. (ed.), *The Middle East: Quest for an American Policy*, State University of New York Press, Albany, 1973.

Bhutani, Surendra, *Israeli Soviet Cold War*, Atul Prakashan, Delhi, 1975.

Bober, Arie (ed.), *The Other Israel: The Radical Case Against Zionism*, Doubleday, New York, 1972.

Bose, Tarun Chandra, *The Superpowers and the Middle East*, Asia Publishing House, New Delhi and London, 1972.

Chaliand, Gérard, *The Palestinian Resistance*, Penguin Books, Harmondsworth, 1972.

Confino, Michael, and Shamir, Shimon (eds), *The USSR and the Middle East*, Israel Universities Press, Jerusalem, 1973.

Cooley, John K., *Green March, Black September: The Story of the Palestinian Arabs*, Frank Cass, London, 1973.

Copeland, Miles, *The Game of Nations: The Amorality of Power Politics*, Weidenfeld & Nicolson, London, 1969.

Dagan, Avigdor, *Moscow and Jerusalem: Twenty Years of Relations between Israel and the Soviet Union*, Abelard-Schuman, London and New York, 1970.

Dann, Uriel, *Iraq Under Qassem: A Political History, 1958–1963*, Pall Mall, London, 1969.

Davis, Uri, *Israel: Utopia Incorporated*, Zed Press, London, 1977.

Dawisha, Karen, *Soviet Foreign Policy Towards Egypt*, The Macmillan Press, London, 1979.

Dimont, Max I., *Jews, God And History*, New American Library, New York, 1962.

Eveland, Wilbur Crane, *Ropes of Sand: America's Failure in the Middle East*, W. W. Norton, New York, 1980.

Freedman, Robert O., *Soviet Policy Toward the Middle East since 1970*, Frederick Praeger, New York and London, 1975.
Gabbay, Rony, *Communism and Agrarian Reform in Iraq*, Croom Helm, London, 1978.
Gendzier, Irene L. (ed.), *The Middle East Reader*, Pegasus, New York, 1969.
Ghilan, Maxim, *How Israel Lost Its Soul*, Penguin Books, Harmondsworth, 1974.
Golan, Galia, *The Soviet Union and the Arab–Israel War of October 1973*, The Hebrew University of Jerusalem, Jerusalem, 1974.
Halliday, Fred, *Arabia Without Sultans*, Penguin Books, Harmondsworth, 1974.
Heikal, Mohamed, *Nasser: The Cairo Documents*, New English Library, London, 1972.
Heikal, Mohamed, *The Road to Ramadan*, Fontana, London, 1976.
Hirst, David, *The Gun and the Olive Branch: The Roots of Violence in the Middle East*, Futura, London, 1978.
Howard, Harry N., *The King–Crane Commission*, Khayats, Beirut, 1963.
Hudson, Michael C., *Arab Politics: The Search for Legitimacy*, Yale University Press, New Haven and London, 1977.
Hussein, Mahmoud, *Class Conflict in Egypt: 1945–1970*, Monthly Review Press, New York and London, 1973.
Ismael, Tareq Y., *The Arab Left*, Syracuse University Press, Syracuse, 1976.
Ismael, Tareq Y. et al., *The Middle East in World Politics*, Syracuse University Press, Syracuse, 1976.
Kazziha, Walid W., *Revolutionary Transformation in the Arab World*, Charles Knight, London, 1975.
Kerr, Malcolm, *The Arab Cold War*, Oxford University Press, London and New York, Third Edition, 1975.
Khadduri, Majid, *Republican Iraq: A Study of Iraqi Politics since the Revolution of 1958*, Oxford University Press, London and New York, 1969.
Khadduri, Majid, *Socialist Iraq: A Study in Iraqi Politics since 1968*, The Middle East Institute, Washington, DC, 1978.
Knauerhase, Ramon, *The Saudi Arabian Economy*, Frederick Praeger, New York and London, 1975.
Koury, Enver M., *The Super-Powers and the Balance of Power in the Arab World*, Catholic Press, Beirut, 1970.
Krammer, Arnold, *The Forgotten Friendship: Israel and the Soviet Bloc, 1947–53*, University of Illinois Press, Urbana and London, 1974.
Lackner, Helen, *A House Built on Sand: A Political Economy of Saudi Arabia*, Ithaca Press, London, 1978.
Laqueur, Walter Z., *The Soviet Union and the Middle East*, Routledge & Kegan Paul, London, 1959.
Laqueur, Walter Z., *Communism and Nationalism in the Middle East*, Routledge & Kegan Paul, London, 1961.
Laqueur, Walter Z., *The Struggle for the Middle East: The Soviet Union and the Middle East, 1958–68*, Routledge & Kegan Paul, London, 1969.
Lederer, Ivo J., and Vucinich, Wayne S. (eds), *The Soviet Union and the Middle East: The Post World War II Era*, Hoover Institution Press, Stanford, 1974.
Lenczowski, George (ed.), *The Political Awakening in the Middle East*, Prentice Hall, Englewood Cliffs, 1970.
Lenczowski, George (ed.), *Political Elites in the Middle East Arab World*, American Enterprise Institute for Public Policy Research, Washington, DC, 1975.
Lenin, V. I., *Collected Works: Volume 7*, Foreign Languages Publishing House, Moscow, 1952.
Lewis, Bernard, *The Arabs in History*, Hutchinson, London, Fifth Edition, 1970.

Lucas, Noah, *The Modern History of Israel*, Weidenfeld & Nicolson, London, 1975.

McLaurin, R. D., *The Middle East in Soviet Policy*, Lexington Books, Lexington and London, 1975.

Magnus, Ralph M. (ed.), *Documents on the Middle East*, American Enterprise Institute for Public Policy Research, Washington, DC, 1969.

Mangold, Peter, *Superpower Intervention in the Middle East*, Croom Helm, London, 1977.

Mansfield, Peter, *The Arabs*, Penguin Books, Harmondsworth, 1978.

Mansfield, Peter (ed.), *The Middle East: A Political and Economic Survey*, Oxford University Press, London and New York, Fourth Edition, 1973.

Ma'oz, Moshe, *Syria Under Fafiz al-Asad*, The Hebrew University of Jerusalem, Jerusalem, 1975.

Ma'oz, Moshe (ed.), *Palestinian Arab Politics*, Jerusalem Academic Press, Jerusalem, 1975.

Mirsky, Georgi, *Arab Peoples Continue the Struggle* (in Russian: *Arabskie Narody Prodolshayut Borby*), Mezhdunarodnya Otnosheniya, Moscow, 1965.

Naamani, Israel T., *Israel: A Profile*, Pall Mall, London, 1972.

Nahas, Duniya, *Israeli Communist Party*, Croom Helm, London, 1976.

Nakhleh, Emile A., *The United States and Saudi Arabia: A Policy Study*, American Enterprise Institute for Public Policy Research, Washington, DC, 1975.

Page, Stephen, *The USSR and Arabs*, Central Asian Research Centre, London, 1971.

Pennar, Jean, *The USSR and the Arabs: The Ideological Dimension*, Hurst, London, 1973.

Peretz, Don, *The Government and Politics of Israel*, Westview Press, Boulder, 1979.

Petran, Tabitha, *Syria: A Modern History*, Ernest Benn, London, 1978.

Pomerance, Michla, *American Guarantees to Israel and the Law of American Foreign Relations*, The Hebrew University of Jerusalem, Jerusalem, 1976.

Quandt, William B., *Decade of Decisions: American Policy Toward the Arab–Israeli Conflict, 1967–1976*, University of California Press, Berkeley and London, 1977.

El-Rayyes, Riad N., and Nahas, Duniya (eds), *Guerrillas for Palestine*, An-Nahar Press Services SARL, Beirut, 1974.

Rodinson, Maxime, *Israel and the Arabs*, Penguin Books, Harmondsworth, 1968.

Ro'i, Yaacov (ed.), *The Limits to Power: Soviet Policy in the Middle East*, Croom Helm, London, 1979.

Safran, Nadav, *Israel: The Embattled Ally*, Belknap Press of Harvard University Press, Cambridge and London, 1978.

Said, Edward W., *The Question of Palestine*, Routledge & Kegan Paul, London, 1980.

Seale, Patrick, *The Struggle for Syria: A Study of Post-War Arab Politics, 1945–1958*, Oxford University Press, London and New York, 1965.

Segre, V. D., *Israel: A Society in Transition*, Oxford University Press, London and New York, 1971.

Shaw, Ralph, *Kuwait*, Macmillan, London, 1976.

Sid-Ahmed, Mohamed, *After the Guns Fall Silent*, Croom Helm, London, 1976.

Smith, Colin, *The Palestinians*, Minority Rights Group, London, 1975.

Smolansky, Oleg M., *The Soviet Union and the Arab East under Khrushchev*, Bucknell University Press, Lewisburg, 1974.

Stephens, Robert, *Nasser: A Political Biography*, Allen Lane: The Penguin Press, London, 1971.

Stevens, Richard P., *American Zionism and the US Foreign Policy*, Pageant Press, New York, 1962.

Stocking, George W., *Middle East Oil: A Study in Political and Economic Controversy*, Vanderbilt University Press, Nashville, 1970.

Stookey, Robert W., *America and the Arab States: An Uneasy Encounter*, John Wiley, New York and London, 1975.

Tomkinson, Michael, *The United Arab Emirates*, Tomkinson, London, 1975.

Torrey, Gordon S., *Syrian Politics and the Military*, Ohio State University Press, Columbus, 1964.

Walichnowski, Tadeusz, *The Tel Aviv–Bonn Axis and Poland*, Interpress, Warsaw, 1968.

Yodfat, A., and Abir, M., *In the Direction of the Persian Gulf: The Soviet Union and the Persian Gulf*, Frank Cass, London, 1977.

Zander, Walter, *Soviet Jewry, Palestine and the West*, Victor Gollancz, London, 1947.

## NEWSAGENCIES, NEWSPAPERS AND PERIODICALS

*Al Ahali* (Cairo)
*Al Ahram* (Cairo)
*Arab Dawn* (London)
*Arab News* (Jeddah)
*Arab World File* (Beirut)
*Arabia: The Islamic World Review* (London)
Associated Press (New York)
*Aziya i Afrika Segodnya* (Moscow)
*BBC Summary of World Broadcasts* (Reading)
*Chicago Sun-Times* (Chicago)
*Daily American* (Rome)
*Daily Star* (Beirut)
*Daily Telegraph* (London)
*Daily Telegraph Magazine* (London)
*Economic and Political Weekly* (Bombay)
*Economist* (London)
*Economist Foreign Report* (London)
*Egyptian Gazette* (Cairo)
*8 Days* (London)
*Emirates News* (Abu Dhabi)
*Events* (London)
*Financial Times* (London)
*Guardian* (London)
*Al Hadaf* (Beirut)
*Ike* (Beirut)
*International Herald Tribune* (Paris)
Iraqi News Agency (Baghdad)
*Izvestia* (Moscow)
*Jerusalem Post* (Jerusalem)
*Jordan Times* (Amman)
*Keesing's Contemporary Archives* (Edinburgh)
*Khamsin* (London)
*Krasnaya Zvezda (Moscow)*
*Kuwait Times* (Kuwait)
*Le Monde* (Paris)
*Literaturnaya Gazeta* (Moscow)
*L'Orient-Le Jour* (Beirut)
*Mainstream* (New Delhi)
*Mezhdunarodnaya Zhizn* (Moscow)
*Middle East Economic Digest* (London)
*Middle East International* (London)
*Middle East Monitor* (Washington)
Middle East News Agency (Cairo)
*Middle East Research and Information Project* (Washington)
*Mirovaya Ekonomika i Mezhdunarodnie Otnosheniya* (Moscow)
*Mizan Newsletter* (London)
*Monday Morning* (Beirut)
*Al Mustaqabal* (Paris)
*Al Nahar* (Beirut)
*Nation* (New York)
*New Left Review* (London)
*New Society* (London)
*New Standard* (London)
*New Statesman* (London)
*New Times* (Moscow)
*New York Times* (New York)
*New York Times Magazine* (New York)

*Newsweek* (New York)
*Novoe Vremia* (Moscow)
*Now!* (London)
*Observer* (London)
*Palestine* (Beirut)
*Peace, Freedom and Socialism* (Prague)
*Al Rai al Aam* (Kuwait)
*Al Safir* (Beirut)
*Sovietski Flot* (Moscow)
*Sunday Telegraph* (London)
*Sunday Times* (London)
*Sunday Times Magazine* (London)
*Tareeq al Shaab* (Baghdad)
Tass (Moscow)
*The Middle East* (London)
*The Times* (London)
*The Times Higher Education Supplement* (London)
*Time* (New York)
*Trud* (Moscow)
United Press International (New York)
*Washington Post* (Washington)
*World Marxist Review* (Toronto)
*Yediot Aharonot* (Tel Aviv)
*Za Rubezhom* (Moscow)

# INDEX

*For a name starting with Al, El or Ul, see its second part. A person's religious or secular title has been excluded.*